ATHENS IN JERUSAI

THE LITTMAN LIBRARY OF
JEWISH CIVILIZATION

MANAGING EDITOR
Connie Webber

'*Get wisdom, get understanding:*
Forsake her not and she shall preserve thee'
PROV. 4:5

ATHENS IN JERUSALEM

———

CLASSICAL ANTIQUITY AND HELLENISM IN THE MAKING OF THE MODERN SECULAR JEW

———

YAACOV SHAVIT

Translated by
CHAYA NAOR AND NIKI WERNER

London · Portland, Oregon
The Littman Library of Jewish Civilization

The Littman Library of Jewish Civilization

Published in the United Kingdom by
Vallentine Mitchell & Co. Ltd.
Newbury House, 900 Eastern Avenue,
London IG2 7HH

Published in the United States and Canada by
Vallentine Mitchell & Co. Ltd.
c/o ISBS, 5804 N.E. Hassalo Street,
Portland, Oregon 97213–3644

Hebrew edition © Am Oved Publishers Ltd., Tel Aviv 1992
First published in English 1997
English edition first issued in paperback 1999
English translation © The Littman Library of Jewish Civilization 1997, 1999

A catalogue record for this book is available from the British Library

The Library of Congress catalogued the hardback edition as follows:

Shavit, Jacob
[Yahadut bi-re'i ha-Yavanut ve-hofa'at ha-Yehudi ha-Helenisti ha-moderni, English]
Athens in Jerusalem: classical antiquity and Hellenism in the making of the modern secular Jew /
Yaacov Shavit; translated by Chaya Naor and Niki Werner.
p. cm.
Includes bibliographical references and index.
1. Judaism—Relations—Greek.   2. Greece—Religion   3. Jews—Civilization—Greek influences.
4. Judaism—Modern period, 1750– —Historiography.   I. Title.
BM506.G7S513 1997   296.3'7—dc21   97-9809 CIP   r97

ISBN 1–874774–36–6

Publishing co-ordinator: Janet Moth
Design: Pete Russell, Faringdon, Oxon
Copy-editing: Leofranc Holford-Strevens
Proof-reading: Connie Webber and Chaya Naor
Typeset by John Waś, Oxford
Printed in Great Britain on acid-free paper by
Biddles Ltd., Guildford & King's Lynn

Then too, 'twill chance
That mirror unto mirror may hand on
A single image, till e'en multiplied
Five or six-fold the likeness will appear.

LUCRETIUS, *De Rerum Natura*, iv. 326–7,
trans. Chas. E. Bennett, 183

―――――

Since that day when many of our maskilim began to look only to the
outside, they began to fashion all the sights they saw there beyond
the boundaries of their nation, into a pattern and a programme for
all the affairs of Israel.

ZE'EV JAWITZ, 'Olamot overim ve'olam omed'
('Worlds Pass and a World Remains')

―――――

And then the judges began to judge the ways of this people and to
compare them with the Greeks. And it would not be surprising if there
were many among them who gave the Greeks preference.

PERETZ SMOLENSKIN, 'Et lata'at' ('A Time to Plant' [Eccl. 3: 2])

―――――

PREFACE

THIS book is more than a translation of my Hebrew book, published in 1992. In preparing the English version, I not only expanded and improved on it in several aspects; I also corrected those points that required correction, and tried to be more precise in the concepts and terms I used. In consequence this is in many respects a vastly different book from that published in Hebrew.

When I began writing this book, almost six years ago, its general structure, scope, and central ideas were quite clear to me; I was familiar with some of the literature dealing with its main topic and related topics, but it had not occurred to me that the relevant literature was so vast. I am not referring only to academic works but to all those numerous texts in which the world of Judaism is linked, in one way or another, with classical antiquity and Hellenism. I very soon found myself as the reverse of Hemingway's old man: I had a skeleton, but in order to put skin and bones on it, I had to throw my net into the large ocean of texts. In the course of the years during which I wrote and rewrote this book, I cast my net again and again—and each time I discovered how full the sea is. I also had to resolve to throw back into the sea many fish that already were or subsequently became familiar to me; for example, I had to forgo citing many works of philosophy, theology, semantics, and psychosemantics. On the other hand, I tried to haul in those fish that were not so well known, or were dispersed in different waters. But I have no doubt that the number of references to the subject is immense and many fish still remain in the large sea of texts. While I believe that a few more of these texts could enrich the evidence presented in this book, they would not change its skeletal structure or its key ideas.

The main subject of this study is Jewish history, but I truly believe that even a zealous classicist may find it interesting and enriching to see the diverse, and often strange, fields to which the classical heritage was borne and in which it was transplanted. It also seems to me that anyone interested in the history of classical culture and its heritage will be intrigued by the question of how these were reflected in the world of images of Judaism, which is after all the only culture to accompany classical antiquity in all its many transformations and ramifications, from the time of Homer to the present day.

I was fortunate to have Dr Leofranc Holford-Strevens as my editor. He not only read the manuscript with a critical eye, saving me from many errors, but also made available to me the treasurehouse of his phenomenal knowledge in so many fields. Since classical antiquity was for me in many respects an alien sea, he was my Lynceus, guiding me through these boundless waters. Many references to classical literature (but not only to classical literature) are the fruit of his generous contribution. I do hope he will not object to my saying that in many respects the book is his hardly less than it is mine. I really regret that now that the work is completed, our prolonged exchange of e-mail queries and answers, which enriched me in so many regards, has come to its end.

Tel Aviv University   YAACOV SHAVIT
1996

ACKNOWLEDGEMENTS

I FIRST began writing this book during my stay in Bonn and Bad Godesberg (1986–7), and I am pleased once more to express my gratitude to Edith and Dr Heinrich Pfeiffer for their hospitality. In the summer of 1989, Dr Barbara and Professor Peter Schäfer not only extended me their warm hospitality in Berlin but also allowed me the use of their rich library, which was of indispensable help in broadening my knowledge of the Second Temple period. I owe thanks to my colleagues and friends who read the manuscript and made invaluable comments, and even saved me from falling into the grave errors that anyone venturing to grapple with this complex issue is likely to commit. In particular, I am grateful to Professor Aharon Oppenheimer and Nili Oppenheimer, who were always willing to spare the time to help me resolve questions relating to talmudic literature. To Professor Itamar Even-Zohar I am grateful for intellectual input and for friendship, to Professor Uriel Rappaport for his comments on Part III. My thanks go to Professor Aryeh Kasher for putting at my disposal the manuscript of his translation of *Against Apion*; he too also encouraged me and was ready to answer my queries concerning the literature of the Second Temple period. I am indebted to Professor Avraham Shapira for his assistance and encouragement. To Dr Nicholas de Lange I owe a debt of gratitude for the initiative that gave me the opportunity of rewriting this book for an English version. Mrs Connie Webber closely followed my work on the book throughout in detail; I am grateful to her for her attention and interest, but above all for her faith in its merit.

Deserving of special mention are Professor Benjamin Harshav and Barbara Harshav, who encouraged me to put pen to paper; I should also like to thank Mr Stanley Holwitz for his kindness and interest, and Professor David Shavit (De Kalb, Ill.) for his valuable bibliographical assistance. I am also grateful to Professor Dan Amir, the Rector of Tel Aviv University, for his assistance, and to Professor Yoram Dinstein, the President of Tel Aviv University, from whom I received the most precious of all gifts: moral support.

I also wish to thank Chaya Naor and Niki Werner, the translators, for their excellent translation, as well as for their untiring patience in the face of the additions and changes I repeatedly introduced into the text. Tragically, Niki died without seeing the book published. I am also grateful to my wife Zohar, who has always been a source of support and encouragement;

in my work on this book, which extended over a very long period, and was beset by many difficulties, her constant support was invaluable; I could not have done without it. Last but not least, I am indebted to Mrs Colette Littman for her generosity.

Rabbi Yehoshua ben Perachyah said 'Acquire a teacher and gain a friend' (*Mishnah Avot* 1: 6); Socrates asks in Xenophon's *Memorabilia* (2. 4. 5) 'But compared with what other possession would a good friend not appear far superior?' While writing this book, I have learnt how much truth there is in both the words of the Sages and the wisdom of the ancients.

CONTENTS

Translators' Note　　　　　　　　　　　　　　　　　　　　xiii

Introduction　　　　　　　　　　　　　　　　　　　　　　　I

PART I

THE FIRST MIRROR

1　Waking the Dead—Greece as an Ideal and an Exemplar　　21

2　Hellenism and Hebraism: The Two Poles of the World　　40

3　Israel and Greece: Reviving a Legendary Past　　58

4　'Greek Wisdom' as Secular Knowledge and Science　　79

5　Japheth in the Tents of Shem: The Reception of the
　　　Classical Heritage in Modern Hebrew Culture　　119

6　The Moral Dimension: Commonality and Particularity　　155

7　Worlds without Compromise: Reconstructing the
　　　Disparities　　188

8　Have Jews Imagination? Jews and the Creative Arts　　220

PART II

THE SECOND MIRROR

9　The Nature of the Hellenistic Mirror　　281

10　Judaism and Hellenism in Palestine and Alexandria:
　　　Two Models of a National and Cultural Encounter　　306

11　Homeric Books and Hellenistic Culture in the World
　　　of the Sages　　337

PART III
ATHENS IN JERUSALEM

12 Back to History: The Secularization of the Ancient
Jewish Past   355

13 The Children of Japheth (Aryans) and the Children of
Shem (Semites): Race and Innate Nationalism   381

14 The People and its Land: Country, Landscape, and
Culture   403

15 A 'Polis' in Jerusalem: The Jewish State   432

16 The New Jewish Culture: Ideal and Reality   449

Conclusion: What has Athens to do with Jerusalem?   473

Bibliography   481

Index   547

TRANSLATORS' NOTE

TRANSLATING this book has been for us an enlightening journey through Jewish cultural and intellectual history in its reciprocal relations with its European counterpart. Along the way we encountered a corpus of works that ranged from classical antiquity to modern times. This occasionally presented us with challenges and difficulties as well as rewards.

Many passages from Hebrew works are included in this book, some of them lengthy. We have used existing translations wherever possible (the translations used are noted in the Bibliography), but where no such possibility existed, we had to translate the material ourselves; when no note on the source is given, the translation is ours. The poetry excerpts were translated by Niki Werner. Many of the excerpts we translated ourselves were from works written during the period known as the Haskalah—the equivalent in the Jewish world of the Enlightenment—when Hebrew as a modern secular language was still in its formative stages; many words did not exist, and authors created their own diction. Since the Hebrew words used by Haskalah writers are sometimes unfamiliar to today's Hebrew-speaker, we have attempted to render them in English in a similarly archaic style.

As the author notes in his Preface, this book is not a direct translation of the Hebrew edition. Much material was added and many changes made, some as we were working on the translation itself. Every effort was made to make the text fully accessible to an English-speaking readership not necessarily familiar with Jewish history or scholarship; for example, we have included biographical information about people mentioned in the text that was not considered necessary for the Hebrew edition.

Since many of the works cited are in Hebrew, we had to decide how to refer to them in the text: whether to transliterate the Hebrew title or to translate it. For this purpose, we distinguished between primary sources, whose titles might conceivably be familiar to readers, and scholarly books and articles. In the case of the former, the Hebrew title is given in transliteration, followed at first mention by an English translation in parentheses, to give the non-Hebrew speaker an idea of what the work is about. In the notes such works are referred to by a shortened form of the transliterated Hebrew title, while the full title and its translation are given in the Bibliography together with other bibliographical data. However, for those primary sources available in English translation, we cited the translated title only (as with some of Ahad Ha'am's essays).

In contrast, the titles of scholarly works and articles in Hebrew are cited only in English translation; since readers are unlikely to be familiar with such works it was considered preferable to give them an idea of the subject-matter rather than a transliteration of the Hebrew title, which could in any case be ascertained fairly easily by the reader curious enough to follow up a reference. In most cases, the English title given is the one that appears in the book or article; this has been done to help readers who may wish to search for the work in a catalogue. Since so many of the works are in this category, we have indicated that they are translations only in the Bibliography, by the addition of '(Heb.)' after the title. However, since our use of shortened forms for titles throughout the notes means that readers will in any case have to check the Bibliography to ascertain full details of the works in which they are interested, this should not present too great an obstacle to scholarship.

In transliterating Hebrew titles we decided to adopt the system that seemed to be most helpful to the general reader, a system that would convey the sounds of the Hebrew and help the reader approximate a correct pronunciation with a minimum of confusion. Connie Webber's advice in this regard was invaluable, and we are grateful for her assistance. Note that both 'ch', representing the letter *chet*, and 'kh', representing *khaf*, are pronounced like the 'ch' in 'loch'.

In spelling proper names, we have used the *Encyclopaedia Judaica* as our prime reference, except in transliterating Hebrew names, where we followed the guidelines outlined above.

Those Hebrew words that are basic to an understanding of Judaism and likely to be part of the vocabulary of people reading this book have not been italicized, on the grounds that such italicization would be more intrusive than helpful. Other than that, we have wherever possible tried to avoid using Hebrew terms. One important exception is the Hebrew word *chokhmah*, usually translated as 'wisdom'. Unlike the English 'wisdom', *chokhmah* may refer to a discrete entity and be used in the plural *chokhmot*, which sometimes corresponds to English 'sciences', but also has a wider meaning. Since 'wisdoms' is not a customary usage in English, it has seemed better on some occasions to retain the Hebrew word.

Most of the biblical citations are from the Revised Standard Version, published by Oxford University Press. A few, however, are from the King James Version; in each case we chose the translation closer to the sense of the original Hebrew. All the excerpts from rabbinic literature are from published translations. A list of the translations used is included in the Bibliography.

In general, whenever English translations were available of works published in other languages, we have cited the translation.

We have had the advantage of Professor Shavit's readiness to respond to our numerous queries and to accept many of our suggestions. The results, we trust, make the book and its subject more accessible to the English reader.

CHAYA NAOR
NIKI WERNER

INTRODUCTION

'WHAT THEN HAS ATHENS TO DO WITH JERUSALEM?'[1]

The aim of this book is to try to answer Tertullian's rhetorical question and to deal with the dichotomy between Athens and Jerusalem from a new point of view, namely: did Athens (classical antiquity and Hellenism) have any impact on the shaping of modern Jewish culture?

Athens and Jerusalem, Greeks and Jews, represent two distinct and different human entities. Here are but a few examples.

In his lost book *On Sleep*, Clearchus of Soli in Cyprus, a pupil of Aristotle, referred to the Jews as a 'philosophical race' and described a Jew from Judaea who had met Aristotle during the years he was teaching in Asia Minor as a perfect Greek 'not only in his language but also in his soul' (Josephus, *Against Apion*, i. 181).[2] By that, writes Werner Jaeger, he meant:

Not what modern historical or philological scholarship tries to grasp in Homer, Pindar, or in Periclean Athens, of course; a Greek soul is for him the intellectualized human mind in whose crystal-clear world even a highly gifted and intelligent foreigner could participate and move with perfect ease and grace.[3]

Clearchus' definition of a 'Greek soul' was different from what Heinrich Heine had in mind many generations later when he wrote about the 'Hellenic soul', in contrast to the 'Jewish soul'. The Greeks in Heine's

---

[1] Tertullian, *De praescriptione*, 7. 9: 'Quid ergo Athenis et Hierosolymis?' Jerusalem, of course, symbolized faith, Athens philosophy. Tertullian continues: 'or the Academy with the Church?', and elsewhere asks: 'What is there in common between the philosopher and the Christian, the pupil of Hellas and the pupil of Heaven?' (*Apologeticus*, 46. 18). See Cochrane, *Christianity and Classical Culture*, 213–60, esp. 222–3; Alexander, 'Quid Athenis et Hierosolymis?', 101, 120 n. 1.

[2] Or 'also his soul was Greek'. The passage is fragment 6 of Clearchus in Wehrli, *Die Schule des Aristoteles*. The first known 'Hellenized' Jew, according to an inscription discovered in Greece, was a slave whose prospective freedom is recorded in an inscription of 300–250 BC, Moschos son of Moschion, who like his father bore a Greek name and was so far assimilated to his pagan environment to have sought (and received) a dream in the Amphiareion at Oropus; see D. M. Lewis, 'The First Greek Jew'; M. Stern's review of Y. Gutman, *The Beginnings of Jewish Hellenistic Literature*, in *Studies in Jewish History*, 573.

[3] Jaeger, *Early Christianity*, 30; J. Levy, 'Aristotle and the Jewish Sage'; Y. Gutman, 'Clearchus', 91–4; Bickerman, *Jews in the Greek Age*, 15–16, who believes that the story may well be true. According to Morton Smith, by *philosophia* the Hellenistic writers meant not 'philosophy' but 'cult of wisdom' ('Palestinian Judaism in the First Century', 79), or, better, 'religion', for which the Hellenistic and Roman world had no general term. It is worth recalling that Aristotle was impressed by the self-restraint of the Jew and the fact that he abstained from eating certain foods. This idealistic image of the Jews as philosophers by race also appears in Theophrastus, *On Piety* (fragment 584A. 26. 3 Fortenbaugh *et al.*) and Strabo 16. 2. 35–40 (perhaps from Poseidonius of Apamea), contrasting with the negative image: see Modrzejewski, 'L'Image du juif'.

perception were far from being gifted philosophers with 'intellectualized human minds'. For him, they represented an entirely different human type. In contrast to Clearchus' view, an excess of intellectuality and abstraction was considered a negative trait by Heine as well as by those Jewish thinkers who adhered to the doctrine of vitalism. A 'Greek soul', that is, a pagan soul, was a symbol of a vibrant, robust entity, possessed of youth, spontaneity, and energy.[4]

In a similar vein, M. J. Berdyczewski (1865–1921), the Hebrew radical writer and thinker,[5] wrote in his personal diary in May 1905: 'When the Jews return to the Land of Canaan and settle there as a people, they must again grasp hold of the thread that the prophets had already broken by their overzealous morality. A political and spiritual renewal of the Jews as a people, but as a Hellenic people . . .'.[6] And when the eminent French orientalist Ernest Renan (1823–92) came to visit Athens after a stay in Palestine (1860–1), he was so overwhelmed by the sublime manifestation of pure beauty and pure reason that he saw in his mind's eye, that he uttered an enthusiastic prayer: his 'Prière sur l'Acropole', in which he addressed Athene, as the goddess of truth and beauty, the opposite of Jerusalem. For him, a 'Greek soul' was the longed-for unity of sublime beauty and pure reason.

When the author of the Second Book of Maccabees tells in disgust how the establishment of the gymnasium in Jerusalem under Jason's rule (and the city's conversion into a *polis*) immediately imposed a Hellenic character upon his fellow Jews (2 Macc. 4), it is clear that by *akmē tis Hellēnismou* (v. 13: 'a climax of Hellenism'), *ton Hellēnikon charaktēra* (v. 10: 'the Greek way of life') and *tas Hellēnikas doxas* (v: 16: 'the Greek scale of values'), he is referring to a way of life which is decidedly different from that intended by Clearchus or by Heine. Here a 'Greek soul' is the soul of an amoral idolater. 'The ways of the Hellenes' in traditional Jewish literature mean the abandonment of the Torah and the ancestral tradition; the abandonment of both religion and culture. Throughout the whole of Jewish literature, as we shall see, 'the ways of the Hellenes' always carry a negative connotation.

From these two polar points of view, *Athens* and *Jerusalem* represent two different and contradictory worlds.[7]

---

[4] See Ch. 1.

[5] His views will be described in detail in the following chapters.

[6] In Holzman, *Ginzei Mikhah Yosef*, vi. 58.

[7] Jaeger, *Early Christianity*, 3–4; Highet, *The Classical Tradition*, 454, 687 n. 44. In describing Paul's visit to Athens, Renan also finds an excellent occasion to contrast Greek and Christian sensibilities. The Greeks are said to have little care for the profundity of death but are an artistic people who take

What, then, has Athens to do with Jerusalem?

Jerusalem and the Jews, Athens and the Greeks (Hellenes), the 'Greek soul' and the 'Jewish soul'—these few instances are the product of different perceptions; Athens and Jerusalem, Jews and Hellene, are conceptual twins in a binary model. If this is so, how can one speak of 'Athens' in 'Jerusalem', of 'Athens' as an integral part of 'Jerusalem'? Of the 'Greek soul' as an integral component of the 'Jewish soul'?

This question is at the core of my study. I have chosen not to write under the heading of 'Athens *and* Jerusalem', which would imply that Jerusalem and Athens (as well as Rome and Alexandria) belonged to the same historical-cultural sphere.[8] Nor am I writing under the heading of 'Athens *versus* Jerusalem', representing the notion that there was— and still is—an irreconcilable opposition and struggle between the nature of 'Athens' (Greek culture) and 'Jerusalem' (Jewish culture). These two headings have in fact served as the titles of quite a few studies; I, however, have chosen to write this book under the heading of 'Athens *in* Jerusalem', namely, on the manner in which cultural traits or values characterized as 'Greek' became an integral part of the Jewish collective soul in the modern era, altering its nature and identity. By 'Athens in Jerusalem' I am not merely suggesting that there are gymnasia or stadia in the new Jerusalem. Neither do I accept the Orthodox view that the modern secular Jew is a Hellenizing Jew like those in the time of the Hasmonean revolt. My intention in this book is to examine the impact 'Greek' values had in the making of the 'new Jerusalem', that is to say, modern secular Judaism. I am using 'new Jerusalem' as a metaphor for the new Jewish culture which emerged from the dawn of the Jewish Enlightenment or Haskalah in the last quarter of the eighteenth century, inspired modern Jewish nationalism, and nurtured the creation of modern Jewish (Hebrew) culture in Palestine from the 1880s and thereafter. This is, of course, only one possible road to take in exploring the complex terrain of the modern history of Judaism, but it is a major thoroughfare.

Why 'Athens' and not 'Greece'? Because 'Athens' symbolizes 'Greece', or 'classical antiquity', as it does in most of the texts I am dealing with. Those who lived in the Hellenistic era also knew very well that Athens did

---

an immediate joy in the present; their art is always a modification of nature (Shapiro, 'Nietzsche contra Renan', 208).

[8] 'Thus Rome gave us the framework, as Athens and Jerusalem on the whole gave the inner content of our living Christian civilization', Murray, *Hellenism and the Modern World*, 19. In the same vein, see W. T. Harris, in his introduction to Davidson, *The Education of the Greek People*: 'Thus Greece educated all modern nations in the forms of art and literature, while Rome educates them in civil law' (p. viii).

not represent all of Greece, but the idealization of the classical past nearly always was the idealization of Athens. Thucydides, for example, made Pericles call Athens 'the school (*paideusis*) of all Greece', and Isocrates traced the origin of all culture in Attica, making Athens the founder of all civilization.[9] And why 'Athens' and not 'Western culture'? The truth is, of course, that 'Athens' stands for 'Europe' since Greece was perceived, both by Jews and Europeans, as the *alma mater* of Europe, and it served as a metaphor for modern 'secular' Europe and secularization. The image of Greece as a pagan or 'secular' entity became a code by which the Jews symbolized, signified, and defined hopes and fears, as well as the familiar and the alien. They also applied this code to various concepts and traits that in their minds were different and opposed to those they thought were inherent in them, defined them, and were represented by them. By means of this code and its various signals, Judaism made known its attitude towards the world outside. A cultural value or trait was identified as 'Greek' in order to approve of it or, conversely, to attach a stigma to it. The changes that took place in the image of Greek and classical antiquity are but reflections of the changes in the Jews' attitude both towards their ancient past and towards 'Europe'. Some Jewish writers, as we shall see, have argued that 'Athens' and 'Jerusalem' signify the two forces of a primal duality (*Urzwei*) that have been contending with each other in Judaism since its inception, creating within it a tension, as well as a dynamic and enriching multiplicity. However, duality also creates a disintegrating tension, or one which in the final analysis causes the totality and the unity to alter their nature.

The reception of the classical tradition in Russia from the time of Peter the Great's reign was one aspect of 'Russia's orientation towards Western Europe in general'.[10] Taking the Russian case as an analogy, one could also say that the reception of the classical heritage by the Jews from the dawn of the Haskalah movement was one aspect of Judaism's orientation towards Western Europe. Greek philosophy first became known to Jewish philosophers in the Hellenistic period and the encounter with it became intensive and influential from the Middle Ages up to the modern era, but classical antiquity was an almost unknown world to the Jewish public at large. Only during the nineteenth century did Jews become more familiar with it, and this was one aspect of their acculturation or 'Europeanization'.

---

[9] Thucydides, *Histories*, 2. 41. 1; for Isocrates see esp. *Panegyricus*, 23–50. Matthew Arnold echoed these authors when he declared: 'The Athens of Pericles was a vigorous man, at the summit of his bodily strength and mental energy' ('Modern Element', 45), with 'the utmost energy of mature manhood, public and private, the most unprejudiced and intelligent observation of human affairs' (ibid. 60).

[10] Wes, *Classics in Russia*, 4.

But the modern encounter of Judaism with classical tradition was far more than the reading of Greek literature or the translation of Greek literature into Hebrew, thereby exhibiting cultural openness and tolerance, as well as sensitivity to the depth and otherness of human and cultural movements. It was a process by which 'Greek values' permeated and changed the value system of Judaism and the cultural reality of the Jews in nearly every sphere. 'Athens' became an integral part of 'Jerusalem', or, if we prefer a different metaphor, 'Jerusalem' became a new reality in which 'Athens' and 'Jerusalem' are integral parts. This, then, was a process of more than becoming acquainted with the 'other', or even of borrowing certain values and traits from its culture. The Jews and Judaism have always borrowed traits and values from other cultures, changing them while assimilating them (by 'Judaizing' them), or modifying them in one or another sphere. This time, the change was more sweeping and substantial than in previous instances.

Jews often redefined their identity and its nature by looking into the Greek mirror. The prominent Islamist G. E. von Grunebaum wrote that 'the tendency to utilize the "other" civilization in order to understand one's own is clearly to be distinguished from mere recognition of another civilization as an entity of some value'.[11] Polarization had been a way to define the world beyond the borders of one's own culture, and to define, or redefine, one's own culture. The 'other' was utilized in order to represent it as foreign and inferior, in order to reinforce one's sense of self-value (though occasionally as a model of a superior type of person or society). In the fifth century BC, the consciousness of the polarization of barbarian and Hellene became a popular *topos* in Greek tragedy. A 'discourse of barbarism' was created as a component of the Panhellenic ideology; this discourse comprised 'a complex system of signifiers denoting the ethnically, psychologically, and politically "other": terms, themes, actions, and images'.[12] This was the case with the polarization between Jews and Gentiles (*goyim*), and is so too with 'Judaism' and 'Hellenism'.

Frequently the 'other' serves as an oppositional model, an external *Gegenpol*; such a structure must be contrasted with an immanent polar duality in which the two contradictory but mutually enriching forces are inherent in the specific entity itself, so that the *Gegenpol* is not external. This principle of dual polarity, which finds in the tension between the

---

[11] Grunebaum, 'An Analysis of Islamic Anthropology', 43.

[12] Hall, *Inventing the Barbarian*, 2, cf. 11; Herodotus, writes Lateiner, already showed an 'impulse toward discovering polarities' (*The Historical Methods of Herodotus*, 150). See also G. E. R. Lloyd, *Polarity and Analogy*; Romm, *The Edges of the Earth*, 45–81.

poles a universally immanent *polare Natur* of society, first appeared in the historical philosophy of the German Enlightenment or *Aufklärung*, and then developed in the Romantic and conservative philosophy of history. Often the immanent *Gegenpol* is signified by external phenomena that are in a sense its metaphor and manifestation, as when 'the Orient' stands for supposedly 'Oriental' elements in the West. However, in the case of the Jewish–Greek polarity, Judaism was not only a manifestation of an innate *Gegenpol* in Western culture and in the nature of Western man; it was also a real external *Gegenpol*, constituting a complete essence in polar opposition to Westernism. Jews utilized it for purposes of self-observation and self-definition and in order to establish a new relationship with the world of the 'other', which was perceived as different from the 'old' Christian world or the Gentiles as defined in the traditional point of view.

The appearance of a new 'other'—side by side with the traditional 'others'—resulted from the change that took place in the status of Jews in the surrounding European society and their attitude towards it, as well as from the fact that Jews began to define and regard Judaism as a culture: an all-encompassing life experience, no longer corresponding and identical with religion. By the start of the Haskalah, this tireless effort had already begun: to depict Judaism as a culture and Jews as a nation of culture (*Kulturnation*), who carried with them, wherever they went, a rich cultural heritage of great attainment that bore its own distinctive stamp and which they continued to enrich and enhance in every locale. This definition made it necessary not only to examine the features and exclusive qualities of Jewish culture, but also to draw the portrait of this culture in full detail, and to elucidate the patterns of contact that existed between it and the surrounding culture. The 'other' is turned into an inverted mirror in which Judaism examines itself using the method of opposition. I use the term 'method of opposition' in its simplest sense, as a method of comparison and analogy.[13] For many it was not enough to identify the idea or content of Judaism; it was also necessary to place it in opposition to another entity in order to delineate its nature the more precisely. Jews have done this throughout history when comparing Judaism and Christianity. Now, in modern times, they had begun to compare it with the classical heritage as well. 'Jews, who for centuries had fiercely defended themselves against Christianity, were now occasionally tainted by pagan imagery'.[14]

Many Jews looked into the Greek mirror and in order to prove the

[13] It should be noted that an analogy is 'never an absolute likeness; it points to a similarity in certain respects shown in context which will differ in other respects', *Encyclopaedia Britannica* (1962), i. 863–4.

[14] Manuel, *The Eighteenth Century Confronts the Gods*, 3.

superiority of Judaism paraphrased the question asked by the queen in the famous fairy-tale:

> Mirror, mirror, on the wall,
> Is not our culture the finest of all?

Others looked there not merely to see the opposite of their own image and essence but to discover in it essential attributes which, in their view, their own culture lacked. In this way, they could discern the absence of attributes and elements of culture that they now felt they needed. Not only did such mirror-inspection create an all-encompassing and stereotypical portrait of the 'other'; very often, as in the subject of the present study, it also obliged Jews to ask new questions about their own identity, to ascribe different emphases and meaning to various fundamental elements in their tradition and their historical experience, to effect radical changes in that tradition, to internalize new criteria and tools for self-judgement. In other words, the meeting with an 'other'—one that has the status of a close and oppositional culture—engenders conflict, while at the same time generating a complex and dialectical process of self-discovery and even of self-rebuilding and of defining the desirable and the actual relationship between these two worlds. It was the cause and the result of the discovery of both the world outside and the 'inner world'.

When Ahad Ha'am (1856–1927), one of the main exponents of the idea of modern Jewish nationalism, approached the task of writing a work of summation of the treasures of Jewish culture that would demonstrate its unity and uniqueness in all spheres, he proposed, among other things, using the method of comparison: 'It will be necessary, in my opinion, to choose the method of comparison, that is, to compare every experience in the life of Jews and Judaism to those experiences close to it in the lives of other peoples, so that all issues may be understood in their general contexts, which are grounded in the nature of man, and Judaism will no longer be an upside-down world that survives by a miracle and has no relation to life at all'.[15] The Jewish scholar Leopold (Yom Tov) Lippmann Zunz (1794–1886), one of the founders of the *Wissenschaft des Judentums* or 'science of Judaism', wrote ironically in May 1836: 'I search desperately to find some positive content for Judaism, in contrast to non-Judaism, in other words, the taste of an apple is nothing other than the opposite of the taste of a non-apple.'[16] Neither Ahad Ha'am nor Leopold Zunz contemplated

---

[15] Ahad Ha'am, 'Al devar otzar hayahadut', 213–14.

[16] Glatzer, *Leopold Zunz*, 85. A 'Western man', educated in Christian and classical traditions, wrote Toynbee, 'came to look upon history as a comparison in two terms' (*A Study of History*, ii. 387).

comparison with the cultures of the Far East or of Islam, but rather with
Western culture and its progenitrix, the culture of classical antiquity. This
was not because they excluded those cultures from humanity as a whole,
but because they, like many of their contemporaries, adopted a distinctly
Eurocentric point of view; for them, Europe represented progress. The
fact that Jews and Judaism existed in the midst of a European society whose
secularism grew ever more intense called for a new approach in studying
the relations between Judaism and modern secular culture, of which the
idea and essence of classical antiquity, which we shall call Greekness, was the
quintessential metaphor. In fact, the antinomy of Judaism and Greekness
was, at one and the same time, a chapter in the old-new Judaeo-Christian
polemics and in the confrontational encounter of Jews with the modern
secular culture around them. This chapter has precursors and parallels in
Hellenistic Alexandria, in Islamic Spain, in Europe of the Renaissance.[17]

The method of comparison clearly requires a knowledge of the culture with which one is drawing a comparison, and a culture capable of
comparison, that is to say not entirely foreign and disparate. However, this
does not necessarily mean that the object of comparison is relativized. The
danger of relativization exists, but the comparison can also strengthen the
absolute value that one assigns oneself. It seems that both Zunz and Ahad
Ha'am were aware of the fact that, in the words of Bakhtin, 'in the realm
of culture, outsidedness is a most powerful factor in understanding. It is
only in the eyes of another culture that foreign culture reveals itself fully
and profoundly . . .'.[18] Although the outside observer may understand or
err, feel identity or identification, owing to his point of view he will necessarily see things differently from someone on the 'inside'. The tension
between the two viewpoints—the inner and the outer—is an inseparable
part of the history of culture.

However, more is involved here than a process of comparison and analogy. It is also a process of shaping a world-picture based on a binary model
in which two opposites confront one another. Thus 'Greece' became the
Gegentyp of Judaism in such a model. A binary model is one of the available options for organizing and constituting a diversified and multifaceted
world. Every such model calls for the choice of an opposite, whether it be

---

[17] The interchanges between Islamic civilization and Judaism are the subject of many studies and lie
outside the scope of this book. On the impact of Persian culture and religion on Judaism see Gafni, *The
Jews of Babylonia*, 149–76.

[18] Bakhtin, 'Response to a Question', 1–7. Christopher Herbert writes: 'In order not to be paralyzed
by these and analogous questions, cultural analysis has no option except to proceed by means of what by
its own axioms it ought not to allow, a process of comparison with some point of reference external to
the "culture" under study' (*Culture and Anomie*, 8).

the sole existing opposite or one selected from among several possibilities; in general, it is not a distant and alien culture that is chosen as the opposite, but rather a familiar culture, often one with which there are common links. The paradox is that there is no point in drawing an antithesis with anything totally different. The antithesis draws its vitality and strength from the fact that by constituting the world according to a binary model one incorporates the power of myth into various aspects of life. The antithesis is powerful because oppositions do exist in various spheres of life, that is, they are not inventions, but really do exist.[19] Greece and the Greeks of classical antiquity became a model of a human *typos*, a prototype, and an ideal type of society and culture; as a result, from a Jewish point of view, they became a counter-type. Obviously, these are generalizations and abstractions, but without them no opposition is possible. In Weber's definition, an ideal type is 'formed by a synthesis of a great many diffuse, discrete, more or less present and occasionally absent concrete individual phenomena, which are arranged according to those one-sided emphasized viewpoints into a unified analytical construct (*Gedankenbild*)'.[20] Thus Greece as an ideal type could present a clear collective human entity and culture, an encompassing entity whose complex traits add up to a coherent whole. Only when plurality is transformed into unity, can this unity serve as an 'opposition', as a mirror, or as the 'other'. The 'Greek soul' and the 'Jewish soul', the 'Greek mentality' and 'Greek spirit', as much as the 'Jewish mentality' and 'Jewish spirit', are but presupposed imaginary abstractions,[21] but they were, as we shall see, very powerful and useful abstractions.

The method of comparison and analogy does not only call for some familiarity with the object of this comparison; it can also attest to the internalization of some of the values of the 'other', culminating in self-change. Again, what von Grunebaum has to say on the phenomena of acculturation in modern Islam is very relevant to modern Judaism: 'Arab writers of more recent days are concerned with fighting Westernization by means of a self-image that is itself very largely a result of acculturation'.[22] And indeed, the impact of the tradition and heritage of classical antiquity and of Hellenism on modern Judaism has two aspects: it induced Jews to fight against Westernization by reinforcing their self-image in order to resist acculturation; and it caused them to internalize 'Greek values' in the course of their struggle. The Jewish historical consciousness underwent a

---

[19] Lotman and Uspenski, 'Binary Models'.
[20] Weber, 'On the Methodology of the Social Sciences', 90.
[21] Momigliano, 'Introduction', 298–9 and see Ch. 7.
[22] Grunebaum, 'Acculturation and Literature', 350–60.

profound change, at the end of which many of its layers are closer to the 'Greek soul' than to the 'Jewish soul'.

An ancient culture and an ancient world can serve as a store of components that one can and should borrow from. Matthew Arnold, for example, dealt 'with specific and well-defined areas of Greek life rather than with general phenomena or an extracted Hellenic essence',[23] while German philosophers believed in the binding powers of Hellenic analogies.[24] The Greek heritage was viewed not only as one *topos* but also as a broad congeries of items from which one could select the components one desired and required. In European literature, Greece and Hellenism (as much as Judaism) are often generalizations and abstractions.[25]

In Jewish historical memory, Hellenism (*tarbut yevanit*) was perceived as the enemy of Judaism, and the Jews' struggle against it in order to hold on to their own tradition and preserve its singularity symbolized the conflict between them and a hostile world. Hence the name given to the enemies of Judaism from within was 'Hellenizers' (*mityavnim*), which became a derogatory term. In many instances, the use of the name 'Greek' (or Hellenizer) in a text was the exploitation of a *topos* intended to serve *ad terrorem*. In modern times Greece became a *topos*, but at the same time it was split up into a set of cultural signals, images, and models; that is, into a set of *topoi*, 'a set of references, a congeries of characteristics that seems to have its origin in a quotation or a fragment of a text or a citation from someone's work'.[26] By *topoi* I refer to a congeries of conventions used in the literature to describe Greece, its inhabitants, and its culture, which became its conventionally accepted characterization. In turn, the concept of 'Greece' became a source of a store of *topoi*. 'Greek' and 'Hellenic' could be applied as labels to things that had no connection with historic

---

[23] Turner, *The Greek Heritage*, 9.

[24] A. Stephens, 'Socrates or Chorus Person?', 259.

[25] Momigliano, 'Time in Ancient Historiography'. He claims that as abstract ideas they are of interest to epistemologists, not to historians, unless their significance is fixed in a concrete time and place. By the same token, one might add that it is the task of the historian to uncover the way in which these abstractions have been understood and used.

[26] Said, *Orientalism*, 177. In Greek rhetoric *koinos topos* (*locus communis*), that is, commonplace, was a source of argument applicable to more than one case; *koinoi topoi* are 'a mass of general, all-purpose ideas which it was very easy to re-use for almost anything and everything' (Marrou, *History of Education in Antiquity*, 191). In the theory of poetics it is a mode of thought according to defined characteristics. If several motifs form a stable configuration, that is, are often repeated in literature, it is designated as a *topos* (Decrot and Todorov, *Encyclopaedic Dictionary of the Science of Language*, 206). *Topos* is 'Any of a stable disposition of motifs that frequently appears in (literary) texts' (Prince, *Dict. of Narratology*, 98). See also E. R. Curtius, *European Literature and the Latin Middle Ages*, 70; *New Princeton Encyclopedia of Poetry and Poetics*, 1294. It is clear then that we can speak of the *topos* of 'Greece', but also describe 'Greece' as a set of *topoi*.

Greece.[27] For example, the general term 'Greek culture', names such as 'Sparta', 'Athens', 'Alexandria', or 'Socrates', and concepts such as 'Greek wisdom', became codewords whose use transmitted a clear message to readers and listeners.[28] The growing familiarity of the educated Jewish public with these terms and concepts clearly made them widespread *topoi* in Hebrew culture as well.

My assertion in this work is that from the late eighteenth century onwards two modes of historical comprehension and insight were created. The first was an idealistic mode, the fruit of a confrontation between two abstract entities—Judaism versus classical Greece (Greekness). Both Greece and 'Judaism' represent 'ideal cultures'. The second was an empirical historical mode, in which Hellenism was perceived as a historical-cultural reality, syncretistic and diversified. Historical research addressed the complex relationship and cultural interferences between the cultural (and political) reality in the Hellenistic era (and later the relations between Jewish philosophy and the heritage of Greek-Hellenistic philosophy). This led to a new understanding of Jewish history and Judaism; Judaism was perceived as a pluralistic, dynamic, even syncretistic, entity. The binary model mainly served the Jewish quest for the essence of the idea of Judaism, while the examination of Jewish history in the Hellenistic-Roman world served mostly those who wished to explore a concrete, empirical-historical model of contacts and influences between Judaism and another culture, with which it conducts a close and extensive historical discourse. These two functions differ in their nature; for this reason, I have made a clear and schematic division in this book between the discussion of the way in which Jewish historical consciousness understood, utilized, and interpreted the opposition between Judaism and the classical world, on the one hand, and the way it interpreted the relationship between it and the Hellenistic culture (including its classical heritage), on the other.

It is quite clear, I believe, that in this study I am singling out one element of the Jewish picture of the past and the way in which it contrasted its world with the world of the Gentiles, particularly from the end of the eighteenth century. In doing so, I believe that, from this special vantage-point, I am casting light on several fundamental issues of intellectual history and the history of Jewish culture in modern times. The emphasis is, therefore, on historical reflections and perceptions and images of the past and their role

---

[27] Jenkyns, *The Victorians and Ancient Greece*, 173. He adds that the 'usefulness of Hellenism as a metaphor reveals its decline as a living and complex force'.

[28] Naturally the term *topos* can also be applied to a stock sentiment, as by Jaeger, *Early Christianity*, 114 n. 3 to 'Disunity and Strife have often destroyed powerful states and great nations' (Clement of Rome, *I Corinth.* 6. 4).

in collective historical memory and in directing the future. It is not my aim
in this book to provide even a brief description of the relationships between
Judaism and paganism in ancient times or between Judaism and Western
civilization in modern times, nor is it a book on Jewish philosophy. My
interest lies in the way in which a historical understanding and historical
images were created, disseminated, and received, becoming conventions in
a culture and helping to shape it. Therefore, I briefly sketch the nature of
the Greek mirror and the Hellenistic mirror, and pass through reference-
points of the relatively slow stages in which the Jews encountered and
became familiar with all levels and facets of Greek culture, accepting them
into their own. In some cases, this was a re-encounter, in others it was
a new appearance. Later in the book I examine how the *maskilim*—the
exponents of the Haskalah—utilized classical antiquity and Hellenism. I
explore in particular the new configuration of the symbol 'Greek wisdom'
as a symbol for enlightenment and the so-called non-Jewish world-views,
as well as of Greek morality (or rather the absence of Greek morality) as
a symbol of decadent secular culture. Then I describe the overall binary
model (or pattern of antinomy) and its repertoire, as well as the manner in
which Jews tried to define the content of their own culture and what it
lacked and to depict a Jewish culture that was whole, complete, original,
and ideal.

The relations between Judaism and Hellenism, as they evolved from the
first appearance of the Hellenistic civilization on the stage of history, are
presented briefly in Part II. The intent is not to describe cultural history 'as
it really was', but rather to focus on the popular images of this relationship
as they developed in historiography and in culture, and on the conclusions
and ideas that can be drawn from them: what can we learn from the
history of the encounter between Judaism and Hellenism, and how did
this encounter and clash become a model of the relations between Judaism
and other cultures in the modern era? This will serve as a background
for an understanding of the phenomenon I shall metaphorically—and
only metaphorically—term the Hellenization of the Jewish world-view, in
particular of secular nationalistic Judaism and of Jewish culture. I am fully
aware that in Hebrew this term has negative overtones, but I am employing
it here to define the process of modernization or of Europeanization
in the last two hundred years, mainly in the realm of modern Jewish
Enlightenment and modern Jewish nationalism—both as an idea and as
a cultural reality. I then focus on the way in which modern Judaism
understood itself as it gazed into the mirror of Hellenism, as well as the
way in which it tried to define itself as a whole and complete culture.

This definition compelled it, as we shall see later, to determine all the components of this cultural congeries as well as to determine its character as a cultural unity. This is the impetus for the intellectual and creative effort to establish the norms of the ideal modern Jewish culture, as well as to create it in reality.

In Part III, I describe the process in which the Jewish world-view and culture absorbed and internalized values and items from 'the outside', which were identified by Jewish writers as 'Greek' and whose absorption determined and shaped the character of the Jewish intellectual world— particularly its modern national existence—and the nature of Jewish culture as a reality.[29]

My historical point of departure is the period of the Haskalah and the *maskilim* (most of them *Gebildete* and not *Gelehrte*,[30] men of letters, not scholars). This is because the *maskilim* and the Haskalah mark a turning-point in Jewish history. In our context, they were the first to become more deeply acquainted with the classical heritage and its images; it was they who conducted a new discourse with the contemporary European culture, with the medieval Jewish philosophical tradition, and with the talmudic (and rabbinical) tradition. They—especially the early generation—tried their best to establish an accord between the different Jewish heritages and the new trends in European intellectual and cultural life. In their literature, one can find most of the seeds and options of the future, sometimes even contradictory developments.[31]

The second group of men of letters whose writings I used is that of the spokesmen of the modern Jewish nationalism that developed from the 1870s. Although the national ideology absorbed a great many of the values of the Haskalah, it differs from it fundamentally. While the moderate *maskilim* tried to initiate some means to control and regulate the processes of Jewish acculturation into Gentile society, in order to establish a cultural coexistence, and the radical *maskilim* encouraged profound acculturation, and even assimilation, the aim of the national movement was to achieve

---

[29] It turns out that in this instance I was following Momigliano's words (which I read only after writing this book): 'If Judaism is to be appreciated by restoring [it] to categories drawn from a different system of thought, it is inevitable that one ends up realizing that its truth lies in the thought that provides the criterion for such appreciation' ('An Apology of Judaism', 66).

[30] Dülmen, *Die Gesellschaft der Aufklärer*.

[31] Among the many studies on the history of the Haskalah movement in western and eastern Europe see: Barzilay, 'The Italian and Berlin Haskalah'; Etkes, *The East European Jewish Enlightenment* (with an annotated bibliography, 456–7); Frankel, *Prophecy and Politics*; Feiner, 'Isaac Euchel'; id., *Haskalah and History*; J. Katz, *Tradition and Crisis*; M. Levin, *Social and Economic Values*; Lowenstein, *The Berlin Jewish Community*; Miron, *When Loners Come Together*; Pelli, *The Age of Haskalah*; id., *Struggle for Change*; Raisin, *The Haskalah Movement in Russia*; Sorkin, *The Transformation of German Jewry*; U. Shavit, 'What is Haskalah?'; Werses, *Trends and Forms in Haskalah Literature*.

the modernization of Judaism by absorbing Western values and making them an integral part of the national culture. For this purpose, it also had to search through the Jewish historical tradition to find values corresponding to modern national values, and to infuse them with new content and new meaning. As a national ideology, it employed a rhetoric that underscored the national culture's singularity and uniqueness which eschews foreign influence. But in fact its aim was to prevent the assimilation of Jews into Western society, by incorporating Western values into the new Judaism.

My choice of texts or writers was not necessarily based on their importance or influence, but on the fact that they reflect representative views. It may be argued that my choice of authors was fortuitous and that I have cited secondary and marginal authors, rather than renowned philosophers. That claim would have carried some weight had this book been a history of Jewish philosophy. In fact, however, it addresses what is known as 'public thought' and public consciousness; in this context, secondary authors and texts are no less important—perhaps even more so—than great philosophers. It is 'secondary texts' that disseminate opinions and values to the public at large, and the secondary writer in the domain of philosophy, history, and the like becomes the mediator between philosophical thought and the general public; he actively participates in creating a climate of ideas and a collective consciousness and in imparting values, images, and concepts to that public.[32] What Paul Hazard wrote on the climate of ideas in eighteenth-century Europe fits as a description of Jewish intellectual history during the nineteenth century: 'Ideas that had been slowly maturing out of sight suddenly burst forth into the light of day; theories that had hitherto been confined to an exclusive élite became the property of the many.'[33]

This book, then, deals with the perception and reception of classical Greece and Hellenism (meaning Hellenistic civilization) in and by modern culture. Although in literature the boundaries between these two are frequently blurred, since they are in any case separated by very fine lines, it is worth while explaining the distinction made between them in the writings I deal with here.

Those who spoke of classical antiquity, or of the Hellenes and Greekness (or *Griechentum*, in German), in contrast to Judaism, were generally referring to what they described as the culture of classical Greece. And by classical Greece, they meant the totality of the Greek cultural heritage as it took shape from its inception until the time of Alexander the Great.

---

[32] Darnton, 'The Social History of Ideas'; Walicki, *The Slavophile Controversy*, 1–15.
[33] Hazard, *European Thought*, p. xvii.

Obviously they knew that this heritage was never lost and that sections of it had become an indivisible part of the heritage of the generations that followed. However, in speaking of classical antiquity, they were also referring to a historical period and its heritage. They believed the classical world was a different historical entity from the world that followed it. More precisely, they had in mind the culture of Athens at its zenith during the fifth century BC. Of course, they were aware of the existence of Greece outside Athens, but Athens at its pinnacle symbolized the classical world. In the Bible (Gen. 10: 12), Javan is the son of Japheth[34] and the grandson of Noah. This name appears in Assyrian sources as early as the eighth century BC, and refers to the population of *Iōnes* which settled in Asia Minor, and later on to the Greeks of Hellas.[35] According to Josephus, Javan was the son of Japheth and the father of all the Ionians and the Hellenes (*Antiquities*, i. 124). The Sages spoke about Javan or the kingdom of Javan (*malkhut Yavan*), referring to the Hellenistic kingdoms,[36] but they never used the term 'Hellenism', speaking instead of 'Greek wisdom', by which they meant both classical Greek and Hellenistic philosophy (and science). Hence when I use terms such as 'Greek wisdom' or 'Greek ethics', I shall do so in the framework of the discussion about the attitude of the Jews towards the classical heritage.

In precisely the same way, the distinction between Judaism and Hebraism is very obscure and susceptible to various interpretations. Those who spoke of Hebraism (in English) were frequently referring only to the Judaism of the biblical period, while Judaism was the term used for the Second Temple period and thereafter. In many instances, there is scarcely any discrimination drawn in European texts between the various phases of the development of Judaism. Even those who knew that Judaism was not a uniform and one-dimensional religio-cultural entity presented it schematically, counterpoising it with the world of the 'other'. The term 'Hebraism', then, could relate to a special, defined period in Jewish history, or could simply be identical with Judaism in general. In this book, I shall use the adjective 'Jewish' and the noun 'Judaism', rather than 'Hebrew' and 'Hebraism' (other than in quoted material). Hebrew culture is defined as that culture which is written in the Hebrew language

---

[34] On the speculative connection between the Titan Iapetos and the biblical Japheth see J. P. Brown, *Israel and Hellas*, 82–3.

[35] The Sanskrit transcription is *yavana*, the name applied in Indian works to Ionians or Greeks and foreigners generally (McCrindle, *The Invasion of India*, 122 n. 1).

[36] Cf. Gen. Rabbah 2: 4 (ed. Theodor–Albeck, 16): 'And darkness symbolizes Greece, which darkened the eyes of Israel with its decrees.'

or that which developed in the framework of the secular Jewish national movement.[37]

In English, the term 'Hellenism' (derived from Hellenes, the name given from the fifth century BC to the Greek-speaking world, from Sicily to the Black Sea) denotes both Greek culture and the culture of the Hellenistic era. Hence some scholars prefer to use 'classical antiquity' or 'Greekness' to describe the world that existed prior to the conquest of Alexander the Great. In this study 'Hellenism' denotes the civilization created in the East following the conquests of Alexander the Great, a period which was perceived as a new historical era. The classical heritage persisted in the Hellenistic and Roman periods, and some parts of it never disappeared even after the demise of the ancient world. However, the Hellenistic period (336–31 BC), which in certain cultural aspects continued until the fall of the Western Empire, was carried on in the East in the Byzantine Empire until its overthrow in AD 1453.[38] In medieval Muslim (and Jewish) civilization, the cultural heritage of Greece consisted in the various philosophical and scientific traditions as they developed from classical Greece until the demise of pagan philosophy, no distinction being drawn between the different stages of their development.

The term 'Hellēnistai' is derived from the verb *hellēnizō* ('to speak Greek'); in the New Testament it is used for the Greek-speaking element among the Jews, but implies an accommodation to pagan ways of thought and conduct. It sometimes coexists with a textual variant 'Hellenes', which however generally bears the sense 'pagans', the Greeks being in both Jewish and Christian eyes the pagans *par excellence*; this sense is adopted by the Church Fathers. Under the pagan Emperor Julian 'Hellenism' was the pagan religion, Hellenists its adherents; so intimately in Julian's view

[37] Y. Shavit, *The New Hebrew Nation*, 1–20. In late antiquity *Hebraïsmos* and *Ioudaïsmos* became identical. Eusebius described Philo as a 'Hebrew' (*Ecclesiastical History*, ii. 4. 2); the Emperor Julian in *Against the Galilaeans* employs the terms *Ioudaioi* and *Hebraioi* interchangeably: 'It is worth while to recall in a few words whence and how we first arrive at a conception of God; next to compare what is said about the divine among the Hellenes and Hebrews; and finally of those who are neither Hellenes nor Jews' (42 E, trans. W. C. Wright, iii. 319, 321). See also Isaac, 'Ethnic Groups in Judaea', 204–7.

[38] After 31 BC (the battle of Actium), Hellenism indicates not a political entity but the cultural tradition of the Greek-speaking part of the Roman Empire and Greek cultural traits in its other parts, mainly Rome. See Burstein, 'The Greek Tradition'; Jones, 'Graecia Capta'; Wilson, *Scholars of Byzantium*; Bolgar, *The Classical Heritage*, 59–90. Werner Jaeger writes, in response to Hermann Diels and Wilamowitz: '. . . . I have also spent a whole life on the study of Christian tradition, especially in its ancient Greek and Roman phase. I therefore am deeply impressed by the continuity of the fundamental forms of thought and expression which triumphantly bridges the chasm between these antithetic periods of the human mind and integrates them into one universal civilization' (*Theology of Early Greek Philosophers*, 9). For different views on the nature of the continuity of the Greek and Hellenistic cultural legacy in the Islamic civilization, see the illuminating survey by Kraemer, *Humanism in the Renaissance of Islam*, 135–64.

was it connected with classical culture that Christians were forbidden to teach Greek literature.[39] It was the German historian Johann Gustav Droysen who turned 'Hellenism' into a signifier of the era that began with Alexander the Great's conquest of the East, for the first time in a letter written in 1831, and then in his book *Geschichte des Hellenismus* (1836–43). The opening sentence of his book about Alexander, *Geschichte Alexanders des Großen* (1833), states: 'Der Name Alexander bezeichnet das Ende einer Weltepoche, den Anfang einer neuen' ('The name Alexander denotes the end of one historical era and the beginning of a new era').[40] It refers mainly to a *kulturelles Reichtum*, a cultural entity, rather than to a political entity. Usually the term 'Hellenism', from the point of view of Greek history, applies to the period between Alexander and Augustus, but from the standpoint of cultural history and the people affected by the Greek heritage, it extended well down to the seventh century AD, when the study of Greek finally had come to an end in Latin Europe.[41]

[39] On the history of the names Hellas and Hellene see Finley, *The Legacy of Greece*, 1–9; Herzfeld, *Ours Once More*, 3–5, 124–8. Hellene was conceived of as a common outlook; a consciousness of membership in a single body of Hellenes (Thucydides, *Histories*, 1. 3). In the East the Christian word for non-Christian was 'Hellene' (H. Chadwick, *The Early Church*, 17); indeed, for Christians the word 'came exclusively to mean, as it did in the Jewish tradition, "pagan"' (Rawson, *The Spartan Tradition*, 118). For Julian see Athanassiadi-Fowden, esp. 1–12; Pelikan, *Christianity and Classical Culture*, 12.

[40] *Geschichte Alexanders*, 3; Avi-Yonah, *Hellenism and the East*, 2. J. Burckhardt, *Griechische Kulturgeschichte*, iv. 348, defines Hellenism as 'die große Verwandlung des Hellenentums aus einer politischen in eine Kulturpotenz'. Droysen, writes Jaeger, 'was motivated . . . by his Christian faith and dogma, because he had perceived that without this postclassical evolution of Greek culture the rise of a Christian world-religion would have been impossible' (*Early Christianity*, 5). See also Hengel, *Judaism and Hellenism*, 1–5, and Schneider, *Kulturgeschichte des Hellenismus*, i. 2, and Momigliano, 'Droysen between Greeks and Jews', 309–10. Momigliano himself saw the Hellenic civilization (and the Hellenic atmosphere) as the place where 'the Latins and the Jews acquired the Greek language, assimilated Greek ideas, and questioned the Greek way of life. But the fusion of Greek, Latin, and Jewish tradition is Christian' ('The Fault of the Greeks', 17). See more on this subject in Ch. 9.

[41] Goitein, 'The Intermediate Civilization', 56. On the term in the Jewish sources see Ch. 9.

PART I

THE FIRST MIRROR

May the beauty of Japheth dwell in the tents of Shem.
BABYLONIAN TALMUD, *Megillah*, 9b

The history of the Jews shows what God does for men;
the history of Greece shows what man does for himself.
ERNEST RENAN

Judah is the heart of humanity, just as Greece is the mind of humanity.
ÉTIENNE VACHEROT,
cited in Moses Hess, 'Die drei großen mittelländischen
Völker und das Christentum' (1865)

The Greek tradition is not Greek civilization;
it is man's interpretation of the civilization.
GEORGE BOAS, *The Greek Tradition*

I am the Jew: your eternal adversary!
Neither the breadth of the heavens nor the vastness of the plain
can span the rift that separates the legacy
of my forebears from the religion of your worshippers.
SAUL TCHERNICHOWSKY, 'Lenokhach pesel Apollo'
('In Front of the Statue of Apollo') (1899)

I

WAKING THE DEAD—GREECE AS AN IDEAL AND AN EXEMPLAR

The real Hellenism is more important to me than the entire Orient.

JULIUS WELLHAUSEN to Theodor Nöldeke

Schöne Welt, wo bist du? kehre wieder,
Holdes Blütenalter der Natur!
Ach! nur in dem Feenland der Lieder
Lebt noch deine goldne Spur.
Ausgestorben trauert das Gefilde,
Keine Gottheit zeigt sich meinem Blick,
Ach! von jenen lebenwarmen Bilde
Blieb nur das Gerippe mir zurück.

FRIEDRICH SCHILLER, 'Die Götter Griechenlandes'[1]

O ye vain false gods of Hellas,
Ye are silent ever more!

Get to dust, as common mortals,
By a common doom and track!
Let no Schiller from the portals
Of that Hades, call you back . . .

ELIZABETH BARRETT BROWNING,
'The Dead Pan'

Das sind sie selber, die Götter von Hellas,
Die einst so freudig die Welt beherrschten,
Doch jetzt, verdrängt und verstorben,
Als ungeheure Gespenster dahinziehn
Am mitternächtlichen Himmel.

HEINRICH HEINE, 'Die Götter Griechenlands'[2]

A new spirit arose in the land of Ashkenaz . . . This spirit was the
Greek spirit, which they aroused and clung to with all their might, for it
was a smiting rod for Catholicism and the spirit of polarity that their
priests spread throughout the land . . .   PERETZ SMOLENSKIN, 'Et lata'at'

---

[1] 'Beauteous World, where art thou gone? Oh, thou | Nature's blooming youth, return once more! |
Ah, but in Song's fairy region now | Lives thy fabled trace so dear of yore! | Cold and perished sorrow
now the plains, | Not one Godhead greets my longing sight; | Ach, the shadow only now remains | Of
your living image bright!' (trans. Bowring, 74).

[2] 'It is they themselves, the gods of Hellas, | who once so joyously ruled the world, | but now, expelled
and extinct, | they move across the midnight | as giant ghosts' (trans. P. Branscombe).

GREECE AND GREEKS AS SYMBOLS OF PERFECTION

WHY GREECE?

When asked why he went to the trouble of digging up inscriptions and coins, the first Renaissance archaeologist, Cyriac of Ancona (*c.*1391–1450), replied: 'To waken the dead.'[3] 'Homines maxime homines' ('men who are in the fullest sense men') was how the younger Pliny described the Greeks of Greece proper (*Epistulae*, viii. 24. 2), and Cicero wrote with a devotee's admiration: 'Athens, the source whence civilization, knowledge, religion, agriculture, justice, and law are thought to have sprung and spread into all lands' (*Pro Flacco*, 62).[4] Generations later this admirable land and those imaginary people of the distant past rose fom the dead to become a symbol of human and 'almost godlike' perfection. Greece was to wake from the dead and was seen not as a mother who had completed her task but as one who could still sustain and nurture her children's children as well.

Wake from the dead, yes, since even if the pagan gods were always alive in European culture during the Middle Ages, Europe of the Renaissance and after was fully aware of the historical distance which separated her from classical antiquity.[5] For that reason it was not enough to waken the dead; they had to be given a new life and a new vitality.

There was no culture more esteemed by Europe than that of Greece. The *Idealbild* of Greece was that of an Arcadian vision, a 'heavenly city', a shimmering fantasy on the horizon,[6] a paradise lost;[7] in the nineteenth century it became a cult of romantic passion, 'since the image of the beloved one is a creation of the lover'.[8] 'In all history there is no analogy of one Culture making a passionate cult of the memory of another', wrote Oswald Spengler in *Der Untergang des Abendlandes*.[9] In Germany this Greece ruled over philosophy, literature, and art. Friedrich Schiller

---

[3] Burckhardt, *The Civilization of the Renaissance*, i. 128; see also Kent-Hild, 'Archaeology and the Idea of Classical Antiquity'.

[4] In his essay 'On the Fortune of the Romans' Plutarch wrote of Athens: 'This city, as we all know, has been the mother and kindly nurse of many other arts, some of which she was the first to discover and reveal, while to others she gave added strength and honour and embellishment' (§2, *Moralia* 345 F, trans. Babbitt). On Roman ambivalence towards Greece see Gruen, *Hellenistic World*, 250–66.

[5] Seznec, *The Survival of the Pagan Gods*, 322.

[6] Jenkyns, *The Victorians and Ancient Greece*, 13. See also Turner, 'Why the Greeks and not the Romans?'; Z. Yavetz, 'Why Rome?'.

[7] Montesquieu writes with sharp irony on this nostalgia for a 'promised land' and a 'golden age' which are always in another place, another time: 'It is known that Hesperia, the ideal country that was so famous among the ancients, was originally Greece, which its neighbours regarded as an abode of bliss. The Greeks, failing to find this happy land in their own country, went to look for it in Italy . . .' (*Persian Letters*, no. 131, p. 234).

[8] Muller, 'The Romantic Glory', 100.

[9] Spengler, *The Decline of the West*, 30 (*Der Untergang des Abendlandes*, 41).

responded in derisive verses to the excessive Hellenic cult of the Romantic movement: 'Hardly has the cold fever of *Gallomania* left us | Then there breaks out a burning fever, *Greekomania* (*Gräkomanie*).'[10] It was, according to Elizabeth M. Butler, a tyranny: the 'tyranny of Greece over Germany'. The changes that took place in its representations were manifestations of the changing mood in the spirit of Germany itself—from Apollonian classicism to Romanticism and to the obscure, neo-pagan, daemonic Orphism or Dionysian mysticism.[11] According to Martin Bernal (the author of a highly critical and provocative study on the influence of the Indo-European myth on the study of ancient antiquity), it was a Hellenic obsession: *Hellenomania*.[12] Its fruits were the speculative theories that German scholars (for the most part) spun around the history of Greece (in Bernal's words, the 'tyranny of Germany over Greece') in order to hide its 'Eastern roots'.

So, why Greece? Because for the Enlightenment 'the primacy of Greece meant the primacy of philosophy',[13] and because it was perceived by the New Humanism as an entity that steps out of the circle of history: 'Even if their destinies belong to the general chain of events, yet in this respect they matter least to us', wrote the great statesman and philologist Wilhelm von Humboldt (1767–1835), in his essay *Über das Studium des Altertums und des Griechischen inbesondere* (1793). 'We fail entirely to recognize our relationship to them if we dare to apply the standards to them which we apply to the rest of world history. Knowledge of the Greeks is not merely pleasant, useful or necessary to us—no. In the Greeks alone we find the ideal of what we should like to be . . .'.[14] The Antique is classic, so Goethe told his faithful companion Eckermann, 'not because it is old; but because it is strong, fresh, joyous and healthy.'[15] Classicism, in Grunebaum's interpretation, 'discovers in the chosen past an absolute model, and implies that this model must be emulated and recovered'. The

[10] B. Feldman and Richardson, *The Rise of Modern Mythology*, 302. What he really meant by *Greekomania* was *Mythomania*. In 1805 he wrote to Goethe that 'only as a past must antiquity appear to us' (cit. Behler, 'The Force of Classical Greece', 127). Of course, especially in Protestant countries, the Bible also played a part: the relation between the Bible and Homer in 19th-c. discourse merits a study of its own.

[11] Butler, *The Tyranny of Greece*; Feire, 'The Greek Tradition in Germany'; Highet, *The Classical Tradition*, 367–90; Behler, 'The Force of Classical Greece', 127.

[12] Bernal, *Black Athena*, i. 280–336.

[13] Gay, *The Rise of Modern Paganism*, 72.

[14] In Cowan, *An Anthology of the Writings of W. von Humboldt*, 79. He even went so far as to claim that slavery was among the external circumstances which favoured human development in Greece (Vogt, *Ancient Slavery*, 171).

[15] Goethe, *Conversations with Eckermann*, 305. Trevelyan commented that 'Had he [Goethe] known the Greeks better, they might have lost half their power over him': *Goethe and the Greeks*, 29; cf. id., *The Popular Background to Goethe's Hellenism*.

classical tradition could, for some, justify stability, while for others it could justify change. Indeed, 'Nostalgia is the most sophistic, most deceptive form regression can take',[16] but it is not only a form of regression but also a way, often a naïve way, to criticize the present and envisage the future. 'To the rising post-Renaissance West the Greeks were often but a mirror in which contemporary ideals of beauty and freedom, of *humanitas* and naturalness, were made to shine.'[17] Ancient Greece, writes Richard Jenkyns, 'preoccupied many of the finest minds of the last century and thus directly and indirectly it became a pervasive influence, reaching even the edges of popular culture'.[18] 'Classical literature—philosophy, mythology and history—' writes Frank M. Turner 'provided a means for achieving self-knowledge and cultural self-confidence.'[19]

Indeed, Hellenomania, or Greekomania, it was; an obsession, but an obsession with a noble cause. The imaginary Greece and Greeks were Europe's longed-for image, with which it conducted a profound, fervent, incisive, and ramified discourse. This Greece, Spengler wrote, was a mere phantom, an idol, composed by belated Romantics who lost themselves in the cloudy realms of an antiquity ('Sie verlieren sich in den Wolkenregionen eines Altertums') that is really no more than the image of their own sensibility in a philological mirror.[20] But although the Greece that was born of and nourished by obsession was but a fictitious entity, a creature of the imagination, its images played a prominent part in shaping the culture of modern Europe; the process of forming these images and their functions aptly reflects the character and trends of that culture. Primarily, 'Greece' signifies the intense desire to seek the origin and paradigm of a perfect and complete secular world. Its creation was the result of a poignant yearning that grew out of the recognition of a lack, and out of an aspiration for redemption. The ideal of ancient Greece was a central part of the different ideological, political, and aesthetic streams and sub-streams which were active in the spirit of Europe of the time. It was not only the philosophical heritage of classical antiquity that inspired the intellectual life of Europe; it was classical antiquity whole and entire, as a living entity. Different cultural and social trends gazed at the Greek mirror in order to understand their

---

[16] Gay, *The Science of Freedom*, 92.

[17] Grunebaum, 'The Concept of Cultural Classicism', 121.

[18] Jenkyns, *The Victorians and Ancient Greece*, p. vi.

[19] Turner, *The Greek Heritage*, p. xii.

[20] *The Decline*, 28 (*Der Untergang*, 38). Spengler notes that the image of classical Greece is based on a very small group of Greek works and the rest, including the whole wealth of Hellenistic literature, was rejected and had been almost lost. On the different approaches of Nietzsche and Burckhardt see Salin, *Jacob Burckhardt und Nietzsche*.

nature and essence, to be inspired, to seek a model, whether positive or negative. The image of Greece was thus interwoven into the ideological reactions and responses to industrialization, nationalism, mass society, and secularization. It could serve both liberals and conservatives, a longing for aesthetic values, resistance to modern alienation, and yearning for the imagined 'natural man' and 'natural society'. In the Greek mirror one saw a lost golden age, a spiritual anchor, or a warning and an omen.

The humanist Cardinal Aeneas Sylvius Piccolomini wrote despairingly to Pope Nicholas V in July 1453, after the fall of Constantinople: 'How many names of mighty men will perish! It is a second death to Homer and Plato. The fount of the Muses is dried up for evermore.' Precious manuscripts were saved and Homer and Plato were 'disinterred for evermore'.[21] From the Renaissance onwards, antiquity was reborn and became a Golden Age. Many agents were actively involved in shaping the image of the almost 'godlike' Greece and in disseminating Greek heritage and its ideals: scholars and laymen, craftsmen and artisans, schools and textbooks, poetry and prose and the arts; philology and *Altertumswissenschaft*, ideology and travelogues, song and drama, paintings, sculpture, translations of classical literature, and publications of scientific books and manuscripts.[22] As a result of the advent of printing and engraving the 'antique has been continuously with us',[23] and this was true mainly after the heritage of Greece 'crossed the Alps' during the Renaissance period and later.[24] Classical Greek was now rediscovered,[25] and numerous classical literary works of every kind were

---

[21] Eisenstein, *The Printing Revolution*, 125–6.

[22] Among the many studies on this subject see Bolgar, *The Classical Heritage*; id. (ed.), *Classical Influences, 500–1500*; id. (ed.), *Classical Influences, 1500–1700*; Bowen, 'Education, Ideology and the Ruling Class'; M. L. Clarke, *Classical Education*; *Graecogermania 1469–1523*; Griffith, 'Classical Greece and the Italian Renaissance'; Gay, *The Rise of Modern Paganism*, 73–94; Haskins, *The Renaissance of the Twelfth Century*; Highet, *The Classical Tradition*; Kristeller, *Renaissance Thought*; Langlois, *The Persistent Voice*; O'Leary, *How Greek Science Passed to the Arabs*; Peters, *Aristotle and the Arabs*; Prescott, 'The Greek Tradition in the Hellenistic Age'; Riche, *Education and Culture*; Sandys, *A History of Classical Scholarship*; Stephens, *The Italian Renaissance*, 151–75; Thompson, *A History of Historical Writing*; Tsigakou, *The Rediscovery of Greece*; Walzer, *Greek into Arabic*; Wilamowitz, *History of Classical Scholarship*; Wilson, *From Byzantium to Italy*. On the study of Homer see Spiegel, *Homer*, 435–40.

[23] Eisenstein, *The Printing Revolution*, 122.

[24] Toynbee, *A Study of History*, ii. 267.

[25] See Highet, *The Classical Tradition*, 1–21. On Greek manuscripts in Italy during the 15th c. and the translations of the Greek and Roman classical authors before 1600 see Apps. I–II in Bolgar, *The Classical Heritage*, 455–541. As Athanassiadi-Fowden reminds us, the fact that in Byzantium many classical Greek manuscripts were preserved, crucial as it was for the Greek revival in the Muslim Middle Ages and in the European Renaissance, even that Hellenism 'lived through Byzantium as a hidden underground current' (*Julian and Hellenism*, 11), should not banish from our minds the armies of 'imbecile monks' who 'still in the eleventh century were running throughout Greece destroying whatever remained of the ancient temples' (ibid. 4 n. 9).

translated into different European languages.[26] In a mighty outpouring, the past came to life again, and took part in the process in which 'Europe' itself came into existence not as a religious Christian identity but as a 'European way of life' and explored its roots in the classical world.[27] Classical antiquity and paganism became contributory factors in Europe's transformation. 'What distinguishes the Renaissance from the Middle Ages in the field of Greek studies is a shift of interest from scientific (or what was held to be scientific) knowledge to literature, morality, and politics.'[28] The remembrance of Greece was infused into the collective memory and into diverse strata of culture, and Greece became a system of enduring and popular signs and symbols. 'Jupiter had returned in triumph to the realms of the most Christian kings of Europe',[29] and soon enough pagan deities appeared everywhere, in middle-class homes and in exterior decorations.

Some scholars, we have just seen, claim that much of the Greek legacy had been made available to the educated public during the Renaissance,[30] and the classical heritage had passed into the common stock of European thought. Others argue that 'Only since the late eighteenth century did ancient Greece commence on a significant scale',[31] and only then 'Greek literature for the first time re-entered the blood stream of European Civilization in an undiluted form.' Therefore the eighteenth century marks the beginning of a new era.[32] Not only literature: historical and factual knowledge increased; genuine Greek history burst through the mists of legend and fragmentary information. Of course, there had been previous revivals, but only then and above all during the nineteenth century did comprehensive histories of Europe become available to readers in the various European languages, when a veritable flood of books and articles

[26] Highet, *The Classical Tradition*, 104–26.

[27] On the emergence of the idea of Europe see Hay, *Europe: The Emergence of an Idea*; Hazard, *European Thought*, 438–68.

[28] Bolgar, 'The Greek Legacy', 452.

[29] Manuel, *The Eighteenth Century*, 3.

[30] Wilson, *From Byzantium*, 157; Bolgar, *The Classical Heritage*, 265–301, esp. 301: 'At the end of the fourteenth century, the cultural tradition of the West bore the recognisable imprint of the Middle Ages. By the end of the sixteenth, the medieval elements had been replaced by others drawn from the Graeco-Roman heritage . . .'.

[31] Turner, *The Greek Heritage*, p. xii.

[32] Lloyd-Jones, *Blood for the Ghosts*, 168–9. Cf. Bolgar, 'Greek Legacy', 462: 'In the field of Greek studies, the eighteenth century marks the beginning of a new era. The discovery of fresh information in classical sources was now no longer an essential precondition of cultural advance. The philosophical and scientific concepts, the literary, mathematical, and technological procedures that Athens, Alexandria, and Byzantium could readily contribute, had been absorbed into the European traditions, and an impressive superstructure of new ideas and techniques was rising on the foundation antiquity had supplied. In this changed situation, Greece came to be seen as a world remote from ours, whose virtues constituted a challenge to the imperfections of the present.'

were printed, aimed at reconstructing its chronicles. As Manuel notes, it was only during the course of the eighteenth century that the voluminous literary heritage from antiquity on the nature of the gods was made more accessible to gentlemanly readers who had an interest in philosophy but little Latin and less Greek, by a steady outpouring of new translations from the classics.[33] 'Greek, sir,' said Dr Johnson in 1781, 'is like lace: every man gets as much of it as he can', and 'Classical quotation is the *parole* of literary men all over the world.'[34] Antiquity became a source of 'prescriptive values and of illustrative moral and political allusions',[35] but it was more than a store of examples and quotations; it was a model of perfect human existence.

Was not this Greece a benevolent ghost that hovered over the mind of Europe; or was it rather a burden, a ghostlike and oppressive shadow?

In the eyes of the 'moderns', classical antiquity was but a burden, not a help. The debate on the significance of the classical past was opened when the French scholar Charles Perrault (1628–1703) published his poem *Le Siècle de Louis le Grand* (1687) and his *Parallèle des Anciens et des Modernes* (1688–96), reviving the controversy between antiquity (Graeco-Roman heritage) and modernity (*la querelle des anciens et des modernes*).[36] He was followed by Fontenelle's *Dialogues des morts* (1683) and *Digression sur les Anciens et les Modernes* (1688), William Temple's *Essay on Ancient and Modern Learning* (1690), and many others. Those who initiated the idea of 'progress' in the seventeenth and eighteenth centuries viewed the Renaissance 'worship of the ancients' as an obstacle to progress and modernity. The ancient past is not an ideal, they argued; it is a burden that one must cast off. Maturity learns no lessons from infancy: so argued Francis Bacon in his *Novum Organum* (1620), which represents the 'moderns' in its dispute with

---

[33] Manuel, *The Eighteenth Century*, 8.

[34] *Boswell's Life of Johnson*, ed. G. B. Hill and L. F. Powell, iv (Oxford, 1934), 23, 102; cf. Bolgar, 'The Greek Legacy'; Gay, *The Rise of Modern Paganism*, 39.

[35] Turner, *The Greek Heritage*, 4.

[36] Bury, *The Idea of Progress*, 76–126; Highet, *The Classical Tradition*, 261–88; Cherniss, 'Ancient as Authority'; Gay, *The Rise of Modern Paganism*, 279–321. See also Jonathan Swift's satire: *Full and True Account of the Battle fought . . . between the Ancient and the Modern Books*: 'The Army of the Antients was much fewer in Number: Homer led the Horse, Pindar the Light-Horse, Euclid was chief Engineer . . .' (ed. Herbert Davis with *A Tale of a Tub*, Oxford, 1967, 169; cf. Toynbee, *A Study of History*, 281–2). The French debate over the merits of Homer began after the appearance of the new translation by Antoine de La Motte Houdar (1713), accompanied by a *Discours sur Homère*. Montesquieu, in *Persian Letters*, no. 36 (pp. 89–90), ridicules the argument between the 'new' and the 'ancient': 'Everyone wanted to decide on his rating' (of an 'old Greek poet', sc. Homer). See too Mill, *Spirit of the Age*, 47. On the debate about Homer see Bolgar, 'The Greek Legacy', 462–3. Also see Gay, *The Rise of Modern Paganism*, 279–321; Barash, 'The System of Arts', 74–5. For the Jewish version of this dispute see Yuval, '"Rishonim" and "Aharonim"', and for the Russian version see Walicki, *The Slavophile Controversy*, 22–63.

the 'ancients', and the supremacy of progress over the cyclical or nostalgic conception of the ritual of the ancients. The Greeks, after all, he wrote, lived in the youth of the world, therefore people in the new era are wiser, for they have the added experience of all the generations.[37] They (the ancients) 'flew at once to the most general conclusions'.[38] Others held the view that the ancient world was not nearly as wise, happy, and glorious as their own world, and even a Romantic like J. G. Herder (1744–1803) was not convinced that the Greek age was any better, and certainly was not of the view that one should, or could, return to it.[39] One must, however, remember that the main point of the dispute was about the development of literature, art, and science, rather than of ethics or the connection between social morals and happiness on the one hand and the development of science (civilization) on the other. In the eighteenth and nineteenth centuries, this issue became a key theme, once progress and happiness—in relation to the morality of society and the individual—became the central issue.[40]

Nevertheless, the projected pictures of future paradise and redemption were drawn in clearer and more perceptible lines, while in the background, the vision—or the fantasy—was usually a picture of the future as it had already taken place in the past. Therefore this distant historical past was vital. 'It needed a guide, and found one in the ancient civilization, with its wealth of truth and knowledge in every spiritual interest', wrote the great Swiss historian of culture and founder of the modern history of art,

---

[37] Becker, *The Heavenly City*, 130–5.

[38] P. Urbach, *Francis Bacon's Philosophy of Science*, 36.

[39] Lovejoy, 'Herder and the Enlightenment', 166–82. See too Kapitaza, *Ein bürgerlicher Krieg*. Gay writes that the philosophers of the Enlightenment 'appealed from Christianity to classical thought and then, having made their polemical point, they mitigated their classicism with modern confidence in this world' (*The Science of Freedom*, 87). The German *Aufklärer*, however, were fully aware that those who 'became enlightened by the classics became atheists, if not real heathens', and spent 'considerable time combating anti-Christian assumptions' (Reill, *The German Enlightenment*, 174–5). Amos Funkenstein rejects Gay's reinterpretation of the Enlightenment and claims that its ties to the Christian past overshadowed all traces of the spirit of ancient antiquity: 'The Enlightenment was, it seems to me, through and through a post-Christian phenomenon.' One of the main Christian features he finds in the Enlightenment is its ideal of missionary and pedagogical-social motives, which were taken from Christianity ('The Threshold of Modernity', 235). Indeed, it was a post-Christian phenomenon, but it took its missionary spirit from the Greek and Hellenistic belief in the role of *paideia* (which was taken by Christianity from 'pagan' humanism). It did not offer redemption through the acceptance of a religious dogma; instead it proposed enrichment of the mind and creation of a new man through education and the acquisition of knowledge. The Enlightenment, it seems to me, was a return to the classical notion of *paideia* and *humanitas*. (On the Muslim case see Kraemer, *Humanism in the Renaissance of Islam*, 155–6.)

[40] The historians of the *Aufklärung* argued that classical literature improved only forms of expression, but failed to generate the visceral reaction of great moral impulses (Reill, *The German Enlightenment*, 175).

Jacob Burckhardt (1818–97), in his *Die Kultur der Renaissance in Italien*. 'But culture, as soon as it freed itself from the fantastic bonds of the Middle Ages, could not at once and without help find its way to an understanding of the physical and intellectual world.'[41] The expectation was to find in classical antiquity essential truths in all regions of the spirit: a complete living model of perfect humanity (*Humanität*). The ability of the 'new world' to rekindle for itself the wisdom of the ancients, and to transform it into a living and active part of its heritage, was considered by many an essential requirement of progress itself. Instead of approaching the unknown and depicting an entirely new utopia, it was preferable to try to sketch a future based on a past described as utopia. In this way, the future is not seen as something that needs to be realized, but as a future that already has a past. The *Aufklärer* were 'forging a new future anchored upon the sound tradition of the past'.[42] However, one ought not to forget that the past, particularly the distant past, can often serve as a model for a revolutionary future, since the more distant the past, the more its values and principles are perceived as being strenuously opposed to the values and principles of the present. In other words, models from the past have a revolutionary potential.

Needless to say, Greece was also a vivid political example. As a result of living in cities, the men of the Renaissance were concerned to discover the best form of civic urban life.[43] Thus in Toynbee's opinion, 'The late Medieval Italian renaissance of Hellenism exerted a more enduring influence on Western life on the political plane than on either the literary or the artistic'; above all it 'propagated a cult of constitutional government'.[44] The history of Greece and Rome, wrote Thomas Arnold in the introduction to his Greek edition of Thucydides (1830–5), 'is not an idle inquiry about remote ages and forgotten institutions, but a living picture of things present, fit not so much for the curiosity of the scholar as for the instruction of the statesman and the citizen, and as a clue to the study of history'.[45] The

---

[41] Burckhardt, *The Civilization of the Renaissance*, i. 123. 'The classical past', writes Gay, 'supplied the men of the Enlightenment with illustrious ancestors and models' (*The Rise of Modern Paganism*, 31–2). For Burckhardt, writes Momigliano, Greek civilization represented the conflict between material power and spiritual culture, between masses and individuals, religion and humanism ('Introduction', 300–1).

[42] Reill, *The German Enlightenment*, 200. See too Gay, *The Rise of Modern Paganism*, 263.

[43] Bolgar, *The Classical Heritage*, 381–2: 'The life of the Italian cities was dominated during that period by the needs of the rising middle class. The new capitalists wanted to consolidate their mastery of the material environment, and so set great store by accurate means of expression and calculation. They lived in cities and so were concerned to discover the best forms of civic life.'

[44] Toynbee, *A Study of History*, 268–9. For further discussion see Ch. 15.

[45] Turner, *The Greek Heritage*, 26–7.

studies of Turner, Jenkyns, and Reinhold[46] provide illuminating examples
of the influence of the political heritage of classical antiquity. These and
other studies show how vital ancient Greece was as a political model. Some
found in it the noble ideals of heroism and patriotism; some, on the other
hand, saw division and fragmentation rather than political unity: a schism
between the élite and the masses, between aristocracy and democracy,
between philosopher and mob, between good leader and demagogue—a
breach that led to destruction and devastation. In the main, Greece and
Rome provided Western societies with ideals and values to guide their
political behaviour and political values—mostly positive, but occasionally
negative as well. But it was not only Greek democracy that served as an
example. From time to time, Greece was a negative model of anarchy, of
mob rule, and of the breakdown of organized systems. There were those
who considered Sparta as an exemplar.[47] Wes provides an illuminating example of how the political heritage of Greece could be perceived: when
the Russian scholar Aleksandr Uvarov translated some Greek and Latin
inscriptions into Russian, conservative advisers reminded the Tsar that the
Parisian revolutionaries of 1789 had already idolized Greek and Roman
heroes of freedom. It was necessary to allay fears and reply that there
was nothing in Homer, Pindar, Greek tragedy, Demosthenes, Virgil, and
Cicero that could be used by atheists and anarchists.[48]

SHIFTING PERCEPTIONS AND IMAGES
IN THE NINETEENTH CENTURY

Since Jewish writers of the nineteenth-century Haskalah movement were
inspired mainly by German literature we shall concentrate mainly on
the image of classical Greece in it. The *Aufklärung* and later intellectual
developments from 1770 to 1830, writes Hans Kohn, drew their strength
'not only from modern England and France but also from a rediscovery
of classical antiquity and a reassertion of its perennial value as a universal
standard and guide'. And this was a genuine German discovery. Kohn
asserts that 'No one was more deeply inspired by classical antiquity than
Goethe: with his almost Greek confidence in the all-encompassing security
and unity of the cosmos, he was the last European "universal man"',

---

[46] Reinhold, *Classica Americana*.

[47] Will, *Doriens et Ioniens*; Rawson, *The Spartan Tradition*; Turner, *The Greek Heritage*, 195–7.

[48] Wes, *Classics in Russia*, 247–50. Thomas Hobbes had famously blamed civil strife on reading of
anti-monarchical 'Greek, and Latine Authors' (*Leviathan*, Part II, ch. 21); Napoleon sought to have
Tacitus taken off the syllabus of the École Normale (Lloyd-Jones, p. xxiv, repr. 152). See too Alexis de
Tocqueville, *De la démocratie en Amérique*, book 2, ch. 7.

and points out that while in Lessing's *Nathan the Wise* it is a Jew who 'transcended the traditional limitations of his faith and tribe', in Goethe's *Iphigenia in Tauris* it is a Greek woman who in a supreme moment of crisis transcends her Greek inheritance: 'His Iphigenia saved the Greeks, not by the help of a god who interceded for them, but by her humaneness . . . Thanks to Iphigenia a world separated by hatred and suspicion became one bound by friendship.'[49]

The *Griechenbild* of Johann Joachim Winckelmann (1717–68), the influential creator of this idealistic image, conjured up a Greece of noble simplicity and quiet grandeur (*edle Einfalt und stille Größe*).[50] Winckelmann represented the Greeks, not the Romans, as reflecting the ancient world, and Greek culture as the redemptive model of future art. 'We learn nothing by reading him, but we become something', Goethe told Eckermann.[51] In Butler's view, Winckelmann's Greece represents the 'hopeless passion for the absolute'.[52] The great German philologist Friedrich August Wolf (1759–1824), the writer of the epoch-making study *Prolegomena ad Homerum* (1773–95), summed up the image of Greece in the Germany of his time in the following words: 'The Greek ideal is this: a purely human education and elevation of all the powers of mind and soul to a beautiful harmony of the inner and outer man . . . As long as there exists in the world a generation who make this elevation their aim, so long will they turn to the ancients for instruction and encouragement in prosecuting it. The simplicity, the dignity, the grand comprehensive spirit of their works, will ever make them a source from which the human soul will draw perpetual youth.'[53] And Goethe told Eckermann in 1827: 'But a noble man, in whose soul God has placed the capability for future greatness of character and elevation of mind, will, through knowledge of and familiar intercourse with the elevated natures of ancient Greeks and Romans, develop to the utmost, and every day make a visible approach to similar greatness.'[54] The Greece of Wilhelm von Humboldt was a harmonious blend of morality and sensuality (*Sittlichkeit* and *Sinnlichkeit*), while the

[49] Kohn, *The Mind of Germany: The Education of a Nation*, 23, 31–3.

[50] Winckelmann, *Writings on Art*; Hatfield, *Aesthetic Paganism*; id., *Winckelmann and his German Critics*; L. Curtius, *Winckelmann und seine Nachfolge*; Pater, 'Winckelmann'; Behler, 'The Force of Classical Greece'; Kristeller, 'The Modern System of the Arts'; Barash, *Winckelmann as a Theoretician*; Uhlig, *Griechenland als Ideal*, 7–19. On Lessing's criticism of Winckelmann see in Hazard, *European Thought*, 420–33.

[51] Goethe, *Conversations with Eckermann*, 173.

[52] Butler, *The Tyranny of Greece*, 3.

[53] Delaura, *Hebrew and Hellene*, 118.

[54] Goethe, *Conversations with Eckermann*, 186 n. 52. His reaction to Wolf's work was that whereas he could never equal the single poetic genius Homer whom Wolf had apparently demolished, he could aspire to parity with the bards whose songs had been combined to form the great epics: 'Doch Homeride

Greece of the Romantic philosopher Friedrich von Schlegel (1767–1845) symbolized the harmony of an organic totality and perfection. The Greece of all these German philosophers and men of art was also a Greece that spawned immortal gods and heroes, human Titans, as well as restless and illimitable philosophers who rebelled against the gods and attempted to conquer Nature for man's sake and to uncover all her secrets.

George Brandes (1842–1927), the Danish Jewish historian of literature, described the Greek renaissance as 'the great Pan's awakening from his long slumber', and regarded this 'perpetual Greek youthfulness' as a distinctive product of German Romanticism. In his view the Germans had invested Greece with too ponderous and sombre a nature, whereas in fact it had a lighter spirit, like that of France, a 'spirit of the south', without the German heaviness.[55] According to this view there is a wide gulf between the deep and ponderous Germanic spirit and that of the Mediterranean, the spirit of the classical world, reviving in Italy and Greece, that sent so many Germans southward to the shores of the Mediterranean, to imbibe the atmosphere of a sensual, spontaneous, rather superficial, and yet vibrant and joyful world.[56] 'The German enjoyed speaking of Hellas in religious language', writes Jenkyns, 'but in a manner less of pilgrims than of visionaries.' The German love of Greece is different from the English, French, or Italian, wrote the Italian philosopher and historian Benedetto Croce (1866–1952), since it is given to the Greece of an everlasting mysterious race described and designed by German classical philology: 'even in their interest for other people the Germans mirrored their own tendencies and imagination.'[57] But the fact is that Victorians themselves had different visions of Greece, a variety of images which was 'inherent in the Greek experience itself'.[58] Pilgrims or visionaries—Greece was seen by almost all of them as an ideal type.[59]

zu sein, auch nur als letzter, ist schön' (elegy 'Hermann und Dorothea' on his epic of the same name, 30). See too Maass, *Goethe und die Antike*; Trevelyan, *Goethe and the Greeks*.

[55] Brandes, *Main Currents in Nineteenth-Century Literature*, i. 159–60. Brandes was very influential in his day; his aesthetic views were clearly affected by Nietzsche.

[56] On the differences between the German and the French perceptions of classical antiquity see Highet, *The Classical Tradition*, 367–99; Camus, 'L'Exil d'Hélène'; Pemble, *The Mediterranean Passion*.

[57] Jenkyns, *The Victorians*, 13; Croce, *History of Europe*, 79. 'German, French and English cultures illustrate the quite different ways in which ancient Greece was viewed and employed by later cultures' (Thomas, introd. to *Paths from Ancient Greece*, 3).

[58] Turner, *The Greek Heritage*, 19.

[59] Among the books I found helpful on this subject are: Boas, *The Greek Tradition*; id. (ed.), *Classical Influences* (both titles); Bowra, *The Greek Experience*; Brink, *English Classical Scholarship*; Butcher, *Some Aspects of the Greek Genius*; Butler, *The Tyranny of Greece*; G. W. Clarke (ed.), *Rediscovering Hellenism*;

In 1819 the German Romantic and Catholic author Joseph von Eichendorff (1788–1857) published his story *Das Marmorbild*, in which the hero grapples with the tension between Christianity and Greek antiquity.[60] In Edward Bulwer-Lytton's historical novel *The Last Days of Pompeii* (1834), the Christian Glaucus writes to Sallust, ten years after the destruction of Pompeii: 'Visit me, then, Sallust; bring with you the learned scrolls of Epicurus, Pythagoras, Diogenes; arm yourself for defeat.'[61] For most Christian writers, Greece and Rome (Rome even more than Greece) were the historical manifestation of immoral paganism (and they shared this same view with the Jews). More moderate Christians suggested that it was a conflict between striving for a perfection rooted in reason and striving for a perfection that aspires to love; between an ideal addressed to the élite and an ideal related to all men. Thus, 'While Greece is the mother of political democracy, Christianity brought spiritual democracy into the world.'[62] The quarrel between Christianity and classical antiquity did not die out in the nineteenth century. On the contrary. Was it not Christianity which destroyed and buried the classical world? Both Greek rationalism and Greek folk-religion were perceived mainly as antitheses of the Christian faith of the Middle Ages and strict Protestantism, and this modern paganism met with the resistance of faithful Christians and anti-rationalist writers.[63]

M. L. Clarke, *Greek Studies in England, 1700–1830*; Davis, *English Neo-Classical Art*; Delaura, *Hebrew and Hellene*; Gay, *The Rise of Modern Paganism*; id., *The Science of Freedom*; Hadas, *The Greek Ideal*; Hamilton, *The Greek Way*; Henderson, *The Revival of Greek Thought*; Highet, *The Classical Tradition*; Jenkyns, *The Victorians and Ancient Greece*; Kitto, *The Greeks*; Livingstone, *Greek Genius*; id., *Greek Ideals*; id., *The Legacy of Greece*; Lloyd-Jones, *Blood for the Ghosts*; id., *Classical Survivals*; Pfeiffer, *History of Classical Scholarship from the Beginning*; id., *History of Classical Scholarship from 1830 to 1850*; Reill, *The German Enlightenment*; Reinhold, *Classica Americana*; Richard, *The Founders and the Classics*; Rosenthal, *The Classical Heritage in Islam*; H. Schneider, *Deutsche Idyllentheorien*; Schröder, *Germanentum und Hellenismus*; Snell, *The Discovery of Mind*; St. Clair, *That Greece might Still be Free*; Stobart, *The Glory that was Greece*; Thomas, *Paths from Ancient Greece*; J. A. K. Thomson, *The Classical Background*; Toynbee, *Greek Civilization and Character*; Turner, *The Greek Heritage*; Uhlig, *Griechenland als Ideal*; Waddell, *The Wandering Scholars*, pp. ix–xxvii, 1–22; Waetzoldt, *J. J. Winckelmann*; Weiss, *The Renaissance Discovery*; Wes, *Classics in Russia*; Woodhouse, *The Philhellenes*. See also Peter Green's review of Jenkyns and Turner in 'Victorian Hellas', 31–44.

[60] Glaser, *The German Mind*, 59–63. The American author John Jay Chapman, in *Greek Genius and Other Essays* (New York, 1915) 'decried not only the English scholars' "limp Grecism" (!), but also the German use of Greek as a stalking-horse for Teutonic psychology' (cit. Herzfeld, *Ours Once More*, 4–5).

[61] Bulwer-Lytton, *The Last Days*, 407; in his introduction he wrote: 'The creed of that departed religion, the customs of that past civilization, present little that is sacred or attractive to our Northern civilization.' However, the message contained in the novel is not one of a fanatical Christianity. Glaucus adds that he 'can share not the zeal of those who see crime and eternal wrath in men who cannot believe as they', because 'some mixture of the soft Greek blood still mingles with my faith' (ibid. 408).

[62] Livingstone, *Greek Ideas*, 144–75. Thus, 'While Greece is the mother of political democracy, Christianity brought spiritual democracy into the world.'

[63] See Gay's discussion of the tension with Christianity, *The Rise of Modern Paganism*, 207–419.

Greece or the example of Greece was perceived as the antithesis of Christianity, often its bitter enemy. This conflict, according to Delaura, was the 'conflict of Apollo and Christ, Rome and Jerusalem, intelligence and belief, the secular and the sacred impulse in society'.[64] Highet distinguishes between two attitudes which he calls 'Parnassus' and 'Antichrist'. Parnassus (or the Parnassian trend) strove to assert the beauty of Greek and Latin aesthetic ideals in opposition to those of the nineteenth century. The Antichrists loved paganism 'for every thing that was not Christian in it. They hated Christianity because it was not Greco-Roman, or was a perversion of Greco-Roman ideas.' In their view, Christianity means repression; it is timid and feeble; it is not part of the European tradition. On the other hand paganism is strong and intense and means liberty.[65]

The ideal perception of Greece as a symbol of perfection or youth or as a uniform entity was challenged from different directions. There were those who explored the dark, irrational side of Greece. Already by 1830 Goethe was aware that Romanticism glorified the dark side of Greece; as he told Eckermann: 'Instead of the beautiful subjects from Grecian mythology, there are devils, witches and vampires, and the lofty heroes of antiquity must give place to jugglers and galley slaves. This is piquant!'[66] Were the Greeks so happy or so reasonable? 'No period of their history could be described as an age of optimism', writes J. B. Bury, and the truth of the matter is that the Greeks were driven by an instinctive pessimism.[67] August Boeckh (1785-1867), the founder of the historical school in the study of Greek literature, wrote that amid the brilliance of their art and the flowering of their freedom the Greeks were a much less happy people than we imagine ('Die Griechen waren im Glanze der Kunst und in der Blüte der Freiheit unglücklicher, als wir glauben').[68] 'The truth of the matter is that the Greeks were the most restless and least moderate people in history', Herbert J. Muller asserts in the same vein in his study of 'the uses of the past'.[69] According to the founder of the Slavophile doctrine, Ivan Kireevsky (1806–56), Greek civilization in patriarchal times was less

[64] Delaura, Hebrew and Hellene, 11.

[65] Highet, The Classical Tradition, 437–65; Gay, The Rise of Modern Paganism, 207–419; and see Ch. 2. The view that Christianity was the cause of the decline of the European artistic impulses was expressed by John Addington Symonds (1840–93), who wrote in his Renaissance in Italy that when Christianity triumphed the gods were sent into exile and the mind was imprisoned in dogma, the flesh entombed in 'hair shirts and cerements' and pleasure smothered by the concept of sin (cit. Pemble, The Mediterranean Passion, 199).

[66] Goethe, Conversations with Eckermann, 356.

[67] Bury, The Idea of Progress, 17.

[68] L. Curtius, Winckelmann und seine Nachfolge, 15; and see Momigliano, 'Introduction', 300–2.

[69] Muller, 'The Romantic Glory', 116–19.

infected by rationalism; custom and tradition had retained their authority, and patriarchal social bonds had not entirely disappeared, while the Athens of Pericles was infected by it.[70] William James asserted that the Greeks, even in Homeric times, were full to the brim of the sad morality of the sunlit world: 'the moment the Greeks grew systematically pensive and thought of ultimates, they became unmitigated pessimists. The difference between their pessimism and the modern (or "oriental") pessimism is that the Greeks had not made the discovery that the pathetic mood may be idealized . . .'.[71] E. R. Dodds writes in his study *The Greek and the Irrational* that 'the men who created the first European rationalism were never— until the Hellenistic age—"mere" rationalists; that is to say, they were deeply and imaginatively aware of the power, the wonder and the peril of the irrational'.[72]

Thus one unidimensional perception was replaced by another. As a reaction some proposed a more dynamic approach and invented a divided Greece. According to it, Greece was divided and ruled by two inner souls: the fundamental 'Apollonian' and 'Dionysian' forces. Greece's existence was not forged by only one, but rather by two elements struggling against one another, at times achieving marvellous harmony. These two concepts emerged as a means of controlling the inner oppositions in human nature and as metaphors of the dual nature of Greek existence. Nietzsche, who popularized this pair of opposites (and, according to Stephens, effected a revolution in German Hellenism),[73] believed that the Apollonian element was stronger in Greece and therefore was capable of restraining the Dionysian element. In Glaser's view this 'longing for a mankind still close to divine origins was the goal both of Apollonian sublimity, which "overlooks" the world, and of Dionysian descent, which becomes one with the world in its depth'.[74] What Nietzsche really longed for desperately was the

[70] Walicki, *The Slavophile Controversy*, 136.

[71] W. James, *The Varieties of Religious Experience*, 142.

[72] Dodds, *The Greeks and the Irrational*, 256. 'The general opinion is that the Greeks of the Classical age were happily free from superstition. I am sorry that I am obliged to refute this opinion' (Nilsson, *Greek Folk Religion*, 111). The decline of the idyllic image of classical Greece and the discovery of its 'shocking perversities' had already begun in the late 19th c.: see Pemble, *The Mediterranean Passion*, 181–2.

[73] A. Stephens, 'Socrates or Chorus Person?'

[74] Glaser, *The German Mind*, 37. See also W. Kaufmann, *Nietzsche*, 120–5; Dodds, *The Greeks and the Irrational*, 103–22. The dualistic concept of Dionysian and Apollonian as two 'Typen der Weltanschauung' (to use Wilhelm Dilthey's terminology) was accepted by anthropologists. Ruth Benedict, for example, defines the South-West Pueblos as Apollonian, and even that 'Apollonian institutions have been carried much further in the Pueblos than in Greece', since 'Greece was by no means as single-minded. In particular, Greece did not carry out as the Pueblos have the distrust of individualism that the Apollonian way of life implies, but which in Greece was scanted because of forces with which it came in conflict'. On the other hand, the American Indians as a whole, including those of Mexico, were passionately

revival of new existence (*neue Daseinsform*) with metaphysical depth and redeeming harmony; then man would be saved from his *polare Natur* and gain his *Einheit*. From this point of view, Greece was neither a unity nor a diversity, but a split collective soul, where rival forces were struggling endlessly: Apollonian Greece versus a Dionysian Greece, or an Olympian Greece against Orphic Greece,[75] that is to say, a rationalistic Greece versus a Greece replete with passions and awash in mysterious beliefs and rites, youthfulness and decadence, freedom and tyranny, the rational and the irrational, nature and culture; all the parts of the whole, or all the elements of human dualism and pluralism were present in Greece.

There were also those who claimed, and rightly so, that all these were nothing but fictitious entities, mirrors of European ideals and not a historical reality. The real historical 'Greece' had many faces; 'Greece' is plurality (*Vielheit*). In the words of R. W. Livingstone: 'We are apt to speak as if "the Greeks" began with Homer and ended with Aristotle and were almost as homogeneous as the Victorians . . . rather than a continent where we travel from one geological formation to another through ever-changing scenery.'[76] This 'Greece' is plurality: it was archaic Greece, the Greece of mythology, the Greece of Orpheus and of Apollo and Prometheus, of Lycurgus and Solon and the tyrants, and of the philosophers; it was an élite Greece and a common Greece, the Greece of Corinth and Thebes, of Sparta and Olympia, of the Olympic games and the oracle at Delphi; Greece was a slave society, an exemplary democracy, an imperialistic *polis*, and so on. It embraced lofty heights as well as the depths of degeneration. 'In view of such variety, no single classification can properly embrace the whole . . .'.[77]

GREECE AS A CULTURE AND COUNTER-CULTURE

R. Johanan Bar Nappaha (3rd c. AD), in commenting on the story of Noah and his sons, stated that Shem obtained the *tallit*, the prayer-shawl, and Japheth (the Greeks) the *pallium*, the philosopher's mantle (Gen. Rabbah

---

Dionysian. They valued all violent experiences, all means by which human beings may break through the usual sensory routine, and to all such experiences they attributed the highest value' (*Patterns of Culture*, 56–8).

[75] 'By Olympian we mean the humanizing, immanentalist attitude, characteristic of Homeric theology; by Orphic we mean the mystical transcendentalist attitude characteristic of the religious service of the sixth century B.C.' (Hinks, *Myth and Allegory*, 21).

[76] Livingstone, *Greek Ideas*, 116; see too id., *Greek Genius*. For him Greece was a prototype for a moderate conservatism (Turner, *The Greek Heritage*, 33–6).

[77] Hadas, *The Greek Ideal*, 12.

36: 3, ed. Theodor–Albeck, 339). The Sages, who were far removed in time from the confrontation with Hellenism, could relate to 'Greece' not only as a 'wicked kingdom' or as a symbol of paganism, but also as representing high culture, and hence spoke of it in the same spirit as the Enlightenment and the nineteenth century did: the most important function of 'Greece' in the nineteenth century's historical consciousness was its image as a great (and secular) high culture. Greece was perceived chiefly—but not exclusively—as a 'nation of culture'. Hegel wrote that 'among the Greeks we feel ourselves immediately at home . . . for we are in the region of spirit',[78] and Goethe told Eckermann that he was not 'much charmed by the history of Greece'.[79] Culture (*Kultur*) was severed from political or social history and was conceived as an autonomous phenomenon. Greek culture was understood as a product of reason and as a man-made culture—a human creation that developed in local conditions and by the creative spirit of the Greeks. It was a culture with an inner code, a content that organized its world and determined its mores, not only its laws of aesthetics. At its peak, it was a mature, inspired culture, striving for the heights, a culture symbolized chiefly by Apollo, Orpheus, and Prometheus—not Dionysus,[80] a human culture that places man at its centre—his sovereign reason, his liberating curiosity, his spiritual openness, his resoluteness, his daring, his readiness to struggle against blind fate, his incessant efforts to conquer nature and to restrain his irrational drives.

By this account the 'Greek' is a totally different person from the impulsive and passive 'Oriental', and he also differs from the 'Jew', who blindly obeys a transcendental divinity, submitting to its arbitrary demands through acceptance of a heavenly decree, supported by theodicy. Greece's bequest to humanity was rationalism, science, art, literature, philosophy, her moral and political code, the wisdom of strategy and diplomacy. Greece bestowed

---

[78] Hegel, *The Philosophy of History*, introd. to Part II, p. 233. It is interesting to note that in Jewish historical consciousness Rome stood for power, authority, law, and administration, while Greece stood for culture, philosophy, science, and arts. This is illustrated by the 3,000 words and terms Hebrew absorbed from Greek and the 250-odd words and terms from Latin (the same process of absorption of Greek words took place in Arabic). Rab Huna (*c.* AD 250) said: 'The Greek kingdom was superior to the Roman in three things: in law, science, and language' (Gen. Rabbah 16: 4, ed. Theodor–Albeck, 148), and the *amora* R. Jonathan of Eleutheropolis said that the Greek language was excellent for poetry, Latin for war (yMeg. 1: 71b and parallels). To 16th- and 17th-c. humanistic Jews the Greeks also represented the cultural achievement of mankind, while the Romans represented political and military affairs and superiority (Melamed, 'The Perception of Jewish History', 56–7). The German historians of the *Aufklärung* were interested in the interplay between the political conditions and the state of literature (Reill, *The German Enlightenment*, 63–5, 256 n. 51).

[79] Goethe, *Conversations with Eckermann*, 72.

[80] Glaser, *The German Mind*, 36–73. The permanent feature of Greek thought is that 'the universe, both the physical and the moral universe, must be not only rational, and therefore knowable, but also simple' (Kitto, *The Greeks*, 179).

beauty; she was a culture, moreover a universal culture, the fruit of inspiration, not of revelation. The Greeks had no priestly caste, no scribes of the law; as Edith Hamilton wrote, they 'had no authoritative Sacred Book, no creed, no ten commandments, no dogmas. The very idea of orthodoxy was unknown to them. They had no theologians to draw up sacrosanct definitions of the eternal and infinite.'[81] The Greek set himself to answer questions with no revelation from God to guide him. Thus he became an example of the man who wishes to find revelation in human nature itself.[82]

The Greeks had religious ideas, of course, but they never made them into a system.[83] There was a dominant ideal, which all could acquire and internalize if only they acknowledged it. Different people saw it in a different light. It meant one thing to the artist, another to the warrior. '"Excellence" is the nearest equivalent we have to the word they commonly used to describe it' (namely *aretē*).[84] The Greeks, Hamilton writes, 'could never wander very far from the spirit of Apollo'—what Winckelmann had characterized as 'noble simplicity and quiet greatness'—since they knew 'that freedom is freedom only when controlled and limited'.[85]

Here, then, in this common image, is a Greece all too aware of the limits of man's ability and ambition, and mindful of the dangers awaiting him owing to his insatiable conceit. Greece stood for 'rationalism', 'humanism' (Humboldt's *Humanität*), and 'secularism', but 'humanism' and 'secularism' can be understood in different ways and take on different meanings: they may represent the peak of the cultural achievements of an advanced liberal society, or express a primitivistic longing for a 'return to nature'. Some argued that 'Greece' stood for 'paganism', not 'secularism', but longing for 'paganism' does not mean a 'return to nature', to heathen cults, primitivism, and the like; and if by 'secularism' we understand emancipation from religious institutions, free thought, love of art, and in particular, a view of 'culture' as a focus of human identity, then 'Greece' did indeed signify 'secularism'. As Werner Jaeger writes,

Greece is much more than a mirror to reflect the civilization of today, or a symbol of our rationalist consciousness of self-hood. The creation of any ideal is surrounded by all the secrecy and wonder of birth; and, with the increasing

---

[81] Hamilton, *The Greek Way*, 208.

[82] Livingstone, *Greek Genius*, 247–8. Immanuel Wolf, in his programmatic article 'On the Concepts of a Science of Judaism' (1822), 196, expressed a similar opinion, but reached an opposite conclusion: 'In Judaism the divine idea is present as a given, revealed idea. In Hellenism all knowledge has developed from the human spirit itself. Both in their very different ways are the most momentous factors in the cultural history of the human spirit.' See also Ch. 16.

[83] Nilsson, *Greek Folk Religion*, 4.

[84] Hamilton, *The Greek Way*, 209.

[85] Ibid. 214.

danger of degrading even the highest by daily use, men who realize the deeper values of human spirit must return more and more to the original forms in which it was embodied, at the dawn of historical memory and creative genius.[86]

And again, 'it is because humanism as realized by ancient Greece has a permanent importance for the mind of man that modern education is essentially and inevitably based on the study of antiquity'.[87]

Jewish writers adopted not only the image of Greece as an immoral pagan world, one they shared with the traditional Christian view, but also the image of Greece as the mother of culture. Hence they internalized the portrait of Greece as a creator of culture as well as the typological system which was ascribed to it. Moreover, when Jewish writers and men of letters turned to their own ancient and classical past, seeking to find there what 'Europe' sought to find in classical antiquity, namely a living whole and an ideal model for new Jewish secularism and nationalism, they also envisaged several types of this Jewish 'secularism' and 'humanism'.[88]

---

[86] Jaeger, *Paideia*, i, p. xviii. Cf. ibid. 37, on the deep dependence of European literature on Greek literature: 'Most of the literary forms created by Greek literature are unparalleled in any other language and civilization. Tragedy, comedy, philosophical treatise, dialogue, scientific manual, critical history, biography, forensic, political, and ceremonial oratory, travel notes, memoirs, collections of letters, autobiographies, reminiscences, and essays—all of these literary types were created and bequeathed to us by the Greeks.'

[87] Ibid. 301.

[88] The Black American Afrocentric view stresses the major impact of the Greek and Hellenic paradigm of Western civilization: the classical revival, according to West, *Prophesy Deliverance*, 51, 'infuses Greek ocular metaphors and classical ideals of beauty, proportion, and moderation into the beginnings of modern discourse'. Indeed, the notion that modern Europe is but a reflection of ancient Greece has reached as far as China. The Chinese man of letters Liang Ch'i-ch'ao, for example, in *The New History* and *A Short History of Athens* (1902), declared that Athenian civilization was the prototype and spiritual father of modern British civilization. See Levenson, *Liang Ch'i-ch'ao*, 91. Some radical Afrocentrists (e.g. Ani, *Yurugu*) condemn the Western world-view as based on Graeco-Judaic principles, from which they argue for a total break; others (see Ch. 3 n. 60) derive both Greek civilization and Jewish religion from the culture of Black Africa and 'black' Egypt, so allowing them to be called 'African'! But both parties regard the Graeco-Judaic heritage as a single unity.

2

HELLENISM AND HEBRAISM:
THE TWO POLES OF THE WORLD

Hebraism and Hellenism—between these two points of Influence moves our world.
MATTHEW ARNOLD, *Culture and Anarchy*

For Jews demand signs and Greeks seek wisdom.
1 CORINTHIANS 1: 22

N O W that we have the answer (or answers) to the question 'Why Greece?', the next question to ask is what it was that made 'Hellenism' and 'Hebraism'—in contraposition to one another—'terms of common literary and cultural usage',[1] or conceptual twins. Why did not the various uses made of the Greek historical-cultural model or the conflict between it and Christianity suffice? Why was it also necessary to place the Greek ideal in opposition to Hebraism (Judaism)? To answer this question, we ought first briefly to describe the appearance of the pattern of antinomy, its repertoire, and their reception.

'All men are either Jews or Hellenes' ('alle Menschen sind entweder Juden oder Hellenen'), Heinrich Heine (1800–56) stated in his commemorative essay *Ludwig Börne: Eine Denkschrift* (1840), and went on to contrast the two: men who are ascetics, despisers of the flesh, yearning for spiritual enlightenment, or men content with their earthly existence, building their lives in the practical, realistic world. There were Hellenes (in spirit) in the families of German pastors, and Jews (also in spirit) who were born in Athens and perhaps were descendants of Theseus. Jewish and Christian Nazarenes are 'men of ascetic instincts, enemies of artistic representations and bent on the life of the mind and spirit' ('mit asketischen, bildfeindlichen, vergeistigungssüchtigen Trieben'); Jewish and Christian Hellenes are full of life, realistic, and proud of their capacity for exposition ('Menschen von lebensheiterem, entfaltungsstolzem und realistischem Wesen').[2] Expressions like 'Nazarene' or 'Jews', Heine hastened to explain,

---

[1] Turner, *The Greek Heritage*, 7.

[2] In Heine, *Sämtliche Werke*, xi. 15–16. See W. Kaufmann, *Nietzsche*, 377. On Heine's ambivalence see Gilman, *Jewish Self-Hatred*, 167–88. On Ludwig Börne see ibid. 148–67 and 176–88. Similarly, in 'Shakespeares Mädchen und Frauen' (1839) Heine wrote of the 1,800 years of struggle between 'Jerusalem' and 'Athens' (*Sämtliche Werke*, x. 147): 'Ah yes! this hatred between Jerusalem and Athens, between the holy shrine and the cradle of art, between life in the soul and the soul in life, has continued

designate not a particular people but a cast of mind and a way of looking at things: 'I say "Nazarene" to use neither the expression "Jewish"
or "Christian", although those expressions are synonymous for me.' In
other words, this is a new division of the human race (that is, Western
civilization) which supplants the split into 'Jews' versus 'Christians'. The
aim of these expressions, he assured his readers, was not to suggest a racial
division instead of the religious one but a metaphorical one: of two types
(*Typen*) of human nature.

Heine set the Olympian, natural world of the Hellenes in opposition to
the world of the God of the Jews (and Christians) who, in his opinion, is a
'zealous and tyrannic god, who oppresses the free emotions and confines
them with bonds of harsh and fastidious spirituality'. The religion of the
Jews, in his view, is wholly a dialectic exercise which separates the material
from the spiritual, the absolute existing solely in the form of the spirit
(*Geist*). Heine envisaged a duel (*Zweikampf*) between Jewish spiritualism
and the Hellenic glorification of life ('judäischer Spiritualismus gegen hel-
lenische Lebensherrlichkeit').[3] Thus he expunged the distinction between
'Jews' and 'Christians' and replaced it with a distinction between two new
abstract types of human entity. Heine found in Hebraism and Hellenism
two faces of Western civilization, two universal categories: the ascetic spiritualism of the Jews in contrast to the glorification of life and the sensuality
of the Hellenes. This riven world is both the cause and the expression of
the crisis; hence redemption will only come when a new harmony is established. And one can only ask: when will harmony reign again, when will
the world recover from one-sided aspirations? ('Wann wird die Harmonie
wieder eintreten?'). He expected redemption to come through liberation
from one-sidedness and reconciliation between Hebraism and Hellenism
(Greekness).

This internal dichotomy or duality that Heine posits in *Ludwig Börne*
was not an innovation for him. It reflects a method he himself employed
in other instances as well: he viewed Plato and Aristotle not only as the
founders of two diverse philosophical methods but also as representatives
of two disparate types of human being, whose tug-of-war charted the
history of the Christian Church; he also distinguished between talmudic

---

for the past eighteen hundred years' (*Heine on Shakespeare*, 13). Keshet, 'Al Heine', suggests that Heine
used the term 'Nazarener' because he had a vague memory of the Hebrew word *nazir*, 'monk'.

[3] Heine, *Sämtliche Werke*, xi. 14–15. In 'Elementargeister' (1837) he claimed that early Christianity
had to choose between Hellenism and Judaism (x. 45–6): 'The question was whether the gloomy, lean,
anti-sensual, over-intellectual Judaism of the Nazarenes or Hellenic cheerfulness, love of beauty, and
flourishing joy of life should prevail in the world.'

Judaism and biblical Judaism, stating that talmudic Judaism was 'Jewish Catholicism' (*jüdischer Katholizismus*) which Mendelssohn, the 'German Socrates', 'overthrew', founding in its stead 'a pure Mosaism'.[4] As Luther overthrew the Papacy, so Mendelssohn overthrew the Talmud by a similar process. He discarded tradition and declared the Bible the wellspring of religion.[5]

This idealistic morphology fell on fertile soil,[6] in an age in which the search for the quiddity of a social group (its *Volksgeist*)—that is, for that content which has a historical source, but is stable and unchanging and determines the group's character—was on the intellectual agenda, and was soon transformed into a racial morphology. It also fell on fertile soil in an age when immanent duality was seen as the dynamic and creative force. Heine coined metaphors, abstract categories, but he signified them with names which were identified with historical entities. Soon Jews and Hellenes would become not only symbols or signals of universal immanent duality, but two antithetical human realities.

Heine's intellectual and emotional life, and no less so his image, may personify the fate of this polarization and the fact that it was not free of contradictions, inner tensions, and conflicts. He vacillated between the different poles, heightening contrasts and changing moods. In his essay 'Die Götter im Exil' (1853), he recounted with great sarcasm the fate of the gods of Greece and Rome after Christianity became dominant: these gods underwent a metamorphosis when Christianity achieved supreme control of the world and the gods were declared to be myths, exiled spirits, inventions of falsehood and error.[7] Already in his 'Elementargeister' of 1837 he had lamented that the Greek way of feeling and thinking, its love of beauty, the old Greek joy of life which appeared to the Christians as sheer diabolism, was destroyed by Christianity and the emaciated, ascetic, over-spiritual Judaism of the Nazarenes.

All this joy, all this gay laughter has long been silenced, and in the ruins of the ancient temples the old Greek deities still dwell, but they have lost their power through the victory of Christ, and now they are mere devils hiding by day, among owls and toads . . .[8]

---

[4] Heine, 'Religion and Philosophy', in *The Prose Writings of Heine*, ed. Ellis, 166–7.

[5] See Prawer, *Heine's Jewish Comedy*, 251–4. For an anthology of Heine's writings on Judaism and the Jews, see Heine, *Not a Kadish Will They Say*.

[6] On the dualistic view of history in the mind of the Enlightenment see Gay, *The Rise of Modern Paganism*, 32–8.

[7] In *Prose and Poetry by Heinrich Heine*, ed. Rhys, 306 and *The Prose Writings of Heine*, ed. Ellis, 259.

[8] In 'Elemental Spirits' (1837), in *The Poetry and Prose of Heine*, ed. Ewen, 565–6. Similarly, in *Reisebilder*, 'Die Stadt Lucca', ch. 6 he writes of the world that became 'grey and dark. There were no

In one of his most famous poems, 'Die Götter Griechenlands', he wrote that the gods of Greece were giant ghosts, but in the war of the gods he now took the side of the defeated gods (*der besiegten Götter*). Yet earlier in the same poem he confessed that in fact 'I never loved you, ye gods | For the Greeks are repugnant to me' ('Ich hab euch niemals geliebt, ihr Götter! | Denn widerwärtig sind mir die Griechen'), words reminiscent of Byron's declaration that Greece is 'the land of the lost gods'. The Homeric tales are no more than pictures, while nature with all its force is found in the Holy Scriptures. However, we must not forget that his Judah was 'Western': 'a piece of the West that lost its way in the East'.[9] The world must be eternally grateful to the Jews for giving it the Bible, which it transmuted into Protestantism. They rescued the Bible from the bankruptcy of the Roman Empire and preserved the precious volume intact during all the wild tumults of the migration of races.[10] The Bible served the whole Germanic world as a textbook and that is why not only Germany, but the rest of the world too, 'is raising itself up to the Jews'.[11] Having discovered, as he put it, the original (biblical) Judaism, he recognized that the gods of the 'naturalists' (Schelling, Goethe, Spinoza) were not redeeming gods. In his *Geständnisse* ('Confessions') of 1854, he wrote that although he had formerly felt little affection for Moses, because the Hellenic spirit dominated him, now at the end of his life, he realized that Moses was a great artist, who shaped his people as an exemplar to the entire human

happy gods any more, Olympus became a hospital' (vi. 28); Kohn remarks that 'Nowhere in European literature have the ancient Gods in their downfall and degradation come so alive through the deep love and compassion bestowed on them by a suffering Jew' (*The Mind of Germany*, 105). And in his 'Nachwort' to *Romanzero* he describes 'Unsere liebe Frau von Milo', the statue that seems to wish to say: 'Cannot you see that I have no arms and therefore cannot help?' And see also the same theme in 'Die Götter im Exil'.

[9] Heine, *Geständnisse*, 'Judäa erschien mir immer wie ein Stück Okzident, das sich mitten in den Orient verloren' (*Sämtliche Werke*, xiii. 131). His belief in a spiritual kinship of Germans and Jews is expressed in the remark that Palestine could be considered 'an oriental Germany' ('Jessica', in *Shakespeares Mädchen und Frauen*, x. 227). Nietzsche wrote in *Human, All Too Human*, i, §475 that the Jews were responsible for the Westernization of culture: 'In the darkest medieval times, when the Asiatic cloud had settled heavily over Europe, it was the Jewish free-thinkers, scholars, and doctors, who, under the harshest personal pressure, held fast to the banner of enlightenment and intellectual independence, and defended Europe against Asia . . . If Christianity did everything possible to orientalize the Occident, then Judaism helped substantially to occidentalize it again and again, which, in a certain sense, is to say that it made Europe's history and task into a *continuation of the Greek*' (trans. Faber and Lehmann, 229). And see Low, *The Jews in the Eyes of the Germans*, 387. This idea had an influence on Nietzsche and the pro-European strand in Zionism (for example, on Jabotinsky, who repeated the idea several times in a similar vein). See the discussion in Yovel, *Spinoza and Other Heretics*, 51–72 and Kaufmann, *Nietzsche*, 346, 353–76. See too Eldad, 'Nietzsche and the Bible'; Golomb, 'Nietzsche's Image of the Jews'.

[10] In *The Prose Writings of Heine*, ed. Ellis, 312 and *The Poetry and Prose of Heine*, ed. Ewen, 353–76.

[11] In Prawer, *Heine's Jewish Comedy*, 287–8.

race.[12] In a newspaper article of 1849 he called himself 'an old sick unto death Jew', and elsewhere he stated that 'it is better to be good than to be beautiful'.[13]

Nevertheless, Heine never ceased to agonize and waver between the Hellenic element and the Jewish element inside him. Between 1853 and 1856, tormented by his debilitating disease, lying on his 'mattress tomb' ('Auf der Matratzengruft'), Heine wrote his last poem, 'La Mouche'. In this requiem-poem relating his dream 'on a summer night' ('Es träumte mir von einer Sommernacht'), the world of unequivocal antinomy became a locus of confused feelings; he describes a magical dream of a dead man with features gentle in their suffering, lying in a marble sarcophagus, ornamented with reliefs showing Jewish and Greek motifs: side by side stand Apollo and Vulcan, Mercury and Diana, with the patriarch Abraham, Moses and Aaron, and Balaam's ass.

> So, in a contrast glaring and grotesque,
> Judea's Godward yearning was combined
> With the Greek sense of joy! Its arabesque.
> The clinging ivy about both had twined.
>
> Oh, well I know they never will agree;
> Beauty and truth will always be at variance,
> The army of mankind will always be
> Split in two camps: the Hellenes and Barbarians.[14]

These shifts in Heine's mood and consciousness, as they surfaced in the tension between his 'Hellenic' spirit and his 'Jewish' spirit, in his uncertainty about which he truly was in his authentic innermost being and which was the acquired outer veneer, are not just the subject of a central chapter in his biography. What is important in this case is that, on the one hand Heine became in the following years a symbol embodying the conception of the idealistic, unequivocal dualism endorsed by so many

---

[12] *The Prose Writings of Heine*, ed. Ellis, 307–8.

[13] Augsburg *Gazette*, Apr. 1849: 'I am no longer a divine biped, nor am I "the free German" after Goethe . . . Nor am I the Great Pagan No. 2 who was likened to Dionysus wreathed in vine leaves. . . . Nor am I a well-fleshed Hellene who enjoys his life and smiles down on melancholy Nazarenes—all I am now is a poor Jew sick unto death (*ein armer todkranker Jude*), an emaciated image of wretchedness, and unhappy man.' According to Prawer's interpretation, Heine's new Jewish identity as a 'poor Jew sick unto death' is presented by him as a defeat: *Heine's Jewish Comedy*, 531. For the second quotation see *The Prose Writings of Heine*, ed. Ellis, 313.

[14] 'Die Gegensätze sind hier grell gepaart, | Des Griechen Lustsinn und der Gottgedanke | Judäas! Und in Arabeskenart | Um beide schlingt der Efeu seine Ranke. . . . O, dieser Streit wird enden nimmermehr, | Stets wird die Wahrhiet hadern mit dem Schönen, | Stets wird geschieden sein der Menschheit Heer | in zwei Partei'n: Barbaren und Hellenen': 'For the Mouche', trans. by Margaret Armor in *Prose and Poetry by Heinrich Heine*, ed. Rhys, 166–70, and Heine, *Selected Verse*, ed. Branscombe, 246–53.

after him, on the other he personified the inner struggle and the spiritual and cultural qualms of a broader public, its perception that Hellenism and Judaism interacted, contended, and became reconciled, creating a perpetual tension and constant dynamic even when one overpowered the other. He set up Goethe as the archetype of the Hellene, and he himself became the archetype of a man in whom two souls are vying with each other.

Heinrich Graetz (1817–91), the great Jewish historian, for example, was surely referring to Heine when he wrote that 'not a few poets and thinkers mourn the demise of a paganism bursting with life, of an Olympian serenity in whose stead comes a nervous churchliness which through its constant awareness of death no longer lets one imbibe the foamy cup of joy'.[15] For many, Heine became the archetype of the ancient, biblical Hebrew: 'Did Heine really once walk the earth as a little Greek? . . . that same Heine, the Greek, the Hellene, in the past, never existed . . . Heine never was a harmonious Greek, just as the aesthetic Nietzsche was never a Dionysus . . .'.[16] Others saw clearly that Heine personified a state of dual nature. In the view of Matthew Arnold, who made Heine well known to the English reading public, he intended to 'make the superiority of Hellenism more manifest',[17] but 'himself had in him both the spirit of Greece and the spirit of Judea . . . Both these spirits reach the infinite, which is the true goal of all poetry and all art—the Greek spirit of beauty, the Hebrew spirit of sublimity. By his perfection of literary form, by his love of clearness, by his love of beauty, Heine is Greek; by his intensity, by his untenableness, by his longing which cannot be uttered, he is Hebrew.'[18] Heine epitomized the 'Hellenic Jew', or the Jew within whom two souls—that of the 'Hellenic Jew' and that of the 'Jewish Jew'— were wrestling and contending. M. L. Lilienblum (1843–1910), one of the leading figures in the Hebrew revival and the Jewish national movement Hibbat Zion in Russia, wrote at the end of a long letter to his friend the poet Judah Leib Gordon (1830–92): 'in this, I see a reincarnation of Heine's ideas. I will make myself clear. Heine said that although he himself was an Israelite, in his spirit and nature he was a Hellene.' Heine possessed an extra soul, a Hellenic soul, side by side with his Jewish soul.

[15] H. Graetz, 'The Correspondence', 229–30.

[16] Marcuse, *Heine*, 291.

[17] Arnold, 'Culture and Anarchy', 275, and see also his 'Heinrich Heine' in *Essays in Criticism*, 119–47.

[18] Id., 'Heinrich Heine', 142. Moses Hess wrote that the two primal types of 'Hebrew' and 'Hellene' no longer had classical nations as their representatives, and only a few individuals represented their typical genius in its purity; Goethe and Schiller represented the Greek type, Heine and Börne the Jewish (*Rome and Jerusalem*, Epilogue, 184–5).

These two souls existed in him side by side, but never intermingled. 'You also have two souls—an Israelite soul and an Hellenic soul. When you are moved by the Hellenic soul, you have no peer among the poets of Israel'; that is because Gordon has a 'good taste for beauty', the legacy of the Hellene.[19] Since Gordon knew very well that Lilienblum's view of Hellenism was utterly unfavourable in all respects except the aesthetic,[20] it is no wonder that this letter was not pleasing to its recipient. He firmly rejected the Heinian model; on receiving his reply, Lilienblum hastened to write apologetically: 'I can see from your letter that the things I wrote, that the spirit of Heine . . . wounded your heart or at least displeased you, as if those words were meant to be provoking or to do you some injustice.'

It is even more important that the two eternal universal metaphors that Heine coined have become an enduring legacy of the intellectual history of nineteenth- and twentieth-century Europe, not only of Christian or post-Christian Europe, but also that of the Jews. Many adopted and used the antinomy he had coined, disseminating and internalizing it in their perceptions of human culture—past and present.

Among the English reading public it was Matthew Arnold who made known Heine's distinction between Hebraism and Hellenism; his essay gained renown far beyond its intrinsic value or originality. His pattern of antinomy ought to be understood against the background of the Victorian era, although he borrowed both its repertoire and its pseudo-scientific foundation directly from Heine and Renan.[21] For Arnold, as for Heine, Judaism and Hellenism are two categories that constitute the nature of European civilization. He has no interest in Judaism *per se*, but rather in Judaism (abstract Judaism, I may add) as an aspect of Europe's soul and culture. Arnold believed that European civilization would be redeemed when the harmonious blend between the two elements, or points of influence, which together maintained a dialectical tension throughout the centuries, should be realized.

The uppermost idea with Hellenism is to see things as they really are; the uppermost idea with Hebraism is conduct and obedience. Nothing can do away with this ineffaceable difference. The Greek quarrel with the body and its desires is that they hinder right thinking, the Hebrew quarrel with them is that they hinder

---

[19] *Igrot M. Lilienblum*, ed. Brieman, 202. Lilienblum found in Gordon what Heine found in Shakespeare (*Sämtliche Werke*, xi. 43): 'Shakespeare is at once Jew and Greek, or rather in him both elements, spirituality and art, have fused in reconciliation with each other and developed to a higher wholeness.' On Heine's reception in Hebrew see Bar-Yosef, 'The Heine Cult in Hebrew' and Gelber, 'Heine, Herzl, and Nordau'.

[20] On Lilienblum's perception of Greekness see Ch. 6.

[21] Delaura, *Hebrew and Hellene*, 139–99; Turner, *The Greek Heritage*, 15–36.

right acting. . . . The governing idea of Hellenism is spontaneity of consciousness; that of Hebraism, strictness of conscience. . . . Both Hellenism and Hebraism arise out of the wants of human nature, and address themselves to satisfying those wants. But their methods are so different. . . . The discipline of the Old Testament may be summed up as a discipline teaching us to abhor and flee from sin; the discipline of the New Testament, as a discipline teaching us to die for it. As Hellenism speaks of thinking clearly, seeing things in their essence and beauty, as a grand and precious feat for man to achieve, so Hebraism speaks of becoming conscious of sin, of awakening to a sense of sin, as a feat of this kind.[22]

In the second half of the nineteenth century, a deterministic link was postulated not only between a social group's racial origin and its world outlook, but also between the group's origin and its capabilities and achievements in art and the sciences. The Jews, Gladstone told his audience in his rectorial address of 1865, fulfilled their particular God-ordained mission, but there was other work to do; it was done elsewhere, by the Greeks, and the world thus created was different from the 'Hebrew world'. They developed their language and philosophy—'the secular counterpart of the Gospel'—which later permitted the diffusion of Christianity throughout the Mediterranean world. They also nurtured certain fundamental potentialities in human nature that the messianic mission of the Hebrews prevented the Chosen People from realizing. 'These included the capacity of art, science, philosophy, commerce, government, and all other activities that provided for the quality of life on earth.'[23]

In his *Harvard Lectures on Greek Subjects* (1904), S. H. Butcher repeated, like a faithful echo, the Arnoldian model: 'Two nations, Greece and Israel, stand out from all others in the history of the world, and form a striking contrast as representing divergent impulses and tendencies of human nature, different ideals of perfection.'[24] He also presented the same redemptive formula of the fusion of these elements into a single unity:

the Hebrews preoccupied, dominated by a single idea, and that a religious one; the Greeks moved by the impulse for manifold culture. Two distinct individualities stand out in clear relief. To the Hebrews it was committed to proclaim to mankind the one and supreme God, to keep alive His pure worship, to assert the inexorable moral law in a corrupt and heathen world. For the Greeks the paramount end was the perfection of the whole nature, the unfolding of every power and capacity,

---

[22] Arnold, 'Culture and Anarchy', 273–300. And see Barrett, *Irrational Man*, 61–80, esp. 64: even though we know considerably more about the 'real Greeks' than Arnold knew, he 'is fundamentally right in his distinction between between the Hebrew and Greek, as is shown by the gifts bestowed on humanity by the two races'.

[23] Turner, *The Greek Heritage*, 169; cf. below, Ch. 8.

[24] Butcher, 'Greece and Israel', 1.

the complete equipment of the man and of the citizen for secular existence. The Hebrews had no achievement to show in the purely secular sphere of thought and conduct. . . .[25]

R. W. Livingstone also echoed this characterization and the view that the importance of Greece's contribution to European history immeasurably outweighed that of the Jews. However, he rejected the notion that the substantive difference between Greece and the Jewish people stemmed from the Greeks' having no religious spirit. The difference lay in their respective conceptions of God and of man:

In their approach to the problem of life the two civilizations start at opposite ends. Greece starts at the human end . . . Palestine begins at the opposite end and works from God down to man . . . the centre of Judaism was not as Arnold thought, a passion for abstract righteousness, in which the Bible shows no interest. Righteousness attracted the Jew not for its own sake, but as the will of a personal God. The Judaism of Arnold is not Judaism at all.[26]

'The Hebrews', writes Muller in the same vein, 'had a passion for justice on this earth, demanding the final establishment of terrestrial peace and order . . . The Greeks could fight bravely for their city-state, but they had no passion for the cause of justice or an ideal state on earth.'[27]

Most of the dichotomies quoted here[28] are static and monolithic in nature. They invent 'Greeks' and 'Jews' as unchanging, one-dimensional, uncomplicated general entities, which in actual fact never existed. Most of these dichotomies relate to the Greeks of the classical era or the Israelites of the biblical era on the assumption that the Europeans and Jews of later periods are an unmistakable embodiment of ancient peoples. These few examples, a mere drop in the ocean, will suffice to illustrate the antinomy.[29]

[25] Butcher, 'Greece and Israel', 12–13. See also Prickett, '"Hebrew" versus "Hellene"'.

[26] Livingstone, *Greek Ideas*, 157.

[27] Muller, 'The Romantic Glory', 108–11, 119–21.

[28] And see further the discussion in Chs. 7–8, where I present the Jewish point of view.

[29] There is of course a vast literature on this subject, written from theological, ethno-psychological, and metahistorical points of view; needless to say it is impossible to try to cover even a small part of it. From an ethno-psychological point of view Boman writes: 'it can be said that the Israelites gave the world historical religion and the Greeks gave it historical science' (*Hebrew Thought Compared with Greek*, 11); 'The Greek most acutely experiences the world and existence while he stands and reflects, but the Israelite reaches his zenith in ceaseless movement. Rest, harmony, composure, and self-control—this is the Greek way; movement, life, deep emotion, and power—this is the Hebrew way' (205). On this see Barr, *The Semantics of Biblical Language*, 8–45. See also Herberg, *Judaism and Modern Man*, 47–57, comparing the Hebraic world outlook with the 'outlook of the very different type of religion manifested in Greco-Oriental spirituality'; Barrett's scheme of the antinomy, *Irrational Man*, 68–9; Shestov, *Athens and Jerusalem*; Eidelberg, *Jerusalem vs. Athens*. On a similar pattern of thought, which described the African and African-American man as a unique ontological human entity, as well as his specific traits, see among many others Diop, *Civilization or Barbarism*, 211–28.

HELLENISM, CHRISTIANITY, AND GERMANISM

Heine was the most important source of the antithetical picture drawn by Nietzsche of the struggle between paganism and Christianity and between these two and Judaism.

Nietzsche pungently criticized the literary praise of Greece as superficial and void of content. Various intellectuals and non-intellectuals, he wrote,

play with impotent phrases such as 'Greek harmony', 'Greek beauty', 'Greek cheerfulness'. And those very circles whose dignified task it might be to draw indefatigably from the Greek reservoir for the good of German culture, the teachers of higher educational institutions, have learned best to compromise with the Greeks easily and in good time, often by skeptically abandoning the Hellenic ideal and completely preserving the true purpose of antiquarian studies.[30]

His Hellenism, on the other hand, aspired to turn Greece into an analogy of new human existence. Heine had declared that the Greeks were only beautiful youths, while the Jews had always been men, powerful, inflexible men; Nietzsche writes in the same vein of the heroic Jewish character, having found in the Old Testament 'great men, heroic landscape and something of that which is most rare on earth, the incomparable naïvety of the *strong heart*', and speaks of 'their energy and higher intelligence, the capital of spirit and will, which accumulated from generation to generation'.[31] They were martyrs who gave the world a god and a morality and fought and suffered on all the battlefields of thought. However, Nietzsche primarily contended with Christianity, as well as with its Jewish component, preferring ancient Greece to both Christianity and 'ancient Germanism'.

Indeed, Nietzsche is a notable example of the way in which European thinkers contemplated the Greek heritage of Christianity and the West in order to understand it and its debt to classical antiquity. What are the links between *Christenheit* and *Europa*, between *Deutschtum* and *Hellenentum*? What is germane to our discussion is the fact that the inevitable result

---

[30] Nietzsche, *The Birth of Tragedy*, §20, trans. Kaufmann, 122. By contrast (§19, p. 120), 'For to us who stand on the boundary line between two different forms of existence, the Hellenic prototype retains the immeasurable value that all these transitions and struggles are imprinted upon it in a classical instructive form, except that we, as it were, pass through the chief epochs of the Hellenic genius, analogically *in reverse order . . .*'.

[31] Heine, *Geständnisse*, 'Ich sehe jetzt, die Griechen waren nur schöne Jünglinge, die Juden aber waren immer Männer, gewaltige, unbeugsame Männer, nicht bloß ehmals, sondern bis auf den heutigen Tag, trotz achtzehn Jahrhunderten der Verfolgung und des Elends' (*Sämtliche Werke*, xiii. 126); Nietzsche, *Zur Genealogie der Moral*, §22, trans. Diethe, 114; *Human, All Too Human*, i, § 475, pp. 228–9. Nevertheless, the ancient Greeks were also portrayed as full of the 'strongest instinct, the will to power' and 'the will to life': *Twilight of the Idols*, trans. Hollingdale, 115–21.

was to reinterpret the influences of Judaism and classical antiquity (and Hellenism) on Christianity.

In the climate of ideas of the nineteenth century the question of the role of Judaism versus that of Hellenism in moulding Christianity became a key question in shaping attitudes towards Christianity (and Western civilization) itself.[32] The question became sharper and more intense following the appearance of the Romantic nostalgia for the medieval period and the introduction of the element of race and racism (Semitism against Aryanism). If Christianity also had a Jewish source, which meant it had a Semitic origin, what conclusion must this lead to regarding the place of Christianity in the Indo-European civilization of Europe? This became a burning issue in the Germanic context, and the problem of the relationship between Christianity and *Germanentum* was intensively debated. Particularly in Germany, 'Greekness' became a metaphorical mirror in which Christianity, Judaism, and Germanism were all reflected.[33] The Hellenic ideal could have been—but generally was not—utilized to accentuate both the deep opposition between Christianity and Judaism, and that between Europe and the Jews. By the same token, however, it could have served as a rein on anti-Jewish sentiments. The Hellenic ideal apparently became not

---

[32] Harnack, *History of Dogma*, vols. i–iv; see too Tal, *Christians and Jews*, 176–22. Graetz wrote: 'The school of Schleiermacher made this intense contempt of Judaism its password and the basis of its orthodoxy' (*History of the Jewish People*, 426–8). In Pelikan's words, 'Especially since the Protestant Reformation, charges and countercharges of whether Hellenization represented "apostasy" or "progress" have shaped theological controversy, philosophical speculation, and historical interpretation': *Christianity and Classical Culture*, 21, noting that Harnack strove to purify the Gospel of 'alien elements'. See too Nock, *Early Gentile Christianity* and Armstrong, 'Greek Philosophy and Christianity'.

[33] See Highet's discussion of 'Parnassus and Antichrist' in *The Classical Tradition*, 437–65. *Germanentum* is the idea of a unique *deutsches Volkstum*, based on the nature and essence (*Volksgeist*) of the ancient Germans (*Germanen*) of Tacitus, medieval mystics, and racial memories. Goethe considered the German Middle Ages, though officially Christian, as pagan, and rejected the practice of comparing the *Nibelungenlied* with the *Iliad*: in the *Nibelungenlied* there was no contact with God, no reflection of the divine, while Homer was truly in touch with the gods (Kohn, *The Mind of Germany*, 41). Thus racialist writers like Paul de Lagarde and Julius Langbehn rejected traditional Christianity and blamed St Paul for 'having enveloped untainted Christianity in sterile Hebrew law', and claimed that the German *Volk* was endowed with a particularly vital spiritual revelation. Some claim that the Teutonic people had been the carriers of all that was best in Greek and Roman civilization; some transformed the ancient Greeks into Germans, and some replaced the Greek gods with Nordic gods, and in their zeal to recapture the roots of Germanism displayed a marked trend towards a committed heathenism, and transformed Christ into the Germanic sun-god. These ideas became those of the German *Zeitgeist*: 'By the end of the nineteenth century the ideological foundations of Volkish thought were securely laid': see Mosse, *The Crisis of German Ideology: Intellectual Origins of the Third Reich*, 149, on whose account this summary is based. Nietzsche rejected the positive idea of *Germanentum*, though it is well known that he also sharply criticized Pauline Christianity: *The Will to Power*, §175, trans. Kaufmann and Hollingdale, 106: 'The song in praise of love that Paul composed is nothing Christian, but a Jewish outburst of the eternal flame that is Semitic': §198 'The founder of Christianity had to pay for having directed himself to the lowest class of Jewish society and intelligence. They conceived him in the spirit they understood' (p. 116).

only part of traditional antisemitism but also a part of anti-Christianism; however, it seems to have served the latter purpose more than the former.[34]

Does Judaism stand in irreconcilable contradiction to the Germanic spirit because of their disparate nature—as so many antisemitic authors claimed—so that there is neither any place nor any possibility for Jews to become assimilated into the national German culture, or is there a correspondence between the 'Germanic' spirit and the Jewish spirit? There were, of course, faithful Christians, Pietists and opponents of rationalizing religion, who did not share the general mood of the Romantic movement and its worship of pagan Greece. In their view, it was Judaism that endowed pagan and barbaric Europe with its religious and moral sense. Similarly, so far as Heine was concerned, the fact that Germanic Christianity had absorbed and internalized the pantheism of the early Germans was not to its credit. From a liberal Christian point of view—'liberal' being understood in its theological sense of accommodating Christianity to the current secular ideology—it was a conflict between striving for the perfection that is rooted in reason, and striving for the perfection that aspires to love; between an ideal addressed to the élite and an ideal relating to all men. Thus, 'while Greece is the mother of political democracy, Christianity brought spiritual democracy into the world'.[35] But the Romantics and the advocates of an organicist outlook desired to purge the Jewish elements in Christianity (if they wished to adhere to it), or failing that Germany, and turn to Greece or the German Middle Ages. As a result, stress was laid on medievalism and Teutonism in order to enhance the cultivation of *Volkstum*.[36] According to the *völkisch* ideology, Germanism is the offspring of the 'healthiest' branch of the Indo-European race, the Teutonic branch. Not classical Greece, but the Germanic tribes and the German Middle Ages are the preferred cultural heritage.[37]

The historical fact, which could not be ignored, is that a deep and complicated interplay took place between early Christianity, Greek myths, Greek philosophy, and the Jewish heritage.[38] The complex concepts of Judaism as Semitic-bred, of Christianity as descended from this Jewish-Semitic stock, yet also of Greek origin, and the ambivalent attitude of Aryanism towards Christianity (rejecting it as 'Semitic' or embracing it as

---

[34] Tal, *Christians and Jews*, 279–89.

[35] Livingstone, *Greek Ideas*, 167.

[36] Marr, *Der Sieg des Judenthums*; Low, *The Jews in the Eyes of the Germans*, 169; Tal, *Christians and Jews*, 225–34. On the attitude of Hamman, Herder, and Goethe to the Jews and Judaism, see now at length Z. Levy, *Judaism in the World View*.

[37] Delaura, *Hebrew and Hellene*, 111.

[38] Finley, 'Christian Beginnings: Three Views'.

'Aryan') have caused the heads of many writers to spin, giving rise to a
plethora of speculative pseudo-scientific writings of all types.[39]

A well-established argument was that early Christianity was indeed a
continuation of Judaism, since it inherited its historical narrative and
cosmology as well as religion and its institutions, endowing them with
the validity of a message of universal–personal redemption. Christianity
was therefore a new and 'true' interpretation of the Jewish tradition (*verus
Israel*), mainly its prophetic universal moral message. Having become liberated from the national and legalistic nature of the old Judaism, Christianity
emerged as a new phenomenon that was appropriate to the European spirit,
and shaped that spirit.[40] Nevertheless, Christianity inherited the positive
elements of Judaism, which had made a substantial contribution to mellowing the primitive qualities of paganism, and had also endowed it with
a lofty system of ethics and values. Furthermore, as Friedrich Nietzsche
wrote, Judaism had not only imbued Europe with a deep moral sense, it
had also rescued the scientific heritage of Greece for Europe's sake. Judaism
had made Europe the continuation of Western civilization. However, as
stated, Western civilization ought to return to the true classical antiquity,
not to Christianity or to 'ancient Germanism'.[41]

From another point of view, it was argued that Pauline Christianity was
Hellenized Christianity. Without this Hellenization of the Christian religion, it could not have spread all over the Greek-speaking world within
the Roman Empire.[42] Hence, its main and substantive foundations were
not Jewish but rather classical (or pagan). Christianity was mainly a continuation of Hellenism, but it was neither a cancellation of nor a declension
from Hellenism but a development and completion of it; it enlarged the
Greek conception of man, and emphasized more justly the place of religion
in life.[43] Under the impact of the new racial doctrines, some argued that
there are both Jewish (Semitic) and Hellenistic (non-Semitic) elements in
Christianity. Therefore it was necessary—and possible—to divest Christianity of all its alien Semitic features and endow it with the more open,
more flexible Indo-European genius. In other words, it was possible and
necessary to rescue Christianity and Europe from Semitic Judaism by turn-

[39] See in Olender, *The Languages of Paradise*.

[40] See M. Simon, *Verus Israel*. The Emperor Julian wrote that the Christians 'have not accepted a
single admirable or important doctrine of those that are held either by us Hellenes or by the Hebrews
who derived them from Moses' (*Against the Galilaeans*, 43 A, trans. W. C. Wright, iii. 321).

[41] W. Kaufmann, *Nietzsche*, 337–90; Low, *The Jews in the Eyes of the Germans*, 377–86. See Nietzsche's
characterization of the Jews in *Morgenröte* (*The Dawn of Day*), §205, trans. Kennedy, 211: 'their heroic
spernere se sperni that surpasses the virtues of all the saints'.

[42] Jaeger, *Early Christianity*, 5.

[43] Livingstone, *Greek Ideas*, 174. On Christian and anti-Christian antisemitism see Tal, 235–89.

ing to either its medieval or its Hellenic sources. Jesus must be 'rescued' from Judaism or else Jesus must be given up.[44] Christianity, according to Renan, was a rupture with Judaism, the abrogation of the Torah (while according to Nietzsche, it was not the overcoming of the Jewish *Ressentiment* but its superstitious extension).[45] To save Europe from Judaism, Europe must turn to its own roots. 'Progress will consist in constantly developing what Greece has conceived, in executing the designs which she has, so to speak, traced out for us.'[46]

According to Kant, for example, in his *Die Religion innerhalb der Grenzen der bloßen Vernunft* (1793), Judaism is in no sense a religion, for it makes no claim upon man's conscience; if Judaism had any religious characteristics (meaning ethics), these were foreign imports derived from Greek wisdom.[47] Hence he denied any affinity between Christianity and Judaism. On this view, not only Second Temple Judaism, but biblical Judaism as well, laid stress on external, mechanistic acts, and not on inner faith. Christianity was born in Greece (or from a 'Greek mind') and therefore was Aryan from its outset. 'Athens and Judaea—Should Judaea be the Teuton's Fatherland?' was the title of an essay written by Hegel in his youth, in 1795. Later he wrote that the Jewish religion appeared as a 'religion of sublimity', the Greek religion as 'one of beauty', and the Roman religion as 'one of utility'.[48] Hegel viewed Judaism as a severe, bleak religion, created out of tribulation for the sake of tribulation, not for joyful play—the God of the Jews is too serious—and as a religion that separates nature from the worship of God, the secular from the spiritual. He also criticized the 'lack of freedom in Judaism'. Hegel's view of the history of the Jewish religion can only be properly understood—wrote Wilhelm Dilthey—if we bear in mind the idealized picture of Greece as it once was.[49]

From a *völkisch* point of view, the fact that Christianity was the heir of Judaism meant that it had absorbed many negative Jewish elements totally out of keeping with the singular spirit of the European peoples (and above all that of the German *Volkstum*). Consequently, it was necessary to sever

---

[44] Olender, *The Languages of Paradise*, 69.

[45] Shapiro, 'Nietzsche contra Renan', 196–7, 203.

[46] Renan, *History*, i, p. vii.

[47] Michael A. Meyer, *Response to Modernity*, 64–5. See also Rotenstreich, 'Kant's Image of Judaism', and Low, *The Jews in the Eyes of the Germans*, 93–9.

[48] On the changing attitudes of Hegel towards Judaism see the discussion in Low, 274–8; on his and Nietsche's perceptions of Jews and Judaism (often in contrast to Hellenism) see Yovel, *Dark Riddle* (which I was able to read only after this book had been completed).

[49] Wilhelm Dilthey wrote in the same vein that the Jews and the people of the ancient East excelled in the religious motif, the Greeks in the aesthetic motif, and the Romans in the motif of will, in the sense of government, law, and jurisprudence (*Weltanschauung und Analyse*, 1). Quoted in Friedman, *Julius Wellhausen*, 29–31.

the ties between Aryan Europeanism and Semitic Christianity. Christianity had vitiated the original cultural traits of the Aryans as well as their physical and spiritual vitality. The growth of Christianity had destroyed the great Indo-European pantheons. Taken to its extreme, this entails the conclusion that one must totally eradicate by *Entjudung* the 'Judaization' or *Verjudung* of the Aryan world through Christianity. Since there is no possibility of redeeming Christianity from its Jewish origin, Christianity must be fought against.[50] If monotheism is regarded as a supreme stage of faith and as the root of ethics and the message of universal redemption—whether it came into Christianity from a Jewish source or there exists an independent and distinctly Aryan monotheism—the identification of an Aryan monotheism has inexorably liberated Christianity from Judaism. P. J. Proudhon (1809–65), for example, the French journalist who founded modern anarchism, believed that monotheism was a product of the Indo-Germanic spirit; according to Gustave Tridon (1840–71), the antisemitic French writer and leader of the Paris Commune, this Indo-Germanic spirit esteems the family, values of beauty, humanity, and freedom, which are opposed to the values of Judaism: 'the desert was in the brain of the Semites'. The Semitic God appears in his book *Du molochisme juif* (1884) as a 'murderous, hypocritical and perverse god, aiding and initiating all crime'.[51] According to Eugen Dühring, in *Die Judenfrage als Frage der Rassen* (1881), Judaism has Semitic elements and an Asiatic heritage and should therefore be repulsed. The same view was expressed by another Young Hegelian, Ludwig Feuerbach (1804–72) in his *Das Wesen der Religion*.[52] In all the anti-Jewish literature of the late nineteenth century, Judaism was depicted as a religion representing God as a supernatural, tyrannical, and selfish divinity. This God of the Jews created Judaism and the Jews in His image (or vice versa) and is responsible for all the afflictions of modern Western society.[53]

The point relevant to this discussion is not the attempt to unravel the tangled web of the disparate elements in what is called the Judaeo-Christian civilization. Instead it is the new repertoire that has been added to the old repertoire of anti-Jewish barbs (or, in some cases, a reuse of an old repertoire). The new–old repertoire depicted Judaism as a faith and a way of life and described the innate collective character traits of the Jews and

---

[50] Tal, *Christians and Jews*, 205–34.

[51] Wistrich, 'Radical Antisemitism', 172–3.

[52] Ibid. 174–83; Kamenka, *The Philosophy of L. Feuerbach*, 15–32.

[53] For a comprehensive discussion of the image of Jews in 19th-c. German literature, see Liebeschütz, *Das Judentum im deutschen Geschichtsbild*.

their origins. According to this view, a Jew cannot be born or raised in Athens since he is a 'Semite'.

There were those, like Heine and Arnold (and Renan), who believed that the European heritage was the product of cross-breeding between Jewish-Christian-Semitic and Hellenistic-Aryan traits. This cross-breeding had created the basic components that caused internal tension and reconciliation in the European existence. Redemption could be achieved not through the total separation of these elements, but through a new harmony between them. European civilization was a product of several heritages; hence it had a non-integralist nature and yearned for a redemptive synthesis. Ernest Renan, for example, believed that only 'the God of Israel was capable of becoming a universal God, and this cannot be said of the Grecian gods, even of Jupiter'. But it was Greece that had bequeathed to the world the marvellous treasures of progressive and rational humanity: 'Our science, our arts, our literature, our philosophy, our moral code, our political code, our strategy, our diplomacy, our maritime and international law are of Greek origin.' Judah, on the other hand, gave the world the doctrine of a zealous God of absolute human justice. Greece gave beauty, Judah gave ethics; Greece universalism, Israel tribalism. The Jews acted according to the will of God; the Greeks acted without the guidance of a revelatory deity, but only of their own courage and reason. It was Rome that created the conditions to turn Hellenism and Jewish prophecy, as well as its heir Christianity, into elements contending amongst themselves over the civilization of the West: the zenith of human culture. These were not two alien, distant cultures, indifferent to one another, but rather two inter-related beings that together made up a common civilization. Renan did not limit his remarks to a spiritual antinomy. He described the ancient Semites as 'an inferior race'; their spirit derived from their race, and it was a spirit of intolerance, jealousy, and fanaticism, of greed, narrow-mindedness, selfishness, and the like. It was not at all difficult to blur the distinction Renan made between the ancient Hebrews and the Jews of his time,[54] and to conclude that the Jews were the 'negative side of humanity', and that all the despicable attributes they had ever exhibited from time immemorial were eternal and everlasting. The European peoples had inherited from Greece the values of beauty, humanity, freedom, and brotherhood; they had a sense of respect for the family, nature, women, the earth. Greece had been the apogee of humanity's childhood, Europe was the apogee of its maturity. All humanity (meaning Europe) needed for its redemption was

---

[54] e.g. in his essay *Le Judaïsme comme race et comme religion*. See Almog, 'The Racial Motif', and below, Ch. 8; also Y. Shavit, '"Semites" and "Aryans"'.

not to reject the positive heritage of Judaism, but Judaism itself had no role to play in it since its universal message had been absorbed long ago by Christianity.

The popularity and frequent use of the human-cultural morphology and its foundations—Jewish, Greek, and Roman—in Russian nineteenth-century thought may show how widespread this pattern of antinomy and its repertoire were even in cultural contexts other than those of Western Europe. The Russian Slavophile school of thought was preoccupied in examining its attitude towards the Russian Orthodox Church, the Greek heritage, and Western culture; however, the Judaism–Hellenism antinomy also played a role in it. Nikolai I. Danilevsky (1822–85), believed that every successive 'historical-cultural type' selected particular clusters of culture for emphasis and elaboration: the Hebrew, being a mono-elemental religious type, concentrated on monotheistic religion, the Greek on art, the Roman type on law and government.[55] Aleksei Khomyakov (1804–60), in his bizarre universal morphology, asserted that the Greeks lacked any kind of genius in the religious sphere and their beliefs were an amalgam of Iranian and Kushite elements. They worshipped in man not his freedom, but his external 'plastic' beauty. At the other extreme, the religion of the Israelite was a pure expression of the inspired spirit of freedom.[56] According to Ivan Kireevsky (1806–56), Russia was spared the agony the West suffered since it lacked the antagonistic dual heritage of Christianity and the juridical rationalism of the Roman state.[57] For many Slavophiles, Judaism embodied prophetic revelation not created by human beings, the antithesis of theoretical science and rationalism, which was the fruit of reason that broke human existence into its separate parts and revoked its unity.[58]

We may return now to our question. What was it that elicited the need to formulate a pattern of antinomy between 'Europe', represented by classical antiquity, and the Jews and Judaism?

The first reply is, needless to say, that the antinomy of Judaism and Hellenism was the heir of the antinomy between Christianity and Judaism. Heine and Arnold, to mention only these two, did not mean to contrapose Judaism and Christianity as two separate and real historical entities,

---

[55] Vucinich, *Darwin in Russian Thought*, 345; see too Walicki, *The Slavophile Controversy*, 515–17.

[56] Walicki, *The Slavophile Controversy*, 208–22.

[57] Id., *History of Russian Thought*, 93–4.

[58] In 1938 the Russian Jewish philosopher L. Shestov (Schwarzmann) (1866–1938) published a book in Paris entitled *Athens and Jerusalem* maintaining that biblical truth was revealed and not created by man: 'Reason and its by-product, scientific method, have their proper use, but they cannot and must not be allowed to determine the directions of man's metaphysical quest or to decide on the ultimate issues.' See Martin's introduction to the English translation. Franz Rosenzweig expressed almost the same ideas in his *Star of Redemption*.

proposing instead a universal cleavage. However, almost inevitably their intent was obfuscated, and the pattern of antinomy became one of Judaism versus the 'Hellenic West'. Many felt the need to redefine the nature of 'Europeanism' and of 'Westernism' against the backdrop of the internal oppositions; but this did not become a search for a model of emulation like the utopian Hellenism of Nietzsche, who believed that one could learn the essence of the new desired form of existence both from an inner sense and on the basis of Hellenic analogies.

In order to learn from a historical precedent, it is best to set up a *Gegenbild*—a mirror-image—which will show the opposite of the positive precedent. Judaism, of course, was such a mirror. There were other possible opposites, for instance the antinomy between 'West' and 'East', but the world of the Orient—the Near East and the Far East—was far more foreign, indistinct, and obscure.[59] Hostility to Judaism, on the other hand, was deeply imprinted in the European tradition; hence it could change its content and appear in new garb. While continuing the repertoire of images and prejudices, it created a new model of two types of man and culture, adding a new repertoire to it.

Before describing how Jews from the mid-nineteenth century reacted to the appearance of the pattern of antinomy, I shall first consider three prior issues: the legendary traditions of the relationship between Greece and the people of Israel; what the Jews knew and learnt in the course of the nineteenth century about classical antiquity and its cultural heritage; and what interpretation they gave to the traditional concept of 'Greek wisdom', turning it into a modern signal.

---

[59] On the discovery and function of the image of the 'Orient' and the 'Far East' in the European world-view see Schwab, *The Oriental Renaissance*; Willson, *A Mythical Image*; Baird, *Ismael*; Said, *Orientalism*; Lach, *Asia in the Making of Europe*; Singhal, *India and World Civilization*. Heine, incidentally, derided this 'discovery' when he wrote that he knew full well that he was 'descended from Brahma's head and not from his corns': *Reisebilder: Ideen. Das Buch Le Grand*, ch. 5 (*Sämtliche Werke*, v. 117).

3

ISRAEL AND GREECE:
REVIVING A LEGENDARY PAST

My first thought is one of intense astonishment at the current opinion
that, in the study of primeval history, the Greeks alone deserve serious
attention, . . . For in the Greek world everything will be found to be
modern, and dating, so to speak, from yesterday or the day before . . .
Surely then, it is absurd that the Greeks should be so conceited as to
think themselves the sole possessors of a knowledge of antiquity and the
only accurate reporters of its history . . .

JOSEPHUS, *Against Apion*, i. 6–7, 15 (trans. H. St J. Thackeray)

THE COMMON ORIGIN OF CULTURE:
MYTHOLOGY AND EUHEMERISM

THE interest in the origin of nations (*origines gentium*), in the origins of
culture, in its stages of progress, and in the ways in which cultural traits
were transmitted and diffused was shared by many ancient peoples, and the
problem of how man acquired the arts became a focus of reflection.[1] Greek
(and Latin) authors examined the conditions which favoured the genesis
and progress of culture and civilization, linguistic and cultural patterns,
and the connection between habitat and habits, national character and
institutions, and the variety and diversity of humanity. Ethnography was
regarded as an access to history.[2] Even though they never used the term
'culture' in the modern sense, there is no doubt that they had great interest
in the phenomenon of culture and in cultural history.[3]

---

[1] Bickerman, 'Origines Gentium'; see too Kroeber, 'Explanations of Cause and Origin'; Dowden,
The Uses of Greek Mythology, 72–92; van Steres, 'The Primeval Histories', who notes that Greek traditions
origins are primarily concerned with the origins of particular states, tribes, and peoples, rather than with
that of the human race in general.

[2] Lateiner, *The Historical Methods of Herodotus*, 145–62; see too Havelock, *The Liberal Temper*, 25–
124.

[3] When, for example, Isocrates, the Panhellenist Athenian orator, wrote *c*.380 BC: 'the title "Hellenes"'
is applied rather to those who share our *paideusis* than to those who share a common *physis*' (*Panegyrikos*,
50), Norlin rightly renders 'our culture' (i. 149), though he wrongly renders *physis* 'blood' instead of
'physical nature'. For him rhetoric was not an isolated technique, but the crown of a complete system for
training and educating the mind and spirit, a conscious ideal of human perfection, of culture. *Paideusis* is
the acquisition of education, a universal principle accepted by all mankind and a foundation of universal
human culture. 'Originally the concept paideia had applied only to the process of education. Now
its significance grew to include the objective side, the content of paideia—just as our word *culture* or

Aeschylus (if he is the author) describes in *Prometheus Bound* the stages of cultural development: the gift of fire, the use of animals for transport, the invention of the sailing-ship, the discovery of medicine, of divination, of metals.[4] In *Antigone* the figure of Prometheus disappears and Man is now truly a self-taught inventor. In Lucretius' *De Rerum Natura*, v. 1241–57, the genesis and evolution of culture is the product of necessity, skill, and a sense of utility. Isocrates stated that '. . . we have come together and founded cities and invented arts . . .'.[5] Man has done the work for himself; 'he taught himself' each new knowledge. In the words of Xenophanes in the sixth century BC:

> Knowledge came not to men from the first divine revelation,
> But man's search, with time, all things more clearly reveals.[6]

Here progress is a result of common human effort and not of a god's intervention. In the mytho-historical tradition, which was created by the Greek mythographer Euhemerus (*c.*300 BC), the gods were turned into heroes and thus rationalized myths as reflections of history. According

the Latin *cultura*, having meant the *process* of education, came to mean the *state* of education; and then the *content* of education, and finally the whole *intellectual and spiritual world* revealed by education, into which any individual, according to his nationality or social position, is born' (Jaeger, *Paideia*, i. 300) According to Marrou, *paideia* 'comes to signify "culture"—not in the sense of something active and preparational like education, but in the sense that the word has for us today—of something perfected; a mind fully developed' (*History of Education in Antiquity*, 98–9); he defines Hellenism as 'The Civilization of the *Paideia*' (95–105). What is the meaning of this 'civilizing education', or the 'ceaseless striving for wisdom and knowledge, and the higher education or culture that is the result of it' (Jaeger, *Early Christianity*, 134–5 n. 34)? Gay writes that Jaeger 'credited the Greeks with the invention of the idea of culture' (*The Rise of Modern Paganism*, 466). In the narrow sense *paideia* meant training in the liberal arts, but in its wider sense it constituted the entire corpus of Greek literature and included norms of human social behaviour (Jaeger, *Early Christianity*, 18), which might rightly be understood as 'culture'. Jaeger speaks of 'Greek culture' and 'Greek cultural ideas' and identifies culture in the true sense as *paideia* of humanism; cf. Kraemer, *Humanism in the Renaissance of Islam*, 140. Under Julian Greek *paideia* became a religion and an article of faith. Anyone brought up on philosophy or literature in a particular language is also imbued with the world of thought typical of that language and that literature; cf. Davidson on Greek culture as the result of Greek education, *The Education of the Greek People*, 168. As Athanassiadi-Fowden notes, for Julian, who regarded Graeco-Roman culture as the product of divine revelation, *paideia* included the study of epic, lyric, and dramatic poetry, philosophy, rhetoric, and history (*Julian and Hellenism*, 122–4; and see the whole chapter on the Julianic *paideia*, pp. 121–60.

[4] On early Greek anthropological thought see Havelock, *The Liberal Temper*, 25–124. On *Prometheus Bound* see ibid. 52–86. One might perhaps find in several biblical mythological stories some interest in ethnography: for example, in the story of Cain and Abel (the tension between nomads and farmers) or the Tower of Babel (the phenomenon of the multiplicity of languages). It is interesting to note that in bPes. 54*a* and Gen. Rabbah 11: 2 (ed. Theodor–Albeck, 89) the Almighty is said to have given intelligence to the first human being, who took two tiles, banged them together, whereupon light issued from them.

[5] Droge, *Homer or Moses?*, 169; see too Edelstein, *The Idea of Progress in Classical Antiquity*.

[6] In Livingstone, *Greek Ideas*, 62–3.

to Diodorus Siculus' *Library of History* (i. 15–16), Osiris (equated with Dionysus) encouraged agriculture and technology, and his scribe Hermes, whose advice he most relied on, articulated the common language, invented writing, 'made the lyre with three strings', and taught the Greeks the art of expressing their thoughts (*hermeneia*).[7] This tradition was exploited in Christian polemics against the pagan apologists; as a result the pagan gods became a personification of traits and symbols of culture, a tradition that carried on during the Renaissance as well.[8] Jewish writers had no hesitation in utilizing it.

The Greeks also developed a minor genre of literature devoted to the 'first discoverers' (*prōtoi heuretai*) of art, technique, objects, and ideas. 'The inventions that are recognized as such in concrete science are more likely to be ascribed to mythical or legendary gods or heroes than to figures securely framed as what we should call historical personages—though we should note that the Greeks' "first discoverers" also include plenty of the latter as well as the former . . .'.[9] These first discoveries were described as a result of a series of miraculous inventions and inventors.[10]

In the mythological traditions deeply embedded in the Book of Genesis, Jubal is 'the father of all those who play the lyre and pipe', while Tubal-Cain is the 'forger of all instruments of bronze and iron' (4: 21–2). In the Book of Jubilees (ix. 11) Tubal is the son of Japheth, and settles in a place connected in fact with the origins of the Iron Age. In other words, the two great inventions, iron and the arts, belong to the generation before the Flood and to all humanity. The Bible fails to tell us how these skills were preserved after the flood; later aggadic and midrashic tradition fills this void with several different stories. According to one, it was the sons of Seth who discovered and recorded the science of the heavenly bodies (Josephus, *Antiquities*, i. 69–70); according to another, it was the first man himself who learnt the various crafts and wisdom from the fallen angels.[11] The Jewish legends reveal both a negative and a positive

---

[7] Edwin Murphy writes that although Diodorus relates the mythological tales about the heroic culture-bringer, he prefers the natural explanation, which views the development of culture as men's reaction to external stimuli (trans. of *The Antiquities of Egypt*, 11 n. 12); see too Havelock, *The Liberal Temper*, 83–4. Diodorus also relates (v. 4–5) that Demeter rewarded the men who treated her well with 'the gift of the fruit of wheat' and also 'taught mankind how to prepare it for food' (trans. C. H. Oldfather, iii. 107–11).

[8] And as a result Euhemerus was permissible in orthodox Christian Europe. Seznec, *The Survival of the Pagan Gods*, 11–36. On the Euhemerist historicized myth in the 18th c. see Manuel, *The Eighteenth Century*, 85–125.

[9] G. E. R. Lloyd, *The Revolution of Wisdom*, 51–2.

[10] Thraede, 'Erfinder II', in *Reallexikon*, v. 1191–1278.

[11] See in Ginzberg, *The Legends of the Jews*, i.

attitude towards 'culture', and, among other things, describe inventions such as weapons of war in the most pejorative manner (1 Enoch 69: 6).[12]

It can be argued that both Genesis and the later Midrashim (exegeses on specific books of the Bible) show that the primary elements of human culture were created by men, not by gods, so there was no need for their authors to transform gods into legendary heroes.[13] However, in the biblical and midrashic mythography the inventors of culture are gods or distinctly mythological figures (unless we assume that Seth and Noah are historical figures, but Mercury, Jupiter, and Prometheus the fruit of mythological imagination). The fact remains that the creators of human culture—even when disguised as gods or mythological figures—were great men possessed of genius, reason, and creative forces.[14] In the biblical period and in later Jewish traditions, however, the inventors of culture are the ancestors of mankind in general, since neither Seth, Tubal, or Jubal had a distinctive nationality. In other words, the emergence of culture is not linked to any specific land or nation; it is universal. The Christian apologist Tatian, in his *Oratio ad Graecos* (*c.*AD 155–77/8), ascribed the inventions not to heroes but to barbarian nations.[15]

While the biblical author and the writers of many of the Midrashim were interested mainly in the origin of mankind and universal culture, Jewish writers during the Hellenistic period were more specific in their interest. They wanted to show that the Hebrews were an integral part of the history of the eastern Mediterranean basin from its dawn, and that the Jewish ancestors were the possessors of primeval wisdom and the inventors and disseminators of culture in the ancient world; that is, Egyptian and Greek culture. Not only were Israel's ancestors men of great learning, they were the teachers of the Greeks and instructed them in every skill. Some of these fabricated stories were ethnological legends, claiming that the ancient Hebrews and some of the ancient Greeks shared the same common stock.

Hellenistic Jewish literature fabricated legendary traditions and used

---

[12] S. D. Luzzatto explains that the Bible did not see fit to relate who invented most of the crafts necessary for human existence (*Igrot Shadal*, i. 70). In the Jewish pseudepigrapha a 'clear distinction is made between true wisdom received by Enoch and pagan culture deriving from the fallen angels': Stroumsa, 'Myth into Metaphor', 318.

[13] M. D. Cassuto, *A Commentary on the Book of Genesis*, 155.

[14] Y. Gutman, 'Hecataeus', 48.

[15] This was an important part of the theme of *laudatio barbarorum* in Graeco-Roman literature. See Droge, *Homer or Moses?*, 86–96.

the technique of euhemerism. Its interest was to prove that the various traits of culture were disseminated by historical figures who belong to Jewish history. While the Bible and the Midrashim do not mention the region of the world in which cultural traits were invented, the Hellenistic Jewish literature specifies the location in which the Hebrew Sages taught their wisdom to the Egyptians and the Greeks. It is the soil of ancient Egypt. In the popular legend in the talmudic literature, the encounters between Jewish Sages and Greeks take place in Athens or in Jerusalem. The Hellenistic Jewish literature written in Alexandria followed native Egyptian, Greek, and Hellenistic historians who designated Egypt as the mother of the human race and the cradle of human civilization: for instance Herodotus, who in his long account of Egypt made it the source of many of the elements of Greek culture; Hecataeus of Abdera, who claimed in his *Aegyptiaca* ('On Egypt') that Egypt was the source of all elements of human culture, and Diodorus Siculus' *Library of History* (i. 28–9).[16] This view was very prevalent in the Hellenistic era and later on during the Renaissance.[17] The interest of Hellenistic Jewish literature written in Egypt was to reveal both Egypt's and Greece's cultural debt to Israel; in doing so, it attempted to prove the existence of influences, and hence a type of fruitful dialogue.

Do these legends preserve any historical facts?

'The Greeks', wrote Arnaldo Momigliano, 'lived happily in their classical age without recognizing the existence of the Jews',[18] and Bickerman points out that 'the Chosen People and its heroes are never mentioned in classical Greek literature'.[19] The Bible does not suggest that the people of Israel really knew the Greeks before the conquests of Alexander the Great. Greece is mentioned only in the Later Prophets. Isaiah couples 'Javan' and 'the isles afar off' (66: 19), Ezekiel 'Dan also and Javan going to and fro occupied in thy fairs' (27: 19), and Zechariah foresees an apocalyptic war between the children of Zion and the children of Javan: 'and raise up thy sons, O Zion, against thy sons, O Greece . . .' (9: 13).[20]

---

[16] See Sterling, *Historiography and Self-Definition*, 51–9, Y. Gutman, 'Hecataeus', 45–51. Diodorus Siculus (i. 9. 6) writes: 'Therefore, since the myths place the origins of the gods in Egypt, and the earliest observations of the stars are said to have been made there; and since, in addition, many remarkable achievements of mighty men are there preserved, we shall begin our history with the affairs of Egypt' (trans. Murphy, 12).

[17] Godwin, *Athanasius Kircher*; Bernal, *Black Athena*, i. 121–223.

[18] Momigliano, *Alien Wisdom*, 78, and see Bickerman's chapters: 'The Greeks Discover the Jews' and 'The Jews Discover the Greeks', *The Jews in the Greek Age*, 13–25; M. Stern, 'Chronological Sequence of the First References to Jews in Greek Literature'. See too Gabba, *Greek Knowledge of the Jews*, and Y. Gutman, 'Pseudo-Allusions to Israel in Greek Literature'.

[19] Bickerman, *The Jews in the Greek Age*, 14.

[20] However, it seems that the Jews in the 7th c. BC had some knowledge of Greeks and Greek

Undoubtedly, there were commercial and other links; the prophet cursed the men of Tyre and Sidon for having sold the children of Israel to the Greeks as slaves: 'You have sold the people of Judah and Jerusalem to the Greeks, removing them far from their own border' (Joel 4: 6). There is no substantial evidence that Greek oral tradition (as against material culture) exerted any influence on Israelite culture before the monarchical period, and scholars disagree as to the range of its influence even then.

The Greeks of the classical period, as far as we know, showed no interest in the Jews and knew next to nothing about them. If they had, they might not have distinguished between them and the Canaanites—the Phoenicians. Herodotus, whose interest in ethnography is well known, never mentioned the Israelites of his time, and no Greek traveller in the Orient paid any attention to Jerusalem or its Deity.[21] It was mainly the native Hellenistic writers who began to show an interest in the Jews, their religion and historical traditions, and while authors of Hellenistic fictitious biographies were prepared to recognize the intellectual debt of the Greeks to Egyptian culture, they did not pay any attention to the fabrications and claims of the Jews. Some Hellenistic authors, however, did fabricate ancient legendary historical links between Greeks and Jews. Hecataeus, for example, linked the story of Exodus to the myth of Danaos and claimed that both the Hebrews and the *Danaoi* were descendants of foreign peoples—expelled from Egypt by the autochthonous Egyptians—who wandered in the Mediterranean region, each going its own way: the Greeks under the leadership of Danaos and Cadmos to Greece; the Hebrews, under the leadership of Moses, to Palestine.[22] Hence a link was established between the legend of Samson and the legend of Hercules. Another source (from about 143 BC) invented a common origin for the Jews and the Spartans: the race of Abraham.[23] Other authors, such as Artapanus and Pseudo-Eupolemus (who was a Samar-

myth (see Ch. 5). On the Cadmus legend and its historical background see Edwards, *Kadmos the Phoenician*.

[21] Bickerman, *The Jews*, 14; see too Momigliano, 'Jews and Greeks', 11.

[22] Friedrich Jacoby, *Fragmente der griechischen Historiker* (FGrH), 264 F 6; Y. Gutman, 'Hecataeus', 49–50; J. Levy, 'Hecataeus', 52. Yigael Yadin even suggested that there could be some links between the Danai and the tribe of Dan: certain sections of the Danai had settled in Palestine 'and at the beginning of the twelfth century drew near to the tribes of Israel (again?) and were admitted to the amphictyonic covenant and given the status of one of the tribes of Israel' ('And Dan, Why did he Remain in Ships?', 307); Margalith, 'The Parallels'; id., *The Sea Peoples in the Bible*, 235–50.

[23] 1 Macc. 12: 21; Y. Gutman, 'The Negotiation with Sparta'; Bickerman, *From Ezra*, 155–6; Ginsburg, 'Sparta and Judea'; Rawson, *The Spartan Tradition*, 95–6. Bickerman writes that the forgery is

itan), combined biblical stories with Greek myths: Enoch was identified with Atlas, and the children of Abraham were described as those
who helped Heracles in the war against Libya.[24] This was a practice,
widespread in the Hellenistic period, of linking, through genealogical
and etymological tables, the fathers of the Jewish nation with various
cities and peoples in the Mediterranean world.[25] Hellenistic writers (and
Roman, e.g. Tacitus) used this practice to denigrate the Jews, while Hellenistic Jews did not hesitate to connect biblical events with non-Jewish
events.

This was because, as Josephus stated (*Against Apion*, ii. 152), every nation
tries to trace its own origin to the remotest antiquity so as not to appear
to be an imitator of other people.[26] In this context a sense of antiquity and
originality imparted and reinforced self-awareness and self-worth, and no
less than that, provided a sense of superiority in the context of a political
and cultural world, in which antiquity and ancient roots added honour
and glory, and even 'truth', to the religions and teachings of a particular
culture. In the Ptolemaic period, the native Egyptians began to stress
their antiquity in contrast to their Greek conquerors. Since the Greeks
regarded themselves as a nation of a new culture that had no memory of its
distant past, they were more than willing to accept the Egyptians' claims
of their own antiquity—a claim which was, of course, well founded—
and to accord it honour. The Ptolemaic dynasty had its own reasons for
nurturing the literature that supported the Egyptian claim of antiquity
and superiority, since it accorded Hellenistic Egypt a status of honour
and prestige. Thus, just as the native Hellenized Egyptians turned to the
annals of their priests and rewrote the history of Egypt, so the Jews turned
to the Bible and 'Graecized' the fathers of the nation, making them an
inseparable part of the history of the ancient world. The biblical chronology
was adapted to the accepted chronology of Egypt and Greece. Therefore
biblical stories were combined with Greek myths, biblical figures with the
heroes of historical mythologies, in order to create a 'common history'
in which the Jews had a prominent place. It was an effort to Hellenize
Hebrew traditions in order to establish the identity of the group within the
setting of the larger world.[27] In the Hellenistic age, more than ever before,

---

perfectly consonant with the spirit of the time: 'Men were eager to "discover" ancient evidence as a
basis for most recent friendships.'

[24] Pseudo-Eupolemus, *FGrH* 724 F 1. 9; Josephus, *Antiquities*, i. 241.
[25] Bickerman, *From Ezra*, 155–7; id., 'Origines Gentium'.
[26] Cf. Bickerman, 'The Jewish Historian Demetrius', 348.
[27] Sterling, *Historiography*, 17.

some Jews had good reason to retell the story of their past to their non-Jewish audience.[28] In any event, the attempt to create a correspondence between biblical and foreign legends was secondary in comparison to the attempt to prove that the Jewish patriarchs were the creators of human culture.

It is important to note that the use of these tactics does not indicate assimilation, for the writers' intent was to overturn the Hellenistic Egyptian traditions; to prove through them the validity of the Jewish historical tradition. As Bickerman wrote: 'As long as they continued to be attached to native traditions the Hellenistic Jewish writers (like the other Oriental intellectuals) could not become Hellenes spiritually. One had to choose between Athens and Jerusalem, or Memphis, or Babylon.'[29] They all wrote, says Sterling, *ad maiorem Iudaeorum gloriam.*[30] However, at the same time, by creating an imaginary link and planting it in a common past, or, by going even further and describing the Jewish culture as the source of the desirable and prestigious elements of the surrounding culture, they could justify cultural borrowings and even acculturation into the foreign culture. This, then, was a response in kind to the Hellenistic sense of superiority, and no less so to the Egyptian 'national' anti-Hellenistic attitude. It expresses a desire to integrate Jewish intellectual and cultural history into the civilization of the surrounding world (*oikoumene*). It was an explicit attempt to portray Jewish culture as an integral part of the ancient Mediterranean world, and to assign the Jews a central place in it, a place of honour, based primarily on their antiquity and their function as bringers of culture.

HOMER AND THE BIBLE

The legendary historical traditions of the Hellenistic era about the link between Jews and Greeks enjoyed some success in later generations. In the course of the centuries, quite a few works purported to provide incontrovertible evidence that 'Greek literature and Greek theologies are nothing but inferior translations or facile versions of the Hebrew', as Ignaz (Yitzhak) Goldziher (1850–1921), the eminent Jewish Hungarian Orientalist, a pioneer in the field of Islamic history and the comparative history of religion, ironically stated. Goldziher, of course, was mocking these theories about borrowing, but his mockery and scepticism did not help to

[28] Collins, *Between Athens and Jerusalem*, 25.
[29] Bickerman, 'The Jewish Historian Demetrius', 355.
[30] Sterling, *Historiography*, 223; see too Momigliano, 'An Apology of Judaism'.

put an end to them.[31] On the contrary, when remnants of ancient epics, mainly Ugaritic literature, were unearthed among archaeological finds in 1929, they constituted a fertile field for the flowering of theories both by scholars and by dilettantes about the ties between Greece, Phoenicia, Israel, and Egypt at the dawn of history. The derogatory attitude towards ancient traditions gave way to the conviction that they preserved genuine evidence, and that archaeology was authenticating tradition and giving it support. A new picture of the ancient past emerged: that of ramified cultural exchanges. The inner Mediterranean basin was now portrayed as a stage, featuring the incessant activity of settlers and immigrants, of conquerors and seafarers, of consumer goods and of language, mythology, science, and ritual. The common ground between the Homeric and the biblical worlds was described not only as a consequence of the adoption by the Homeric or the pre-Homeric world of the Phoenician–Hebrew alphabet, but also as the result of numerous parallels in every sphere of culture: in rituals and religious practices, social patterns, literary motifs, and material culture.[32] This is a story which will take us far from the main path.[33]

THE THEFT OF WISDOM

It was not the legendary stories about the mythological heroes and tribes that attained the greatest success and endured for the longest time. Rather, it was the traditions about the ancient Jews being the source and origin of philosophy and the sciences. Jewish writers were anxious to find a connection in the intellectual and cultural era between two worlds. Well versed in Hellenistic traditions, their aim was to present Judaism to their readers as a 'universal wisdom' (as well as to emphasize its unique qualities).

[31] Goldziher, *Mythology among the Hebrews*, pp. xx–xxi. He refers to books such as Zachary Bogan, *Homerus Hebraizon sive Comparatio Homeri cum Scriptoribus Sacris* (Oxford, 1658) and Jacobus Dupurtus, *Homeri Gnomologia* (Cambridge, 1660). In 1823 one author even suggested that Homer and Moses were the same person (Turner, *The Greek Heritage*, 156–7 n. 30). Gerhard Croeses interpreted the whole of the *Iliad* as a pagan rewording of Joshua's assault against Jericho and the adventures of Odysseus as a transformed account of the wanderings of the patriarchs from the destruction of Sodom to Moses (Manuel, *The Eighteenth Century*, 115). Such claims appear already in the writing of an anonymous Christian apologist of the 3rd c. who produced a number of 'Homeric parallels' to the book of Genesis (Droge, *Homer or Moses?*, 1).

[32] See Tchernichowsky's afterword to his translation of the *Iliad*, 630–8, and the *Odyssey*, 464–80 (his main inspiration came from the works of the French historian Victor Bérar). See Shavit, 'Hebrews and Phoenicians'; C. Gordon, *Before the Bible*; id., *Ugarit and Minoan Crete*; Damon, 'Troy and Canaan'; Burkert, *The Orientalizing Revolution*, 139–43; J. P. Brown, *Israel and Hellas*; Diop, *Cultural Unity of Black Africa*, 199–208; Brown, *Semitic Influence*. There is no doubt that the Greek language absorbed words from Hebrew or Phoenician.

[33] See further Y. Shavit, *The New Hebrew Nation*.

In their encounter with Hellenism, they asserted the antiquity of Jewish wisdom as the source of Greek philosophy and science and described it as a science 'returning to the source', and as 'lost property restored to its owner'.[34] In this way they legitimized the influence on them of 'alien' Greek philosophy and science (very much as the Iranian intellectuals also did). However, it was apparently more important to them to stress the role of the Patriarchs as creators of culture than as creators and teachers of philosophy.

According to Josephus, Abraham introduced arithmetic and the laws of astronomy to Egypt: 'For before the coming of Abraham the Egyptians were ignorant of these sciences, which thus travelled from the Chaldaeans to Egypt, whence they passed to the Greeks' (*Antiquities*, i. 167–8). According to Aristobulus (2nd c. BC), Socrates, Pythagoras, and Plato read the Torah in Greek translation, which existed even before the Septuagint:

. . . the Greeks begin from the philosophy of the Hebrews . . . It is evident that Plato imitated our legislation and that he had investigated thoroughly each of the elements in it. . . . It seems to me that Pythagoras, Socrates, and Plato with great care follow him [Moses] in all respects. They copy him [Moses] when they say that they hear the voice of God, when they contemplate the argument of the universe, so carefully made and so unceasingly held together by God. And further, Orpheus also imitates Moses in verses from his (book) on the Hieros Logos.[35]

Artapanus the romancer asserts in his *Judaica* that Abraham, Joseph, and Moses were the creators of the ancient Egyptian culture (which according to Greek and Egyptian writers was the progenitrix of Greek culture). Abraham taught the Egyptians astronomy and Joseph was the first to divide the land and distinguish it with boundaries. He also discovered measurements and accounts. Moses is presented as a perfect Hellenistic man: a successful general, the inventor of ships, cranes, weapons, and machines for drawing water, as well as a philosopher. Eupolemus designates Moses as a wise man, the inventor of astrology and the originator of the alphabet, the first lawgiver. According to Eusebius, '. . . Eupolemus says that Moses was the first wise man and was the first to impart the alphabet to the Jews; and that the Phoenicians received it from the Jews, and the Greeks from the Phoenicians . . '.[36] Pseudo-Eupolemus (before 1st c. BC) wrote that 'Abraham lived in Heliopolis with the Egyptian priests and taught them

---

[34] Roth, 'The Theft of Philosophy'; S. Shaked, 'Persia as a Model', 110.

[35] Cited by Eusebius, *Praeparatio euangelica*, xiii. 12. 4; cf. Y. Gutman, 'Aristobulus'.

[36] Bartlett, *Jews in the Hellenistic World*, 59.

much; he explained astrology and other sciences to them . . .'. He says that the Greeks claim that Atlas discovered astrology; however, Atlas is 'the same as Enoch'.[37]

Philo of Alexandria, on the other hand, takes a different view. For the very same purpose, he turns the picture upside-down. In his legendary history, he describes Moses as the student of Egyptian and Greek teachers: Moses learnt arithmetic, geometry, and the arts of metre and music from Egyptian scholars, together with the philosophy conveyed by hieroglyphs; both they and the Chaldaeans taught him astrology, but it was the Greeks who taught him the rest of the regular syllabus, the so-called 'encyclopaedic subjects' (*De Vita Mosis*, i. 21—5).[38] Philo clearly differentiated between the version that Moses learnt 'various wisdoms' from the Egyptians and the Greeks and the version that the Greek philosophers were influenced by the Mosaic law; at the same time, he believed that philosophy was a divine gift to the Greeks.

The formula aptly stated by Norman Roth as the 'Theft of Philosophy by the Greeks from the Jews' was the prevalent one; it was accepted by the Church Fathers, who were not interested in the history of writing, in astronomy, and the like, but primarily in philosophy and the legendary traditions related by Josephus (*Against Apion*, i. 168; *Antiquities*, i. 168) and

---

[37] Aristobulus in A.-M. Denis, *Fragmenta Pseudepigraphorum quae supersunt Graeca*, 217–28; Eupolemus, *FGrH* 723; Pseudo-Eupolemus, *FGrH* 724; Artapanus, *FGrH* 726. This summary is based on the translations in Charlesworth, *The Old Testament Pseudepigrapha*, ii (Aristobulus, 831–42, Pseudo-Eupolemus, 882–3, Artapanus, 889–903, Eupolemus, 861–72) and on Sterling, *Historiography and Self-Definition*, 137–225; Rappel, *Seven Wisdoms*, 46–50; Collins, *Between Athens and Jerusalem*; Bartlett, *Jews in the Hellenistic World*; L. H. Feldman, *Jews and Gentiles*, 177–96; Droge, *Homer or Moses?*, 12–48; Momigliano, 'Jews and Greeks'; Conzelman, *Gentiles, Jews and Christians*; Y. Gutman, 'Demetrius the Chronographer'. There is no need here to discuss the question of the historical credibility of these legends; and see Momigliano, 'The Origins of Universal History'; Hadas, *Hellenistic Culture*, 73; Scott, *Hermetica*, 90–1; Bickerman, *Jews in the Greek Age*, 13–14, who writes that 'Plato, however, never sat at Jeremiah's feet' (cf. St Augustine: 'Plato could not have seen Jeremiah', *City of God*, viii. 11), but at the same time argues that, since in the Persian period Jews were part of a universal Aramaic-speaking Levantine civilization, the 'Jewish (and later Christian) forgers had more historical sense than those German professors who denied the possibility of biblical influence on classical Greece'. Another interesting question is why Greek and Hellenistic writers were ready to admit the Greek indebtedness to ancient Egypt (see, for example, in Diodorus Siculus, *Library of History*, i. 69, 77, 96–8; trans. Murphy, *The Antiquities of Egypt*, 88, 97–8, 122–7). On Jews in the science of the 3rd–1st cc. BC see M. Stern, 'Philosophers and Men of Science'. It is interesting—and important—to note that while the Church Fathers (and the Jewish Hellenistic writers) were eager to establish the dependence of Plato on "Jewish sources", Jewish writers in the Middle Ages were eager to establish Aristotle's dependence as a response to the revival of Aristotle from the 13th c. onwards and the central place attained by his philosophy. On the pagan view of Moses see Gager, *Moses in Greco-Roman Paganism*.

[38] *The Life of Moses*, trans. F. H. Colson, vi. 286–9. Also see Mendelsohn, *Secular Education in Philo*; Kahn, 'Philo's Secular Education'; Roth, 'The Theft of Philosophy', 64; Wolfson, *Philo*, i. 141–3. See too Ch. 4.

Aristobulus that Abraham and Moses were the teachers of philosophers. Early Christianity's need to claim antiquity led it to adopt some of the Hellenistic Jewish apologetics as well as the Jewish and Egyptian traditions. The aim of the Christian apologetics was to represent Christianity not as a new, rootless religion (since nothing could be both new and true),[39] but as one rooted in historical religion, and to permit the classical heritage to be absorbed into the new religion. Thus the Church Fathers gave a seal of approval to the adoption and internalization of the philosophical teachings of the idol-worshipping Greeks by asserting that they came to the Greeks through the Jews! They wavered between the pan-Egyptian outlook that viewed Egyptian culture as the source of all wisdom and the pan-Jewish outlook that viewed Moses as the source of wisdom, making him the father of both Egyptian and Greek wisdom. Since in the Greek culture there was no concept of divine revelation in history, it was important to claim that the religious truths were revealed to Moses by God and were then borrowed by the pagans.[40] Justin Martyr was willing to connect Plato with Moses, and Clement of Alexandria argued that the Old Testament was much older than any part of Greek philosophy, which must be borrowed from it.[41] Since Christian apologies, in particular that of Origen (185–254), wished to explain the unity of the works of God in the world and Christianity as a *triton genos*, they needed to link Christianity with both Jewish history and Greek tradition, Moses and Homer, in one historical mould.[42]

This tradition found its way into the literature of Islam, as well. Thus we find the medieval Spanish Muslim scholar Ṣāʿid al-ʾAndalusī stating in his *Kitāb ṭabaqāt al-ʿumam* ('Book of the Categories of Nations') in 1068: 'Pythagoras studied philosophy in Egypt under the disciples of Solomon, son of David.' The Arab philosophers of the Middle Ages had no difficulty in admitting that Muslim civilization had learnt most of the elements of its culture from Hellenistic civilization through Christian intermediaries, and they did so with full awareness.[43] The guiding principle of this receptiveness to 'foreign wisdom' was expressed by al-Kindī, the Arab philosopher who lived in Baghdad in the second half of the ninth century: 'We ought not

---

[39] Droge, *Homer or Moses?*, 9.

[40] Stroumsa, 'Moses' Riddles'.

[41] Sarton, *Hellenistic Science*, 246; Droge, *Homer or Moses?*, 145–6.

[42] Jaeger, *Early Christianity*, 36–7, and see Droge, *Homer or Moses?*, 157–67. Christian apologists compared their use of the pagan heritage to the Israelites' despoiling of the Egyptians (e.g. Augustine, *De doctrina Christiana*, ii. 40. 60–1 (144–7) with Green's note, p. 124 n. 117) or their going down to the Philistines to sharpen their blades (Gregory the Great, *In librum primum Regum*, v. 84, pp. 471–2 Verbraken, on I Reg. [= 1 Sam.] 13: 20). See Waddell, *The Wandering Scholars*, p. xvi.

[43] al-ʾAndalusī, *Science in the Medieval World*, 21. See also Ibn Khaldûn, *The Muqaddimah*, vi. 23; *Rasāʾil al-Kindī al-falsafiyya*, cit. Kraemer, *Humanism in the Renaissance of Islam*, pp. xix, 2–3.

to be ashamed of appreciating the truth and of acquiring it wherever it comes from . . .'.[44] 'The religion of Islam was once purely Arab. Science was once Greek, and then became Arab too.' In this succinct saying Shaykh Muḥammad 'Abduh (1849–1905), in his book *al-'Islām wa' l-Naṣrāniyya ma'a 'l-'ilm wa 'l-madaniyya* ('Islam and Christianity in Respect of Science and Civilization'), summed up the history of Islam as a civilization which knew how to internalize 'alien science' and to benefit from it.[45]

Not so the Jews. They were writing out of a sense of inferiority, and that is why they had to resort to apologetics and were not satisfied merely to act as intermediaries between ancient antiquity and Europe. From a Jewish standpoint, the role of a people who preserved the Greek treasures of wisdom and passed them on to the West was not a sufficiently meaningful one.

The Spanish Jewish poet and thinker Judah Halevi, in his great work of apologetics the *Kuzari*, i. 63, gives precedence to the Persians and the Chaldaeans in order to deny it to the Greeks:

There is an excuse for the Philosophers. Being Grecians, science and religion did not come to them as inheritances. They belong to the descendants of Japheth, who inhabited the north, whilst that knowledge coming from Adam, and supported by the divine influence, is only to be found among the progeny of Shem, who represented the successors of Noah and constituted, as it were, his essence. This knowledge has always been connected with this essence, and will always remain so. The Greeks only received it when they became powerful, from Persia. The Persians had it from the Chaldaeans. It was only then that the famous [Greek] Philosophers arose, but as soon as Rome assumed political leadership they produced no philosopher worthy of the name.[46]

To Judah Halevi, the main rationale for the development of Greek philosophy was not only that it borrowed from the wisdom of the East—after Greece conquered the East by force and thus inherited its wisdom—but also that Greece was a great kingdom, capable of preserving that wisdom. Yet 'from the day the dominion passed to Rome, not one famous philosopher arose among the Greeks', he claimed. What he meant in this case, of course, was 'wisdom' in the sense of metaphysics. But this was not enough for Judah Halevi. Wisdom, as we shall soon see, meant to him also a system of knowledge which included natural sciences like agriculture, zoology, the science of spheres and their courses (astronomy), the art of making music, and more. The Greeks received all of these ('the wisdom of

---

[44] Quoted by Kraemer, *Humanism in the Renaissance of Islam*, 149.
[45] Quoted by Haykal, *The Life of Muhammad*, 579–80.
[46] *Kuzari*, 46–7.

Solomon')—not just metaphysics—from the Semites: 'Now the roots and principles of all wisdom were copied from us, first to the Chaldaeans and then later to Persia and Media and then to Greece, and after that to Rome. But because of the distance in time and the numerous copiers, it is not written in the books that they copied from Hebrew—they only mention that they are copied from Greek and Latin' (ii. 65). Halevi also wrote that the Sanhedrin had to possess a broad knowledge in astronomy, agriculture, zoology, and so forth (that is, in the *chokhmot tiviyot*).[47]

Thomas Blackwell the younger (1701–57), professor of Greek at Marischal College in the University of Aberdeen, who read Johannes Buxtorfius' Latin translation of *Liber Cosri*, published at Basel in 1660, and also produced the most radical and influential re-evaluation of Homer,[48] refers to Judah Halevi as the originator of the claim that the Jews were the source of superior wisdom—not only all the sciences, but also the philosophy of Pythagoras, Plato, and others.[49] Indeed, his apologia appears again and again in medieval, Renaissance, and post-Renaissance literature as a true historical account; already in the fourteenth century Meir ben Solomon Alguadez from Castile declared in the preface to his Hebrew translation of the *Nicomachean Ethics* that Aristotle was explaining the precepts of the Torah.

Isaac Fernando Cardozo (1604–83), a court physician at the palace of Philip IV of Spain and a forced convert to Christianity who escaped to Venice and returned there to the faith of his fathers, wrote in *Las excelencias de los Hebreos* (Amsterdam, 1679) that 'The philosophers of Athens saw with their own eyes wonderful philosophers worshipping only one god, and inspired by them, some abandoned their idolatry.'[50] Cardozo followed the Christian apologists in asserting that 'the journeys of Pythagoras, Plato,

---

[47] Ibid. 108–9, and see Ch. 4. Maimonides, by contrast, wrote that the various branches of science (particularly speculative science) 'were once cultivated by our forefathers, but were in the course of time neglected especially in the consequence of the tyranny which the barbarous nations exercised upon us' (*Guide*, I. lxxx, pp. 107–8); he did not claim that Greek philosophy originated with the Sages of Israel.

[48] B. Feldman and Richardson, *The Rise of Modern Mythology*, 99–103.

[49] Blackwell, *An Inquiry*, 220–1.

[50] Cardozo, *Las Excelencias*, 35–8. The story of Aristotle's learning from the books of King Solomon and converting to Judaism at the end of his life was apparently composed in Spain in the 14th c., appearing for the first time in Meir ben Isaac Aldabi (*c.*1310–*c.*1360), *Shevilei emunah* (*Paths of Faith*: 1360, first published in Riva de Trento, 1518). Aldabi, a religious philosopher with a strong leaning towards kabbalah, relates that Aristotle took the treasures of Solomon's library and copied his book, and then hid them in order to banish from mind the source of his wisdom. He also recounts Aristotle's meeting with the Jewish sage and states that Aristotle sent Alexander a letter telling him that after this meeting he came to the conclusion he should burn all the books he had written since now he recognized the truth of the Torah and the fallacies of 'invented philosophy' (viii. 82). Other Jewish writers repeated this story, which travelled from Spain to Italy and reappeared in the *Bibliotheca Magna Rabbinica* of Giulio Bartolocci (1613–87).

and other Greek sages to Egypt, Phoenicia, and Babylonia, helped them to know the Hebrews better and to arrive at the true knowledge of the First Cause.' He also repeats the Italian Peripatetic philosopher Liceti (1577–1656), who in his *De Pietate Aristotelis erga Deum* ('On Aristotle's Piety') went so far as to tell his readers that at the end of his life Aristotle converted to Judaism. Cardozo gives another reason for using this motif: the meetings between Jewish Sages and learned Gentiles outside Palestine justify the existence of the Diaspora, because only there could the Sages of Israel disseminate the knowledge of the Holy Books among the Gentiles. 'Owing to this dispersion of the Jews among the nations, the latter became well acquainted with the holy books.'[51]

David Nieto, a rabbi and physician (1654–1728), writes in *HaKuzari hasheni–Matteh Dan* (1714): 'it is known that the source of wisdom came from us and that our holy Torah encompasses it all'. This viewpoint can be found in various forms in the writings of the rabbi and preacher Judah ben Joseph Moscato (c.1530–c.1593), and of Tobias ben Moses Cohn (1652–1729), a physician and man of letters, in his encyclopaedia *Ma'aseh Tuviyah* (Venice, 1707). According to the statesman, philosopher, and biblical exegete Don Isaac ben Judah Abrabanel (1437–1508), Plato was the pupil of Jeremiah. The same view was expressed by Manasseh ben Israel (1604–57), the Polish rabbi and codifier Rabbi Moses Isserles (1525–72), and the Italian rabbi and author Simone Luzzatto (1583–1663), who, continuing the old tradition, could justly and proudly declare that the mouths that maligned the Jews as being alien to 'wisdom' had been stopped.[52] Gedaliah ibn Yahya (1553–87), a physician and philosopher, writes in his book *Shalshelet hakabalah* ('The Chain of Tradition') (Venice, 1586) that many Athenian scholars went to study in Jerusalem and that accounts of their wisdom travelled far and wide. He tells again how Hippocrates learnt Torah from Achitophel and the sons of Korah, that Pythagoras studied with the Jews in Babylon, and that Plato was in Egypt with Jeremiah, where he first mocked the prophet and then learnt from him about the living God and other things. Ibn Yahya was familiar with the works of Eusebius, and through them, as well, he learnt the motif of 'the theft of wisdom'. The Jewish Italian historian Azariah de' Rossi (1511–78), who was in fact the first 'modern' Jewish historian, dedicates a special chapter in his *Me'or einayim* to the reiteration of Judah Halevi's statement that most Christian

---

[51] Ruderman, *Science, Medicine and Jewish Culture*; Melamed, 'Philosophical Commentaries'. On Babylonian 'first discoverers' see Reiner, 'Etiological Myth'.

[52] On Simone Luzzatto's *Sefer elim* see Ruderman, *Science, Medicine*, 17; id., *The World of a Renaissance Jew*, 77; id., *Jewish Thought and Scientific Discovery*. 153–84; on Isseles ibid. 69–76.

knowledge came from Hebrew sources.[53] These examples represent but a select few links in the long chain of this tradition.[54]

Hellenistic Jewish writers and Jewish scholars in the Middle Ages and the Renaissance and Baroque periods had much in common. They all lived between two cultures, and in the light of the great esteem in which the 'ancients' were held in their cultural milieu they turned to the ancient sources of their own people to search for an accord between them and the ancient sources of the Gentiles. In doing so, they mounted a strong defence of the cultural contribution made by their people, and found a very useful vehicle for their apologetics in the claim of the 'Jewish source', and 'the restoration of wisdom to its owners' (thus also spurring a renewed study of the Jewish sources). But while the Hellenistic Jewish authors 'made this claim to make Judaism respected among the gentile philosophers, the wheel had turned full cycle by the time we come to Nieto who made the same claim in order to make philosophy respected among the Jews'.[55]

In fact, Jewish intellectuals of that period tried to achieve three goals by using these legendary traditions. The first was to give legitimacy to the study of subjects considered outside the Jewish cultural tradition which called for close contact with the Christian world (like medicine and astronomy). The second goal was to defend 'philosophy' against its opponents. This is the logic behind the claim that philosophy is not alien to the Torah, but rather that its source is Israel and that it is a product of Israel's wisdom. The third goal was to give legitimacy to Jewish involvement in different fields of art. Renaissance and post-Renaissance Jews lived in a society which ascribed great importance to the various elements of cultural creation, and Jewish writers thought it necessary to prove not only the virtues of the Jewish religion but also the virtues of Jewish culture in spheres such as norms of behaviour, political conduct, music, and theatre. Just as writers in the Italian Renaissance turned to the historical past to learn and gain legitimacy from it, so Jewish writers turned to the Jewish past to gain legitimacy from it and to moor their actions in antiquity,[56] and to claim

---

[53] See Bonfil's Introduction to *Azariah de' Rossi*, 57. On this view in rabbinical literature in 16th-c. Poland see Elbaum, *Openness and Insularity*, 159–60.

[54] Other examples are Abraham bar Hiyya (d. *c.*1136); Shem Tov ben Joseph Falaquera (*c.*1225–95), *Sefer hama'alot*; Levi ben Avraham ben Chayim (13th c.), *Chaiyei hanefesh vehalechashim* on the history of the sciences; Profiat Doran (*c.*1414), Spanish scholar and physician, *Ma'aseh efod* (Vienna, 1865); Simeon Zemah Duran ('Rashbaz'), Spanish rabbi, philosopher, and scientist, *Magen avot* (Livorno, 1785). This view was also accepted by Christian scholars such as Roger Bacon, *De arte cabalistica*, who believed that Plato learnt from Jeremiah, Johannes Reuchlin, and the Italian humanist Marsilio Ficino, *De religione Christiana* (Paris, 1559), 48. In the 17th c. the Italian rabbi and scholar Leone Modena (Judah Aryeh, 1571–1648), observed in his *Arie no'hem* (1840), 34 that this was groundless nonsense.

[55] Petuchowski, *The Theology of Haham David Nieto*, 54–5.

[56] Bonfil, 'Expressions of the Uniqueness of the Jewish People'; id., *As by a Mirror*, 119–36; Melamed,

(as we shall see in Ch. 8) that not only were Jewish science and philosophy the root of Western knowledge but also Jewish music and drama were the source of Western art.

It was probably Isaac Satanow (1732–1804), one of the most prolific of the early *maskilim*, who revived in the Hebrew literature of the Haskalah the claim that the Jews were the source of all wisdom, and that all 'the wisdom being revived today was known to our forebears in ancient time'.[57] Not all his colleagues were swayed by this tradition and tactic. Under the influence of deism and the doctrine of natural philosophy—hence not out of feelings of superiority but rather from a desire to profess equality—they asserted that every culture developed its 'wisdom' out of its own innate powers and that the 'wisdoms' were equal in all cultures. Typifying this outlook was a short poem published in the journal of the Berlin Haskalah, *Hame'asef*:

> Like us, all the nations are called to serve God,
> They are all His handiwork, created in His image.
> There was no nation void of wise people,
> Socrates brought wisdom to the north, Confucius to the East.
> Doors a frame to wisdom, and through them,
> From one sea to another, man's philosophy is heard.[58]

Thus Socrates did not learn Torah from Moses or from the prophets of Israel, and did not 'steal' from them; the prophet is not superior to the philosopher. As Isaac Euchel (1756–1804), Hebrew author, biblical commentator, and the 'entrepreneur' of the Haskalah in Germany, who named himself 'the Jewish Socrates', wrote with biting sarcasm in 'Igrot Meshulam ben Uriyah ha'eshtemo'i' ('Epistles of Meshullam son of Uriah of Eshtemoa'): 'Socrates the Greek and Zarathustra the Indian [*sic*] were both happy men, even if they did not keep the commandments of Judaism.'[59] Greek philosophy should therefore be studied without the need to seek authorization and approval through tactical disguise or masquerade.

However, it was Isaac Baer Levinsohn (1788–1860), the central figure in the Haskalah movement in Russia in the first half of the nineteenth century, who exhibited the broadest erudition regarding the 'tradition of the theft of wisdom', and wove almost all the traditions into the web of

---

Wisdom's Little Sister, 18–27, 99–104. In order to use the argument of the 'source of wisdom', an allegoristic reading of the Bible was necessary.

[57] See Razler-Bershon, 'Isaac Satanow'; Pelli, *The Age of Haskalah*, 157–70; Werses, 'On I. Satanow and his Work *Mishlei Asaf*'.

[58] *Hame'asef*, 1 (1784), 176.

[59] 'Igrot Meshulam', 40. See Pelli, *Struggle for Change*, 13–14 and Feiner, 'Isaac Euchel'.

his apologia. In his book *Te'udah beYisrael* ('A Testimony in Israel', Vilna, 1828), he draws legends from every source: from the lore of the Sages, that Greek philosophers came from Athens to learn in Jerusalem; from Zachary Bogan's *Homerus Hebraizon* that Homer borrowed from the Bible; and from medieval literature that Greek philosophy came to Europe from the Jews (and the Arabs), including the works of Josephus, Judah Halevi, and Maimonides, as well as Fathers of the Church like Origen. Thus Levinsohn transmitted the chain of the legendary tradition to the world of the Jewish *maskilim* in eastern Europe, giving it substantial scholarly support. In this way, he enhanced the notion that the Jews had made an invaluable contribution to Western culture—i.e. to philosophy and the sciences—and that Western civilization was greatly indebted to Jewish intellectual achievements.[60] He also repeated the tradition that Socrates 'recognized his Creator in his wisdom and sanctified His great name', and that he learnt from Achitophel and Asaph the Korahite, but notes that Socrates lived in a later period and that the reference is probably to another Greek philosopher.[61] The prolific writer Judah Leib Ben-Ze'ev, the 'typical *maskil* of his generation', [62] wrote in his popular reader *Beit hasefer* (Vienna, 1802) that 'it is said of Aristotle that he was a pupil of a Jewish sage who taught him the wisdom of Egypt, and that this sage was Simon HaTsaddik (the Pious), the High Priest at the beginning of the Second Temple Period'.[63]

SOCRATES' SECRET

I shall approach the conclusion of this chapter by way of a 'Socratic novel', *Sodo shel Socrates* ('Socrates' Secret', 1955) by the Hebrew writer and poet Avigdor Hameiri (1890–1970), which is written in the form of Socratic dialogues. Its plot is simple: a Greek officer comes to Socrates in Athens bringing him a gift from his beloved pupil, Alcibiades—a boy named

---

[60] See Sarton, *Hellenistic Science*, 246–8; and cf. n. 50. Similarly, in his historical novel *Akiva* (1881), Marcus Lehmann writes that although the renowned astronomer Edmund Halley claimed to have observed a new planet, the erudite Rabbi Rappaport of Prague had already proved that this planet had been discovered by Rabbi Joshua, of Rabbi Akiva's generation! On the modern African American version of this tradition see G. James, *Stolen Legacy*; Lefkowitz, 'The Myth of a "Stolen Legacy"'; ead., *Not Out of Africa*. We may note the similarity between the claim that Alexander the Great robbed the libraries of the Egyptian temples and took the books to Greece, where they were the source of Greek philosophy and science, and the medieval legend that Alexander moved King Solomon's library from Jerusalem to Greece, thus enabling the transfer of Jewish wisdom to the Greek world.

[61] Levinsohn, *Te'udah beYisrael*, 113.

[62] Klausner, *History of Modern Hebrew Literature*, i. 189.

[63] The book has two parts: *Mesilat halimud* and *Mesilat hameisharim*. It was published in nine editions.

Hanun ben Adin, a native of Phoenicia, of a tribe called 'Ivrim'. In the dialogues that Socrates conducts with his friends during the course of the novel, the youth, Hanun, does not shy away from engaging in a philosophical discussion with Greek's greatest philosophers. With a sharp tongue and keen intelligence, the Hebrew youth places the Jewish mirror in front of the Athenian philosophers, so they can see in it the weaknesses and faults of Greek culture and recognize the undisputed superiority of the Torah of Israel over the philosophy of Greece. Naturally the Greek philosophers fail to understand the boy's words and react with curiosity and astonishment. But one of them, Socrates himself, is deeply impressed, particularly by what the boy has to say about the essence of the fundamental difference between the philosopher and the prophet. The prophet of Israel expresses eternal truth, the fruit of revelation, and is ready to lay down his life for that truth, unlike the philosopher who searches for truth but is not prepared to die for it. It is the indelible impression of these words on Socrates, as they reveal to him an unknown world of absolute truth, that moves him to reject the suggestion that he escape from prison and certain death and to choose instead to drink the cup of hemlock. To one of his pupils, the imprisoned philosopher says: 'If anyone ever asks who Socrates was, do not say a philosopher, but rather the first Hellene who knew how to die willingly and fearlessly for his truth', in other words a prophet. This is Hameiri's retort to Christian critics who asserted that Socrates did not suffer for his beliefs as the prophets or the apostles did.

It is not surprising, of course, that Hameiri chose Socrates, the man who from the beginning of the Haskalah and even earlier in the Jewish Renaissance was regarded as the philosopher closest to the 'Jewish spirit'. His major inspiration probably came from Judah Halevi's *Kuzari* (iv. 16), in which the King of the Khazars explains the distance between the God of Abraham and the gods of Aristotle. A Greek philosopher, he says, would not lay down his life for his truth (he overlooked Socrates' statement that 'the unexamined life is not worth living', Plato, *Apology*, 38 A), whereas a believer in the religion of Abraham is prepared to die in sanctification of the Divine Name. Although Halevi did write about the 'gods of Aristotle', it is very likely that he was referring to Socrates, the only Greek philosopher prepared to die for the sake of his truth—which was not prophetic truth. Later scholars regard Socrates as equivalent to a martyr dying for the sake of religious faith, or at least, as the first 'secular martyr', but it is the distinction between dedication to philosophical truth and dedication to religious faith—even when in both cases there is a willingness to sacrifice one's life—that influenced Hameiri. Inspired by Halevi, he depicted dedication to a faith and its principles as the most sublime.[64] His intention was to show the preferability of Judaism, embodied in prophecy; and it would seem that not only the recollections of ancient traditions were his literary inspiration, but also historical or pseudo-historical theories of his own time that referred to contacts between Phoenicia and Greece, between the Phoenician-Canaanite culture and the Aegean cultures of the eastern basin of the Mediterranean.

THREE TACTICS OF INTELLECTUAL ACCULTURATION

These legendary traditions and their uses illustrate three tactics (or devices) which were used by Jewish scholars and men of letters from the Hellenistic period onward to legitimize cultural borrowing from 'alien cultures'. The first may be defined as the 'legendary tactic', a web spun of imaginary threads connecting the Jewish culture and the foreign culture, actually turning the Jewish culture into the source of the foreign culture. The second may be defined as the 'tactic of disguise', the use of fictitious connections to legitimize the cultural contact with the surrounding culture as well as the borrowing from it of new components. Through these tactics, borrowed components can be represented as originating from a Jewish source or as old components. The third may be defined as the 'tactic of appropriation', the tactic of labelling cultural traits or ideas as Jewish in their nature and content. In this manner, a cultural idea or component can be identified as 'positive', because it is compatible with an idea or component in the Jewish tradition. To employ this tactic, it was necessary to reread the Jewish intellectual and literary tradition—first, to find in it suitable components, and, secondly, to determine which values and components from the surrounding culture could be adopted.

The legendary traditions also afforded their users an opportunity to draw an 'open' picture of the history of Jewish culture—a history of reciprocal relations with its cultural environment. By means of these tactics, Judaism is not only described as creative and as a 'source' but also as a self-sufficient culture which has no need to learn from anything else. The Jews are capable of creating everything alone—and in fact have always done so. This tradition, or chain of traditions, could be used as a bridge over the deep chasm between the notion of profound, total alienation, and eternal

---

[64] On Socrates as a paragon in Jewish literature, see Ch. 5. Hameiri may also have been influenced by Klausner ('Jeremiah', 116), who describes Socrates as a 'holy man' who gave up his life for the sake of an idea, although Hameiri regards Socrates as a 'prophet'.

hostility on the one hand and that of affinity, reception, and even common ground on the other, but it could easily encourage a sense of superiority. The same ambivalence towards the world outside and the debt owed to it is also to be found in Greek literature.

These legends were indeed useful, but the *maskilim*, as we shall see in the next chapter, preferred the traditions which described the Sages and the Rabbis as educated in 'alien wisdom', that is, as students of 'Greek wisdom' and not as the teachers of the Greeks.

4

'GREEK WISDOM' AS SECULAR KNOWLEDGE AND SCIENCE

Ben Damah, the son of R. Ishmael's sister, once asked R. Ishmael: May one such as I, who have studied the whole of the Torah, learn Greek wisdom? He thereupon read to him the following verse: *This book of the law shall not depart out of thy mouth, but thou shalt meditate therein day and night* (Joshua 1: 8). Go then and find a time that is neither day nor night and learn then Greek wisdom. This, however, is at variance with the view of R. Samuel b. Nahmani. For R. Samuel b. Nahmani said in the name of R. Jonathan: This verse is neither duty nor command, but a blessing (for the Holy One, blessed be He, promised Joshua that 'this book of the law shall not depart out of thy mouth').

BABYLONIAN TALMUD, *Menachot*, 99*b*

R. Eleazar ben Hisma said: Astronomy and geometry are like the savouries of wisdom. *Pirkei Avot*, 3: 23

If the reading of your own scripture is sufficient for you, why do you nibble at the learnings of the Hellenes?

JULIAN, *Against the Galilaeans*, 229 C (trans. W. C. Wright)

Be not troubled with fears, my Father,
for I will learn the secular tongue only to enhance knowledge
and to introduce the beauty of Japheth into the tents of Shem.

The wisdom will not be inimical to our Torah;
Our fathers and their fathers before them
also sought it throughout the generations:
and who knows as you do, my father and teacher,
that only men of learning sat in the Sanhedrin
and that all of our Sages were wise men?

JUDAH LEIB GORDON, *Shenei Yosef ben Shimon*

Only a fanatical believer like Omar would assert that all the *chokhmot* are in the Koran, but we know that not all the *chokhmot* are found in the Torah, and it is not opposed to all the *chokhmot* and all the systems, since it did not inquire into and interpret philosophy, but rather the life of the people.

PERETZ SMOLENSKIN, 'Mishpat ami' ('The Fate of my People')

THE GATES TO 'WISDOM' ('CHOKHMAH')

IN the biblical epic *Shirei tiferet* ('Songs of Glory', 1789), by Naphtali Herz Wessely (Hartwig Wessely, 1725–1805), Amram sends his son Moses to Pharaoh's palace, reassuring his wife Yocheved: 'There he will learn the manners of the rulers, the wisdom of Egypt and the wisdom of the ancient sages, but will not be inclined to the ways of falsehood.' Wessely followed Philo (*Vita Mosis*, i. 21–5), who relates that Moses received the very finest education: teachers were commissioned from all parts of Egypt, from Greece, and from Babylon to teach him: 'arithmetic, geometry, the lore of metre, rhythm, and harmony and the whole subject of music as shown by the use of instruments or in textbooks and treatises of a more special character, were imparted to him by learned Egyptians. These further instructed him in the philosophy conveyed in symbols [sc. the hieroglyphs] . . . He had Greeks to teach him the rest of the regular school course, and the inhabitants of the neighbouring countries for Assyrian letters and the Chaldean sciences of heavenly bodies . . .', but 'His mind was incapable of accepting any falsehood . . .'.[1] From Philo, Wessely could learn that neutral knowledge (as one may call it) belongs to all mankind and is also essential for the Jews, but is inferior to philosophy, i.e. an understanding of the divinity. Scientific knowledge about the created world was, in his view, merely a springboard to lofty philosophy, and also encompassed many unnecessary matters.

In Wessely's epic, in contrast to the Hellenistic Jewish legendary traditions (except for Philo), Moses is not the teacher of the Greeks, but rather their pupil; he was the first among the Jews to learn alien wisdom and was later followed by the Sages. The members of the Sanhedrin were bound not to let any science—real, fictitious, or conventional—escape their knowledge. 'Who can count all the rabbis who taught languages and wisdom?' asks Levinsohn. The Sages were not narrow-minded theoreticians, but men well versed in the customs of their time. Wessely recalls the

---

[1] Philo, *The Life of Moses*, trans. Colson, vi. 287–8. St Augustine was ready to ascribe to the ancient Egyptians a considerable amount of learning 'which might be called wisdom . . . Otherwise it would not be said in the holy Scriptures that Moses was "learned in all the wisdom of the Egyptians"' (*City of God*, xviii. 37, citing Acts 7: 22). Gregory of Nyssa wrote that Moses not only learnt but used the wisdom of the Egyptians (*De vita Moysis*, ii, ed. Musurillo, pp. 66–7); cf. Basil the Great, *De legendis libris Gentilium*, 3. 11–15 (ed. Wilson, pp. 21–2), who goes on to say that like Moses, 'in later times, they say that the wise Daniel at Babylon had learnt the Chaldaeans' wisdom before he touched the divine teachings'. Discussing the dimensions of the Ark, Augustine writes, following Origen, that Moses was 'versed in all the learning of the Egyptians', and infers that since they were 'addicted to geometry', he must have been conversant with it. On 'wisdom' see Wolfson, *Philo*, ii. 211. See too Kahn, 'On Philo's Secular Education'; id., 'The Status of Secular Education'; A. Mendelsohn, *Secular Education in Philo*.

old days of glory when Jewish wisdom flourished in almost every field: Judah Halevi had stated (*Kuzari*, ii. 63–6) that Jews since biblical times have had knowledge in all branches of science, and Maimonides had stated (*Guide*, i. lxxi) that 'many sciences were once cultivated by our forefathers, but were in the course of time neglected'. Alas, in Judaea, unlike Greece, there were no schools or academies; wisdom was not recorded and therefore was forgotten. This was indeed the declared mission of the Haskalah movement: to rediscover and recover this lost and forgotten wisdom. But in order to fulfil this mission, the Haskalah needed legitimization for its endeavour, and what better legitimization could there be than that which was part of the internal Jewish tradition, and could convince even the most conservative? Wessely was ready to use Egyptian wisdom not because he preferred it to Greek (Egyptian wisdom had a very bad reputation in the Bible and the Talmud), but because he could use Moses, the Law-giver, as a prototype of a man who acquired alien wisdom but kept his moral purity.

'External wisdom' (that is, knowledge external to the Torah) was not always described in the Haskalah as 'Greek wisdom'; this was probably deliberate, owing to the negative connotation of the term. Wessely himself preferred to talk about *torat ha'adam*, literally 'the Torah of Man', wisdom developed by man, as opposed to the wisdom of the Torah that the Jews had received from God. The *chokhmot limudiyot* (theoretical sciences) and the *chokhmot tiviyot* (natural sciences), he wrote in *Divrei shalom ve'emet* ('Words of Peace and Truth', Berlin, 1782–5), are not Greek wisdom, but are the wisdom of the sages of all nations. There was no state in which some did not engage in these sciences, hence they are universal, and not identified with one single people or any one culture. This universal wisdom is even prior in time to the Mosaic laws. Hence Satanow writes: 'Buy pearls from whoever sells them, and knowledge from whoever is knowledgeable. Respect wisdom and ask for it from anyone. . . . The sages also said that the truth should be accepted from whoever tells it . . . "Who is the wise man? He who learns from everyone." '[2] This type of knowledge could be

---

[2] See Razler-Bershon, 'Isaac Satanow', 85; Kraemer, *Humanism*, 4–5, 76–7; Pelli, *The Age of Haskalah*, 51–70. Cf. *Avot* 4: 1: 'Ben Zoma says: "Who is wise? He who learns from everyone."' It was said that R. Meir found a pomegranate, ate its inside, and threw away its outside (*Chagigah* 15: 10). Cf. the famous *hadīth* exhorting Muslims to seek *'ilm* (wisdom, knowledge) even in China; for Muslim philosophers also distinguished between 'the human sciences' (*al-'ulūm al-'insāniyya*) and the 'divine science' (*al-'ilm al-'ilāhī*). In his *Introduction to the Study of Aristotle*, al-Kindī wrote: 'We ought not to be ashamed of appreciating the truth and of acquiring it wherever it comes from, even if it comes from races distant and nations different fron us.' They were aware that these 'ancient sciences' (*al-'ulūm al-'awā'il*) were the common heritage of mankind. See Kraemer, *Humanism*, 148–50, and on the concept of *'ilm* and *ḥikma* in Islam Franz Rosenthal, *Knowledge Triumphant*, esp. 35–69. On the other hand Qadir, *Philosophy and*

classified as Greek wisdom, but it could just as well be regarded as universal knowledge (belonging to all—Jews, Greeks, Egyptians, and Persians). This is neutral knowledge, 'external wisdom', but there is no reason to stamp it as particularly Greek wisdom, and by doing so, to prevent both *maskilim* and the common man from acquiring essential knowledge, not for the sake of philosophical studies but for their everyday needs. However, since the term 'Greek wisdom' had a long history, the *maskilim* turned to it to seek support and legitimization for their views in the Jewish intellectual tradition. The term 'wisdom' was the main—perhaps even the only—positive signal with which the Jews marked part of the Greek-Hellenistic culture, and the one with the longest and most consecutive history; it was generally identified with Greek wisdom. It meant the heritage and legacy of classical antiquity and Hellenism in philosophy, sciences, and the arts; it also symbolized a lost Jewish heritage and the proper relationship between the Jewish world and the world of the Gentiles. A recent example was provided by the Israeli minister of education, Zevulun Hammer, the leader of the National Religious Party, who in an interview given after entering office, declared: 'Judaism is founded on ethics, while Hellenism was founded on aesthetics . . . We shall not be human beings on an aesthetic basis alone.'[3] Moreover, wisdom became a multipurpose and multivalent concept that in the intellectual utopia of the *maskilim* was intended to serve as a bridge and intermediary between the Jewish intellectual tradition and the outside world.

Until the twentieth century, the word 'wisdom' in Jewish literature encompassed all branches of philosophy and science. Needless to say, it is not my intention, nor is it within my ability, to deal with the history of Jewish philosophy and the many attempts to attain a reconciliation between faith and philosophy. Nor is it possible to discriminate between science and philosophy, for science has, or can have, implications for the fundamentals of faith, particularly when it seeks to offer an explanation of the Creation or touches upon sacred historical traditions. To be sure, the dispute between faith and science does not centre on the validity of the various laws governing nature, but on their source; however, it is not always

---

Science in the Islamic World, 18–20, claims that whereas the spirit of Greek science was manifested in a deductive method, leading to neglect of observation and experiments, Muslim science was inspired by the inductive method, long before Bacon: 'The spirit of the Quran is dynamic and hence anti-classical. . . . As against Greek philosophers, the Quran attaches great significance to sensory knowledge'; hence a unique Islamic philosophy and science do exist, and Muslims should acquire modern scientific knowledge. See too ch. 6, 'Muslim Philosophers and their Problems', 70–88, and ch. 8, 'Science in the Golden Period of Islam', 104–21.

[3] *Ma'ariv*, 2 Mar. 1996.

possible to distinguish between neutral or applied science and science that makes a statement about the nature of the Creation and the forces that govern and guide the world. These are very weighty subjects, which have all been on the Jewish agenda since at least the Middle Ages, and have given rise to several main patterns of response.[4]

During the sixteenth to eighteenth centuries, Jewish thinkers took an increasing interest in science and scientific discoveries; scientific knowledge was diffused within the Jewish community.[5] However, some members of the Jewish élite seem to have been mainly concerned with adapting European scientific works, commenting on them, and attempting to prove that there was no contradiction between them and the Torah of Israel, even that some (in particular those dealing with astronomy) made a contribution to its understanding, rather than making a real contribution to scientific research. In any case the acceptance in élite circles of science and scientific knowledge as possessing utility was not the prevailing view.

Furthermore, Jewish thinkers distinguished between science on the one hand and metaphysics and philosophy on the other. Rabbi Moses Isserles replied to his critics that the rabbis 'only feared the study of the cursed Greeks like the book of physics together with the metaphysics . . . However, they did not forbid the study of the scholars and their investigations of the essence of reality and its nature. On the contrary, through this, the greatness of the Creator of the world, may He be blessed, is made known.'[6]

While in the Middle Ages and the Renaissance there were voices calling for a total break with secular learning and an anti-rationalistic creed, and others rejecting the medieval idea of the essential unity of physical and metaphysical worlds and the authority of the Aristotelian system of knowledge,[7] in the Haskalah the situation was totally different. There was a zeal for scientific knowledge both among observant and 'free-thinking' Jews; from the end of the eighteenth century the Haskalah never doubted the

---

[4] Macy, 'Hellenistic Influences on Islam and Judaism', proposes a typology of four theological and philosophical approaches to the relationship between philosophy and pure science and theology: (i) fundamentalistic theology; (ii) intellectual theology; (iii) 'religious' philosophy; and (iv) 'extremist' philosophy that suppresses free thinking and progress in the interest of dogma. On the nature of Jewish philosophy see among others Sirat, A History of Jewish Philosophy; Schweid, Ta'am vehakashah; Z. Levy. Shem and Japheth; Neumark, Toledot hafilosofiah hayisraelit; J. B. Soloveitchik, The Halakhic Mind. Rabbi Soloveitchik affirms (pp. 100–1) that Jewish philosophy, being rooted in Greek and medieval Muslim thought, 'despite its accomplishment and merit, has not taken deep root in Jewish historical realism and has not shaped religious world perspective . . . It is impossible to reconstruct a unique Jewish world perspective out of alien material . . there is only a single source from which a Jewish philosophical Weltanschauung could emerge: the objective order—the Halakha.'

[5] See Ruderman, Jewish Thought and Scientific Discovery.

[6] Isserles, Responsa, 31, cit. Ruderman, Jewish Thought, 73.

[7] Bonfil, 'Preaching as Mediation'.

value of science as an explanation for natural phenomena. It was also free of the conservatism that viewed new ideas as dangerous. This led to attempts to reconcile science and faith, to argue that there was no connection whatsoever between the two, or to castigate faith in the light of science, even to the point of rejecting its key principles.[8] Nineteenth-century science, in particular materialism and positivism, posed a new intellectual challenge; in its wake a rich literature came into being, that gave expression to these three modes of thought.

This, of course, is a complex subject; my main interest in this chapter is the history of the word 'wisdom' as a signifier for everything that is an intellectual product of the non-Jewish world, as in 'Greek wisdom', 'alien wisdom', or 'external wisdom'. I shall also attempt to briefly describe here the manner in which 'wisdom' (particularly science) received total legitimation, not only as a permissible occupation for Jews but also as one in which they could demonstrate their special talents.

Jewish intellectual history offered the *maskilim* several traditions concerning the nature of wisdom and the attitude to it: the biblical and wisdom literature of the Second Temple period, the talmudic literature, and the philosophical traditions of the Middle Ages and the Renaissance. The *maskilim* and Jewish scholars of the nineteenth century had the option of choosing one of them or trying to reconcile them. Needless to say, for the moderate *maskilim*—the *maskilim* who were practising Jews but also believed in acquiring a general education—the most important tradition was that of the Sages' notion of 'Greek wisdom', since it represented an 'authentic tradition'.

(a) The Wisdom of the Sages

The question of what the Sages meant in speaking of 'Greek wisdom' has spawned diverse interpretations. Differing views were found in their words, depending greatly on the changing circumstances in which they were uttered.[9] The Midrash says 'Should a person tell you there is wisdom among the nations, believe it' (Lam. Rabbah 2: 13) and Rabbi Judah Hanasi felt that in certain matters—he was referring to the orbit of the sun—'Their view is preferable to ours' (bPes. 94b). However, elsewhere there were strict prohibitions against too close a cultural contact, and even a vehement objection to the study of logic ('Restrain your sons from *higayon*', bBer. 28b,

---

[8] Barzilay, 'The Italian and Berlin Haskalah'.

[9] Lieberman, 'The Natural Sciences of the Rabbis'; id., 'The Alleged Ban on Greek Wisdom'; Wiesenberg, 'Related Prohibitions'; Herr, 'Greek Wisdom'; Hallewy, 'Concerning the Ban on Greek Wisdom'; Rappel, *Seven Wisdoms*; *Encyclopaedia Judaica*, xvi. 558–63; M. Greenberg, 'The Sages and Alien Wisdom'; Rappel, '*Chokhmah Yevanit*: Rhetoric'.

52).[10] The reason why the meaning of 'Greek wisdom' in the writings of the Sages lacks clarity is probably that it changed constantly throughout the generations. Many of these statements are temporary measures, reactions to a historical situation or a personal stance. That, for example, is how one should understand a doctrinaire statement such as 'Accursed is a man who raises pigs, and accursed is a man who teaches his son Greek wisdom' (e.g. bSot. 49b), or contradictory statements.

Minimalist commentators have argued that by 'wisdom' the Sages meant only the art of rhetoric, or particularly astronomy. Others were of the opinion that the Sages were not speaking of wisdom as *sophia*, in the sense of metaphysics, theology, understanding of the world, or knowledge about the natural sciences, but only of *techne*, various practical skills in the area of crafts and applied arts (the medieval *ars mechanica*), in particular astronomy and arithmetic, which in the language of the Haskalah were known as 'useful (or applied) *chokhmot*'.[11] There is another view that interprets 'Greek wisdom' as the 'wisdom of the occult', which originated in the allegorical literature of Philo and continued in mysticism and kabbalah. In the fourteenth century, for example, R. Isaac bar Sheshet stated that the Sages had pronounced Greek wisdom the 'wisdom of allusions and riddles'. This shows that his objection to Greek wisdom was an expression of the rationalistic mainstream of Judaism.[12] However, it seems safe to assume that by 'Greek wisdom' the Sages were referring to the 'rationalistic' aspects of Hellenistic civilization.

It therefore appears that 'alien wisdom' denotes wisdom from a foreign

---

[10] *Higayon* is usually understood as 'idle reading', but some commentators take it as 'logic': thus Lieberman translates it 'Prevent your children from (engaging in) the sciences of logic' ('The Alleged Ban on Greek Wisdom', 103). In my view, however, there is no reason to believe that the Sages did not know the importance of logic.

[11] Werblowsky, 'Greek Wisdom'; Kadushin, *The Rabbinic Mind*; Shalit's notes to Josephus' *Antiquities*, books vii–x (vol. ii, pp. a–b n. 1a); Wolfson, 'The Classification of Sciences'. See too Origen, *Epistola ad Gregorium* (PG 11. 87–91), calling on his pupils to prepare themselves by studying Greek philosophy, geometry, and astronomy, as well as the words of the philosophers on music, grammar, and rhetoric, which assist philosophy. According to David Nieto it is 'impossible to believe that the Sages of Israel should have discouraged the study of the very sciences which are essential to civilized life. All they prohibited was the reading of such books which could lead to heresy, immorality, or the kind of idleness which induces mental disturbances' (Petuchowski, *The Theology of Haham David Nieto*, 51). Among the many studies on Jews and sciences see W. H. Feldman, *Rabbinical Mathematics and Astronomy*; Friedenwald, *The Jews and Medicine*.

[12] According to Sh. Rubin, *Milchemet hanigleh vehanistar*, 'Greek wisdom' is esoteric wisdom, mysticism, which began with Philo's allegorical literature and continued in kabbalah. In his view, there was an ongoing struggle in Jewish intellectual circles between those influenced by the external world of esoteric and those adhering to original Jewish rationalism. This struggle was waged by ignoring, attacking, and mocking the esoteric views. The idea did not originate with him: already in the Middle Ages some Jewish writers had understood 'Greek wisdom' as magic or mythology. See Dov Schwartz, '"Greek Wisdom"'.

(non-Jewish) source, or wisdom which is not an integral part of the Torah. In any event, the Sages never viewed astronomy or mathematics as *propaideia* for the Torah in the sense of 'spiritual preparation' or even as intellectual skills required for its defence. As far as they were concerned, Greek wisdom was anything that assists one in learning about the universe and the surrounding society and maintaining vitally necessary communications with it. Hence 'wisdom' was interpreted in the Talmud as 'secular studies', 'neutral knowledge' that did not impair faith and the Torah; for example, R. Eleazar ben Hisma said 'astronomy and geometry are like the savouries of wisdom' (*Pirkei Avot* 3: 23).[13]

For the Sages, then, Greek wisdom is not *sophia*, an independent authority of comprehension of the world, theology, and metaphysics; nor is the scientific knowledge acquired through the study of 'external wisdoms' intended to support and validate the words of the Torah and historical tradition. The Sages made no attempt to reconcile philosophy with their contemplations. They did not search for a common denominator between them and rationalistic philosophy, nor did they believe that wisdom is derived from observing a theoretically universal human nature. A knowledge of astronomy, physics, and the rest assisted comprehension of a world order and its organization, but for the Sages it did not prove—as it did for the philosophers—the existence of a God who created and governed the universe. Thus they accepted God's admonition to Job and did not 'inquire into the miraculous'.[14]

From the Talmud, then, the *maskilim* were able to avail themselves of one interpretation of wisdom literature: an acknowledgement of the importance of useful 'neutral knowledge'. That pragmatic outlook was adopted both by orthodox scholars and moderate *maskilim*. The legitimation accorded by the Vilna Gaon (Elijah of Vilna, 1720–97, the great Lithuanian scholar and leader of the *mitnagedim*, opponents of the hasidic movement) to some branches of science such as geography, algebra, geometry, and music was, as in the Talmud, instrumental in nature: they assist in achieving an understanding of the Torah and are as it were a savoury relish to bring out its full flavour. Two disciples of his, Rabbi Israel Zamosc and Rabbi Baruch Shklov, both employed arguments originating in the

[13] Some modern scholars see here a reference to numerology (*gematria*), but medieval commentators understood the text as it is translated here. See Wasserstein, 'Astronomy and Geometry'; Samhursky, 'The Term Gematria'. On mathemetics as propaedeutic see Jaeger, *Paideia* ii. 301–9; Marrou, *History of Education in Antiquity*, 176–85.

[14] Ruderman goes too far, in my view, when he writes that the rabbis 'not only endorsed the mastery of naturalistic knowledge; they were open to improving nature, to mastering its forces, and even replicating it' (*Jewish Thought and Scientific Discovery*, 376).

medieval tradition to explain the necessity of learning the 'alien wisdoms'. Baruch Shklov wrote in the introduction to his *Euclid* that the Gaon had told him: 'To the degree that a man is lacking in knowledge and secular sciences, he will lack one-hundredfold in the wisdom of the Torah.' In the case of the Vilna Gaon, one obviously cannot speak of the reconciliation of Greek wisdom with the Torah or the subordination of the Torah to Greek wisdom. For him sciences had no value in their own right, nor did he believe that they contributed to the wholeness of the Jew in respect of faith. The 'practical' legitimation was most commonly found in the literature of the moderate Haskalah—the benefit to be gained from general knowledge in understanding the halakhah or the Bible. The various subjects covered by the 'natural sciences' or general scientific learning were understood in the sense of 'seasoning added to wisdom', not necessary to an understanding of the Torah but a useful addition to general knowledge. Thus Smolenskin was wrong to accept the claim of some conservative scholars that the Vilna Gaon was the 'father of the wisdom and Sages of Jewry'.[15]

(b) The Bible and Wisdom Literature

In the Bible and in the literature of the Second Temple period the *maskilim* found different meanings of 'wisdom'. It is no wonder that they began translating the Jewish wisdom literature of the Second Temple period, in which 'wisdom' means mainly a moral code of behaviour, but also useful skills.

First, we shall briefly consider the meaning of wisdom in the Bible. In 1 Kings the wisdom of Solomon, which surpassed 'the wisdom of all the people of the east, and all the wisdom of Egypt' (5: 10 Hebr.; 4: 31 in English versions), was the wisdom to compose proverbs and songs, but it was also an encyclopaedic knowledge of the world of nature, the ability to solve riddles and answer hard questions.[16] In the Book of Proverbs, wisdom is ethical instruction for righteous conduct, but also a divine attribute: 'The Lord by wisdom founded the earth; by understanding he established the heavens' (3: 19). In his foreword to Wolf Meir's translation

[15] Smolenskin, 'Et lata'at', 194. This remark was part of his sharp criticism of Mendelssohn and his concept of emancipation, which, in Smolenskin's view, was anti-national. Therefore he preferred to present the Gaon (that is to say, an 'authentic' inner tradition) as the forerunner of Haskalah—for it was important for him to stress that one can be against Mendelssohn but at the same time not reject 'sciences'. Hence Smolenskin was wrong because he misunderstood the different conception of 'wisdom' in 'modernized traditional Judaism'; for a truer view see Etkes, 'The Question of the Forerunners'; id., 'The Gaon of Vilna and the Haskalah'.

[16] Wood, *Wisdom Literature*, 49–51. In later tradition the 'hard questions' put to Solomon by the Queen of Sheba (1 Kgs. 10: 1) were understood as riddles.

of Proverbs (Prague, 1834) Isaac Euchel, following in Wessely's footsteps, interpreted the concept of wisdom not only as practical wisdom, or as rules of proper conduct, but as an abstract force, which is not found in reality but offers an ideal of perfection. In his view, the wise man is one who approaches this perfection. Every kind of knowledge that brings man closer to this perfection is wisdom, and the verse in Proverbs 'Wisdom crieth in the street' (1: 20) refers to the entire range of wisdom.[17] In the Book of Job, wisdom is mainly the fear of God ('The fear of the Lord, that is wisdom', 28: 28).[18] But wisdom is also the knowledge acquired by old age ('Wisdom is with the aged', 12: 12), and it also indicates human skill and ingenuity. Thus in the Bible, wisdom is at once a philosophy of life and an accumulated lore of rules for life; 'Wisdom may be a special divine gift granted by God to men, subsequent to and apart from their creation.'[19]

As to the Second Temple period, in the Wisdom of Jesus the Son of Sirach or Ben-Sira, traditionally known in the West as Ecclesiasticus, and the Wisdom of Solomon, wisdom is not only a system of neutral and pragmatic knowledge, i.e. secular studies, but it is as it were a cosmological entity that came into being before any thing was created and is found in all the acts of creation; it is universal and transcends all boundaries. It has endowed man with the abilities required to create the various sciences (Wisd. 7: 17–20). In any event, wisdom, that is to say science, is limited in its ability to understand the secrets of the world and the ways of the Lord.

[17] Euchel, *Hakdamah lesefer Mishlei*, 15.

[18] Ramhal (Moses Chaim Luzzatto) writes that in Job 'the fear of the Lord is thus identified with wisdom, and declared to be the only true wisdom. The term "wisdom" presupposes the use of the intellect' (*Mesilat yesharim*, 6). The alien sources of the notion of wisdom in the Bible are clearly reflected in Ecclesiastes, and Job polemicizes against it. 'Thus, the wisdom books—Proverbs, Ecclesiastes, Job— are not only witness to a cultural history, but a theological controversy over the profoundest question of human existence, the question of the understanding of God and man, world and life': Würthwein, 'Egyptian Wisdom and the Old Testament', 148. In Würthwein's view, the way Kohelet (Ecclesiastes) conducts the debate shows him to be a 'thinker of great individuality whose spiritual attitude one might want to make intelligible by reference to Greek spirituality. But, repeated attempts to prove conclusively a Greek source for Ecclesiastes have not yet succeeded' (ibid. 144) In Bickerman's view Kohelet, who 'is Job who failed the test', wrote in Ptolemaic Jerusalem and may have heard a Greek debater in Palestine, but his despair was a unique Jewish type of despair: 'for the Jewish sage the discovery of the vanity of the world was not a step to liberation but a confession of despair. . . . The absence of retributive justice—shrugged off by a contemporary Greek dissenter—was the basic evil of all that happened under the sun.' Thus 'Ecclesiastes could have been written only by a devout Jew who discovered that there was no Providence, and that he was alone in a world foreign to him.' See the chapter 'Koheleth (Ecclesiastes) or The Philosophy of an Acquisitive Society' in Bickerman, *Four Strange Books of the Bible*, 141–67. R. Gordis also rejects the different theories concerning an alleged Greek influence on the spirit of the book and writes that 'What is most striking, however, is not his familiarity with some popular ideas drawn from Greek philosophy, but his completely original and independent use of these ideas to express his own unique world-view' (*Kohelet—The Man and his World*, 56).

[19] Rylaarsdam, *Revelation in Jewish Wisdom Literature*, 55–6; see too Wood, *Wisdom Literature*, 63–6; Gilbert, 'Wisdom Literature', 283–324.

'All wisdom is from the Lord; wisdom is with Him for ever' (Sir. 1: 1). The beginning and end of all wisdom, Ben-Sira preaches, is the fear of God, as he relates that '. . . from my youth I followed [Wisdom's] steps' (51: 15); 'Do not pry into things too hard for you or examine what is beyond your reach', for '. . . .what the Lord keeps secret is no concern of yours' (3: 21–2). 'If you long for wisdom, keep the commandments' (1: 26). All this wisdom was given to the Jewish people in a revelation through the Torah.[20]

Long before it was endeavoured to translate the wisdom literature of the Hellenistic period into Hebrew, de' Rossi had defended the reading of it. In his *Sefer me'or einayim: Imrei binah*, ch. 2, he dealt with the attitude of the Sages towards Ben-Sira and the other Apocrypha, attempting to prove not only that their rejection of these works was not absolute, but that the Sages themselves employed the words of Ben-Sira.[21] In his youth Wessely translated the Wisdom of Solomon from French and German,[22] adding to it an amateurish philosophical commentary called *Ruach chen* ('The Spirit of Grace', Zech. 12: 10). He also published another work, *Gan na'ul* ('A Garden Locked', S. of S. 4: 12; Amsterdam, 1765/6), which discussed the concept of wisdom in the Bible.[23] J. L. Ben-Ze'ev translated *Mishlei Ben-Sira* (Breslau, 1798) through the German translation. (A free and inferior translation of this work was also made in 1820.) The Wisdom of Ben-Sira and the Wisdom of Solomon were thought of as one work. The fact that the *amora'im*—the rabbis active from the period of the completion of the Mishnah (c.AD 200) until the completion of the Babylonian and Jerusalem Talmuds (end of the fourth and fifth centuries respectively)— forbade the reading of Ben-Sira (which was apparently no longer extant in Hebrew after the tenth century) obviously did not prevent it from being accepted by the Haskalah. It is not surprising that Menahem Stein

[20] There is a scholarly dispute concerning the alleged Hellenistic influences on Ben-Sira. See Rylaarsdam, *Revelation in Jewish Wisdom Literature*; Wood, *Wisdom Literature*; Schnabel, *Law and Wisdom*; M. Z. Segal, *Sefer Ben-Sira hashalem*. According to Di Lella, in his introduction and commentary (The Anchor Bible edition), 49, the 'dependence of Ben Sira on several non-Jewish writings seems beyond question'. In his view, wisdom in Ben-Sira 'may be considered as either speculative or practical. Speculative wisdom has the intellect as its focus . . . Practical wisdom . . . includes what we would call today secular, ethical, and spiritual concerns and choices in daily life' (p. 79). See also Charles's introduction, *Apocrypha and Pseudepigrapha*, i. 268–315, esp. 270: 'Ben-Sira has here and there thoughts which at first sight look like traces of Hellenic influence, but are not so in reality: they are independent parallels, but have not otherwise anything to do with Greek culture.'

[21] Bonfil, *Azariah de' Rossi*, 217–33.

[22] Kahanah, *Hasefarim hachitsoniyim*, ii/2. 472–63.

[23] *Ruach chen* is literally 'the spirit of grace' (Zech. 12: 10), but *chen* was also understood as an acronym for *chokhmat hanistar*, the 'hidden wisdom' of mysticism. *Gan na'ul*, 'a garden locked' (S. of S. 4: 12), implies secrecy and mystery.

regarded Wessely's translation of the Wisdom of Solomon as a work on the very threshold of the new Hebrew literature.[24] Both these books were eminently suited to the new intellectual world of some of the *maskilim*.

It is clear why this particular Jewish literature served as an exemplar for the early *maskilim* and a source of inspiration for their view that wisdom from a divine source endows man with a recognition and an understanding of the world. 'He himself gave me a true understanding of things as they are: a knowledge of the structure of the world and the operation of the elements; the beginning and end of epochs and their middle course; alternating solstices and changing seasons; the cycles of the years and the constellations . . .' (Wisd. 7: 17–19). Here the wisdom of God is manifested in the order of creation; it represents the entire spectrum of nature and teaches all human arts and crafts (vv. 14–21). Hence wisdom is parallel to *technē*, the ability of man to master things that affect his life. It is also 'wisdom' that guides one to proper ethical conduct, since 'the fear of the Lord is wisdom and discipline; fidelity and gentleness are his delight' (Sir. 1: 27). Hence the catechism literature and the didactic ethics of the Haskalah are suffused with a pietistic spirit. Ethical conduct, a key part of the *Bildung* of the 'new man', is therefore not the fruit of obedience and enslavement to an obscurantist tradition, but is rather an outcome of ever-expanding knowledge. In the Wisdom of Solomon, as in the Haskalah literature that emulates it, wisdom is personified and depicted as a mediator between God and man: its source is divine and it does not conflict with or contradict the commandments.

Nevertheless, the reference to Ben-Sira appears to have constituted a deviation from the tradition, and even an opposition to it. Although one can show that the Sages were familiar with Ben-Sira and even used it without direct quotation, their attitude towards it was ambivalent. In the view of some Sages, the book did not 'sully the hands' (that is, was not sacred, so that one could touch ordinary objects after handling it); Rabbi Akiva was said to have declared with vehemence that whoever brings Ben-Sira into his home brings with it confusion and compounds unnecessary and harmful prattle and tedium.

Wisdom is also the source of ethics. As ethics and as knowledge, wisdom is important to mend and modernize society, and to improve its attributes and its image. Hence Ben-Sira and the Wisdom of Solomon were regarded as a source of support for the world outlook of the Haskalah and for its programme. In Chapter 8 we shall see how the *maskilim* used the model of the wisdom literature to create a new didactic literature of their

---

[24] See Sarton, *Hellenistic Science*, 237–8.

own; in Chapter 10 we shall follow the emergence of the new image of Hellenistic Jewish culture in Alexandria. At this point, it is important to note the resemblances that some scholars have found between the Sages and the sophists in technique and in goals, mainly 'in their concern with the education of the youth for practical life and in their culmination in philosophical skepticism'—resemblances also to be found in the age of the Haskalah and after—but perhaps most importantly in the fact that the wisdom literature is 'the most secular branch of ancient Hebrew literature, being concerned with broadly human rather than with specifically Jewish problems'.[25] Thus the Hebrew *maskilim* could find in this literature not only a guide to Wisdom but also a texture of religious feelings and human concerns.

(c) The Medieval, Renaissance, and Post-Renaissance Intellectual Traditions

These intellectual traditions followed both the talmudic and the Jewish-Hellenistic outlook and created a dual or ambivalent position towards wisdom. Judah Halevi, in his famous and pithy maxim, 'Do not exalt Greek wisdom, which has no fruit but only flowers', did not intend 'flowers' to mean aesthetic value, just as he was not using 'wisdom' in the Sages' sense. He was referring first and foremost to Greek philosophy, i.e. to metaphysics, which deals with the essence of the world and the purpose of its existence, a discipline he regarded as utterly sterile. It was metaphysics against which he issued his warning; by contrast, he did not reject out of hand Greek wisdom in the sense intended by the Sages, i.e. all those areas of knowledge about the world and the applied professions, such as astronomy, medicine, and zoology, which are not injurious to faith and the Torah of Israel. He even maintained that the Greek knowledge of nature is extremely valuable, and he himself made use of the theories of Galen and Hippocrates (although, unlike Maimonides, he did not believe that the 'wisdom of Aristotle' was necessarily always the correct understanding of nature). Thus Judah Halevi's view was that one ought to accept the natural sciences (agriculture, zoology, anatomy, etc.) as well as the science of the celestial spheres and their movements (astronomy), i.e. the 'auxiliary wisdoms', about which there was general agreement. His conception of the hierarchical division of sciences was as follows: supreme were philosophy and metaphysics; in the second class came astronomy, mathematics, and medicine; in the third class the arts and crafts. The difference between the natural sciences and metaphysics, he writes, arises from the fact that

[25] Gordis, *Kohelet—The Man and his World*, 30–2.

in the former there is general agreement, which is not the case in the latter; this demonstrates the limits of human wisdom. It is no wonder that a religiously observant *maskil* like Shadal (S. D. Luzzatto) was deeply impressed by Judah Halevi and regarded him as an exemplary figure: 'He studied Greek and Islamic wisdom but his heart was not seduced by it.'[26]

The term *chokhmah*, writes Maimonides, 'is used for four different things. 1. It denotes the knowledge of those truths which lead to the knowledge of God . . . 2. The expression *chokhmah* denotes also knowledge for any workmanship . . . 3. It is also used for the acquisition of moral principles . . . 4. It implies, lastly, the notion of cunning and subtlety . . .' (*Guide*, III. liv).[27] Maimonides demonstrated a positive attitude towards *chokhmah* as knowledge (science) that is at the very limit of human experience, establishes incontrovertible laws, and perceives the relationship between the theoretical and natural sciences, on the one hand, and divine science (metaphysics) on the other. For instance, he believed that through the science of astronomy and the science of nature, man learns that this world has a God who not only created it, but also governs it, according to a primal will expressed in the laws of nature. In a vivid image, Maimonides describes those engaged in a study of the mathematical sciences and logic as simply walking around the walls of a palace and seeking the gate, while those who embark on a study of the natural sciences pass through the forecourt:

My son, so long as you are engaged in studying the Mathematical Sciences and Logic, you belong to those who go round the palace in search of the gate . . . When you understand Physics, you have entered the hall; and when, after completing the study of Natural Philosophy, you master metaphysics, you have entered the innermost court, and are with the king in the same palace. You have attained the degree of the wise men, who include Men of different grades of perfection. (*Guide*, III. li).[28]

There is a lengthy dispute about the nature and meaning of wisdom in Maimonides' writings;[29] it is well known that his idea of creating harmony between Aristotelian metaphysics and the Jewish concept of creation and revelation was the object of copious criticism, not only on the part of the anti-Maimonidean orthodoxy but also on the part of secular Jews. They viewed Maimonides as the negative model of a seeker of a harmony that

[26] In his *Betulat bat Yehudah* ('The Virgin Daughter of Judah', Lam. 1: 15, but also 'of Judah Halevi'; Prague, 1840), 4. See in Werses, 'Judah Halevi in the Nineteenth Century', 269. On Shadal see Ch. 6.

[27] See Maimonides, *Guide*, 393–7.

[28] Ibid. 385. Pines, 'The Philosophical Sources of the *Guide*', 15–35. See also Hartman, *Maimonides: Torah and Philosophy*.

[29] Wolfson, 'The Classification of Sciences', 172–3; Pines, 'The Philosophical Sources'.

contradicts the 'spirit of Israel'. One of his first critics, Rabbi Judah ibn al-Fakhar (a physician and leader of the Jewish community in Toledo in the second half of the thirteenth century), denounced Maimonides with the words:

> Hence the Torah will face a dark night
> and its law will not come to light;
> Into its sacred places are come a Gentile horde
> and Greeks have defiled the Temple of the Lord
> And wherever God's name is profaned, no honour is bestowed on a rabbi.[30]

In the same vein, Rabbi Hasdai Crescas (d. 1412?), the Spanish philosopher and theologian, criticized Maimonides for straying from the truth:

> And many members of our people pretended to conjure up a vision and words of prophecy, vague and sealed off by dreams and idle fancies . . . until some of our greatest sages were drawn to their words and preened themselves in their writings, and adorned themselves with their proofs; and among them and at their head was the esteemed Rabbi Moses ben Maimon (of blessed memory) who with his great intellect and superlative comprehension of the Talmud and his generous heart, understood the books of philosophy and their essays. They tempted him and he was enticed and from their weak hypotheses, he made pillars and foundations for the secrets of the Torah in a book called *The Guide of the Perplexed*.[31]

Nevertheless, as was already noted, a lengthy attempt was made to find some correspondence between the world-view of Judaism and Aristotelianism: '. . . and there is no one except only the blessed Almighty, who is above human intelligence, and all this was demonstrated through indisputable proofs in Aristotle's books on divinity [i.e. metaphysics]', wrote Rabbi Yosef ibn Caspi (14th c.). 'Therefore Maimonides was greatly vexed when he found that Aristotle had ventured to interpret the commandments and attributed interpretations to himself, which he had stolen from books written by another. That is the reason Maimonides found it necessary to write the *Guide of the Perplexed*.'[32]

In his defence of the use of external *chokhmot* in the second chapter

---

[30] al-Fakhar, *Igrot hakana'ut*, 1. Cf. Ross, 'Spinoza and the Interpretation of the Bible', and Gottschalk, *Ahad Ha'am*, 147–52. See also Sarachek, *Faith and Reason*; Silver, *Maimonidean Criticism*.

[31] M. Kellner, 'Inadvertent Heresy', 401; Julius Guttmann, *Philosophies of Judaism*, 224–41.

[32] In J. Dan, *Hebrew Ethical and Homiletical Literature*, 100; see also 94–102. A totally different view was expressed by Saadiah ben Maimun ibn Danan (Dannan), the grammarian, philosopher, poet, and halakhist of Granada who defended *The Guide of the Perplexed* in a satirical poem attacking the view that philosophy was a dangerous wisdom and that the ancient Greeks were no more than idolaters: 'The Greeks do not only have carved idols made by their forefathers that they inherited; | For their sages in their wisdom explored the truth and found the true religion' (cit. Zinberg, *History of the Literature of Israel*, ii. 220).

of *Imrei binah*, de' Rossi refers mainly to philosophy. He quotes, among others, the words of Rabbi Menahem Recanati, of the fourteenth century, who wrote that 'the ways of the kingdom of Greece are close to those of faith, namely to the path of the Torah', and interpreted that as a reference mainly to the philosophers who preceded Aristotle and in their opinions tended towards the view of the Torah. He added evidence to show that from the twelfth century on the rabbis were thoroughly familiar with Aristotle: 'These external wisdoms, which we shall use for the purpose of the internal ones, the children of God shall see that they are good.'[33] Furthermore, we have already noted his use of the continuous tradition that Aristotle, or Plato, was a pupil of Moses, Jeremiah, and others.

If we summarize all the things that were described as 'Greek wisdom' in medieval literature, particularly in Spain, we shall find that in general it was identified with everything that is not Torah. The identification of sciences as external to the Torah remained as a signal of a conservative and traditional nature, rarely positive (associated with a positive attitude towards Greek philosophy), generally bearing the character of a stigma, for the purpose of cautioning Jews to keep their distance from them. Greek wisdom was generally understood to mean all branches of the natural sciences, study of which became more widely tolerated as useful and necessary, both for an understanding of the Torah and the halakhah, and also for professional and social activity, but not necessarily as a basis for faith. Although there were those who regarded a knowledge of the sciences as an essential contribution to knowledge of the Torah, a fierce and deep-seated dispute raged about the attitude that Jews should take to Greek philosophy, its purpose, and its link to faith. However, one must bear in mind that this argument was conducted in the élite circles of Jewish society; the traditional Jewish society from which modern Judaism sprang in the West generally exhibited distinctly conservative, and even extreme, attitudes in its opposition to Greek sciences.

Obviously, in order to adopt the positive attitude of medieval Jewish philosophy towards the 'external wisdoms', one first had to have a positive attitude towards Jewish philosophy in general,[34] mainly since Jewish philosophy, from its inception in the tenth century, was frequently regarded

---

[33] In Bonfil's edition of Azariah de' Rossi, 222. No wonder this book was published by the Berlin Haskalah (1794). On the debate about the attitude towards 'external wisdoms' among Ashkenazi rabbis in the 16th c. see Elbaum, *Openness and Insularity*, 156–74; Ruderman, *Jewish Thought and Scientific Discovery*, 54–99.

[34] See Funkenstein, 'Haskalah, History, and the Medieval Tradition'.

as the fruit of 'alien influences',[35] and as 'heresy incarnate'. Only under the impact of Hellenistic and Islamic philosophy did Jews begin to philosophize about their faith. Indeed, the moderate Haskalah attempted to differentiate between wisdom (as knowledge and science) and philosophy, because it understood all too well the dangers of philosophy; possibly also to avoid being dragged into the medieval dispute between philosophers and anti-philosophers, a dispute that could only harm and hinder the educational aims of the Haskalah. Nevertheless, the *maskilim* carried on the polemic surrounding Maimonides. In the end, their attitude towards Maimonides (towards Aristotle's influence upon him, and through him, towards Aristotle) became the essence and the expression of the internal debate amongst the *maskilim* in favour of and against philosophy in general and Jewish philosophy in particular. More importantly, the *maskilim* found in the writings of their sixteenth- to eighteenth-century predecessors not only a corpus of scientific knowledge but above all legitimation for its acquisition, and set out to make it available to the general Jewish public as one manifestation of modern Jewishness.

THE DEFINITION AND CLASSIFICATION OF WISDOM IN THE HASKALAH

The controversy concerning the nature of wisdom and the attitude to be taken towards it entered a new phase in the late eighteenth and the nineteenth century. In modern Jewish literature from the Haskalah onward, wisdom was understood as philosophy, professional skills, pragmatic knowledge, and science.

In considering philosophy, science, secular studies, general education, neutral knowledge, and various professional skills, the *maskilim* attempted to find their way amidst the various German and Hebrew intellectual terms in use (*Erkenntnis, Vernunft, Verstand, Verstehen, Wissen; chokhmah, binah, da'at*).[36] What is the difference between abstract cognition (*Erkenntnis*) and objective knowledge (*Verstehen*)? What is the role of scientific knowledge and what is the relationship of Torah and faith to the philosophy and science of the eighteenth and nineteenth centuries? This was the crucial question. In other words, the *maskil* was confronted by two challenges: first to distinguish between philosophy and other fields of wisdom, and second to define the various fields of wisdom and their domains, and

---

[35] Guttmann, *Philosophies of Judaism*, 42–3; J. Katz, 'Halakhah and Kabalah as Competitive Subjects of Study'. See also Sirat, *Jewish Philosophical Thought*.

[36] The parallel terms in Renaissance literature are *prudenza, intelletto, scienza,* and *sapienza*.

to indicate which are desirable and which are to be avoided. Medieval and Renaissance Jewish writings offered several classifications of the 'alien wisdoms', and the *maskilim* followed this path. We have already seen that from the Talmud and from medieval and Renaissance philosophy they inherited a positive attitude towards wisdom in the sense of knowledge about the world as part of a man's education. None of the traditions ignores the need for a knowledge of natural sciences, medicine, and the like. The *maskilim*, however, show a partiality for those sayings that grant permission for the study of foreign languages and contact with the outside environment, while rejecting all those that prohibit them. On this point, moderate and radical *maskilim* are in complete agreement, in contrast to the negative attitude of conservative Orthodoxy. From the biblical and Hellenistic Jewish wisdom literature they borrowed the concept of Wisdom as a personification of the logic of the Creation and world-orders that mediates between faith and the world.

Thus the *maskilim* were aware of the manifold areas and types of wisdom. Two of the founders of the Haskalah categorized the different areas, based on earlier traditions. Wessely, in *Divrei shalom ve'emet* and *Gan na'ul*, tries to explain the difference between wisdom (*chokhmah*), understanding (*binah*), and knowledge (*da'at*). He holds wisdom to be a discrete faculty that is not a concrete reality, but is an abstraction unconnected to its subject in the process of our thinking. A wise man (*chakham*) is one who does not transgress against the laws of God and of common sense, who comprehends the ways of wisdom and moves closer to it. Perfection is wisdom and one who approaches it will be called wise. Wisdom is also an amalgam of all sublime knowledge. Anything that achieves perfection is wisdom.[37] Understanding or intelligence, in Wessely's view, also signifies a discrete faculty that is not a concrete reality. It is the faculty that distinguishes between truth and falsehood. Every wise man is intelligent, but not every intelligent man is wise. The third concept, knowledge, stands for all the education, the teachings, the laws and acts that the human intellect can acquire through learning and through trial and error. In his analysis, Wessely further distinguishes between *chokhmot tiviyot*, *chokhmot nimusiyot*, and *chokhmot limudiyot*.

Chokhmot tiviyot are the positivistic sciences, which are learnt empirically, through observation. The term encompasses the knowledge of nature, botany, medicine, chemistry, and the like. In other words, they deal with phenomena that fulfil certain conditions, such as natural laws, or that

---

[37] Wessely, *Divrei shalom ve'emet*, 62.

belong to the world of the Creation; in contrast, things created by man are not natural.

Chokhmot nimusiyot are the manners and virtues that are found in every human being whoever he may be, and which, in a Jew, exist even before he takes on the yoke of the Torah. The influence of deism and the Protestant evangelical revival can be recognized here in the claim that every human being has an inherent moral instinct. In Wessely's view, 'the perfect man' as well as 'the Jew as a perfect man' must first fulfil the universal rules of ethics and only after that, the particularistic commandments. All human society, and the Jew is no exception, draws on the same fundamental moral code. These *chokhmot nimusiyot* also include a knowledge of local customs; hence Wessely counted history and geography among them.[38] They are sometimes described as *chokhmot to'altiyot* or 'useful wisdoms'.

Chokhmot limudiyot—and here the influence of Kant is evident—are categories of thought implanted in the human intellect. They include mainly geometry and astronomy, which are based on 'axioms'. They are that same 'divine influence' without which man could not attain an understanding (*Verstehen*) of the essence of things. (To the above list, we should add the *chokhmot nitsrakhot*, which are the various kinds of practical skills.[39]) It is through the *chokhmot tiviyot* and *chokhmot limudiyot* that the eternal laws of the world are learnt and understood, for they were established by God and cannot be altered by man's knowledge or deeds.[40]

In his *Te'udah beYisrael*, the Russian *maskil* Isaac Baer Levinsohn, known as 'Ribal' (1788–1860), offers a detailed catalogue of Jewish literature through the ages and its attitude to *chokhmot*. The manifest objective of this list is to proffer solid evidence in support of his Haskalah programme. Not content with compiling a collection of essays in favour of Greek wisdom, he also tries to discover allusions to it in the writings of sages, philosophers, and rabbis. Levinsohn concludes that, in the context of Jewish intellectual tradition, nothing separated Judaism from the world around it, and that it was the rabbinical community which deviated widely from the tolerance

---

[38] In the Talmud the word *nimus* appears several times referring to the 'laws of the state'; it is derived from the Greek *nomos*, 'law, custom', and may also mean 'etiquette', 'manners', and 'customs'. In the Talmud the word does not refer to *musar* (ethics), but in the Haskalah literature it could be used for *musar*, laws, or manners. English 'law' is too narrow, since it does not cover custom.

[39] Wessely, *Divrei shalom ve'emet*, 63.

[40] See Wolfson, 'The Classification of Sciences'. On the classification of the sciences ('*ulūm*) in Muslim writings see Ibn Khaldûn, *The Muqaddimah*, ch. vi; Kraemer, *Humanism*, 150–5; Rosenthal, *The Classical Heritage in Islam*, 54–74; *Encyclopaedia of Islam*, iii. 1133–4; Melamed, *Wisdom's Little Sister*; Rice, *The Renaissance Idea of Wisdom*; Sarton, *The Appreciation of Ancient and Medieval Science*. On al-Fārābī's treatise *'Ihṣā' al-'ulūm* ('The Enumeration of the Sciences') see Rahman, *Islam and Modernity*, 32–4; Netton, *Al-Farabi and his School*, 34–54.

shown by Judaism and Jewish history.[41] In his view, and in the opinion of
those on which he bases his conclusion, the natural sciences and astronomy
are not prohibited by the Sages, for 'these are branches of the principles of
our faith'. What the Sages prohibited is 'also not the wisdom of allegory',
which is nothing other than the wisdom of the proverb and the image, but
the perusal of mythology. A study of all the *chokhmot* does not lead to an
abandonment of religion, not even the study of Aristotle, for his writings
contradict neither the Torah nor the words of the prophets (since, in any
case, the origin of philosophy is in Judaism). He believed that the Sages
directed men to approach a study of the *chokhmot* via a middle path: not to
aspire to be wise in matters beyond our grasp, nor to be too lazy to attain
whatever is possible from the *chokhmot* after diligent study and search. The
study of metaphysics is likened to a light lit within man that guides him
in learning those things that his intellect is capable of grasping in order to
know the deeds and glory of God.

Not only did Isaac Baer Levinsohn take matters much further than the
German Jewish *maskilim*, it would appear that he was also more radical than
those who came after him among the east European *maskilim*. One can
find continuity in the programmes of Wessely and Levinsohn—who were
separated by a fifty-year interval—but there are also palpable differences
between them. Levinsohn mobilized all levels of Jewish intellectual tradition to support his theory of 'correspondence', and to help open wide
the gates of Jewish society to all types of enlightenment. Like Wessely and
the Berlin *maskilim*, Levinsohn saw in wisdom not only a utilitarian need,
but also a value of universal human significance. There can be no Torah
without wisdom, and no 'great scholar of Torah' who is not also a 'great
scholar of wisdom'. However, the ostensibly traditional character of the
programme was made manifest in the theory of correspondence: enlightenment is in harmony with tradition and is an indispensable and essential
part of it. In other words, it was the rabbis who undermined tradition, and
not the *maskilim*, who neither denied it nor rebelled against it, but were
actually traditionalists themselves!

Levinsohn followed the path of the Berlin Haskalah, but in contrast to its
outlook his arguments had deeper underpinnings in the Jewish philosophical tradition of the Middle Ages and the Renaissance. Nevertheless, he is
closer to Mendelssohn and the Berlin Haskalah than he is to the medieval
philosophers. His struggle within traditional Jewish society would not have
been successful had he preferred the medieval philosophical tradition to
the world of the Sages; but indeed they had far more to contribute for his

---

[41] See the long list of Sages and rabbis who spoke in favour of sciences, 113–51.

purposes. In contrast to the philosophers, Levinsohn was interested in comprehensive sociocultural change, and not in a change in attitude towards metaphysical questions. He did not oppose a strict study of metaphysics, but his main interest was to encourage and to give full legitimation to the study of the modern sciences. Therefore he assigns far greater pragmatic utility to the *chokmot nitsrakhot* than to attempts at proving the relevance of Aristotelian metaphysics, and places them at the top of the list, because it was these for which the fathers of the Jewish nation—Moses, David, Solomon, and others—were noted. Without them it would be impossible to understand the meaning of the commandments. After the *chokhmot tiviyot* come geography, historiography, and so on, which comprise the *chokhmot limudiyot*. In answer to the assertion that these studies led 'to forsaking religion', Levinsohn based his reply on references both from the Sages and from Maimonides.

WISDOM AS PHILOSOPHY

While a *maskil* like Satanow did not need Maimonides in order to preface the second part of *Mishlei Asaf* with the statement that the book's spirit is that of Aristotle's *Ethics*, a moderate *maskil* like Wessely wrote that Aristotle's metaphysics was constructed out of 'spiders' webs' and 'chaos' and was of no significance.[42] In any event, the fact that Aristotelian views occasionally found their way into books about nature and might lead to heresy was no reason to reject the various *chokhmot* (since these were 'quarried from the rock of Israel and came forth from the days of Judah'). The prohibition in the Talmud against learning Greek philosophy, he wrote, arose from the belief that faith needs no help from philosophy, and that philosophy might impair faith. These views were totally disparate from those expressed by Isaac Samuel Reggio, rabbi of Gorizia (1784–1855), who in 1827 wrote a pamphlet entitled *HaTorah vehafilosofiah chovrot ishah el achotah* ('Torah and Philosophy are Intertwined'), in which he asserted that the Sages did not forbid the study of philosophy in general, and that only Aristotelian philosophy is not the true philosophy.[43]

---

[42] Wessely, *Divrei shalom ve'emet*, ii. 76–7. He accepts logic, which, is, in his view, a Greek innovation, and rejects metaphysics. In medieval Jewish writings, 'wisdom', as philosophy, is mainly Aristotelian philosophy, which is preferable to Neoplatonism. For Delmedigo (1591–1655) the way of harmonization adversely affects both the Torah and wisdom; hence the correct way is a theory of dual truth, namely, a view that posits the existence of two different levels of understanding that ought to be separated from one another (*Sefer bechinat hadat*, ed. Ross, 48–54).

[43] And see the same view in Krochmal, *Moreh nevukhei hazeman*, 120.

Shadal (S. D. Luzzatto) described Maimonides and the other medieval
Jewish philosophers as those 'whose vine grew from the vine of Greece';
Shai (Sha'ul Yisrael) Hurowitz (1861–1922), the radical *maskil* and Hebraist, wrote in 1885 that anyone seeking to reconcile the faith of Israel with
the 'debauchery of the ancient Greek philosophers' is misled and misleads
others: such were the *maskilim* and their great mentor Maimonides.[44]
Smolenskin's view of Maimonides' writings was that 'an evil spirit [had]
descended, leading him to graze in foreign pastures and to espouse Aristotle as a teacher superior to all teachers', thus directing the Torah of Israel
according to the ways of the Greeks.[45] However, these anti-Maimonidean
views, Orthodox and secular, were lonely voices.[46] Meir Eleazar Rappaport, for example, in his introduction to Ben-Ze'ev's book, *Chakhmei
Yavan* ('The Greek Sages', Munkács, 1795), wrote about the permission
granted for the study of Greek philosophy. In his introduction, he enu-
merated all the familiar reasons, mentioning the legendary traditions that
Judaism was the source of Greek philosophy, the names of the Sages who
permitted the study of Greek philosophy, and the fundamental harmony
between Greek philosophy and the wisdom of Israel. The wise men of
Greece, he wrote, have an advantage over those of other nations, because
'the course of their ideas and their theories are very close to the words of
our Sages' (and not only because they learnt from them). Hence he rejected
the words of Joseph Solomon Delmedigo (Yashar of Candia) that 'he who
searches for God and His divine words in the books of the philosophers
is like him who searches for the living in a cemetery' and conversely, he
who interprets the words of the Law and the Scripture according to the

[44] Nash, *In Search of Hebraism*, 70–1. It is ironic that he censured Mendelssohn, whom he called
the 'German Socrates' ('down with the German Socrates', he declared), and praised Krochmal as an
original thinker (despite his being influenced by Hegel), while at the same time admitting that he himself
was writing under Pan-Slavic and Pan-Germanic influences, 75. On Shadal's attitude see Rosenbloom,
Studies in Torah Judaism, 31–9. S. L. Steinheim, the German Jewish philosopher, defined Mendelsohn as
a man 'with pagan mind and Jewish body' (*Moses Mendelssohn und seine Schule*, Hamburg, 1840).

[45] 'Et lata'at', 209. His opposition stemmed from his objection to the codification of Jewish law as
creating a stultified and dogmatic halakhah which did not permit any development in keeping with
the spirit of the time. Hence philosophy exerted a negative influence because it became a 'burdensome
weight'. It seems that he blurred the distinction between Maimonides' principles of faith and philosophy,
on the one hand, and the principles of faith and the codification of the halakhah, on the other, which
certainly did not come to Maimonides from Greek inspiration. It would seem that he vented his anger
upon Maimonides as a student of Aristotle, for the wrong reasons; see his polemic at pp. 209–16.
Hamman also described Mendelssohn's philosophical rationalism as 'Greek', Z. Levy, *Judaism in the
World View*, 65.

[46] The Galician *maskil* Judah Leib Miesis (1798–1831), in his anti-hasidic satire *Kin'at ha'emet* ('Zeal for
the Truth', Vienna, 1828), depicted Maimonides as if he were a modern scientist. See Y. Friedlander's
edition in *Hebrew Satire*, iii; id. 'The Status of the Halakhah'. On Ahad Ha'am's attitude towards
Maimonides and his critics see Gottschalk, *Ahad Ha'am*, 150–5, and see Ahad Ha'am's essay 'Shilton
hasekhel'.

ideas of the philosophers is seeking the dead among the living'.[47] Meir Rappaport had only one cautionary remark: young *maskilim* whose faith is not secure and who are like innocent, impulsive chicks, liable to be blinded and to desecrate everything sacred, ought not to enter the *pardes* of philosophy.[48] Rappaport summed up all the expressions of apologetic and legitimation familiar from the intellectual tradition by saying that Jewish sages and philosophers alike not only expressed themselves in the spirit of the words of Greek sages, but also 'learnt lessons from the mouths of the sages of the nations . . .'. And if that were not enough, 'the sages of the nations' whose teachings are closest to the Torah of Israel are the sages of Greece.[49]

Whatever our viewpoint may be regarding the nature of Jewish philosophy and the affinity between it and faith, one thing cannot be doubted: since the end of the eighteenth century, intensive attempts have been made to explain Judaism according to philosophical principles and to establish harmony between them and 'the dogmas of Judaism'. In this way, Judaism was tested and evaluated according to insights 'borrowed from the outside world'. These tests and evaluations did not remain the province of a small group, but infiltrated and were absorbed into the world outlook of an ever-expanding Jewish communal entity.

SCIENCE AND FAITH

While philosophy was a matter of concern, science was accepted by the *maskilim* without many hesitations.

'[T]wo generations of philosophers, anxious to poison relations between science and religion', writes Gay, 'found that, whatever Newton's own religious convictions, they could do without them.'[50] The truth is that the German *Aufklärer* and the first generations of Jewish *maskilim* did their best to establish harmony between faith and science. Here they followed

---

[47] Quoted in Barzilay, *Joseph Solomon Delmedigo*, 180. However, Delmedigo, the first Jewish scholar to use logarithmic tables, was far from rejecting the study of philosophy or science (ibid. 169–219).

[48] *Pardes* is literally an orchard, but in the Talmud appears (though this is disputed) to be used for the fruitful but thorny world of kabbalah, to be approached only with caution.

[49] Ben-Ze'ev also translated Saadiah Gaon's *Emunot vede'ot* ('Beliefs and Opinions') from the Berlin edition of 1789, and distinguished between three components in religion: the divine, which relates to beliefs and views; the intellectual, which relates to the knowledge of the Deity; and the political, which relates to the obligations of a citizen in the society and the state.

[50] Gay, *The Science of Freedom*, 142. The philosophers claim that 'Reason needs not Authority, it is self-sufficing' (Hazard, *European Thought*, 26–43). It is also important to remember that 'the Newtonian Enlightenment was intended by its participants as a vast holding against materialism . . . against what is best described as the Radical Enlightenment': Jacob, *The Cultural Meaning of the Scientific Revolution*, 97. See also Westfall, *Science and Religion in Seventeenth-Century England*.

the Jewish medieval philosophers who used the speculative cosmological proofs (and in fact also ontological proofs) for the existence of God,[51] and saw in modern science an ally, not an enemy. Here enlightened piety conflicted with narrow-minded obscurantism.

Josephus, under the influence of Hellenistic philosophy, stated in *Antiquities* that Abraham 'was thus the first boldly to declare that God, the creator of the universe, is one, and that, if any other being contributed aught to man's welfare, each did so by His command and not in virtue of its own inherent power. This he inferred from the changes to which land and sea are subject, from the course of sun and moon, and from all the celestial phenomena . . .' (*Antiquities*, i. 155–6). The Hellenistic categories of cosmological thinking offered Josephus new justification for the monotheism of the Bible. In the same spirit, Shadal, who in his efforts to refute materialism found it useful to claim support from Socrates, Xenophon, Cicero, Galen, Newton, and the Scottish philosopher Dugald Stewart (1753–1828), as well as from Maimonides, displays great expertise in contemporary sciences and uses anatomy, physics, Copernican astronomy,[52] and other sciences to arrive at the conclusion that the orders of the universe—the microcosm and the macrocosm—are irrefutable evidence of the validity of the cosmological argument: harmony extant in all parts of creation proves the existence of a Divine Providence.[53] In his *Lezioni di teologia dogmatica* he writes about the 'strength of the teleological claim', which, in his view, 'is the most real, the most powerful, and the most ancient of all the arguments that were raised to prove the existence of a Deity'. Everything extant in nature is evidence of forethought and the Creator's intention, and proves the existence of a Creator of unlimited wisdom.[54] He follows here also Philo's view that the task of wisdom is 'to investigate all that nature has to show', and this nature (cosmos) is the creation of God, who governs the whole heaven and earth.[55]

[51] Wolfson writes that 'of the many historical proofs for the existence of God . . ., the cosmological, the ontological, and the teleological . . . only the cosmological type of argument was pressed into service by Jewish theologians . . . It is the cosmological argument, therefore, based upon the principle of causality, that became the standard proof of the existence of God in Jewish Philosophy' ('Notes on Proofs of the Existence of God', 575, 584). On attempts during the Renaissance to reconcile contemporary science with the Bible see Petuchowski, *The Theology of Haham David Nieto*, 60–3, and on the use of teleological and cosmological proofs see pp. 106–11.

[52] The *maskilim* of the 18th c. did not oppose Copernicus (or Newton), as their predecessors had done. See Levine, 'Paradise not Surrendered'.

[53] S. D. Luzzatto, 'Ha'emunah beTorat Moshe'. This is an 'argument from design' (see Cicero, *De Natura Deorum*, ii. 15). Wolfson, 'Notes on Proofs', 582–3.

[54] S. D. Luzzatto, *Lezioni di teologia dogmatica* = *Selected Writings*, i. 84–9.

[55] Philo, *On Providence*, 1 (trans. Colson, ix. 457); *De opificio mundi*, 9, 171–2 (trans. Whitaker, i. 11, 135–7).

Shadal also stated that the purpose of the Torah is not to teach natural sciences but to instil in men's hearts faith in the Almighty; if anything in the Torah from heaven contradicts the natural sciences, that in no way detracts from the values of the Torah, and hence the scholar ought not to misconstrue the Scriptures in order to make them conform to the natural sciences.[56] In other words, Shadal believed there could be some incompatibility between the Torah and the laws of nature, and therefore wished to separate the two, but insisted that the biblical concept of a world created according to a divine plan retains its metaphysical validity.

Most of the *maskilim*, even the religious among them, tried not to separate faith from science but to reconcile the two; however, their main interest was to reconcile belief in the Creation with the new scientific discoveries. In the writings of the *maskilim*, including their textbooks and their catechism, which dealt with the benefit derived from a knowledge of natural sciences, there were clear traces of the principle of the 'predetermined harmony' of the immanent revelation (from within the world) and of the sacred cosmology of writers like the botanist and physician Nehemiah Grew (1628–1711) and the naturalist John Ray (*The Wisdom of God Manifested in the Works of Creation*, 1691). One learns about the Creation from the nature of the world and the correspondence between form and function in the organic structures. Sacred cosmology serves as evidence of the existence of a Creator. They also were influenced by the arguments of Bishop Joseph Butler (*Analogy of Religion Natural and Revealed to the Constitution and Course of Nature*, 1736) and the apologist William Paley (*Natural Theology*, 1802), which claim that 'over and above the evidence of design in nature there were simply too many parallels between the law of civilization as discovered by impartial science and the teaching of the Bible to leave room for reasonable doubts.'[57] In the conceptual and spiritual world of the *maskilim* we shall also find an accord between previous internal traditions and the spiritual world of the German Enlightenment (which was less radical than the French Enlightenment). Very few of the German *Aufklärer*, as Reill observes, lost their faith or their confidence that hidden springs direct external events.[58] They believed in revelation and divine

---

[56] S. D. Luzzatto, 'Perush leBereshit 1–2', 135: the believer is not entitled to take the Scriptures out of context in order to agree with the natural sciences (*chokhmot tiviyot*), nor to reject the Torah from heaven (*Torah min hashamayim*) if he finds stories in it that cannot be reconciled with scientific research.

[57] Marsden, *Fundamentalism*, 16; cf. Willey, *The Eighteenth-Century Background*. These writers were influenced by the Stoic arguments reproduced by Cicero in his *De natura deorum* (see J. M. Ross's introduction, 58–60); cf. David Hume's *Dialogues concerning Natural Religion* (see N. K. Smith, *Hume's Dialogues*).

[58] Reill, *The German Enlightenment*, 190; cf. Hazard, *European Thought*, 127: 'The whole object of

intervention in history, and accepted that the Jewish people was chosen and unique. The more conservative among them distinguished between 'reason' (*Verstand*) as a negative and destructive agent, and *sophia*, which according to Gottfried Arnold is 'an inner light that transcends all rational exposition because it is a hypostasis in God', and directs and guides human beings.[59] Most of the *Aufklärer* believed in reason, which was capable of achieving a recognition of universal truth and revealing the causality that operates in human society as it does in nature. Hence they accorded a central role to education as a means of *Bildung*, of creating the new man. On the other hand, reason was considered by the conservatives to be a satanic tool. The distinction between knowledge and reason, in favour of knowledge, arose from the conception of reason—speculative philosophy—as an autonomous factor that undermined the validity of faith. Even more important was their conception of *sophia* as an illumination of the intellect that leads to and strengthens faith.

Moses Chayim Luzzatto (1707–46), known in Jewish sources as Ramhal, gives expression in his play *Layesharim tehilah* ('Praise to the Righteous', Amsterdam, 1743) to the outlook of a post-Renaissance Jew who anticipated the Haskalah in viewing the natural sciences as a means by which to achieve 'knowledge close to the truth about the magnificence of the Creator'. In the drama, all areas of natural science known at that time are attacked by Folly, who believes they serve no practical purpose:

> Weighing the wind with a scale
> Measuring water in the hollow of a hand
> They will be haughty, and there is no bread in their homes.

According to Ramhal, the world and its creatures attest to the wisdom of the Creator; only a Supreme Power, the Creator of the universe, could have brought into existence such a world of exemplary order and system. The enquiry into the miraculous arouses fervour for the works of the Creator. He believed that Wisdom and Enquiry do not impair Faith. For Enquiry states that:

> Here I go to explore
> The wonders of intelligence and they are unfathomable
> Our Creator and Maker reveals all . . .[60]

the German *Aufklärer* was to establish, not atheism, far from it, but "eine vernünftige Erkentnis Gottes", a rational knowledge of God.' A religiously observant *maskil* could not of course accept the deist view that God does not engage in the affairs of the world.

[59] Reill, *The German Enlightenment*, 27.
[60] M. Ch. Luzzatto, *Leyesharim tehilah*, 42.

Wisdom, then, does not give rise to doubts, but rather to certainty and faith (and morals). Hence there is no need to fear it as long as faith remains steadfast. This then is the basis for the permission to open Jewish society to the spirit of the time and to modernity—a desire which is both social and intellectual. In other words, all Jews can learn, as Moses did, various *chokhmot* in the 'palace of Pharaoh' without impairment to their faith or morals.

In the world of the Sages, there was no room for this kind of rationalization, namely that the knowledge of alien wisdoms did not present a danger to faith or piety, or that on the contrary alien wisdoms only intensified and strengthened faith and reverence, and actually prevented impiety by relating divine deeds with grandeur and praise. And yet this became the principal argument of the *maskilim*. From the eighteenth century the cosmological argument functioned as perhaps one of the most powerful barriers against apostasy.

In the first manifesto of the Berlin Haskalah, *Nachal habesor* ('The Brook Besor', 1 Sam. 30: 9–10), we read: 'When Wisdom sings out-of-doors, and lifts up her voice in the streets, hasten to call her, hurry to bring her home.' By no means did this advocate free-thinking, nor did it intend to encourage a loss of faith. What it did suggest was that faith and the commandments should be complemented by wisdom (meaning 'general knowledge' and science). Such universal knowledge, offering a full and clear picture of the cosmological system (and the pre-determined harmony inherent in the nature of the world and directing it), and of human society, would in any case engender the awareness of a Supreme Power who had created and continued to direct these complex and harmonious systems. Hence the natural sciences are mentioned here not as a body of knowledge by which one might understand natural phenomena, but as a vital source for understanding the divine purpose and origin of these phenomena.

Not so is man, who is created in the image of God: wisdom and science are God's gift to him, so he may observe His mighty deeds and comprehend His truths. Wisdom is a ladder set upon the earth with its highest rung reaching the heavens. The spirit of mankind ascends . . . Do not say that wisdom is far removed from us. Whatsoever you turn to you will understand. The gates [of wisdom] are open to every man for all eternity.[61]

Such declarations are characteristic of the new mode of thought, that encompassed not only apologetics but also the Newtonian use of science

---

[61] F. Baer, *Sefer toledot Yisrael*, 57.

to prove the existence of a Deity, as well as the perfect faith that bridged the gap between 'faith' and 'science'. Shadal wrote in similar vein:

Every man of Israel must know and believe that there is a Primal Being, ancient and eternal, and it is He who has devised and still devises everything in existence, and He is God, blessed be He . . . It is impossible, in any event, that there should not be a Primal Being who transcends all nature, its laws and its boundaries, who is void of every deficiency, every multiplicity and compositeness, every relationship and attribute, every human condition, for Him not to be the true cause of all who exist and all who will be born of them. For otherwise, that which we see existing now and that which will continue to exist, would be impossible.[62]

And here is the song of praise that Judah Leib Ben-Ze'ev offers at the beginning of his *Mesilat halimud* ('The Path of Study', 1802):

How majestic and great is [man's] superiority of training in science and erudition! He constructs for himself a telescope through which he looks to a place which the human eye never saw. Through proficiency in writing, he knows what is taking place on the other side of the world. He prepares for himself a balloon to lift him to the sky. All that he sees and observes he studies, to learn its qualities. He gauges every substance, taking all measures and dimensions: length and width, height and depth, density and area, round and square, from every angle and circumference—and that is geometry. He calculates ratios and degrees, computations and amounts, numbers and digits—and that is arithmetic. He studies the history of all living creatures, according to their kind: animals and beasts and fowl and reptiles and insects and worms. He studies and examines every plant, every seedling, every vegetable and herb, every blade of grass, every root, every tree trunk, every bough and every branch, every twig, every leaf, every blossom, every fruit. From some he prepares his food and from others his drink; from still others he brews remedies and potions, prepares bandages and whatever else he needs to heal any ailment and soothe any pain, practising the art of medicine.

And far wider and greater is man's capacity (*chokhmah*) for ideas and sciences. The spirit of his understanding spreads its wings to the ends of earth, and divides it into separate sections, into nations and their languages, and sets the boundaries for each and every state, for each district, each province, each elevation, unto each city and each village. He demarcates the places: here a city and there a village, here a valley and there a mountain, here a field and there a forest, here a sea and there a river. He probes deep into the nether regions of the earth and what is hidden deep within the mountains he explores. From the bowels of the earth he extracts water and salt, gold and silver and other treasures. He rises to the heavens, and in his wisdom measures the highest and utmost limits of the sky. He knows the orbits of the sun and the moon and the stars in their established order. According to them he keeps the laws of the special days and the festivals, for the jubilee and

---

[62] S. D. Luzzatto, 'Ha'emunah beTorat Moshe', 26–7.

the sabbatical year, for the years and the seasons, for the months and the Sabbaths, for the days and the hours. Thus he studies all that is in the heavens above and the earth below. He knows the arrangement of voices and will blend them into a melody, either to sing songs or to play on a musical instrument: violin, harp, drum, flute, and trumpet. He trains his tongue to speak sweetly in song and in poesy to recount the wonders of the Almighty, because He is a living and omnipotent God who has the greatness and might, the blessing and the glory.[63]

Ben-Ze'ev was repeating a commonly held idea: there is nothing accidental in the order of the world. 'Although we cannot see the Creator with our own eyes, none the less when we look upon His great and awesome deeds, His grandeur and understanding and goodness, we recognize that all that He did is good and comely, great and wondrous.' In other words, a knowledge of nature became a part of the Jewish intellectual's catechism. Ben-Ze'ev found support for the claim he made in the introduction to his book of catechism, *Yesodei hada'at* ('Foundation of Knowledge', Vienna, 1810–11), in the Book of Proverbs, 16: 4: 'The Lord has made everything for its purpose.' He interpreted this to mean that all parts of the Creation have a purpose and a logic to them. 'For all things, from the very height of the stars to the fine dust on the earth, have an intent in the Creation and a purpose for which they were created.' It is also not difficult to discern that in the nineteenth century new disciplines, such as geography, history, technology, etc. were added to the classic professions of astronomy, medicine, chemistry, and the like.

The hierarchical ordering of the universe that instates man as the lord of Creation represents a clear correspondence between Jewish tradition and the image of the 'vast chain of being' which Alexander Pope made so popular in his *Essay on Man* (1733–4). Mendelssohn greatly esteemed this work and wrote an essay about it called 'Pope the Metaphysician' (1755). Man, according to Pope and Mendelssohn, is 'the crowning glory of all living creatures', a noble link in the endless chain of beings midway from nothing to deity—an ancient concept found both in Hellenistic philosophy and in the Talmud.[64] The Haskalah extravagantly lauded man's intelligence, which educates him to recognize and decipher the codes of nature and the world, and enables him to mobilize science and technology for his own needs. This is an optimistic paean of praise to progress, which is a deliberate act of Divine Providence. Science is instrumental, but scientific progress, when it means understanding the world and its workings, is not neutral knowledge or a neutral act from the standpoint of faith. What mattered

[63] Ben-Ze'ev, *Mesilat halimud*, in *Beit hasefer*, i. 69–71.
[64] Gilon, *Mendelssohn's* Kohelet musar, 77.

was not the fact that the new picture of the world shattered the picture of
the biblical-talmudic world—and the Platonic-Aristotelian world as well.
The picture of the world, after all, was not the determining factor: it was
rather the fact that there was *order* to it. We must not forget, however,
that the spirit of Proverbs and Ben-Sira also hovered nearby, like the spirit
of pessimistic, righteous pietism—all too often chilling enthusiasm and
calling for restraint:

> The wise man does not seek wisdom
> In the hope that it will suffice to the end,
> But will seek it out so there shall be no
> Folly, and the *maskil* needs nothing save that.
> Man is wise while still he quests
> For wisdom, and when he thinks
> That he has reached his destination, he is
> A fool.[65]

Haskalah literature brims with a plethora of flowery praises for the
achievements of science and the new world—which is described as a world
of good, being created every day for all to see. From the Jewish point of
view, it appeared that modernity and progress promised civil liberties and
tolerance, and would therefore allow Jewish roots to be struck in European
society.

From a more general and inestimably more optimistic point of view,
the Enlightenment and the sciences promised the creation of a beneficent
world. Enlightenment would banish ignorance and dark fanaticism, would
link distant and different parts of the globe, would open wide the gates of
countries that were until then closed to the outside world, would spread
its light among them, and would bring a better, more moral life to all the
earth's inhabitants.

From the eighteenth century onward, praises were not only lavished on
the eternal cosmic order. The activities of human beings—'Promethean
humans'—who change primal orders were also praised, although it was
always remembered that it was God who imbued man with the intelligence
and the ability to change the world. God has placed man in a 'spacious and
well-furnished world', wrote Ray, and it is man's duty as well as privilege
to exploit and improve it as much as he can.[66] The Hebrew newspaper
Hamagid summarized the prevailing tone of the period in a series of articles
called 'The Spirit of the Times' (1858):

[65] Ben-Ze'ev, *Mesilat halimud*, 274.
[66] Willey, *The Eighteenth-Century Background*, 41.

With a mighty hand and an outstretched arm, Wisdom will reign in our generation. She will extend her royal sceptre like the dawn to cover the land, and day after day her strength and might will grow and drive out her foes: ignorance and evil folly, the children of the inferno and the mists of obscurity . . . Her many achievements are frequently renewed, always generating wonders. There is no end to the many undertakings of the scholars of our day and to the exploits of the nations in general, who are influenced by the spirit of the times, and act according to their generation. Indeed, the ways of the European nations are not miserly. They do not hide the treasures of their wisdom in the depths of the European soil alone, but are ready to fill the whole world with the fruits of their exploits. They will send the fountains of knowledge to water even the alien lands at the ends of the earth and the far corners of the world. In the spirit of wisdom, the borders of India, China, and Japan will be erased; it will be like the dew to those countries as well, and will revitalize even those distant regions.[67]

In the same vein, David Zamosc included in his literary miscellany of 1821, *Resisei hamelitzah*, a song of praise entitled 'Toledot yemei olam' ('History of the World'), by Mordekhai Rakh, eulogizing Columbus, Franklin, Herschel, and Newton, each of whom in his own way contributed to an expansion of the world and a more profound understanding of it.[68]

This optimism was as much an attempt at self-persuasion as a response to criticisms from traditional society and Orthodoxy. Haskalah literature—at first that of western Europe, later, more urgently and more frequently, that of eastern Europe—found it increasingly necessary to convince itself and its readership that wisdom by no means had the power to undermine faith or to invalidate the Torah. Decisively and with great confidence, it contended that not only did wisdom and science lack the power to shake the foundations of faith, they actually had the power to reinforce them. It was wisdom and science that were the instruments of faith and devoutness; they were the strongest and most convincing testimony to the truth of the faith and the Torah. The Haskalah adopted the Enlightenment's goals of edifying and educating society and all mankind, and of creating a being who approaches the ideal of human perfection (*Humanität*). These objectives were absorbed into their moral outlook:

Cast your eyes about you and see: the sciences will extend their boundaries every day, and wisdom will be perfected from one day to the next. And as the boundaries of science are extended, and the perfection of wisdom is increased, so will man's perfection grow and increase towards the Torah and the Law, towards truth and

---

[67] Y. Shavit, 'Window on the World'.
[68] Zamosc, *Resisei hamelitzah*, ii. 31–2.

insight; and God's light—His illumination and His truth—explores the innermost recesses of religion and the law.[69]

Furthermore, wisdom itself—the achievements of the sciences—is God's work. It is He who implanted wisdom into human beings, and directed their achievements in all the diverse fields. The telegraph, a technological accomplishment which greatly impressed that generation, was perceived as the consummation of Creation, under the tutelage of the Omniscient One.

Here wisdom arouses no doubts, only wonderment and awe. The wisdom of man, wrote Satanow, cannot arrive at the solution of the secrets of wisdom, but can only make man open his eyes and see what is revealed and what is hidden: 'Honour the Lord, let your eyes look upon God's work and see His deeds. Know Him with your intelligence and your knowledge. Not everyone is founded on wisdom. If they are reconciled with Him, they have no faults' (*Mishlei Asaf*, xxi. 15–16). For wisdom is the loyal handmaiden of faith and of reverence. 'There is no science to knowing God and there is no entry except through the path of wisdom. And there is no wisdom like that which God established through His deeds' (ibid. v. 18–19). When God wished to improve the lot of His creatures, He called Wisdom to appear before Him and sent her to walk about the land for the love of man. Declarations of this kind permeate Haskalah literature, which thus denies the existence of no neutral science or neutral history. All the works of wisdom and knowledge were instituted by God in order to serve man and engender piety. In any case, in no wise whatever are wisdom and knowledge in contradiction with faith.

Against this background, it was also possible to claim that it was the Judaeo-Christian myth, based on the monistic perception of an ordered universe—in which an omnipotent God determined its laws, which human understanding was capable of grasping—that actually spurred the development of modern science, and not the polytheistic perception of a multiplicity of forces and a Prime Mover or divinity immanent in nature. Thus, years later, as part of his collected translations of Greek and Latin poetry, Yisrael Rall introduced a polemical poem titled 'Da mah shetashiv!' ('Know What to Reply'), which counters Lucretius and his Epicurean philosophy:

> For we know it is the will of the all-merciful God,
> That all laws should be founded *On the Nature of Things*
> For without laws, thought and knowledge,
> No laws would ever come into being.

[69] *Hamagid*, Aug. 1857.

Without a plan, no system could be born,
And without an overseer, it would turn into disorder . . .
Any philosophy that is ignorant and false,
Will say: This is not a divine masterwork.
Denying the Creator of the world is false, and more:
For above and beyond nature, faith rules![70]

Lucretius was unable to attain faith, not only because he was an idolater, but also because of his arrogant reliance on intellect alone. At this point, Rall does not follow Ramhal's path and does not differentiate between the sensualistic and the rationalistic viewpoints. His criticism is turned against Lucretius and against the followers of nineteenth-century positivistic or materialistic outlooks, which introduced into the world a multiplicity of forces in order to explain the state of law by which it is governed. In that case, Rall characteristically asserts, the deeper one probes to investigate reality and the more one understands its complexity, the clearer it becomes that human intelligence is limited in understanding the inner rationale of things and that the physical laws cannot be a satisfactory explanation. The positivistic philosophers, he wrote, explain only the external factors, by the laws of gravity, magnetism, and so on. However, they cannot arrive at an enquiry into the first and only truth—the Primal Cause.

The self-evident conclusion is that:

Only the reverence of God is a fortress, a staff—
Happy is the man whose covenant with it is true!
How goodly and how pleasant it is for one who embraces
Refined faith, purified sevenfold—
Reverence for the God of wisdom! And His spirit spoke out,
'Turn away from bad understanding.' Truth will endure, Selah!

It is clear, then, that the *maskilim* expressed optimism about the possibility of bridging the gap between faith and science. This approach remained valid almost until the final quarter of the nineteenth century, when Haskalah optimism was replaced by sociopolitical radicalism or by nationalism. In the 1860s, Kalman Schulman sketched the portraits of what he viewed as the two polarized negative types: the secular, free-thinking *maskil* on the one hand, and the reclusive Orthodox Jew on the other. The first turns his back on religion, the second turns his back on wisdom:

And all the more so, that in this generation most of our people have been divided into two streams: one which seeks not wisdom, and decides that there is no piety in the language of God and the language of the Torah, and that all who immerse

[70] Rall, *Shirei romi*, 72–84.

themselves in it contravene piety. And the second, which makes a pretence of honouring wisdom, decides that there is no wisdom in it [religion] or in all its books, and that all who immerse themselves in it are not wise. And any *maskil* who seeks God will toil in vain to demonstrate to the one group that this language is a holy treasury and the fear of God is its treasure, and to make the second group understand that its nation is a source of wisdom and a fountain flowing with knowledge. For the first was not eager to see, and the second had no heart to understand—and the Lord gave us only scattered remnants whose eyes could see and whose hearts could understand that the Holy Tongue upholds all the honour of the House of Israel. Without it the honoured name of Ivrim—Hebrews—is not appropriate to us, for every people is called by the name of its language, and if the Hebrew language [Ivrit] is not used by us, how can we be called Ivrim? If this language is forgotten, so will Israel's Torah be forgotten, for the Torah is written in this language, and without knowing its ways, how shall we know the Torah?[71]

The need to find support in earlier traditions and the search for a correspondence between these traditions and the science of the time characterize the moderate *maskilim*, which found the ancients to be the best source of support for their interest in science. On the other hand the *maskilim* believed in scientific progress (although some tempered the enthusiasm with the proviso that scientific progress does not necessarily mean moral progress).[72] They asserted that since there had been many developments in science that the Sages knew nothing of, it is impossible to state that all wisdom is found in the Sources. Hence one must learn the new sciences, and they can be learnt only from the 'books of the Greeks'. This implicitly recognizes the fact that Jews are sadly lacking in their education, but primarily it acknowledges the fact that science is a process of discovery, and that old wisdom must give way to new. This view, and the new image of man as changing the fundamental order of the universe, were two of the important contributions of the Haskalah.

It was not enough to shower praises upon the values and benefits to be derived from the sciences that reveal the world and its laws to mankind: the task of the *maskilim* was to produce popular literature on science for the general Jewish public. From the close of the eighteenth century, through the nineteenth century, and onwards, the *maskilim* provided abundant articles and information in all areas of science.[73] General encyclopaedias were written covering every type of subject-matter. Many textbooks focused on imparting knowledge compiled by the *maskilim* in various disciplines:

[71] Schulman, *Divrei yemei olam*, iv. 22–38.
[72] See Ch. 6.
[73] On the *Sachschriften* in Germany during the 18th c. see Brüggemann and Ewers, *Handbuch*, 957–1216.

mineralogy and botany, zoology and anatomy, physics and geography.[74] This popular scientific literature in its Hebrew garb won accolades for giving the reader of Hebrew an opportunity to acquire 'wisdom and knowledge' without recourse to 'the languages of the nations'. In other words, the *maskilim* wanted Hebrew to be the chief language in the modernization process. The history of the Haskalah in the course of the nineteenth century is the record of the great endeavour made by many to fill the void in the cultural world of the Jews and to publish—in Hebrew (but also in Yiddish)—both serious and popular scientific literature. With time, there was less and less need to obtain legitimation for this endeavour, until finally the study of the sciences achieved an autonomous and independent status, and no longer had to contribute to an understanding of the Bible and the Talmud, or to provide evidence of God's works in the world.

THE CHALLENGE OF MODERN SCIENTIFIC THEORIES

The Haskalah was both a historical turning-point in Jewish intellectual history and a new phase in Jews' active involvement in the different fields of science. We have seen that the moderate *maskilim* believed that a Jew desiring to be modern and to integrate into his surroundings must acquire a fluent knowledge of the vernacular, of commerce, geography, history, government, etc. This is useful knowledge or *chokhmot nitsrakhot*. In other words, a modern Jew is one who, in addition to being devout in obeying the commandments, acquires a 'neutral system' of pragmatic and useful knowledge. It is a complementary system, one that reinforces faith rather than one that casts doubt on it. From the vantage-point of the moderate Haskalah, thanks to this kind of knowledge the Jew becomes a man in addition to being a more 'complete Jew'. It is not merely a pragmatic necessity, but a personal and collective existential need. Wisdom is a weapon in the struggle against prejudice, against a decaying tradition and stagnating conservatism. Thus the Haskalah was the harbinger of two historical options.

The first was the continuation of medieval philosophy under completely different historical circumstances. It offered the option of regarding the Torah and the sciences as completely separate authorities, but, at the same time, it followed medieval philosophy in its attempt to describe Israel's Torah as a world-view that also included the knowledge of natural sciences. The problem with this view was that since the laws of nature are universal

---

[74] Raisin, *The Haskalah Movement*, 82–110. In the 19th c. the adaptations to the popular scientific encyclopaedias in Hebrew generally lagged behind scientific achievements by at least one generation.

laws, these universal laws and the cosmogony and 'knowledge of natural sciences' in the Bible should be in harmony. This view accepted philosophy and science as an integral part of modern Jewish culture but separate from the principles of Judaism. In other words, it regarded philosophy and science as systems of explanation and outlook that have no connection whatever to the commandments and the principles of Jewish faith.

Moderate *maskilim* and observant Jews did not wish to relinquish science and philosophy, but, on the other hand, were apprehensive of knowledge and its implications. This inner tension was manifested in the essays of Rabbi Jacob Emden, who lists a long series of 'neutral [but important] sciences', but also states that anyone venturing into the modern-day *pardes* must do so with the utmost caution, in order to avoid the danger of succumbing to its seductions. A Jew who read philosophical works might possibly forfeit the secure bastion of his faith and start to err in his way of life. For this reason, Orthodoxy emphasized the stern admonitions against Greek wisdom from among the normative prescriptions to be found in the talmudic and rabbinical world and proscribed the learning of any sort of secular wisdom even for pragmatic needs. The chief reason Orthodoxy adopted a conservative stand of this kind was its awareness that in modern times the preoccupation with philosophy is not the province of the élite, as it had been in the Middle Ages. Furthermore, there was undoubtedly a fear that the questions raised by philosophical study were the very ones into which Jewish tradition prohibited any enquiry, fearing their destructive influence on faith. The enquiry into the Creation, for instance, or 'what was outside the world and what came before it', which is forbidden according to *Chagigah 2a* and Saadiah Gaon's *Sefer hagalu'i*, was not in their view pursued by the *maskilim* for the purpose of metaphysical-speculative study, but as a scientific test of the validity of sacred traditions that are the basis of religious faith.

Moreover, modern scientific theories, in particular the theories of progress and evolution, often posed a grave challenge. The *maskilim's* optimistic vision of the possibility of creating a harmonious reconciliation between modern science and faith proved utopian: since the mid-nineteenth century the dispute between 'science' and 'faith' has raged amongst the Jewish intelligentsia. To some, science was a destructive means by which to challenge sacred traditions; for others, it was a means of validating them. When Ahad Ha'am, for example, declared that he could 'even adopt that "scientific heresy which bears the name of Darwin", without any danger to my Judaism',[75] he had no intention of claiming that faith and Darwin-

---

[75] 'Slavery in Freedom', 194.

ism were two discrete and mutually exclusive ways of thinking. Going even further, he maintained that Darwinism could be used to help explain Judaism, that is, according to the concept of evolution. It was possible, according to this view, 'to replace the wine in the cask, filling it with new wine from alien vines, provided that the cask itself would be preserved'.

Moses Lilienblum was more radical in his attitude and wrote about the 'absolute advantage of the natural sciences'. He went so far as to claim that the natural sciences and the scientific knowledge of the universe are the source of true ideas. As if to defend Jewish faith, he claimed that the Jewish religion is based on the belief in the Creator of the Torah from heaven and that this belief cannot be affected by any scientific theory:

That way, a great benefit will accrue to religion as well, for it will no longer be profaned by someone who comes to prove that the world was created several million years ago; and that man was not actually created in the form he has now and had to go through many stages until he gradually evolved; and other things like that.

By separating science (that is, theories concerning the creation and evolution of the cosmos) from faith in this way, Jews will be spared the dilemma of choosing between the two, and the subsequent despair. In Lilienblum's opinion the natural sciences enjoy absolute superiority since only by gaining a knowledge of reality through science can one arrive at valid ideas.[76]

No wonder then, that observant Jews regarded both Ahad Ha'am and Lilienblum as 'Hellenic Jews'. 'Those who wish to combine Torah with external wisdom', wrote the ultra-Orthodox writer Akiva Schlesinger, 'are worse than heretics; they are in the same category as idolaters.'[77] From this ultra-Orthodox point of view, any other exposition of wisdom apart from neutral knowledge, crafts, and arts, was considered one form or another of the Hellenization of knowledge, hence in all cases heresy. The main ground for this negative attitude was that every attempt to generate a correspondence between the normative world of Jewish thought and scientific knowledge could ostensibly demonstrate that the Jewish concepts would not conform to the new sciences. Thus the radical ultra-Orthodox

---

[76] Lilienblum, *An Autobiography*, iii. 143–4; ii. 45–6. Here he echoes Ibn Ezra, who claimed that the Torah could not serve as a substitute for Greek science, since it contained neither scientific proofs, nor an explanation of the way the cosmos came into being. See Funkenstein, *Styles in Medieval Biblical Exegesis*, 37 and id., 'History and Accommodation'.

[77] *Beit Yosef Hahadash* (title-page). In another book, *El ha'adarim* ('To the Herds'), he wrote: 'The halakhah is clear: whoever engages in the study of "external books" is a sinner and an apostate [*mumar neged kol haTorah kulo*], because who is there in our time who has mastered the Talmud and the *posekim* [the post-talmudic writers on halakhah]? And even he would be permitted only to study natural sciences [*chokhmat hateva*].' See M. K. Silver, 'The Emergence of Ultra-Orthodoxy'.

response is to regard 'Greek wisdom' not even as neutral, indifferent to the question of faith, but to reject it totally. In the ultra-Orthodox yeshivot there are no secular studies whatsoever.

There is, however, another type of Orthodox response, and that is the Orthodox fundamentalist response. Fundamentalism is aware of the danger of temptation that lurks in 'the beauty (wisdom) of Japheth', but it strives to reach the 'totality of Judaism', that is, to depict Judaism as supplying its own answers to all questions of existence—or in the dictum of the Lubavicher Rebbe, to portray a Judaism whose Torah is not divorced from life. In this approach, Judaism must be presented as a cosmogony as well as a scientific theory;[78] hence the revived practice of reading the Bible and the Talmud to seek therein astronomy and physics, botany and anatomy, medicine and law. However, it is worth remembering that such fundamentalism does not necessarily imply a contradiction between the laws of science and the scientific laws which are revealed in the traditional Jewish sources. It levels no charge against the laws of physics and chemistry, for example, but rather against any theory which denies that the source of these laws and the reason behind them, from the moment they 'came into the world' during Creation, is Almighty God. Modern Jewish fundamentalism, better perhaps called 'scripturalism', is characterized by a desire to demonstrate the harmony prevailing between modern science and the Bible. A corollary of this approach is, of course, the necessity to determine which modern scientific theory is acceptable, and then to draw a correspondence between it and an alleged biblical concept. Paradoxically, this implies a recognition of the value of science under the guise of fundamentalism. This testifies to the dialectical victory of the Haskalah, since it transpires that fundamentalism, supposedly the arch-enemy of modern science, provides the most convincing evidence of the value of science.

When the spirit of research was revitalized, from the period of the Renaissance onward, the Jewish genius was also interwoven in it: from Spinoza to Einstein, from Freud to Paul Ehrlich and Hertz, from Marx to Robert Oppenheimer and Edward Teller. How did this come about? And does it disprove the claim that the basic Jewish spirit is anti-scientific? Or perhaps one of the dominant expressions of the secularization of the Jewish spirit was that Jews now allowed themselves the Aristotelian amazement that alerted curiosity and engaged in an untiring quest for answers and solutions? Already in the 1860s Kalman Schulman was able to include Jews' achievements in science (a modern catalogue of inventors) as part of the

---

[78] Ravitsky, *Messianism, Zionism, and Jewish Religious Radicalism*, 253–7. Cf. the recent example of Muslim fundamentalism in Bucaille, *The Bible, the Qur'an and Science*.

broad picture of their achievements in culture. In fact, Jewish involvement in the natural sciences grew slowly during the second half of the nineteenth century (being mainly confined to medicine and related fields),[79] but this picture changed radically in the following generations.[80] This involvement by Jews in the realm of universal sciences may be regarded as an expression of the revolutionary change in parts of the Jewish world and its release from a theology that prevented its engagement in the natural sciences.[81]

On the other hand, nationalism also kindled among Jewish men of letters the baseless notion that there is such a thing as a 'national science', namely that the national genius is expressed not only in the intensiveness of scientific creativity, but also in the nature of scientific thinking. In this, those writers moved another step away—far away—from the attempt to disprove the claim that the Jewish genius lacked the necessary qualities for scientific thought to an attempt to prove there is a 'uniquely Jewish science'.[82]

In a lecture delivered in April 1933 on the future of the new Hebrew University, Chaim Weizmann, who was not only a statesman but also a renowned chemist, stated that while no one could doubt that the study of the humanities would be stamped with the national imprint, scientific methods in fields such as chemistry and physics, generally thought to be totally international in nature, also differ since the mode of enquiry is a national trait. 'An example of this', he said, is that 'the English genius is the empirical genius in science, following in the path of Newton, Faraday, and others . . . and there is the way of the French, the way of Descartes, Laplace, and their like. They took the path of logic, the way of rationalism, and the experiment came after the logic. We the Jews have studied in all corners of the world. We have no methods of enquiry of our own. Perhaps our university will bring about the discovery of the specific Jewish method, and through a special Jewish way of investigation we shall discover new laws . . .'.[83] To Weizmann's credit, he spoke only in general terms about a 'Hebrew scientific way', as a phenomenon that would develop in the future, but he did not know how, or did not try, to characterize it in any way.

Often, however, the result of this search for a 'Jewish scientific method'

[79] Y. Toury, *Between Revolution, Reaction and Emancipation*, 125–6. A. Ruppin, *The Sociology of the Jews*, iii/iv. 240 also provides a list of Jews in modern science.

[80] Volkov, 'Soziale Ursachen des jüdischen Erfolgs in der Wissenschaft'.

[81] Weiler, *Jewish Theocracy*, 250–69. He, of course, identifies 'Judaism' with halakhah and hence presents a limited view.

[82] See Ch. 8.

[83] Weizmann, 'Al darkah shel ha'Universitah ha'Ivrit', 516–17.

was that the nature of the Jewish scientific genius was characterized in contradictory ways. One writer claimed, for example, that Einstein's theory of relativity could only have evolved in a Semitic brain; Aryans could not have understood the postulate of unity, since in their world-view 'nature' consisted of variety and not of unity. The laws of nature are not (he maintained) 'natural laws' but depend on the point of view of the observer; thus, since the Jewish genius is characterized by observing unity, only a Jew was able to come forward with a postulate of unity. The concept of the unity of the Creator came into the world through Moses; the theory of nature's unity with the Creator, through Spinoza; and the theory of the unity of the laws of nature, through Einstein:

These three theories, which join together into one perfect whole—their power came out of the deepest thoughts of the sons of Shem! And the war against these theories is a war, indeed an 'antisemitic' one, but not in the usual meaning of the word. Not out of animosity and not out of malice will these fighters do battle, but simply out of the inability to grasp the notion of unity.[84]

David Ben-Gurion believed that the Jewish genius, from the days of the prophets to those of Einstein, did not accept the dualism of material and spirit that (he claimed) had influenced thinkers from the Greeks and Persians down to Descartes and his disciples. The Jewish genius was marked by a unified view of the world, of the universe, and of existence.[85]

Others adopted the widespread anti-Jewish claim that Jewish thinkers had made an unmistakable contribution to the breakdown of the unified world: Freud and Kafka and Einstein, each in his own field, were depicted as the prophets of modernism, which was fragmenting the organic unity of the universe and human experience. The originators of these theories were assigned the role of Semites who wished to destroy and fragment the unity of the world as emissaries of the forces of evil. Others claim that these theories were the product of a Jewish genius which was Aryanized (or Hellenized). Needless to say, the search for a 'national science' is no more than a crude or distorted product of nationalistic and racist thought. In our case the important fact is that scientific creativity became one of the accepted manifestations of the 'Jewish genius'.

[84] Sh. Urbach, 'Hate'oriah shel Einstein veha'antishemiyut'.
[85] Ben-Gurion, *Medinat Yisrael hamitchadeshet*, 13–14.

5

JAPHETH IN THE TENTS OF SHEM: THE RECEPTION OF THE CLASSICAL HERITAGE IN MODERN HEBREW CULTURE

Said Rabbi Jonathan of Bet Gubrin: Four languages are appropriately used in the world and these are: Greek, for song; Latin, for war; Sursi [Aramaic], for wailing; Hebrew, for clear speech.

JERUSALEM TALMUD, *Megillah*, i. 9, 71*a–b*, tr. Neusner, xix. 49

For wisdom sometimes is the key to the holy books,
a knowledge of the stars to the proclamation of the months
and the language of Greece and Rome to the Mishnah and the Midrashim.

J. L. GORDON, *Shenei Yosef ben Shimon*

A CULTURE THAT WENT BEGGING

FROM a traditional Jewish point of view the modern revival of ancient Greece was indeed seen as an effort to waken the dead. 'A culture that went begging from door to door': that was the picturesque and mocking phrase with which the religious *maskil*, writer, and historian, Ze'ev Jawitz (1842–1927) described the culture of nineteenth-century Europe.[1] The culture of Europe, he wrote, is a 'medley of Hebrew ideas, Indian imagination, Roman culture'; in other words, not an organic and original culture but an eclectic one. This is the reason, in his view, why Europe was going begging: because her mind and soul were made up of rags and tatters, opposites and contradictions, filled with anguish and dissatisfaction. As a result of this distorted mental state, Europe was induced to yearn for her lost wholeness and to search for it in the irretrievable past. This quest led her 'to visit the graves of cultures lost to the world', first and foremost among them, of course, the culture of Greece. These wanderings called forth a Hellenic ideal, the portrait of a lost and longed-for golden age, but they ended in disappointment and disillusion. This was not only because such a golden age never really existed, but because attempts to resurrect an ancient long-gone past and to infuse it with the lifeblood of the new world, thus to

[1] Jawitz, *Sichot mini kedem*, 6–7.

renew its lost vitality and organicity, were doomed to failure. They were but an expression of a culture that had lost its faith and had revealed itself to be an empty vessel. Even if one might appreciate these yearnings in and of themselves, in the final analysis they were a manifestation of futility. Here he is echoed by Spengler, who declares: 'We have projected our deepest spiritual needs and feelings on the Classical picture', and continues: 'Some day a gifted psychologist will deal with this most fateful illusion and tell us the story of the "Classical" that we have consistently reverenced . . . Otto III was the first victim of the South, Nietzsche the last.'[2]

A religiously observant Jew yet a supporter of the Enlightenment, Jawitz had no reservations about preferring Christian Europe to pagan Greece or secular Europe, for he conceived of Christianity as based on monotheism and moral laws, in contrast to the polytheistic (and secular) paganism so devoid of all moral obligations and conscience. From this vantage-point, the Middle Ages were better than the Hellenic paganism of the past and the secular paganism of the present.

Judaism, in Jawitz's view, in contrast to the European ideal of ancient antiquity, is not an illusory ideal, but a living, continuous entity, whose past is an integral part of its present and future. This is the immense advantage of Judaism over Greekness. Judaism has earned eternal life thanks to its externality, whereas Greekness has sunk into the chasm of oblivion, where it wanders like a spectre. Western civilization, which has lost its faith, has no source from which to draw new faith. Hence it searches desperately for a panacea in Greece or, alternatively, in the Orient, in the Middle Ages, or in various theories of redemption, all of which have the one thing it lacks: organicity. Judaism, on the other hand, is protected against crisis and calamity, nor does it have any need of a renaissance. It lives and exists, whole, complete, vital, and perfect as it has always been and always will be. Reflected in this Jewish mirror, Europe looks split, divided, haunted, vacuous, alarmed at its own emptiness, searching for peace in realms of the past and in foreign lands. This is by no means a desirable and enticing image. In contrast, the reflection of Judaism perfectly matches the image beheld by the observer: as a continuous and consummate whole. This will be one of the basic arguments of those who pressed the claims of Judaism as being superior both to the culture of Greece and to the culture of the West.

Jawitz turned again to the Greek revival at the turn of the century to present the yearning for an imaginary classical antiquity as a clear manifes-

---

[2] Spengler, *The Decline*, 30 (*Der Untergang*, 41).

tation of the emptiness of the modern European soul and to warn against
its dangerous consequences:

When European man awoke at the end of the Middle Ages from the deep slumber
in which he was enveloped by the culture of India, the favourite daughter of the
spirit of Japheth, Greek culture approached his cradle, offering him the icons
of her delight, while his eyes were still bound up in the bonds of sleep; and
she began to sing sweetly to him the ancient songs and to compose new ones
in the same fashion, trying to revive his spirit by showing him the figures of
Apollo Belvedere and Laocoon that she dug up from the mounds of earth and
polished and presented to the assembly, and to delight his soul with her singing,
well-arranged in her beautiful style, and the ancient flavour could be found in
song and rhetoric and in venerable works of art and in the literature of the times.
But sadly, the delight of the works of art turned the gaze of the multitude towards
her, but only momentarily did they feast their eyes upon their hearts' desire, for
the noble spirit of the cold, still, and pallid marble did not come to life, and the
melodies that were not of their time did not touch their hearts or the hearts of
their generation, and were not pleasing to them. And when men of Japheth saw
this they added to the art of sculpture the art of painting, which brings its creations
to life in a profusion of colour . . .

Furthermore, the negative influences of the Greek revival were not
limited to art or literature; they had their destructive impact on political
behaviour. From the French Revolution onwards, the literature of Japheth
became a synonym for 'French literature', which the *maskilim* in eastern
Europe thought of as light. This 'Greek influence' cast Europe into a
maelstrom of violence, because the subject of ancient Greek literature was
lawless violence. Thus Greek literature become a reckless, capricious, and
sinister adviser that led Europe to the very edge of the abyss and to a
reaction: a return to the Middle Ages.[3]

This is not how things looked to a radical *maskil* like Peretz Smolenskin
(1842–85), who on several occasions examined the nature of 'the Greek
renaissance in Ashkenaz' (i.e. Germany). He believed that Greece was
reborn in order to function as a smiting-rod to strike at zealous Catholicism and drive it out. The Greek and Roman cultures inspired the new
humanism, which played a leading role in Germany's spiritual liberation
from theology, and also in the process of creating a German self-identity.
In that event, it was simple to deduce from this the role reserved for the
Hebrew renaissance: to achieve national 'secular' liberation from the onus
of rabbinic tradition and authority. Nevertheless, Smolenskin thought that

---

[3] Jawitz, 'Olamot overim', 47. The unfavourable view of French literature was influenced by the
Russian Slavophiles; see e.g. Dostoevsky, *Winter Notes on Summer Impressions*.

in the profusion of textual and philological studies the pervading spirit
was sometimes forgotten, and scholarly research became an end in its own
right. Learning ancient languages became a heavy burden, a torment.
Even so, he concluded, the status of Greek and Roman literature, as a
yardstick by which to gauge contemporary literature, was not impaired.
German writers 'suckled the milk of life from breasts that had been dry
for thousands of years', and it gave them renewed vitality.[4]

Here Smolenskin echoes Friedrich Paulson's statement that: 'In the
Greek ideal, the new age found the image of the God who became
man . . . Hellenizing humanism is a new religion, the philologists are
its priests; the university and schools, its temple.'[5] This statement could
just as well be translated into the modern Jewish cultural context. Here
too philologists, historians, literary men, and schoolteachers inherited the
place of the previous spiritual authority. They all were asked to take part—
and did take part—in the attempt to create a 'new Jewish man' and a 'new
Jewish people'.

No matter what the Jewish response was to the driving forces behind
the vital presence of the 'ideal of Greece', this ideal became a living
historical entity; and hence the revival and presence of the classical past
became a challenge and an inspiration, an example, and an incentive to the
trend towards reviving the Jewish classical past, both in scholarly research
and as part of culture. From the eighteenth century onwards, the Jewish
intelligentsia, with many deep-seated reservations, began to acknowledge
what Jacob Burckhardt called 'the rediscovery of antiquity'. This was a
slow and gradual process, beset by many impediments. Their discovery
of Greece and their perceptions of it of course took different paths, had
different motivations, and produced different results. It compelled them
to relate themselves not only to the ideal Greece and to its function in
European culture, not only to the Greece of Jewish historical memory
(and not only to Greek philosophy), but also to both the 'real' Greece
and the imaginary Greece that was resurrected in literature, polemics, and
historical scholarship, as well as to Greece as the 'other', that Greece which
was contraposed to Judaism and represented as its complete opposite. Once
they became acquainted with classical antiquity, there were two attitudes
that they could take to it. One was to continue viewing it as a distinctly
idolatrous culture (although some, at the end of the nineteenth century,
would assign a positive interpretation to this paganism); the other was to
view it as a classical culture and to find positive cultural values in it.

[4] Smolenskin, 'Et lata'at', 197–8.
[5] Quoted in Delaura, *Hebrew and Hellene*, 187.

THE JEWISH DISCOVERY OF CLASSICAL ANTIQUITY

In 1903 David Neumark (1866–1924), a scholar and philosopher of Reform Judaism, explicated the fundamental difference between the knowledge of philosophy and the knowledge of literature:

The Greek spirit was revealed in philosophy only in a fragmented manner. During the Renaissance, when the arts and sciences of antiquity were discovered, when the spirit of Greece began to breathe upon its myriad treasures, out of all the discoveries of life in the ancient world, the contradiction between the spirit of Greece with its blind basis of existence, and the spirit of Judaism with its cosmic knowledge, received a marked emphasis.[6]

What Neumark meant is that the 'Greek spirit' was not truly embodied in the philosophical works, but rather in 'culture' in the widest sense of this concept; Greek culture in its historical context often differed in nature from Greek philosophy. At the same time, Neumark makes it clear that it was only at the dawn of the modern era that the European nations actually became acquainted with the entire body of Greek culture, and that all they knew of it beforehand—other than Greek thought—was merely bits and pieces. This was not the case only with Jewish scholars; the Muslim world in the Middle Ages was also unfamiliar with Greek literature and historiography.[7]

Thus it was only during the nineteenth century that Jewish scholars, and the Jewish public at large, had the opportunity to know and to read the Greek epic, lyric, comedy, and tragedy, and to become familiar with Greek deities and mythological heroes. In the realm of 'culture', as it was manifested in literature and art, Jews did not revive their knowledge of classical antiquity but had to learn about it almost from the start.

'The study of Greek literature is rare among Jews', declared Origen, who lived in Caesarea for twenty years in the third century AD and knew its Jewish inhabitants well (*Contra Cels.* ii. 34).[8] Origen pointed to this lack

---

[6] Neumark, 'Hashkafat olam vehashkafat chayim'.

[7] Kraemer, *Humanism in the Renaissance of Islam*, pp. xxx–xxxii; Rosenthal, *The Classical Heritage in Islam*, 10, 256–66. On the familiarity of medieval Jews with Greek literature see Dinur, *A Documentary History*, 190–202, 227–57; for rabbis in Poland and Germany see Elbaum, *Openness and Insularity*, 154–82. The first Yiddish–Hebrew–Latin dictionary was published in 1542. It is interesting to note here that Homer's *Iliad* was translated into modern Greek in the mid-19th c. (Dakin, *The Unification of Greece*, 268), into Arabic in 1904, and (in part) into Turkish only after 1914 (Malečková, 'Ludwig Büchner versus Nat Pinkerton'). Tchernichowsky's translation into Hebrew was published in 1924–9.

[8] But he also recounts that he conversed in Caesarea with Jews and the Midrash records dialogues between R. Hoshaya and a philosopher. The controversy centred on the meaning of the prophecies about Jerusalem. The library Origen established in Caesarea contained no tragic, comic, or lyric poetry, and no works of Aristotle: Droge, *Homer or Moses?*, 191.

of knowledge among the Jews since he himself encouraged the Christians
to study not only Greek philosophy but also Greek natural sciences, music,
rhetoric, and so forth. The situation he describes was true not only for
his own time but also for the entire period of the Second Temple and
thereafter. Throughout this period, there were undoubtedly Jews living
in Palestine who could speak Greek, and also some who could read it,
but very few could or did write in Greek. According to Rabban Simon,
the son of Rabban Gamaliel the Patriarch, 'There were a thousand young
men in my father's house, five hundred of whom studied the (Jewish) law,
while the other five hundred studied Greek wisdom' (*Bava kama*, 8: 3*a*, ed.
Lieberman, 242), a grossly exaggerated statement; in the Tosefta one also
finds that 'permission was granted to the House of Rabban Gamaliel to
teach the children Greek owing to its relation with the [Roman] government' (*Sotah* 15: 8).[9] Although scholars differ about the scope and depth
of the knowledge of Greek culture among Jews in Palestine,[10] it seems
that few educated Jews read Greek literature as part of their education and
learning.[11] The Sages, as we shall see later, banned the reading of Greek
philosophy, but apparently adopted an attitude of disdainful forbearance
towards Greek mythology, since they believed its power was too feeble to
cause any harm.

Learned Jews in the Middle Ages were familiar with Greek philosophy
and science, but they were unable to read Greek and were dependent on
Latin or Arabic translations.[12] Even humanist Jews in the Italian Renaissance and after, who viewed the Jewish heritage as a distinguished part of
the classical tradition, did not read Greek (or Arabic) and relied on translations into Latin or Italian. They nevertheless could, for example, absorb
mythological motifs in any number of ways, mainly through the manuals
'which had their place in the library of every men of letters',[13] just as the
Sages had acquired a second-hand familiarity with Greek mythological
motifs. Azariah de' Rossi (1511–78), the first modern Jewish historian, is
an example of a Renaissance Jew who read not only Greek and Roman

---

[9] Lieberman, *The Alleged Ban on Greek Wisdom*, 102–4. Rabban Gamaliel the Elder died *c.*AD 50.

[10] Bentwich, for example, holds the view that knowledge of Greek in the rabbinical circles was banned
from the 2nd c. AD because at that period Hellenism ceased to rely on reason and contemplation and
was identified with fantastic trinities, theosophies, etc.: 'The Rabbis instinctively recognized a canker in
this medley' (*Hellenism*, 287–90). See too Ch. 11.

[11] See Herr, 'External Influences', 86. On the use of Greek in the Byzantine period see de Lange,
'Shem and Japheth'.

[12] On mythological motifs in Jewish literature see Ginzberg, *Halakhah and Aggadah*, 255–6; Idel, 'The
Journey to Paradise'; Liebes, *The Sin of Elisha*, 22–5; Lachs, 'The Pandora–Eve Motif in Rabbinic
Literature'. On Muslim knowledge see Rosenthal, *The Classical Heritage*, 5–21, and with reference to
art ibid. 256–66.

[13] Seznec, *The Survival of the Pagan Gods*, 279–323.

historical and philosophical works, but also Homer, Virgil, and Ovid, in addition to an array of folk-tales and legends.[14] Authors like Abraham ben Samuel Mordecai Zacuto (1452–1515), an astronomer and historian, who advised Columbus and Vasco da Gama and wrote *Sefer yochasin* ('Book of Lineage'), or Joseph Solomon Delmedigo, were familiar with Greek mythology. In the parts of his book dealing with the time of the Patriarchs and the First and Second Temple periods, Zacuto interposed names from Greek mythology and history for the purpose of synchronization.[15] Another example is that of David de Bene (d. 1635), an Italian Jewish rabbinical author and preacher in Mantua, who, 'earlier in life, had shown an excessive tendency to use in his sermons mythological motifs' and caused bitter dispute.[16]

And what about the modern acculturated Jew?

A familiarity with classical antiquity was considered an integral part of European education and of culture, particularly in the nineteenth century, and it was an integral part of the *humanistisches Gymnasium* and the English public school. No wonder that the members of Chevrat Dorshei Leshon Ever (Society for the Promotion of the Hebrew Language), the founders of *Hame'asef*, the first modern Hebrew literary periodical, introduced themselves to their mentor Naphtali Herz Wessely in 1783, as 'a group of intelligent fellows, some who were Torah scholars, and some who knew the foreign languages of Greece and Rome, and others who were conversant with both practical and noble sciences'.[17] The *Hame'asef* circle was but a small group of autodidacts, but by the middle of the nineteenth century Latin became a required subject in 'modern' Jewish schools in Germany. This aroused harsh criticism on the part of traditional and Orthodox Jews in eastern Europe:

And even worse than that is the study of Torah in Ashkenaz, which is done this way: they bring the young child aged five or six to the school and they begin to read to him and teach him the script and language of Ashkenaz, France, Italy, and Britain, and the language of Greece and Rome, the books of Homer, Virgil, Horace, and many of their kind . . .[18]

---

[14] See Bonfil's introduction to Azariah de' Rossi, *Selected Chapters*, 28–30.

[15] Michael, *Jewish Historiography*, 20–1. According to Zacuto, Jupiter lived in the time of Abraham, Minerva in the time of Jacob, and so forth. Cf. Barzilay, *Joseph Solomon Delmedigo*, 31–2. Delmedigo wrote that 'whatever precious knowledge there was in the (Arabic) language was taken from the Greeks', whose books the Arabs had 'strangely' distorted by additions and subtractions (ibid. 33).

[16] D. Kaufman, 'The Dispute about the Sermons', 513–17. In his sermons, 'The Gods of the Greeks and the Romans were to explain the dicta of the Agada', 514.

[17] Tzamriyon, *Hame'asef*, 37–40; Pelli, *Struggle for Change*, 48.

[18] Hilperin, *Teshuvot anshei aven*, 35, cit. Eliav, *Jewish Education*, 319 n. 40.

Latin (and to a lesser extent Greek) became part of the acculturation process of the modern educated Jew. From the point of view of their Orthodox opponents this was one more step towards assimilation. It bred terrible licentiousness. The Jewish pupil, his parents' pride and joy—mocked the critic sharply—finishes school full of everything good, without leaving out any wisdom in the world 'except the wisdom of the Torah, which he did not learn'.[19] Two generations later, in the 1880s, Smolenskin was angered by both the German Jewish *Wissenschaft des Judentums* and by modern German Jewish Orthodoxy; both of them, in his opinion, had deserted the national culture and the Hebrew language as well, for the sake of foreign language and classical antiquity:

. . . and almost all the sages of Israel in Ashkenaz, even the rabbis and the sermonizers, humiliate the Hebrew language. I do not exaggerate too much when I say 'humiliate', for indeed, they do humiliate this language. For only what is written in Greek or Latin is wisdom, whereas in Hebrew, it is nothing more than nonsense, words which to them are without logic. And also those who have knowledge of the languages of Greece and Rome will yet spurn their knowledge of the Hebrew language, and they too will boast of their lack of knowledge in the Hebrew language in order to be considered wise in the 'languages of the canon of shame'.[20]

Smolenskin also did not spare Mendelssohn, whom he detested, commenting that in fact Mendelssohn did not know Greek and Latin well, although he had done his utmost to disseminate Greek wisdom among the Jews. He certainly did not mean by that anything in the spirit of Heine's sarcastic remark in *Reisebilder* ('Travel Scenes') that 'The monks of the Middle Ages were not very much in the wrong when they asserted that Greek was an invention of the Devil.'[21] If Smolenskin felt Greek was 'of the Devil', it was not because of its grammar but because of the grave effects the 'spirit of Greece' had had on the national Jewish spirit. In the last decade of the nineteenth century, the Rabbi of Prague, Eliezer Falklash, spoke out, with no less exaggeration, against the changes in the reading habits of Jewish readers: no longer did they take up a book of ethics, but only books in foreign languages and on philosophy.[22] This was a far cry from the reality. The critics were actually referring not to the study of classical culture, but to the growing popularity of 'secular studies'; only

[19] Eliav, *Jewish Education*, 155.

[20] Smolenskin, 'Et lata'at', 200. According to Ruppin, among 3,307 Jewish students in Germany in 1929/30, only 26 took their degree in classical languages. However, obviously others studied Latin and Greek as part of their studies in other fields (*The Sociology of the Jews*, i. 113).

[21] Heine, *Reisebilder: Ideen. Das Buch Le Grand*, ch. 7 (*Sämtliche Werke*, v. 128).

[22] Eliav, *Jewish Education*, 319.

the élite was receptive to classical culture through Greek or Latin. But as in the Second Temple period and thereafter one did not need to read Homer in order to know something about the Homeric heroes. Clearly, many learned Jews were familiar with classical literature through translations into German (or Russian).[23] From the Haskalah literature it is obvious that the *maskilim* were acquainted with a large body of classical literature through translations, but one must bear in mind that, owing to changes in the development of the German language, they drew their knowledge primarily from the new translations made from the eighteenth century onwards (the *Odyssey*, for example, was translated into German in 1537, but only became highly popular after J. J. Bodmer's 1778 translation).

There were other views. For example, the philosopher and historian Nachman Krochmal (1785–1840, known by the acronym Renak), a spiritual leader of the Haskalah in eastern Europe, wrote in his *Moreh nevukhei hazeman* ('Guide to the Perplexed of Our Time', Lvov, 1851) that the commentators erred in concluding that the Sages had forbidden the reading of the books of Aristotle and other philosophers, for the simple reason that they were not familiar with them, while on the other hand 'it is clear that they permitted the reading of *sifrei hamiros*, which are all the books in the Greek language'. He himself read classical literature and according to the testimony of his pupil Meir Halevi Letteris (1800?–1871), a Hebrew poet and editor himself, the works of Aristotle stood on his desk, next to Horace and Lucian.[24] Classical works became part of the literary baggage of the Jewish *maskil* and men of letters: Solomon Loewinsohn (1789–1821), a brilliant scholar who was to commit suicide at the age of 31, studied Latin and read classical literature at the University of Prague; Shadal knew Latin and a little Greek, at the age of 11 began to write a book on Aesop, and translated Ovid's poem *De Remedio Amoris* ('On the Remedy against Love') from the Latin in 1816–17;[25] Simon Dubnow (1860–1941), the eminent Jewish historian born in Belorussia, stated that in his youth he knew no Hebrew literature and was brought up on Homer, Virgil, Plato, and other such authors.

A representative literary figure of the generation of Jews who felt at home with classical Greece, almost to the point of caricature, is Reb

[23] See Michael, 'Solomon Lewinsohn'; Zinberg, *History of Jewish Literature*, vi. 93; Dubnow, 'Autonomy—The Basis of the National Plan', 70; Klausner, *History of Hebrew Literature*, ii. 49, 75; T. Cohen, *The Melitzat Yeshurun of Shlomo Levinsohn*, 22–3. On translations of classical works into Russian see Wes, *Classics in Russia*.

[24] Zinberg, *History of Jewish Literature*, vi. 93.

[25] According to Alexander Neckam, a Christian scholar of the 12th c., a learned Christian should be familiar with this poem (Waddell, *The Wandering Scholars*, p. xx).

Ephraim Walder, the scholarly bookseller from Berlin, in I. J. Singer's novel *The Family Carnovsky*. Walder, an autodidact *par excellence*, who is inimitably erudite in Greek philosophical literature, had been immersed all his life in writing his great work, which would prove there is no contradiction between learning the wisdom of the Gentiles and the Torah of Israel:

This is what Reb Ephraim is doing in his great book, which he has been writing for several years, to bring peace between Shem and Japheth. In thousands of pages written in his cramped handwriting, he reviews and examines all the theories of philosophy, from the Greek philosophers up to the most recent ones, and he proves that everything that had been said about wisdom and ethics in the tents of Japheth, was originally said in the tents of Shem.[26]

Reb Walder, who compared himself to Philo but denied any apologetic tendencies, is the imaginary descendant of medieval Jewish philosophers, but he is also a descendant of the generation of Jewish men of letters and scholars whose definitive beginning was in the Berlin Haskalah and its educational activities. The same kind of positive attitude towards familiarity with Greek culture is amply reflected in the way Fritz Baer describes the enlightened Palestinian Jew of that time:[27]

And ever since the kings of Greece ruled over Syria and Egypt and over all their environs, many Greeks came to live there and became intermingled with the other nations. And the Greek language overpowered the languages of the other nations and the whole country was one language . . . And the Jews also began to learn the Greek tongue and its literature, the language of the people amongst whom they lived; and they read the books written by Pythagoras, Socrates, Plato, and Aristotle, the sages of Greece. They expounded and explored and delved into these books and began to interpret and elucidate the Torah in accordance with them . . .

We have already alluded to the erudition of Isaac Baer Levinsohn, who could be considered the prototype of this kind of *maskil* with a wide-ranging breadth of scholarship. His familiarity with Graeco-Roman litera-ture was gained mostly through translations into German, as demonstrated by his prodigious reading, evidence of which is interwoven through the various chapters of his book *Te'udah be Yisrael* (1828): Pliny and Aristotle, Homer and Xenophon, Hesiod and Dionysius of Halicarnassus, and others besides. Levinsohn is without question a direct Jewish descendant of the

---

[26] I. J. Singer, *The Family Carnovsky*, 64–5. The Yiddish original was published in 1943; this paragraph was omitted from the English translation.

[27] *Sefer toledot Yisrael*, ii. 8.

'Greek renaissance' in Germany.[28] 'An educated Jew', wrote Lilienblum, 'must learn classical languages and not the languages of the Ancient East.' However, he complained in a letter to the poet J. L. Gordon in December 1878 that Latin grammar was very difficult, and 'the Greek language is even more laborious'.[29]

However, the process of reception was very slow and met with many reservations.[30]

Not very long ago a critic reviewed the stage-setting in an Israeli television programme starring a Greek singer. The scenery included the 'requisite' ruins of Greek columns, which reminded the critic of a precocious little 6-year-old girl to whom she had once read Aesop's fables. The child had said: 'I don't want to hear about him!' 'Why not?' 'Because he's a bad Greek, and all the Greeks are bad and he destroyed our Temple.'[31] This little anecdote does not merely show the innocent manifestation of the eternal hostility to Greeks, deeply stamped on the Jewish historical consciousness: it is also an example of the product of Israeli schooling, in which classical culture is almost unknown. One can often read laments about the 'lost generation' of students versed in the classics, which refer mainly to the students at the Jewish or general *gymnasia* in Europe, particularly in Poland, who were at home in classical culture. This 'lost generation' made its appearance at the dawn of the Haskalah, yielding a bounteous harvest, especially between the two world wars, and then vanished in the Holocaust.[32]

Thus despite the translations made from Greek into Hebrew during the last generations—comprising about one hundred partially or completely translated works—it was still possible not long ago to state in the foreword of a literary periodical devoted to classical translations that Israeli culture is still deplorably lacking in this field, in comparison with the literatures of Europe. This is because, so the editors claimed, 'in the not too distant past, it was impossible even to consider discussing ancient Greek writings as long as religion was the prime foundation of Jewish life. How could we

---

[28] See Etkes's introduction to the new edition of Levinsohn's *Te'udah beYisrael*, 3–19.

[29] Lilienblum, *An Autobiography*, ii. 171.

[30] For example, Günzburg, in his preface to *Galut ha'eretz hachadashah*, quoted Cicero's statement (*Academica Posteriora*, i. 10) that he had translated Greek philosophy into Latin since readers of Greek would enjoy his translation, while the less educated reader would learn from it.

[31] *Ha'aretz*, 17 Feb. 1989. In the 6 Dec. 1994 issue of *Yediot Aharonot*, it was reported that the Prime Minister of Israel, Yitzhak Rabin, in a meeting with the Greek Minister of Defence during Chanukah, had 'settled accounts' with his guest regarding the Greek wars against the Jews. This misperception, which identifies the Seleucids with Greece, is very prevalent among the Israeli public.

[32] See in Shimron, 'Farewell', and in his Introduction to *Classical Civilization*, 139. For a profile of the major figures in Jewish classical studies in Poland between the two world wars see Rosenthal's introd. to M. Stein's *Relationship between Literatures*, 5–25; Shemueli, 'Diokano shel historion le'umi'.

bring together Cronos who swallowed his children, or Zeus who raped Europa, under the same roof as the Holy Ark and the Torah?'[33] In their view, the heightened momentum of translations in Hebrew literature—by Saul Tchernichowsky, Sarah Dvoretzky, Yitzhak Silberschlag, Yosef Libes, E. E. Hallewy, Shlomo Dykman, Aharon Shabetai, Natan Spiegel, and others[34]—hinges upon the return of the Jews to the shores of the Mediterranean (a dubious argument to my mind) but mainly on the fact that there is more than one 'Hellenic facet' to secular Israeli culture. Their example of the 'Hellenic facet' is that Hebrew poetry shifted 'from the narrative to the lyric tone'. The shift to lyricism was in any case a turn to the Greek. Ignorance—it is further argued—lies at the root of the Hebrew reader's inability to decipher the background, the code, and the connotations of considerable layers of European literature, all of them imbued with Greekness.

From the early twentieth century, the endeavour to translate works from European languages into Hebrew was described as a deliberate attempt to transfer the 'literature of Japheth' into the 'tents of Shem'. In 1912 a literary periodical that printed various translations was founded in Palestine under the name *Yefet* ('Japheth').[35] What had been called the 'books of Homer' in the past became in the twentieth century the 'literature of Japheth'. Although there was some disagreement about the desirable ratio between translated literature and original writings, as well as debates about what ought to be translated, from the time of the Haskalah there was no doubt that works translated into Hebrew would constitute an inseparable part of Hebrew literature. The modern Hebrew reader is inordinately more familiar with the literatures of the world than even the most learned readers in past generations, owing to the sheer quantity of translated works. The translator and the reader in Israel no longer need the legitimation that their counterparts in the Haskalah period required. 'Greekness' became an icon symbolizing the entire realm of *belles-lettres* in foreign languages

---

[33] *Proza*, 60–2 (1982).

[34] For an (incomplete) bibliography of translations of classical works into Hebrew see Kollmann and Roisman-Maslowski, 'Hebrew Translations of Greek and Roman Literature'; Dykman, 'Check-List of Greek and Latin Classics Rendered into Hebrew'; Spiegel, *Homer*, 543–69; Y. Shavit, *Judaism in the Greek Mirror*, 417–24.

[35] Shavit and Shavit, 'Translated vs. Original Literature'. The term 'the beauty of Japheth' was also assigned to the aesthetic side of European culture in Palestine: thus it was applied to the colonies of the German Templars (*Tempelgesellschaft*), settlers who came from Württemberg after 1868, and more generally to the principle of studying Western culture and incorporating it into the national, Hebrew culture. Conversely, the Centralverein Deutscher Staatsbürger jüdischen Glaubens, representing liberal German Jewry, named the publishing-house it established in 1919 in Berlin 'Philo-Verlag'; Philo, who represented the ideology of bridging between Hellenistic (German) and Jewish culture, served as a symbol for German Jews searching for a symbiosis with German culture.

(the literature of Japheth) and certain motifs and themes in literature. What is more important, to my mind, is the fact that in the twentieth century, prohibitions against reading Greek were replaced by laments about the dearth of Greek knowledge among Israeli intellectuals and their ignorance of classical literature in comparison with the Diaspora-educated modern Jews of the nineteenth century.

AFFINITY THROUGH KNOWLEDGE

Hebrew culture did not easily accept classical literature into its midst. A deeply internalized traditional cultural barrier inhibited, delayed, and obstructed the transfer of Greek and Roman literature into the Hebrew language. (Yiddish, to the best of my knowledge, offered next to nothing either.)[36] Thus the reader of Hebrew who could not read translations into European languages was left with a lack of knowledge, and therefore perhaps with preconceived ideas as well. For the most part, 'the books of Homer' exemplified classical and modern literature. Indeed, the Sages did permit the reading of *sifrei hamiros* (ySanh. x. 28a; cf. Mishnah Yad. 4: 6); in the modern era, the question of what they meant by *sifrei hamiros* has turned into—or become once again—a topical issue.[37] Despite this apparent latitude, classical literature was perceived as literature which, in its entirety and by its very nature, was charged with dangerous pagan values. This called for endless apologetics on the part of translators and editors, supported by a goodly amount of evidence from the distant past—evidence that purported to prove that the Sages did not refuse to acknowledge Greek literature and that ignorance lay at the root of the hostility and eternal enmity between Jews and Greeks. In this way a new motif was born, which we can call the motif of affinity through knowledge.

At the outset of the Haskalah, there was already a trend of introducing—at an unhurried pace—the 'literature of Japheth' into the tents of Shem. Here and there, mythological motifs were interspersed into Hebrew literature, or excerpts of classical works were translated. For example, David Zamosc (1789–1864) dared to mention Mars, the god of war, in the same breath with King David, in the collection *Resisei hamelitzah* (1821); J. L. Gordon (1830–92) freely translated one of the *Anacreontea* along with a

---

[36] Meir Dick (1814–93), a prolific writer of Yiddish popular literature, published at Vilna in 1864 a book in Yiddish with a Hebrew title, *Sipurei chakhmei Yavan* ('Stories of the Sages of Greece'), in which, following Ben-Ze'ev, he presented figures from ancient Greek history as models of wisdom and morals worthy of emulation.

[37] Gordis, 'Homeric Books'; Lieberman, 'The Greek of the Rabbis', in *Greek in Jewish Palestine*, 15-28.

motto from Isaiah 22: 13, and also rendered 'Das verschleierte Bild zu Sais' with a motto from Exodus 33: 20; the poet Micah Joseph Lebensohn (1828–56), in 1849, at the age of 19, translated ninety-seven stanzas from Schiller's German version of book ii of the *Aeneid* (a translation that established his reputation in the literary world of Vilna).[38] In 1868 Israel Rall (1838–93) published in Odessa the first collection in Hebrew of Roman poetry (*Shirei romi*), in which he drew a distinction between Ovid's *Metamorphoses* and Lucretius' *De Rerum Natura* ('On the Nature of Things'): in the *Metamorphoses* he discerned a deep-seated link to the cosmogony of the Holy Scriptures, for in both books the act of creation is described as the work of a divine demiurge (a similarity he explained by deriving Greek mythology from ancient Egyptian sources!); by contrast, *De Rerum Natura* was a heretical poem, one that demolished all the foundations of faith by denying the existence of a divine providence that directs the world.[39] In 1888 Aaron Kaminka (1866–1950), a rabbi, scholar, and translator, published a collection of translations entitled *Zemurot nokhri'ot* ('Alien Sprigs'). Saul Tchernichowsky (1875–1943) began to publish his translations in the early 1920s and made the most valuable contribution to the translation of classical literary works into Hebrew in the first half of the twentieth century.

However, even these occasional references needed legitimation. Isaac Baer Schlesinger (1773–1836), a teacher and scholar from Bohemia and a devout Jew, who wrote a monograph on Pythagoras, did not shy away from declaring in the introduction to his drama *Hachashmona'im* ('The Hasmoneans', Prague, 1816) that 'from between its lines, the faith of the ancient Greeks will shed its light'. About half a century later, Kalman Schulman (1819–99), perhaps the most prolific Hebrew popularizer in the nineteenth century, apologized in the introduction to the first volume of *Divrei yemei olam* ('Universal History', Vilna, 1867) for including in his book a long description of pagan Hellenic culture, namely an account of the Greek gods.[40] He anticipated criticism: that was his payment and that was his reward! Yet the description, as he explained, was intended only to point out the immeasurable distance that lay between the faith of Israel

[38] Zamosc also included several short poems on the wisdom and integrity of Socrates. Gordon's poem, 'Neginat shoteh shekhar' ('The Music of a Winebibber'), is a free adaptation of *Carmina Anacreontea*, no. 8 West. Lebensohn's translation of Schiller was published under the title 'The Ruins of Troy', accompanied by a preface in which he said that the book moved him since it described Aeneas' longing for his homeland Troy (*Shirei Mikhal*, 212–42).

[39] He also edited a literary periodical called *Shem ve Yefet* (Lvov, 1887–8, 4 vols.); M. Zohar, 'Between Shem and Japhet'. See more in Ch. 8.

[40] Based on George Weber, *Allgemeine Weltgeschichte* (1857–81).

and the abominations of the idolaters; the Greek sages too had tried to unravel the secret of the oneness of the divinity.[41]

When Judah Leib Ben-Ze'ev (1764–1811), one of the most prolific *maskilim*, the 'typical *maskil*' according to Klausner,[42] included short biographies of 'Greek sages', Hellenic and Hellenistic philosophers, along with short excerpts from their ethical works (wise sayings) in his Hebrew chrestomathy *Limudei hameisharim* ('The Learning of the Righteous', Vienna, 1802), the second part of his reader *Beit hasefer*, he too felt the need to apologize by remarking that in the words of the Greek sages there is no mention of the fear of Heaven, while the Sages of Israel conjoin the rules of moral behaviour with a fear of God.[43] One generation earlier, David Friedländer (1750–1834), a leader of the Jewish community in Berlin, a member of Mendelssohn's circle, a patron of the Haskalah, and a forerunner of Reform Judaism, did the same in his German reader.[44] Joseph Perl (1773–1839), the radical *maskil* and satirist from Galicia, in his work *Luach hashanah* ('Calendar', 1813), which attempted to bring the traditional camp closer to the issues of enlightenment, interspersed 'what I saw in the Greek books'—that is, stories that dealt with Greek sages.[45] These were mere drops from the ocean of classical literature.

Ahad Ha'am wrote, with some naïvety, that if the works of Plato and Aristotle had been translated for the Jews in Palestine, those Jews would have been familiar with the great literature of Greece and would not have been seduced by its abominable and common pagan literature. 'If those Elders, who translated the Bible into Greek for the benefit of the Egyptian Jews, had also translated Plato into Hebrew for the benefit of the Jews in Palestine . . . there would have been no "traitorous enemies of the covenant" among our people, and perhaps there would have been no need of the Maccabees and all the spiritual history . . .'.[46] On this view, a knowledge of Plato's writings would have prevented Jews from becoming Hellenists, because (like the modern Jew) they would have been warmed by the light of philosophy. In a similar vein, Smolenskin wrote in his essay 'Et ledaber' ('A Time to Speak', Eccl. 3: 7) that after the Great Revolt, the Sages issued a decree against learning Greek wisdom. This decree, however, came 'not from the edicts of faith', but rather

from the edicts of the people; after this language and this wisdom caused harm to

[41] Schulman, *Divrei yemei olam*, i. 7–8.
[42] Klausner, *History of Hebrew Literature*, i. 178–90.
[43] See Spiegel, *The Wisdom of Ancient Greece*.
[44] Friedländer, *Lesebuch für jüdische Kinder*.
[45] See Mahler, *Hasidim and Haskalah*, 187–207.
[46] Ahad Ha'am, 'Imitation and Assimilation,' 118–19.

the people, they decreed against it. Such a decree is meant to be only for its own time, but then came Rabbi Akiva, who hated the Gentile with the utmost hatred, and when he saw that the other did not persist from Greek song or Homer, he affirmed that whoever reads the Apocrypha denies God's existence and that the Almighty's legacy would be taken away from him.

In other words, the decree against reading Greek literature was a reaction to a historical situation; it was the outcome of popular national awareness and not dictated by some religious principle. Undoubtedly under the influence of Ahad Ha'am, David Ben-Gurion wrote that if Sophocles, Thucydides, Plato, and the other great Greek philosophers had been translated into Hebrew, the face of Jewish history would have been different. How unfortunate it is, he added, that the Sages did not know how to distinguish between the worthless facets of Hellenistic culture and the spiritual treasures of the Greek genius in its days of glory.[47]

In the same spirit as Ahad Ha'am, but of course far more radical, was the introduction to a selection of stories from Greek mythology published in Warsaw in 1919, which stated that this Hebrew translation would confirm the affinity between the Jewish and Greek cultures. And this time it referred to their mythologies! If the Hellenizing Jews had succeeded in showing our people the glory of Hellenism—it is asserted in the introduction to what is usually considered the most abominable part of Greek literature, the mythology—and not just revealing its indecency and corruption, they would have brought the cultures closer instead of engendering eternal enmity between them. The historical mistake—which the Polish Jewish lover of the classics sought to change—was that the Hellenizing Jews threw away the healthy contents of Greek culture, and retained only its shell.[48]
Another example is I. A. Trezek's *Misterei hagoyim hakadmonim (hamitologiah) beshalosh tekufot* ('The Mysteries of the Ancient Peoples (Mythology) in Three Ages [sc. Babylonian, Egyptian, and Greek]', Warsaw, 1875). In order to justify his work, he presents evidence that the Sages knew Greek mythology and even alluded to it. He found similarities between mythological and biblical heroes: Noah brings to mind Saturn, Samson was the origin of the tales of Hercules, and so on. And so after many hundreds of years, this Hellenistic Jewish tactic makes its reappearance in Warsaw![49]

---

[47] Ben-Gurion, *Yichud veye'ud*, 123.

[48] Mitelponski, *Hagadot Yavan*. See also Rosenstein, *Mi'agadot Yavan*. The first Hebrew translation of a Greek mythology book published in Palestine was by Yehuda Gor-Grasovsky, *Me'agadot haYevanim* (1915). They were based on Polish adaptations.

[49] These books are some examples of the collections and adaptations of Greek mythology published in various European languages. The fact is that Greek mythology was translated or adapted into Hebrew at a very late date, compared to the situation in European literatures. Three adaptations into Hebrew

There were other views. M. J. Berdyczewski expostulated against Ahad Ha'am's views: how strange it was to believe that a translation of Plato into Hebrew could change the course of history! After all, he stated, it was not an error on the part of the God of Israel in designing the mission of His people to send them not translators who would introduce the beauty of Japheth into the tents of Shem, but those who decreed 'Accursed is the man who teaches his son Greek!' The prohibition against translation, Berdyczewski argued, is not a deviation but an integral expression of the spirit of Judaism, one to which he, of course, was opposed.[50]

David Ben-Gurion, who truly believed in the possibility of combining Greek science and art with Judaism (but also believed the Greek philosophers longed for justice and good) might be described as a Zionist and Israeli Reb Walder. While spending the early months of the Second World War in London, in May 1940 he began studying Greek from books purchased (for over £15) from Blackwell's at Oxford ('the bookstore he always dreamed of'): at the very time when total Nazi victory appeared most probable, the head of the Jewish Agency was preoccupied with Greek poetry and philosophy and conducted long discussions with his English companions on Greek history and Greek ideals, wondering whether these Greek ideals could become in the future the ideals of the Jewish state. He himself wrote that the study of Greek helped him to forget both the enemy air raids and the failure of Zionist diplomacy in London; later that year he continued it in New York.[51]

J. H. Brenner hailed the Hebrew translation of Plato's *Symposium* published by Yefet (Jaffa, 1914). At the outset of the First World War, he wrote, the beauty of Japheth, who has become a Christian, is being consumed by the flames of the war, and no compassion is shown him. Brenner

---

were published in Warsaw in 1901 (an adaptation from Polish of the story of the Argonauts), 1909, and 1921, and one in Palestine in 1915. Edith Hamilton's *Mythology* was translated in 1967 and Charles Kingsley's *The Heroes* (1856) was translated only in 1934.

It is well known that 'Greek mythologies in the sense of a homogeneous system of myths did not exist . . .', Edmunds, *Approaches to Greek Myth*, 4, and see also Dowden, *The Use of Greek Mythology*, 13–17; Kirk, *Myth*, 8. However, during the 18th and the 19th cc. adaptations of mythological stories became very popular. To name only a few: G. A. Scheppach, *Mythologisches Lesebuch für die Jugend* (1785/86); M. G. Hermann, *Handbuch der Mythologie aus Homer und Hesiod* (1789), with a foreword by C. G. Heyne; W. Hempel, *Mythologie für die Jugend* (1802); M. G. Hermann, *Mythologie der Griechen* (1801–2); Thomas Keightley, *The Mythology of Ancient Greece and Italy for the Use of Schools* (11th edn., 1845); George Fox, *Tales from Greek Mythology* (1861), and many more (*Lexikon der Kinder- und Jugendliteratur*, ii. 526–7). Also see Turner, *The Greek Heritage*, 77–134; Feldman and Richardson, *The Rise of Modern Mythology* (and the extensive bibliography, 528–54); Manuel, *The Eighteenth Century*. All these books were preceded by the manuals of the 16th and 17th cc. See Seznec, *The Survival of the Pagan Gods*, 279–323.

[50] Berdyczewski, 'Mishnei ha'avarim', 109–10.
[51] Teveth, *Ben-Gurion: The Burning Ground*, 750–5, 770–1.

commended the translation and went on to discuss Socrates, the 'finest of the sons of Greece', a 'sacred satyr, insolent and wanton, but also adored and a source of [man's] aspiration for good'.

To the Hebrew reader, who in the main has only learned about classical Greece from hearsay, books of this kind are an eye-opener. Now that the Symposium is written in Hebrew, he has the opportunity—if only he is sufficiently developed to understand it—to obtain some slight notion of the greatness of Greek wisdom. Here he will be introduced to a pure culture of the spirit, a lofty view of life, a classical Greek work. The justified hate he may harbour in his heart towards the Greek people in the past and in the present—towards this corrupt and faithless nation—will not blind his eyes so that he cannot see the great light in the place where it shines. And the light is great.[52]

The prejudice against the Greeks exists here too—but Socrates rises above the 'Greek people' and his philosophy and exemplary life are a great light.

There can be no better words than these of Brenner's to move us ahead to the next section.

SOCRATES AS PARAGON

In the pantheon of Jewish historical figures, there were martyrs, but these were martyrs in sanctification of the Holy Name, not of a philosophical idea or freedom of opinion (with the exception, of course, of Uriel da Costa and Spinoza). Consequently, great interest was shown during the Haskalah in Socrates' character and fate, and he became a modern Jewish hero.

Even before then, in 1651, the Venetian Rabbi Simone (Shimon b. Yitzhak Simchah) Luzzatto published a philosophical fantasy entitled *Socrate, overo dell'humano sapere esercitio seriogiocoso* ('Socrates, or on Human Wisdom: A Serio-Comic Exercise'), in which, according to the title-page, it is shown 'how feeble is human understanding so long as it is not guided by divine revelation'. The setting is an 'Academy for the Reform of Human Knowledge' sitting at Delphi, to which Reason, imprisoned by Authority, submits a petition for her release; this is opposed by Pythagoras, whose dicta are credited on his mere say-so, and Aristotle, who has done very well from the notion that it is almost sacrilegious to disagree with him. As an example of the damage done by the flouting of Authority he cites Aristarchus of Samos, who had imagined that the earth revolved round the sun; the allusion to Galileo is patent. Nevertheless, Reason is released, and

---

[52] *Sedeh hasifrut*, ii. 336–8.

Authority forbidden to interfere until the Academy shall have determined how the two shall be blended; at the same time, in true Venetian style, a receptacle is opened for anonymous denunciations of any harm that unauthorized doctrines may have done. Socrates is accused of having attempted to demolish the marvellous edifice of human learning; Xenophon objects that even if the charge were true, any attempt at repression would merely draw attention to the doctrines under attack, but the Academy takes the view that error may be fought in other ways, and its own business is to determine the merits of the case. Socrates is therefore invited to defend himself; his plea, which occupies the greatest part of the book, recounts the failure of the various philosophers he consulted to assuage his doubts, and in particular contrasts Hippias' view that philosophy was a power for good, and a better understanding of the Creator's works, with Timon's assertion that it led to harm, and the justification of gross immoralities: 'this rash wisdom, not guided by a greater light, claiming to destroy superstition, puts religion itself to flight' (p. 287). Socrates inclined to the latter view, but without committing himself, and preferred to follow what was probable. Many of those present declare that Socrates should be not only acquitted but publicly honoured; Alcmaeon the Pythagorean is for condemnation, but Plato persuades the Academy that as Socrates suspends judgement on philosophical questions, so should judgement be suspended on him. Here the work ends, having demonstrated (in the words of the title-page) 'quanto sia imbecile l'humano intendimento', and touched in Timon's speech on the qualification 'mentre non è diretto dalla diuina riuelatione'. By treating a philosophical question in dialogue form, an author may encourage his readers to seek their own solutions without stating his own; this is evidently the case with Luzzatto, whose work, long neglected, has recently received various interpretations.[53]

---

[53] Despite brief discussion in Graetz, *History of the Jews*, v. 80–7; Lachower, *A History of Hebrew Literature*, i. 9–10; Bonfil, 'Preaching as Mediation', 78–9, the first serious studies of the background, content, and meaning of Luzzatto's book are Ariel Viterbo, 'Socrates in the Ghetto of Venice', and Ruderman, *Jewish Thought and Scientific Discovery in Early Modern Europe*, 153–84, who observes 'No scholar has even described the work fully, let alone mentioned reading it in its entirety' (p. 154). Viterbo takes the book for Luzzatto's intellectual autobiography, revealing the range of his learning, and expressing his scepticism about the possibility of achieving knowledge by reason and the value of the evidence one can offer in order to justify any assertion; he suggests that the book was written in Italian for educated Italian readers and shows the popularity of learning and science among this public. Ruderman does not exclude a Jewish audience, more familiar at that date with Italian than Hebrew (p. 155), and suspects Luzzatto of doubting that very divine revelation he professes to vindicate. Dr Holford-Strevens, to whom I am grateful for examining this microcosm of Italian Jewish classical and scientific learning in the British Library, points out that Luzzatto's Timon is primarily the Athenian misanthrope, rather than the sceptical pupil of Pyrrho; nevertheless, he connects Plato's second-order suspension of judgement with the radical Pyrrhonian scepticism that rejected certainty even in uncertainty. Pyrrhonians refuted

The outlook of humanism, which viewed Socrates as Jesus' precursor in his quest for the path to spiritual redemption, was that the human being must learn to know his inner soul. Socrates taught the humanists that scepticism could serve lofty ends: he was 'the first great apostle of intellectual and moral freedom . . . a supreme example of intellectual and moral integrity. However, he was not spiritual enough and offered no guarantees of life eternal.'[54] Socrates, then, could be a representative *par excellence* of both faith and agnosticism; he could be both a liberal reformer and a doubting rationalist. A lone and solitary figure within his community, he was ostracized by a conservative, superstition-ridden society and was a victim of his struggle with it.

In the wake of European rationalism, which viewed him as a martyr on the altar of intellectual truth, Socrates was widely represented as one who was devoted to learning and studying in order to draw nearer to the wellsprings of the human soul; he was the lone intellectual of his time, who had fought for his truth in a hostile milieu. Although Socrates assailed prejudice and tyranny, he was not a nihilistic sophist seeking to undermine the foundations of faith. Hence, unlike all the Greeks before and after him, it was Socrates alone who understood the unity of the Creator and His Providence, as well as the mechanism of reward and punishment. We should also bear in mind that Socrates was not a philosopher who held himself aloof from society. He was a loyal son of his city, who served in Athens' army and strove to introduce a proper social order there. He was after all the archetype of the philosophical and civic paragon of the intellectual utopia. In 1759 J. G. Hamann wrote his *Sokratische Denkwürdigkeiten*, in which he expressed his objection to intellectualism and stated his view that Socrates was the thinker who believed that faith is in no way dependent on reason.[55] In 1772 J. A. Eberhard, in his book *Neue Apologie des Sokrates*, tried to use the figure and life of Socrates to prove that it is ethics and good deeds—not philosophical study—that elevate man to the highest spiritual plane.

---

the Academic doctrine of probability, but conformed with common custom as a basis for action; it would follow that for Luzzatto a Jew should walk in the ways of his fathers without accepting arguments either for them or against them.

[54] Muller, 'The Romantic Glory', 140–3. Cicero, *Tusculan Disputations*, v. 10, described Socrates as the Greek sage who was the first to bring philosophy down from the heavens to the cities of men and into their homes. On the Socratic tradition as a source of the Renaissance's *humanitas* see J. Stephens, *The Italian Renaissance*, 23–9.

[55] 'Socrates was the philosopher who took pride in not knowing and trusted his daimon rather than his reason' (Blackall, *The Emergence of German*, 437; cf. M. Schwarcz, 'Mendelssohn's "Jerusalem"'). Indeed, in Judah Leib Miesis's anti-hasidic satire *Kinat ha'emet*, Socrates is described as a mysticist who embraced vain beliefs.

We have already seen that in Jewish philosophy, as well of the Hellenistic as the medieval period, the great Greek philosophers are alluded to with approval as having, under the influence of Jewish teachers, come closer to recognizing the unity of the Creator. Even before the Haskalah, therefore, the Judaizing of Socrates was a vehicle of prime importance in giving legitimacy to the study of philosophy. It was Moses Mendelssohn, in *Phädon oder über Unsterblichkeit der Seele in drei Gesprächen* (1767), who assigned Socrates his central position in the consciousness of the Haskalah. Wessely, in his introduction to the Hebrew translation of Plato's *Phaedo* by S. Baer, *Fedon hu sefer hisharut hanefesh* (Warsaw, 1785), exalted Socrates and several other lofty Greek personages as: 'singular people, men of reputation in every wisdom, in every science, like Pythagoras, Socrates, Plato, and their friends and disciples, who rose above the beliefs of the masses, and promulgated the existence and unity of God, the existence and immortality of the soul'.[56]

The profound interest in Socrates must be understood against the backdrop of his image in the nineteenth century, and via the diverse messages it conveyed to the historical consciousness. Indeed, the nineteenth century is sometimes hyperbolically called 'the century of Socrates', to indicate his status as a paragon in the contemporary consciousness. Frank M. Turner, for example, writes that in Victorian England Socrates was the most famous citizen of Athens.[57] He appears not only in philosophical writings, but also in popular didactic-moralistic books, which include, for the most part, biographical episodes and important sayings. In many works, Jesus and Socrates represented two antipodal archetypes of human resolve—the messiah versus the teacher—in relation to the world. Jesus' crucifixion and Socrates' death by hemlock became two constitutive events of symbolic stature, two pivotal events in the history of European and world civilization.[58]

---

[56] Tertullian, *Apologeticus*, 22. 1, interprets the 'daimonion' that deters the Platonic Socrates from actions in the Christian sense of the word as a demon or devil subordinate to Satan, and maliciously alleges that it deterred Socrates from doing good. (Elsewhere in the same speech, at 14. 7, Tertullian, ever the advocate eager to have it both ways, makes Socrates tell the truth in undermining pagan religion, and the Athenians confess the fact when they posthumously rehabilitated him, a legend widely believed by Tertullian's day.) Cf. Feiner, '"History" and "Historical Images"', 122–4.

[57] Turner, *The Greek Heritage*, 264–321. On Socrates as a folk-hero in the Enlightenment see Gay, *The Rise of Modern Paganism*, 81–2.

[58] Of these and other reinterpretations Ernst Cassirer was to write: 'the facts of the philosophical past, the doctrines and systems of the great thinkers, are meaningless without an interpretation. And this process of interpretation never comes to a complete standstill. . . . No example is perhaps more characteristic and instructive in this respect than the change in our portrait of Socrates. We have the Socrates of Xenophon and Plato; we have a Stoic, a sceptic, a mystic, a rationalistic, and a romantic Socrates. They are entirely dissimilar. Nevertheless they are not untrue; each of them gives us a new

This debate is an echo of another, far earlier in time. Justin Martyr, in his *First Apology*, described Socrates as a man who tried to lead men away from falsehood into truth; in other words, his work was a preparation for the complete work of Christ. For Tertullian, by contrast, Socrates was self-confessedly guided by a demon.[59] In the context of the Patristic period, this is, of course, an argument about the link between Christianity and Greek philosophy.

It is evident why Jewish intellectuals found it almost impossible to avoid turning to the figure of Socrates. Mendelssohn, who was called 'the Jewish Socrates', was asked by J. C. Lavater, his polemical adversary, to explain why he viewed the pagan Socrates in a positive light, yet did not divulge what his real attitude was towards Jesus.[60] In the contemporary intellectual climate, however, there were a number of criteria that were applicable to Socrates, just as 'in reality', Socrates himself had been a multifaceted personality. Rationalists and anti-rationalists alike inscribed his name on the banners waved in the lively controversy that raged between them.[61] Hence we have another instance of correspondence between the internal Jewish position and one of the positions prevalent in the wider cultural climate. Socrates was the model for studying either metaphysics or ethics, as the case might be. It was through Socrates that the study of Western philosophy was given the stamp of approval, because an outstanding aspect of his thinking was its search for a transcendental element. Socrates, after all, made every effort to understand the secret of immortality. Moreover, from the Hellenistic period on, he was already the universal philosopher-hero. In biographical legends, Socrates encounters the wise men of many different nations throughout the world. For example, in the *Life of Socrates* written by Aristotle's pupil Aristoxenus of Tarentum, the Athenian philosopher meets a wise man from India. When Socrates explains that he is 'inquiring into the

---

aspect, a characteristic perspective of the historical Socrates and his intellectual and moral physiognomy' (*An Essay on Man: An Introduction to a Philosophy of Human Culture*, 179–80).

[59] Justin, *Apol. I*, 5. 3, Tertullian, *Apologeticus*, 22. 1; Copleston, *A History of Philosophy*, vii/1, 31–2. See also Jaeger, *Early Christianity*, 28.

[60] Altmann, *Moses Mendelssohn*, 194–263. See Kreeft, *Socrates Meets Jesus*.

[61] For Nietzsche he was the type of the theoretical man, a theoretical optimist 'who, with his faith that the nature of things can be fathomed, ascribes to knowledge and insight the power of a panacea, while understanding error as the evil *par excellence*' (*The Birth of Tragedy*, §15, trans. Kaufmann, 97). On Nietzsche's view see the chapter 'Nietzsche's Admiration for Socrates', in W. Kaufmann, *Nietzsche*, 391–441. See also Sandross, *Sokrates und Nietzsche*; Jaeger, *Paideia*, ii. 13–17. Lev Shestov compares Socrates with Abraham, a true believer who goes forward, without looking to the right or left, without asking where he is going, without calculating, while Socrates wished to know beforehand where he would arrive (*Athens and Jerusalem*, 396–7).

life of man', the Indian mockingly retorts that it is impossible to understand the life of man without first understanding the idea of Godhead; that is, without dealing with natural philosophy, a topic that Socrates rejected.[62]

If that is the case, Socrates could have inspired faith. In his *Lezioni di teologia dogmatica*, Shadal calls him the first man to use a teleological or physical argument to prove the existence of a God: 'the most real, the most powerful, and the most ancient of all the arguments that were raised to prove the existence of a Deity'.[63] That is, Socrates was coming closer to Jewish monotheism. Just as Western thinkers wanted to Christianize Socrates (and Muslim thinkers to Islamize him),[64]there were Jewish writers who wanted to Judaize him. In diametrical opposition, Isaac Euchel in 'Igrot Meshulam' also used the example of Socrates to show that it was possible to live a happy life without observing the Commandments. Socrates thus became a prototype of the modern non-observant Jew, who, so Euchel maintained, can be happy (and the goal of happiness was one of the main innovations of the Haskalah!) without keeping the Jewish laws.

Socrates served as the paragon of a true believer and the ideal of human perfection. His place in Paradise is well deserved, because he sacrificed his life for the truth. At one and the same time, he was a rationalist who examined faith according to rational criteria, and a righteous man who was persecuted by a conspiratorial environment, permeated by ignorance and illiteracy. In *Luach hashanah* (1814), Joseph Perl wrote that Socrates was 'nobler than all the philosophers of Greece because he was growing ever closer to the notion of monotheism'.

He was a very wise and righteous man, who has no equal among all the wise men of the world and their followers. Among the Greeks, he was the first who studied and was able, through his understanding spirit, to know the existence of one God, the Creator of heaven and earth and all they contain. But because of his righteousness and his faith, Socrates perished. (May he be blessed! For he died an honourable death and his end was an everlasting blessing!) When Socrates turned away from the other gods, whom the people of Athens worshipped, the priests conferred about him in secret, and brought him to trial . . .[65]

To J. L. Ben-Ze'ev, Socrates

was the most magnificent of all the Greek sages in ethical justice . . . and at first he

---

[62] Aristoxenus, fr. 53 Wehrli; cf. the tales at Pseudo-Plato, *Axiochus*, 371 A; Diogenes Laertius, ii. 45 (Aristotle, fr. 32 Rose).

[63] S. D. Luzzatto, *Lezioni di teologia dogmatica*. I used the Hebrew translation, *Shi'urim bete'ologiah dogmatit*, 82.   [64] I. Alon, *Socrates in Medieval Arabic Literature*.

[65] This survey is indebted to Feiner, '"History" and "Historical Images"', 122–5.

studied wisdom and science with his teacher, Anaxagoras. When he saw that most of these sciences did not educate man in the path of morality and righteousness, so as to improve his ways, doing right and abstaining from evil, then he set his heart upon learning the virtues of morality and justice so that he would be a good example in his studies. He was the first to carry out what he himself learned of ethical ways, and he was firm in the stronghold of his purity and righteousness, all the days of his life.[66]

In his *Sefer toledot Yeshurun* (Prague, 1817), the historian Marcus Fischer wrote that Socrates was one of the righteous men of the world and resembled one of Israel's prophets; 'he sought for God's closeness daily, and preached morals and a knowledge of God, hence he was persecuted'. There were conservative *maskilim* who rejected the positive image of Socrates, which exalted him above believers: he was, after all, an idolater, wrote Schlesinger, who himself preferred, as we have already noted, the world of the devout Christian to secular Western culture. Socrates, in the guise of an exemplary figure, was not acceptable to those who believed that in the final analysis, 'philosophical monotheism' was not a guarantee of morality.

As a loyal subject of his city, Socrates was a model for the Haskalah concept of citizenship, which advocated that Jews ought to profess loyalty to the countries they live in, for he had even served as a soldier in Athens' army. As a citizen who symbolized the clash between free-spirited man and the governing authorities, Socrates became part of Jewish public discourse only in the context of political tensions in the State of Israel from the 1960s onwards. He served as a symbol of conflict between the intellectual and the state. Frequent reference was made to Socrates' self-image in the *Apology* as a 'gadfly to a horse that is large and well bred but rather sluggish because of its size so that it needed to be aroused'. Socrates and the prophets of Israel who admonished the people at the gates were a useful symbol. For example, in February 1959 the author S. Izhar wrote a letter to Ben-Gurion, then Israel's Prime Minister, in which he compared the Hebrew writers to Socrates. Socrates, Ben-Gurion replied, exaggerated in his description of the sins and flaws of Athens but he unquestionably played a positive and essential role. 'Even today, all is not lost, and if there is no Isaiah around, there are many Socrateses who in their wisdom, sense of justice, and striving for the sublime, the good, and the beautiful, do not fall short of Plato's great teacher.'[67]

---

[66] Ben-Ze'ev, *Mesilat halimud*, in *Beit hasefer*, i. 255.
[67] Keren, *Ben-Gurion and the Intellectuals*, 132–6.

GREEK MYTHOLOGICAL SYMBOLS IN HEBREW

In itself, a knowledge of 'alien' literature and the reception of a translated literary corpus into one's own literature does not indicate the acceptance of its cultural norms and values. But very often this reception brings along with it a whole world of concepts, categories of thought, inherited metaphors, and subtle connotations of meaning, such as the Greek *paideia* brought along with it.[68] Literature is not only a gate into culture, it also creates values. And indeed, at the dawn of the Jewish Enlightenment there were already those who recognized the danger; and since they identified classical literature with mythology and idolatry, they did their best to combat it.

Greek mythology, wrote Goethe, offers 'einen unerschöpflichen Reichtum göttlicher und menschlicher Symbole'.[69] This wealth of mythology survived even during the 'dark' Middle Ages. Heine finds it most remarkable that the beautiful beings of the Greek world of legends ('die schönen Wesen der griechischen Fabelwelt') had survived in Europe for so long and in such disguises;[70] but this rich *Fabelwelt* was never an integral part of Jewish culture, even when well known to it. In the Bible one can find few traces of Greek mythological motifs or names, though the *benei Elohim* and *nefilim* of Gen. 6: 2, 4 correspond to the Titans and Giants; but if there had indeed been cultural contacts between ancient Israel and Greece, one might wonder why the Bible should reveal no direct use of Greek mythology. The situation was of course different during the Second Temple period: Philo was well acquainted with Greek mythology, and in sectarian works, such as the Book of Enoch and the Sibylline Oracles, we find traces of familiarity with it, reference to it, and use of its motifs.

In Ch. 11 I shall deal with the Sages' use of a few mythological motifs; I have already mentioned (see above at n. 12) a few examples of their sporadic appearance in Jewish literature from the Middle Ages to the eighteenth century. From the late eighteenth century onwards Greek mythology infiltrates into Jewish literature for children as well as for adults.

In the introduction to the first issue of *Hame'asef*, in 1783, Naphtali Herz Wessely warned the writers of modern Hebrew poetry against being carried away by the prevailing fashion in contemporary European poetry:

In translating the poems and songs do not mention the names of the ancient gods to which the Greeks and Romans referred in their poems and ethics, and

---

[68] Jaeger, *Early Christianity*, 6.
[69] Goethe, *Dichtung und Wahrheit*, ii. 258.
[70] Heine, *Ludwig Börne*, 'Helgoland, den 1. August' (*Sämtliche Werke*, xi. 47).

to which all the European poets of our times are drawn, for Jacob supped not of things like these. They should not be heard from your mouths.[71]

But the writers of *Hame'asef* did not heed Wessely's warning; they wrote songs of nature, drinking songs, as well as 'songs of debauchery', and even interspersed mythological motifs in their writing. The Hebrew poets of the Haskalah in eastern Europe carried on the same trend, and the most salient example is that of Isaac Baer Levinsohn. Not only did he not follow Wessely's advice, but his book is perhaps the most 'Hellenic' of all the Hebrew literature written in the nineteenth century. His polemical book *Te'udah beYisrael* bears the imprint of his uncompromising and unflagging effort to affirm the affinity between Jewish tradition and various aspects of the legacy of classical antiquity. It is not at all surprising that he chose to begin his book with a quotation from Virgil, and also to preface the first section with a short poem he wrote, called 'To Wisdom', addressed to Pallas Athene, whom he apostrophizes:

> Awaken daughter of the gods! Awaken mother of wisdom!
> Put on your armour and don your helmet,
> Take up your spear, and descend from on high to my aid;
> Deliver me from foolish authority, that rushes to rout me,
> And from abusive tongues, that are ready to condemn me,
> For I have come to bear a libation in Jeshurun.[72]

This radical enlightened Hebrew writer was calling upon Pallas Athene, the Olympian goddess of wisdom, to assist him in his struggle to spread Haskalah values among his Jewish brethren in Tsarist Russia! Such a writer would certainly pay no heed to the warnings of Wessely, nor would he find any fault with the acknowledgement of mythology. He sees nothing wrong in using the Greek metaphors merely because they are anchored in Greek mythology. He allows that the 'Greek wisdom' forbidden by the Sages was Greek mythology, but believes that there is no longer a connection between the signified and the signifier. If that were not the case, he writes with barbed irony, Jews could not mention, for instance, the names of the continents 'Europe' and 'Asia'—'for these are the names of gods'—or the names of certain towns and cities, the months of the year, and the days of the week. Levinsohn went even further in supporting his case with usages suggesting Eros, which he found in the writings of the Sages. There is also 'hymn' or 'hymeneal', that is 'epithalamion', he argues—aiming directly

---

[71] Tzamiriyon, *Hame'asef*, 38.

[72] Heine had ironically wondered only a few years earlier in his 'Die Götter Griechenlands' why Pallas Athene, with her shield and wisdom, was unable to prevent the destruction of the gods.

at the vulnerable spot of the 'guardians of the wall'—and those words originate with the Greek god Hymen, who presided over mating and matrimony. (This argument may be extended: the names of the planets are also mythological in origin, as are the Hebrew months, which are named after Babylonian and Persian gods, as well as perfectly acceptable Hebrew first names such as Esther.)

In consequence, Levinsohn believes Jews may use mythological symbols because there is no longer any significance or substance to the names and they no longer attest to 'any authority or divinity'. He argued that the Hebrew writer may not only acknowledge the mythological heroes as non-divine, but also make use of mythological metaphors and allegory without any fear of apostasy.[73] In the same way, Levinsohn also rejects on principle the criticism of the Hebrew poet Micah Joseph Lebensohn by Shadal, who in a letter of 1851 had complained of his including in his poem 'Shelomo veKohelet' ('Solomon and Ecclesiastes') 'depictions of Minerva and Medusa': 'It seems quite unreasonable to me that a young Lithuanian Jew—who as a boy was raised at the knees of the Prophets, the *tana'im*, and the *amora'im*—should preach about the foolish idols of the ancient pagans, there to learn the secrets of wisdom.'[74]

As a matter of fact, Lebensohn was to a great extent following the example of medieval Christian literature that turned the gods into allegorical figures and mere ornaments, as was done by Fulgentius (AD 5th–6th cc.) in his *Mythologiae*. But for him the mythology became not a *philosophia moralis* or a collection of fables with hidden meaning, but simply part of the culturally accepted repertoire of symbols and names. However, from the 1920s onwards, the mythological (and biblical) symbols took on greater meaning. Kirk writes that mythological symbols are 'bearers of important messages about life in general and life-within-society in particular'.[75] This is the most convincing explanation for the fact that pagan divinities and ancient mythological heroes continued, throughout history—even in the Middle Ages—to be the bearers of ideas and messages, and this is why they never disappeared and were never forgotten.[76]

---

[73] *Te'udah*, 61–2. He also refers to some of the bizarre theories which attempt not only to prove the existence of Greek mythological motifs in the Bible (like the parallel between Samson and Hercules or between the sun standing still in Gibeon and Homer's words in the *Iliad*, ii. 412–13: 'Zeus . . . Grant that the sun may not go down . . .'.) Boman compares the Homeric passage with Josh. 10: 12 and Ps. 19: 5 ff., and writes that in the Bible it is an expression of God's power and glory, while in Homer it is an indication of time (*Hebrew Thought Compared with Greek*, 133). On mythological motifs in Jewish mosaics in the late Roman and Byzantine period see Ch. 11.

[74] Werses, 'Judah Halevi in the Nineteenth Century', 72–4.

[75] Kirk, *The Nature of Greek Myths*, 28–9.

[76] Seznec, *The Survival of the Pagan Gods*, 147.

The infiltration of mythological motifs and themes into modern Hebrew literature did not come about simply by way of translations of poetry or drama of mythological content, but also by their absorption, through various intermediaries, into Hebrew culture.[77] In this history of absorption and acceptance of mythological themes it is possible to discern two layers: in the first, 'mythological man' is the symbol of the 'natural man', a hero and conqueror; in the second, he is the symbol and example of 'modern man', inwardly riven and dogged by fate.

Here are but a few examples.

The idyllic-romantic image of the Greek, a symbol of youth and a dauntless warrior who sacrifices himself for his homeland and tempts his fate, is deeply embedded in numerous Hebrew texts as the *alter ego* and exemplar of the young revolutionary Hebrew who changes the world. 'He must be young, a young Greek, and he must know how to brandish his spear and stand boldly against fate . . . to conquer life with one thrust, to seal his fate . . . and if he reaches his goal—then will he rule over life, the laurel wreath fluttering on his brow; and the trembling youth will become a strong man, an achiever, a conqueror . . .'.[78] These *chalutzim* (pioneers), young radical socialist Zionists in Palestine in the early twenties, likened themselves to the coterie of gods in 'Olympic Spring', who awaken from a long winter's hibernation and with mighty steps ascend from the 'hell of the Diaspora to the Land of Israel, a veritable Garden of Eden, in the freshness of their youthful vigour and with youth's imagination'. They are filled with an inner radiance that is reflected in their *risus gratus*—the Horatian 'pleasant laughter'. They are imbued with faith in the Orphic power of the dream, the desire, the vision, the love, the poetry. There is also a Dionysian base to their existence, which they express in dancing: 'This is the Dionysian act, this is man's reincarnation: flight and descent.'

This is of course an extreme example that does not typify the overall community of *chalutzim* in their spiritual-intellectual world, permeated as it was by the allusions and symbols of classical culture. For after all, they were—by their own testimony—'ragged pioneers who studied Plato and Nietzsche'. On a wall in one of the huts occupied by such *chalutzim* hung Anselm Auerbach's well-known picture *Plato's Symposium*. This picture, according to one of the writers in the collection of confessions and meditations *Kehiliyatenu* ('Our Community')—symbolized the life force of the *kevutsah* (collective settlement): '*Plato's Symposium* . . . was the actual every-

---

[77] Spiegel, *Homer*, 548–63.   [78] Zur, *Kehiliyatenu*, 46–7.

day, routine vision' in people's lives.[79] However, the reader of this unusual collection can discern the other layer in which the young revolutionary was symbolized by the Greek youth, who boldly goes out to confront his fate, unflinching in the face of punishment for his hubris, prepared to end his life tragically, but never to flee from his destiny.

Ze'ev Jabotinsky (1880–1940), the Zionist leader, who was also a poet and translator, saw in the 'Homeric man' the archetype of the modern Hebrew man. In one of his literary feuilletons, written in 1904, he describes a group of young Jewish men of letters who meet somewhere at a summer resort (probably on the shores of the Black Sea), and hold a lively discussion on literary matters. They try to compose a list of the ten books which, in their opinion, deserve to be counted with the best in world literature. Each of the participants had selected a list of his own and not everyone there is enthusiastic about Homer, but one fervent champion, defending Homer's right to be added to the 'ten greatest books', makes an eloquent speech praising the 'Homeric man'. No, argue the dissenters, that is not modern man, for the man of the future will be much more complex and many-sided, much richer and wiser than the archaic Greek. The supporters of Homer, however, claim that the utopian man of the future will possess—in fact must possess—the same healthy and perfect natural splendour as the Homeric man. In this feuilleton, a profile of the 'Homeric man' is sketched along the lines of his image in German Romanticism: young, indestructible, naïve, 'natural', robust in body and in spirit, like the 'beasts of the wild'. And that is just what the new Hebrew man will be, when liberated from the fetters of religion that enchain him and distance him from life and from nature. Hebrew youth must be as 'naïve as nature, as the songs of Homer, as the Ten Commandments'. He is the equivalent of the modern man, but modern man would not be perfect without the dimension of the Homeric man.[80]

Jabotinsky may have borrowed this idea from Slavophiles like the fanatic Ivan Kireyevsky or from Konstantin Aksakov (1817–60), who in the mid-nineteenth century described the Homeric ideal as 'simplicity and *naïveté*'. Kireyevsky, in writing about the Russian translation of the *Odyssey* (1845), stated that 'The living expression of the spirit of the Greek people will make it easier to understand our own national character, which survives but weakly in our disappearing folk epics.'[81] The 'Homeric man' has become a utopian human model: the biblical 'ancient Hebrew', who is

---

[79] Ibid. 135, 214; for *gratus risus* see Horace, *Odes*, i. 9. 22 (of a playful girl).

[80] Jabotinsky, 'Aseret hasefarim', 46–7; id., 'Dr Herzl'.

[81] Walicki, *The Slavophile Controversy*, 291.

none other than the twin of the 'Greek man'. The paragon, however, is not wise Socrates, who strove for divine perfection, but rather the beautiful, pure-spirited Greek youth.

THE HEBREW APOLLO AND THE HEBREW PROMETHEUS

Prometheus and Sisyphus, Orpheus and Odysseus, Oedipus and the rest, were all accepted into Hebrew symbolic language. I shall illustrate the process of absorption of mythological figures by examining the way in which Apollo and Prometheus penetrated into Hebrew literature.

In *Kehiliyatenu*, 'the Act of Apollo' is an achievement of contentment with oneself, the yearning for balance and the golden mean. This image of Apollo—who descended in his golden chariot to put an end to depravity on earth—was consistent with the Nietzschean picture of the great god who was given the title of 'god of moderation'. In Tchernichowsky's poem, 'In Front of the Statue of Apollo' (written in Odessa and Heidelberg in 1899), the poet comes to kneel before the statue of the Greek god, clearly reminding his critics of the Hellenizing Jews who brought the 'idol into the Temple' in the time of Antiochus' decrees. But who really is Tchernichowsky's Apollo? It is quite clear that he is not an impulsive, sensual, permissive god, but rather a 'youth-god, sublime and free, the acme of beauty', who rules the sun and the mysteries of life. His statue is the 'symbol of the light of life'. Hence it is surprising that the poet compares him with or places him alongside the ancient Hebrew God of the desert, 'God of gods, of the wonders of the desert, the God of those who stormed Canaan in conquest'.

Now, let me ask, was Tchernichowsky's Apollo intended to be disguised as Dionysus, or perhaps as Ares? Unquestionably, Tchernichowsky was very familiar with the image of Apollo in Greek mythology and in European literature.[82] It seems that he wrote his poem under the influence of Nietzsche's *Birth of Tragedy*, and his Apollo is indeed a symbol of spontaneous 'life' and vitality. But Apollo is primarily the god of light, of restraint, intelligence, and measure, whose commandments called for

---

[82] It is interesting to compare this poem with one in the first book of Heine's *Romanzero*, 'Der Apollogott', where Phoebus Apollo is depicted as Faibisch, a former cantor in the synagogue, who has dismayed his parents by falling into bad ways: 'Haben kein Pläsier am Sohne. | Diese spielt sehr gut die Leier, | Aber leider noch viel besser | Spielt er oft Tarock und L'hombre. || Auch ein Freigeist ist er, aß | Schweinefleisch, verlor sein Amt, | Und er zog herum im Lande | Mit geschminkten Komödianten' (trans. Untermeyer: 'And their son gives them no pleasure. | True, he plays the lyre not badly, | But he plays taroc and omber | And such games of chance much better. || He's become a non-conformer, | Eaten swine and lost his pulpit; | And he troops about the country | With a lot of low comedians').

moderation and discipline, purity of soul, and the meting out of justice. H. J. Rose describes him as 'the most Greek of all gods, in art the ideal type of youth, but not immature youth . . . He is often associated with the higher development of civilization, approving codes of law . . . inculcating high moral and religious principles and favouring philosophy.'[83] In Shelley's poem 'Hymn of Apollo' the god declares

> I am the eye with which the Universe
>   Beholds itself and knows itself divine;
> All harmony of instrument or verse,
>   All prophecy, all medicine is mine,
> All light of art or nature;—to my song
> Victory and praise in its own right belong.

Hence Apollo might have served as a Hellenic antithesis to the God of Judaism, not in the image of a jealous and impassioned god, but more as a human god, bestowing goodness on human beings and giving them not laws but the things most needed for human existence. Now did Tchernichowsky choose Apollo, as some have claimed, because he preferred his depiction in the Homeric hymns as a grim, avenging deity? It seems to me that his Apollo is indeed an eternal youth, but he is the god of tamed nature, not a deity of desert *Sturm und Drang*. The Hebrew poet did not intend to replace the God of the Jews with a Dionysian deity, or the divinity 'tied up with the straps of phylacteries' with a frenzied Dionysian Bacchanalia. Therefore his Apollo reveals Tchernichowsky's own dualism: he possesses a fresh and perfect beauty in contrast to the absence of beauty in Judaism. But this is a restrained beauty of purity of soul, not of vibrant instinctuality. Is not Apollo in his familiar image, as the carrier of justice and morals into the world of men, actually close to the image of the God of Israel?

Berdyczewski had embraced this approach even before Tchernichowsky. A brief article he wrote in reaction to the account of Achilles' revenge in the *Iliad*, which appeared in 1888 in Kaminka's translation, may have inspired Tchernichowsky. Berdyczewski admitted that he had never learnt Greek and therefore was unable to read the epic in the original. Now, having read book xxi in Hebrew translation, he discovered that its subject was a collision of forces: 'A giant son of Japheth raged in the voice of the sons of Israel!' The Homeric epic poem not only extends the narrow band of the Jewish spirit, it also opens up a new channel for an understanding of

---

[83] In the *Oxford Classical Dictionary*, 81–2; see also Muller, 'The Romantic Glory', 139; Hamilton, *The Greek Way*, 214.

biblical poetry. Thus the Book of Numbers is revealed, in the light of the Homeric epic, not as a book dealing only with sacrifices and laws but as one replete with grandeur and sublime poetry. In it is reflected the Hebrew man bringing animal sacrifices. The hand of the poet thus tears down the partition that separates the generations, Berdyczewski wrote. 'We the sons of Shem also pray to Apollo, son of the curly-haired Leto; with all the oppositions of the Prophets that were planted in our hearts we stand only a step away from the entrance of the Tabernacle of the Congregation, which is in the prophecy of the Pentateuch, bringing an offering to the tents of the altar . . .'.[84]

Far more than Apollo, it was Prometheus who underwent a process of 'Judaization'. He was crowned as the typical example of the Greek spirit, the prototype of the modern spirit. His reception into Hebrew culture may have been encouraged by the similarity many tried to find between the story of Prometheus and the midrash in bPes. 54a (cf. Gen. Rabbah 11: 2): 'The Holy One, blessed be He, inspired Adam with knowledge of a kind similar to divine knowledge, and he procured two stones and rubbed them one against each other, and fire issued from them, and he blessed it.' In Louis Ginzberg's view, there is a parallel here between the mythological story of Prometheus bringing light to human beings and the legend that the first mortal was the father of human culture,[85] but we should not be misled by this superficial similarity. It is true that in Genesis Rabbah the first man is the creator of culture, but what he does is not done against the will of the Almighty, whereas in the Greek myth the Titan Prometheus, 'clever above all others' as he is (Hesiod, *Works and Days*, 54), is punished by Zeus for his act. Aeschylus in *Prometheus Bound* endowed him with high moral standing as the helper of human beings against the arbitrariness of the gods and the embodiment of intelligence; he is the inventor, the researcher.[86] Following this tradition, the sophist Protagoras in Plato's dialogue makes

---

[84] Berdyczewski, 'Divrei bikoret', 261.

[85] Ginzberg, *Halakhah and Aggadah*, 255; id., *Legends of the Jews*, v. 112–13 n. 104.

[86] See Havelock, *The Liberal Temper*, 64, and A. Shabtai's introduction to his new translation of *Prometheus* (1994); man thus also acquired agony and pain, and awareness of his limited power. In this play the traditional Greek pessimism (which resembles the pessimism of Genesis) was reversed and man is perceived as 'worth preserving and worth loving' (Havelock, op. cit. 54). On the other hand, Sophocles' *Antigone*, dispenses with Prometheus to provide, as Havelock observes (pp. 66–7), the supreme expression of humanism, crediting mankind with inherent genius: 'The world has marvels exceeding strong | But the miracle thing these marvels among | Is the creature man' (332–4); 'Quick speech and wind-swift thought, | The usage and moods of the town, strong walls that warm in the night, | The builded roof, retreat from driving rain, | These are his self-taught arts | The total resources of man' (353–7). See too Havelock's description of the changes in the perception of the idea of progress, ch. 3, pp. 52–86.

Prometheus steal from Athena and Hephaestus, on men's behalf, the *technai* together with fire, but not political wisdom, which was too well guarded by Zeus (*Protagoras*, 321 C–E). In later authors he creates man from clay—and from parts of other animals, adds Horace (*Odes*, i. 16. 13–16). None of these roles was assigned to Adam in Genesis or the Midrash.

The story of Prometheus took the form of a metaphor in the Hellenistic period and is embedded in two Jewish texts of the Middle Ages.[87] Its presence there indicates that the Jews were familiar with myths other than those embedded in the Talmud, in Midrashim,[88] and in later literature. In writings of both Rabbi Isaac ben Samuel of Acre from the early fourteenth century and Rabbi Abraham Yagel of the sixteenth, Prometheus appears in different modes and diverse adaptations. Obviously there is a great difference between the appearance of mythological motifs in writings of limited circulation and their appearance in the broad cultural discourse. In the latter, Prometheus became a symbol of the spirit of modern man, the being who gave man the tools with which to extricate himself from his primitive state, in keeping with Shelley's description of him as typifying the highest perfection of moral and intellectual nature.

> This, like thy glory, Titan, is to be
> Good, great and joyous, beautiful and free;
> This is alone Life, Joy, Empire, and Victory.
>
> ('Prometheus Unbound', Act IV, ll. 576–8)

For Goethe, Prometheus shaped man in his own image; he is a man who has forced the gods to enter into a covenant with him.[89] For Nietzsche, Prometheus is a Titan of heroic aspirations, attempting to express universality and to become the sole universal entity:

Man, rising to the level of the Titans, acquires his culture by himself, and compels the gods to ally themselves with him, because in his self-sufficient wisdom he

---

[87] Idel, 'Prometheus in Hebrew Garb'.

[88] The Midrash *Agadat Bereshit* tells of the angels Uzza and Azzael, who were shackled with iron chains to the mountains of darkness for teaching humans the magic arts. There is probably also some connection between the legend of the Titans' rebellion against Zeus and the biblical giants (Herr, 'External Influences', 86).

[89] 'Prometheus', ll. 51–8: 'Hier sitz' ich, forme Menschen | Nach meinem Bilde | Ein Geschlecht, das mir gleich sei, | Zu leiden, weinen, | Genießen und zu freuen sich, | Und dein nicht zu achten, | Wie ich.' ('Here I sit, forming mankind | In my own image | A race resembling me— | To sorrow, to weep, | To enjoy, to have pleasure, | And to take no heed of thee, | Even as I': trans. L.A.H.-S.). On the dispute concerning the character of Prometheus between Lessing and Jacobi in the wake of Goethe's poem and centring on interpretation of Spinoza, which led to the anonymous publication *Prometheus und seine Rezensenten* (Frankfurt, 1775), see Goethe, *Dichtung und Wahrheit*, book 15.

holds in his hands their existence and their limitations. The most wonderful thing, however, in the Prometheus fable . . . is the Aeschylean yearning for *justice*.

The myth is 'an original possession of the entire Aryan race, and is documentary evidence of its capacity for the profoundly tragic'.[90] Following in Nietzsche's footsteps, Berdyczewski described Prometheus as the archetype and symbol of the modern man who demands a reply from the gods, and is not prepared to submit to arbitrariness or to the argument that knowledge is beyond his reach.

In *Kehiliyatenu* the young Jewish pioneers are likened to Prometheus who willingly bound himself to the rock (in this case, the rocks of the Galilee) which is his destiny and fate: 'To me, all of our people are like Prometheus, chained to the rock cliff, where an eagle devoured his liver. And where is the redeeming Hercules who will cut our bonds and release us from our suffering?'[91] Here Prometheus' tragedy is regarded as the archetype of Greek culture. Abraham Stern ('Yair', 1907–42), the leader of the Lehi underground in Palestine, was described by his devoted disciples after his death as a heroic Hebrew Prometheus: 'He was not like all men, who live and die. He was Prometheus, who appears once in many generations and brings fire to the human race . . . the fire is always reminiscent of the great maker of fire, of Prometheus who sacrificed himself . . . after two thousand years of exile, Yair rekindled the flame of passion for freedom.'[92] Although the Lehi, in its philosophy, placed great emphasis on the world of Jewish symbols, it found no archetypal character in Hebrew literature more worthy of symbolizing the leader of the Jewish underground organization!

A figure akin to those of Prometheus (and Faust) in Jewish literary tradition is Cain—at least as Byron portrays him in his poem. The Hebrew author, critic, and translator David Frischmann (1859–1922), who translated Byron's *Cain* and also Nietzsche's *Also sprach Zarathustra*, saw in Cain a characteristic Romantic hero, who is stirred by a powerful passion for rebellion, for knowledge, and for life; whose spirit is torn, who is full of doubts about all that concerns good and evil, and who questions the Divine intentions. Such rebellion, in Frischmann's view, cannot end in redemption, but is expressed in an immanent state of tragic pain, reflecting a deterministic-pessimistic view of the world. Unlike Cain, Job is a totally

---

[90] *The Birth of Tragedy*, §9, pp. 66–72. Butcher sees in Prometheus a symbol of supreme moral valour; a combination of tenderness and magnanimity. He demonstrates that 'physical power without wisdom is ephemeral' ('Greece and Israel', 17–29).

[91] Zur, *Kehiliyatenu*, 138.

[92] Heller, *Lehi*, 152.

different type, who forgives God for His deeds and nullifies himself and his doubts before Him.[93]

As Hebrew literature came to integrate all branches of modernism, the use of Greek symbols was supplanted by that of others needed by modern man: a sceptic, a wanderer, a man struggling against his fate, an eternal pilgrim in time and place. Whereas the *maskilim* had seen Socrates as the symbol of a universalist-humanist partnership between Judaism and classical antiquity, now Orpheus, Odysseus, and Prometheus became the symbols of this partnership in the world of modern man. They were symbols representing modernity, very far removed from the world of the Midrashim of the Sages, for whom the stories of the mythologies were nothing but fairy-tales, but far closer to the world of allegorical interpretation of Hellenistic Jewish literature.[94] Although on more than one occasion the mythological heroes were 'Judaized' before being introduced into Hebrew prose and poetry, this 'Judaization' could not blur their Hellenic nature, nor could it disguise the very fact of their use and the world from which they were taken.[95]

As the Hebrew literary corpus grew over the years, the basis of the partnership underwent changes. In the Haskalah movement it had a humanistic and moral base, frequently supported by the philosophy of natural religion and faith in reason shared by the entire human race, which leads it toward a better world. Romanticism, nationalism, and radical socialism replaced the attitude of the *maskilim* with a radically integrative view of society, culture, and mankind that combined modernity and 'naturalness'. The crisis of Romanticism created a picture of man's anguish in the modern era. Now, at the end of this long process, the modern Hebrew reader shares a repertoire of symbols and images with readers of other Western literatures: a mythological repertoire borrowed both from the Bible and from classical mythology. The literary heritage of Japheth dwells in the tents of the new Hebrew, son of Shem.

The modern educated Jew's repertoire of symbols includes stories such as those of Pandora, Tantalus, Sisyphus, Penelope, Orpheus, Ariadne, the Argonauts, and the Trojan War. They do not represent pagan or mythical conceptions, but are stories representing various kinds of human, social, and political situations.

Of course, many Jews in the late eighteenth and nineteenth centuries

[93] Frischmann, introduction to translation of Byron's *Cain*, in *Kol kitvei David Frishman*, 9–45; see too Gilboa, *Between Realism and Romanticism*, 51–71.
[94] Stroumsa, 'Myth into Metaphor'; Raggio, *The Myth of Prometheus*.
[95] Ben-Porat, '"Japheth's" Appearance'; Abramson, 'Hellenism Revisited'.

were indifferent to the presence of classical antiquity in the mind and
heart of Europe. They knew next to nothing about ancient Greece, and
whatever little they knew came from the recollection of Greeks as idolaters.
But for those who involved themselves in European culture, the heritage of
Greece became part of their own culture. They saw nothing wrong with
adopting motifs from classical literature, even mythological motifs, into
Hebrew literature. In doing so, they were expressing the new openness of
Hebrew culture, and to no less a degree they were revealing a subjective
awareness that Hebrew literature and Hebrew culture needed these motifs.
They believed that Greekness possessed vital elements lacking in Judaism.
Hence, it is maintained, modern Jewish culture should be and is permitted
to borrow ingredients of Hellenic culture, to appropriate them, and to
make them an integral part of itself. But this is on condition that it shall
know how to establish proper criteria of culling and choosing before it
begins to borrow, accept, and assimilate these elements. Thus Greece was
perceived as a rich and diversified cultural domain in which one might
find universal human values.

6

THE MORAL DIMENSION: COMMONALITY AND PARTICULARITY

'They that sit in the gate talk of me'. This refers to the nations of the
world who sit in theatres and circuses . . . Another interpretation . . . is
that it alludes to the Israelites who sit in the Synagogues and Houses of
Study . . .   Lamentations Rabbah, Proems XVII

ATTICISM (HELLENISM) AND JUDAISM

KNOWLEDGE, or 'Greek wisdom', could be regarded as 'neutral' or 'universal', but what about morals and morality? Are moral rules also universal, or are different social groups characterized by particular rules of morality? Is there such thing as a unique Jewish ethics, not in the narrow sense of manners, but in the deeper sense, of rules that shape the entire spectrum of man's attitude to the world and to society?

The great interest shown by the *maskilim*, men of letters and thinkers, in the contents and origin of Jewish ethics was, to a great extent, a reaction to the portrayal, in the extensive anti-Jewish literature, of Jews and Judaism as amoral. In contrast to the prevalent description of Jews in this literature as possessing negative moral traits, the *maskilim* of the nineteenth century portrayed them as possessing lofty moral qualities. In contrast to the anti-Jewish literature and its negation of the existence of Jewish ethics and its value, ethics was represented by Jewish writers as the supreme value of Judaism. Their object in stressing the ethical aspect of Judaism and of Jewish life was to present a different portrait of Jews and Judaism from that painted in anti-Jewish literature.[1] However, their interest also stemmed from the fact that ethics—moral qualities and moral behaviour—should be regarded as a singular expression of the national character. The Torah was now appraised according to the ethical rules it lays down, and Jewish history was judged according to the ethical values it represents. The essence of ethics was not only a question of image or self-awareness; it was also a practical question. Since ethical rules determine social behaviour (and the legal system as well), one can only believe in the coexistence of Jews with

---

[1] See e.g. Grégoire, *Essai sur la régénération*, ch. 6. This is, needless to say, only one example out of many; the literature containing negative images of Jews is too broad to be surveyed here.

non-Jewish society, or in the integration of Jews into their non-Jewish environment, if there is some sort of human basis of morality shared by all.

In this chapter I do not propose to conduct an inquiry into the nature of Jewish ethics but to emphasize, first, that it was the ethical (moral) basis of Judaism that was now seen as separating Jews from non-Jews, and, secondly, that the Greek mirror played an important role in shaping the image of Jewish morality. Greek morality (or better non-morality) was perceived as antinomical to Judaism; even when Jewish writers were ready to agree that Greek ethics did exist, they found them fundamentally different from (and inferior to) Jewish ethics.

Greeks and Jews alike distinguished between themselves and other nations on a moral basis. Some Greek writers believed that Greek ethics was what separated the Hellenes from the barbarians, since they had different *nomoi*, which were given expression in a moral code of conduct and virtues; one of the most important in the eyes of the fourth-century philosophers was *sōphrosunē* (restraint), which tempered all the passions and made possible the observance of measure (*mesotēs*) in all actions of society and its laws of justice.[2] The dominant view in Jewish tradition is similar, and also stressed the deep chasm between the moral behaviour of Jews and that of Gentiles. The Sages did not discuss the ethical ideas of Greek philosophy, but judged Hellenistic society as a social and cultural reality and condemned it as amoral; however, while Greek and Roman ethical philosophy deals with humanity at large, Jewish ethical writings are aimed specifically at Jewish society.[3] Pagan writers in turn accused both Jews and Christians of being amoral; Christian writers, on the other hand, described the new Christian people (*ethnos*) as a moral community. The Athenian Christian Aristides, for example, in the time of the emperor Hadrian, included in his defence of his faith 'some extraordinary claims for Christian morality', and the traits upon which he focuses to distinguish between Christians and other nations are both theological and moral— 'beliefs about the divine and human worlds and consequent practices'.[4] The central role of moral behaviour in early Christianity stands against the

---

[2] Hall, *Inventing the Barbarian*, 121; on the *sōphrōn* (and the *dikaios*) see Dover, *Greek Popular Morality*, 46–50. On the development of Greek humanism see Baldry, *The Unity of Mankind* and Hunt, *The Humanism of Cicero*. On the genetic inheritance of moral qualities see Ch. 13.

[3] Jewish ethical literature (*sifrut hamusar*) includes the ethical tractates *Pirkei avot*, *Derekh eretz rabah*, and *Derekh eretz zuta*, and the ethical literature of the Middle Ages and after. On the development of the Jewish doctrine of ethics see J. Dan, *Hebrew Ethical and Homiletical Literature*.

[4] Meeks, *The Origins of Christian Morality*, 8–11, citing *Apol.* 51. 3–7.

Jewish argument we shall meet later in this chapter that morality was not a major component of early Christianity.

From the time of the Haskalah many Jews began to regard ethics as the paramount content of Judaism and to assert that morality stems from a natural sense of justice inherent in Jews. From this view, one could conclude that a commonality of ethics was possible between Jews and non-Jews; but, as we shall see, it was also possible to reach the opposite conclusion— namely, that ethics is the main trait that distinguishes between Jews and non-Jews. However, the fundamental difference between the traditional stance and that of the early *maskilim* was that the latter were searching for a universal philosophical base of morality, and hence attempting to impart a pre-eminent status to those elements in the tradition that stress the existence of a shared human basis. Here they followed the wisdom literature, in which the evildoer, the sinner, the immoral man, is not identified as non-Jewish, but is associated with general, universal concepts. The evildoer and the sinner can themselves be members of Jewish society.[5]

Samuel David Luzzatto (1800–65), frequently referred to by his acronymic abbreviation Shadal, the Italian Jewish scholar, philosopher, and Bible commentator who was one of the central figures of the moderate Haskalah, is important in this context, not only because he was the first Jewish author to turn the antinomy between classical Greece and Greekness into the keystone of his world-view, with Jewish morality and Hellenic amorality in the centre, but also because he was a man of his time, so that his thinking on the nature of ethics encompassed diverse elements from diverse sources.[6] He distinguished between ethical philosophy—a natural moral sense—and a moral sense which has its roots in faith and in *mitzvot*, commandments of transcendental laws. In 1841, a year after Heine published his *Ludwig Börne*, Shadal published his poem 'Derekh eretz o Atikismus: Shirat Shadal le doro' ('The Way of the World or Atticism: Shadal's Poetry for his Time'), in a pamphlet called *Il falso progresso*; in 1879 it was republished in *Kinor na'im* ('The Sweet Lyre [Ps. 81: 3]').[7] His article

---

[5] M. Greenberg, 'Mankind, Israel and the Nations'; Kaufmann, *The Religion of Israel*, ii. 1, 557–646.

[6] See Rosenbloom, *Studies in Torah Judaism*, 17–39, who observes: 'It seems that in Atticism, Luzzatto saw the anti-Judaic forces which were operating in Jewish life in the nineteenth century' (p. 33). In 'Yesodei haTorah', 31, Shadal claims that in contrast to the Greeks, who defined as *barbaroi* anyone who did not attain their cultural level and treated them as beasts, the Jews treated the "other" as human beings, and dissociated themselves from them through their laws and commandments, owing to their disparate beliefs, and not as a result of a superior attitude towards them. When Shadal seeks to define the virtues of the Jew—abstinence from pleasures, the control of passions and urges, and the readiness to suffer sorrow and poverty in pursuit of these virtues—the example he cites is the Greek philosopher Epictetus' teaching *sustine et abstine*, 'bear and forbear' (p. 32).

[7] The poem can be found in *Luzzatto's Selected Writings*, ii. 41–73.

on the same subject, 'Atticisme et judaïsme', was published in Hebrew with a French summary in 1863/4.[8] Although it seems that he never read *Ludwig Börne*, he anticipated Heine in several private letters that reveal this topic to have occupied his thoughts. Luzzatto can be regarded as Heine's counterpart not only because their works were published in such close proximity, but also because his notion of 'Atticism and Judaism' is almost a mirror-image of Heine's 'Hellenen und Nazarener'.

In a letter written in 1839 Shadal presented Hellenism as diametrically opposed to Judaism: 'Our culture[9] derives from two elements: Atticism and Judaism. What is evil comes from the first, what is good in us (and I speak of morals) comes from the second.'[10] In the same spirit, he concluded that the civilization which the nineteenth century was so proud of had a dual soul: 'Sinai' was the source of 'compassion, justice, honesty, and charity between man and his fellow, between one nation and another'; Greece was the source of 'excessive rhetoric, of sterile, theoretical trenchancy, the pursuit of pleasure, the contempt for the simple honest man'. What came from Greece was 'the ignominy of our generation, our corruption, not our glory!' To sum up, Greece was responsible for the negative face of European culture. 'Hebraism', added Shadal in a letter written in July 1839 to the German Jewish historian Isaac Marcus Jost (1793–1860), 'will not cease to exist because it is essential to human society, and when the enlightenment shall increase and spread, then the need of human beings for Hebraism will grow, but Hebraism will not exist if its priests, the men of Judaism, perish.'[11] In another letter, written in May 1840, he adds another thought: 'Human society will not be redeemed through the ways of Greece but rather through the ways of Moses and Abraham, which is the way of the Lord who judges men with righteousness.'[12] He hoped for the redemption of European civilization, since this is the civilization the Jews have to live with,[13] but in contrast to Heine he was not struggling with intense and troubling inner doubts. He devoted much of his scholarship, intellectual energy, and emotions to demonstrating the strength and depth of the spiritual content of Judaism, not only to prove Jewish moral superiority but mainly to fight the trends

[8] S. D. Luzzatto, 'Atticisme et judaïsme'; discussed by Klausner, 'Yehudah veYavan—shenei hafachim?'; id., *History of Modern Hebrew Literature*, ii. 84–96. On Philo's comparison of Greek and Jewish ethics see Sandmel, 'The Confrontation of Greek and Jewish Ethics'.

[9] By 'our culture', he meant not only Jewish culture but also Western culture!

[10] In Klausner, *History of Modern Hebrew Literature*, ii. 95.

[11] *Igrot Shadal*, v. 633. He used the term 'Hebraism' (*ebraismo*) rather than 'Judaism' (*giudaismo*), since in Italian the word for 'Jew' is *ebreo*.

[12] To Leopold Löw in Vienna, 17 May 1740, ibid. 698.

[13] S. D. Luzzatto, *Mahut hayahadut*, 56.

of acculturation and assimilation and to protect traditional values. Nevertheless he was not seeking a total separation between Western culture and Judaism. In a letter dated 21 January 1864, almost the last year of his life, he admitted that 'nothing is absolute'; even though in Judaism one element is prominent and in Hellenism the other, Judaism does not prevent the development of human intelligence and Hellenism does not prevent the development of objective emotions.[14] It is therefore clear that Shadal did not oppose the tendency to throw some bridges of mutual relationship between the world of the Jews and Gentile society, but he was also anxious to keep some walls between the two societies. These walls must be built of morality and ethics. As a result of this need, he established an uncompromising distinction between 'Judaism' and 'Atticism' on the basis of morality.

This is how he portrays the dual nature of Western (Judaeo-Christian) civilization:

Present-day world culture is the product of two different elements: Atticism and Judaism. From Athens the world received philosophy, the arts, the sciences, the development of the intellect, order, the love of beauty and grandeur, and intellectual, calculated ethics. From Judaism, the world received religion, the ethics of the heart, devoid of bias (*désintéressée*), and the love of goodness. Atticism is progressive, for the intellect is capable of continuous development and of constantly making new discoveries. Judaism is a fixed element; its teachings will not change. The heart may be corrupted but not attain perfection. Goodness is innate, evil is acquired. Judaism can cleanse itself of alien appendages that have clung to it; it may return to its primitive state, but it cannot perfect itself. Atticism, being progressive, assumes new shapes all the time and therefore pleases, charms, attracts. Judaism, eternally immutable, looks older and uglier every day, and therefore bores, disgusts, repels. Hence the apparent superiority and triumph of Atticism over Judaism. However, man's nature has an inextinguishable need for goodness. Beauty and grandeur cannot be a substitute for goodness. Society craves emotions, but reason and Atticism do not inspire emotions; they enfeeble or extinguish them. That is why human nature reacts and will always react in favour of the heart, of goodness, of Judaism.[15]

Another formative text of Shadal's in framing the pattern of antinomy is his long poem, 'Derekh eretz o Atikismus'. In it he describes a debate or dialogue between the Torah of Israel and Atticism, that is, Greekness or secularism. Here, too, Western culture has two aspects, or two souls, and its positive aspect has its origins in Sinai. The source of this positive aspect

[14] Klausner, *History of Hebrew Literature*, ii. 95.
[15] 'Atticisme et judaïsme', 131–2, quoted in Artom's introduction to *Luzzatto's Selected Writings*, i. 28–9.

is not in reason but in a good heart, which is the essence of Judaism. The poem opens by listing the great advantages of Atticism:

> Atticism! Atticism,
> Who performed wonders as you did?
> All my life shall I give thanks to you,
> For e'er shall I bless and bow down to you,
> Atticism, I will champion you,
> Then shall I succeed, then shall I prevail!

Atticism is not necessarily identical with Greek philosophy. It is the world of arrogant vanity:

> Atticism, your commandments,
> Your laws,
> If a man fulfils them, he will live by them.
> How pleasant, how dear,
> How pure . . .
> I, Atticism, took you out
> Of the darkness of folly into the light of reason,
> Into the light of civilization.
> You shall have naught supreme but me,
> You shall have no other god before me . . .

Atticism also shames and humiliates Judaism:

> . . . Judaism is an abomination:
> Whatever touches it will never be clean.
> Judaism is a villain, the father of villains.
> Hold honour far from them: the meanness of the soul . . .
> Only darkness, only fear of their endeavours;
> Only darkness, only fear is in their ways,
> Poverty, indolence, flightiness,
> Meanness, cheapness, shamelessness,
> Madness, and folly.

In the third part of the poem, a dispute takes place between the 'Attic' and the Jew. The Jew, whom the Attic describes as a misanthrope, defends himself by listing his merits. Countering the Attic, who claims that the source of the world's good qualities is Greece, the Jew responds:

> Yes, you were right, I too shall not deny it.
> Government of law, dominion of honesty,
> Equality of young and old, that is good, that is felicity,
> It is the blessing of God Almighty from above.
> But these did not come to us from Greece,

They are not from Athens, nor Atticism:
From Sinai they came, they are Judaism,
Equality of master and slave, laws of justice
For strangers, and together, for our foe,
This was lacking in Plato, in Cicero . . .
This we learnt from Sinai, not from Greece:
The root of brotherly love, the Law of Justice from Zion,
From Jerusalem comes civilization.[16]

A philosophical debate then takes place between the Attic and the Jew
on the question of the relationship between 'reason' and 'heart'. The Attic,
of course, admires the merits of intelligence; the Jew, on the other hand,
esteems the merits of the 'heart' that is implanted in mankind and is the
source of morals and ethical conduct. In so doing, he also defines the
nature and substance of the commandments, as

. . . flesh, bone, sinews and skin for the soul,
Tools with which to work upon them.
As the heavens are high above the earth,
The soul will soar and be carried aloft.

Western culture, in that case, is not entirely 'non-Jewish'. It has a Greek
facet that is wholly negative, and it has an ethical facet that is wholly
positive, which originated in Judaism:

Civilization, people of our generation,
Half of it is good, half evil.
From Sinai came kindness, justice, honesty, and charity . . .

The negative attributes

. . . came from Greece.
They are the disgrace of our generation;
They are our defilement, not our glory.

Shadal here delineates the divided spirit of European culture; Jewish culture, in contrast, is whole and undivided.

Shadal often expressed deep despair at the inability (as he saw it) of European culture to redeem itself, because when Europe accepted Christianity
(and through it Jewish elements), it had not succeeded in liberating itself
from its pagan heritage. If this were the case, the crucial question was: could
Judaism be part of an amoral culture such as that bequeathed to Europe

---

[16] The poem appears in *Luzzatto's Selected Writings*, ii. 41–73. In the autumn of 1851, the young poet
M. J. Lebensohn wrote from Berlin to Shadal in Padua that he had read the polemical poem, which
touched his heart because 'he heard from it a Jewish voice' (*Shirei Mikhal*, 246).

by classical antiquity? Was there any hope for the future? Could Jews live in cultural isolation, cut off from modern society, or must they find a new mode of coexistence? Shadal did not disclaim Greece's contribution to humanity, but claimed that 'Greece' engendered cultural decadence, which in European culture was represented, in his view, by Balzac, Charles-Paul de Kock, and Jules Janin! This 'decadent' literature he placed in opposition to ancient books containing the words of Plato and Aristotle, on the one hand, and the Mishnah, the Midrash, and writings of the Geonim, on the other. The mark of the modern decadent world was that it did not care about the books of wisdom and the Torah, but about cheap novels. Plato and Aristotle are mentioned here not as teachers of morals but as men who contributed to wisdom. In order not to forgo the great contributions of Greece to European culture the solution was to split Europe into good and evil. European culture had a positive side (under Jewish influence, of course) and a negative side; hence it was clear that if it was permissible for Judaism to be influenced by Europe, it might be influenced only by its positive side, and must reject its negative, decadent side.

Since Shadal could not deny the existence of Greek (and Roman) ethical philosophy,[17] he distinguished between the philosophical plane and the moral code of social conduct; morality is not the product of philosophical writings but of an inner feeling. He repudiated the value of Greek ethical philosophy for two reasons: first, because it was confined to a small group and did not mould the way of life of Greek society; secondly, because the ethical philosophy itself did not excel in its moral values.

When I began to spend much time reading the books of the wise men of Greece and Rome and others, and saw their words and deeds, I found no philosopher or wise man in the world who demonstrated such signs of integrity and honesty and such desire to do good to others, without seeking personal benefits, as did the sages of the Mishnah and the Talmud. For although moral sensitivity is a human quality, without commandments that set out reward and punishment and fix the fear of God in men's hearts morality cannot exist.[18]

[17] In referring to such philosophical writers as Seneca, Epictetus, and Marcus Aurelius (see Sandbach, *The Stoics*), Shadal ignores the fact that, as we have seen, philosophical ethics are universal and deal with Everyman, whereas the ethical literature of the Sages relates to morals within Jewish society. On Stoic ethics see Sandbach, *The Stoics*, 28–68.

[18] 'And if anyone says he is not among the pupils of the sages of Greece, but rather among those of Kant', Shadal adds, 'this is of little benefit, since study and progress serve only to weaken the moral feelings that exist solely in the books of Israel, not in those of the Gentiles or the Jewish philosophers, whose soul was not a true Jewish soul': *Igrot Shadal*, vii. 1030–1, letter to M. Steinschneider. This view was shared by H. Steinthal, who asserted that 'all the splendor and vigor of ancient Greco-Roman civilization proved incapable of giving Western morality the warmth which radiated from the preaching of life and justice by the Psalmist (33: 5, 101) and the great Jewish prophets . . . In the Greco-Roman

According to Shadal, Greek moral philosophy was only an abstract doctrine and not a real way of life. He went even further and claimed that
Greek philosophy accustomed people to behave only on the basis of reason
and cold logic, and that this destroyed man's sensibilities and his compassion; it made him egotistical, hypocritical, hedonistic. On the other hand,
the Pharisees and the Sages did not view ethics as a conceptual system,
formulated by philosophers, but rather as a normative system developed by
and within society.[19] Like other Jewish writers, Shadal rejected the image
of Judaism as escapist, spartan, lacking any understanding for the ordinary
needs of man, despising corporeality, and so forth; on the contrary, he
maintained, Jews possessed an understanding and sensitivity for the physical needs of the individual and of the ordinary people. His aim was both
to declare the superiority of Jewish ethics and to show that they were
not rigid or harsh but 'human', open and sensitive to man's needs, full of
understanding and compassion.

This became conventional wisdom. Judaism, wrote David Neumark, is
a 'life-outlook', based not on a cosmological system but on internal observation, which attempts to understand good and evil and does not pose any
cosmological questions.[20] On the other hand, the Greek 'world-outlook'
is based on external observations, which attempts to clarify cosmological
laws. Neumark did not mean to say that Judaism had no world-outlook
of its own, namely its own cosmology; rather he argued that it is not the
cosmology that is the keystone of Judaism, but rather its outlook on life;
hence Jewish ethical doctrine is not the result of an intellectual observation of the cosmic order but the consequence of an inner sense and a
recognition of the moral order of the world.

Heine, wrote the rabbi and scholar Simon Berenfeld (1860–1940), erred
in assuming that Judaism is distinguished by a 'hatred of the flesh'. Heine
confused the Pharisees with the Essenes. The Pharisees did not withdraw

table of virtues love is lacking' (quoted from *Allgemeine Ethik* (1885), 108 by Baumgardt, 'The Ethics of
Lazarus and Steinthal', 208).

[19] Kadushin, *Worship and Ethics*, 20. See also id., *Rabbinic Mind* and J. Dan, *Hebrew Ethical and
Homiletical Literature*. See also M. M. Kaplan's introduction to Ramhal's *Mesilat yesharim*, pp. xi–xxxvii:
Jewish ethics points to the system of rewards and punishments according to tradition meted out by God,
and on the whole 'did not feel the need of engaging in philosophical speculations concerning the nature
and source of duty, because the assumption from which it proceeded was that the only authority to which
the human being would voluntarily defer was God'. See also Nieto's view on the 'Rabbis' advantage
over the Philosophers in the Moral Realm': 'despite the fact that both the Rabbis and the philosophers
try to find the distinction between Good and Evil, the Truth sought by the Rabbis is that of Divine
Revelation, which means: absolute certainty' (Petuchowski, *The Theology of Haham David Nieto*, 95).
He follows Philo's distinction between philosophical ethics and revealed ethics, considered at length by
Wolfson, *Philo*, ii. 165–321.

[20] Neumark, 'Hashkafat olam vehashkafat chayim'.

from real life, they did not despise the life of this world and did not encourage asceticism. There is a profound difference between a war against 'temptations of the body' and 'rejection of the body'. The Jews were not haters of nature, nor did they alienate themselves from it or exploit it. Judaism was a vibrant doctrine of life 'which did not allow the material to dominate the spirit, but gave the body its due'. Greek philosophers wished to uproot the negative attributes from their people, but since they were unbelievers they lacked the spirit of education without which it is impossible to purify hearts and instil virtues; the Greeks did create enlightenment and art, but from those sprang a 'dominion of the flesh' with all its concomitant flaws.[21]

Just as Shadal had denied the value of ethical philosophy, arguing that it possessed neither feeling nor positive commandments, he now rejected Jewish ethical philosophy even though it did indeed possess positive commandments. He rejected medieval Jewish philosophy and especially Maimonides' rational ethics, which he believed were an attempt to formulate a doctrine of morality, while in Judaism morality is internalized into the consciousness and 'real life'. His own 'Moral Theology' does not subordinate ethics to any metaphysical end whatsoever, nor is it dependent upon metaphysical concepts. He rejected the ethical-theological tendency cultivated by those Jewish thinkers who came under the influence of Aristotelian thought. He wrote that in subordinating social and ethical goals to the metaphysical, Maimonides was not following the teaching of biblical Judaism and the Sages, but rather the teaching of the philosophy of his time, the dogmatic theology of Arabic Aristotelianism.[22]

However, Shadal himself wrote under the impact of European ethical philosophy. From the eighteenth-century philosophy of Natural Morality,[23] he accepted the notion of 'moral sense' which derives from 'an immediate feeling and finer internal sense'. Thus in his *Lezioni di teologia morale israelitica* (1862), and in many of his articles and letters, he asserted that the moral sense is a general human phenomenon and as a result the Greeks had a natural sense of morality; it is impossible to divest the Greeks

[21] Berenfeld, *Kore hadorot*, i. 9–10. And see also Jellinek's book *Der jüdische Stamm* (Vienna, 1868). According to Shadal, the restrictions decreed by the Sages were not an expression of anti-social tendencies but rather were intended to protect Judaism from the environment which was anti-moral in its character and behaviour ('Ahavat haberiot bayahadut').

[22] S. D. Luzzatto, *Lezioni di teologia dogmatica* = *Selected Writings*, 71.

[23] Shadal states that in 1831 he made a thorough study of ethical philosophy including Cicero, Francis Bacon, Samuel Pufendorf, Leibniz, Hume, Locke, Christian Wolf, and many others, and rejected the moral doctrines of these philosophers (*Lezioni di teologia morale israelitica*, pp. vi–vii); and see Rosenbloom, *Studies in Torah Judaism*, 22–6. On the natural morality of the 18th c. see Willey, *The Eighteenth-Century Background*, 60–77; Hazard, *European Thought*, 160–77.

of this natural sense, which is universal. His explanation of the Hellenes' lack of morality was that a natural sense does not suffice in itself, and that the Greeks had failed to give it expression because they did not take upon themselves the yoke of Torah and commandments. As a result the pagan society of classical antiquity at large lacked morality, and a 'popular morality' never existed among the Greeks. Greek as well as Hellenistic society was in its essence an idolatrous society: a permissive paganism awash in cruel depravity—hedonistic, irrational, Dionysian, daemonic. All the good qualities ascribed to it were nothing but an illusion, a pipe-dream, an ephemeron. Greek divinity is a blind divinity as opposed to the 'living God' of Judaism. The people of the classical world lacked a knowledge and sense of sin and therefore were incapable of providing a moral basis rooted in the faith in one God. The Graeco-Roman cult was fundamentally amoral. The Greek strives to satisfy his inclinations, and does not shrink from any act. Opinions based on reason alone expunge from man's heart the two elements upon which Judaism is founded and which it teaches: compassion for one's fellow man and the belief in the doctrine of reward and punishment. Modern culture is corrupt because it is ruled by 'Atticism'. Shadal did not believe that the pagan world could be moral, owing to the world outlook that governed it. As believers in many gods, pagan society as well as the pagan philosophers could not behave morally. There can be no ethics without a belief in *Torah mishamayim* ('Torah from heaven') and there can be no ethics without compassion. Without preparatory education, he declares, natural ethics cannot be given effect.[24] The unique feature of Judaism is the commandments that set forth the moral obligations as part of human behaviour and the belief that morality originates in divine truth.

Needless to say, these views are a far cry from the modern portrayal of Greek society as a moral society, precisely because it did not have a written, binding system of laws; a far cry from the view that saw in the life of the religion of the ancient Greeks intense seriousness and deep morality and eagerness for justice.[25]

THE MORAL SCALE

Shadal's representation, not fundamentally new, struck roots and acquired the status of a useful and popular model. But while he appreciated various

[24] 'E finalmente la Legge di natura manca di Propedeutica, ossia di un ammaestramento preparativo': S. D. Luzzatto, *Lezioni di teologia morale israelitica*, 7. This training is contained in the revealed law of God (ibid. 8).

[25] Jaeger writes of the 'will to justice which grew up in the communal life of the city-state'; see *Paideia*, ch. 6, 'The City-State and its Ideal of Justice', i. 99–113 at 105.

layers of the classical heritage and of Western culture, others saw only the decadent and dark side, so that what they wrote was a mirror-image of the attacks on the Jewish tradition and Judaism.

Ze'ev Jawitz compiled a scale of 'outlooks and moral attributes', ranging from the 'Law of Moses' on the one hand to the 'teachings of Greece' on the other:

The Torah of Israel	*The Teachings of Greece*
Knowledge of God	Knowledge of nature
Volition	Compulsion
Love	Might
Ethics	Instinct and passion
Righteousness	Forcefulness (Virtus)
Justice	Utilitarianism
The path of maintaining and sustaining oneself and others	The path of conquest and sustaining oneself and wasting others[26]

And Jawitz adds: 'And now anyone who has a brain in his head, feeling in his heart, and taste in his palate will please answer me: Is it worthwhile for us, the children of Israel, to exchange the old book, that is, the Torah of Moses and the words of his pupils, our prophets and rabbis, for some other literature? . . . After all, the Torah of Israel has found what is good and correct in human culture for the last four thousand years, without changing its tune according to every wind that blows, nor is it like someone "dancing to the sound of every pipe" . . .'. Jawitz sketched the pattern of antinomy under the influence of Krochmal and Shadal, but at the outset of his article 'Olamot overim ve'olam omed', he also explains the vitality of the motif of the mirror which urges modern Jews to look at themselves through the mirror of the Greek other:

This overzealousness, as the imagination hastens to compare and adapt, instead of allowing intelligence to discriminate and single out, has existed in the Jewish character and scholarship for about a century. Since that day when many of our *maskilim* began to look only to the outside, they began to fashion all the sights they saw there beyond the boundaries of their nation into a pattern and a programme for all the affairs of Israel . . .[27]

The paradox here lies in the fact that Jawitz used the pattern of antinomy

---

[26] Jawitz, 'Olamot overim', 50. And compare the list of virtues (universal virtues!) in the wisdom literature: Rylaarsdam, *Revelation in Wisdom Literature*, 57.

[27] Jawitz, 'Olamot overim', 43.

even though in his view there is no foundation for attempting to understand Judaism through an analogy to Greekness, for they are two disparate entities. Greek culture is based on a knowledge of nature, and hence it is a culture of instinct, of violence, and of a deep-seated psychological flaw. It does not provide all the needs of the soul but only those of the senses. Hence, in his view, European culture finds itself in a profound spiritual and existential crisis. In contrast, the Torah of Israel is a stable and complete doctrine, which knows its Creator and provides all the needs of the soul. It is a doctrine of the totality of existence. Based on this view, the Torah of Israel grants man happiness and freedom and thus ensures his moral character.

The same view was expressed by the historian Joseph Klausner (1874–1959). In 1890 he wrote that the Jewish people was notable for its simple life, its family purity, its scrupulous morality. Although the Greeks did, in fact, succeed in probing the mysteries of nature, they were inherently an amoral people that depicted its gods as avaricious, cruel, and profligate.[28] The morality of Jewish society is portrayed by him in idyllic colours, in the manner in which many farming communities were pictured in contemporary European literature. It is not surprising that a radical historicist like M. J. Berdyczewski, a 'Dionysian Jew' himself, responded with sharp sarcasm to this scale of moral attributes. In Berdyczewski's caustic words, Jawitz is trying to describe himself as a 'man' or a 'mature human being' and Plato as a 'youth'. However, writes Berdyczewski, if Jawitz describes the Jews as an 'ancient, honourable, and magnificent people, and the Greeks as a band of youths dancing to the music of a reed pipe', then he (Berdyczewski) can only pity him for his narrow-minded naïvety.[29]

A DEBATE BETWEEN OLYMPUS AND SINAI

The pattern of moral antinomy permeated deep into the Jewish collective consciousness, even though for the most part it was the Gentile—the non-Jew as an inclusive type, not necessarily the Greek—who prevailed there. The pattern of antinomy between Judaism and Greekness exists with great intensity because of its deep roots in historical tradition. One short example will suffice. An ultra-Orthodox newspaper published a satirical and didactic ode in honour of Chanukah. Headed 'The Culture of Olympus and the Torah from Sinai', it was actually an adaptation of Shadal's poem. Arrogant Olympus says:

[28] Klausner, 'Milchemet haruach'.
[29] Berdyczewski, 'Tziyunim', 22–3.

> From the heavens I returned and brought down
> Physical culture, a teaching for all,
> I created a new generation:
> Proud and erect and standing tall.

To which the humble 'Sinai', confident of its superiority, then responds:

> My people espouse spiritual wealth,
> Which is eternal, exalted, sublime.
> For what value has material wealth
> Against the vision of Torah for all time?

This polemical dialogue continues through many stanzas. Although 'Olympus' tries to prove that displays of vacuity and cruelty are not the primary and sole expression of his culture, 'Sinai' concludes the discussion by deciding that in order to judge an entire culture, one iota suffices. If that is the case, what is left of 'Olympian culture' but the empty 'culture of leg-kicking' whose 'heart's core is like a football'?[30]

Among ultra-Orthodox circles, this is the pervasive image of Greek culture and of the Western civilization that it symbolizes.

THE UNIVERSALITY OF MORALS

An essay by a German scholar, E. Bussler, 'Hiob und Prometheus', published in 1897, prompted Ahad Ha'am to write a short article under the same title, which was primarily a delayed response to Shadal's 'Atticisme et judaïsme'. In his view, Shadal represented the new nationalistic trends; he did not interpret his words as expressing the traditional Orthodox position, but rather the views of his time, which stressed the uniqueness of the national genius.

Since the time when national awareness also became intensified in our midst, the well-known view, which Shadal in his day often uttered, has been promulgated amongst us—that the Hebrew moral sense is actually something intrinsically distinct, the like of which cannot be found in all the other nations of ancient culture before they came into contact with Judaism. And it was already the subject of people's everyday conversations, that the genius of the Jews is morality

---

[30] *Erev Shabat*, 2 Dec. 1993. The two mountains had already been counterposed by Heinrich Gross in a very different spirit: he concludes: 'We are like the earth, which moves about a double axis. The one axis is the spiritual property that we have inherited from our fathers, to which we hold fast unshakably, the other axis is the general culture of humanity, for which we strive in honourable competition. In this double motion, in this twofold manner, in which we engage as Israelites looking back to the past and as human beings staring into the future, lie the roots of our strength' ('Olymp und Sinai', 620).

and the genius of the Greeks—beauty. This view is indeed true in a certain sense, but not absolutely so.[31]

What evoked this response? Bussler believed that Prometheus was struggling against the tyranny of the gods and was prepared to pay for his revolt and his desire to change the face of the world. Hence he was a great moral figure. Job, on the other hand, was reconciled to his fate and did not demand a change in man's existence; he is the archetype of the passive man who accepts the fate decreed for him. Berdyczewski accepted this interpretation and viewed Prometheus, as we have already seen, as the archetype and symbol of the modern man. If Ahad Ha'am is really speaking in the name of human freedom, then he is a 'Greek' and not a Jew, since it is pantheism, and not monotheism, which expresses the freedom of man. But Ahad Ha'am had something else in mind. He saw in Prometheus a mythological figure representing the moral dimension in the Greek world-view and thus corroborating the claim that the ancient Greeks were a moral people, or at least strove towards morality. Since his basic assumption was that mythological figures are the product of a certain world-view, which they express, he understood the figure of Prometheus as the product of a world-view seeking justice. Ahad Ha'am, then, agreed with Shadal that the essence of Judaism is its moral content, but at the same time expressed his reservations about the notion that the Greeks lacked any sense of morality:

It is very true that the sublime monotheism of the Prophets paved the way for a special development of the moral feeling of the Jews, in which it attained a perfection which the polytheistic Greeks could never achieve. But it is an error to think that there is some discrete difference rooted in the nature of these peoples from their very creation, as though a particular 'moral sense' had been instilled only in the Jews, in which they sensed the existence of the moral world, with all its visions, obligations, and problems, while the Greeks were lacking in that same sense and were incapable of seeing and understanding that world.

In fact, Ahad Ha'am's opinion about the moral reality in the ancient world was no different from that of the Sages or Shadal. His view was that there is no inevitable correspondence between the 'inner spirit' (or ethical philosophy) and the behaviour of society in the sphere of ethical norms. Society, in his view, can behave against its 'inner spirit', but since he found moral tendencies in Greek literature, he could not negate the

[31] Ahad Ha'am, 'Iyov vePrometheus'. In his notes he refers also to Schmidt's *Die Ethik der alten Griechen* (1882). And see Gottschalk, *Ahad Ha'am*, 162–4.

existence of a moral sense among the Greeks. In their literature he found evidence that the Greeks suffered the pain of knowing the deep abyss between the moral ideal and the reality of life. What Prometheus and Job had in common, in his view, was the fact that they were both heroes of folk literature who reflect moral man rebelling against the injustice prevailing in the governance of the world and striving to fathom divine justice and its motives.

From all this, one must inevitably reach the conclusion that from a Jewish point of view the decline of Christianity and the revival of the 'pagan values' of classical antiquity were seen as a dangerous process. And indeed, in the introduction to his drama *Hachashmona'im* ('The Hasmoneans', 1816), I. B. Schlesinger (1773–1836), an observant *maskil* who, among other works, wrote a monograph on Pythagoras, gives one example of this attitude when he writes that it is a mistake to seek a parallel between the new Europe and classical antiquity since the Greeks were 'walkers in darkness' and idolaters, whereas the Christians of his day were 'sages of Torah and ethics' who believed in the Mosaic laws and their ancient divine origin. While Greece totally lacked morality, he wrote, Christian Europe, whose religion derives from the Mosaic laws, is totally different.[32] In other words, from this point of view, the decline of morality results unequivocally from the decline of religion.

Heinrich Graetz viewed Christianity in a different light: its starting-point, he wrote in his Twelfth Letter, was not morality but redemption; in contrast, Judaism was a moral religion, distinguished from all others by its moral basis. Paganism had not discovered the importance of ethics till too late; Christianity had done so only after a long development, and then simply because it was a child of Judaism. His conclusion was that Christianity had 'not remained free from some heathen contamination' and that the amorality of modern European society was a direct and unavoidable consequence of the deep pagan layer embedded in its spirit. Now that the theological layer was weakened and the shackles of religious ethics had become loosened and fallen away, the anti-humanistic, pagan elements of Christian society were surfacing from the depths, in the fullness of their repugnance and cruelty. Thus it seems very clear that Graetz did not pin any hopes on modern liberalism, but saw in it a grave moral danger as a result of the rise of modern paganism.[33]

---

[32] In the late Middle Ages a few 'enlightened' rabbis stated that Christianity also had a praiseworthy level of morality and distinguished between 'nations that accepted the Almighty' and pagans. See J. Katz, *Exclusiveness and Tolerance*, 156–68.

[33] H. Graetz, 'The Significance of Judaism for the Present and Future', 283, cf. 290.

This view of pagan morality and Greek and Roman philosophy was shared by Jews and Christians. The philosophers had been too ineffectual to change the morality of society since they lacked divine authority; the examples set by the gods were more influential than the arguments of philosophers.[34] The pagan gods had never sanctioned a doctrine of right living and never helped men to restrain their desires; in fact they had assisted the process of depravation and corruption. The defenders of the Christian faith in the eighteenth century held to the same old view that ethical philosophy was unable to restrain men's desires and lusts;[35] similarly, in his *Jerusalem* (1783), Mendelssohn declared: 'Nowhere in their mythology, poems, or other records of early times can we find a trace suggesting that the pagans attributed even the smallest amount of love and mercy for humans to any of their deities.'[36]

But was it not incongruous for Jews to lament the decline of 'Christian values', the waning of its bitter enemy? Did not the emergence of the new humanism and universal liberalism provide a better ground for understanding, free from the long years of religious hatred and prejudice? Indeed, Moses Mendelssohn searched for common ground not with Christianity, but with the humanism of his time. His ideas were close to the European ideal of humanism, that is, to the ideal originating in Roman philosophy that posits the unity of all creatures. This ideal, as is well known, was revived during the Renaissance and became the humanistic ideal of the eighteenth century (in fact, from a historical point of view, it was not a 'Greek ideal' in origin, but rather a 'Hellenistic-Roman ideal'). Therefore, Mendelssohn tried to find a correspondence between the value concepts in the tradition of the Sages on the one hand, and the humanistic ideal (the Hellenistic-Roman ideal), on the other.[37] As a result, he had to recognize the existence of immanent hu-

---

[34] St Augustine, *The City of God*, ii. 6–7. On the other hand the Emperor Julian wrote in his *Letter to a Priest* that 'philosophy alone will be appropriate for us priests; and of philosophers only those who chose the gods as guides of their mental discipline, like Pythagoras and Plato and Aristotle, and the school of Chrysippus and Zeno. For we ought [to heed only] those philosophers and those of their doctrines that make man god-fearing . . .' (300 D–301 A, trans. Wright, ii. 325–7).

[35] Gay, *The Science of Freedom*, 195.

[36] Mendelssohn, *Jerusalem*, 92–3.

[37] Heinemann, 'The Unity in Mendelssohn's Philosophy', 216: 'This concept [*humanitas*], which has its roots in Roman philosophy, encompasses two ideals: that of humanity (faith in the oneness of all beings) and that of humaneness: an appreciation of the intellectual, ethical and aesthetic endowments which separate man from other creatures. And the two are interconnected; the oneness of humanity is based on the human estate, shared by all beings. This dual ideal was abandoned in the Middle Ages, first because Aristotle's teachings contained only its beginnings; second, because Christianity and Islam placed their faith, not in our natural faculties, but much more in the Divine

man ethics that originates in the essence of the human being and is based on human reason. From this point, it was easy to reach the assumption that there is such a thing as 'pagan ethics' or 'humanistic Hellenism' and that this pagan morality and Jewish morality have common foundations.

The *maskilim* had to make a choice: they could believe it was possible to find a basis common to Jewish ethics and the contemporary Christian ethical movement, or they could believe that it was more fitting to find this common basis not with Christianity but with humanism, with its classical origins separating ethics from religion. Most of the *maskilim* were far from this radical view. They tried instead to reach an accord between the talmudic moral precepts and the moral outlook of the eighteenth century, and sometimes between all three components: Christian, Jewish, and humanistic ethics. And indeed, during the eighteenth and the early nineteenth century, German pietistic moralism and *Philanthropismus* viewed the Bible as a guide to moral conduct. Religious textbooks (*Religionsunterricht*) became very popular, and many adaptations of biblical stories with a moral content appeared. The collection of *Zweymal zwey und funfzig auserlesene Biblische Historien aus dem Alten und Neuen Testamente, der Jugend zum Besten abgefasset* (1714), by Johann Hübner, is an outstanding example of a work that had a great influence on Haskalah circles. Books on ethics (*Moralische Geschichten, Moralische Elementarbücher, Methodischer Catechismus*),[38] such as Johann Georg Sulzer's *Versuch einiger moralischer Betrachtungen über der Werke der Nature* (1741), Johann Bernhard Basedow's *Methodischer Unterricht der Jugend in der Religion und Sittlenlehre*, 2 vols. (1764) and *Vorbereitung der Juden zur Moralität und natürlichen Religion* (1766), Joachim Heinrich Campe's *Kleine Seelenlehre für Kinder* (1780), and many others of the same kind,[39] had a formative influence on the Jewish Enlightenment and its approach to education and morality.[40] About a hundred Jewish catechisms were published in the course of the nineteenth century in Germany alone.[41] In almost all of them faith was perceived as the origin and source of morality, and only a few radical *maskilim* were prepared to sever morals from faith. It was imperative for them to combine the faith of their forefathers

Revelation.' The definition of *humanitas* is taken from *Real-Encyklopädie der classichen Altertumswissenschaft*, vA. 282 ff.

[38] *Lexikon der Kinder- und Jugendliteratur*, ii. 493–5.
[39] Brüggemann and Ewers, *Handbuch zur Kinder- und Jugendliteratur*, 480–679.
[40] Eliav, *Jewish Education*, 257–70; Michael A. Meyer, *Response to Modernity*, 39–42.
[41] Rappel, 'Jewish Education'.

with the new faith in wisdom (reason) and in a natural sense of morality.

> So long as you have not bought knowledge and wisdom,
> You cannot hope to buy morals and justice.
> For without knowledge there can be no morals;
> Good and evil are entangled in a bush of thorns.[42]

The new seed of humanism and natural philosophy penetrated even the works of the moderate *maskilim*. In his book for young readers, J. L. Ben-Ze'ev, without any hesitation whatsoever, equated ethical maxims from the Talmud with ethical maxims from Greek philosophy. He thus antedated by a century the school of thought that found a parallel between the ethical world of the Jewish Sages and the spiritual, literary world of the Greeks.[43] In this way, he was following a medieval tradition. For example, *Muserei hafilosofim* ('Ethics of the Philosophers'), translated from the Arabic into Hebrew by Rabbi Judah ben al-Harizi, presented aphorisms of Socrates, Diogenes, Pythagoras, and others.[44] Ben-Ze'ev expressed reservations only about Epicurus, about whom he wrote 'his qualities and deeds are very desirable but his views and his teachings are very bad indeed; hence we will take of his good and ban the bad, for he despised our eternal Torah . . .'. Solon, he wrote, was a moral man who claimed that the middle road is the right one in all circumstances, whereas Socrates was an exemplary man because he not only taught the virtues of ethics and justice, but also led his own life in accordance with them; this refuted the claim that the everyday life of Greece was one of total licentiousness and moral corruption.

Such comments signified a trend to create a common universal human basis for both bourgeois and mass culture. The *maskilim* of the early nineteenth century found in Socrates and Aeschylus, in Seneca and Marcus Aurelius, and in others, incontrovertible evidence of a moral sense and moral precepts in Greek culture. They adduced this evidence not only in ethical philosophy, but also in drama and lyric poetry—in all expressions of popular sentiments and in the moral reflections on life of the Greek common people.[45] Clearly, it was the tactic of correspondence that

---

[42] Ben-Ze'ev, *Beit hasefer*, ii: *Limudei hameisharim*, 185.

[43] Ibid. 220–60.

[44] The original work, *Nawādir al-falāsifa*, was written in 873 by the Christian translator Ḥunayn ibn 'Ishāq, who lived in Baghdad; the Hebrew translation, *Muserei hafilosofim*, was edited by A. Löwenthal (Frankfurt am Main, 1896). On the Muslim use of 'Wise Sayings' during the Middle Ages see Rosenthal, *The Classical Heritage*, 118–44. Plutarch was translated into German by J. F. S. Kaltwasser in 1779 (Plutarch, *Moralische philosophische Werke*).

[45] Dover, *Greek Popular Morality*; Nilsson, *Greek Piety*.

was at work here, namely the tactic of establishing a similarity between
the ethical values of the moderate German Jewish Haskalah and German
bourgeois society on the one hand, and the traditional Jewish ethical values on the other. The trend of calling attention to points of similarity
between Jewish and Greek ethics underwent a process of radicalization,
and there were those who tried to find an absolute identity between the
two.

The popular religion (*Volksreligion*)—wrote Aaron Kaminka, a leading
spokesman of this approach—was not a religion of immorality and riotous degeneration. Like Ben-Ze'ev, although long after him, Kaminka
drew an analogy between the outlook on ethics and society of the Roman philosopher-emperor Marcus Aurelius and the beliefs of Rabbi Judah
Hanasi. Kaminka even argued the existence of a certain reciprocal influence between the Mishnah and the Stoa.[46] Accordingly, Marcus Aurelius
merited esteem, as Kaminka declared in a poem first published in 1919 and
then appended to his translation, *The Ideas of Marcus Aurelius Antoninus*
(1922):

> And I say, I will raise up your memory from the ashes,
> And to the treasure of Jeshurun's language your words will be added!
> For what shall be written in Hebrew in a book,
> Will never be effaced or forgotten and will never cease to be.

In other words, as far as Kaminka was concerned, there was no such
thing as a separate Jewish ethics; there is only human ethics or divine
ethics that share the same basis. Once again we come across the view
that the chasm between Judaism and Hellenism originated not in their
dissimilar and uncompromising substances but rather in ignorance and
preconceptions on both sides. The Jews had not succeeded in fostering
among the Greeks a correct opinion of their morality, but in addition, 'no
man ever tried to give the Sages of Israel a true conception in Hebrew
of Greek ethical principles'. What was initiated by a small number of
early *maskilim* became the mission of the modern *maskil* who was not
prepared to reject out of hand the classics, and in fact, Western culture
as a whole. Kaminka and those who thought as he did represented the
pole of optimism. From this it was almost natural to reach the radical
historical conclusion that 'One cannot speak about talmudic Jewish ethics,
since these ethics, in essence, are nothing other than the morals of the

---

[46] See his afterword 'Ethics in Seneca and Jewish Ethics' to his Hebrew translation of Seneca, *Kitvei
Seneca*, 359–69 and also his introduction to his translation of Marcus Aurelius' *Meditations* (*Raiyonot
Marcus Aurelius*). On the Stoic philosophy see Rist, *Stoic Philosophy*.

Hellenistic world (and the sages of Greece and Rome debated questions of morals much more than we think and assume).'[47] The response to the notion that morality and moral precepts based on monotheistic faith, i.e. on transcendental metaphysics and on an absolutist concept, which impose transcendental sanctions (of reward and punishment), are loftier and more powerful than a concept of ethics based on a 'natural sense', or on a systematic theoretical philosophy of a subjectivist nature, was that it is not necessarily the halakhah as a code that had made the Jews a moral nation, but rather the doctrine of rewards and their faith. It is also well known that norms of conduct in Greece were established not by myth nor by philosophical education, but by written laws of the state and by *ethē*, customs handed down by ancestors, which are like an 'unwritten legal code' (*agraphoi nomoi*) or an internalized social code—and not like the Jewish Oral Law, which expounds the pre-existing written law.

The eminent Israeli historian Yitzhak (Fritz) Baer (1888–1980), motivated by his organic approach to the social and cultural history of the Jewish people, drew a startling comparison between Jewish society and the Greek *polis*:

As historians and humanists, we acknowledge the greatness of classical Greek culture, the greatness of its original religion despite the abominations that adhere to it, the greatness of its sages and its poets. Athens' great tragedians had a profound grasp of the problems of mankind, but they themselves sang their songs while struggling against the fear of pagan tradition.

What is more astonishing is that he compares Jewish society at the time of the Mishnah with the fifth-century Greek *polis*: in each case one can find a natural and pre-rationalistic society, governed by laws and civic ethics which stem from the real experience of life and not from rationalistic or theoretical considerations. In other words, Jewish society and the *polis* were two organic societies, where 'law' and 'life' constituted a living whole. However, even he, a 'humanist historian', could not depart from the traditional and conventional view that this organic society of the *polis* was deficient and could not survive for a long period because it lacked transcendental faith.[48]

---

[47] Hallewy, *The Values of the Aggadah and the Halakhah*, iv. 14–17. The Jewish Oral Law, it should be remembered, in fact constitutes written rules to which the Sages imparted a status of sanctity. See E. E. Urbach, *The Sages*, i. 268–314.

[48] Baer, 'Problems of Religion in the Hasmonean Period', 49–52, 62–4 (= 56–9, 59–71); 'The Historical Foundations of the Halakhah', 307–8. Momigliano writes that in Greece thought about religion caused people to be less religious, whereas in Judah it made them more religious ('Religion in Athens, Rome, and Jerusalem').

PROGRESS AND MORALITY: THE
APPEARANCE AND GROWTH OF DESPAIR

In the 1860s Kalman Schulman described the decline of Christian faith
and the rise of corruption in Western society in the following words:

And here it is, the new Enlightenment which with one hand has thrown down
the wall of fanaticism and its morals of vanity, and with the other has smitten the
foundations of the Christian religion, destroying them and turning the Christians
away from them. They also despised its virtues and moral instructions, for they
followed the teachings of Plato and Aristotle, and trod underfoot every religion
and faith. Even the chief priests (the cardinals and the prelates) cast aside their
religion for the sake of this enlightenment, for they also clung to the wisdom
of Greece and the wisdom of all ancient sages, and were struck with wonder
at the loftiness of their understanding and the depth of their thought, and they
learnt their tongue so they could speak just as they did and think their thoughts,
until they should become as one with them in speech and in heart, and trample
with contempt on all religious studies and on belief as well as moral lessons
about proper conduct between man and his fellow . . . From that time, religion
remained only in the hands of the simple folk and the superstitious masses,
and when these ignorant people began to believe even more devoutly in empty
vanities and in elusive chimeras, the *maskilim* drew further away from faith, denied
everything, and despised all Torah, all religion and any belief. In the end, those
maskilim who destroyed the basis of fanaticism and forsook its vain morals and
great wickedness, also annihilated the institutions of their religion which their
forefathers had bequeathed to them, along with every virtue and every just and
honest act of proper conduct. Avarice and a covetousness for honour became the
watchword for all their deeds, and to gold they said, 'You are my god'; and to
pleasures of the flesh they said, 'You are the life of our spirit and the purpose of
our lives.'

However, Schulman could not unqualifiedly censure and condemn enlightenment and progress. He therefore drew a distinction between the
Haskalah proper and the *maskilim* who adhered to it only in order to find
justification for abandoning religion. This was for him and his generation a convenient and necessary distinction between the principles of the
Haskalah and the destructive effect that, in its superficial mode, it had on
a large segment of the public. To a distant observer, living in Vilna, it was
Germany that demonstrated that the Haskalah could make an impact on a
broad sector of a people's culture and not only affect the élite few. For after
all, even the most modern of the *maskilim* could not remain indifferent to

the 'youthful vigour and light' that the Haskalah brought to the world or ignore its wonderful social-cultural creations.[49]

'Light will shine forth from now onwards not from Babylonia, but from Germany—from our homeland, whose people share the qualities of patience and energy, reason and *naïveté* in a wondrous blend. And in step with the legal freedom and the true refinement of forms of culture, the emancipation of Jews, both civil and spiritual, strides forward unswervingly.' With these optimistic words of prophecy, which read now like a bitter mockery, Leopold Zunz, the leader of the Jewish Reform movement, ended his great work, *Die gottesdienstlichen Vorträge der Juden* (1892).[50] This was an optimistic outlook, based on the notion of the universality of morals and on progress. From this vantage-point classical antiquity could be seen both as the origin and the mirror of modern Europe.

In the course of the nineteenth century, this mirror underwent a major change of focus. More and more, during the second half of that century, contemporary Europe was perceived as a likeness of the morally corrupt pagan-Hellenic world and not as the realization of a moral philosophy or a popular sense of morality. Humanism was fading and romanticism and nationalism were taking its place. In view of this process, the author of a series of articles in the Hebrew newspaper *Hamagid* in 1857 stressed the barbarism and lack of a moral sense among the ancients, since they were not 'savage and ignorant' peoples.[51] After all, he wrote, the archaeological excavations in Mesopotamia, which uncovered remnants of a splendid culture, also show that the achievements of material culture did not suppress people's inclinations to believe in superstitions. The same holds true in regard to all of Greek culture. In order to uproot error 'from the hearts of the Hellenists who only sought teachings from Greece and Rome', the writer asserts that those nations who were outstanding 'in every wisdom and science . . . became stupid and erred, in dreadful disgrace and eternal shame'. He cites various instances of Greek barbarity: human sacrifices, cruelty for its own sake, and others. At the same time as 'they reached the peak of intellectual qualities', they continued to offer human sacrifices, and to amuse themselves by watching gladiators and athletes. And even the wise Seneca, the writer continues, was attracted like a brute by the *Zeitgeist*, that is, by the cruel customs of Rome, and saw nothing wrong with the cruel and inhumane laws enforced in Imperial Rome. All this, of course, was diametrically opposed to the spirit and character of the

---

[49] Schulman, *Divrei yemei olam*, iv. 19–20.
[50] Zunz, *Die gottesdienstlichen Vorträge*. I used the Hebrew translation, *Haderashot be Yisrael*, 220–1.
[51] *Hamagid*, 10 Sept. 1857.

Jewish people, which was 'like a wanderer in the heart of the turbulent sea and like an upright pillar of moral purity (*die sittliche Reinheit*); a pure and holy paragon for all who look upon it . . .'. Between 'ethics' (morality) and 'culture' (civilization) there is neither congruence nor identity. Thus it was again Greek culture which served as an example and as irrefutable evidence that even a glorious culture does not guarantee virtues, a sense of justice and morals. The author's aim in this article was to claim that the progress of civilization does not necessarily concur with the state of morality, nor do Western culture and progress guarantee moral perfection.

Heinrich Graetz expressed himself in a similar vein in 'The Correspondence of an English Lady on Judaism and Semitism' (1886), where he describes European culture as plummeting to the depths of moral and cultural degeneration. As conclusive evidence, he cites statistics on the number of people in Europe with syphilis and the alarming rise in the number of bastards in Germany born out of illicit love-affairs. Europe is a 'hospital for the incurable', a ghastly monster, dangerously ill. Antiquity—writes Graetz—'was little more than a public brothel, and modern civilization has merely transformed it into private houses', that is, made licentiousness available to all. The cult of Aphrodite still attracted enthusiastic adherents, against whom the powers of morality moved in vain, and 'now, in addition, [there are] the filthy novels à la Zola!' Hence, in matters of faith and morals, the forward march of time is not important at all. What is important is the power of faith. Only one who supposes 'that from decay will come regeneration'[52] can believe in the revival of Europe.

Graetz wavered between rationalism and Romanticism, between a belief in emancipation and a longing for the 'regeneration of the race'. 'Can you de-Europeanize us?' wonders Graetz's fictional English lady friend, his 'other voice', for at the turn of the century, Europeanism filled the enlightened Jew's entire field of vision.[53] But what was this Europe? The positivists and the materialists emptied the heavens of their gods. People like Heine regretted the decline of high-spirited paganism in the tranquillity of Olympus. In its place came a nervous ecclesiasticism, which deterred human beings from sipping from the effervescent cup of life, replacing it with its *memento mori*. But this venerated Greek (and Roman) culture was neither concerned nor associated with ethics, and in the words of the liberal Catholic J. J. I. Döllinger: 'The gratification of sexual lust was one of the cornerstones of the religious rite.' Greekness is a culture of licentiousness and depravity. Jewish monotheism, to Graetz,

[52] See H. Graetz, 'Correspondence', 169–99.   [53] Ibid. 213.

and not to him alone, was founded first and foremost on ethics. Moral corruption and licentiousness were identified with polytheism and hence could be interpreted as a negation of secularism and atheism. The exalted ethical precepts, especially chastity (meaning the repressive sexual ethic), incorporated in the Commandments are, in Graetz's view, the essential principles of Judaism as well as its universal message.[54] In contrast to those who discerned a yearning for moral perfection in Greek popular religion, Graetz saw in it a manifestation of the moral decay and corruption in Hellenic culture. The Greek *Volksreligion* is indeed the true 'embodiment of the Greek spirit'. Plato and Aristotle, Sophocles and Euripides craved moral perfection, as did Goethe and Schiller. But this aspiration was, and always remained, the province of a narrow élite. The *Volksgeist* ('spirit of the people') on the other hand, was permeated by moral corruption and depravity. Hence one must differentiate between abstract ethical norms on the one hand, and moral values as they are realized in society on the other. Consequently, Hellenism and 'Europeanism' are doomed to unmitigated condemnation.

Smolenskin shared the same view; even Greek philosophy did not redeem the Greeks from spiritual inferiority. They were ruled by flesh-and-blood gods who dwelt on Mount Olympus, and not by a wise, mighty, and just king. Polytheism implies relativistic ethics, which opens wide the door to nihilism, cruelty, and destruction. Simon Dubnow held that on the philosophical plane the Greek spirit approximated the spirit of Israel. But philosophical thought was the domain of the élite alone; in Israel, on the other hand, the Torah and its ethics belonged to the entire nation.[55] From a socialist point of view, Nachman Syrkin (1878–1918) claimed that the Greeks conceived of the world as a 'garden of art and play', while the Hebrews saw it as a 'holy place where the universal idea must triumph'. This universal idea is, of course, the commitment to social justice and co-operation.[56] Jewish socialist thinkers stressed that the Prophets are the primary source of the yearning for social justice and that the Bible and the Talmud are the source of the most progressive social ideas and laws.

In the second half of the nineteenth century this pessimistic mood led to revolutionary messianism and to nationalism. Emphatic voices of disillusionment—with the Europe that emerged after the 1848 revolutions, with the domination by barbarism, with secularism and materialism—resounded with ever greater frequency. The more recently the spokesman

---

[54] Ibid. 230–83.
[55] Dubnow, *The World History of the Jewish People*, ii. 4–5.
[56] Frankel, *Prophecy and Politics*, 305.

had joined the ranks of the devotees of progress, the greater were his disappointment and bitterness, and hence also the intensity of his radicalism.
Expressions of disillusionment with the Haskalah and with progress re-
curred constantly in writings from the mid-nineteenth century and grew
stronger towards the end of the century. The utopia turned out to be a
mere will-of-the-wisp. After statements like 'We were intoxicated with
great joy' and 'In our eyes the land became a paradise and its inhabitants
supermen', now came the sober awakening:

We were grievously mistaken in regard to the very nature of man's enlightenment!
Enlightenment does not improve the character and temperament of man, but only
develops his talents and endows him with the ability to become better or worse
with greater zeal and ambition, and whenever hate and jealousy have found a nest
in man's heart, his enlightenment will turn into snake-venom and will only act
to increase the numbers of those he despises and persecutes, for he will use it as
an instrument of evil to corrupt and to increase crime through wicked scheming
and cunning wile.[57]

Ashkenaz (Germany), which Schulman then viewed as the land in which
the values of the Haskalah would be realized, is described in the Hebrew
newspaper *Hamelitz* in an article in 1896 entitled 'Hahaskalah shel hame'ah
ha-19 vetikvat Yisrael' ('Nineteenth-century Haskalah and the Hope of
Israel') as the nadir of degradation: 'And this bitter and rash fate [modern
antisemitism], now at the end of the nineteenth century, is widespread
throughout the land of wisdom and science, which leads in the enlightenment of the time, the land of Ashkenaz!' There is thus no inevitable connection between intellectual understanding and moral perfection; rather,
these two are light-years apart.

In the very same year—1896—the Russian radical positivist *maskil*,
Judah Leib Levin (1844–1925), who called for social changes in Jewish
society, came to a similar grave conclusion. He wrote that science did not
perfect human society, but rather endowed the wicked with new forces.
'Brute force that suppresses the weak is in a state of decline, but the craving
to subdue the weak has not been expunged by wisdom and the sciences.'
Levin expressed disillusionment with nineteenth-century progress in his
poem 'She'elot hazeman' ('Questions of our Time'):

> The living, enlightened, edified time,
> The nineteenth century praised and sublime,
> Is thrilled and amazed by every crime.

[57] *Hamelitz*, 7 Mar. 1896.

This was not a century of education and morals but rather a time when pagan barbarism was re-emerging: ' . . . A time of force, the oppressing fist raised | the nineteenth century much lauded and praised.'[58] In 1883 he bitterly criticizes the opinion of the English historian Henry Thomas Buckle (1821–62) that Progress is determined not by moral faculties but by the intellect; this theory, maintained by Mill, Comte, and others, had greatly influenced the Russian Jewish intelligentsia through its popularization by Buckle, whom Smolenskin awarded the title 'the prince of the wise men'. Levin claimed that a distinction should be drawn between the progress of civilization and the degeneration of morality. The fact is that the negative aspect of European culture was encouraged by scientific and technological inventions and innovations, since instead of serving the cause of morality, they served as new and powerful tools for injustice, oppression, and brutality. 'Would a knowledge of astronomy, chemistry, and physics prevent someone from stealing from my pocket or my plate?' Science and technology placed new and ever more powerful tools at the disposal of evil.[59] 'The nineteenth century, which began with a wave of glowing youthful hopes, came to a close worn and enfeebled, in the aesthetic and ethical condition described by the term *fin de siècle*': with these words Simon Dubnow summed up the close of the century. 'One of the powerful antitheses of Jewish history created by this turbulent century is now gradually drawing to its close.'[60] When these pessimistic words were written in December 1901, obviously neither Dubnow nor his contemporaries could have known what the future held. But later, even after 1945, the ambivalent attitude towards Europe remained as it was prior to 1939 and prior to 1914.

I shall give one example of an intellectual biography that can serve as an illustration of the Jewish ambivalence towards the West as embodied by Greece: that of Joseph Klausner. At the close of the nineteenth century, Klausner adopted Shadal's teachings, both in letter and in spirit. Judaism and Greekness, he wrote in 1896, are two opposing forces operating in history. And whenever they meet, they struggle fiercely against one another, since an irreconcilable opposition inheres in them. Many years later, far removed from the pessimism and extremism of the *fin de siècle*, Klausner retreated from this first stance and adopted Ahad Ha'am's view. He reached the conclusion that anyone familiar with the writings of

---

[58] Y. L. Levin, 'She'elot hazeman'.

[59] Y. Shavit, 'The "Glorious" Century', 206, 209. On Buckle and his influence on the Jewish intelligentsia see Y. Shavit, 'The Works of H. T. Buckle'.

[60] Dubnow, 'Autonomy—The Basis of the National Plan', 131.

Socrates, Plato, Aristotle, or the Stoic philosophy in all its ramifications, with Posidonius, Epictetus, and Seneca, the works of Aeschylus, Euripides, and Sophocles, would acknowledge the loftiness of Hellenic morals and the marvellous pagan humanism, which in its own way had also created the concept of mankind. Hence, they err who see in Greekness naught but unrestrained mythology; did not the humanist philosophers themselves deride the mythological tales, viewing them as mere fantasy and diversion?[61] Klausner put forth this approach in 1937, that is, in the fourth year of the Nazi regime in Germany; a year in which a bitter civil war was raging in Spain, in which purges were being carried out in Moscow; a year of bloody 'incidents' in Palestine, and more signs of the time. It is more than somewhat odd that it was at this time that he reached the peak of humanistic optimism.

Klausner also learnt about the existence of pagan humanism from scholarly literature, in particular from a Russian version of the book written by the renowned Polish classical philologist Tadeusz Zieliński (1859–1944) *Hellenizm a Judaizm* ('Hellenism and Judaism', 1927) and perhaps also from Dimitri Merezhkovsky's novel, *Smert' bogov: Julian Otstupnik* ('The Death of the Gods: Julian the Apostate', 1896).[62] Zieliński was regarded as an out-and-out antisemite by his Jewish antagonists in Poland, who attempted to refute his harsh reproaches against Judaism, whereas in Klausner's view he was an exemplar of a distinguished humanist. What many viewed as a dangerous and terrifying rise of nihilistic mythic paganism, Klausner regarded as a manifestation of pagan humanism.

Was this a deep-seated naïvety, a naïvety for which Klausner had been taken to task on more than one occasion, or was it appalling blindness in the face of danger? Or, perhaps, the pathetic attempt of a Jewish scholar, whose utopia envisioned a marriage between Judaism and mankind, to hang on to the coat-tails of a European humanism that was fast disappearing from the scene? It was hard for a Jewish man of letters, who grew up on European culture, to reach the conclusion that beneath the veneer of European humanism there lurked a monster, and hence that the alleged Jewish moral heritage had no impact at all on the fundamentally amoral pagan nature of Western culture.[63] The poem 'Yerushalayim shel matah' ('The Earthly Jerusalem', 1925), written by Uri Zevi Greenberg (1894–1981)—perhaps the greatest Hebrew poet after Judah Halevi—a year after he emigrated

[61] Klausner, 'The War of the Spirit'.

[62] Published in English as *Julian the Apostate*, trans. Charles Johnston (1899); other translations appeared in 1901 (as *The Death of the Gods*) 1929. See Rosenthal, 'Stages of Nietzscheanism'.

[63] Yevin, 'Legion hazarim'.

to Palestine, is a powerful and illuminating example of this ambivalent attitude towards Europe:

> We ought to go
> The lands cried under our feet . . .
> We ought to hate what we loved so dearly,
> We have loved the wood, the stream, the well, the mill,
> We have loved the falling leaves, the fishes, the bucket, and the bread, and in deep secrecy we have loved their bell-ringing.
> We have loved the harmonica, flute, and Ukrainian folk-songs, the village girls in their dancing ribbons . . .
> We have loved deeply the smoky hours in the coffee shops,
> And operas, parks, a perfumed head, and dancing-places. Opium. Ballet, boulevards, and brothels, And electricity, museums of antiquities, and city libraries.[64]

Despite his Europhobia this is a desperate and painful love-cry to both the bright and the dark sides of Europe.

A circle was closed: the radical *maskil* started down the path of faith in a common universal morality and the belief that Jewish existence ought to be reformed according to general principles of ethics. His world picture was optimistic and confident in the progress that would result from reforms and would manifest itself in tolerance. The radical *maskil* who became a nationalist cast aside this naïve faith with bitter disappointment.

Having endured disillusionment and suffering, the *maskilim* returned to the tradition that viewed the cultural isolation of the Jews as a necessity and their moral superiority as an indisputable fact. Many of them considered the moral side of Judaism its purest, most sublime expression. For the early *maskilim* and for liberal Jews, common morality was perceived as the underpinning of the coexistence between Jews and Gentiles. But the stress on the centrality of morals and ethics in Judaism was also an effort to create a barrier between Jewish society and Gentile society. In view of the decline of religion and the process of acculturation which had blurred many of the deep-rooted differences between the Jews and the surrounding society, a new fundamental element was urgently needed to distinguish between them; this element was the element of morality. Their gazing into the Greek mirror, which began with the search for a common human denominator, ended with the reinforcement of the old notion of Jewish moral superiority. Morality became a central element of the Jewish essence separating and distinguishing Jews from Gentiles in the

---

[64] My translation of 'Yerushalayim shel matah' in *Eimah gedolah veyare'ach* ('The earthly Jerusalem' in *Great Fear and the Moon*, Tel Aviv, 1925).

modern European world. But, as we shall see, it was not in itself considered sufficient to ensure this separation.

THE SECULARIZATION OF MORALITY AND THE NATIONAL ETHICS

Let us go back to the early Haskalah as a turning-point.

We saw that many of the *maskilim* did not lose their faith, but some were influenced by the European Enlightenment, which distinguished between 'faith', 'religion', 'theology', and 'church'. In his *Characteristics of Men, Manners, Opinion and Time* (1711), Lord Shaftesbury, we recall, made an influential distinction between morals that derive from positive law and morals that derive from an 'immediate feeling and finer internal sense'. He regarded the church and theology as an external expression, while morals were conceived of as an inner expression of the free individual. In Shaftesbury's view, the weakness of the Renaissance lay in the fact that its 'enlightenment' was totally devoid of moral content. Classical literature in itself does not enlighten or educate unless one adds to it a 'great moral impulse' (the *instinctus moralis*).[65] This notion made it possible to turn religion into a product of the moral sense, and not the other way round. The list of virtues remained the same, but their origins and sanctions dramatically changed.[66]

This is the main reason why many Jewish thinkers turned to biblical prophecy to locate the main spirit of Judaism. One could conclude from it not only that there is a common denominator for human ethics, but also that moral precepts are above the precepts of faith and religious behaviour, and are a product of intelligence and immanent human quality. Biblical prophecy, on this view, was transcendentally based and bore both a universal and a national character that assigned greater weight to precepts than to ritual. In the talmudic and biblical tradition, the purpose of prophecy was to caution against any deviation from the Torah, whereas in the modern conception of prophetic morality, prophecy was severed from the system of precepts—the ritual law—and became a codified world outlook and a system of rules of social and human conduct. By placing prophetic morality at the very centre of Judaism, both the 'mission theory'—that the Jews'

---

[65] See in Reill, *German Enlightenment*, 58; Willey, *The Eighteenth-Century Background*, 60–77.

[66] On the concept of immanent morality in Judaism see Rosenbloom, *Studies in Torah Judaism*, 252–6 (which deals with the great influence of Kant's ethical philosophy on Shadal); and on M. Lazarus's view of the immanent morality of the Sages see E. E. Urbach, *The Sages*, i. 317–19; Baumgardt, 'The Ethics of Lazarus and Steinthal'.

mission is to disseminate montheistically based moral values amongst the nations—and the nationalist ideology seemed to be adopting the Christian outlook; in that outlook, as is well known, an immanent link was created between the prophetic moral message and Jesus' universal message. Since faith has lost its power of appeal, wrote Graetz, morality becomes the tugboat to pull theology.[67] And, indeed, 'ethics' became an essential and fundamental characteristic of Judaism. As a result, efforts were made to give it new foundations. Quite a few Jewish thinkers since Mendelssohn have proposed various concepts of the relationship between religion and ethics as well as of the essence of Jewish ethics. Religion was seen as only one sphere in which ethics is expressed, and ethics was endowed with an autonomous basis.[68]

Not everyone was so sure that morality could indeed take the place of religion as the core of Jewish existence, or even that Jewish morality and ethics as a conceptual framework and historical tradition existed at all. In April 1904 Shai Ish-Hurwitz published a provocative article, 'Leshe'elat kiyum hayahadut' ('On the Existence of Judaism') in the Hebrew periodical *Hashilo'ach*, in which he levelled the harshest criticism against the assumption that the content of Judaism is expressed in Jewish ethics. In his view, ethics is universal in its essence and there is no such thing as a special national ethics. In differing circumstances, ethics undergoes changes and no national ethics exists as a metahistorical entity. The Jewish people is itself a good example of ethical dynamics, since in different periods it behaved in contradiction to the moral standards preached to it. Anyone sketching an idealistic depiction of Jewish virtues is unfaithful to historical truth, which demonstrates how different the reality was from the scale of virtues attributed to the Jews. Furthermore, the nations of the world possess a great ethical literature—Kant, Spencer, Rousseau, and Tolstoy—for which the Jews have no equivalent.[69]

This radical view was rejected, and the belief in Jewish ethics became a conventional wisdom and the basis and cornerstone not only of scholarly writings but also of the self-image of the Jewish public. 'We have become accustomed to think', wrote Ahad Ha'am, 'that from its very creation ethics has been a part of religion, that it only came into the world with religion and through religion and is based upon it—and cannot be imagined without it.' From Lecky's *History of European Morals* (2 vols., London, 1869),

[67] H. Graetz, 'The Correspondence', 231.
[68] Julius Guttmann, *Philosophies of Judaism*, 350–2.
[69] On him see Nash, *In Search of Hebraism*.

from Draper's *History of the Conflict between Religion and Science* (1874),[70] and especially from Comte, he had learnt that the moral behaviour of a society is linked to various circumstances and factors. Sometimes there is a conflict between the demands of ethics and the requirements of religion, and at times the rules of religion clash with the moral sense: 'Thus we find the Greek and Roman authors (Plato, Lucretius, and others) constantly deploring the state of religion in their time, which sets before its believers a divine ideal which is much inferior to them in its moral development.' And in a similar fashion, the prophets reproach religion and its priests, whose conduct is far from moral, or even completely immoral.[71] The appeal to ethical prophecy, like that to wisdom literature, was an appeal to the universalistic layer in the Bible and in later Jewish literature, a literature that does not give prominence to religious ritual, but rather views man's moral obligation as a supreme value and the Torah first and foremost as an ethical doctrine independent of any religious rites.[72] If this is the case, ethics and moral sense develop in a people in the course of its history. Judaism not only created a monotheistic faith, but also created a unique collective genius and collective national morality (*musar le'umi*) as an integral part of it.[73] It is, however, not religion that produces the ethics enveloped in the commandments. The various normative texts represent one organic whole that does not depend upon religious ritual. There is also no need to accept the metaphysical assumptions of medieval Jewish philosophy, and the rational moral idea should be extricated from 'under the wave of the old metaphysics'.[74] The moral precept became a human creation, the fruit of a people's spirit and genius, which creates ideals and, by internalizing them, turns them into a positive historical force which shapes the entire experience of life. Hence the national utopia of a new Jewish moral society emerged: a utopia of a national society (and state) that should be the creation of a people with a unique moral sense.

Here the dialectical pattern is very evident: the secular concept of 'national ethics' was to a great extent a continuation of the Second Temple

---

[70] O. Chadwick, *The Secularization of the European Mind*, 229–49. See also Henry Sidgwick, *Practical Ethics* (1874), and Sutherland, *The Origins and Growth of the Moral Instinct*.

[71] Ahad Ha'am, 'Derekh haruach'. See also id., 'Hamusar hale'umi', 'Past and Future', and 'The Transvaluation of Values' (a response to Berdyczewski, 'Shinui arakhim').

[72] The paradox here lies in the fact that the idea of the Christian critics of Judaism, who regarded the Talmud and talmudism as a departure from the prophetic morality and from the original Mosaic ethics which were fully realized in Jesus' teachings, was actually adopted and internalized.

[73] Ahad Ha'am, 'Hamusar hale'umi'.

[74] Gottschalk, *Ahad Ha'am*, 159–99. Ahad Ha'am often expressed the intention to write a comprehensive study of Jewish ethical principles and Jewish ethical philosophy, but never in fact tried to fulfil this wish.

era and wisdom literature. In the latter, we recall, the source of ethics lies in universal human reason and is not part of the covenant between the nation and its God. But more than that, it is a continuation of the concept of ethics in biblical prophecy, in which both the individual and the nation had clear ethical obligations. This strongly emphasized the ethical dimension of Christian criticism, which averred that Judaism had forsaken the universal-ethical dimension (and stressed, for example, the figure of Moses as a legislator, not as a prophet).[75] Ethical prophecy, which had been taken from the Jews and appropriated by Christianity, or had become, at the hands of liberal Jews, the basis for an a-national ideology, was restored to Judaism by the national ideology. The national body—the nation—is the bearer of the prophetic moral mission, which claims there is no contradiction between national existence, ethical national existence, and universal moral values.

Again, a circle is closed. The Sages judged Hellenistic society according to its behaviour, not according to its norms of behaviour; the Jewish society and the Jewish state is also judged according to its conduct, not according to its abstract principles of ethics.

[75] Z. Levy, *Judaism in the World View*, 51–9.

7

WORLDS WITHOUT COMPROMISE: RECONSTRUCTING THE DISPARITIES

> The purpose of the Romans was to give great honour to physical strength, which could at any moment be returned to dust; the purpose of the Greeks was crafts to enhance the glory of the body, which is an act of futility. But the purpose of the Hebrews was exalted above the dust and the beauty of Nature, a purpose which will reach to the heavens and which could be proclaimed in few words: intellect and a knowledge of God. To inform other nations of His glory would be their joyful path. Not in the name of a wisdom that is above Nature, but in the name of God and in the spirit of our faith . . .
>
> PERETZ SMOLENSKIN, 'Am olam' ('Eternal People')

THE JEWISH TRADITION OF POLARITY

THERE was nothing new in the notion that Judaism and Greekness represent two different absolute moods of human nature. Therefore it is no wonder that some Jewish writers responded to the binary model in kind: by formulating a new absolute and abstract Jewish binary model.

In the Jewish tradition an uncompromising opposition by Jews and Judaism to 'the nations of the world', 'the foreigners', or the 'Gentiles' (goyim) was deep-rooted. The Jewish traditional view from the biblical era onwards intensified and brought into sharp focus the disparity between the Jews and the Gentile world, describing it as a world suffused with horrifying immoralities:

And the LORD spake unto Moses, saying, Speak unto the children of Israel, and say unto them, I am the LORD your God. After the doings of the land of Egypt, wherein ye dwelt, and after the doings of the land of Canaan, whither I bring you, shall ye not do; neither shall ye walk in their ordinances. (Lev. 18: 1–3)

Josephus was very well acquainted with the claims made in anti-Jewish propaganda, in particular those criticizing Jews for an insularity resulting from their feelings of superiority. He also was familiar with the complaints about the contempt they showed for pagan cults. Hence, in this matter as well, he wrote in a spirit of apology: the Jews are not by nature devoid of humane feelings and do not hate those who belong to another race. On the contrary, they would like all human beings to enjoy the blessings the Creator bestows upon His creations. He rejected the claim that the God of Israel is not a universal God, because He does not permit non-Jews to participate in the Jewish rites, whereas the pagan religion does not set up any barriers. In his reply to Apion, he wrote that the pagan faith ought not to be despised but rather should be the object of philosophical criticism. The religion of Israel is actually a universal religion, whereas the Greeks describe their gods as human beings, a description which does not befit the greatness of One who set forth the orders of the universe. In other words, Josephus reconfirmed the existence of the contrast between the two; he made no attempt to urge the foreigners to worship the God of Israel, but rather tried to defend Jewish uniqueness, without inciting any rebellion in the tents of the Greeks. The religion of Israel is described as a religion with universal moral authority and the desire to maintain particularity as a universal phenomenon.[1]

The approach to the problem of antinomy and antagonism in the literature of the Sages was different. There the heritage of classical antiquity and Hellenism signifed a totality of properties, and in their centre, the value-laden term idolatry. It was not only a conflict between different modes of faith, the worship of one God versus the worship of idols. The conflict also encompassed daily life and folk wisdom. It is worth noting that the Sages did not identify Greece with aesthetics, that is, literature and art. They asserted the existence of an all-embracing, deep human cultural-religious disparity, and told folk-tales about the differences in character and intelligence. One example is the anachronistic popular story in Lam. Rabbah 1: 4 mocking the stupidity of the Athenians and lauding the wisdom and cleverness of the Jerusalemites who spend the night in an inn at Athens.[2] A more colourful and detailed fable is narrated in bBek. 8b, about R. Joshua b. Hananiah, who boasted to the Emperor that the Sages of Israel were wiser than those of Athens, and was ordered, 'If you are wise (more than they are), go and defeat them [in argument] and bring them to me'; R. Joshua did indeed go to Athens, where he demonstrated his cleverness and

---

[1] *Against Apion*, ii. 164–296; see esp. §§168–9, 209–10; 280–1, 287; cf. *The Letter of Aristeas*, 129–71, and Philo in *Vita Mosis*, ii. 22–5. This seems to be a response to popular accusations and unfriendly characterizations such as reappear in Tacitus, *Historiae*, 5. 4. 1: 'Profana illic omnia quae apud nos sacra, rursum concessa apud illos quae nobis incesta': among the Jews, all that is sacred for Romans is deemed profane, but what is immoral for Romans is permitted to the Jews, who thus are not only different from other people, in the normal way that peoples differ from each other, but manifest a reversal of values. See also M. Greenberg, 'Mankind, Israel and the Nations'; L. H. Feldman, *Jews and Gentiles*, 177–96, 288–415; Machinist, 'Question of Distinctiveness'.

[2] Shinan, *The World of Aggadic Literature*, 83–4. On the cycles of stories praising the wisdom of the Jerusalemites and of R. Hananiah, see Yasif, *The Hebrew Folktale*, 116–17, 196–8.

wisdom in a series of exploits, and brought the [Greek] sages before the Emperor, totally defeated and humiliated. In the same chain of folk-tales it is related that R. Joshua competed with the sixty wise men of Athens in another confrontation. The wise men ask him to build a house in the sky, and he 'recalls the name of God' and flies up to a column high in the sky and calls the wise men of Greece to bring him some bricks and mortar. They reply that they have no wings. To that he replies scornfully: 'Then wait until you sprout wings in order to build a house high in the sky.'[3]

In the talmudic literature there are both explicit and tacit disputes with Greek philosophy. For example, when a philosopher poses a provocative question to R. Gamaliel asking him why the God of Israel did not destroy the idols, the Sage replies that if God were to destroy and eliminate all the idols, then he would have had to destroy the sun and the moon, the stars, the trees, the beasts, and so on, since the pagans have made them into gods and worship them (e.g. bAv. Zar. 54*b*). Another type of confrontation is not related to questions of theology but rather, as we have seen, to the wisdom of life (common sense and wit). A third type of total antinomy is expressed, for example, in the words of R. Levi: 'All Israel's actions are distinct from corresponding actions of the nations of the world: this applies to their ploughing, their sowing, their reaping, their sheaves, their threshing, their granaries, their wine-vats, their shaving, and their counting' (Num. Rabbah 10: 1). At the very most, there was a common denominator in the most basic human affairs. A similar attitude was expressed in Deut. Rabbah 7: 7:

It is related that once a Gentile put a question to R. Yohanan b. Zakkai, saying: 'We have festivals and you have festivals; we have the Calends, Saturnalia, and Kratēsis, and you have Passover, Pentecost, and Tabernacles; which is the day whereon we and you rejoice alike?' R. Yohanan b. Zakkai replied: 'It is the day when rain falls.'[4]

In the literature of the Sages, Yavan (Greece) is the world outside—the alien, the different, the threatening, the negative, and the seductive[5]—but it

---

[3] Bialik and Ravnitzky, *The Book of Legends*, 187; the building of a city in the sky forms the plot of Aristophanes' *Birds*, commemorated in the English word 'Cloudcuckooland'. E. E. Urbach writes that 'Even those sages who considered the Jewish concept of religion to be fundamentally different from those of other people recognized that certain mental attitudes and predispositions are common to all men.' Thus the sharp differentiation between Israel and the Gentiles 'was not intended to ensure self-isolation' ('Self-Isolation or Self-Affirmation').

[4] Ed. Lieberman, 111; see Hallewy, *The Biographical-Historical Legends*, 322–5. 'Calends' here mean not the first day of each month, but specifically the Calends of January or New Year; 'Kratēsis' is the celebration of the current emperor's accession, his *dies imperii*, of which some emperors made more than others.

[5] Heschel, 'The Heresy of Japheth in the Tents of Shem'.

also represents high culture from which much can be learnt. Yet at the same time one can discern in this antithesis a self-evident recognition that Greece and Israel are the two great peoples of culture, who have created universal spiritual resources that endure even after their sovereignty has lapsed. The Mishnah, out of a sense of superiority, expressed a consciousness of this many-layered antithesis. For example, it states that a child and a craftsman of Israel possess Torah and beauty that outweigh the wisdom and science of the nations: 'Do not say: I have learnt the wisdom of Israel, I will learn the wisdom of the nations of the world.' 'Nor shall you follow their customs, the things engraved in their hearts, such as theatres and circuses and stadia' (*Sifra*, 'Acharei mot' 9: 13, ed. Weiss, 86*a*). It seems right to say that the Sages acknowledged the pre-eminence of the Greeks in the various sciences and drew a distinction between idolatry in the sense of ritual and those traits of culture that were not directly connected with pagan ritual but belonged to their morally lax lifestyle.

This popular attitude towards the Gentiles as 'Greeks' was deeply imprinted in the Jewish historical awareness and collective memory. In the everyday language of east European Jews, Greeks signified all the Gentiles, as the words of a folk-song showed: 'Alle Yevonim hobn di zelbe ponim' ('All the Greeks have the same face'). They also represented the negative and the threatening: children kidnapped from the *cheder* to serve as 'Greeks' in the Tsar's army: 'From the *cheder* they tear away the babes so weak | And dress them up in the clothes of a Greek.'[6] *Yevonim* was used as a sobriquet for the Russians, recalling the Byzantine Greek origins of the Russian Orthodox Church, but also associated in the popular mind with the characteristic Russian name Ivan, in contemporary Hebrew literature often applied metonymically to Russia.

Against this background it was not difficult at all for Jewish writers, thinkers, and creative artists of diverse viewpoints to adopt the binary model as an appropriate historical code. Nevertheless, the modern era formulated new conditions and inspired new meanings within tradition, or aroused protest against it for reasons new in nature. Since the eighteenth century—and to a greater extent in the centuries that followed—the confrontation or encounter with Greekness (as a metaphor for modern European culture) has neither exhausted nor diminished the debate in matters of philosophy or theology, but rather extended it to all areas of human existence. It was no longer just a small circle of *maskilim*, or circumscribed

---

[6] 'Kleine oyfalach reist men fun cheder | un men tut zei on Yevonishe kleider': Vital, *The Origins of Zionism*, 39–40. His translation is: 'The children are turned away from school | And are dressed up in soldiers' uniforms.'

groups who had social and cultural contact with the outside world, who faced this confrontation. Gradually, all strata of Jewish society faced the new European culture, and became involved in the process of building and creating the new Jewish world. In the process, the validity of the antinomy was strengthened, its roots grew deeper, its horizons broadened, and it became all-embracing—a historical and cultural challenge that had constantly to be faced. The pattern of antinomy became a self-explanatory and fundamental pattern, useful in different circumstances and for different needs. Paradoxically, as the desire to be regarded as a nation of culture became more intense and the broadening of the antinomy became more pronounced, the process that I define as the 'Hellenization' of thought-categories and criteria deepened. In order to reject European culture *in toto* and build a new Jewish culture, it was necessary to describe Jewish civilization as a totally different type from that of Greece and the West. Here too—in the radical Jewish antinomy—Greekness and Judaism become ideal types, all-encompassing, unchanging, and one-dimensional, dominating all areas of life. In this way, the self-affirmation of Jewish superiority acquired new garb and a new content. As a response to the Greek utopia, a Jewish utopia was put forth.

This does not mean that the utopia of the *maskilim* disappeared. Certain Jewish circles responded to modernity in a radical way, reaching the radical conclusion that there was no difference, in any sphere, between Jews and Gentiles, and held that coexistence, emancipation, and symbiosis were possible, and even desirable. This conclusion was far removed from the utopia of the first generation of modern Jews, from whose viewpoint uncompromising and total antinomy could not have been entirely acceptable; after all, they had been seeking a bridge to European culture, and did not attempt to establish and intensify the separations. They held, as we have just seen, that the Gentiles also had not only wisdom but ethics as well, and for that reason believed in the possibility of harmonious co-existence. Radical Jews who accepted this view went one step further—but this additional step took them from acculturation to the brink of assimilation. A different type of response came from a national point of view. The response of the nationalist Jews from the 1870s and 1880s to antisemitism, as well as to the growth of Gentile nationalism, was to abandon the utopia of the early *maskilim* and their successors, who believed in integration and even active involvement in European society, in favour of an ideology of separation and diversity. This Jewish outlook characterized 'Europe' and 'Greece', its model, as the antitype of Judaism: a collective entity, or an organic unity of world-view, rules of behaviour, and patterns of character, standing opposite another eternal collective entity, that of the Jews. The opposition of Judaism–Greekness thus both continued the old conflict and expressed another of a completely new type.

The new binary model subdivided into four main forms, each reaching its own conclusions:

(i) Greekness and Judaism are two separate and different entities from the spiritual as well as from the 'natural' point of view. They represent not only two different religions, but two different collective human characters and ways of life. There can be no reconciliation, no partnership, and no affinity of any kind between the Jewish world and the Greek world. The conclusion is that Judaism and the Jewish people should separate these worlds from each other.

(ii) Judaism and Greekness are indeed two dissimilar cultures, but they share some fundamental elements that can serve as a basis for mutual understanding and dialogue. Moreover, harmony can reign between Judaism and Greekness, not as two components of Western culture, but as two cultures existing side by side.

(iii) Judaism, like European culture (and Greek culture), is a riven culture; it has a 'Greek' basis as well as a 'Jewish' one, and it will be revitalized once there is an inner harmony between these two.

(iv) Greekness is preferable to Judaism as a world-view and as a view of life. Modern secular (liberal) Judaism can only exist if it adopts the 'Greek' world-view.

THE TOTAL ANTINOMY: SEMITISM AND ORIENTALISM

The adaptation of the new Western categories began with Nachman Krochmal, who, following in Maimonides' footsteps, wrote *Moreh nevukhei hazeman* ('The Guide of the Perplexed of Our Time'). In it he argued, under the influence of Hegel, that every nation is distinguished by spiritual attributes it has internalized; however, the various nations differ in the way in which the basic attributes that express their spirit are manifested. All the good attributes of the Jewish nation are fully realized and determine its metahistorical status. Such finer qualities are diminished during the decline of a nation; however, in Krochmal's view, what makes the Jewish people unique in comparison to other nations is the fact that its immanent and absolute attributes have not disappeared, but rather continue to thrive.[7] One commentator on his book argues that Krochmal wished to reconcile

---

[7] Krochmal, *Moreh nevukhei hazeman*, vii. 34–9.

the 'Jerusalem of heaven with the Athens of heaven',[8] but it seems that his aim, like Shadal's, was to give the traditional antinomy a new interpretation according to the Idealistic philosophy. Although Krochmal did not draw an analogy between the nature of the higher human qualities of the nations and of Israel when they were at their peak, he apparently ascribed a superior status to the good qualities of the Jewish people in every era, since he did not address only the ideological content of Judaism but all spheres of Jewish life as constituting an organic whole. However, he did not describe the spiritual attributes of the Greeks, but only the qualities of the absolute Jewish spirit (*absoluter Geist*).

About thirty years after Heine (and Shadal), the German Jewish socialist philosopher and political leader Moses Hess (1812–75) adopted the antinomic pattern and placed it at the heart of his scheme of history.[9] For Hess (who at the same time, as a forerunner of modern Jewish nationalism, journeyed between the two worlds of universal socialism and organic nationalism) the antithesis between Judaism and Hellenism lay not only in such manifestations as ethics or social behaviour, but rather in innate collective character traits, in the collective genius. In his *Rom und Jerusalem* (1862), Hess presents one of the most powerful formulations of the pattern of antinomy between 'Hellenen und Israeliten':

The Greeks had sanctified and worshiped Nature in their religious cult only in its finished and harmonious form, but not in its creative and becoming aspect. Man, also, had been deified in the Grecian world only as a complete organization, as a being who stands at the height of organic life, but not as the representative of a new life sphere; not as a moral and social being, who is to be looked upon as in the midst of becoming and developing, as is the case with Christianity, the descendant of the historical religion of Judaism. The Jews, on the other hand, had turned the tables, deifying the *becoming*; worshiping the God whose very name expresses past, present and future. Even the cosmic and organic life spheres, which are already completed in this universal epoch, are not considered by the Bible as eternal and unchangeable, but viewed from the creative standpoint. The Bible begins with the creation of the world and the declaration of the natural Sabbath, but the prophets have gone further and completed the process, embracing as they did the

---

[8] Rawidowicz in his introduction to *Moreh*, 145. See Julius Guttmann, *Philosophies of Judaism*, 321–44.

[9] See 'Briefe über Israels Mission', Third Letter, 22: 'And just as the creative genius of the Indo-European races achieved its classical expression in Greece, so the creative genius of the Semitic races was revealed in Judah'; id., 'Ein charakteristischer Psalm', 126: 'The Israelites and the Greeks were not acquainted with one another for a very long time, and when they finally came to know one another, there were conflicts and clashes between them which led to the destruction of the entire ancient culture and its world-view, because these two chosen peoples, each in its own way, had its justified universal historical mission, and only after a war that raged between them for two thousand years, were they reconciled in modern humanism.'

entire history of human development and foreseeing the final historical Sabbath. The tendency to view God in history, not only in the history of humanity, but also in the history of the cosmic and organic world, is an essential expression of the Jewish spirit. This striving after the recognition of God is developed in historical studies, through observation of historical facts; but in nature-study it posits a certain mental direction as a starting-point, one that is totally unknown to modern scientists. Goethe and Humboldt were utterly opposed to the tendency of spiritualizing Nature, which is so closely united with the Jewish God-idea.

The Greeks sanctified the totality of Nature, including man as a complete product; the Jews sanctified the totality of history, including that of organic and cosmic life; and the Christians deified and sanctified the individual. Individuality had thus found its complete expression through Christian apotheosis. Such a view does man both justice and injustice; for in order to delineate the rights of the individual, man must be conceived abstractly and not as he really exists, united with Nature and history, family and country. The fall of the ancient world and the entry of the Germanic race upon the arena of history have brought about both the strengthening of individuality and its one-sidedness, which today is undermining individuality, but true personality will rise again when individualism will be united with other higher tendencies. The realization of this higher unity can be made possible only by viewing the Jewish historical religion in a scientific manner. The religion which will be raised to a science is none other than the Bible religion, which preaches the genesis and unity of cosmic, organic and social life, and to the development and spread of which, the genius of the Jews after their regeneration as an independent nation, will be devoted.[10]

From his organic and evolutionist starting-point, Hess, who adopted the racially based outlook prevailing among his contemporaries, regarded the Hebrews and the Hellenes as two racial types, each with its diverse cosmology, and in the Hellenic–Jewish antithesis saw the peak of racial opposition, reflected in the disparate cosmology: the Hellenes proceeded from a recognition of the multiplicity in life, the Jews from a recognition of the unity in life:

The languages of these nations with whom our civilization originated belong to two primal races, the Indo-Germanic and the Semitic. The ancient culture of the former reached its culminating point in Greece; of the latter, in Judea. In these two countries, the typical antithesis between the Indo-Germanic and Semitic races reached its highest point, and the fundamental differences in the view of life of these two races were expressed in the classical works of the Hellenes and Hebrews. We see, from those works, that the former viewed life as a multiplicity and the latter as a unity; the one, looked upon the world as eternal being, the other, as eternal becoming. The spirit of the one expressed itself in terms of

[10] Hess (trans. Waxman), *Rome and Jerusalem* (note VI), 249–51; cf. Avineri, *M. Hess*, 171–208.

space, that of the other, in terms of time. In the expression of the Greek spirit, there is the underlying idea of a perfectly created world; the Hebrew spirit, on the other hand, is permeated with the invisible energy of becoming, and the world, according to it, is governed by a principle which will begin its workday in social life, when it has arrived at a standstill in the world of Nature. The classical representatives of the natural Sabbath no longer exist as a people, and the God of history has dispersed his people, which foresaw the historical Sabbath, among the nations. But the two primal types of spirit, which no longer have classical nations as their representatives, still have many such individuals among civilized nations. The two giants of German literature, Goethe and Schiller, are the German representatives of the two types of genius—the Greek and the Hebrew—of the natural and historical Sabbath. And when Heine divides all men into Hellenists and Nazarenes, he designates, unconsciously, these two types of spirit. Modern Jews, like the Indo-Germanic nations, have in Heine and Börne their representatives of these two types of cultural life.[11]

This pattern of antinomy never gave Hess any respite; over the years he only added new motifs to it. He asserted that what the Hellenes cherished most of all was freedom in its broadest sense, freedom that develops and enriches all the psychological forces of the spirit.[12] This is then, in Hess's opinion, the root of the Hellenes' unquenchable preoccupation with meta-physics and the nurturing of science, beauty, and wisdom. However, it is also the source of their negative traits—jealousy, impatience, and intol-erance. The Hellenes did not succeed in becoming a nation and they disappeared as a race; Israel dedicated all of man's finer qualities to the highest goal—the realization of universal justice. Hess's theory rests on the principle of a sole supreme being, which contains within itself all the aspects and spheres of life. This does not entail enslavement to God, but rather sublime freedom; the relationship between God and the people is a bond of a voluntary covenant, and this bond is eternal. The Jewish race—as well as its world-view—is firm and abiding. Thus the Hellenic race has disappeared, but its heirs, the Germans, exist. They, according to this view, continue to embody and express the diametrical opposition between the Semites and the Indo-Europeans.

In his own notes to *Rome and Jerusalem*, Hess declared that he did not deny the existence of a racial difference between the Germans and the Jews, or between the Indo-European peoples and the Semites, nor did he deny Jewish nationalism. On the contrary, he wrote, he based his entire world outlook on this fundamental antagonism that has existed from the outset

[11] Hess, *Rome and Jerusalem* (Epilogue), 183–5.
[12] Id., 'Die drei großen mittelländischen Völker', 72–3.

(*ursprünglich*) between the historical peoples (*Geschichtsvölker*). In Greece and Judaea—the classical lands of the primeval spirit—the Indo-European race created the distinctive Natural Religion reflected in the multiplicity of hues in its development, as well as the circle that closes after its perfection. Art and science are the mature fruit of this genius. On the other hand, the spirit of the Semitic people is expressed in prophecy and literature alone, which will be truly appreciated only after the development and education of the human race are perfected. The Jewish world-view is intrinsically genetic, while the Greek is pantheistic and polytheistic.[13]

Hess himself returned to this eternal theme, engaging in an incisive argument with Renan: the Hebrews, whom he described as the classic representatives of the sons of Shem, strove to introduce ethics and holiness into human life, whereas the Aryans strove to beautify and explain life. The Hebrews' interest in life was practical and purposeful, the Greeks' only theoretical and philosophical.[14]

Heinrich Graetz seems to echo Hess: 'The sharp opposition of Judaism to a paganism sunk in idolatry and immorality, traits which are conspicuously evident at a single glance, is nothing but the broad antithesis between the religion of the spirit and the religion of nature, divine transcendence and immanence.'[15] 'Paganism rests on the prior assumption that nature in its broadest sense, operates on the immanent force. The pagan notion of God is identical with nature . . . Pagan immortals are subject to necessity no whit less than mortals.'[16] Graetz clearly accepted Solomon Ludwig Steinheim's view in his famous debate with Zunz that idolatry cannot lead to religious awareness, which can only be attained through revelation, whereas Zunz believed that idolatrous consciousness can also lead to religious awareness.[17]

Hess's idea found a more crystallized expression in the writings of the German Jewish philosopher Hermann Cohen (1842–1918), the founder of the Marburg school of Neo-Kantianism, who drew a distinction between the Jewish and the Greek concept of history, its course, and its purpose;[18] but Cohen's intentions were different since he hoped for a German–Jewish symbiosis. In a critical review of Cohen's *Deutschtum und Judentum* (1915), the writer and philosopher Jacob Klatzkin (1882–1948) strongly rejected

[13] Na'aman, 'Hess Explains'. This conception, in various forms, will appear many times in Jewish literature. It asserts that the abstract Greek world outlook is implied by the concrete and is not antithetical to it. The body is not external to the spirit and there is no split or conflict between the two. In contrast to this perception of the essence of Greekness, in Christianity there is a profound breach and struggle between body and spirit.   [14] Hess, 'Eine charakteristischer Psalm', 124–7.

[15] H. Graetz, 'The Structure of Jewish History', 43.   [16] Ibid. 67.

[17] Julius Guttmann, *Philosophies of Judaism*, 344–9.   [18] See Karl Löwith, *Meaning in History*.

the theory that Germans and Jews shared a common base stemming from their affinity to Greekness. The cardinal point in the relationship between Judaism and Hellenism lay not on the theoretical-philosophical but on the religious plane: the religion of Israel was totally different from the Greek religion of myth, for it had a moral knowledge of God. Christianity, he added, never succeeded in effacing German paganism, which remained embedded in it; hence there was no affinity between Germans and Jews.[19]

Martin Buber (1878–1965), the Jewish existentialist philosopher, was influenced in his early years by Hess, by German conservative Romanticism,[20] and by the fashionable German mystical Orientalism of the turn of the century.[21] His 'Europe' is not exclusively Hellenic but Indo-European, and his Jews are not the sons of Shem (Semites), but sons of the East (an obscure geographical and cultural definition, which Buber preferred to 'Semites'). The East does not have racial connotations, for in Buber's East, Semites and Aryans existed without division. Under the influence of mystic German Orientalism, Buber sought to define Judaism as an Eastern phenomenon in order to grant it the deep-rooted character and the irrational aspect which he believed was so necessary to it.[22] Orientalism was a reaction to an excess of Jewish intellectualism, to a spirituality which was lacking in vitality, and also to the absence of the myth as the foundation of intuitive vitality. Thus Buber set out, particularly in his early essay 'Ruach hamizrach vehayahadut' ('The Spirit of the Orient and Judaism'; 1912), to describe the Eastern Jew as a unified being. The Greek was presented as a sensory type, whose senses 'are separated from each other and from the undifferentiated base of organic life', while the Oriental was a motor type whose senses were 'closely connected with each other and with the dark life of the organism'. Western man grasps the world in a stratified and divided way, Eastern man dynamically. The intention of the Jewish or Hebrew revival was to liberate the Jew from the objective circumstances forced upon him, through which he had become heedless of the image of God in him.

---

[19] Klatzkin's review appeared in *Hatekufah*, 11 (Warsaw, 1921), 493–502. Cohen believed in the total integration of German Jewry into German society; he responded to Treitschke's polemic, *Ein Wort über unser Judentum* (1879) in *Ein Bekenntnis zur Judenfrage* (1880). He also believed that the idea of the unity of mankind was essentially Jewish in origin. On his ethical philosophy see Schwarzschild, 'The Theological-Political Basis of Liberal Christian–Jewish Relations', and Dietrich, *Cohen and Troeltsch*.

[20] A. Shapira, 'Buber's Attachment to Herder'; Mendes-Flohr, 'Buber between Nationalism and Mysticism'.

[21] Mendes-Flohr, '*Fin de siècle* Orientalism'. See also Schwab, *The Oriental Renaissance*.

[22] On the 'invention' of the Eastern Jews by Buber and others see Gilman, *Jewish Self-Hatred*, 270–86.

Moreover, the divided external reality shattered and destroyed his inner unity.[23]

Buber posited the unequivocal contrast between Eastern and Western man with arguments clearly and recognizably reminiscent of Moses Hess some fifty years earlier:

From this point it can be seen that of all the Orientals the Jew is the most obvious antithesis of the Greek. The Greek wants to master the world, the Jew, to perfect it. For the Greek the world exists; for the Jew, it becomes. The Greek confronts it; the Jew is involved with it. The Greek apprehends it under the aspect of measure, the Jew as intent. For the Greek the deed is in the world, for the Jew the world is in the deed.[24]

Hence, according to Buber, the salvation of the world could not come out of the spirit of the West; it could only come out of the spirit of the East. Keen critics have already discerned that here Buber actually disguises his romantic-mystic yearning for the organic man—in the style of conservative German Romanticism—by dressing it in Eastern garb. Buber's East is nothing but a concretization of utopia, a creature of his spirit of conservative-mystic idealism. The 'flight from the West' is not truly an escape from it; it is actually a flight on a labyrinthine path in order to return there through the back door. Buber also added another antithesis, already mentioned in Chapter 3, between the philosopher and the prophet. He found (using the example of Plato) that the difference between the communal mission of the prophet and that of the philosopher was that the latter wished to draw the picture of a perfect society, while the prophet (Isaiah) was content to censure the evils and flaws of existing society and confront the people with moralistic demands. Buber believes that the prophet sees before his very eyes a singular nation within which a utopia will be realized through the prophet. Unlike Ahad Ha'am in his well-known essay 'Kohen venavi' ('Priest and Prophet'), Buber asserts that the prophet is not the possessor of a universal abstract truth, but rather receives from time to time a special mission, a temporary assignment.

Another version of this idealistic-organic antinomy has led to the idea that the Greek world was based on the sense of sight, and Judaism on that of hearing. Buber also presents the argument, which was to reappear many times in the future, that the Jew of antiquity (the Hebrew or the Semite) was a hearing man more than a seeing man; a man of time, not of space. In the world of Greece, it was alleged, the dimension and dynamics of time are not

---

[23] Buber, 'The Spirit of the Orient and Judaism'.
[24] Ibid. 66, and see Werses, 'Nahman's Last Speech'.

important. In the Greek consciousness, time does not begin with Genesis, nor does it proceed towards a specific objective. In the Jewish view, on the other hand, time is dynamic, comes from a defined source, and moves towards an objective that is known in advance. Israel Eldad (Scheib) (1910–96), a nationalistic and messianic thinker whose writings were inspired by Nietzsche, Schopenhauer, and Eduard von Hartmann,[25] expressed ideas suggesting more than a few parallels to the Slavophile philosophy in mid-nineteenth-century Russia and later. He argued that the Greek view of history was a cyclic one, while the Jewish view of history (and emanating from it, the Christian view) was teleological: moving towards a preordained purpose and destiny. In Greece, the 'dimension of sight' prevailed. Hence the expansive detail of epic description and the price it exacted, in the want of perspective and depth. Greek literature was not attentive to the inner meaning of things. Judaism gave the world the notion of creation through speech: with a word, God created the world and brought the Israelite people into being. Eldad borrowed this duality, perhaps through Buber, even though he totally rejected Buber's political outlook.[26] It is worth citing the main points of the text epitomizing this speculative and idealistic scheme:

This difference does not signify polarity. Not that Greek culture was entirely a *tarbut ha'ayin* (culture of the eye) and aesthetics, without any *tarbut ha'ozen* (culture of the ear) and ethics. And not that Jewish culture was wholly of the ears without any feeling for the beauty of nature and form, without aesthetics. Time, by its very nature is unidirectional. That is not true of place. What you looked at a moment ago, you can look at a second and third time. But when something is heard—sound is unidirectional—you cannot hear again what you heard a moment ago . . . Therefore, that sense of responsibility for every deed, and that anger at idlers of the world when the world is the biblical one, in the sense of time, not of space. Hence the succinctness of biblical literature; therefore every word is a rock, and therefore it is all the choicest of the choice, a treasure. . . . It was not by chance that art and theatre developed in Greece and not in Judah. There are also profound reasons linked to content: the tragic perception of Greece was not possible in Judah. Possibly that too is linked somehow to the difference between the cyclical perception—which is better suited to space and the orbits of the planets—and the linear perception that is suited to Him who created the world out of volition and knowledge, and created man in His image. There is the eyeball and it can rotate this way and that. But the ear has no such ball. It hears sounds

[25] Y. Shavit, *Jabotinsky*, 155–61.

[26] Despite similarities in their idea of nationalism, and the shared influence of conservative Romanticism, but while in the historical and political context Eldad developed a nationalist and messianic ideology, Buber proposed far-reaching compromises in order to avoid a Jewish–Palestinian conflict. See Tal, 'Myth and Solidarity' and Shavit, 'Uri Zvi Greenberg: Conservative Revolutionarism'.

from the unseen depths of the soul, from the immeasurable heights of God. This is a vertical perception, starting from that same 'Let there be light' through 'I [am the Lord]' in the Ten Commandments and to *Shema Yisrael* ['Hear O Israel'] and the prayers from below to above. Performance and dialectics on the one hand, prophecy and prayer on the other. Horizontality as opposed to verticality.[27]

The number of texts in which I have found an explicit or implicit reference to the antinomy between the visual culture and the auditory culture is astonishing. This shows how an a priori claim can be embedded in the consciousness and become conventional wisdom. Here the inchoate psychology of the eighteenth century and the spiritual German epistemology of the nineteenth century left an ineradicable stamp. Orthodox and radical nationalist Jews alike, therefore, adopted the unfounded assertion that the Greeks were notable particularly for their ability to see and to describe sights. The German philosophers saw in this an expression of a 'pre-logical characteristic', while the Jews saw in it a clear expression of polytheism that cannot spiritually and intellectually come anywhere close to a knowledge of reality, and at the close of the nineteenth century Jewish literature adopted the categories of national genius and race.[28]

Perhaps the most detailed picture of the antinomy in nineteenth-century Jewish literature came from the pen of Lilienblum, who in December 1887 wrote to his friend the poet J. L. Gordon using the categories of racial differences as a basis for an 'empirical' historical profile. He followed Shadal in claiming that the Jews are serious-minded men of moral virtues, pursuing peace and preferring inner spirituality, while the Greeks are men of vast imagination, hedonists, sensual, and devoid of moral principles. This character is manifested in their culture:

The children of Israel pledge their hearts to one thing (as Heine put it), so that the forces they see are united in their case into one God, but in the case of the sons of Japheth into various things. The children of Israel nobly investigate the affairs of nature and take a moderate interest in history and legends. The sons of Japheth approach both of these with a daring and capricious imagination (without noting that recently their sages have been analysing and learning from the things they observe). The children of Israel are meticulous about keeping the pure virtues,

---

[27] Eldad, 'Tarbut ha'ayin beYavan'; cf. McGrath, *Dionysian Art*. Heinrich Graetz also wrote that 'the fundamental difference between the Jewish and the pagan form of perception is evident' ('The Structure of Jewish History'), 79.

[28] Boman writes that 'In the entire Old Testament, we do not find a single description of an objective "photographic" appearance . . . for the Hebrew the most important of his senses for the experience of truth was his hearing (as well as various kinds of being), but for the Greek it had to be his sight; or perhaps inversely, because the Greeks were organized in a predominantly visual way and the Hebrew in a predominantly auditory way, each people's conception of truth was formed in an increasingly different way' (*Hebrew Thought*, 74, 206). See Ch. 12.

about the inner content found in everything and its inherent spirit, and are distant from false pleasures. The children of Japheth have paid greater heed to beauty and taste, so much so that beauty for them has become idolatry, and to this very day the outer appearance is the main theme in their poetry and stories, and they eagerly pursue pleasures. If I suspected that our forefathers knew this, I would say they deliberately called the father of the Aryan race Japheth, in the name of its love of beauty. The Bible is the book of the people of Israel, just as the book of Homer is the book of the Greek people. How vast a difference between the two, how disparate the spirit that animates each of them, and how far apart are their aims! From these books, we can see what matters engaged the attention of each of them!

The children of Israel observed the years of the Second Tithe when they went up to Jerusalem and bought with their money cattle and goats and whatever their hearts desired, whereas the Greeks had the Olympic games, the chariots, the races, the sights and spectacles; the Romans had the animals in their colosseums, the theatres and the circuses, the likes of which still remain in Spain and exist in a modern form among all the European peoples. How ardently eager are the children of Europe for spectacles. We see what the hungry folk cried out for in ancient times: *panem et circenses*. (I was always seized by nausea when I recalled this odd pair of words in the mouths of the starving masses!) And the enormous amounts of money that they invest even now in theatres, when they have no proper schools, hospitals, and charitable institutions. Thus in Odessa they have just built a large theatre for a million and half a million roubles (even though it already has other medium-sized theatres), while the hospital in that city is in need of repair and there is no money for that, and there are not even half the number of schools that are needed and no funds for the medical faculty . . .

The Romans despised and cursed the poor, they never practised charity and mercy, and even now the poor man who begs is liable to be arrested for that. The Romans had no understanding of modesty, and in the Middle Ages and even today, the peoples of Europe are thoroughly shameless. Is it at all possible that what happened to Pushkin regarding his love-affairs and his demise could happen to a Jewish poet? I am not speaking of poets of ancient times, like Ibn Gabirol and Judah Halevi, but about our contemporaries: Almanzi, Shadal, Adam Hakohen of blessed memory, Yalag,[29] and others, may they live on. The Evangel did not bring about any change in the lives of its Aryan hearers. The holidays, rulers, and law-code of the Romans have remained on the same foundations. . . . The leopard may change its spots but not its nature . . . The Jewish writer said: 'Be rather a tail to the lions and not a head for the foxes', and the Roman writer said: 'It is better to be the first in the village than to be the second in the city.'

The children of Israel did not mark the events of their history on columns,

---

[29] Almanzi Joseph (1801–60) was a Hebrew poet in Italy; Adam Hakohen (Abraham Lebensohn) (1794–1878) was a Hebrew poet during the Haskalah period and author of the allegorical play, *Emet ve'emunah* ('Truth and Faith', 1867); 'Yalag' was J. L. Gordon himself.

tablets, and images, but rather with *matzot*, tabernacles, Chanukah candles, and the like. It was through observing the Commandments that the children of Israel remembered those events and realities to which the children of Japheth were awakened by pillars, idols, and paintings. The songs of Israel are very far removed from the songs of the Aryans. The children of Japheth, who are bloodthirsty and lovers of war, could not sire a man who would envisage a time when men would no longer raise their swords against each other. On the contrary: one of their finest sons, when he came to the tomb of Alexander the Great, wept and said: 'In such and such a year of his life, he had already conquered half the world, and I have not yet done a thing!' How despicable these words are, as if it is the duty of every man to ravage, at least, half of the world! Whether or not Julius Caesar really spoke these words is irrelevant. I will not judge based on an individual, but rather on the story so widespread among the people about its hero, and it is in this story that we can see the spirit of the people itself. The children of Israel have never told such tales about their heroes.

The children of Israel do not go out hunting simply for pleasure or to occupy their leisure time. All types of games, devised as pastimes, are the fruit of the children of Japheth.

The children of Israel are far removed from order and laws, whereas the children of Japheth are very meticulous about order, so much so that owing to the patterns and methods that they introduced into the various *chokhmot*, we forget that the originators of these *chokhmot* were actually the sons of Shem, the Babylonians, and the Assyrians. So very numerous are the differences between the children of Israel and the children of Japheth, and perhaps all these differences are but various branches stemming from one source and one cause. To unite the different natures, to create in the sons of Israel the spirit of the sons of Japheth, or vice versa, or to bridge the gap between the two, is neither necessary nor in my view possible. To decide which of them is the better, is not for me to judge, as a man of Israel and a party to the dispute. However, I do say, as Lessing did, each one will believe that his nature is the true one.[30]

Lilienblum, as a radical *maskil* who became one of the leading figures in the national movement in the last quarter of the nineteenth century, concluded from this detailed description of two totally antithetical cultures that the European Enlightenment, which the Jews had so warmly embraced, had caused them incalculable damage; as a result of it, they internalized negative attributes totally at variance with the singular Jewish spirit. The Jewish intelligentsia had assimilated European values, whose source was Hellenic and Roman, and thus had lost their individuality. On the face of it, he accepts Shadal's negative perception of Europe.[31]

---

[30] *Igrot Lilienblum*, ed. Brieman, 198–203, and Lilienblum, *An Autobiography*, ii. 50–6. Cf. Cardoso, *Las Excelencias*, 126.

[31] *Igrot Lilienblum*, ed. Brieman, 201.

However, we ought not to be misled by Lilienblum's rhetorical pathos: he was far removed from the anti-Western attitude of the Russian Slavophiles of his time.[32] His vision of Jewish national redemption also favoured a fusion of European enlightenment and nationalism. He did not regard European culture as totally negative—indeed, he found much about it that was positive: 'I cling to my view that the wisdom of Israel is in need of the classicism of the Greeks, the Romans, and the Persians, rather than the language of Chaldaeans, Arabs, and Syria', he wrote to Gordon in another letter in 1877.[33] He also added elsewhere that without Europeanism it would be impossible to open the windows of Judaism wide to let out the 'musty smells'. Hence once again we encounter the inner tension between the desire to emulate and adopt Europeanism and the urge to spurn it with scorn, for fear of assimilation. The metaphor of Hellenism enabled Lilienblum, at least theoretically, to distinguish between what was a foreign spirit, i.e. the Hellenes' spirit of taste and beauty, and the spirit of Israel. However, at the same time, it enabled him to see in Hellenism, as if in a mirror, a reflection of everything lacking and so sorely needed in the spirit of Israel: an enlightenment of logic, true criticism, pure virtues, and a love of natural sciences. Despite this negative image of 'Greece' (i.e. Europe) he was not totally opposed to 'Europeanism', nor could he reject modernity. Like many modern nationalist Jews, he believed that only within the setting of a national culture in Palestine could windows to Europe be opened. Only there can 'the beauty of Japheth dwell in the tents of Shem' and only there 'can we graft this alien corn on to the vine of Israel'.[34]

Lilienblum also expressed his ambivalence in another letter to Gordon. In December 1878, he wrote to him that the wisdom of Israel is not the philosophy of the Middle Ages, but rather the spirit of the Talmud and the Midrash. Philosophy was the province of only a small number of individuals and made no impact on the spirit of the nation. However, at the same time he writes that the spirit of the Talmud was influenced by the classicism of the Greeks and the Romans, and also of the Persians, under whose rule that spirit was created. Ostensibly this suggests that the spirit of the Talmud, which is the 'culture' of the Jewish people, bears the imprint of a foreign influence. However, Lilienblum hastens to equivocate and states that the Greek and Roman influences underwent great changes when they were absorbed by Judaism, taking on totally disparate meaning

---

[32] Frankel, *Prophecy and Politics*, 89–90; see also Kelner, 'Attempts at Reviving'.

[33] *Igrot Lilienblum*, ed. Brieman, 159.

[34] Ibid. 201–2.

and nature. Despite this opposition, one cannot understand the spirit of the Talmud without a knowledge of the languages of Greece, Rome, and Persia![35]

It is in the very same vein as Lilienblum's words that the fictitious English lady who serves as Graetz's 'other voice' writes in her third letter: 'Public buildings, railway stations, parliamentary buildings for those who represent the rights and welfare of the people, halls of scholarship, temples for the art of Thespis and Melpomene and even houses of worship by their very size induce amazement and by their symmetry please our still very demanding aesthetic sense. . . . And now to discover that all these marvels are only hospitals in which tenants, builders, and visitors alike suffer from secret, ravaging diseases!'[36] Graetz's bitter diagnosis represented culture as a thin veneer that concealed human beings heading towards utter destruction. 'Is it not an oppressive thought . . .?' asks the English lady. There is then no compromise between the Jewish spirit and the 'European spirit', that of the sons of Japheth. To prevent the Jews from being swept up and engulfed by this evil spirit, it is incumbent upon them to cut themselves off from it and to give expression to their own nature.

Another radical *maskil* and nationalist thinker, Peretz Smolenskin, spoke in the same language. In his view, the Greek dimension existing in Judaism is not necessarily a result of a sterile spirit, but rather the outcome of objective conditions: 'If Israel were still settled on its own land instead of suffering so many tribulations, such agony, anger, and pain each day, then perhaps it would have differed from the Greek people only in its knowledge of God, for then the people of Israel would also have rejoiced in its land, in its work, in the harvest of its land, and in all the delights of life, but now it has become in every way the opposite of that people.'[37] In other words, it is the Diaspora and not its immanent world-view that has cut the Jewish people off from earthiness, from a life of action. On the face of it, it would thus appear that Smolenskin was trying to erect a bridge between Hellenism and Judaism, while turning Hellenism into an analogy of real life, of which the Jews were forcibly deprived. However, that is not the case. For him too, Hellenism is identified with a lack of values, materialism, and decadent permissiveness. Christianity, according to Smolenskin, who here echoes Heine and Nietzsche, is a combination of the two doctrines: the knowledge and Torah of God with the doctrine of life and the earthly man. These are the two constitutive elements of Western civilization: 'And from then to this day this war between the

---

[35] Lilienblum, *An Autobiography*, ii. 169. [36] H. Graetz, 'Correspondence' 199–200.
[37] Smolenskin, 'Et lata'at', 169–74.

Jewish spirit and the Greek spirit has never ceased.' The historical difference between the fate of classical Greece and that of Judaism is that
there is no people keeping the Greek spirit intact in itself (Greekness is
only one element of Christianity), while the Jews maintain Judaism in a
state of purity and wholeness.

Smolenskin thus believed that from a radically nationalist vantage-point
it made no difference to the Jewish people which element was now dominant in Western culture, the Greek or the Israelite (i.e. the Christian).
Both these elements gave rise to antisemitism: on the one hand, the Jews
were threatened by the Church, and on the other by secular antisemitism
of the variety propagated by Voltaire, 'whose heart was filled by the Greek
spirit'. Hence the search for the Greek aspect in Judaism was an attempt to
rehabilitate Judaism by exposing dormant layers and hidden veins in it, and
to breathe a *joie de vivre* into it by means of elements regarded as Hellenic.
This tendency developed into an identification of traditionally non-Jewish
elements as distinctly Jewish. And it developed even further—into appropriation of the Hellenistic strata in the tradition of the Sages and their
transformation into a distinctive embodiment of the spirit of Judaism.

Smolenskin, however, like Lilienblum, was by no means a fervent adherent of 'old Judaism'; therefore, unlike the religious nationalist Jawitz,
he could not take the view that Judaism was a spiritual and organic unity
in the old way. He turned to a one-sided generalization of another kind:
the Greeks had lost their vision and their utopia and had sunk into the
real, material essence of life, and therefore they declined. The Jews, on
the other hand, had lost contact with the reality of life from the time they
lost their sovereignty and were exiled from their land. No innate defect in
character or spirit had caused their decline, as we have noted, but rather
external circumstances of life. Two universal human entities were in antithesis. However, the absolute contrast between them was perceived as
deriving not only from a divergent metaphysical outlook and cosmology,
but also from the deepest wellsprings of their world-view. A fundamental
affinity did exist between them, in that both Judaism and Hellenism asked
similar questions about the essence of the world and its orders. But the answers they gave were totally different and postulated a completely different
relationship between man and the superhuman. The essence of Judaism
lay in understanding man's relationship to God, not to nature. The Jew
did not want to understand God's works; his concern was reverence of the
Lord for its own sake.

Hence (Smolenskin declares) one must not recoil from the pattern of
antinomy, and one may readily confess with no hint of apology that it is

indeed immanent and eternal: all one needs to do is to admit it and to be aware of it. This awareness is vital not only to bolster the nationalistic and messianic idea, but also to create a new, all-inclusive Jewish nationalistic culture. Judaism champions the spirit, Greek culture might; Judaism inheres in content, Greece in form; in Judaism the good determines what is beautiful, in Greece beauty determines what is good; Judaism forgoes the present in favour of the future, Greek culture forgoes the future in favour of the present; Judaism adheres to ethics and for its sake gives up utilitarianism, Greek culture seeks utilitarianism and for its sake gives up ethics; Judaism espouses unity and wholeness, Greek culture espouses multiplicity and division; Judaism esteems the perfection of the soul and sees the true substance in spiritual values and in something above nature, Greek culture esteems the perfection of the body and recognizes only the natural and tangible substance.

Yehezkel Kaufmann (1899–1963), the eminent Bible scholar who spoke out against the school of Protestant biblical criticism in his monumental study of the origins of Jewish monotheism, *Toledot ha'emunah hayisraelit* (translated in abridgement as *The Religion of Israel*), assigned the antithesis a central place in his scheme of history. The uniqueness of the Israelite nation, according to Kaufmann, has its source in a singular metaphysical notion of an absolute, supreme, divine revelation in history. In contrast, the idea that shaped the 'Greek age' (the sixth to fourth centuries BC), which was parallel to the Second Temple era, is a scientific world outlook that aspires to liberate man's spirit from its ties to tradition. It desires to free the spirit and establish its right to determine beliefs and opinions on the basis of rational and sensory observation. The Greek intellectual revolution is not manifested in the anticipation of divine salvation and the redemption of the world by a just and righteous God, but in the fact that for the first time, the spirit recognizes itself as the source of knowledge and creation. Thus reflective thought was engendered in fifth-century Greece, and the spirit became the object of knowledge and inquiry: the philosophy or science of nature, the philosophy of the spirit and of culture. We are dealing therefore with two world outlooks which are totally and irreconcilably different from each other:

The elementary idea of the Jewish outlook was: the origin of all things is an exalted divine volition, a good, benevolent, purposeful and rational will which is the source of every natural and ethical law. It included belief in the revelation of God's word as absolute truth, in the giving of the eternal, living Torah to mankind; it included the belief in divine retribution; it included belief in miracles and in the kingdom of heaven, which will appear as a miracle in years to come. Its most eminent requirement was knowledge of the Torah. The elementary idea of the Greek outlook was: the rule of natural law in all of existence, in the animate, the inanimate and the divine—if there is a divine. It included the awareness that the spirit of man had the ability to comprehend existence and its laws and mysteries, and also to choose the way of good and evil by its own power, without depending upon the tradition of revelation. It aspired to establish the knowledge of realistic, rational and moral truth and also the cultural and social actions of man on the basis of systematic scholarship, of sensory observation and informed examination. It also required systematic inquiry into the capacity of the spirit to comprehend concepts and to establish values. Its most eminent requirement was free scientific thought. It believed that scientific thought could teach man the way of life and goodness.[38]

Greek and Jewish philosophy were completely different from each other. On the one hand, there was dogmatism, submission to tradition, prohibition against investigating the miraculous, reliance upon the manifestation of God's grace. On the other hand, there was inquiry, freedom of spirit, bold inquisitiveness, intelligent search for scientific truth.[39] Both these idealistic fundamental outlooks, he concludes, converged during the Hellenistic period—as well as in the Christianity that followed it—and shaped the character of the world. According to Kaufmann, during the Persian period these two polar worlds were separated and unknown to each other; only after the beginning of the Hellenistic period did Judaism meet the Hellenic world, and mainly not its idols but its *paideia*. As a result a prolonged confrontation emerged.

Jacob Klatzkin shared the opinion that they were inimical to one another, and intensified and exacerbated their conflict.[40] On the philosophical plane too, Greekness was no more than pagan rationalism or 'rational idolatry'. In Greekness redemption hinged on the strength of the intellect; Judaism believed in the divine revelation and the holy spirit of God, which gave mankind the Torah and its commandments. There is no real difference between élite and vulgar Greekness, for both popular paganism and Greek philosophy were anchored in moral nihilism; both of them advocated a relativistic attitude to life and both lacked an obligatory system of commandments.

After the Second World War, the antinomy served to impart a metahistorical interpretation to the Holocaust. Not always, it is true, was Japheth identified with ancient Greece; very often the name Japheth was the

---

[38] See the chapter 'Israel and Greece', iv/1. 487-495 and also i/2. 221-54.

[39] See ibid. v. 493. And see the whole sub-chapter entitled 'Greece and Israel', 487-95.

[40] Klatzkin, *Kera'im*, 136-46. In 1921, Klatzkin published a monograph dedicated to Hermann Cohen, besides the review cited in n. 19.

metaphor for medieval Europe and its continuation in modern Europe. But Europe would always be characterized by a congeries of characteristics, which were usually attributed in Jewish literature to Greece, that is to the original Japheth. From recent speculative theory, for example, we find Nazism interpreted as an inevitable consequence of the historical and metahistorical (and metagenetic) confrontation between Graeco-Teutonic culture and Jewish culture: German culture (but no other European culture!) represents the Sisyphean type, while Judaism represents the idyllic unified Tantalic type. These are collective, total, and deterministic types. Buber's analysis, or the contraposition of Job to Prometheus (or Antigone), is exchanged for a scheme that rests upon the ideas of the French Jewish scholar Solomon Reinbach, author of the monumental study *L'Origine des aryens: histoire d'une controverse* (Paris, 1892), which contrast the Sisyphean and the Tantalic (Western) human types. In the past, these antithetical types had precipitated an inescapable confrontation between Judaism and Hellenistic civilization; and in modern history they had precipitated a confrontation between Judaism and Germanism. Because ancient Teutonic society did not actually absorb the Tantalic elements in the European spirit which Judaism had internalized through Christianity, Germany remained fundamentally Graeco-Teutonic. Such a society is characterized by its absolute amorality. The connection between the Olympian gods and the Teutonic pagan deities—between Homer and the *Nibelungenlied*—produced an untamed, bloodthirsty, and blood-drenched culture. Greek divinity did, in fact, possess an element of beauty and moderation, but when it joined with the Teutons, this moderate element disappeared entirely, creating a savage, primitive, and murderous being, devoid of all restraints. Because Greek culture lacked the concept of man's creation in God's image, every moral sense was obliterated from it. The conquest of the world by science and technology brought about a situation in which the *golem* (science) began to govern its monstrous creator. Hellenic-Teutonic Western culture is then a Frankenstein's monster stalking the earth. By its very nature and creation, it is genetically programmed to attempt the destruction and annihilation of the Jews.[41]

THE SEARCH FOR A POSITIVE SYNTHESIS

We have already seen that this subject greatly preoccupied Joseph Klausner, who struggled with it while attempting to link a positivistic historical

---

[41] Shoham, *Walhalla, Calvary, and Auschwitz*, 120–48; see also Rivka Schaechter, 'Revival'.

study to the prevalent idealistic, speculative categories. Having in youth espoused almost without qualification the antinomic model, Klausner, in the course of his life, dissociated himself in turn, from the pattern, from this moderation, and from the quest for a utopia of Judaism and humanity. In the earliest stages of his thinking, he believed that Judah and Greece were two opposites.[42] Later, he found in Greek philosophy and literature clear signs of pagan humanism that esteemed goodness, honesty, and justice no less than Judaism did. It is ironic, as we have seen, that he borrowed the concept of pagan humanism from the Polish philologist Tadeusz Zieliński, the adversary of Judaism as well as Christianity.[43]

Klausner also signalled the universal duality with which we are concerned, by using the metaphor of Greekness and of Judaism. He identified Jewish elements (moral ideals) in Greek philosophy, and Greek values (aesthetics and a plastic sensibility) in Judaism. However, he was not satisfied with this simplistic view, but in his writings elucidates the internal contradiction between these elements and the quest for their reconciliation, exhibited in different measure in the words of all advocates of secular nationalism: a quest for reconciliation between the new and the traditional, between the objective and the subjective, between universalism and nationalism, between Judaism and Europeanism (Greekness). Klausner is enthusiastic about the etching of Hellenic traits into Jewish life, but at the same time he recoils in apprehension, wondering whether Jewish nationalism had not gone too far in its secularism and become more European than necessary. Like his contemporaries, the young Klausner also had to separate advances in civilization which were of Hellenic origin from moral progress and improvement. Both of these, he posited, like Judah Leib Levin before him, are completely autonomous realms. There is no connection between science and values. Therefore, one can praise and glorify Judaism; although it is backward in matters of civilization, it has been outstanding in its moral greatness through the ages. Jewish society was always an ethical society, simple in its ways, and pure. The fact that it had not studied the mysteries of nature, nor engaged in crafts, nor written poetry does not impair its perfection. Using Shadal as a point of departure, he states that the Greeks, in contrast, were an amoral people by nature. In the same spirit as Hess, he asserts that in the Jewish soul the subjective dimension is strong; it struggles for self-realization, against extremism and zealotry. Hence its inability to ob-

---

[42] Klausner, 'Yehudah ve Yavan—shenei hafachim?'

[43] Id., 'Milchemet haruach'; Perush, 'Judaism and Europeanism'. See M. Stein's reply in 'Judaism and Hellenism'.

jectivize things, to profess scepticism, liberalism, and diversity. All the traits that critics of Judaism considered negative here merit unbounded praise.

In that case, are all those who aspire to take goods from Japheth and place them in the tents of Shem assimilationists who have 'abandoned the Torah' and become depraved Hellenists? If the young Klausner was an enthusiastic adherent of total antithesis, then the mature Klausner, desiring a synthesis between Judaism and humanism, speaks in a different spirit and in another style. First of all, he bases his work on Ahad Ha'am (and not on Shadal) by distinguishing between different levels of the spirit of Greece. He espouses the old *maskil*-like distinction, which gives the Greeks an advantage over all the pagan peoples and expresses veneration, not only for Aristotle and Plato, but also for Homer, Virgil, Euripides, and Ovid. The Jewish spirit needs all of them and will therefore borrow them from the Greeks and their Roman heirs: 'We shall surrender to the spirit of Greece, and later we shall rule over it.' The antinomy is mellowing; even rapprochement of a sort is developing. There is in Greece something of Judaism, namely a moral sense; there is in Judaism something of Greece, namely an aesthetic sense. Klausner, it is worth noting, does not seek in Judaism Greek values like heroism or national zealotry. For him these exist in Judaism and always have. His point of departure is clearly cultural. Hence he posits that 'Greece and Judaea are not really two opposites. Greece sought goodness and righteousness and justice, to a certain extent, although not to the full extent that Judaea did; and Judaea loved beauty and harmony to a certain extent, but not as fully as Greece did.'[44]

What we are dealing with, then, are two spiritual propensities or two opposed human qualities, which, in different nations, are present in different measure. The Jews are characterized by subjectivism, that is, by the contemplation of the inner world of nature as against the observation of its outer world. In Judaism, the world exists for the sake of mankind; society and nation are central to it, not the individual. Judaism is noted for demanding total morality, but it lacks the skill of objectivization. For that reason, it never developed sculpture and painting; it has no epics or drama; it did not conceive philosophical or scientific doctrines. The contrast exists in content, in the way of contemplating the world, in the social and cultural order of priorities, not in capacities or potential; if Jews have not done things, it is not for want of qualifications or of skills.

[44] Klausner, 'Yehudah veYavan'.

It is quite clear that Klausner, the historian, does not offer a static picture of the spirit such as the thinkers and writers mentioned earlier had done. His dynamic historical picture was necessary to a thinker who strongly desired that Judaism should revive and rehabilitate elements and attributes that it lacked, and without which it could not be a complete nation of culture. The Judaism of the biblical era is not identical with Second Temple Judaism, and the latter is different from the Judaism of the Middle Ages. A quality does not produce a sealed totality of attributes that cannot change or diversify: it produces propensities, emphases, a different mix of components, but not a closed and unchanging totality of propensities and preoccupations. Judaism, in that case, is not one-sided or one-dimensional. Hence the difference between Judaism and Greekness is not fundamental and unbridgeable. Judaism can see in various elements of Greekness a source from which to make selective borrowings, or a mirror displaying what it lacks in order to be complete. Thus the antinomic model does not decree absolute estrangement between Judaism and the West, but offers a basis for balanced and positive cross-fertilization.

David Ben-Gurion was among those who followed in the path of Ahad Ha'am and Klausner. It is not true, he declared, that Greece was lacking in morality and it is not true that ancient Judaism was lacking in beauty:

We shall be denying the truth if we say that the greatness of ancient Greece was confined only to the sphere of reason and beauty. In the writings of Plato, Aristotle, Plotinus, and other Greek sages, we find a deep yearning for goodness and justice. And we shall be denying the truth if we say that the greatness of ancient Judaism was only in the religious and moral message of the prophets of Israel. A number of the biblical books are rich in consummate beauty and profound wisdom.[45]

And in a letter to the philosopher Samuel Hugo Bergman, in October 1960, Ben-Gurion wrote that the philosophers and the prophets both believed in the existence of a cosmic order, but the prophets felt no need to explore the secrets of the cosmos, and accepted it unquestionably.[46] He was chiefly concerned with the possibility of reconciliation between ethics and science, and with offering evidence that Jews are also able to be pioneering men of science.

[45] Ben-Gurion, *Medinat Yisrael hamitchadeshet*. In 'S. Freud: Das Unbehagen in der Kultur', published in the organ of the Zionist Socialist party, Achdut Ha'avodah, in 1930 A. Zeligman wrote that although people often say that the Jews tend towards monism, the contrary is true; they have a talent for casuistry that grinds every subject into fine dust.

[46] Letter of 1 Nov. 1960, published in *Ha'aretz*, 7 Nov. 1986.

THE DUALITY IN JUDAISM AND
THE SEARCH FOR A NEW HARMONY

Under the unmistakable influence of Berdyczewski, Abba Achimeir (1896–1962), a philosopher from the radical wing of the Revisionist movement, protested at the prevalent use of this pair of commonly accepted opposites, arguing that they denied Judaism attributes that are essential to a political and territorial nation. The nature of a nation is an obscure concept, he wrote. For him, Hellenism only served as a *topos*, not as a real historical description of classical Greece. In the spirit of Israel, the two elements constantly battled between themselves; the Jewish element— Pharisaic, theocratic, lacking in any feeling for nature, for country, for state—got the upper hand mainly because of external influences. The Jewish element is the one that was dominant in the Jewish people until the destruction of the Temple and the establishment of rabbinical Judaism by R. Johanan b. Zakkai. Achimeir regards ben Zakkai as the founder of negative, anti-nationalistic Judaism, and hence describes him in the most caustic terms. Judaism was then deprived of the Greek element, i.e. the secular, country-state element, becoming rabbinical Judaism, which Achimeir depicts in the spirit of Christian historical theology. Zionism came into the world, he believes, in order to strengthen the anti-theological element in the spirit of the Jewish people; in other words, to revitalize and rehabilitate immanent qualities that were doomed by rabbinical Judaism to a state of deep anaesthesia. Consequently Achimeir adopted, in letter and in spirit, the Protestant theological image of talmudic Judaism, so rife with contempt and bitter animosity towards everything that R. Johanan b. Zakkai and other Sages represented.

Achimeir's dualism was in fact an adaptation of the Nietzschean antinomy, and he cherished a vision of the resurrection of the Dionysian element of Judaism. Dionysian here means a militantly activist political and national renewal.[47] In later writings, Achimeir sketched a broader speculative antinomy, in which authors like Dostoyevsky, Nietzsche, and Kierkegaard represent the subjective, theological, Dionysian (!) Jewish world-view, whereas Kant, Hegel, Goethe, Pushkin, and Tolstoy represent the objective, philosophical, Apollonian Greek world-view.[48] Applying this same method, he was also able to contrapose Ahad Ha'am, as the representative of Apollonian secular Judaism, to Berdyczewski, the yearner for Dionysian secular Judaism, who maintained that Hellenism was char-

---

[47] Achimeir, '"Yavan" beYehudah ve"Yehudah" beYavan'.
[48] Id., 'Aman venavi', 64–5.

acterized by its aspiration for power and by its immoral vitality. In his view, that was the nature of Hebraism, before it was suppressed by rabbinical Judaism. Berdyczewski's imaginary Hebrew of the time before the Babylonian Exile was a replica of the imaginary Hellene. It is against this background that one can understand Berdyczewski's endeavour to reveal the Hellenic Jew, motivated by will-power and the impulse for life, and to present the gamut of the various and changing notions of Judaism, as they existed together in the synchronic and diachronic dimension of Jewish history. For Berdyczewski and his disciple Achimeir, the biblical man is not the farmer tilling the soil in the pastoral Arcadia of the Land of Israel, sitting under his vine and his fig-tree, but rather a man of powerful instincts, whose soul is one of unplumbed depths and mystery.

The Hellenic Jew was contrasted with the Jewish Jew, both as a two-dimensional picture of the Jews and as a reflection of the split personality of the inventors of this perception of a double image. They aspired to a utopian figure of an organic Jew, but until it came into being, they described Judaism as moving between two poles, enticed and entangled. Their Hellenic mirror reflected a split image: Hellene and Jew were synonymous with Dionysian and Apollonian; hence in turn with Jew and Hebrew. But where was the Dionysian phase in Jewish history? When was a Dionysian dimension created in the Jewish spirit? Menahem Soloweitschik (1883–1957), one of the pioneers of modern Jewish biblical research, believes, for example, that the period of the desert was the Apollonian chapter while the period of settlement gave rise to the Dionysian chapter, the religion, in which the Dionysian element played a major role. In the Dionysian world, the Apollonian desert life, when viewed with nostalgia, was transformed into a picture of golden days and an ideal of purity and innocence.[49] Achimeir, on the other hand, whose writings were strongly influenced by Spengler, turned this notion upside-down. In his view, it was the period of the desert which was actually the Dionysian era—an age of heroism, brutality, sternness, and puritanism. The desert imposes on its inhabitants a life of hardiness and forbearance, while life in towns and cities makes men lapse into self-indulgence and decadence, seeking an easy life. The desert and the mountain are the cradle of nationalism; the plain and the city are the focuses of anti-nationalistic cosmopolitanism.[50] He is not concerned with the foundry in which the Jewish people was forged,

---

[49] Soloweitschik, 'The Desert in the History and in the World-View of the People of Israel', and see the discussion in Ch. 13.

[50] Achimeir, 'Milchemet ha'or vehachosekh baNegev', 12–13.

but rather with pointing out that these two elements have been immanent in the Jewish soul and the Jewish being since the dawn of history.

Out of an uneasy feeling, radical secularists made a distinct and deliberate attempt to escape from the prevailing clichés of the antinomy. This pattern attaches a stigma to Jews with which nationalists—and not only they—do not feel comfortable; they cast it off and replace it with a different repertoire. It is surely symptomatic that most of those meeting the challenge of the antinomy in this manner, who seek Greek elements in Judaism, are the very people whose intellectual biography reveals a life of attempts to reconcile diverse aspirations and different insights in order to attain individual perfection and an accord between themselves and the world outside. Nathan Birnbaum (1864–1937), a capricious thinker, is a good illustration of this trend. The course of his life ran from the extreme of nationalism to the extreme of Orthodoxy; he also adopted the pattern of antinomy and accepted its racial basis. He created a system which encompassed both negative and positive attributes, in which Greece symbolizes aesthetics, scientific revolution, and the Renaissance, but also represents the pursuit of wealth, class war, and historical materialism. Europe's redemption will come if it succeeds in embracing Jewish moral and social values, whereas the revitalization of national Jewish culture will only be possible if it embraces the Greek (or as he calls them 'Aryan') qualities of Europe.[51]

Birnbaum further elaborated his utopian notion of a future reconciliation between Judaism and classical Greece in an article stating his view that the Jews embodied solemnity of life, the pain of the world, and spiritual asceticism, the Greeks the joy of life and the pleasure of the world.[52] The acme of Judaism and its values was represented by Isaiah and Jesus, that of classical Greece by Homer, Sophocles, and Phidias. Judaism had conquered the world through Christianity, but the latter declined during the Middle Ages to moral degradation and narrow-minded dogmatism; classical Greece was defiled by Rome and revived in the Renaissance. The gap between them became deeper in consequence of the French Revolution and the emergence of anti-Christian nationalism; the redemption of mankind would come in the wake of a synthesis between the two cultural inheritances, each with its own high value. This synthesis would also lead to a revitalization of Judaism, which would reabsorb the Greek values it had not always found alien (there is 'truly Greek' eroticism in the Song of Songs); thus it would descend from the heights of abstract

[51] Doron, *The Zionist Thinking of Birnbaum*, 86–8.
[52] 'Judaismus und Hellenismus'; see Doron, *The Zionist Thinking of Birnbaum*, 130–2.

metaphysical thought and express its new vitality in spontaneous life and dramatic creation. Since Birnbaum took a negative view of the Hellenizers as assimilationists, and was strongly opposed to modern attempts in that direction, it is clear that he drew a sharp distinction between 'imitative' Hellenism and the vital, creative synthesis of the future.

In David Neumark's view, the enriching confrontation between the Jewish view of life and the Greek view of the world, which at the time gave birth to Christianity, is likely to create a new synthesis, whose nature is difficult to predict.[53]Or, in the words of Norman Bentwich (1883–1971), who served as Attorney-General to the British authorities in Palestine (1920–31) and taught international relations at the Hebrew University (1932–51):

The harmony of Hebraic and Hellenic ideas, which was not accomplished in the transplanted Hellenism, may be achieved in the future by a self-conscious Jewish people which will imbibe those elements of outside that are ennobling, but will transmute them by the dominating Hebrew spirit. Our civilization, which is based partly on Hellenic, partly on Hebraic creations is continually progressing to such a harmony.[54]

Without such harmony, he concludes, the perfection of humanity will not be achieved. Bentwich's redeeming formula appears to be an Arnoldian blending of the two: Judaism (or Protestantism) and Hellenism (or the Renaissance). While Arnold 'does not look forward to a harmonious fusion of two equal elements, and his ideal Greekness absorbs the impulse of Hebraism into its own ideal of the harmonious development of all human powers',[55]Bentwich absorbed the impulse of ideal Greekness into his own ideal of Hebraism and humanity.

The messianic era is represented as a harmonious union between nationalism and socialism. After a period of stormy and painful pre-messianic tribulations, the millennium will arrive and there will be no disparity between Jew and Hellene. This was the view of the the socialist thinker Chaim Zhitlovsky (1865–1943), a spokesman for Jewish nationalism in the Diaspora. Until then, he wrote, Jews and Hellenes are duty-bound to come to some arrangement so that they can live together.[56] Only by a combination of logic and ethics, Hermann Cohen wrote in his article, 'The Social Ideal as seen by Plato and the Prophets', can the ideal future be established. The prophets, on the one hand, and Plato on the other,

---

[53] Neumark, 'Hashkafat olam vehashkafat chayim'. Rosenzweig too writes 'A way of looking at life (*Lebensanschauung*) confronts a way of looking at the world (*Weltanschauung*)' (*Star of Redemption*, 11).

[54] Bentwich, *Hellenism*, 358–9.   [55] Delaura, *Hebrew and Hellene*, 73.

[56] Frankel, *Prophecy and Politics*, 269–70.

were regarded as the spiritual mentors of mankind. The Greeks, he stated quite erroneously, were not familiar with the concept of friendship and humanity, and that came into Protestanism through the Book of Psalms. Only through a intermingling of the two can the social ideal be fulfilled.

THE REDEMPTION OF JUDAISM THROUGH GREEKNESS

According to Berdyczewski, the fundamental difference between Judaism and Hellenism lay in the fact that

for the children of Israel one god sufficed in later times, while the Greeks were not even content with numerous gods. To what can this be likened? Someone sacrifices all of his strength, his very life, to constructing one large building, which he beautifies and perfects; he toils only for that and his thoughts are distracted from all else. His friend builds many towers, plants gardens and orchards, bridges and ferries; his strength is dispersed in many directions and in different colours. This is the difference between the children of Israel and the Greeks. The latter toured throughout the land, enjoying life to the full, paying heed to all that lies in the sea and on the land, in the heavens and the earth and all the host of them; whereas the former knew only how to build one tower, one tower without which all else is vanity. Furthermore, it never occurred to them to stand at the peak of that same tower, in order that their eyes might see the broad square and the world that lay at its feet . . .[57]

Judaism shackles man to the commandments given by God, distances him from nature, including his own nature, deprives him of spontaneity and creative vitality, making him weak and debilitated. Needless to say, the radical Berdyczewski preferred the Greek way. The Jewish way led to a 'fundamental misrepresentation' of nature. The Jews alienated themselves from nature and naturalness and out of a sense of individuality built a world that was opposed to natural conditions. All attempts to restore to Jewish life its primal naturalness were to no avail. In any case, it was clear that a national Hebrew cultural revival meant a return to natural life, i.e. the necessity of abolishing the narrow focus and total concentration on one sole element. Berdyczewski underscored the Apollonian character of traditional Judaism and harshly criticized it. In his view, an Apollonian nature is equated with spirituality detached from life and devoid of vitality. His Hellenism tendentiously stressed the Dionysian in order to strengthen the other, dormant, suppressed face of Judaism.

---

[57] Berdyczewski, 'Machshavot', 33–4.

The process of secularization turned Greekness into a positive model
of human existence. The Greek religion—which in the view of most
Jewish observers engendered a relativization of ethics, moral corruption,
and a lack of obligatory social norms; which created gods at man's level
and not above him—was depicted by the Jewish critics of Judaism as a
tolerant religion, which believed in the existence of superhuman powers,
and also in sin and punishment. At the same time, Greece was portrayed
as a culture that did not intervene in all spheres of life and did not seek
totally to swaddle and constrain them, but wished to bestow freedom.
The Greek religion was tolerant and liberal—tolerant of the presence of
other religions, even while flaunting its sense of superiority over them;
liberal because it allowed a diversity of authorities to exist side by side
with it in absolute freedom. Without trying to impose its ideas and laws,
it admitted the legitimacy of multiplicity and variety. Judaism lacks all this,
and this nature of Judaism explains the absence of a Jewish contribution to
scientific and technological development. This is the root of the immanent
conservatism of traditional Jewish society. What Job symbolizes is not
necessarily a moral order based on recognition of the limits of human
intelligence, but rather the passive submission to tyranny, the acceptance
of things at face value. This oppressive nature of Judaism is the deep
source of the feelings of vengeance that Hellenic Europe harbours toward
the Jews, who gave it an enslaving Christianity and robbed it of its Hellenic
freedom! In this Greek mirror, Judaism was reflected as ugly and wretched,
with a miserable past and a future which was no less hapless. The Jew who
wanted to live must be liberated from Judaism and become a Greek—an
Athenian in Jerusalem![58]

The first of the four approaches outlined above represents a position I shall
call 'closed Judaic', which views Judaism as a totally closed and sovereign
metaphysical cultural entity, uncontaminated by any outside influences.
This Judaism has no need of any outside influence, of any Greek traits; it
can create every trait it needs through its inner forces, in keeping with its
original spirit or its own creative genius. The second approach represents
an 'open Judaic' position, which views Jewish culture as dynamic and open
and as a pluralistic historical phenomenon, absorbing influences, living in
coexistence and even symbiosis with the outside world.

In keeping with the tradition of such disputes, the critic of culture
from a closed point of departure cautions, in a tone of cultural despair,
against an excess of negative Western influences on Israeli society, and

[58] Evron, 'Atunah ve'eretz Utz'.

asserts that these influences lead to the decadence of Jewish culture and the creation of a Hellenized Jewish society. His description emphasizes what he regards as expressions of vacuity and superficiality, of distancing from the sources, etc. Needless to say, critics of this type assign to Hebrew culture the mission and aim of restoring the spirit in Hebrew literature, but they fail to observe that by investing *belles-lettres* with educational and cultural content and with a prophetic destiny, they are internalizing the concept of the status of literature expressed by the Haskalah and European Romanticism. The Westerner in this argument rejects the analogy between Hellenization and the acceptance of influences from Greek culture. In any case, he has a positive attitude towards Greek culture; he even believes that the Greek ladder of culture reaches not only to the heights of Olympus but even higher—to the very heavens, and its rungs are definitely worthy of integration into those of Jacob's ladder. The path of the people of Israel towards complete cultural revival ought to lead it up the rungs of both the Greek ladder and Jacob's ladder, and there is no need to fear the negative effects of Greek culture. Even the Sages knew they had nothing to fear from Aphrodite or Orpheus. The buds of Israeli Hebrew art have begun to flower and give off their fragrance. Owing to whom? To Olympus tenfold! So on the one hand, we have classical Greece as a signal of cultural licentiousness, and on the other, an optimistic picture of harmonious, fertile and creative fusion, in a spirit of individuality.[59]

The third approach represents the idea that Judaism can create all the traits of culture that it requires: the 'Hellenic' dimension, which some say has to be revived and incorporated in Jewish culture, already exists within Judaism. In other words, Judaism can produce its own 'Greekness'. The fourth approach has internalized all the criticism of Judaism from the outside and has a pronounced element of Jewish self-hate. It sees Judaism as a one-dimensional, flawed, closed, and doctrinaire entity, which cannot be changed, and must be replaced.

In the next chapter, we shall see how the adherents of the first and second views observed the development of the new Jewish or Hebrew culture—in language, literature, and art—as they gazed into the Greek mirror to discover what modern Jewish culture lacked.

[59] See the debate between Avraham Kariv and Akiva Govrin in Govrin, *Be'ikvei hamesimot*, 322–6.

8

HAVE JEWS IMAGINATION?
JEWS AND THE CREATIVE ARTS

But (urges Apion) we 'have not produced any geniuses, for example,
inventors in arts and crafts . . .'　　JOSEPHUS, *Against Apion*, ii. 135

The Jews never worshipped the Graces.
HENRI BAPTISTE GRÉGOIRE,
Essai sur la régénération physique,
morale et politique des Juifs

The 'external wisdoms' and the fine arts never occupied a central place
in the national life of our people in most time periods.
AHAD HA'AM, 'Al devar otzar hayahadut balashon ha'ivrit'
('On the Treasury of Judaism in the Hebrew Language')

THE METAMORPHOSES OF A 'FABLE CONVENUE'

THE fact that I am devoting a chapter to the question whether Jews have
imagination, namely whether they have the creativity to produce works of
art, may come as a surprise to anyone familiar with the corpus of literary
and artistic work created by Jews, which encompasses works of art and
literature of all types and reveals a vast and copious creative imagination.
In the nineteenth century, a different image prevailed.

In Disraeli's novel *Lothair* (1870), a conversation takes place, in which
one of the characters repeats Ernest Renan's theory: 'Aryan principles . . .
are calculated to maintain the health and beauty of a first-rate race. In a
greater or lesser degree, these conditions obtained from the age of Pericles
to the age of Hadrian in pure Aryan communities, but Semitism began
then to prevail and ultimately triumphed. Semitism has destroyed art; it
taught man to despise his own body.' The hero of the novel responds to
these words by saying that surely the Italian painters, who produced great
works of art, were inspired by Semitism. His interlocutor rejects that line
of defence by replying that Semitism gave these painters subjects, 'but the
Renaissance gave them Aryan art, and it gave that art to a purely Aryan
race. But Semitism rallied in the shape of the Reformation and swept it
away.' Lord Leighton pungently expressed a similar view: 'Polytheism is

the arch-friend, as monotheism is the arch-enemy, of beauty.'[1] Gladstone, we recall, repeated this conventional opinion when he stated that the Jews lacked the capacity for art, science, philosophy, commerce, government, and so on.[2] Similarly, S. H. Butcher stated:

They [the Hebrews] had no art—if we except music—no science, no philosophy, no organized political life, no civic activity, no public spirit. . . . Poetry indeed they had, unique in its kind . . . The epic and the drama in its strict sense, are wanting.[3]

There was also a reverse image, according to which the Jews totally lacked a capacity for abstract thought: the 'true Jew' and the child of the East engaged in concrete, figurative thought. Their thinking is not abstract or methodical, but rather popular, vibrant, vivid in its expressions, riveted on the detail and lacking the power to dress it in abstract terms or theories.[4] However, it was not this notion, but rather its opposite, that became generally accepted, so that even Jewish men of letters adhered to it and sought to rediscover their true nature in its light. All the laudatory words of Josephus and of the Hellenistic Jewish authors, in which the ancient Hebrews were accorded fame as the inventors of culture, were forgotten and availed contemporary Jews not a whit; instead the opposite claims were revived. According to the Emperor Julian, sciences had come

---

[1] Turner, *The Greek Heritage*, 20–2; Hersey, 'Aryanism in Victorian England'; Jenkyns, *The Victorians*, 167. Disraeli, *Lord George Bentinck: A Political Biography*, 496, wrote: 'The Jews represent the Semitic principle: all that is spiritual in nature. They are the trustees of tradition, and the conservators of the religious element. They are a living and the most striking evidence of the falsity of that pernicious doctrine of modern times, the natural equality of man'; cf. Cheyette, *Constructions*, 59.

[2] Turner, *The Greek Heritage*, 169; the full quote is cited in Ch. 2 n. 23. According to Boman, 'the distinction between what the Israelite finds beautiful and what the Greek finds so is characteristic. The Israelite finds the beautiful in that which lives and plays in excitement and rhythm, in charm and grace, but also and particularly in power and authority. It is not form and configuration which mediate the experience of beauty, as for the Greeks, but the sensations of light, colour, voice, sound, tone, smell and taste . . .', *Hebrew Thought*, 87. Cf. W. T. Harris, introduction to Davidson, *The Education of the Greek People*, p. viii: 'The Greeks invented all the potent literary forms—epic, lyric, and dramatic. They transformed architecture and structure into shapes that reveal spiritual freedom. They discovered, in fact, the beautiful in its highest forms as the manifestation of freedom or self-determination. Beside the beautiful, they also found the true, and explored its forms in science and philosophy . . .'.

[3] Butcher, 'Greece and Israel', 13–14. The Greeks, wrote Nietzsche, had an incredibly precise and unerring plastic power of eye ('bei der unglaublich bestimmten und sicheren plastischen Befähigung ihres Auges'), *The Birth of Tragedy*, §2, 38–9. According to Boman, *Hebrew Thought*, 85, 'the Greeks' beauty lies in the plastic and consequently in the tranquil, moderate, and harmonious expression of the intellectual motive'. But Karl Popper reminds us that Greek philosophers, mainly Plato, were not lovers of Greek art and literature (*The Open Society*, 228–9 n. 29). In the tenth book of the *Republic* (600 A) Homer is said not to have produced any dextrous inventions in the crafts or other matters such as Thales and Anarcharsis had done', and in 605/b the poets are bluntly forbidden to enter into any well-governed city.

[4] Heinemann, *The Ways of the Aggadah*, 3.

from Babylon and Egypt and Phoenicia as well as Greece, but the Jews had contributed nothing: there was not a single meritorious general among them; their competence in politics and the learned professions was dismal and barbaric; in medicine they lagged behind the Greeks.

Is their 'wisest' man Solomon at all comparable with Phocyclides or Theognis or Isocrates among the Hellenes? Certainly not. At least, if one were to compare the exhortations of Isocrates with Solomon's proverbs, you would, I am very sure, find that the son of Theodorus is superior to their 'wisest' king.[5]

Centuries later, the French Jansenist, Abbé Henri Baptiste Grégoire (1750–1831), in his *Essai sur la régénération physique, morale et politique des Juifs* (1789), expressed a different view. To be sure, he derides the notion that Jews in the Middle Ages were 'princes of the science of medicine' and believes that there are 'no discoveries that can be imputed to the credit of the Hebrew people throughout the generations'. In the same derisive tone, he rejects the claim that it was the Jews who brought about the revival of the sciences and fine arts in Europe. However, in earlier ages—in the first four or five hundred years after Christ—the Jews had been engaged in all occupations and all arts without being shackled by vain beliefs and a demoralizing lifestyle. Moreover, after the ninth century they had learnt the sciences from the Arabs and quickly become more highly educated than other nations, especially in law and medicine. The cultural dimension had been excised from Jewish life not by any psychological flaw, but by religion with its ridiculous rituals and insipid nonsense that stifled true piety and shackled the intellect. Hence it was clear that a change in the status of the Jews and the 'reform' of Jewish society, its re-education, could rehabilitate Judaism and the Jews, making them an integral part of the new European culture. He believed that religion and religious tradition, rather than any character traits or psychological state, were the impediment to remaking the Jews into a creative cultural nation.[6] On the one hand, Grégoire claimed, the Jews' contribution to general human culture was meagre; the yeshivot in Tiberias, Babylonia, or France contributed nothing, only turning the follies of a deranged imagination into the principles of faith. The Jews had no talents in music, art, or mathematics. On the other hand, a lack of talent is not an innate flaw and

    [5] *Against the Galilaeans*, 178 A–B, 218 C–224 D, trans. Wright, iii. 369, 381–3; cf. Rokéah, *Judaism and Christianity*, 221, 227–8.
    [6] Grégoire, *Essai sur la régénération*, chs. 15, 25. He wrote elsewhere that the Jews are human beings (*hommes*) who can be reborn, be led to morality, and hence to happiness: Grégoire, *Motions en faveur des Juifs* (Paris, 1789), iii, cit. R. Cohen, introduction to Hebrew translation of *Essai*, p. xx.

may be corrected by education, by a change in the conditions of life, in the attitude of the surrounding societies.[7]

There were many who helped to establish and spread this cliché in the nineteenth century. Perhaps the most famous was Ernest Renan. He, possibly more than any of his contemporaries, was responsible for disseminating the stock view that the Semites (Jews and Arabs) were lacking in the capacities necessary for the creation of culture.[8] In the fifth volume of *Histoire du peuple d'Israël*, Renan made his infamous statement that in comparison to the Aryan race, the Semitic race was inferior, devoid of mythology, science, creative arts, philosophy, and civic feeling. The genetic spiritual cause of this fundamental deficiency lay in the nature of the Semitic languages and in the circumstances of their birth and emergence in the monotonous desert.[9] It was there, in his view, that the world-picture of the Semites was formed: 'the desert is monotheistic' (*Le désert est monothéiste*). The desert is characterized by monotony and has none of the diversity and multiplicity that exist in those parts of the world where the Indo-European race was forged; the monotonous natural surroundings imposed a monotonous, inflexible, and unvaried language on the Semites, who as a result lack *curiosité*, *variété*, and *sensibilité*. Philosophical reflections conducted with great intensity within a narrowly focused area inevitably lead to the development of simple ideas. The Semitic tongue, therefore, as the first intellectual manifestation of the Semites, was born as an inflexible language. The essence of mythology lies in the living power of the words, and the Semitic tongues leave no room for the realization of such power. Thus monotheism is a subjective view of nature and its source; it is a 'minimal religion' and is incapable of creating culture.

This theory permeated endless texts, and resurfaced as an irrefutable truth in works of a scientific nature, as well as in ideological tracts. It became not only a popular *topos* but also a conventional wisdom, and an integral part of antisemitic literature. In Richard Wagner's notorious book *Das Judentum in der Musik* (1850), to take only one example, the Jews are devoid of any aesthetic or artistic talent and ability, and cannot produce transcendental works of aesthetic value since they possess no imagination.[10]

---

[7] Nietzsche wrote that Europe would fall like a ripe fruit into the lap of the Jews, once they began to excel in all spheres of European achievements (*Daybreak*, §205, 124–5).

[8] His theory was first developed in *L'Histoire générale et système comparé des langues sémitiques* (1848).

[9] Y. Shavit, '"Semites" and "Aryans"'; Almog, 'The Racial Motif'; cf. Ch. 13. For one Jewish response to Renan see Sulzbach, *Renan und der Judaismus*.

[10] See Chamberlain, *Foundations of the Nineteenth Century*, i. 418. For a catalogue of the claims about Jewish creativity see Leroy-Beaulieu, *Israel among the Nations*, 225–62, on 'Jewish Genius', who maintains that the Jews' inventive faculty is manifested in music, drama, poetry, medicine, mathematics, and

The most important point to stress here is that these anti-Jewish notions were accepted, as we shall see later, by some Jewish writers. Thus the young Dov Ber Borochov (1881–1917), the foremost theoretician of Marxist Zionism, described the immanent trait of the Jewish mind in contrast to the Greek mind. The Jewish mind strives toward strict monism, namely an understanding of phenomena according to one unifying principle; owing to the subjectivism of Jewish creation, the Jews were almost totally incapable of creating epics and drama, and were poor at art and architecture. Their literature is primarily lyric and they lack the talent to write epics and odes. There are very few Jewish artists. They are also weak in mathematics and the natural sciences.[11]

THE ENTRY INTO CULTURE

Already in the Middle Ages, Jews sought to prove that they were not strangers to 'adab (the Arabic equivalent of paideia or humanitas),[12] an aggregate of attributes whose possessor had to be well versed in rhetoric, poetic theory, ethical treatises and aphorisms, 'Greek wisdom', and the like.[13] During the Renaissance, there were some Jewish writers who attempted to introduce to the Christian world with which they came into contact the beauty and vitality of the Torah of Israel, for this was what gave them the full right to be regarded as a 'people of culture' in the countries they inhabited. It is as if the Jews wished to show that no part of general culture was alien to them.[14] The ravenous hunger, the obsessive avidity, for culture in the modern sense that intensified throughout the nineteenth century found support both in the historical past and in the present. Just as in the past, the Jews were a 'nation of culture' in the present as well. They were taking an active and impressive part in the creation of modern European culture. The narrow concept of Jewish culture of the early Haskalah was expanded in the approach of chokhmat Yisrael or Wissenschaft des Judentums ('science of Judaism'), and in fact among the radical maskilim

philology; however, the creative Jew adjusts himself, physically and mentally, to the genius of the surrounding nations: 'it is obvious that the children of Israel no longer possess a national genius' (256). See too Gilman, The Jew's Body, 128–49.

[11] Borochov, 'O charaktere evrejskogo uma'; he was influenced by the 'empiriocriticism' of R. Avenarius (1843–96; author of Der menschliche Weltbegriff, 1891) and Ernst Mach (1835–1916).

[12] On the meaning of 'adab see The Encyclopedia of Islam, i. 175–6; for humanitas as the equivalent of paideia see Aulus Gellius, Attic Nights, xiii. 17. 1 (one-sided, but decisive for the academic use of the term). Another term is asteïsmos, in Latin urbanitas, used of the wit of sophisticated city-dwellers.

[13] Talmage, 'R. Yoseph Kimhi', 316–17.

[14] Bonfil, As by a Mirror, 128; Twersky, 'Maimonides and Eretz Yisrael', 453–4.

in general, into a far broader concept. In it, the Jew was not only a 'man' (*Mensch*) but a 'citizen of the world'; for this purpose, *Wissenschaft des Judentums* turned to Jewish literature—from the Gemara to the nineteenth century—in order to find in it works and fragments relating to astronomy, mathematics, geography, medicine, and so forth. The same held true for the contribution of Jews to the various branches of technology, industry, and trade, such as the art of printing; the science in which modern Jews should be interested was not a particular, Jewish science, not some form of talmudic study, but a science superior to earthly trivialities, that is to say universal. This did not mean the invention of some new discipline, but the nurturing of what previously existed, a continuation of the same activity in a framework common to both Jews and non-Jews. In other words, Jews should take part in all branches of modern science.

To do this, they must free themselves from the closed casuistic and legalistic world of the Talmud and turn to the free world of scientific inquiry. As Leopold Zunz stated in a private conversation: 'Unless we get rid of the Talmud, we can do nothing.'[15] In this sense, he differed from Graetz, who believed that the Talmud did indeed direct Jews' intellectual engagement to a single area, but counted to its credit that it sharpened their minds and strengthened their powers of reasoning, thus preparing them to be men of knowledge and participants in the modern rational world.[16] However, the range of culture was regarded as being confined to written works. When Ahad Ha'am conceived of the idea of a Jewish encyclopaedia (*Otzar hayahadut balashon ha'ivrit*), he stated that since the contribution of Jews to art (and literature too) was limited, it would suffice to write about the general Jewish outlook on these subjects, and about the contribution of Jews to the culture of the nations of the world.

Like Zunz, but from a slightly different perspective, J. L. Gordon believed that enlightenment was one and the same for all men of intelligence. This was a view he shared with Wessely, who two generations earlier had regarded enlightenment as the 'doctrine of man', not identified with any national culture whatsoever but universal in nature. By enlightenment, Gordon meant culture, which he defined as the 'general spiritual property of all peoples', that is, knowledge and reason alike.[17] This implies that Jews can not only contribute to 'general culture' (*Weltkultur*), but can also be an integral part of that culture. Only in the 1880s did this radical secular *maskil* entertain the option of participating in the general culture, not as

[15] Glatzer, *Zunz*, 13–18.
[16] H. Graetz, 'The Correspondence', 219–20.
[17] Quoted in Elkoshi, 'Gordon as a Critic', 482.

a separate national culture. A summary of this prevailing attitude can be found in words written by Kalman Schulman, who depicts with broad brush strokes the contribution by Jews to all branches of Western culture:

Anyone who sees clearly will gaze with astonishment at the rapid ascent of Jews to the heights in modern times in all areas of wisdom and knowledge, in all arts and crafts. This they achieved in just a short while, whereas other peoples did not succeed in attaining such heights even over a period of many hundreds of years. For no sooner did the kings and counts of the land unloose their bonds and favour them with civil rights and laws, than they opened their treasuries and displayed the precious qualities and fine talents that had lain dormant in their souls during the dark years when they were persecuted by their foes, who gave them no respite until they devoured them.

Before many days passed, there arose proudly from their midst great poets, wondrous rhetoricians, lauded authors in all the finest tongues of Europe, great philosophers and scholars in all realms, renowned mathematicians and engineers, astronomers, chronologists, men well versed in religion and law, and knowledge-able in all branches of the natural sciences, famous physicians, psalmists, musicians, diplomats, sculptors, visionaries. And there is no wisdom, art, or craftsmanship in which the Jews did not engage and become famous in the land for their prowess.[18]

However, throughout the entire nineteenth century, particularly in the second half of that century, the attitude towards the great cultural world that opened up to the *maskil* and to Jewish students was ambivalent. On the one hand the Jewish *maskil*, having discovered that he was, in the words of Lilienblum, a 'wild Asian within cultured Europe' and wishing to be a part of it, was stirred by the world of culture and enlightenment and envious of the cultured nations of the globe. This strong desire turned him, in Lilienblum's metaphorical language, into 'a bird flitting from book to book, anything that I chance upon, and I will learn and read much'. On the other hand, he wished to prove to the Gentiles that the Jews had their own cultural treasures. These attitudes were to a great extent a response to the prevailing mood and opinions.

And indeed, Jewish *maskilim* and men of letters in the nineteenth century argued that from the time they threw off their bonds and the doors of Europe's culture were opened wide to them, there was no area in which Jews did not participate actively, creating, contributing, and even leading. The inevitable conclusion is that the Jews are not by their nature locked into the close confines of theology and casuistry, a claim frequently levelled at them. They have the capacity to engage in any occupation and every creative and inventive art. These views represented an emphatic apologia

---

[18] Schulman, *Divrei yemei olam*, iv. 13–16.

addressed to the European society and its image of Judaism. No less than that, it was an attempt to bypass the normative tradition, to challenge it, and to point to the multifaceted nature of Judaism as a culture. Indeed, in the nineteenth century this tendency no longer represented the apologetics and ideology of a narrow circle, but became a general cultural trend.

Zunz assigned a central role in Jewish culture to the works of non-halakhic literature. He discovered in Jewish culture a multiplicity of forms, but always subject to a general fundamental law, dependent on religion and history, and developing organically. The entry of Jews into Western culture was thus a rediscovery of the vast cultural potential inherent in the Jews. Culture was the Jew's visiting-card and entrance-ticket into Western culture. To make use of it, it was first necessary to reconstruct the entire scope of Jewish culture, and at the same time to establish what singled it out from the surrounding cultures and endowed it with a Jewish character.[19]

Consequently, from the dawn of the nineteenth century, Jews who faced the problem of identifying their culture began to comb the Jewish intellectual and literary tradition in search of dramas and tragedies, satire and legends, lyrics and choral poetry, epics and folk songs, unique Hebrew poetics, and the like. They began to reread Jewish literature according to Hellenic criteria. They began to discover and publish long-forgotten works, to prove that Jews did indeed have a capacity for inventiveness and imagination, and lacked none of the qualities required for the creation of culture—not only literature and philosophy, but also music, science, and the plastic arts.

The revolution here was a dual one: for the first time, Judaism was defined as a culture, and for the first time it had to clarify what aggregate of constituents made up this culture, what gave each of them a Jewish nature, and what determined the singular character of this whole cultural system as a distinctly Jewish culture. As we shall see,[20] this would become the key issue of the new Jewish nationalism that found in culture both its legitimation and its concrete content. It is important to bear in mind that such a concept was unthinkable before the eighteenth century, for the systematic grouping of all the arts into one unity, organized according to the same internal rules, was a product of that century; at first it was conceived as having a universal content, but Romanticism held that each nation grouped the arts together according to principles derived from its

---

[19] See in Mendes-Flohr, *Modern Jewish Studies*, 81–5; Wieseltier, 'Etwas über die jüdische Historik'. German Jewish Orthodoxy saw nothing wrong with participating in German culture but very few Orthodox Jews were involved in German cultural creation. See M. Breuer, *Jüdische Orthodoxie*, 137–90. See also Volkov, 'Soziale Ursachen des jüdischen Erfolgs in der Wissenschaft'.

[20] See Ch. 16.

own national genius and inner life (*Innerlichkeit*) in its specific historical context. The aim was to combine all the arts into one unity and to reveal the underlying principle that creates them and makes them coherent. Hence in the nineteenth century, intellectual and scholarly endeavours were directed towards revealing the existence of most constituents of culture in Jewish history. The purpose of cultural works was, among other things, to demonstrate the existence of the Jews' creative capacity and to prove that they possessed the ability to create a culture, exceptional and original in nature. We shall trace the principal constituents of this culture and the mental capacities that create it.

THE DISCOVERY OF BEAUTY AND IMAGINATION

In the Middle Ages the terms *imago, figura, aenigma*, denoted literary quality and a figurative expression in contrast to the 'real thing' (*ipsa species veritatis*). Imagination was said to give rise to *figura et imago*, a literary type describing future things or engaging in allegorization and conveying inner understanding.[21] 'Imagination provides soul', a picture that illustrates things vividly. In Ramhal's *Sefer leshon limudim* ('Treatise on Rhetorics', 1727), imagination (*dimyon*) is understood as *comparatio*, and divided into such subtypes as metaphor, catachresis, synecdoche, and antonomasia; he was afterwards followed by Solomon Loewisohn (Shlomo Levinssohn, 1798–1821).[22] In the nineteenth century, imagination, or the inventive and creative faculty, was regarded as one of the essential active faculties of the mind, which gives meaning to existing things and creates new ones. Its absence among the Jews or in Judaism was considered a serious deficiency. Jewish apologists ventured forth to search for it and to prove that it existed.

The *maskilim*, and after them the proponents of the *Wissenschaft des Judentums*, strove to represent the people of Israel as a reasonable, rational people, and Judaism as 'the religion of intelligence'. At the same time, they indignantly denied the allegation that the Jews are devoid of a sense

[21] Kamin, 'The Polemics against Allegory'. According to Maimonides, God speaks through the imagination of the prophets ('I spoke to the prophets, it was I who multiplied visions, and through the prophets gave parables' Hosea 12: 10). According to Thomas Aquinas, the Bible uses metaphors and parables in the language of the imagination, but the prophecy of Moses is truth that is seen without the 'vision of the imagination'. See Harvey, 'Maimonides and Aquinas'.

[22] See T. Cohen, *The Melitsat Yeshurun of Shlomo Levinsohn*, 167–227. Levinsohn writes that the imagination and the parable are marked by *Gleichnis* ('similarity'), 'parallel' (*comparatio*). One of the necessary qualities for artistic work is the onslaught of the imaginative faculty (*stürmische Phantasie*). Shadal defined *mashal* as a method used by the Sages of antiquity because it suggested a similarity between disparate things; and when there was no real resemblance, they employed a fictitious one, an 'imaginary *mashal*' ('Perush leShemot 15', 183–4).

of beauty, i.e. aesthetics. Unlike writers of later generations under the influence of Romanticism, the first *maskilim* did not try to uncover in Judaism vital levels of folklore, and certainly did not look for mysticism or magic. So far as they were concerned, the realm of the imagination was limited and well demarcated; their interpretation of imagination was tempered and qualified. Unquestionably, mythology, as an extreme expression of imagination, they totally spurned. Hence they placed an emphasis on rationalistic moral and didactic literature. The German *Aufklärung*, and in particular the *Philantrophinum* school that dominated pedagogical theory in the late eighteenth century,[23] viewed imagination as a profuse, overflowing force, a-normative by nature, destructive, and frequently dangerous. They described mythology, the product of imagination in the salad days of culture, as idle foolishness that corrupts the mind, especially the tender mind.[24] From a more complex point of view, the imagination was conceived as one of the fundamental faculties of the mind: feeling (*Empfindung*), imagination (*Einbildungskraft*), and reason (*Verstand*), of which imagination characterized culture's youthful days.[25] It meant 'thinking in pictures'. The language of the imagination is the language of symbols, poetry, and metaphor. When it is unrestrained, and does not submit to any laws, the imagination may become like a *golem*, turning on its creators. If this is the case, then a sense of beauty (or a sensitivity to beauty) differs from the imagination since it is restrained by rules. Aesthetics is manifested in perfection.

But what is perfection and what is 'perfect beauty', and what is the dynamics of the mind that creates perfection?

The philosophy of aesthetics in the eighteenth century and that of the early Jewish *maskilim* centred on this issue. What is the nature of the poet and the artist who is endowed with creative genius? What is the nature of the imagination that moves him and is moved by him? How can one unravel the secret of creation? What turns a poet into a man drawing near to the secrets of the Creation? Beauty served as a mirror in which to examine what was lacking in Jewish existence, and at the same time as a yardstick with which to measure the acts of God in the world and man's works of art, through which he becomes close to God, by also producing perfect things. The majority of the intellectuals and the German *Aufklärer* of the eighteenth century regarded imagination as a faculty capable of revealing non-existent worlds. However, they rejected the possibility of

---

[23] Doderer, *Lexikon der Kinder- und Jugendliteratur*, iii. 42–4.

[24] Brüggemann, 'Zur Rezeption antiker Mythologie'; Dahl, *Entstehung*; Ewers, *Kindheit als poetische Daseinsform*.

[25] Reill, *The German Enlightenment*, 59–65; Gay, *The Science of Freedom*, 208–15.

art without rules and laws, seeking instead, as J. J. Bodmer put it, one that is not 'wild' and lacking in rules but self-restrained ('eine Imagination, die sich wohl kultiviert hat').[26]

The literature of the Haskalah from its outset is rife with criticism of traditional Jewish society, which in its view lacks an aesthetic sense and a correct attitude towards nature. Longing for a revitalization of the 'sense of beauty' is a central motif in the young Mendelssohn's *Kohelet musar* (1755);[27] he connected 'ethics' and 'beauty' as two types of perfection in presenting a philosophical discussion of the essence of aesthetic pleasure and the nature of 'the spiritual training a person requires in order to appreciate artistic beauty'.[28] Influenced by the aesthetic conceptions of Leibniz, A. F. Wolf, and Shaftesbury, Mendelssohn regarded pleasure as the result of observing perfection; in turn, perfection and a true comprehension of perfection are the fruit of knowledge and prior understanding. Only someone with a prior understanding of architecture can gain pleasure from the beauty of a palace and the harmony reigning between the rules, their implementation, and the final result. Perfection is also the basis for faith in the divine act of Creation, which produced a complex, whole, and harmonious world.

The creation of the world, wrote Solomon Loewisohn, is also a realization of beauty: 'Beauty is the chosen one of the Almighty.' In order to marvel at it, one must observe it closely, not distractedly or fleetingly. Loewisohn wrote: 'And God commanded the void, that is Earth, and to the chaos He said: Let there be, and charged the world to be filled with beauty.'[29] Following Bishop Lowth, he adapts the so-called Longinus' citation of Gen. 1: 3 (the only quotation from Scripture in classical literature), 'the lawgiver of the Jews, no ordinary man, . . . gave suitable expression to the divine power when he wrote "Let there be light"' (Longinus, *On the Sublime*, 9. 9); but his purpose is at once to demonstrate the advantage derived by Hebrew from its brevity and lofty expression—for since God rules the mind of man, only the Sublime (*das Erhabene*) can convey man's astonishment and wonder (*das Staunen and die Verwunderung*)—and to proclaim his radical conception that God created beauty.

Indeed, for Loewisohn beauty is one of the great manifestations of

---

[26] *Die Discourse der Mahlern*, i, beginning of Discours XIX, cit. Reill, *The German Enlightenment*, 61–2; on Johan Jacob Bodmer (1698–1783) ibid. 199–212. Cf. Blackall, *The Emergence of German*, 276. Perfection is a harmony between the 'inner world' and the 'outer world'.

[27] Gilon, *Mendelssohn's Kohelet musar*.

[28] Ibid.; Michael A. Meyer, *Response to Modernity*, 16–18.

[29] T. Cohen, *The Melitsat Yeshurun of Shlomo Levinsohn*, 115; M. Schwarcz, 'The Poetry of the "Sublime"'.

God's Creation. This was a sharp deviation from the well-known words of R. Shimon: 'He who is going along the way and repeating [his Torah tradition] but interrupts his repetition and says, "How beautiful is that tree! How beautiful is that ploughed field!"—Scripture reckons it to him as if he has become liable for his life' (*Mishnah Avot*, 3: 7). Isaiah had emphasized the uniqueness of the Creator and his utter superiority of His creation (40: 12–17):

Who hath measured the waters in the hollow of his hand, and meted out heaven with the span, and comprehended the dust of the earth in a measure, and weighed the mountains in scales, and the hills in a balance? Who hath directed the Spirit of the LORD, or being his counseller hath taught him? With whom took he counsel, and who instructed him, and taught him in the path of judgment, and taught him knowledge, and shewed to him the way of understanding? Behold, the nations are as a drop of a bucket, and are counted as the small dust of the balance: behold, he taketh up the isles as a very little thing. And Lebanon is not sufficient to burn, nor the beasts thereof sufficient for a burnt offering. All nations before him are as nothing; and they are counted to him less than nothing, and vanity.

Philo had likened God to the architect who builts a city according to a plan existing only in his mind (*De opificio Dei*, 17–20); however, in Mendelssohn's conception this image also legitimated man's appreciating the beauty of the divine architect's entire creation (*das Ganze, das Weltgebäude*). He wrote of 'heavenly delight' (*himmlische Wollust*) and 'intoxicating rapture' (*betäubende Entzückung*); in contrast to R. Shimon, he urges on the Jew contemplation (*Betrachtung*) and admiration of the universe's aesthetic qualities: its beauty and perfection and magnificence. God, then, is the architect of the world (*Weltbaumeister*), and the universe is the building of the world (*Weltgebäude*). A feeling for beauty, which arises from observing it even without an understanding of its logic and its laws, is the key to happiness. That same happiness is also the final aim of moral and social behaviour: the world is a complete and hierarchical system of creation, ascending from the 'inferior' to man looking 'up to the heavens . . . marvelling at the language of the creatures standing above him . . . Tell me, have you ever known greater joy than the joy of this sight?'[30]

In the same spirit, Alexander von Humboldt (1769–1859) wrote in his influential book *Kosmos* (1845–62), part of which was translated into Hebrew (Warsaw, 1859): 'One might say that in the 104th Psalm alone the

---

[30] See the description of God as an architect in Philo, *De opificio mundi*, 17–20 (trans. Whitaker, i. 15–19; Wolfson, *Philo*, i. 243). See Gilon, *Mendelssohn's Kohelet musar*, 55–74. My intention is not to examine Mendelssohn's theory of asthetics but to note that his conception is far from the traditional Jewish view.

picture of the entire cosmos is represented.' According to this approach, in the world outlook of monotheism nature is always something created. The psalm to which Humboldt refers describes God as the creator of the world and the One who established the system of creation down to its minutest details. Humboldt, like Herder and Loewisohn, believed that the attitude to the world revealed by the Psalmist is an attitude of veneration and astonishment filled with longing;[31] he cites as a proof-text Ps. 104: 24: 'O Lord, how manifold are thy works! in wisdom hast thou made them all: the earth is full of thy riches.'

If so, what is the creative faculty of the mind that induces comprehension and pleasure, and what is the connection between classical aesthetics and the irrational and riotous imagination? According to Reill, 'the outstanding problem for eighteenth-century aesthetics became that of irrationality'.[32] This question led contemporary thinkers to explore the nature of feeling and the character of judgement, the process of creation, and the phenomenology of the spirit, the light as well as the dark side of consciousness. In this matter, the Jewish Enlightenment lagged behind; in the main, it searched for 'Jewish classicism' and not for Jewish Romanticism. The imagination, in the view of the Haskalah, is legitimate only as a creative faculty that produces images, which the author of parables uses to stir the mind and soul; it is the capacity of figuration, the skill that endows abstract matters with 'physical forms and pictures'. Hence it is of rhetorical value in the process of education. Nevertheless, imagination of this sort belongs to the age of childhood, including that of the people of Israel, because children need pictures. However, the Jews were delivered of the need when they came of age and crystallized their faith according to abstract concepts, becoming the possessors of a rational Torah. According to S. J. Fuenn (1818–90), in his *Divrei hayamim livnei Yisrael* ('The Chronicles of the Children of Israel', 1893),[33] imagination is typical of childhood (*Kindersinn*), hence before the Return to Zion the soul of the people was 'dominated by the imagination and concrete pictures', of which later there was no need.[34] It is clear from this that an abstract conception and understanding of the Divinity is a mark of progress and closer to the truth.

---

[31] Humboldt, *Kosmos*, ii. 28–30, cit. Low, *Jews in the Eyes of the Germans*, 288.

[32] Reill, *The German Enlightenment*, 59.

[33] See Feiner's introduction to *Fuenn: From Militant to Conservative Maskil*, 1–47.

[34] Fuenn, *Divrei hayamim*, 15–16; cf. Reill 65–8. This was already a cliché: Buno stated in the preface to his *Bilderbibel* that 'Kinder haben fürnehmlich an Bildern ihr Gefallen. Daher der allweise Gott dem Kindern Israel, dieweill sie in Erkenntnis der Geheimnisse Gottes in etwa noch Kinder waren, durch das Levitische Priestertum und die Opfer die göttlichen Geheimnisse in diesen Bildern gleichsahm vor Augen stellt.' Similar notions had been expressed by Luther and Calvin; cf. Maimonides, *The Guide*, 247–9.

We have seen that Schulman's pretext for briefly introducing the elements of Greek mythology to his readers was that the intelligent Hebrew reader ought to be acquainted with the faith of the Gentiles, so that he might better understand the superiority of the true Torah. Israel Rall suggested a totally different explanation. Ignoring Wessely's warning of 1783, some eighty years later he translated classical literature with a mythological content into Hebrew. He also, of course, justified his act by saying he was presenting the ancient source of modern materialistic heresy, but he found an additional value in classical poetry:

I have one other thing to say to you! You may be among those who think that in this sorry age there is no need for rhetoric and poetry, for their time has already passed, and this generation has need of nothing but erudition and naturalism. If you really and truly think that, you err; for the soul of man has many faculties, and the most distinguished of these is the intelligence.[35]

Rall could, for example, have cited sources in the Talmud that permit Jews to read Homer, but he did not consider Homer's writings to be a trivial diversion with no other merit than entertainment. As support for his claims, he cited none other than Henry Thomas Buckle, who wrote about the opposition and reconciliation between 'intelligence' and 'imagination' (or 'understanding' and 'emotion'). Rall paraphrased Buckle's words (based on the Russian translation):

The intelligence and the imagination both require food and sustenance, and if you feed only one faculty and starve the other, you will remain deficient and disabled throughout your life, for the essence of perfection is the harmony between all the faculties, so that none harms the other, but they all help one another. Hence they who wish to erase all traces of rhetoric—the food of the imagination—from literature are ignorant, for that will never happen as long as man lives on this globe, unless human nature itself is changed.[36]

The imagination, or poetry, according to Buckle, has 'an insight into the turn and aspect of things which if properly used would make it the ally of science instead of the enemy'. Poetry is not simply the product of capricious imagination, since it obeys fixed laws of order and logic. The man of science who despises poetry has 'only half his weapons; his arsenal is unfilled'. In this way, the imagination gained two types of legitimacy: on one view it was a faculty that activated the emotion, deepened knowledge of the wondrous act of creation, and kindled faith; on the other it was an essential faculty that activated and spurred on reason and understanding.

[35] In Rall's introduction to *Shirei romi*, 3–10.
[36] Rall, *Roman Poetry*, 9–10; Buckle, *Introduction to the History of Civilization*, 846.

This second legitimation was needed since the objection to imagination also arose from so-called realistic considerations: although visionary books (novels) were important and their absence was felt, they would not bring about a real change in Jewish existence; moreover, 'fantasies of the heavens' might provide hollow consolation and escapism, but the natural and social sciences and realistic literature were the source of true enlightenment.[37]

THE HEBREW LANGUAGE AND THE GREEK

> To th'Hebrew tongue, how-ever *Greece* do grudge
> The sacred right of eldership, I judge.
>   SYLVESTER, 'Babilon', 407–8

Language is the tongue of imagination; it is the source of myth and reflects the soul and culture of a people. This was the position taken by the Haskalah even before the age of Romanticism. The *maskilim* regarded Hebrew as an invaluable key to the treasures of the past and one of the most important capacities of a nation of culture;[38] they wished to demonstrate that Hebrew as a classical language is not inferior in its qualities to Greek. They were able to find that the statements of Hebrew grammarians and philosophers regarding its nature, and the value of linguistic purity,[39] exactly corresponded with those of eighteenth- and nineteenth-century philosophers of language. Mendelssohn described the Hebrew language and biblical poetry as possessed of the ability to express the entire gamut of man's emotions: sorrow, joy, anger, etc. In other words, 'Classical Hebrew can serve as a medium of expression in modern times as well.'[40] In this sense, Mendelssohn was following in the footsteps of Thomas Blackwell, whose book on Homer had an important impact on the German Enlightenment in the eighteenth century; Mendelssohn ascribed the same qualities to Hebrew as Blackwell did to Greek. Blackwell characterized the traits of the Greek language by saying that it 'was brought to express all the best and bravest of the human feelings and retained a sufficient quantity

---

[37] Werses, 'The Relationship between Literature and the Study of Judaism', 13–36; U. Shavit, *Poetry and Ideology*, 11–55.

[38] Tsamiriyon, *Hame'asef*, 72–90; Y. Shavit, 'A Duty too Heavy to Bear'; Pelli, *The Age of Haskalah*, 73–90.

[39] Maimonides observed that in the Diaspora Hebrew became mixed with other languages (Twersky, 'Maimonides and Eretz Yisrael', 368–71). Some medieval Jewish grammarians were strong purists who regarded biblical Hebrew as the only 'pure Hebrew' (Talmage, 'R. Joseph Kimhi', 321–3).

[40] Altmann, *Mendelssohn*, 88; Rawidowicz, 'Mendelssohn's Translation of the Book of Psalms', 285. On the debate between Hamman and Mendelssohn on the philosophy of language, see Z. Levy, *Judaism in the World View*, 70–8, and on Herder's philosophy of language, ibid. 100–11; see too Levinsohn, *Te'udah beYisrael*, 58.

of its original, amazing, metaphoric tincture'.[41] (He noted that both in Greece and in the land of Israel poetry was considered a divine gift.)

Nearly a century before Renan, and about two decades after Blackwell, Robert Lowth (1710–88), bishop of London, expressed in his *De Sacra Poesi Hebraeorum* of 1753, later published in English as *Lectures on the Sacred Poetry of the Hebrews* (1787), the view that 'Greek beyond every other language . . . is copious, flowing, and harmonious, possessed of a great variety of measures, of which the impression is so definite, the effects so striking . . .'. Hebrew, on the other hand, he described by saying 'its form is simple above every other; the radical words are uniform and resemble each other almost exactly . . . nor [is it] capable of much variety; but rather simple, grave, temperate'. Lowth, whom the renowned German orientalist and biblical scholar Johann David Michaelis (1717–91) termed an 'Oriental Orpheus', attempted to decipher the essence of biblical poetry, as well as the disparate nature of Greek and Hebrew. Like Blackwell he believed that language is the 'conveyance of our thoughts', and hence is the result and reflection of the psychological state of the speaking individual or group and of the natural environment that produces poetic language and its world of images.[42]

In his *Kohelet musar*, Mendelssohn stated that Hebrew is suitable for the translation of poetry but not fit for scientific works. Wessely relegated secular studies to the province of European tongues; whereas *Hame'asef*, the organ of the Berlin Haskalah, demanded that the sciences that were being 'renewed every day, at every hour, at every moment' should also be attired in Hebrew garb, and every effort made to propose Hebrew terminologies for the various fields of knowledge. The *Wissenschaft des Judentums*, on the other hand, argued just the contrary: Hebrew not only was hardly fitting for scientific matters, but was unquestionably no longer suitable to be a language of literature and poetry.[43] This trend continued throughout the nineteenth century. Notwithstanding the revival of Hebrew in that century, Ernest Renan could still write:

The roots in this family of languages are, if I may say so, realistic and non-transparent; they did not lend themselves to metaphysics or mythology. The

---

[41] Blackwell, *An Inquiry*, 46–7; Reill, *The German Enlightenment*, 203–6.

[42] Robert Lowth, *Lectures on Sacred Poetry*, 70–1. See Freimarch's introduction to the Olms edn. (1969), pp. v–xxxvi. On Lowth see B. Feldman and Richardson, *The Rise of Modern Mythology*, 144–6; Olender, *The Languages of Paradise*, 28–31. Turgot wrote that the Greeks were the first to develop a language made for progress: 'it was euphonious, rich and varied' (Gay, *The Science of Freedom*, 110–11; T. Cohen, *The Melitsat Yeshurun of Shlomo Levinsohn*, 32). The Sages believed that the Greek language fits poetry; see the first motto to Ch. 5.

[43] The same debate took place among German scholars and men of letters. See Blackall, *The Emergence of German*.

difficulty of explaining in Hebrew the simplest philosophical notions in the Book of Job and in Ecclesiastes is something quite astonishing . . . One fails to imagine what Homer or Hesiod would be like if translated into Hebrew.[44]

Many of the German Jewish scholars regarded Hebrew as a dead language like Latin and Greek, and therefore they did not believe in the revival of Hebrew literature. At the very most, they thought, Hebrew could be written according to the classical models, but that would not be true poetry. Hebrew literature had to contend with the different linguistic models it had internalized: the demand for 'linguistic realism' and the claim that since it is an Oriental tongue, stylistic embellishments are an indivisible part of its nature. Insofar as its ability to be a modern language of culture was concerned, Hebrew was not compared with the classical tongues but with various modern languages. The idea that Hebrew is a deficient tongue became a widespread notion:

We all know that for the time being our language is only half a language and lacks several terms and expressions, without which there is no hope that our literature can attain the status of a living and general literature, lacking in nothing.[45]

With these words Ahad Ha'am repeated Renan's claims, despite the revival of Hebrew as a written language of culture. Indeed, he quoted Renan's statement: 'The greatest blunder which this race has made (for it was the most irreparable) was to adopt, in treating the verb, a mechanism so petty that the expression of the tenses and moods has always been imperfect and cumbersome.' Ahad Ha'am believed that the Jews were struggling with the poverty of the language, a deficiency that hampered their ability to translate the multifariousness of the surrounding world into Hebrew. He was referring to scientific subjects, particularly philosophy, and not to poetry.

How far removed Ahad Ha'am was in his views from the optimism of Isaac Baer Levinsohn! Hebrew, Levinsohn wrote in 1829, is not only the epitome of the best qualities of all tongues, it is the language in which were written

all vision and prophecy, the secrets of the Almighty and the covenant of Sinai, adages of wisdom, rhetoric and poetry, ethics and knowledge, riddles, parables, studies of divinity, destinies and recompense, lamentations and consolations, fervent hopes for a return to strength and for the ends of days . . .

---

[44] Renan, *History of the People of Israel*, i. 41.

[45] Ahad Ha'am, 'Halashon vedikdukah': 'Anyone whose thinking has been accustomed to the structure and usage of the European languages, in which one can express a multitude of pictures by making slight changes in the word, will feel at every turn the paucity of Hebrew.'

Hebrew is thus a language in which all types of works were written and the entire range of human experience was expressed: poetry and law, philosophy and eschatology. In other words, Hebrew is a total language and not one that fills only a partial function. For it is, as J. G. Hamann (1730–88) the German mystical philosopher, claimed, the very language of revelation.[46]

Chayim Nachman Bialik (1873–1934), the Hebrew national poet, may stand as the best example of how deeply the conventional wisdom that Hebrew lacked the flexibility needed for poetry was internalized into nineteenth-century Hebrew literature. In a talk on 'Young Hebrew Literature', Bialik asserted that the peoples of the Semitic family, in contrast to those of the Aryan, were not distinguished by their skills in the plastic arts, such as sculpture and oil-painting, but excelled rather in mosaics and arabesque. This is because the Semitic world-picture had clear boundaries, which were expressed in the distinct transition from one square to another and from one verse to another. In Aryan art, on the other hand, the areas were blurred with no sharp transitions of light and shadow. Bialik drew a contrived analogy between Aryan art and Aryan languages, on the one hand, and Semitic art and Semitic languages on the other:

The difference in these traits, between the Aryan family and the Semitic family, does not rest only in the art of painting, but in all the spheres of national creation of each of them. In this sense, their languages also differ. In the Aryan tongues, for example, one can give one verb many meanings by adding letters to it as suffixes. This flexibility of language is akin to the flexibility of colours, from which one can engender stories upon stories upon stories; in the Semitic tongues this is impossible, and instead of one verb with different affixes, one must use different and specific verbs, like the different small bits of colour inlaid in a square.[47]

PINDAR AND DAVID: THE DISCOVERY OF HEBREW POETRY AND PROSE

If so, can a Hebrew poet compose 'Greek poetry'? Can the Hebrew language produce 'Greek songs'?

As the epigraph to his story 'La Busca de Averroes' ('Averroes' Search') in *El Aleph* (1949), concerning the Islamic philosopher who was the most

[46] Levinsohn, *Te'udah beYisrael*, 16–20. See Harshav, 'Essay on the Revival of the Hebrew Language'; Z. Levy, *Judaism in the World View*, 70–8; Blackall, *The Emergence of German*, ch. 9. On Hebrew as the language of Eden see the excellent study of David S. Katz, *Philo-Semitism*. In a book on the study of language, Ramhal states that Hebrew is the first language and split into other languages; evidence of this is the fact that it is the only one called a 'sacred tongue'.

[47] 'Al hasifrut ha'ivrit hatze'irah', 11–14.

important translator and commentator of Aristotle in the Middle Ages (1126–98), Jorge Luis Borges quotes a statement by Ernest Renan (in his *Averroès et l'averroïsme*, 1852) that Averroes 'imagined that the tragedy was nothing other than the lavishing of praises . . .'. Averroes was unable to understand the real meaning of 'Tragedy' and to distinguish between it and 'Comedy'. The much-admired Muslim philosopher encounters a thorny problem on reading Aristotle's *Poetics*: 'Two doubtful words had halted him at the beginning of the *Poetics*: these words were *tragedy* and *comedy*.' After puzzling over the matter a great deal, he wrote, in a flash of inspiration, 'Aristu (Aristotle) gives the name of tragedy to panegyrics and that of comedy to satires and anathemas. Admirable tragedies and comedies abound in the pages of the Koran and in the *mohalacas* of the sanctuary.' In his closing paragraph, Borges relates: 'I remembered Averroes, who, closed within the orb of Islam, could never know the meaning of the terms *tragedy* and *comedy*.'[48]

In 1790, the author of an article about Greek history in *Hame'asef* encountered some difficulty in describing the Olympic Games. In frustration he wrote that he would have liked to depict all the 'amusements of the Greeks' in detail, but was unable to do so since Hebrew lacked the necessary words and it was hard to invent new ones. He, of course, knew the meaning of tragedy and comedy but felt frustrated because his Hebrew lacked many other terms.[49]

But the real question was not whether Hebrew tradition lacks the proper terms, but primarily whether it has the faculty to create tragedies and

---

[48] Borges, *Labyrinths*, 180–8; the *mohalacas* of the sanctuary are the great pre-Islamic odes, called *al-muʿallaqāt*, 'the suspended (odes)', allegedly because they had originally been prize-poems displayed in the sanctuary of the Kaʿba at Mecca. Some Hebrew literary critics have stated that tragedy is foreign to the Jewish spirit because the belief in a divine providence and in the End of Days is antithetical to a world in which the gods rule arbitrarily and men have no freedom of choice. Similar things have been said about the incompatibility of Christianity with tragedy: they are disproved by Tirso de Molina's play (though the authorship has been doubted) *El condenado por desconfiado*, 'Damned for Despair', in which the central figure, an otherwise virtuous man, cannot bring himself to believe he can be saved, and therefore, refusing to repent of his despair, is damned to hell, which of course is the ultimate evil for the Christian, not death. (Contrast Calderón's *El mágico prodigioso*, in which the Roman Catholic insistence on free will ruins the Faust theme when the sorcerer releases himself from his contract by repentance on the point of death; in Tirso, the central figure could have done so too, but is prevented by the tragic flaw in his character—an outcome far closer to Greek tragedy than the inhuman Fate of the German *Schicksalstragödie*.)

[49] Compare Cicero's words: 'A number of people who had enjoyed a Greek education could not share what they had learnt with their fellow citizens because they did not feel confident that what they had learnt from the Greeks could be expressed in Latin. But we now seem to have made such progress in the matter that not even in vocabulary are we surpassed by the Greeks' (*De natura deorum*, i. 8, trans. after McGregor).

comedies, epics and novels. Can a Jew write Hebrew comedy and tragedy? Do Hebrew literature and Greek literature speak in the same language?

If Mendelssohn's intent in translating the Book of Psalms was to prove that Hebrew—like Greek—had marvellous lyric poetry, occupying a place at the zenith of classical poetry, then Solomon Loewisohn's aim was to underscore the deep-seated contrast between Greek poetry and biblical poetry. Typically, when he proceeded to define biblical poetics, in his book *Melitzat Yeshurun* ('The Poesy of Jeshurun', 1816), he found the desired characterization in Greek poetics itself! In other words, he used terms borrowed from the world of classical poetics and rhetoric to show that biblical poetics surpassed Greek poetics. Loewisohn's major inspiration came from Bishop Lowth's book, which acquired its stature largely through the enthusiastic appraisal of Michaelis. The interest in biblical poetry went hand in hand with the great attention paid to Homeric poetics at the time, as a further development of the analogy drawn between Greek and Hebrew. Loewisohn derived from the supposed Longinus the doctrine of the sublime, in this way bringing biblical poetry closer to the Romantic category.[50] The epigraph of his book exemplifies his approach: 'Est Deus in nobis: agitante calescimus illo' (Ovid, *Fasti*, v. 5: 'A god's in us; his stirring makes us warm').

Earlier, Judah Messer Leon had attempted to base biblical rhetoric on the rules of Aristotle, Cicero, and Quintilian in his *Sefer nofet tzufim* (1475), and Ramhal had anticipated Solomon Loewisohn in applying the rules of classical rhetoric to biblical poetry in his *Sefer leshon limudim* (1724).[51] Loewisohn, however, spurned the criterion of classical beauty, preferring that of the sublime, which sets a goal for poetry—to stir the mind and to arouse wonderment at the sublime. Ever since Boileau's translation of 'Longinus' in 1674, the sublime had become a cliché, with increasing emphasis on the liberation that it brought from the normal rules of art; the opposition of sublimity to beauty was famously expounded by Edmund Burke in *A Philosophical Enquiry into the Origin of our Ideas of the Sublime and Beautiful* (1757). Loewisohn—a well-read scholar and master of several languages—does not cite his sources, but quite a few statements are taken directly from Burke. As we shall see, from this concept the argument developed that all types of Hebrew art took shape according to an identical

---

[50] This critical and aesthetic term is taken from the Greek treatise *Peri hupsous* (in Latin *De sublimitate*) of unknown authorship, formerly ascribed to the rhetorician Cassius Longinus (3rd c. AD). See *Longinus*, trans. Dorsch, 25–6; *New Princeton Encyclopedia of Poetry and Poetics*, 1230–3; T. Cohen, *The Melitsat Yeshurun of Shlomo Levinsohn*, 115; M. Schwarcz, 'The Poetry of the "Sublime"'.

[51] See David, *Moshe Chayim Luzzatto's Theory of Rhetoric and Poetry*. It should be noted that Hebrew writers do not make a sharp distinction between poetics and rhetoric.

principle: the sublime or the monumental. Loewisohn found evidence of the sublime in various books of the Bible, in the Book of Psalms as well as in the Prophets and the wisdom literature (Job). Unquestionably, some of the *maskilim* of his time were familiar with the controversy between J. G. Hamann and Michaelis on the evaluation of biblical poetics. However, only later, in the Romantic period, was it possible to find views comparable to that of Hamann, who saw the most sublime expression of poetry in the Bible, and asked: 'Why are we always referring to the Greeks and to the Romans, and not further back to the living springs of real antiquity?' He added that redemption did not come from the Greeks, but from the Jews ('Das Heil kommt von den Juden') and that one could revive it only 'by going on pilgrimages to Arabia, crusades to the East and by regaining that magic which Bacon said consisted in noting the secret relations of things'. Hamann thus opposed the notion of Michaelis—and Mendelssohn—that Hebrew poetry needed to be vindicated by showing that it met Greek standards.[52]

Only rationalists, then, take a dim view of the poetics and the significant symbolical message of the Bible: a message filled with sublime majesty.[53] It is no surprise that Shadal rejected the application of the alien 'Greek' concept of the 'sublime' to biblical poetics, and in the introduction to his commentary on the Book of Isaiah, he criticized the approach taken by Rossi,[54] Mendelssohn, and Loewisohn, in understanding biblical poetry according to the Greek model, for 'their ways are not ours'. Mendelssohn, he wrote, did not understand that biblical poetry is completely free of all metre.[55] In the same disparaging tone, Smolenskin criticized Graetz's interpretation of the Song of Songs, claiming that Graetz had been misled

[52] See Vincent Freimarck, introduction to Olms Verlag edn. of Robert Lowth, *De Sacra Poesi Hebraeorum*; Michaelis, 'Praefatio Editoris' to vol. i of his edition of Lowth (Göttingen, 1758; vol. ii, 1761) = *Thesaurus Antiquitatum Sacrarum*, xxxi (Venice, 1766), pp. cxxxviii ff. He described Lowth as an 'oriental Orpheus'.

[53] Blackall, *The Emergence of German*, 443; Berlin, *The Magus of the North*; Schwarcz, 'The Poetry of the "Sublime"'; Low, *The Jews in the Eyes of the Germans*, 54–60. On Herder's concept of biblical poetry see Z. Levy, *Judaism in the World View*, 112–61.

[54] Who in *Sefer me'or einayim*, ch. ii (ed. Bonfil, 231), counters those who oppose interpreting biblical rhetoric according to classical theories. In his view, these theories only help for a better understanding of the beauty of the Bible.

[55] S. D. Luzzatto, 'Perush lesefer Yeshayahu', ii. 209; Shadal made a point of this several times, vindicating the uniqueness of biblical poetry against the supposed error of Mendelssohn and Rossi in asserting that biblical poetry was also metrical, and even if it did not observe quantities like Greek and Roman poetry, did more or less have an equal number of feet. But in a letter to M. Letteris (Dec. 1836) he criticized the metre employed in German poetry, which in his view was not poetry at all because it does not strictly keep to an 'equal number of syllables', and as a counterexample cited Homer and Virgil, no less accomplished poets, who knew how to remain within the bounds of the metre and 'abided by the rules of long and short syllables' (*Igrot Shadal*, iii. 358–60).

by Goethe into thinking there was a Greek influence in the Song of Songs, and believed that he was thus defending the honour of biblical poetry.[56]

The first generation of *maskilim* was torn between the desire to represent the language of the Bible as a sublime tongue and the desire to view Hebrew as a language of reason; between Classicism and Romanticism; and between Hebrew as a language of imagination and emotion and Hebrew as a language of enlightenment and science. This argument continued throughout the century. The principle introduced by 'Longinus', and transferred by Solomon Loewisohn to an account of biblical poetry, was rapidly adopted as a unique principle of biblical poetics. Thus Lilienblum could write that 'the poetry of Israel is totally removed from the poetry of the Aryans', because its 'amazing effect did not stem from power nor from beauty, but from the sublime'. In a similar fashion, Ze'ev Jawitz took this poetic principle from Loewisohn and used it to characterize the Jewish essence of the poetry.[57] The borrowed attribute thus became a product of the singular spirit of the people of Israel; in other words, it was appropriated into the Jewish culture.

Wessely warned the *Hame'asef* group not to follow in the steps of the neoclassical poets; however, he regarded the absence of poetry in Jewish culture as a profound lack. The Jewish people in Germany and Poland, he wrote, did not produce even one poet, even though biblical Hebrew poetry surpassed that of Homer, Pindar, and Horace. Wessely blamed the lack of poetry on the condition of the Hebrew language and asserted that this situation would be rectified only when children began learning proper Hebrew.[58] But was the revival of the Hebrew language the only prerequisite for the revival of Hebrew poetry? What was the nature of Hebrew poetry? The prevailing idea was that

the sons of India and Greece possess a greater power to rise above their souls when they utter words of poetry; they are able to erase the tablets of their heart and to burnish the force of their imagination in order to imbibe, in its pristine form, the thing they have chosen as the subject of their poetry! When the children of Israel lift their voices in song, they are unable to purge it of an ingrained irrepressible sweetness that always clings to their poetry, for the emotions of their heart which they cannot subdue even for a single moment will attach themselves like fences to the very subject, falsifying it and hampering its purity.

Thus, after inquiring into the nature and function of architecture, sculpture, painting, music, and poetry, and placing poetry at the head of all

[56] Smolenskin, *Et lata'at*, 199.
[57] Jawitz, 'Hashirah vehachakirah beYisrael uba'amim', 1001–5.
[58] Wessely, 'Divrei shalom ve'emet', 30–1.

melekhet machshevet (*schöne Künste*), Ze'ev Jawitz defined poetry, *melekhet hapiyut* (*Poesie*) as the art that expresses 'the spirit in all the profundity of its mysteries'. Jawitz distinguished between figurative poetry (*bildende Poesie*), narrative poetry (*Epik*), and poetry that stirs the soul (*Lyrik*). Prophetic poetry, the typical Jewish poetry, is neither sensual nor narrative, but is poetry of the heart and soul, and therefore sacred poetry. As lyric poetry spoken from the heart, it has no need for description of the outside world and concrete reality, nor for drama and plot, but merely borrows images ('good ingredients to help it in its craft'). Hence, in his view, Hebrew poetry is greater than that of the sons of India and Greece. The beauty of biblical poetry is the beauty of the inner world it expresses. The unique quality of biblical poetry ought to be the exceptional quality of modern Hebrew poetry: an expression of the moral inner beauty of the Jews.[59]

In that very same spirit, Aaron Kaminka wrote that 'The sons of Shem and the sons of Japheth, in their spirit, lives, and minds are as far removed from each other as East from West.' Since the spirit of a people is reflected first and foremost in its poetry, he then proceeded to examine Greek poetry and to compare it with Hebrew poetry. In a departure from the accepted generalization, Kaminka called attention to the fact that Greek literature includes, besides lyric poetry, both epic and a combination of spectacle and dramatic poetry. In Hebrew literature, on the other hand, there is hardly any dramatic poetry:

for among the Hebrews, the lyrical tendency is dominant: poetry of the soul, a powerful outpouring of emotion, the aroused imagination; subjective poetry in which a man pours forth his words in the purity of his heart, and describes the ideals of his soul, his reason and his desire. Among the Greeks, the epic tendency is dominant—poetry of the spirit, the actions of the mind and thought and the observation of life! Objective poetry has no happy or sad protagonist, but rather a calm and composed painter of portraits, wise in his own eyes, who depicts others.[60]

The topics of Greek poetry were legends about their gods and heroes: 'There is no end to the many inanities that have been collected from one generation to another, into legends . . .' But since Kaminka was going to give them Hebrew attire, he was quick to state that 'it is not the material that lends beauty to Japheth, but the form, the building of towers of song from the blocks of legends'. However, despite the enormous divergence, it was still possible to find an aspect common to these two greatly dissimilar poetic worlds:

[59] Jawitz, 'Hashirah vehachakirah'.
[60] Kaminka, 'Mavo leshirat haYevanim', 128–52.

Another fertile ground for poetry is the field in which we also met with the Greeks, and in which all peoples will meet in their songs: the field of personal feelings, love and revenge, war and peace, passion and pleasures, wine and women, nature in its strength and glory, in its changes and ruin, grace and pleasantness . . . [Although the world of the Greeks is different and strange] the spirit animating them, the spirit of the song of the soul, will light up their faces and remind us at all times that they are ours, children of the East, for their origin is from east of the sun and they give voice to the song of the sons of Shem.

Another approach was introduced in a leading article entitled 'Pindar und David: Eine vergleichende Skizze', that appeared in instalments in March and April 1882 in the *Allgemeine Zeitung des Judentums*, the major newspaper of Germany's Jews, and was written by the editor, Rabbi Ludwig Philippson.[61] It also searched for a common denominator between the two components of modern culture and civilization, namely 'the products of the Hellenic and the Israelite mind', for 'despite all difference between Hellenism and Hebraism, despite all the characteristic peculiarities separating these two magnificent phenomena', the very fact of their fusion in modern culture proved that they shared the same foundations. The writer compared the odes of Pindar, 'incontestably the greatest Greek lyric poets', with the Psalms, finding in them a common theme, the expression of the popular religion. Not religious dogma or abstract philosophical views, but religion as it finds expression in moments of real life: Pindar describes athletic victories, which he endows with religious and ethical meaning; the Psalms treat even national matters from the standpoint of an individual's reaction. Nevertheless the Psalms and Pindar reflected two disparate spiritual worlds: Pindar, the Greek, never transcended polytheism or the conception of the gods as possessing human passions; the Psalms present man as the highly gifted and distinguished creature of the One God, whose Providence is concerned with everything that befalls each individual; Pindar's morality is not derived from the knowledge of worship of God, but from purely human drives and needs.

Such analogies between Hebrew and Greek poetry were nothing other than a preamble to a discussion about the status of poetry in Hebrew literature, and even more so to a discussion about the Hebrew dimension in contrast to the European dimension in modern Hebrew literature. The analogy here was not with classical poetry, but with contemporary European literature. The claim that there is a distinctive Hebrew (or Jewish) literature, not only from the thematic standpoint (the topics that it treats, the manner in which it depicts human existence), but also from

---

[61] His authorship is evident from his references to his own works.

the standpoint of genre and values, seems to me to be totally unfounded. The analogy and contrast drawn between biblical and Greek poetics and their themes was not only a deliberation on the history of literature; it also proposed a literary model. However, other questions needed to be asked. What would be the driving force of the new Hebrew poetry? What would produce poets? What would bring about a revival of the poetic talent known in the distant past?

A Hebrew poet, wrote Uri Zevi Greenberg, cannot write sonnets and idylls, that is to say, poetry along the lines of the classic European models. The modern poet has a different role and status, and therefore his poetics must be entirely different.[62] This is even truer in the case of the modern Hebrew poet, whose prophetic or eschatological poems are an expression of a total metamorphosis in the Jewish cosmos:

How can a Hebrew poet write sonnets and idylls? Petrarch yes, Longfellow yes; a Hebrew poet—No! . . . Alas, to those among us who yearn, with Expressionism in the fullest sense of the word, for Pallas Athena, Olympus, and the nine Muses. The Jewish people is a people with a dynamic vitality, and must not be shackled to classicism.

The Hebrew poet is forbidden to write short poems in the style of the classical Gentiles, and if he does write in the classical style, then 'at the very least' he should write a Hebrew *Iliad* or *Pan Tadeusz*. The Homeric epic will place a divide between 'the Jerusalem of Ezekiel and the present-day conquerors of Canaan, on the one hand, and Rome and Athens, on the other'.[63] Thus, paradoxically, Greenberg both rejected the use of classical poetic forms and proclaimed a deep affinity to Expressionism, in the conviction that it was the sole mode capable of conveying the essence of the Hebrew revolution that brought the biblical Israelite closer to the Greek!

So far as we are concerned, it is important to stress that the claim generally put forward was that the new Hebrew literature was entitled, and indeed obliged, to expand the scope of its poetic genres—or more correctly, to select genres that either had not been previously known or at least never used. This should be done in order to create a complete literary corpus (drama, for example). On the other hand, arguments were also voiced that some genres were appropriate to the Hebrew spirit, while others were not and contradicted its world-outlook and its temper. Should Hebrew prose follow the manner of biblical narrative? According to Erich

---

[62] Shmeruk, 'The Call for a Prophet'; Bar-El, 'The National Poet'. On the Slavonic concept of poetry and prophecy see Erlich, *The Double Image*; Weintraub, *Literature as Prophecy*.

[63] U. Z. Greenberg, *Klapei tishim veteishah*, 6, 8, 15, 44; Hurshovski, *The Theory and Practice of Rhythm*.

Auerbach's *Mimesis* (1946) and Heymann (Hermann) Steinthal's lecture 'Die Erzählungskunst der Bibel', biblical narrative has no epic or breadth, while the *indogermanisch* (Indo-European) story-teller depicts the plot, the background, and the situation in great detail; in his narrative, Steinthal claimed, there are many pauses and digressions, whereas that of the Bible moves swiftly ahead towards its goal. Can Hebrew literature really become modern literature without taking the 'Greek literary model' as an example?[64]

It was the poet Saul Tchernichowsky who made the most valuable contribution to the translation of classical literary works into Hebrew,[65] being therefore portrayed as a 'Hellenic poet', writing in 'Greek melody'. The debate about the nature of his 'Hellenism' began with the appearance of his first book *Chezyonot vemanginot* ('Visions and Melodies', 1898–1900). One of his critics wrote that he was a Hellenic poet by virtue of his admiration of beauty and nature for their own sake and his preference for heroism and strength over spirit and morality: 'The people of Israel could not have been Greek . . . nor could the poetry of Israel have been Greek poetry.'[66] A great deal has been written about his 'Hellenic' nature, and a long controversy raged about the features of his alleged 'Greekness'.[67] Some critics claim that Tchernichowsky's 'Hellenism' is not shown only by the mythological symbols he used, but mainly through his 'pagan' or 'pantheistic' world-outlook, or in other words, his adoption of the concept of the cyclicity of nature. Many show deep hostility towards his 'Hellenism'. Ahad Ha'am, for example, wrote that Tchernichowsky's ideas were 'assorted sweets mixed with fly-poison' and that he was shackled by an alien Greek influence![68] Others asserted that in his poetry Tchernichowsky gave preference to 'external sights'. Indeed, a standard motif in the criticism levelled against Tchernichowsky was that he tried to introduce into Hebrew poetry Greek traits which were alien to its nature; it was said, for example, that Greek love-poetry differs from biblical love-poetry (the Song of Songs) in that the Greek has many loves, but the Hebrew has one great and strong one.

Indeed, the question of the different nature of 'Hebrew poetry' as com-

---

[64] Steinthal, 'Die Erzählkunst der Bibel', 3.

[65] His translations proved how mistaken Renan was in insisting that it was difficult, in fact impossible, to imagine Homer and Hesiod in Hebrew attire (above, n. 44).

[66] A. B. Paperna, *Sefer hashanah*, iii (Warsaw, 1902).

[67] Shamir, 'Bialik and Tchernichowsky'; Abramson, 'Hellenism Revisited'; Klausner, 'Tchernichowsky's World View'; Marthan, 'The Question'; 'Tchernichowsky's Response to Myth'; Silberschlag, 'Tchernichowsky and Homer'.

[68] Ahad Ha'am, letter to J. Klausner, 26 Nov. 1901, *Igrot*, ii. 262–4 at 262.

pared with 'Greek poetry', as well as the question of the status of Hebrew
poetry and prose, was the subject of a controversy that raged from the end
of the eighteenth century throughout the nineteenth and even afterwards.
The participants expressed various preferences for the different kinds of
poetic writing. Similar views were expressed, particularly from the end of
the nineteenth century, in regard to the various genres of prose and drama.
These preferences were an obvious result of cultural ideology, but were also
an outcome of the different views about the relationship existing between
the theme and the genre that expresses it. Ahad Ha'am, for example, was
persuaded that Hebrew literature had the right to emulate some of the
different genres of European literature: the national element in it ought to
be expressed not in form, but in theme. Others showed a more selective
attitude and stated that there were genres or poetics not suitable for use in
forging the national spirit.

It was thus ideas of the national spirit that determined preferences in
relation to genre and poetics. Those who believed that Zionism was a
movement of human and social liberation preferred the socially realistic
novel and regarded the historical romance as a decadent literary form.
Brenner, for example, sharply criticized the translation into Hebrew of
Henryk Sienkiewicz's *With Fire and Sword* because it was a novel reflecting
the world of decadent nobility. In Jabotinsky's opinion, on the other hand,
it was a novel with a dramatic, thrilling plot suitable for the young reader.[69]
Those who claimed that Zionism was a movement of *Sturm und Drang*, an
expression of a total revolution in the realm of thought and experience,
were drawn to Expressionism or Futurism as the poetics most appropriate
for expressing the new national dynamics in its totality.

In his article 'Milchemet haruach' ('The War of the Spirit'), Klausner declared that modern Hellenism, which began with the Haskalah in
Germany, to a great extent grew out of the lack of a philosophy and of
belles-lettres that could satisfy the new needs of the current generation:

Where are the Hebrew books that will prove to everyone that our literature is
not inferior to foreign literature? Modern Jewish culture is totally deficient: it has
no translations of foreign 'wisdom literature'; [no] translations of the best writers
on political economics, philosophy of history, biology, anthropology, sociology,
and the like. And there is in it no diversity of belles-lettres. It has lyric poetry
but no epic poetry. Our literature is poorer in epic poetry than on the day it
came into being. Where is the Hebrew Homer, where are the Hebrew Sophocles
and Euripides, Ovid and Virgil? The peoples of Europe did great things with
narrative poetry, prose poetry, and Greek plasticity, the art of drawing, symmetry,

---

[69] Z. and Y. Shavit, 'Translated vs. Original Literature'; Werses, 'The Relationship'.

the richness of the imagination, and the accord of the dramatic personae. All these enhanced the value of fine literature in Europe, until it became the most usual and most satisfying spiritual sustenance to all who knew how to read.[70]

Klausner adopts the view that we have already found in Lowth (who claimed that there was neither drama nor epic in the Bible, except for occasional traces in Job and the Song of Songs), a view which emerges as an established axiom in Renan.

In order to bridge the deep cultural gap, the new culture-hungry generation of Jews was drawn to the exciting literature of Europe, swallowing at the same time both shell and pith, 'fascinated by the spirit of Greece in its new attire'. As long as Hebrew literature did not have its own Faust, its own Werther, some Maupassant of its own, a Hebrew Ibsen, it would not be able to come to grips with the new Hellenism that threatened it. Nevertheless, Klausner did not regard all European literature as negative and Hellenistic, for some works contained a 'pith' that was worth consuming: the fruits of the spirit of Goethe and Schiller, Tolstoy and Carlyle, for example, who blended art with moral demands. Klausner's war against the new Jewish *Hellēnismos* was not directed against Goethe and Tolstoy, but against materialistic rationalism and relativistic atheism. This meant that there were works in European literature which had a Jewish spirit, and the cultural war of the Jews had to be directed only against that part of European literature which reflected the Greek spirit.

In the same vein, Abba Achimeir also divided European writers into artists and prophets. The latter, of course, were closer to the Jewish spirit, and for the most part were Slavs: Tolstoy, Dostoevsky, Lermontov, Gogol, Mickiewicz, and their like.[71] The battle was not against German Romanticism or Russian Slavophilism, but rather against French decadence and materialism. Such a battle could not be won if Hebrew literature, on its own, did not know how to supply what was missing and what was so vital to it:

And therefore we have a war with France. But once again let us repeat the maxim: *imperat Natura parendo*. In other words, when we too shall describe all that the books of Europe describe; when our literature too shall have Greek plasticity; when psychology shall secure a permanent place for itself in our literature, as well; when there shall be proper scientific literature also in Hebrew; when there shall be in our literature too, a description of all passions, aspirations, desires, and dreams—then shall we attract the hearts of our young people to our new literature, then will the European nations also pay attention, then will it be possible for us to

---

[70] Klausner, 'Milchemet haruach'.   [71] Achimeir, 'Aman venavi'.

develop our spirit, the pure spirit of Israel, in the scientific books written by the scholars of Israel, in the stories written by the Hebrews; and our point of view on the passions will surely be different from the point of view of Maupassant and Zola, Novalis and Tieck, Sand and Ibsen . . . We shall surrender to the spirit of Greece and thereafter we shall rule over it! Through it we shall strengthen the spirit of Israel, as our scholars strengthened it in Spain! And there is already a beginning in the 'crumbs' of Ahad Ha'am, in the wonderful monthly publication *Mimizrach umima'arav* ('From East and West'), notable for Professor Shapira's book and for his excellent articles on Tolstoy and Nietzsche; for the stories of I. L. Peretz (but not his angry critiques . . .), Ben-Avigdor, and Goldin;[72] for the poems of Peretz, Bialik, and Tchernichowsky, who knew how to stir the most sensitive heartstrings. Well, then, let us go forward! Remembering our battle against the spirit of Greece, two thousand and sixty-four years ago, remembering the victory we won both in Palestine and in Spain, we shall strive to defeat it today as well, through our new literature, by learning good taste; and if we install the beauty of Japheth in the tents of Shem and in the spirit of Israel, we shall ensure once again that we shall vanquish the spirit of Greece, 'not by might nor by power, but by the spirit'.[73]

This cultural and literary militancy was tempered over the years, as Klausner's aspirations to seek the alchemical secrets of the synthesis between Judaism and humanity became crystallized. To Renan and his teachings he dedicated a long series of articles called 'Mishpatei Ernest Renan al tekhunot benai Shem veruach sefat Ever' ('Ernest Renan's Theories on the Characteristics of the Sons of Shem and the Spirit of the Hebrew Language'). These were published in the Hebrew periodical *Hamelitz* (1895) and later, with many changes, in his book *Yahadut ve'enoshiut* ('Judaism and Humanity', Warsaw, 1904–5) as 'Ernest Renan and Spiritual Anti-Semitism', and later still in a revised edition as 'Ernest Renan and the Theory of Race'.[74] Although Klausner, in his final version, stated that there was a continuity between Renan's outlook and Nazi racialism, he adopted more than a few of the basic assumptions of Renan's anthropo-psychological ontological teachings, as well as his deterministic milieu theory. He angrily rejected the description of the Semitic race as a *com-*

---

[72] Chayim Nachman Shapira (1895–1943), lectured in Semitic languages (1920–40) at the university in Kaunas (Kovno) and published articles on Hebrew literature in the context of European literature. Only one volume of his magnum opus *Toledot hasifrut ha'ivrit hachadashah* ('A History of Modern Hebrew Literature'), which was to have comprised twelve volumes, was published; the manuscript of the second volume was destroyed in the Kovno ghetto. Isaac Leib Peretz (1852–1915) was a Yiddish and Hebrew writer and poet, Ben-Avigdor (Abraham Leib Shalkovich, 1867–1921), a Russian Hebrew author and pioneer publisher of popular literature in Hebrew, Yacob Goldin (1853–1907) a Yiddish playwright and journalist.   [73] Klausner, 'Milchemet haruach'.

[74] Y. Shavit, '"Semites" and "Aryans"'.

bination inférieure, but agreed that the monotheism of the Israelites was born in the desert, and that the desert left its stamp upon their manner of viewing the world. Hence Renan was correct in declaring that for that reason Hebrew culture included no epic poetry, plastic arts, and the like; but the characteristics it lacked were not necessarily innate, fixed, and eternal. A national character and culture were apt to change in the course of history; at any rate, Renan went too far by divesting the Israelites of so many extremely vital traits and abilities. What they wanted during biblical times, for instance, they possessed during later periods. Renan was correct in everything concerning 'the absence of expanse and variety' in biblical literature. But the Talmud and all the rabbinical writings were full of 'keen, noble, and penetrating studies' on the nature of man and the universe. If Renan did not find a sense of humour in the Bible, that shows that he did not read or understand the talmudic jests. One by one, Klausner enumerates the major flaws in the edifice Renan had erected: not only were Semites not lacking in civic spirit, it was they who laid the cornerstone of Greek civic sense and thereby of citizenship throughout Europe.

Nevertheless, Klausner believed that Renan was right concerning the diversity of literary creation: the Jewish world-picture—its cognizance of unity and its moral sense—caused the Hebrews' poetry to be subjective and lyric rather than objective and epic. This quality was unchanged throughout the centuries. That is why there is no Hebrew novel, no Hebrew epic, no Hebrew drama. Here and there one can find hyperbolic or legendary tales that point to a bold imagination, but a creative imagination does not exist. Choral songs are the fruit of a bold imagination; poesy is the product of a creative one, which the Semitic spirit lacks. Epic poetry, dramas, and novels (narrative prose) call for a creative imagination, as well as the willingness of the author to blur his own identity. One consequence of the pure and simple way in which the Hebrews (and not the Semites as a whole!) knew God was the absence of a Hebrew mythology, and the origins of great epic poetry are always in mythology! The Hebrew writer was unable to give real and concrete form to external reality, to nature, for he lacked all plastic sense. Klausner's subsequent remedy for this conspicuous lack in Hebrew literature differs from his suggestion in 1896:

This deficiency can only be overcome if we offer our young readers all the great Aryan classics in Hebrew translation, and first of all—the great Greek poets and dramatists. Then the students of Hebrew literature will also have the proper literary examples, which they can scrutinize and then imitate for themselves. Little by little they will become accustomed to writing stories, dramas, novels, and poems in Hebrew, which will not be inferior to what is written in Aryan languages, yet without losing their specific, singular Hebrew quality—the freshness of feeling and warm-heartedness. To me, this is a possibility, but to Renan, it is not possible, for a very simple reason: he considers subjectivity an innate racial attribute that is impossible to change, while in truth it should be viewed simply as a quality imprinted upon the Israelites in antiquity and which may change a great deal or only a little. And in addition, as has become clear, subjectivity is not always a disadvantage: at times it is an exceedingly great advantage. The eye that sees and the heart that feels—which of the two is preferable? . . .[75]

To some extent, Klausner also accepted Renan's assumptions regarding the nature of the Hebrew language. However, he did reject Renan's generalization that Hebrew lacked the capacity for abstraction, simulation, and detail, and that there was almost no syntax in it, or variety of structure and conjunctions; moreover, he utterly objected to the static and monochromatic picture of the Hebrew language, pointing to its development and stratification. He did agree with Renan that Hebrew lacked a richness of forms and half-tones (*demi-jours*), and that these missing qualities were vital to a language in the process of being revived. Klausner believed, in contrast to the Haskalah view, that modern Hebrew had to be liberated from the influence of the Bible and had to move closer to the language of later Jewish writings in regard to poetic, scientific, and philosophical diction.

PUTTING HEBREW DRAMA ON STAGE

Those who regarded Greek drama as the 'crowning glory of Greek artistic creation' wondered why the Hebrews had no drama. The Italian Jewish dramatist, theatre director, and poet Judah Leone ben Isaac Sommo (1527–92), maintained in his *Dialoghi* (*Dialogues on the Art of the Stage*, 1565), that the Book of Job, written by Moses, was the first drama in history. It influenced Plato to write in dialogue form, and this, in turn, inspired the Greek dramatists. He also asserted that the Greek dramatists divided their plays into five acts to correspond to the numbers of books in the Pentateuch.

As if to show that his imagination had no limits, Sommo traced the Italian word *scena* ('stage', 'scene') to the Hebrew word *shekhunah* ('neighbourhood').[76] This product of creative imagination was revived in modern times; an article written by Noach Chakham, a religious biblical scholar in

---

[75] Klausner, 'Ernest Renan vetorat hageza', 129–30.
[76] Bonfil, *As by a Mirror*, 132–5. See Schirmann (ed.), *Tzakhut bedichutah dekidushin*, 173–6.

Jerusalem, will serve as a typical example of the attempt to kill several birds with one invented stone. First, he claims, the songs of the chorus and drama are themselves of Canaanite or Hebrew origin, and were transplanted into Greek drama, helping it to reach maturity. Despite the changes that Greek drama underwent in this transition, it is impossible 'to cast any doubt on the fact that the one evolved from the other, just as Christianity cannot deny its Jewish origin . . .'. Therefore, it is 'clear that the drama, like all the other arts, has a Semitic and not an Aryan origin, and from the source of Israel it came to the Greeks who perfected it, just as they perfected everything they received from the sons of Shem'. There is no doubt in his mind that 'In the West, in the land of Greece, the poets heard the sounds of the sweet melodies of the God of Jacob and arranged them for their harps.' Secondly, the dramatic elements can be found in Israelite culture, either in the choral songs of 'companies of prophets' or in the dramatic rhetoric of the prophecy ('the polemics of the prophets'). Greek drama only developed and perfected the dramatic devices, 'but did not dare to abolish the song of the chorus or to thrust it into the background, because it was a borrowed element . . .'.[77]

In Chakham's view, the significant difference between the prophetic spectacle and Greek drama is manifested in the ideological gulf separating the two, which the disparate literary form underscores: 'The author of the Book of Job and Plato, the prophets of Israel and the dramaturges, Judaism and Hellenism—how great the chasm that divides them!' Nevertheless, here too he pointed to a common denominator. Greek drama is a religious-ethical work; since it was written under the influence of the prophets of Israel, therefore the pagan gods act according to the notion of reward and punishment. Aeschylus, our author adds, introduced something of the monotheistic view into Greek art, and addresses personal moral-religious questions according to well-known criteria from the Bible and the literature of the Sages. Hence, Hebrew prophecy and Greek tragedy express the principle of human unity—the unity of all men created in His image—which brings worlds far removed from one another closer. 'And here, the demand of the children of Shem for truth and justice and the adoration of the children of Japheth of beauty bond together; moreover, those same first wondrous people who taught the good to human beings also found the suitable garb for it: the lofty forms of the beautiful.' It is

[77] Chakham, 'Shorshei hadramah'. It is interesting that these writers ignored the Alexandrian Jew Ezekiel, who may be called the first 'modern' Jewish poet and whose Greek dramatization of the Exodus, entitled *Exagōgē*, is the first literary attempt to retell biblical stories for different purposes, as has become popular in recent times. (He is briefly mentioned by H. Gross, 'Olymp und Sinai', 620.)

interesting that J. H. Brenner, who normally took a dim view of such speculations, looked with favour on Hakham's article, apparently because it did not create an unbridgeable gulf between Judaism and Greek culture and Europe. This is probably the reason why Brenner believed Hakham to have succeeded in proving that the origin of drama could be found in the choral songs of ancient Hebrew literature and that it is not a distinctive Greek creation. Although it is true that drama grew out of religious choral songs in honour of Bacchus, the god of wine, he pointed out that wine is explicitly mentioned in the Bible as gladdening the heart of man. As far as a love of wine is concerned, Shem does not take second place to Japheth.[78]

In the debate that took place in the Palestinian Jewish community during the 1890s, those who favoured modern theatre in Hebrew used the same arguments to support their case; its Orthodox and conservative opponents spoke of the theatre with contempt, almost as the Church Fathers (and the Calvinists of Geneva) had done. In response to views expressed by Pines and other members of the Orthodox community that since the theatre essentially belonged to Greek culture (and to the culture of the 'natural peoples') and is totally foreign to Jewish culture, theatrical performances in Hebrew in the Land of Israel were 'Hellenic' (here parallel to the 'culture of France') and an imitation of the 'delusionary acts and orgies of the Greeks and Romans', Eliezer Ben-Yehuda wrote that he was not surprised by the objections raised by the extreme Orthodox, but that Pines, who himself had translated into Hebrew a popular book on 'something foreign', namely 'physics', ought to know that if it is possible to 'Judaize' wisdom and sciences, then 'all the more so, theatre plays'. Ben-Yehuda believed that the Hebrew theatre is an important tool for disseminating the Hebrew language and the national ideology.[79] Pines tried to take an example from the struggle of the Catholic church against the theatre, which did not succeed owing to the interference of the rulers, who favoured the theatre; other participants in the dispute, conducted in anonymous articles in the Jerusalem press towards the end of the nineteenth century, defended the theatre and public dancing at celebrations, stating that dance was part of the Jewish heritage, citing as evidence Miriam, Moses' sister, who led the women playing the timbrel and dancing, King David, who leapt and danced before the Ark, and others. The fact that theatre performances in Greece were characterized by cruelty and lechery did not mean that the theatre could not give expression to exalted values.

[78] Brenner, 'Bimkom bikoret'.   [79] Ben-Yehuda, 'Ha'adon Pines vehaginuto'.

THE SHARED TRADITION
OF THE PARABLE AND THE FABLE

The appeal to the treasures of past culture led to a new categorization of literary works and endowed all branches of belles-lettres with new stature and value. Biblical poetry was judged according to 'classical' criteria, while a search was conducted in talmudic literature for traces of various literary genres: parable, satire, folk-tales, humour, fantasy, and the like.

From the inception of the Haskalah, Hebrew literature adopted the genres most popular in the German culture of the time, which they could claim corresponded to genres already existing in Hebrew literature. So far as parables were concerned, a real correspondence of this sort existed; it was contrived in the legend and the folk-tale.

The *mashal* (meaning 'parable'; plural *meshalim*) was the most prevalent literary genre in Haskalah literature both for adults and for children.[80] In it, as we have seen in Ch. 4, the *maskilim* found the perfect accord between message and literary form. It took on different forms: proverbs (*Spruchweisheiten*), parables in the strict sense (*Gleichnisse*), and fables, i.e. short dramatic stories with a moral. Of these, the proverb, or pithy aphorism, which combined imagination with wit and a moral message, and had, as we have already seen, a general human content, has of course strong roots in Hebrew biblical literary tradition and after, and therefore was the most popular in the Haskalah. Writers of that period were much preoccupied with the question of the relationship between the literature of parables and the literature of legends. However, at the same time they also adapted the fable, a short dramatic story with a moral. Indeed, German writers of that period were much preoccupied with the differences between proverb and fable and between fable and legend (even the mythological legend, which may also be used for moral instruction), and Jewish writers of that age were influenced by both the Jewish and the German tradition.

Fables and legends came into German literature from various sources and through various intermediaries—among others, from the 'Orient'; one of the best known was August Jacob Liebeskind's *Palmblätter: Erlesene morgenländische Erzählungen für die Jugend* (1786–1801), with an introduction by Herder. Under the influence of La Fontaine's *Fables*, of which the first collection was published in 1668, Aesop's fables, popularized throughout Europe by numerous translations and adaptations, also enjoyed a revival in

---

[80] On the history of the fable in German literature see Windfuhr, *Deutsche Fabeln*; Brüggemann and Ewers, *Handbuch*; Dithmer, *Das Fabel*. On the universalist nature of wisdom literature see Blackham, *The Fable as Literature*. On the theory of the fable see Noel, *Theories of the Fable*.

Germany.[81] Renowned fabulists like Friedrich von Hagedorn (1708–54) and Christian Fürchtegott Gellert (1715–69), whose books were the greatest bestsellers in the eighteenth century, openly expressed their intention to transmit a moral lesson, and their books usually carried the subtitle: 'moral fables for children and youth', a literary form suitable as a device for conveying abstract ideas or beliefs. It is no wonder then that a *maskil* like Ben-Ze'ev found in Gellert's parable 'Der Maler' ('The Painter') of 1746 an expression of an attitude towards the divine act of creation that corresponds with the traditional Jewish approach in the fortieth chapter of Isaiah. The 'wise man' or the 'knowledgeable man' knows that a work of art is only judged as a whole; an unintelligent man, on the other hand, arrives at a judgement based on the part; herein lies the moral:

> If a man of understanding rejects your words,
> You should pay heed and replace them,
> But if your words are the choice of fools,
> Then you surely can erase them.[82]

In the main, Jewish tradition took a favourable view of *meshalim*, which constituted one of the major genres of Hebrew literature throughout the ages. This long literary tradition, which included both the proverb (often a series of sayings or maxims) and the fable, began in the Bible, continued in Hellenistic Jewish literature as well as in the writings of the Sages[83]—R. Yohanan said: 'When R. Meir delivered his [public] lecture he would divide his lecture thus: one-third halakhah, one-third aggadah, and one-third parables' (bSanh. 38b)—and persisted in the Middle Ages. The *maskilim* found in it authority both for renewing interest in Hellenistic Jewish literature (hence it is no surprise that Wessely should translate the Wisdom of Solomon and Ben-Ze'ev Ben-Sira) and for appropriating the European fable. This literature was appropriate, in both form and content, to the world-outlook and aims of the *maskilim*.

Owing to the similarity between the Sages' parables and those of Jesus in the New Testament, on the one hand, and those from Greek popular philosophy, they became links in a common Jewish–Christian–European

---

[81] Lessing, *Fabeln* (1759); Richardson, *Aesop's Fables* (1750, translated into German in 1757); Huch, *Aesopus* (1769); see Grätz, *Das Märchen*, 125–51. Aharon Wolfsohn Halle (1754–1835, one of the editors of *Hame'asef*) includes them in *Avtalyon*. See Ofek, *Hebrew Children's Literature*.

[82] Ben-Ze'ev, *Beit hasefer*, i: *Mesilat halimud*, 215–16. Cf. Gellert's original text: 'Wenn deine Schrift dem Kenner nicht gefällt, | So ist es schon ein böses Zeichen; | Doch wenn sie gar des Narren Lob erhält, | So ist es Zeit, sie auszustreichen' (*Sämtliche Fabeln und Erzählungen*, 88).

[83] On the fable in the Bible and in the literature of the Sages, see Yassif, *The Hebrew Folktale*, 31–5, 212–35; Hays, *Old Testament Form Criticism*.

corpus of literature.[84] The situation was different in the case of fables (whether in prose or verse), which was almost entirely absent from the literary Jewish heritage but had long been highly popular in German literature, being used for didactic purposes in theology and in moral and political allegory. During the Enlightenment the fable was defined, for example by Lessing, as a fictitious narration of an individual case embodying a general rule, and as an example of practical morality ('Exempel der praktischen Sittenlehre');[85] Herder stressed the 'imaginative' side of the fable more than its moral point or philosophical idea.[86] Applying the name *Äsopische Fabeln* to beast-fables,[87] he underlined in his introduction to Liebeskind's book the important role of the inventive faculty in shaping an individual's personality.

The fable was represented as a literary garb for the truth; Ben-Ze'ev wrote:

> Since Truth had been naked all this while,
> None sought her out and she was estranged.
> Therefore she acted with cunning and guile,
> In a parable's guise she hid and was changed:
> She breathed fire into the very soil
> Gave voices to wind and water and fire,
> To insects and animals, beasts of toil,
> And to birds that flew high and ever higher.

Ben-Ze'ev was adapting Florian's famous poem 'La Fable et la Vérité',[88]

[84] Flusser, 'The Proverbs of Jesus'; D. Stern, *Parables in Midrash*. See also Lieberman, 'Greek and Latin Proverbs'. On classical wise sayings in medieval Arabic literature see Rosenthal, *The Classical Heritage*, 118–44.

[85] Lessing, *Abhandlungen über die Fabel*, ch. 1, end: 'Wenn wir einen allgemeinen moralischen Satz auf einen besondern Fall zurückführen, diesem besonderen Falle die Wirklichkeit erteilen, und eine Geschichte daraus dichten, in welcher man den allgemeinen Satz anschauend erkennt: so heißt diese Erdichtung eine Fabel'; id.,*Schriften zur Geschichte der Fabel*, quoted in Windfuhr, *Deutsche Fabeln*, 124.

[86] E. Bin-Gorion, *The Path of Legend*, 11–35, 214.

[87] He presents it as already in common use: 'die Einkleidungen . . . die man Äsopische Fabeln nennt'; from the sequel it becomes clear that he has in mind the beast-fable, as opposed to the 'morgenländische Erzählung', the Oriental tale in which human beings express a higher morality than can be credibly assigned to beasts. But this sense goes back through standard Western treatises to Isidore, *Etymologiae*, i. 40. 2: 'Fables are either Aesopic or Libystic [i.e. African]. They are Aesopic when dumb animals are imagined to converse amongst themselves, or inanimate objects like cities, trees, mountains, rocks, and rivers. They are Libystic when exchange of speech is imagined of men with beasts or beasts with men.' (This doctrine is quite artificial, with no application to either ancient fables or other classical comments. The ancients held that Aesopic fable was intended to amuse, but also to say obliquely things that if said directly would arouse the wrath of the powerful.)

[88] Ben-Ze'ev, *Mesilat hameisharim*, in *Beit hasefer*, ii. 187; Florian, *Fables complètes*, i. 1. See Sadan 'The Parable of the Parable'; G. Toury, 'An Enlightened Use of Fable'; Y. Shavit, 'The Fable as a Fable'; Pelli, 'The Genre of the Parable in Hebrew Haskalah'. Magnus Gottfried Lichtwer (1719-83), 'Die beraubte Fabel', *Vier Bücher Aesopischer Fabeln in gebundener Schreib-Art* (Leipzig, 1748), cit. Windfuhr, *Deutsche*

translated and adapted into Hebrew several times; it was itself an adaptation from an earlier source. Ben-Ze'ev also added that the teachers of ethics had chosen the parable because it invests everything, be it flora or fauna, with the power of speech, and hence is the best vehicle for transmitting a moral message.

When the *maskilim* began writing didactic literature and stressing the fundamental stylistic difference between their works and the religiously conservative literature of ethics, they were faced with several possibilities. The difference between the terms was not always clear: what was it that differentiated parable and rhetoric from 'words of wisdom', 'wise adages', a 'pointed moral', and so forth? The biblical and Hellenic traditions and their adaptation to the literary currents of the time offered a range of options. Consequently, Haskalah literature included imitations of Hellenistic Jewish ethical literature such as Satanow's *Mishlei Asaf* (Berlin, 1790),[89] and an eclectic combination of the various forms of the fable by Ben-Ze'ev. In *Hame'asef*, Joel Brüll clearly indicated the *maskilim*'s preference for German ethical literature, which they regarded as a model for emulation, over Jewish ethical writing of the Middle Ages and of their own time. Hebrew (and German) literature for the young Jewish reader was a blend of moral fables, narrative parables, popular science, catechism, biblical stories, and the like—taken from the literary inventory of the time and adapted to Hebrew and the Jewish spirit.

Fable became merely a repertoire of symbolic figures and moral examples, and the Haskalah also gave its stamp of approval to this genre, supposedly introduced by Aesop in the sixth century BC. First printed by Heinrich Steinhöwel (Ulm, 1477), the fables transmitted in his name became extremely popular in German translation, being acknowledged as the outstanding exemplar of the genre.[90] A Hebrew version (*Mishlei shu'alim*, 'Fox Fables') by R. Berechiah ben Natronai Hanakdan, who lived in the twelfth and thirteenth centuries in Normandy and England, was republished in Berlin on Mendelssohn's initiative in 1756.[91]

Fabeln, 40–1, made Fable a goddess who when robbers seized her clothes disappeared, giving way to the naked Truth; unable to bear the sight, they restore her clothes to her: 'Die Räuberschar sah vor sich nieder | Und sprach: "geschehen ist geschehn, | Man geb ihr ihre Kleider wieder, | Wer kann die Wahrheit nackend sehn?"' ('The robber band gazed downwards | and said: "What's done is done; | Give her her clothes back. | Who can look on the truth all bare?"').

[89] Professedly presenting fables and legends to cast light on Aristotle's *Ethics* (Werses, 'On I. Satanow').

[90] See Elschenbroich, *Die deutsche und latinische Fabel*; Könneker, 'Die Rezeption'.

[91] Jacobs, *The Fables of Aesop*, pp. xv–xxii; Schwarzbaum, *Fox Fables*, pp. xviii–xxxvii: he notes that 'R. Berechia was thus the first mediaeval Hebrew author who brought a whole corpus of fables onto an admirably aesthetic, artistic plane of literature, as an independent form of writing in its own right.' His fables aimed to please and instruct simultaneously. On the fables in the Talmud see pp. xiv–xviii.

The *maskilim* based their approval of Aesopic fables on the talmudic literature. There one could find not only distinct traces of Aesopic fables, but also a clear legitimation of the genre. This enabled J. L. Gordon, the greatest fabulist of the Haskalah in the nineteenth century, to view the influence of the Aesopic fable on talmudic literature as unequivocal evidence that the Sages did not shrink from 'grafting an alien branch on to the sacred trunk, which produced a beautiful fruit'.[92] In the Talmud, fables of the 'Aesopic' type were called 'fox fables': it was said about R. Yohanan ben Zakkai, Gordon wrote, that he never in his life left off studying 'the speech of palm-trees, fullers' parables, and fox fables' (bSuk. 28a; *Bava Batra* 124a) and about R. Meir it was said that he had three hundred fox fables (bSanh. 38a). Gordon also believed that R. Meir had spent time in Phrygia, Aesop's birthplace, and there learnt the fables popular in the homeland of the legendary fabulist; he was the first to trace the imprint left by Aesop's fables on the literature of the Sages and to look for parallels. The *maskilim* who preceded him were aware of the similarity and the influence, but did not substantiate them with parallel motifs. Naturally, since Aesop's fables ('beast-fables') had a positive social and moral message, they incurred no danger of rejection by moderate *maskilim*: the Aesopic model could complement proverbs and biblical didactic stories without any difficulty.

The situation was different again when it came to the legend.

THE DISCOVERY OF LEGEND AND OF MYTH

The legend was regarded as the 'unmistakable progeny' of the imagination, and therefore akin to the mythological tale. The eighteenth century was divided in its opinion about legend: on the one hand, there was the prevailing moralistic-puritanical approach which held that the legend nurtured negative and harmful emotions.[93] In the eyes of the *Philanthropinisten*, legends were *dummes Geschwätz* and *Schwämerei*. Contraposed to that view was the approach that attributed an educational and moral value to legends. The narrative legends were thought to express the 'age of childhood' of a nation, which is its time of innocence as well as a period marked by a figurative (and hence an anthropomorphic) world-outlook. The Haskalah did not regard the legend with favour. The reasons for its objections were diverse and interrelated: an opposition to imagination in its broader sense, a shrinking away from everything that symbolized and alluded to mythology

---

[92] Y. L. Gordon's introduction to 'Mishlei Yehudah', 174–9. The Midrash also relates that Bar Kappara knew 300 fox fables (Lev. Rabbah 28: 2; Eccles. Rabbah 1: 3).   [93] Dahl, *Entstehung*.

hiding under the umbrella of folk literature, and a preference for moral literature with a didactic lesson. In the nineteenth century, the exposure of elements of mysticism, magic, or even fantastic stories in the Talmud and other Jewish literature still lay in the distant future. At the very most, there was a readiness to find in the Midrash various kinds of stories conveying moral lessons. One should note here that in the eighteenth century, *Märchen*, as such stories would be called, were understood to be literary narratives derived from various sources (including Far Eastern, Arabic, and Jewish literature) or developed under French influence, particularly fairy-tales (*contes de fées*, in German *Feenmärchen*).[94] The conception of the *Märchen* as a creation of the people, put about by thinkers like Herder and collectors of legends like the brothers Grimm, did not become pervasive till the beginning of the nineteenth century.

Legends were accepted into Jewish and Hebrew culture only later. The distinction made in the talmudic scholarship between the halakhic layer and the aggadic layer and the publication of the legends in separate compilations, were intended to rebut the prevalent claim that the Talmud was cut off from life. A second motive was to gain legitimation for dealing with legends as material for literary adaptation. Under the influence of Romanticism and the *völkisch* ideologies that sought after the spontaneous and direct elements of popular life,[95] the legend and the Midrash took on new appeal as a sort of Jewish *Volksmärchen*, a product of the 'innocent imagination'. It was at the turn of the nineteenth century that the aggadah was recognized as a separate unit in its own right within the Talmud, and as a complex genre, containing folktales, legends, parables, and the like.

It is well known that within the Talmud itself, and in medieval Jewish literature, a debate was conducted about the nature and status of aggadah. Words of praise stand alongside words of denunciation, each from different points of departure.[96] 'If you wish to come to know Him who spoke and the world came into being, study Haggadah, for thereby you will come to know Him and to cling to His ways' (*Sifre on Deuteronomy*,

---

[94] Grätz, *Das Märchen*.

[95] Vico (1668–1744) is thought to be the first to describe legends or folktales as a distinct expression of the 'spirit of the people', when in his *Principi di una scienza nuova* (1725, translated into German in 1822) he portrayed the author of the Homeric epic as the spokesman of the 'people of Greece themselves' (B. Feldman and Richardson, *The Rise of Modern Mythology*, 50–4).

[96] Ginzberg, *The Legends of the Jews*; J. Heinemann, *Aggadah and its Development*, 1–16; Shinan, *The World of Aggadic Literature*; Mack, *The Aggadic Midrash Literature*; Hallewy, *The Biographical-Historical Legends*; id., *The World of Aggadah*; Hirschberg, and Marmelstein, *The Attitude of the Aggadah to the Halakhah*; Kadushin, *The Rabbinic Mind*, 59–96; D. Stern and Mirsky, *Rabbinic Fantasies*; Saperstein, *Decoding the Rabbis*; Heschel, *Theology of Ancient Judaism*, i, pp. x–xxxvi; Yassif, *The Hebrew Folktale*, 22–31; Sh. Safrai, 'The Attitude of the Aggada to the Halakhah'.

49, ed. Finkelstein, 115),[97] or 'And delights, these are the Haggadot' (Eccl. Rabbah 2: 8). There are parallels to this source expressing the view that aggadot are meant mainly as a diversion; in contrast one can also find denigrating words stating that aggadot are 'magicians' manuals' and the like. However, apparently in no case was the aggadah—a literary work *sui generis*—regarded as an expression of the 'innocent imagination', intended mainly for the young reader. And it was certainly not regarded as an expression of primal forces or of a mythical level in the faith of Israel. Unquestionably, in the absence of folktales or their literary imitations (*Kunstmärchen*), the aggadah and the Midrash were the only available store of legends, with the exception of the hasidic tales. Maimonides' opinion that the reader of aggadot 'will scorn them and think them laughable' was rejected, whereas positive attitudes of commentators and pietists towards the aggadah took on a modern coloration.

Heine, in the first canto of 'Jehuda Ben Halevy', likened the halakhah to a fencing-school, the aggadah to a fantastic garden in the air, to which, when bored with halakhic debates, the young Jehuda fled for respite:

> the poor youth took to his heels, and
> Plunged into the bright Aggadah,
>
> Where the lovely legends blossom,
> Curious myths, angelic fables,
> Secret stories of the martyrs,
> Apothegms and holy chorals,
>
> Epigrams, hyperboles,
> Farcical but, somehow, fervent,
> Faith-inspiring, faith-compelling,
> Overflowing with exuberance.
>
> And the boy's enraptured spirit
> Soon was captured by the wonder
> Of the unforeseen adventure
> With its wild, romantic sweetness
>
> And the legendary terror
> Of a world of blessèd secrets,
> Of the sudden revelation
> That we know as poetry.[98]

---

[97] Here and elsewhere 'haggadah' is used as a synonym of 'aggadah'; it does not denote the Passover Haggadah.

[98] 'Floh alsdann sich zu erfrischen | In die blühende Hagada, || Wo die schönen alten Sagen, | Engelmärchen und Legenden, | Stille Märtyrerhistorien, | Festgesänge, Weisheitsprüche, || Auch Hyperbeln, gar possierlich, | Alles aber glaubenskräftig, | Glaubensglühend — O, das glänzte, | Quoll und sproß so überschwenglich — || Und des Knaben edles Herze | Ward ergriffen von der wilden, | Abenteuerlichen

So too Zunz, Levner,[99] Jawitz, Berdyczewski,[100] Bialik,[101] each in his own way, assigned the aggadah a special role separate from that of the halakhah. They described it as a spontaneous, liberated facet of the Hebrew spirit, in contrast to the normative and constitutional facet of the halakhah. Spontaneous, but not irrational, expressing and depicting a concrete reality and social and cultural common property.[102] The halakhah represents the law, the haggadah freedom, wrote Zunz in *Die gottesdienstlichen Vorträge der Juden historisch entwickelt* (1892). Hence the aggadic literature is national literature *par excellence* and encapsulates the views and opinions of broad social strata, and not only those of a scholarly élite. The aggadah, he wrote, 'is the monument of the language and history, of religion and poetry, of science and literature. It is the summation of the views and opinions of many thinking minds from the most remote ages.' Unquestionably, the claim that the aggadah was popular literature, a product of the people's spirit, was due to the influence of Romanticism; it ignored the fact that the talmudic aggadah is in large part a creation of sages and commentators. In any event, Bialik, in his well-known essay 'Halakhah ve'aggadah', did not intend to depict the aggadah as irrational literature. He clearly regarded it as a classic work reflecting a certain level of the people's life and spirit, but even this level draws upon a defined world outlook and is neither spontaneous nor lacking in restraint.

No less importantly, the aggadah served as testimony of the pluralistic and changing nature of Judaism, and of the cultural stratum that, more than others, received influence and motifs from various sources: from the literature of India, Egypt, Greece, and so on. In this way, the aggadah was positioned as the opposite—albeit the complementary—pole to the halakhah, as an expression not only of the aesthetic face of Judaism, but also of the richness of its imagination. From the turn of the century, the aggadah also gained in stature in an adaptation of literature suitable for the young reader. It had taken Hebrew culture about one hundred years to accept the opinion of Campe and other German pedagogues that a legend can also carry an educational message; nevertheless, it was still too early to

Süße, | Von der wundersamen Schmerzlust || Und den fabelhaften Schauern | Jener seligen Geheimwelt, | Jener großen Offenbarung, | Die wir nennen Poesie' (*Romanzero*, book 3, 'Hebräische Melodien'); trans. Untermeyer, *The Poems of Heinrich Heine*, 374.

[99] Levner's *Kol agadot Yisrael* (1898–1903) was a very popular retelling for younger readers.

[100] See Berdyczewski's introduction to *Me'otzar ha'agadah*, pp. xii–xvi.

[101] After the publication of Bialik and Ravitsky's *Sefer Ha'aggadah*, teaching of the talmudic aggadah was suppressed in the religious schools of Palestine (and still in Israel) because the aggadah was regarded as 'secular literature'!

[102] Kagan, *Halakhah and Aggadah*; Shamir, *Love Unveiled*; Miron, 'Razei lailah'; Ginossar, 'Bialik, Berl and Brenner: Law and Narrative'.

expect any of the mythical, fantastic, and demonic elements in the aggadah of the Sages to be revealed. Rather the Greek (German) mirror, that is, the once again potent presence of mythology in European culture, as well as an understanding of mythological tales not as a language of fantasy, but as allegorical and symbolical stories about the nature of man and of the universe, were among the driving forces that lent new dimensions of understanding to the talmudic aggadah.

Ze'ev Jawitz explored the negative or qualified attitudes of both the western and eastern Haskalah with regard to the aggadah, which he viewed as a work of folk poetry that uncovered deep layers of the 'Jewish soul'. Under the influence of European Romanticism, he selected and compiled an anthology of the Sages' aggadot especially geared to the tastes of the young reader. This is not a popular work gathered from among the people, but rather a distinctly literary work, the second face of the world of the Sages. To him, aggadah was not merely narrative illustration, a translation of the abstract into figurative or narrative language; it was rather a narrative parable. In the foreword to Jawitz's anthology *Sichot mini kedem* (Warsaw, 1887), Samuel Joseph Fuenn wrote, years before Bialik, that hidden in the aggadot of the Sages were 'depictions of the thoughts, the ideas, and the hopes of the Israelite nation as a whole', which were 'its own singular revelatory vision of the soul and the defenders of the spirit and the genius'. In contrast to the mythological imagination that corrupted morals, the talmudic aggadah was intended to reinforce religious faith: it was the aggadah and not the halakhah that ensured the survival of the nation.

The writer and scholar S. P. Rabinowitz (1845–1910), who translated Graetz's *Volkstümliche Geschichte der Juden* into Hebrew, also appended a preface to Jawitz's anthology, in which he presented the aggadah as distinctive national literature that could inculcate a love of Torah and of the nation into the hearts of the young. In those generations, he wrote, that have a proliferation of ignoramuses whose faith does not lie in the Torah, then there is a proliferation of 'people [who] seek to learn some lesson of Scripture or aggadah' (Song of Songs Rabbah 2: 14). To such people one must introduce the talmudic aggadah after it has been arranged and adapted. Jawitz himself, in an essay called 'Hamikra veha'agadah' ('The Bible and the Aggadah'), which preceded his anthology of adaptations, examined the similarities and differences between the approach of European literature towards mythology and his own towards the aggadah. The great writers of Europe, he claimed, turned to Greek literature and mythology out of a belief that they contained a profound spiritual quality. It was indeed true that Greek mythology is not pervaded by fantasies as,

for example, Hindu mythology was, and it expressed a world of unity;
Jewish literature, however, offered an infinitely greater and more perfect
unity, and was therefore more worthy. According to Jawitz, the talmudic imagination manifested in the aggadah recounts memorable events
of history (*historische Denkwürdigkeiten*), wise sayings (*Gnomen*), and fables
(*Fabeln*), which collectively are light writings (*Epigrammatik*); the haggadot
(*Erzählungen*) are based on folktales, some realistic (*shemuot, Sagen*), others
fantastic (*sichot, Märchen*). Interest is thereby renewed in haggadot as an expression of 'the apperception of the soul' (*Bewußtsein*), the contemplation
of nature (*Natursinn*), and the consciousness of the value of the nation's
history (*historisches Bewußtsein*).[103] The imagination of the Sages was not
disordered but subject to the religious and ethical values of normative Judaism. Not only did the Jews have a rich and creative imagination: it was
a positive imagination. This view may, of course, recall the use made in
Christian literature of mythological figures that became *philosophia moralis*
or 'merely a repertoire of symbolic figures and moral examples'.[104]

J. H. Brenner established that the talmudic aggadah borrowed motifs
from the contemporary world of legends, including Greek mythology.
Legends and folklore, he remarked, are not a distinct expression of a national spirit, for they recognize no borders and wander from one language
to another and from one culture to another: 'The "national" is borrowed
again and again.'[105] Nevertheless, he did not go so far as to ascribe both
a thematic likeness and a similarity of spiritual message to the talmudic
aggadah and Greek mythology or the *Nibelungenlied*. Moreover, although
he believed that the proverb and the aggadah are genres of a universal
nature, he also stated that each people changes the legends it has received
from others according its own collective popular psychology.

We have already noted that Levinsohn (in *Te'udah beYisrael*) discussed
the Sages' objection to mythology and the absurdity of their opposition
to the use of names taken from Greek myth. The prohibition by the Sages
was correct for its own time, but since then the pagan gods had vanished
from the world and their names no longer signified any divinity. 'All the
pagan deities and their worshippers have been uprooted from the world.'
He pointed out that in modern times the logic of the old prohibition
would be to forbid the use of the Hebrew names of the month since those
are the names of the 'Babylonian and Persian gods'. Based on this view,

---

[103] Jawitz, *Sichot mini kedem*, 3–18, and the introduction by Fuenn and Rabinowitz, pp. i–v, vii–xii.

[104] Theodulf, bishop of Orléans, wrote that 'Poets provide false stories; philosophers often turn these falsehoods into truth' (Seznec, *The Survival of the Pagan Gods*, 90).

[105] Brenner, 'Tiyul be'olam hamashal veha'agadah'.

mythology is but a repertoire of symbols representing various concrete things. However, in the nineteenth century, a different view of mythology and mythical thought was predominant.

At its most radical, the search for a 'Jewish mind' or a 'Jewish spirit' in Jewish history and literature claimed to have exposed a mythological component and mythical conceptions. Since nineteenth-century thought regarded myth as the imaginary life of the metaphor,[106] the absence of this element in the Jewish mind, as alleged by Renan, would be considered a grievous want. Some declared that the Jews had never had myths, others argued that there had been a monotheistic myth; this position was taken by Buber, who asserted that myth is an eternal function of man's soul and as central in a Jewish monotheism that views all things as utterances of God and all events as manifestations of the absolute: 'The Jew of antiquity cannot tell a story in any other way than mythically, for him an event is worth telling only when it has been grasped in its divine significance.'[107] Another argument would be that one must not blur the distinction between mythical thought and allegorization and personification of the deity.[108] But the most extreme and heretical of the arguments was that the Hebrews actually did have a mythology, for they had at the outset been polytheists. Thus the conventional wisdom deriving from Renan was rejected by the adoption of its major premiss and the denial of the minor: mythology is the way in which polytheistic peoples look at the world and interpret the world's phenomena; but the Hebrews had been polytheistic; ergo, they too had rich lives of imagination as well as a mythology!

The question whether mythological layers existed in the Bible (or the Talmud) is a subject of wide-ranging controversy, and this is not the place to explore it (see Ch. 11). An account of one turn-of-the-century reaction will suffice, not only because of its revolutionary and heretical character, but also because of its basic assumptions regarding the nature of the cultures embedded in it, biblical and talmudic. This reaction was also a direct response to the theoretical and scholarly challenge of Renan's thesis.

[106] Turner, *The Greek Heritage*, 104–11. Max Müller defined mythology as 'a disease of language. A myth means a word, but a word which, from being a name or an attribute, has been allowed to assume a more substantial existence' (quoted ibid. 107). For Herder, as for Vico, myth was the creation of the *Volksgeist*.

[107] Buber, 'Myth in Judaism'; see Schwarcz, 'M. Buber's Conception of Myths'; Tal, 'Myth and Solidarity'; A. Shapira, 'Buber's Attachment to Herder'; Anon., *Bible Folk-Lore*, 58: 'later Rabbinical writers themselves presented legends, and short sayings, concerning their national lawgiver, which admit of a simple mythical explanation, and which form strong indications of an esoteric teaching among the Rabbis concerning the early heroes of Israel, the key to which is now lost among modern Jews'. There is a vast literature on the nature of myth and its relationship to religion; see Childs, *Myth and Reality*, 13–30.

[108] Y. Kaufmann, *The Religion*, i/2. 400; Amir, 'Monotheistic Problem'.

As a starting-point we should first distinguish between those scholars whose aim is to prove that the laws of human evolution also apply to the Jews, whose world-view thus evolved from mythical to monotheistic conceptions—whereas the Greek mind had evolved from myth to rational thought[109]—and those who believe that a mythical layer or layers remained inherent in the Jewish world-view. The relation of Judaism and myth thus involves other questions than that of Judaism and mythology. The main driving-forces behind these controversies were the need to respond to general theories about the nature of myth, the need to explain the genesis and evolution of the Jewish religion against the background of Near Eastern and Indo-European paganism, and the investigation of Jewish mysticism. The encounter with Greek culture was perceived mainly as an encounter with philosophical thought.

The founders of the school of *Völkerpsychologie* (national psychology), Heymann Steinthal (1823–99) and Moritz Lazarus (1824–1904), and their follower Ignaz Goldziher viewed culture as a collective creation, the product of both objective and subjective faculties and circumstances. Their purpose was to prove that the Hebrews had had a rich life of the imagination, the fruit of a 'sense of imagination' and inventive ability. This was a quest not for the primeval or the pre-cultural, but rather for the normative elements in culture. Having accepted the prevailing theory that mythology is the primal element of the imaginative faculty, Steinthal and Goldziher claimed that the Jews were polytheists when they took their first steps on the stage of history. This, of course, was an execrable heresy against a most sacred principle of the historical Jewish faith. They believed, however, that it did not in any way denigrate monotheistic values, but merely indicated the manner in which the Hebrews had exchanged polytheism for an exalted monotheism, while copying the figurative world of polytheism to the framework of the new faith and changing its essence and its purpose.[110]

Ignaz Goldziher, subsequently the greatest scholar of Islam of his day, devoted his first, very daring book to verifying the existence of an ancient mythological layer in the Israelite culture. Not long afterward, he came to believe that his book evinced immaturity and the follies of youth; it deserved only to be buried and forgotten.[111] The work drew upon the theories of Max Müller and F. F. A. Kuhn, which posited that Semites did not have a mythology. These theories were highly influential in Goldziher's

---

[109] Y. Shavit, '"Semites" and "Aryans"'.

[110] See Sambursky, *The Laws of Heaven and Earth*; G. E. R. Lloyd, *The Revolution of Wisdom*.

[111] Goldziher's *Mythos bei den Hebräern* (1876) was translated into English with the approval of the author, who later disowned this fruit of his youth. See also Olender, *Languages*, 115–35.

day, and served as a direct rebuttal to Renan's challenge. Goldziher's basic assumption was that polytheism and monotheism are not two opposing conditions of human consciousness, but rather two stages in its overall development. No social group and no culture can deviate from this rule of development. Just as it is impossible to deny members of the various races certain common physiognomic features (for example, similar bodily organs which function in similar ways), so it is impossible to deny them certain common psychological characteristics, the first of which is the ability to create a mythology. From Edward Tylor's widely acclaimed book, *Primitive Culture* (1856), Goldziher learnt that a psychological law must apply everywhere.

Goldziher defined myth as a mode of expression that tells us how nature acts; it is the mode of expression by which man understands and interprets, in the first stages of his intellectual development, how the natural forces around him function. Myth, therefore, is the consequence of pure psychological action. As opposed to this, the mythologies of different peoples are cast in different moulds, but the resulting disparities do not derive from a difference in human nature, but rather from a different reaction or response to the environment in which the myth develops. In Goldziher's early writings he claims that in the early days of their history the Jews were a polytheistic people. It is important to note that he differentiates between primal mythology and cosmogony, which is the product of a much later and more perfected development. The primal mythology is embedded in the most ancient layers of the Bible, in its etymological inventory. The cosmogony is found in the story of Creation in Genesis, where Goldziher detects a profound Babylonian and Persian influence, and defers the date of its transcription to the period of the Babylonian exile.

'Myth', Goldziher writes, 'is something universal . . . the faculty of forming it cannot a priori be denied to any race as such, and the coincidence of mythical ideas and modes of expression is the result of the uniformity of the psychological process which is the foundation of the creation of myth in all races.' This, in his opinion, is also the sphere of influence that imbued the aggadah and the Midrash with mythological elements.

Goldziher and Renan agree on one point, that the Hebrews of antiquity were nomads in the desert. In Goldziher's opinion, however, the desert neither destroyed nor desiccated their powers of imagination; it merely clad this natural characteristic in different garb. Thus after broadly reviewing the ancient mythological elements, Goldziher postulated that when the tribes of Israel settled in Canaan, Hebrew myth ceased developing, while Aryan myth continued to flourish. Goldziher's views were contrary to the prevailing opinion, which held that the Israelite tribes came out of the desert, encountered a Canaanite population with a developed culture, and were influenced by it, thus sullying the pure monotheism they brought with them after years of wandering. He believed that the settlement spurred a nationalistic struggle between the tribes of Israel and the ancient Canaanite inhabitants. The Israelite national consciousness fashioned unique historical traditions for itself, in clear contrast to the mythology of the autochthonous Canaanite population. In this way the mythological heroes of the Hebrew Semites became the heroes of an Israelite national historical tradition. The mythical figure of Abram (in Hebrew, 'exalted father') became Abraham: his name was changed by God through the addition of a letter from the Divine Name when he was divinely elected to become the father of the nation. As the Israelite worldview developed, myth became history and theology, and the patriarchs became national heroes, personifying the theocratic idea.

Goldziher was less original and less daring in describing the second stage of Israelite mythological development, which he viewed as resulting from influence and borrowing from the surrounding cultural sphere, including Indo-European mythology (the Hindu and the Persian). In that stage, the stories were given a new setting and new meaning, and the Perso-Babylonian cosmology became the literary infrastructure of its Israelite counterpart. The account of the Creation in Genesis is intended, by its link to the Sabbath, to impart a new rationale for the latter.

Steinthal and Goldziher did not perceive myth as an expression of the irrational aspect of man, as an unmediated link to nature, but rather as a product of perception and comprehension. Thus the symbols created by myth at the dawn of history continue to exist and to function in the human consciousness. Not only the ancient Hebrews but modern Jews as well are no different in any way from the Greeks or the Christian Europeans, and do not lack any natural characteristic of the human race. Jewish history, from its very inception, was subject to laws of universal development. This does not mean, however, that the development was not influenced or motivated by the singular consciousness and understanding of the Israelite. The Hebrews and the Greeks began, therefore, equally and at the same point. Only later did their paths diverge.

Moses Hess proposed an original reply to Renan's arguments: the message of biblical monotheism was that only in the messianic era would the Supreme Being reign as the One God; until that time, the mythological gods would exist subordinate to the One God. The prophets and sacred poets of the Bible, he said, did indeed despise idolaters; however, the biblical outlook in its entirety shows that in those days everyone believed in the transitory existence of these gods. Were we to advance the hypothesis that they were a total fabrication, then we should be perversely misconstruing the entire Bible, from the Ten Commandments to the last Psalms written. The view of those who explained biblical monotheism as arising from the limited inventive and creative faculties of the Semitic race seemed, in contrast, totally ignorant and superficial.[112]

In contrast to this view, Yehezkel Kaufmann believed that Judaism was a-mythological from its inception and by its very nature, but it did not forbid Jews to tell legends about gods. The fundamental belief in monotheism negated the fundamental belief of polytheism; hence the Jewish religion could not contain any mythological elements, certainly not a cosmogony and cosmology, a gigantomachy or a theomachy: since Judaism has no gods like those in Greek mythology, neither could it have wars between the gods. From his broad and detailed comparison between the Jewish faith and the various mythologies, including Greek, Kaufmann arrives at an absolute antinomian conclusion. If so, what is the significance of the mythological layers in the Bible (and in the literature of the Second Temple and the Sages)? In his view these are only fragments of stories, blocks of folktales from foreign sources, which were adapted to the monotheistic idea. Yet even on his showing, not only was Judaism familiar with mythological tales, it also made use of them both in literature and in popular culture. Although he asserts that these stories were fused in the melting-pot of the monotheistic conception, still it is clear that the monotheistic idea itself, not only its popular expressions, had a need for these stories.[113]

The course of events, then, was as follows. Proverbs, legends, and mythology were at first perceived as products of the faculty of creative imagination, and later as an expression of the people's collective spirit. Hence they were understood as a mode of imparting a message or a translation of reality, its representation by a mythological story or a mythological name. However, later, in the nineteenth century, myth was perceived as the most primal vital, creative force, restrained by culture, and hence rendered barren by it. The call for a renewal of this vitality could have been a call for the creation of a new culture, but by the same token, it might have been an awakening of demons.

---

[112] Hess, 'Ein characteristicher Psalm'.
[113] Y. Kaufmann, *The Religion*, i/2. 245–588, i/3. 589–623. On Greek (and Persian) myths in the literature of the Sages, see E. E. Urbach, *The Sages*, 184–213.

SATIRE: A WEAPON IN THE WAR OF IDEAS

Another literary genre worthy of attention is satire, which quickly became a central genre in Hebrew literature. There was an oblique connection between it and mythology, and it too found its way into Haskalah literature as part of the influence of Greek writing on contemporary European satire. Lucian of Samosata, in the second century AD, had employed satire to deride mythology; in Haskalah literature, it was used to mock popular beliefs in the traditional (particularly the hasidic) society.[114] Unlike aggadah, for example, satire was a new genre, and did not share much common ground with earlier Hebrew satires.[115]

The prolific *maskil* Solomon Rubin, who popularized numerous works, translated Lucian under the title *Halatzah kadmonit* ('Ancient Humour'; Cracow, 1897). The translation included his 'Dialogues of the Dead' and 'Assembly of the Gods'. The intention of this work was to ridicule mythology. Its mockery suited the dismissive attitude of Hellenic philosophy towards the 'fallibilities of the gods' and popular beliefs,[116] and resembled that of the Sages in their approach to mythology. Long before this translation, made at the turn of the century, Meir Letteris had begun to translate Lucian, publishing some of his works in the collection *Hatzefirah* (1823). The indisputable influence and echoes of Lucian's work can be found in the satires of the Galician Haskalah, whose barbed arrows were directed at hasidism, primarily in the satires of Erter and Letteris. They became acquainted with Lucian through Wieland's German translation (Berlin, 1788–9). From him, they took the satiric method of metamorphosis (the reincarnation of man as an animal and vice versa), communication with departed spirits, dialogue, and the like, and Judaized it to suit the conflict and contention within Jewish society. Satire was a loyal ally—as in the hands of the French Enlightenment—against the dark ignorance of the religious authorities, superstition, and the craving for the magic and miracles

---

[114] In Wolfsohn Halle's satire 'Sichah be'eretz hachayim', *Hame'asef*, 7 (1794–7), in the tradition of Lucian's *nekrikoi dialogoi* (*Dialogues of the Dead*), Maimonides and Mendelssohn meet in Hades (described in the manner of a *locus amoenus*). At the entrance to the 'land of the living' (i.e. Hades), there is a sign reading 'This is the entrance for the pagan Greek.' A Polish rabbi appears and derides the Greek sages: 'By what measure can they be compared to us? All their days they have walked in darkness. May their name and memory be effaced from the land of the living.' Maimonides replies: 'What is this? Can you think that Greek sages like Socrates, Plato, and their fellows are prevented from sitting with us here, and that they have no place in our midst? How stupid can you be?' He adds that only after the rabbi has unburdened himself of his false opinions will he learn truly to know the Almighty, acquire wisdom and reason, and achieve a place next to himself and Mendelssohn.

[115] See the debate between Gilon and Friedlander in *Zion*, 54/4 (1987), 510–30. See also Friedlander's four-volume *Hebrew Satire in Europe*.

[116] Werses, 'Echoes'; Routledge, *The Dialogue of the Dead*.

worked by rabbis and *tzaddikim*. We learn of familiarity with Lucian from Meir Letteris' testimony that on R. Nachman Krochmal's table, alongside the Talmud, the Zohar, and Spinoza, lay *Sefer Lukianos miSamazata* ('the book of Lucian of Samosata').

It appears that Wessely's warning of 1783 (see Ch. 5) referred not only to the outright use of a mythological repertoire, but also to the use of anti-mythological satire in the style of Lucian. He feared not only that in this indirect fashion mythology would find its way into modern Hebrew literature, but also that the satire itself would undermine religion. In any event, because there was no source in Jewish literary tradition for satiric literature, Lucian's style was adopted by those who regarded satire as a powerful weapon and an influence in the *Kulturkampf* being conducted at that time among the Jews of eastern Europe.[117] The use of mythology and its analogues, the hasidic aggadot, imparted a romantic and imaginative flavour to the satires, which was needed to make them attractive as literature. Erter explained the mythological motifs in the same way as Rall, but in a different context, as vital to a poetic work; hence the distinction between the message of the mythological story and its aesthetic value. Those who believed in mythology, Erter declared, submerged 'the intelligence of their forefathers in the morass of the imagination' and cast them down 'with the speed of folly, hurrying to believe everything alien to nature and distant from reason'. Despite this negative opinion, however, he did believe that mythological motifs play a part in animating a laudable poetic work.

ART, ARCHITECTURE, AND MUSIC:
CLASSICISM VERSUS MONUMENTALISM

Amateur scholars and writers tend to characterize the laws governing Israelite architecture and decoration, sculpture and painting, as the *Gegentyp* of classical rules. We have already mentioned in another connection the comments of Uri Zevi Greenberg, who discerned in classicism an aesthetic contrary to the dynamic and vital rhythm of Israel:

But woe to those among us, the nation of Expressionism, who long for Pallas Athena, Olympus, and the nine Muses! For the rewards will not be forthcoming; they will not be forthcoming! The yearning for them is in vain. The disavowal of the dynamic essence of Israel is in vain! For our existence is one great outcry in the world! How will they bind us, those who tether us to classicism?[118]

---

[117] Werses, 'Echoes', 112.   [118] *Kelapei tishim veteshah*, 8.

In 1923, the poet Avigdor Hameiri wrote in the same spirit:

The difference between the Hebrew perception in antiquity and the Greek perception at the time was monumentalism in architecture—the very same difference in building cities as between the Assyrians and Egyptians on the one hand, and the Greeks and Romans on the other: a pyramid versus a Greek statue. Here, lofty proportions, monumentalism; there, a pleasing beauty, but reduced in size. In this respect, then, the Greeks and the Romans are to the Egyptians and the Assyrians what the Europeanism of today is to the way of the Greeks: decadence.[119]

The Hebrew sculptor or painter must therefore be, at the very least, a pupil of the author of the Song of Songs, for otherwise he will diminish the monumentalism of this song and depreciate its value! Whereas in Homeric poetry the vehicle of the simile (the image) is diminished by the tenor (the subject), in the Song of Songs the vehicles are a part of nature, and therefore magnified: 'Thy nose is like the tower of Lebanon'; 'thy head upon thee is like Carmel'. This, in other words, is monumental poetry; the East is not exotic or Levantine or Oriental—it is monumental. That is a generalized and groundless claim. It is no wonder that others preferred to stress Jewish aesthetics as it is expressed in art in contrast to the sensuality of classic (as well as Byzantine) art. However, the same line was taken by the sculptor Abraham Melnikoff (1892–1960), whose works were inspired by Mesopotamian sculpture:

For many generations, the Jews did not take part in creating portraiture, and there are numerous reasons for this. The chief reason, however, is that European art is founded on Graeco-Roman culture, and the visionaries envisaged and the dreamers dreamed about the fusion of Athens and Jerusalem . . . East and West, men are distant from each other; one does not touch the other even when they meet. So long as Athens was the mother of the Arts in Europe, the Jew instinctively stood on the outside and every attempt to bring him into the palace came to naught . . . Only after Art turned to the East did the Jew not tarry, but came to secure a place for himself that was seemly for him in this movement. A standard for the art current in Europe is an Eastern standard, something close to the heart of the Jew, and that is Expressionism. Expressionism is neither old nor new, Expressionism is eternal, from ancient times, from the earliest of the primeval kingdoms in Babylon until this very day—one continuing golden chain. Art in Babylon, Assyria, Egypt, India and China is one Expressionistic chain, which fascinates the generations and unifies the different Eastern cultures . . . Yes, Expressionism is ours, bone of our bones and flesh of our flesh, and I deeply

---

[119] *Do'ar hayom*, 14 Dec. 1923; of course he ignored Jewish imitation of the figurative-allegoristic art of mosaic in the Byzantine period (Goodenough, *Jewish Symbols*).

regret that even today a noted group of artists in Palestine still roll in the dust of Japheth and see not the gold of Jacob.[120]

Thus, in this rather ironic way, the sculpture of the pagan Semitic cultures of Mesopotamia became the model for emulation and affinity. This resulted from the need to assign to Jewish sculpture and the plastic arts a character other than the classic. European Expressionism became analogous to the monumental Mesopotamian (and Egyptian) sculpture. This was a result of a distorted portrayal of Greek art and of the relics from the Canaanite and ancient Israelite material culture—which, as a matter of fact, was not monumental.[121]

Jewish art from Palestine in the 1920s and early 1930s shows a neo-Classical influence, particularly in the depiction of Palestine as an Oriental Arcadia, parallel to the ideal of contemporary Hebrew poetry.[122]

In some modern Orthodox circles, there was evidence of an openness to art, on the grounds that Judaism does not oppose non-figurative art and that there are artistic motifs characteristic of Judaism. These groups first sought to identify a concept of Judaism, and against that background they determined how that concept should be expressed in art. Hence one could conclude that Judaism had a modern conception of art and even before the advent of modernism had held the view that art need not imitate reality.[123]

It is worth remembering that prior to seeking the 'concept of Jewish art', it was necessary to accord legitimacy to the very existence of Jewish art. To that end, a number of talmudic passages were cited. Many quoted the words of the Babylonian Talmud: 'There is no artist like our God' (*Berakhot* 10a) or Rabban Gamaliel's reply to the philosopher Proclus, who asked the rabbi how he could bathe in a public bath which displayed a statue of Aphrodite. Rabban Gamaliel replied, 'I did not come within her sphere; she came into mine' (Mishnah, *Avodah Zarah* 3: 4). There is a world of difference between a tolerant or neutral attitude to art and a particular outlook on its function and essence. Such an outlook has been alien to Judaism throughout the ages; it does not occupy

---

[120] *Ha'aretz*, 18 Dec. 1925. See Mishori, 'The Rebirth of Hebrew Art'. Indeed, the search for legitimization for Jewish art goes so far as to view Moses as a patron of art (in the building of the Tabernacle) and also his successor Solomon, the builder of the Temple. It even goes so far as to claim that Canaanite art was an integral part of the art of the children of Israel, and that they also made statuettes. See Y. Malkin, 'Moses and Aaron'.

[121] Ziffer, *At that Time the Canaanites were in the Land*.

[122] Efrat, 'The Idyll and Palestinian Painting'.

[123] D. Cassuto, *Jewish Art*; Schwarzschild, 'The Legal Foundation of Jewish Aesthetics'; Z. Levy, 'Esthetical Values and the Jewish Religious Tradition'; Schweid, 'Art as an Existential Problem'.

itself with aesthetic questions, with the exception of scattered observations.[124]

Those subscribing to later theories preferred to view the opposition to
figurative art as a harbinger of modernism. Knowledge about Jewish art
was drastically modified by the discovery of Palestinian Jewish art from the
Second Temple era and the Hellenistic influence that dominated it, which
continued until the Byzantine era—mosaics with mythological figures and
so on. The unique elements in the Jewish art of this period, which were
integrated into the overall framework of emulation and borrowing, have
been widely discussed as a distinctive model of cultural contact in art.

These theories, then, constitute an appraisal according to borrowed
criteria of the art created by Jews, along with an attempt to ascertain
the artistic school and style best suited to the concept of Judaism, of
Hebraism, of Israelism. We are not speaking, of course, only of Jewish or
Hebrew motifs—of subjects taken from the Jewish historical experience—
but rather of a thematic selection and an artistic design of the world and
of reality according to a Jewish world-outlook and the aesthetic derived
from and dictated by it.

Once it had been proved that Jews and Hebrews had a creative imagination—one which produced poetry, parables, and legends—scholars and
men of letters turned to other areas of spiritual and material culture,
including architecture. In a series of articles published in the journal *Keneset
Yiśrael* under the heading 'Miyefiyuto shel Yefet be'ohalei Shem' ('From
the Beauties of Japheth in the Tents of Shem'), Abraham Tannenbaum
uttered a sustained polemic against the idea that Jews had no intrinsic
architectonic perception. To prove his point, he presented as evidence
the house of worship—the need of every Jewish community to build a
synagogue 'using the finest, most discriminating taste, and in a manner that
is pleasant and beautiful to behold'. It is true, he agrees, that one could
not compare the Jews with the ancient Greeks and Romans, because 'in
the annals of fine arts, these nations, especially the former, rose high above
all the rest'. In comparison to other ancient peoples, however, the Jews
were not inferior 'in the quality of their good taste for grace and beauty,
in their desire for every sight of majesty . . . and vision of glory'. This
was true regarding the art of music as well, and there, too, 'the Jews
were not inferior to the rest of the nations'. If they accomplished little in
painting, engraving in stone, and in the techniques of building, this was
due to objective limitations and not because of any prohibition whatsoever

---

[124] Tsafrir, *Archeology and Art.*

'when they foolishly passed judgement on those who studied the annals of fine arts in ancient times'.

Tannenbaum describes in some detail the monuments and relics that had been unearthed in the soil of Mesopotamia, which was, he claimed, the source of material culture and the source of all the arts, including the art of building, architecture, decoration, and the like. This Mesopotamian material culture was the wellspring of inspiration and imitation for Israel, just as it had been for the Greeks. But Israel gave its material culture a singular character, suited to its world-view and the dictates of its religion. In this respect, Renan is highly praised, as in other contemporary writings. Of all the famous thinkers of Europe, none could compare with him, wrote Tannenbaum, for he contributed so much to the recognition of Canaanite and Phoenician culture.[125]

A few words may be said here about music. Music played a very important role in the cultural life of the Jews, certainly in the service in the Temple. King David, as we know, played the harp (or rather the kithara) and was a sweet singer, hence there is no doubt as to the legitimacy of music and the need for it. 'Music was the pride of a nation which distributed their songs in such a way', wrote Judah Halevi, '. . . David and Samuel were its great masters'.[126]

The question then arose: what is Jewish music? and is it possible to reconstruct it from the biblical period? The musicologist Abraham Idelsohn (1882–1933), for example, believed that the Semitic scale had four notes and that the Greeks borrowed their musical scale from it. He also asserted that musical style and melody are linked to the spirit of the people.[127] Other scholars claimed that medieval Jewish music originated from a Christian source.[128] In any event, it is a historical fact that Jewish music in various cultural activities was clearly influenced by the local musical tradition, and consequently there is no one single, uniform Jewish musical style (just as there is no one uniform 'Jewish cuisine'). The search for Jewish music also arises from the desire to prove that a complete Jewish culture, with all its components, existed in the past, and that such a culture could—and should—also exist in the present. However, music is a good example of the process of Judaizing all traits of culture and of the neutral character of some of them. Evidence of this is the use made in Orthodox circles (particularly by the hasidim) of various melodies, including some from

---

[125] Tannenbaum, 'Habeniyah vehagizrah'.
[126] *Kuzari*, ii. 64; trans. Hirschfeld, 123.
[127] See Idelsohn, *Neginatenu hale'umit*.
[128] Golb, 'The Music of Obadiah'; Harrán, *In Search of Harmony*.

European or Latin American popular and commercial music. Here music is not an expression of the soul, but rather provides a musical framework (melody and rhythm) for contents which incorporate a spiritual message.

THE JEWS AND ATHLETICS

The last element in the pattern of antinomy that will be discussed here is the attitude of Jews to sports and physical culture. The Hasidaeans' contention with the Hellenizing Jews and with Hellenism was a struggle against the Hellenistic cult of the body, in which physical culture and its main arenas, the stadium and the palaestra, were paramount. Yet from the outset the Jewish nationalistic movement introduced—as a counter-reaction to the popular portrait of the physically degenerate Diaspora Jew—the ideology of the 'muscular Jew'.[129] This implied not military bravery, but participation in sport, hikes, and physical activities (not necessarily competitive and achievement-oriented). But if it was the Maccabees, the heroes of the people and the heroic paragons of modern Jewish nationalism, who waged the all-out war against Hellenistic physical culture, how was it then possible to foster a positive attitude toward muscles and sport?

Some Jews took a dim view of the Hasmonean policy. A prominent example was Max Nordau, whose ideology, known as 'muscular Judaism' (and its products as 'muscular Jews'), held that even in the past Jews 'would burst into the arena *en masse*', but concealing their Jewish origin.[130] The modern Jew, in contrast, is once again unashamed of his love of sport, and athletes openly proclaim their Judaism. In another context, legends about Bar-Kokhba and his amazing physical prowess exemplified the value of such attributes, but clearly they could not serve to legitimize participation in sports. To confirm that Jews had in fact taken part in sports, the Wingate Institute of Physical Culture had H. A. Harris's book *Greek Athletics and the Jews* translated into Hebrew.[131] Harris, it is interesting to note, refers to the writings of Philo to show that he was familiar with the popular sports of his time, and that along with his basic reservations about competitive sports (which he shared with Greek philosophers and Fathers

---

[129] Almog, 'From "Muscular Jewry" to the "Religion of Labour"'. On the influence of the Greek idea that superior health implies superior beauty, see Mosse, 'Jewish Emancipation', 10–12.

[130] Nordau, 'Yahadut hashririm', 187–8.

[131] Bella, *The World of Jabotinsky*, 133, quotes Jabotinsky as saying that mankind will be eternally indebted to the Greeks for having made sport a means of education. See also Pinczower, *Der jüdische Läufer*; J. Schwartz, 'Ball Play in Jewish Society'; Gardiner, *Athletics of the Ancient World*.

of the Church) Philo was nevertheless a 'sports fan' at heart; the same is true of St Paul, who must have acquired his sporting experience as Saul of Tarsus.[132]

A knowledge of sport and the use of its various branches as metaphors is certainly not convincing evidence that athletics was an acceptable and legitimate activity in Palestinian Jewish society, which in fact identified games with Hellenistic cultural customs, and considered them contemptible. The fact that modern Jewish culture emphasizes and legitimizes the value of physical education can only be interpreted as a clear trend of Hellenization.

Chayim Tchernowitz (Rav Tza'ir), a Jewish traveller to Palestine in 1912, described the attempt being made there to use tales of heroism, rural hikes, and sport to supplement regular educational activities in order to create a new Jewish type: 'The teachers prepare excursions and games on the Olympic pattern, and accustom [the children] to tournaments and celebrations', he observed, not without a hint of criticism.[133] A typical illustration of this situation is the somewhat paradoxical ceremony of lighting the torch on Chanukah at the tombs of the Maccabees at Modi'in. The ceremony was given a traditional interpretation, in that the torch was linked to the motif of light, which is central to the holiday. However, the ritual of lighting the torch and running with it to various parts of the country to announce the arrival of the holiday is associated not only with the nationalist character of the holiday, but with the torch-races of certain Greek religious rituals and with the torch-bearers of the modern Olympics—though not the ancient Games that they profess to revive. History, then, has produced a keenly ironic event: a ceremony which is meant to commemorate the Jewish spiritual victory over Hellenism is bound up with a symbolic act derived from the very heart of Hellenistic culture![134]

[132] Harris, *Greek Athletics and the Jews*, 51–95; id., *Greek Athletes and Athletics*, 129–35; on the place of sport in Hellenistic education see also Marrou, *History of Education in Antiquity*, 116–32. For a more detailed description of Jews' attitudes to Greek athletics and their participation in it in the general context of Hellenization see Chambers, 'Greek Athletics and the Jews'. Professor Hillel Raskin stated recently (*Ha'aretz*, 15 Nov. 95) that Israelis avoid physical activity because of the historical memory of the struggle against Hellenistic sports; he had written a pamphlet encouraging physical education, distribution of which was banned in the religious schools. No wonder the Orthodox press never mentioned the 1996 Olympic Games in Atlanta, even after the act of terrorism committed there, because, as one journalist explained, 'it is connected in the eyes of ultra-Orthodoxy with Hellenism' (*Ha'aretz*, 29 July 1996).

[133] Tchernowitz, 'Rishmei Eretz Yisrael', 3–4, quoted in Frankel, 'The "Yizkor" Book of 1911', 376 n. 58.

[134] We could expand the discussion to include the history of the rediscovery of the Jewish body and sexuality. See Gilman, *The Jew's Body*; Biale, *Eros and the Jews*.

THE SEARCH FOR AN IDEAL HEBREW CULTURE

> The Greeks, who were created, according to this theory, for the sake of
> beauty, produced all those beautiful works of art, wrote all those beau-
> tiful books; and then, when there was nothing more for them to do, al-
> though their mission was not completely fulfilled, and although during
> the centuries which separated then from the Renaissance their beauty
> lay hidden from the world—then history removed them from the stage,
> and left the rest to that progress which proceeded automatically from
> the Greek legacy of works of art and books. Why, then, should not his-
> tory allow *us* to make our exit? We have done all that we could for our
> mission: we have produced the Scriptures. Further there is nothing for
> us to do; why, then, must we live?[135]

Ahad Ha'am did not accept the theory of mission, that every nation has a
specific mission to fulfil, nor did he think that the Jews had and have only
one mission—to disseminate the message of monotheism. He believed, like
most of the national thinkers, that the people of Israel was a living body,
and therefore it could, and should, create a whole body of culture; the
Jewish genius was not restricted to only one narrow sphere, as important
as that sphere might be.

The revolution in the understanding of Jewish history was expressed in
its reinterpretation and in the notion that Judaism is not only a religion
but also a *culture*; a culture which is the main expression of the spirit and
the genius of a nation. The beautiful, the spontaneous, the imaginative,
and the creative were given the status of key values. Poetry and literature
were perceived as the heart and soul, the inner life (*Innerlichkeit*) of modern
Hebrew culture, its reflection and its expression as well as its very essence
and its driving force. Literature was perceived as society's inner voice, con-
juring up the picture of its past and portraying the vision of its future.
Basing themselves on the premiss that culture is a total system that has
several modes of expression for both the inner and outer world, Hebrew
men of letters and artists gazed into the Greek mirror in order to see in it
what the Jews had and what they lacked, as well as what was one-sided, incomplete, and incorrect. In order to rebut claims that the deficiencies arose
from an integral and irreparable flaw, they emphasized the positive characteristics of Hebrew culture. They examined it and found in it expressions
and manifestations whose existence had been unjustifiably denied, out of
ignorance or prejudice. On the other hand, they also found in the Greek
mirror subjects worthy of borrowing or emulating. If anti-Jewish writings
stamped the Jews with an immutable ontological essence, Jewish thinkers

---

[135] Ahad Ha'am, 'Slavery in Freedom', 187.

and literati responded to the assertion in two ways, which were meant to complement each other, but which also created a deep internal tension. They sought to present Judaism as dynamic, as changing immanently as well as in reaction to external stimuli and challenges; hence what it did not possess, it could acquire and assimilate. But they also sought zealously to guard the eternal and unchanging elements of the immanent, unique essence that gave Judaism its abiding character and culture.

The difficult task they—and modern Hebrew culture—faced was how to create in a short period of time all the necessary cultural components, and how to create them in a Hebrew (or Jewish) spirit.[136]

---

[136] See Ch. 16.

PART II

THE SECOND MIRROR

Scholars, be cautious with your words, for you may incur
the penalty of exile and be banished to a place of evil waters.
The disciples who follow you there may drink and die,
and consequently the Name of Heaven will be profaned.

Mishnah Avot, 1: 11

Owing to Zionism, world culture will enter into Israel and will create
a new Judaism, that will be the historical graftage of the most exalted
creations of the world, of the outside, onto the national characteristics
and the most ancient creations of the people of Israel, within the tent.

NACHMAN SYRKIN, 'Min hachutzah ha'ohelah'
('From the Outside into the Tent')

9

THE NATURE OF THE
HELLENISTIC MIRROR

> The Jews have not merely a tendency to imitation, but a genius for it.
> Whatever they imitate, they imitate well.
>
> AHAD HA'AM, 'Imitation and Assimilation'

AND WHAT HAD ALEXANDRIA TO DO WITH JERUSALEM?

On the historical level the answer is simple: with Alexandria, Jerusalem had a real encounter. Indeed, at one time, in the third century BC, it was under the rule of the Ptolemaic dynasty, but one cannot compare the cultural influences of this occupation on the Jews in Palestine with the influences of Hellenistic rule on the Jewish community in Alexandria. However, 'Alexandria' serves here as a symbol for Hellenistic culture as a whole. And this culture is our second mirror—the Hellenistic mirror. One facet of this mirror is the similarity and disparity between Judaism and Hellenistic civilization; the other is the reflection of the encounter between these two in the modern historical consciousness; or perhaps it would be more correct to say the depiction of the way that Judaism adapted to life within the Hellenistic civilization, was influenced by it, and changed while preserving its uniqueness. The Greek mirror did not have to yield its central position when the Hellenistic mirror made its appearance. The latter only added a new dimension in examining the place of Judaism in the modern world.

The following chapters are intended primarily to describe some of the images of the encounter (or discourse) between Judaism and Hellenism from the time of Alexander the Great until late antiquity. These images served as paradigms for the modern discourse between Western culture and the Jews. The modern Europe that was born after the French Revolution was a totally different historical entity from the ancient East refashioned by Alexander (even though one can find a echo of the ideals of *homonoia* and *concordia* in the abstractly universal ideas of the French Revolution). However, in both historical epochs, Jews had to respond to the new world with its new laws, values, structures, opportunities, temptations, and demands. It is not the ways in which they responded that make the two periods similar, but the mere fact that Jews (and Judaism) had to respond, and that they were well aware that they had to. They were forced to respond in the one because they were fully conscious that the Hellenism in which they had begun to live was different from the former Eastern empires; they were forced to respond in the other because they were fully aware that Europe from the late eighteenth century on was a different historical entity from medieval Europe.

The most important fact to note is that the Jews of the Second Temple period in Palestine and in Alexandria on the one hand encountered different types of Hellenism, but on the other both met a new culture, which was different from classical Greece in many fundamental social, political, and cultural traits. Some of these traits were a result of Eastern influences, for example, the divine cult of kings.[1] Thus, for Second Temple Judaism, Hellenism in the East was not as alien and strange as classical Athens.

THE IMAGES OF HELLENISM

In the nineteenth century the Jew had to encounter not only the ideal Greece and the heritage of classical antiquity but also a new image of Hellenism and of Hellenistic civilization.

In classical Greek the term *Hellēnismos* meant no more than 'using pure Greek style' or 'behaving like a Greek', but in actuality it denoted a shared education, which assumed that human beings (both Greeks and barbarians) are equal, according to their intellectual virtues (*dianoia*) and their nature. It was, as already mentioned, Droysen who made an unequivocal division between the classical world and the era of Hellenistic civilization.[2] He borrowed the term 'Hellenism' from the New Testament (Acts 6: 1), not from the Books of Maccabees. In the New Testament the *Hellēnistai* are Greek-speaking Jews, whether because their primary language was Greek, or because they used Greek in worship. Later on the term 'Hellenist' referred to anyone who followed a Greek style of life (Greek manners) or even anyone who did not live according to the Torah and its precepts, whereas the Jew (*Ioudaios*) was anyone who lived according to the Jewish

---

[1] For seven basic differences betwen the classical world and the new Hellenist culture see M. Smith, *Palestinian Parties*, 58–9; cf. Hengel, *Judaism and Hellenism*, 1–5.

[2] Momigliano, 'Droysen between Greeks and Jews', 308–10 (on Momigliano's view of Droysen see Asheri, 'In Memory of A. Momigliano'); Jaeger, *Early Christianity*, 106–7 n. 5; Mendeles, *The Rise and Fall*, 13–34. Among the many works on Hellenism and Hellenistic civilization see: Ferguson, *The Heritage of Hellenism*; Tarn, *Hellenistic Civilization*; Peters, *The Harvest of Hellenism*; Walbank, *The Hellenistic World*; Golan, *History of the Hellenistic World*; Burstein, 'The Greek Tradition'; Grant, *Hellenistic Religion*; Green, *Hellenistic History and Culture*.

tradition ('the perfect manner of the laws of the fathers', Acts 22: 3, and see also Gal. 2: 14).

The originality of Droysen's approach was 'to take Hellenism to mean specifically the way of thinking of Jews under the influence of Greek language and thought, but generally the language and way of thinking of all the population which had been conquered by Alexander and subjected to Greek influence'.[3] According to Droysen, the city-state gave way to a civilization blended out of Hellenic and Eastern elements, cosmopolitan in nature, crossing national and ethnic borders and blurring them. The cult of the city was replaced by multiethnic empires and cosmopolitan philosophical schools. This was a civilization based first on the Greek language and later on Greek 'education' (paideia). But this picture painted by Droysen ignored the heterogeneous character of Hellenism in various Eastern lands, and the difference in character and content of the Hellenistic component from one syncretistic culture to another. It also ignored the continued existence of age-old autochthonous cultures with their own traditions; the manner in which these cultures came to terms with universal (and imperialistic) Hellenism; and the influence of those very cultures upon Greek immigrant settlers and their descendants. Naturally, the culture of a given Hellenistic polis is not identical either with the generalized 'Hellenistic culture' of modern expositions or with Hellenistic philosophy.

In more recent literature, Hellenism has been perceived as a synthesis between the values of classical Greece and the diversified cultural heritage of the East, but the nature of this compound and the relationship between its various components have been the subject of prolonged debate: What part did the Eastern component play? How deeply did the ancient cultures of the East adapt, defend themselves, and survive?[4] To what depth did classical culture really penetrate those of the East? What was the nature of the new cultural syncretism? And what part did it play in preparing the ground for the appearance and success of Christianity?

In its common positive image, Hellenism was perceived as a universal culture that blurred the boundaries between peoples, and also as modern and liberal in its nature. In it 'East and West were brought together'.[5] Some

---

[3] Momigliano, 'Droysen', 310.

[4] See Eddy, The King is Dead, and Peters, The Harvest of Hellenism, 151–84.

[5] Sarton, Hellenistic Science, 4. Tarn wrote that 'In matters of the spirit, Asia knew that she could outstay the Greeks, as she did' (Hellenistic Civilization), 163. And see Davidson, The Education, 177–229 on the contacts of Greece with the Eastern and the Western world, expressing in sum the view that 'Orientalism' added to Greek philosophy new concepts and contents, including the concept of a living, holy, all-knowing, all-powerful God, concepts which were the underpinnings of Christianity, and thus that the Council of Nicaea (325) saved Christianity—and Hellenism. This rests on the notion,

were so confident about the power of classical Greece that they truly believed that 'dwell where he might, the Greek remained a Greek; wherever
he went he carried Hellas with him'.[6] Needless to say, what Edward Freeman meant by this phrase is that America was shaped by England, since the
Englishman carried England wherever he went, be it America or India.
For example, J. W. Draper, in his popular book *History of the Intellectual
Development of Europe* (1861), defined the Hellenistic period as the 'Greek
age of reason', because of the central role it assigned to science, to rational philosophy, and to institutions such as the museums and libraries
that flourished in it for the benefit of the entire public.[7] It was Hellenism,
he wrote, that eradicated the division between Hellenes and Barbarians
and created one humanity. Gilbert Murray wrote with great ardour, 'It
was a liberal civilization: free, tolerant and unprejudiced, highly cultured,
and out of its abundance, generous and helpful to the rest of mankind.'[8]
Hellenism, mature and consummate, abandoned a childish belief in gods
and myths. Its ethos was shaped by philosophical teachings. Different cultures existing within its framework enriched one another through free
exchange, without prejudices; in consequence all spheres of cultural and
artistic creation flourished and prospered. In this boundless joy, there was
only one closed and fanatical religious group that insisted on maintaining
its uniqueness, while regarding all those around it with unconcealed contempt. A religious group, destined by fate and history to have no state of
its own, in contrast to Hellenism, which formed a vastly powerful culture
and a creative state—thus Eduard Meyer, the great German historian of
antiquity, described the lot of Second Temple Judaism.[9]

It is a striking fact that Hellenism was seen in a positive light even by

shared with Christians by believers in history as progress, that the historic mission of the ancient world
was to prepare the way for Christianity, which was until recent the unchallengeable foundation for
its intellectual history; and that because Christianity as we know it is the faith as defined at Nicaea
(and subsequent councils), therefore Nicaea saved Christianity, and with it Hellenism in its highest form.
Without such a historicism, one may allow that consubstantiality of Son with Father, as opposed to Arian
subordinationism, 'saved' Christianity from the strict monotheism of Judaism and Islam; but it is not
intuitively obvious that that was more a victory for Hellenism, interpreted as polytheism, than a defeat,
insofar as the defeated theologies were more compatible with Neoplatonism, and indeed appeared more
logical (Williams, 'The Logic of Arianism'). After all, 'Arianism' in its various forms was strong in the
Greek world, and among intellectuals; 'consubstantialis' was adopted from the theologically backward
Latin West and imposed by a Latin-speaking emperor of no intellectual standing.

[6] Freeman, *Greater Greece and Greater Britain*, 30. See also Fischer, *The Passing of the European Age*,
129–36.

[7] Draper, *History of Intellectual Development*, 171–206. In *The Birth of Tragedy*, §19 (trans. Kaufmann,
114–21), Nietzsche refers to 'Alexandrian cheerfulness' ('the culture of the opera') as opposed to the
tragic depth of the Aeschylean spirit. 　　　　　[8] Murray, *Hellenism and the Modern World*, 40.

[9] Hoffmann, *Juden und Judentum*, 152, citing Eduard Meyer, *Geschichte des Altertums*, iv/1. 782–3 on
the Jews' 'staatlose Kultur'.

those striving to realize an integrative cultural nationalism, for example in Germany. The temporary political unity of the Hellenic world, achieved by a Macedonian king, blurred the fact that this unity was shattered after his demise, as well as the fact that Hellenism was a culture without any political national boundaries. It seems that it was the tendency to stress the Hellenistic element in Pauline Christianity over the Jewish element that gave Hellenism a positive image. This tendency also deepened the antisemitic element of refined intellectual philhellenism. The modern Christian longing for Hellenism was also attended by sharp anti-Jewish tones, as well as a leaning towards the Aryan theory. The Hellenization of Christianity meant cleansing the West of its putative Semitic origin. In other words, the Jewish–Hellenistic opposition was central to the polemic about the origins of Christianity and its debt to Judaism.

But was Hellenism really a cohesive culture? Martin Hengel writes that 'Hellenism, then, must be treated as a complex phenomenon which cannot be limited to purely political socioeconomic, and cultural aspects, but must embrace them all.'[10] Indeed, the generalized image of Hellenism, from Droysen to Wilamowitz and Tarn, obscures the multiplicity and variety of the Hellenistic civilization and the changes that it underwent during the hundreds of years of its existence. Not only uniformity, but also variety characterized the Hellenistic culture which spread from the Mediterranean to the borders of India. Thus the interest of the historian of the Hellenistic civilization is to describe the core that created the unity and uniformity and how the diversity and variety existed within the general framework. Our interest here lies in the fact that Hellenism was marked by special qualities shared by all of its components, but also by great diversity. Consequently, in any discussion of contacts between Judaism and Hellenism, the question that inevitably arises is: how did Judaism fit into this unity, but, at the same time, by which components of the diversity was it influenced and which did it adopt? Here before us is one more constituent in the analogy with Judaism's encounter with the modern world, a world also marked by a new unifying framework which incorporates great diversity and variety of components.

It should be recalled at this point that although scholarship places an emphasis on the Hellenic renaissance in the art and literature of the nineteenth century, there was another renaissance, perhaps a more important one, which was not manifested in art and literature but rather in the world of philosophical thought. The writings of the Hellenistic philoso-

---

[10] Hengel, *Judaism and Hellenism*, 3; A. Momigliano, review of foregoing; id., 'Hellenism'. See also L. H. Feldman's criticism in 'Hengel's Judaism and Hellenism'.

phers were translated and published in annotated editions, reaching a wider public of educated readers than ever before. We can find many traces of the direct and indirect influence of Hellenistic thinking in modern Western philosophy, as well as more than a few parallels. In other words, a great deal has been written on the revival of Greekness, and too little, in my view, about the revival of Hellenism in its philosophical manifestations. This topic is outside the bounds of this work, as well as being beyond my competence. What should interest us here is this: If Hellenism cannot be succinctly summed up and characterized, the question that presents itself is not only what we can compare or contrast 'Judaism' with. A weightier historical question would be: With which Hellenism did Judaism interact culturally? With which Hellenism did it clash? From which Hellenism did it borrow, and undergo influence? What kind of Hellenistic Judaism (or Jewish Hellenism) was it?

HELLENISM IN JEWISH EYES

From a Jewish point of view, Hellenism was not Droysen's Hellenism but the Hellenism portrayed in the Book of Maccabees. In 2 Maccabees 2: 21 the name *Ioudaïsmos* (the Jewish way of life, namely Judaism) appears as the antithetical equivalent of *Hellēnismos* (Greek manners, Greek fashions); these are presented as two general concepts. 'Jews who came up against "*Hellenists*" defined by their culture rather than, or more than by their descent or place of origin (and certainly not by their residence), respond in kind by defining themselves as "*Judaists*", adherents of "*Judaism*".'[11] Hengel writes that the antithetical use of *Hellēnismos* and *Ioudaïsmos* 'shows both the inner affinity of Judaism to the Greek world as well as its opposition',[12] while Jonathan A. Goldstein has suggested that the writer chose deliberately to use a word of this form because it 'induced his literate Greek audience to remember the struggle of the loyal Hellenes against the barbarian Persians'.[13] In other words, the author of 2 Maccabees wished to present a total antinomy, but in order to characterize it, he needed to invent a new noun, equivalent to the noun *Hellēnismos*.

[11] Daniel Schwartz, *Studies in the Jewish Background*, 10–11. Goodman writes that 2 Macc. 2: 21 'specifically compared Judaism to Hellenism' ('Jews and Judaism in the Mediterranean Diaspora', 211). Shaye J. D. Cohen writes accordingly that 'In separate passages Second Maccabees used the term "Judaism" (2: 21) and its antonym "Hellenism" (4: 13)' (*From the Maccabees to the Mishnah*, 35).

[12] Hengel, *Judaism and Hellenism*, 1–5; id., *Jews, Greeks and Barbarians*, 77–9, noting that *Ioudaïsmos* is used in Maccabees 'to some degree as a counterpart' to *Hellēnismos* (p. 77), and discussing the terms' 'antithetical use' (p. 79); Amir, 'The Term *Ioudaïsmos*', and Rajak, *Josephus*, 55–6, and 'The Hasmoneans', 262–3.   [13] Goldstein, *II Maccabees*, 192 n. 21.

It is interesting to note the different way Hellenization in Jerusalem is described in 1 Maccabees and 2 Maccabees. The author of 2 Maccabees—who uses the standard Greek of his day rather than the biblical Greek into which the preceding book was translated—draws a much more detailed picture of the pagan culture and its diverse elements, which is an indication of his familiarity with that culture. He does not confine himself to abstract generalizations, such as 'Greek qualities', but describes the pagan rituals, the gymnasium, and the 'Greek manners'. On the other hand, 1 Maccabees speaks about 'foreign laws' and about the 'people of the land', but not about 'Hellenic qualities'. In any event, what is relevant to our discussion is the fact that the antithetical picture depicts the Jews, their laws and the ways of their forefathers in contrast to the Hellenistic-pagan world.[14] It is also clear that 2 Maccabees, and even more Josephus, who describes the customs of the Gentiles in Herodian times, refer not only to the pagan cults but to various sectors of pagan culture.[15] Hellenism is represented as a culture initially distinct from the barbaric world and perceived not only as paganism, with its attendant customs, rites, and mythological world, or as philosophical study, but as an all-encompassing way of life.

The introduction of the term *Judentum* or *Judaism* in the nineteenth century was unquestionably due to a similar need in the modern era to respond in kind to the challenge of Western culture and to propose an overall definition for the 'Jewish way of life', that is the Jewish culture. The reason for this was that from the eighteenth century onwards Jewish society became immeasurably more open than ever to 'outside' influences, and it is no wonder that the precedent that came to mind was the complex encounter between Judaism and Hellenism. The revival of interest in this encounter was a result of the ever-growing concern of the Jews to regard Judaism as a culture, and thus to formulate both the essence of Judaism as a culture and the patterns of contacts with European culture. The meeting between Judaism and Hellenism became a vivid historical paradigm.

In Jewish historical memory, the image of Hellenism as a civilization had been basically negative. It was regarded as a culture of idolatry and bloodshed, lacking in any moral sense. It was preserved in the Jewish collective memory as a civilization of lawlessness, debauchery, and vulgarity. When Greece came to the East it did not bring culture to the East, but only brought with it the 'external' aspects of classical antiquity which it

[14] Bowersock notes that *Hellēnismos* 'takes on a new meaning in late antiquity' and 'comes to mean "paganism" itself', not merely Greek culture: *Hellēnes* 'are sometimes "pagans" and sometimes simply "Greeks"'; Eusebius (*Vit. Cons.* 2. 44.) employs *hellēnizein* 'transparently in the sense of "to practice paganism"' (*Hellenism in Late Antiquity*, 9–10).

[15] See *Antiquities*, xv. 267–76.

diluted with an 'Oriental mixture', and even these aspects were swept up by the 'East' and swallowed by it. The classical heritage was held captive by those it conquered.[16] A certain positive image of classical antiquity was saved only by the distinction that was made between Greek classical heritage and the Eastern layers in the Hellenistic civilization. According to this approach, the Hellenic elements of Hellenism were no more than a thin veneer or an outer shell. Alexander and the Macedonians were not 'real Hellenes'; the Greeks in the East were quickly vanquished by the East and became Asiatic. The classical spirit rapidly evaporated. Hellenism then is a form of ancient Levantinism. Here we find the clear echoes of the negative and low image of the 'East' which prevailed in Jewish thinking under the influence of Western 'Orientalism'.

Hellenism, in Jewish eyes, was a soulless culture, or rather a muddled mosaic of cultures with an appallingly low moral threshold. According to this view, there is no connection between Hellenistic philosophical thought—the province of the few—and the general mass culture;[17] but a culture is generally determined by its masses, not by its élite. This totally negative image caused some difficulties; some writers tried to find positive attributes in Hellenism, for if such favourable aspects were not found, one could hardly point to any benefit in borrowing from it! If Hellenism were the model or metaphor of Western civilization, then the prudent would do well to keep a safe distance, and there was a terrible future in store for the emancipation and the integration of Jews in the European environment. Hence there were those who found in Hellenism solid evidence of the appearance of a moral pantheism, of pagan humanism and a philosophical moral code, which was not confined only to a small élite circle, but had penetrated all strata of the population.

A distinction was made between a high and a low culture, the former represented by philosophy and good literature. This positive attitude towards certain manifestations of Hellenistic culture (and its Hellenic heritage) is expressed, as we have already seen, in two spheres: in a sympathetic attitude towards Greek wisdom relating to the sciences, crafts, and secular studies, and in any event, an identification of everything 'outside the Torah' as Greek wisdom (that is, Hellenistic science and philosophy); and in a positive attitude towards Hellenistic philosophy. According to this view, the history of Jewish thought is a consequence of the meeting with Hellenistic Greek philosophy that occurred during three periods: the Hellenistic period, the Middle Ages under Muslim influence, and the

---

[16] Fowden, *The Egyptian Hermes*, 73; Tcherikover, *Hellenistic Civilization*, 28–9.
[17] Bentwich, *Hellenism*, 54–5.

nineteenth century. In the latter two cases, the encounter was the result of the renaissance of Hellenistic philosophy.

The traditional, conservative Jewish approach presents the relationship between Judaism and Hellenism as an absolute and uncompromising confrontation between two cultural and spiritual entities. Any attempt to point to Hellenistic influences meets with criticism and objection or an effort to impose narrow limits on the scope of these influences. In contrast to this conception, a major innovative aspect of modern Jewish historiography was the examination of the Jewish people's history and culture in the context of *die großen Zusammenhänge*, the broad human and cultural context and contacts in which it existed. The readiness of scholars to adopt this point of view did not arise merely from the theoretical understanding that no culture can exist in total isolation, that intercultural relationships are a universal phenomenon, or from increased historical knowledge about the period. It resulted mainly from the recognition that within the context of modern civilization Judaism cannot live as an isolated, closed, and autarkic entity. Thus, if the Second Temple era has any validity as a cultural paradigm for modern historical consciousness, it is because that period offers a multifaceted and dynamic historical picture. Consequently, the Jewish–Hellenistic encounter and its impact on Judaism and the Jews may serve as an analogy to the multifarious encounter of the Jews with Western culture in modern times: a picture of dynamic cultural interferences between two stratified heterogeneous entities.[18]

Since our interest here lies with the cultural system and not with religion (beliefs and practices), we are dealing with a very broad and diversified area. As we shall see, our attitude towards the encounter between Judaism and Hellenism will be determined by the reply to the question whether Judaism had an all-inclusive system of norms to the exclusion of Hellenistic traits, or a system of norms that did not encompass the entire range of human activity and thus left room for the acceptance of Hellenistic components, or indeed—a third possibility—that its system of norms provided for a controlled acceptance of allegedly foreign elements.

All branches of historical scholarship as they developed in the last two centuries ran counter to the picture of Jewish cultural isolation. They not only introduced to the Jewish reader an extensive literature to which he previously had no access, but they discovered and published the library of the Second Temple; that is to say, they added to the body of knowledge an abundance of texts of all types. These revealed a rich, teeming, dynamic, and mercurial spiritual and cultural world, comprising a complex web that

---

[18] I. Even-Zohar, 'System, Dynamics, and Interferences in Culture'.

was difficult to depict with accuracy. Moreover, archaeological finds from this period greatly enriched the historical picture, and in many instances exposed the tension between the literary description and the cultural reality.

This was a world open to diverse channels of influences, some of which were given coherent expression, while others constituted an inseparable part of the social and cultural reality of the times. Second Temple Judaism now appeared on the stage of the history as a civilization in its own right. It was not isolated, closed, and one-dimensional, but rather it was a complex and dynamic society with all the aspects and facets of a 'normal' society: a society fragmented into sects and ideological streams, into a 'high' culture and a 'popular' culture. The pregnant image of Second Temple Judaism in the historical and polemical literature as a 'religious community' was anchored in a dogma. That dogma held that the interests of Second Temple Jewry were confined to its religious affairs, that it had narrow cultural horizons and that a clear-cut normative system of laws and regulations determined and shaped the entire sweep of Jewish existence, as well as its scope and boundaries. Historical scholarship, by contrast, had revealed a culture that like any other, is woven of diverse systems, different layers: a changing and developing culture. In other words, historical scholarship cast serious doubt on the validity of unequivocal definitions and generalizations. It transformed Judaism from a self-understood and unidimensional world into a complex cosmos; in it not one single Judaism, but several Judaisms existed. Judaism was always multifaceted, absorbing influences and internalizing them.

This does not mean that the pattern of antinomy was erased or that it disappeared from the world, including the world of scholarship. Jewish scholars, who did their work in the cultural, political, and social context of the turn of the century, obviously did not deny that a fundamental difference existed between the Jewish world and Hellenistic civilization. However, many of them did attempt to challenge the image and the character imputed to Judaism. One approach they adopted was to re-examine the system of links and of cultural interrelations that existed between Judaism and the Hellenistic civilization, a system that was one-directional as far as Hellenism was concerned. The pattern of antinomy remained in force, but at the same time many of its elements were challenged. It turned out that there were diverse points of contact between Judaism and Hellenism; this led to the conclusion that Judaism and Hellenism were not totally alien to one another, and that even between cultures deeply divided by opposing world-outlooks a bridge could be built, over which cultural (spiritual and material) values might pass from one side to the other. Since no culture exists in isolation, and one culture depends on another, it was inevitable that Judaism, as a minority culture, would be influenced by the majority culture around it. No matter how hard it struggled to preserve its uniqueness, and no matter how far it succeeded in doing so, it would always absorb something from its environment.

As a result of this new outlook, the question of contact between cultures, and the attitude of the various currents in Judaism towards the surrounding cultures, the degree to which they were thought to be 'open' or 'closed' to them became an important criterion in the historical description and the ideological judgement of history. The question of the character and intensity of so-called foreign influences and external borrowings on the currents of Judaism became a central and controversial motif in scholarship. Since Judaism was generally defined as a closed culture, the influences on it were depicted as the wholesale transfer of an entire culture from a foreign world outside it into the closed system.

BETWEEN PERSIA AND GREECE

The way in which the historical process in question was studied is abundantly obvious from the frequent use made in Hebrew literature of the term 'Hellenization'. This term was generally employed in the literature to characterize, pejoratively, a process in which Hellenistic cultural elements, represented in derogatory terms, seeped into Jewish culture. A cultural element defined as Hellenistic automatically carried a stigma. One can probably best elucidate the value-laden and tendentious character of the term 'Hellenization' by reviewing the cultural history of the Jewish people before the emergence of Hellenism as a predominant cultural force. A very influential and up to a point convincing historical school asserts that the exiles of Babylonia and those who returned to Zion were influenced by Persian beliefs and that they shaped their religious identity under the influence of Persian conceptions, adapted to the world-order established by the Persian Empire in the time of Cyrus. Some scholars see a Persian influence in many domains of culture; others minimize it, reducing its impact and pointing to the meagre residue that period left in the literature of the time and of the coming generations.[19]

[19] Early scholars like Sh. Rubin and J. H. Schorr, influenced by the West's discovery of the Persian and Indian literature, greatly exaggerated the Persian influence on Second Temple Jewry. On Judaism and Persian culture in later periods see Schorr, 'HaTorah vedat Zaratustra'; Krauss, *Persia and Rome*; S. Shaked, 'The Influence of Iranian Religion'; J. Tabory, 'The Persian Period'. See the short summary in

Historical literature does not necessarily reflect the intensity of the Persian cultural influences of its time. One may even say that precisely because real or alleged Persian influences were accepted, assimilated, and internalized into Judaism, becoming an indivisible part of it, this process was forgotten or repressed, since these influences became elements so ingrained that they were taken for granted. In other words, the process of their Judaization or assimilation was complete. Possible Persian influences were not nominalized with a term such as 'Persianization' or 'Iranization', either in Second Temple literature or in the literature of modern scholarship. In the literature of the period there is no echo of accusations against any Jewish group for having absorbed Persian influence. On the other hand, the noun 'Hellenization' was used to signal every outside influence, in particular any such influence regarded as negative.

One can offer several explanations for this. First, borrowing and assimilation from Persian culture occurred without any outside coercion, without any internal struggles, and hence left no lingering memory of confrontation. The borrowed elements were therefore accepted as an inseparable part of Judaism, while the Hellenizing movement cast a shadow over the ties between Judaism and Hellenism for generations. Second, in the Hellenistic era, Judaism and Persian culture waged a common struggle against Hellenistic influence, which blurred the previous confrontation between the two. Moreover, Judaism borrowed from the Persians several elements of ideological resistance to Hellenistic influence, or at least developed its own resistance in parallel to that of the Persians. Third, paradoxically enough, since the Persian culture transferred to Judaism key components of its content, this transference was for that very reason glossed over and its source denied. Fourth, the Persian empire was essentially different from the Hellenistic civilization. While the former granted full religious and cultural autonomy to the peoples under its rule, and did not attempt to impose its culture on them, Hellenism had a sense of cultural mission and its culture was disseminated not only as the fruit of unavoidable contacts between various segments of the population, but as part of a deliberate policy. Hellenism was an assimilative civilization with a cosmopolitan, a-national, and non-ethnic dimension. In Palestine, the Jews had to contend with Hellenism not only as a political regime or as a pagan ritual; they also had to contend with Hellenism—in all its layers and manifestations—borne not only on the wings of ideas and literature, but embodied in a

---

Gafni, *The Jews of Babylonia*, 161–5. Luzzatto wrote (1840) that he would not deny that the Babylonian Jews acquired false notions from the Babylonians and the Persians, which the Sages could not or would not uproot, or perhaps even believed in themselves (*Igrot*, v. 697).

large, hostile, rival, and alien population, inimical to their own heart and soul. The struggle against Hellenism was a binational struggle for both cultural and physical existence. Hence it is evident why Hellenism—and not Persian culture—became the permanent symbol for a total and eternal adversary.

Morton Smith may be right when he writes that 'Hellenization' cannot be described simply as the adoption of Greek ways by the people of the Near East, since what we have is 'a vast tissue of changes, in which innumerable strands of independent, but parallel, development are interwoven with a woof of influence and reaction',[20] but the fact is that cultural influences were almost always identified as 'Hellenistic'. Since the noun 'Hellenization' expanded until it encompassed all manifestations of life, presupposing a total and uncompromising antithesis, the relevant historical discussion of the contact between the two cultures became an inseparable part of the historical-ideational polemic. One cannot avoid pointing to a historical paradox here: the Sages, unimpressed by the portrait of an ideal Hellenism that appeared in the literature of their time, formed their opinion of Hellenism according to what they saw with their own eyes, that is, based on the nature of the social and cultural reality around them. Modern scholars too do not examine Hellenistic civilization according to its idealized image, but rather according to the complex nature of the social and cultural reality. Paradoxically, as a result of using this same approach, these scholars discover that the division and the polarity the Sages found in all spheres of life blur many of the domains that might be described as the grey areas of commonality and similarity. It often seems that historical scholarship leads one to the radical conclusion that Second Temple Judaism in its entirety was a Hellenistic Judaism, but that its type of Hellenism was expressed in diverse forms.

JUDAISM AS A RELIGION-CULTURE

The reason why advocates of the conservative historical view found it difficult to accept the fact that Judaism had assimilated many Hellenistic traits did not stem only from a religious point of view—namely, the argument that the assimilation of traits from a pagan culture was unthinkable (and if it did occur was always negative). It was also due to the concept of Judaism as an all-inclusive culture, an authentic self-creation of the Jewish people; hence every foreign component was regarded as an impairment of this

---

[20] M. Smith, *Palestinian Parties*, 76.

authenticity and originality, and any cultural dependence was perceived as an admission that Judaism as a *culture* was incapable of producing by itself, for itself, all the items of culture it required.

It is frequently presupposed by the historical discussion that until the Hellenistic period one original authentic Judaism existed, and all the constituents of its faith, ritual, and culture were the product of an internal development, independent of its environment, and even against its environment;[21] only in the Hellenistic era did the power of Hellenism and its temptations exert pressure on Judaism, damaging its original individuality. However, it is well known that Jewish culture in the biblical era (until the destruction of the Temple) absorbed and internalized numerous influences. No one will dispute, for example, that the patterns of government (the monarchy) were borrowed, that Hebrew was the language of the peoples of Canaan, that literary (and perhaps also mythological) motifs were adopted by the Hebrews from the surrounding cultures. The Israelite monarchy—in both Judah and Israel—was influenced by surrounding cultures no less than the Hasmonean kings were, and contained no fewer 'secular' and 'worldly' elements than the Hasmonean state did, when, as Eddy writes, 'Judas and his brothers could not do without secular Hellenism'.[22] Nevertheless, it would follow from the assumption mentioned above that the Jewish community was totally a religious society, and hence that every dimension defined as secular in Jewish life stemmed from a Hellenistic origin, as if the Jews had no worldly interests or as if different worldly interests could not be embellished with religious rationalizations, especially in a period in which no other system of reasoning existed. The kings of Judah were very 'worldly' kings, just like the Hasmonean kings, who had worldly interests for which they could have taken inspiration and legitimacy from the kings of Judah and Israel (who in turn were inspired by the neighbouring kingdoms).

On the other hand, in turning the noun 'Hellenization' into a general, value-laden description, one takes the dogmatic and a priori view that Judaism could have and should have, through its own efforts, developed every trait of its culture independently. There is another assumption here— hidden beneath the surface—that all these traits could and should have been stamped with the impress of Jewish originality and derived from a unique constitutive and amalgamating principle. Such a sweeping approach ignores not only the fact that Judaism, as a way of life and a culture, was always open to influences and was affected by them, willingly or otherwise; it also

---

[21] Wright, *The Old Testament against its Environment*.
[22] Eddy, *The King is Dead*, 226. See also Rajak, 'The Hasmoneans'.

overlooks the fact that the religion as a normative code of behaviour did not lay down mandatory norms in every single sphere of life. It disregards the need to draw a distinction between different strata of culture with different values, meanings, and functions.

The penetration of the Greek language into Jewish society, for example, is basically no different than the penetration into it of Aramaic (or Arabic); but influence on the linguistic level is nothing like that on the world of art and opinions. In the same way, the use of Greek as a language of communication is totally different from its adoption as a language of culture (or ritual). A superficial or even a thorough familiarity with Greek mythology is different in essence from participation in pagan rites or the adoption of pagan symbols: one ought for example to distinguish between influence on religious values and on the legal system (halakhah), between literary influences and the far more radical phenomenon of the imitation and adaptation of a lifestyle, and between an influence on patterns and processes of government and influence in the realm of the plastic arts. Only if one views the Judaism of the Second Temple period and thereafter as a homogeneous religion-cum-culture, all its many parts drawing upon the same source, all possessing a single and special coloration and style, does one arrive at a generalized description of the relation between Judaism and Hellenism. Such a sweeping description also has a static nature that fails to take account of the dynamics of a culture or the different functions of its various constituents, or of the scale of value and importance assigned to them in the cultural framework. The historical fact that Jewish culture, as an all-encompassing but heterogeneous entity, 'required' numerous and diverse cultural traits led it to borrow many of the needed traits from the inventory existing in the surrounding Hellenistic and Oriental culture.

This process of borrowing and acculturation, as we shall see later, was fully understood by Jewish scholars and historians. As a result of this understanding they had to draw, on the one hand, a clear distinction between things that were and were not fundamental to Judaism, on the other between those that were incompatible with Judaism and those that could be tolerated. On the other hand they had to offer a key by which positive influences could be distinguished from negative ones.

The fact that Hellenism was not only a religious cult,[23] but encompassed also education, enlightenment, and a range of other cultural aspects, not

---

[23] 'Hellenism, which is a genuine Greek word for Greek culture (*Hellênismos*), represented language, thought, mythology, and images that constituted an extraordinarily flexible medium of both cultural and religious expression . . . [in the eastern Mediterranean] it provided the means for a more articulate and more universally comprehensible expression of local traditions': Bowersock, *Hellenism in Late Antiquity*, 7, 9.

all of them necessarily connected with pagan cult, made it easier for its neutral traits to seep into Judaism. In principle, one could separate the cult from all those elements that were unrelated to the practice of idolatry, something more difficult for Jews living in Hellenistic cities to do than for those in Jewish cities.[24] One could choose various Hellenistic traits from the whole, without having to adopt the entire system. By neutral traits, I mean those that could be emptied of their value-laden or symbolic meaning in the dominant culture, and those which were devoid of such meaning. As the distance between Judaism and classical antiquity grew and the religious significance of many of the cultural traits blurred, it became easier to divest them of this significance and to regard them as neutral traits. Numerous Hellenistic cultural traits were thus perceived as neutral or as capable of being divested of their Hellenistic content.

Since culture is a complex and stratified system containing many elements and traits, it is essential to clarify, in each case, into which cultural level the outside influence has permeated, and what function it fulfils there. This can be done according to areas of geographical influence (Judaea as against Galilee, Palestine as against Egypt, etc.),[25] or according to social classes, or between the high culture and popular culture, between the influence on the normative centre of cultural authority and that on the periphery. Over the time-period we shall find different patterns of acculturation and assimilation of ideas, motifs, etc. In other words, it is impossible in the historical context of Hellenization to speak in a generalized or a one-dimensional, unambiguous manner. Thus the decisive historical issue is not the identification of every source of influence, but rather the manner in which the absorbed ideas or motifs changed, if they did change, their content and status; that is to say, how they were acculturated and assimilated into a different cultural system from that whence they came.

Not only the Jews, but other nations of the ancient East as well—such as the Persians and Egyptians, who also had a well-developed awareness of their nationality and religion—maintained their singularity and struggled to preserve it; their Hellenization differed in character and had different consequences from one place and time to another. In the Hellenistic era, neither the Egyptians nor the Persians lost their national singularity as an *ethnos* and as a culture.[26] This shows that a nation or a people can be part of a

---

[24] Herr, 'Hellenistic Influences in the Jewish City'; Y. Dan, *The City in Eretz Yisrael*; Fuks, *Scythopolis*.

[25] See e.g. Freyne, *Galilee from Alexander*; Goodman, *State and Society*; Oppenheimer, *Galilee*.

[26] On Hellenistic influences in Persia see Momigliano, *Alien Wisdom*, 123–50; cf. id., 'The Fault of the Greeks', 14: 'both Romans and Jews found a new sense of national identity in measuring themselves with

great civilization without being totally assimilated into it, by consolidating an existence within it of a specific nature. Even those who go furthest in describing the Hellenization of Judaism and Jews do not claim that the Jews lost their ethnic or cultural singularity, or that it was impossible to distinguish between them and the Egyptians, Phoenicians, Persians, and other peoples. They do not even claim that they converted their entire and unique singular religious and cultural system into the dominant one. Such conversion, we must remember, could not be expressed only by adopting forms of government or elements of popular culture and the like. First and foremost, it had to find expression in the formulation of an alternative normative system: in a new historical consciousness, in a new juridical system, and so forth. Failure to observe or to agree on norms is substantially different from apostasy, from forsaking one system in favour of another that is independent, all-inclusive and alternative. One who deviates does not leave his cultural system, but remains a part of it, even if on its periphery or in confrontation with it.[27]

The encounter of Second Temple Judaism was not necessarily with the Greek philosophical heritage, with the classic Greek *polis*, or with a culture that existed without written rules. It was mainly an encounter with a multifaceted and multidimensional culture—for the élite and for the masses, based on written laws as well as on customs, and so on. If the development of contemporary Judaism was in fact an outcome of an encounter that encompassed both rejection of and adaptation to its host culture, then Hellenism in this guise was the world that compelled it to refashion its image and exerted upon it many diverse influences.

CONTACT, INFLUENCE, SYMBIOSIS

It is not surprising that the first scholarly articles devoted to examining the encounter between Judaism and Hellenism were written within the framework of German Jewish culture. Their impetus was the desire to prove that a Jew could simultaneously live under two different cultural systems; or, taking a more radical approach, that a positive symbiosis between Judaism and the surrounding (German) culture was possible. Judaism was

the Greeks'. See also Walbank, *The Hellenistic World*, 60–75; Mendeles, 'Acculturation and Assimilation among Egyptian Intellectuals'; id., *The Rise and Fall of Jewish Nationalism*, 14-15, esp. p. 15: 'far into the Roman period nations kept their ethnic consciousness of what one would call today self-definition and self-identity'; Eddy, *The King is Dead*, ch. 4.

[27] Rajak rightly distinguishes between the steady influx of Hellenistic traits of Greek modes and manners and a conscious adoption of Greek ways ('The Hasmoneans', 266).

portrayed as a pluralistic, dynamic, and open cultural and religious system. On the other hand, nationally oriented historiography laid much greater emphasis on the way in which Judaism had internalized foreign values and on the polarization and confrontation between Judaism and Hellenism (with Hellenistic antisemitism serving as a central theme). No wonder that in 1939 Heinemann wrote that it was not philosophers or scientists who influenced the masses in Alexandria, but rather bushy-bearded masters of rhetoric—and the background to that remark is obvious.[28]

Common to all these historical trends was the perception and reconceptualization of Judaism as a dynamic and multifaceted culture that was not cut off from its surroundings. Pioneering essays and studies by Israel Levy, Saul Lieberman, J. Heinemann, Samuel Krauss, E. E. Hallewy, R. E. Goodenough, Avigdor (Victor) Tcherikover, Johanan Levy, and others, explored Judaism as a cultural whole, by making use of the rich archaeological and literary sources discovered during the previous two centuries.[29] As we have observed, these sources revealed a heterogeneous and changing Jewish world, as well as the disparities between the canonical, normative system and the cultural reality. This pluralistic picture of the distant past bestowed legitimacy upon the ideology of pluralism and change in modern Judaism, but at the same time, it urgently raised the question: What is the stable and immutable factor in Judaism? What is the outer limit of change and the outer limit of influence? What is normative and what is non-normative in Judaism? What is sanctified by religion and tradition? what is added on and what is neutral?

The question of the nature and the practical validity of rabbinic authority over contemporary Jewry was not merely a historical problem. The Jewish world-picture, set against the frame of Hellenistic and Roman civilization, could simultaneously serve not only for protest against rabbinic authority, but also as a basis and a seal of approval for the emergence of other cultural centres of authority. What began in the early years of the Haskalah as an attempt to show that talmudic literature was receptive to the world around it continued after that period as an attempt to prove that the source of rabbinic Judaism's authority—oral teaching and religious institutions (the synagogue, the house of study)—also existed, were created, and were consolidated through symbiosis with the Hellenistic-Roman world.

In his pioneer article, 'Über die Spuren des griechischen und römischen Altertums in talmudischen Schriften' ('On the Traces of Greek and Ro-

---

[28] Heinemann, 'The Attitude of the Ancient World'.
[29] J. Levy, 'New Ways in the Study of Jewish Hellenism'.

man Antiquity in Talmudic Literature', 1878),[30] Israel Levy (1840–1904) asserted that since not everything that derived from the culture of Hellas and Rome was 'of a religious nature', Judaism was able to find common ground with it, and that Jews who came into contact with this culture could accept it without difficulty. This fact, he states, receives 'full affirmation if we delve deeply and properly into talmudic literature'. With these words, he opened the way for studies that shed new light on the literature of the Sages. According to this view, we can find such 'influences' not only in folk culture and in the 'sectarian' world, but also at the core of 'normative Judaism' itself, in the learned literature. Our Sages knew Hellenistic culture and borrowed abundantly from it.

In the following two chapters I shall not even attempt to map out the areas of the real or alleged influences and their pathways. I can only try to suggest a general framework of the model. The historical literature is so rich and so extensive that I have been able to use only a small part of it. The focus will be on two periods, the Hasmonean era and the mishnaic and talmudic era. I intend to examine both from two vantage-points: how they were depicted in historical research, and how their portrait served modern cultural and ideological polemic through new (Hellenic) basic assumptions concerning history. At the start of this brief foray into the vast sea of specific and general essays and studies, I shall attempt to outline a number of principles that characterize the phenomenon of intercultural influence in the historical past as a model of intercultural influence in the historical present.

The purpose of this survey is to present the structural similarity between the complex intercultural relations that existed between Judaism and the Hellenistic civilization in the ancient world and those that exist between Jews and Western culture in the modern age. It is this similarity that motivated the historical study of these past relations between Jews and Hellenists as a model for the relations between Jewish and Western culture in the modern era. However, at the same time, the model emphasizes the

---

[30] I am grateful to Dr C. Hoffmann of the Technische Universität Berlin for taking the trouble to find the text of Israel Levy's lecture for me in the Leipzig library. See E. E. Urbach, 'Attempts at Investigating', and 'Three Teachers of the Talmud', 177–82. The Reform movement dealt extensively with the question of the legitimate appropriation of religious ideas and practices from the non-Jewish environment; see Michael A. Meyer, *Response to Modernity*, 6–7. Earlier Eduard Gans, the founder of the Verein für Cultur und Wissenschaft der Juden, whose four-volume study *Das Erbrecht in weltgeschichtlicher Entwicklung* included treatment of 'Die Grundzüge des mosaisch-talmudischen Erbrechts' ('The Fundamentals of the Mosaic-Talmudic Law of Inheritance'), sought to demonstrate 'the process of westernization that biblical institutions underwent by virtue of talmudic exposition', so that 'studied from the perspective of Graeco-Roman law, talmudic legal practice can be shown to exhibit development, outside influences, and a decided resemblance to the West'; see Schorsch, 'Verein für Cultur und Wissenschaft der Juden', 227.

fundamental difference beween the ancient and the modern encounter: Western culture is not identical with or similar to Hellenistic; hence intercultural relations with it differ from those presented by the ancient model. Moreover, an analogy can be drawn between the cultural field of Hellenistic civilization and that of European culture in modern times: in both cases, we have one inclusive cultural framework that nonetheless encompasses subcultures different in character, divergent streams of thought, and varied cultural phenomena. But again, the character of European culture is not identical with that of Hellenistic culture. However, a description of intercultural relations in the Hellenistic era may contribute to an understanding of those in the modern era because the former constitutes a paradigm for a complex system of relationships. Moreover, this discussion is significant in that the various images of the system of relationships in the Hellenistic era were used in the dispute about the desirability of intercultural relationships in ancient times.

Against the background of my previous remarks, the broad influences of Hellenistic culture on Judaism should be examined according to three categories:[31]

(i) Jewish apostasy through Hellenization, meaning the readiness to forgo basic components of Judaism as well as its elementary symbols. Hellenizing or apostatizing Jews are 'forsakers of the Torah' who adopt not only the surface features of another culture, but also its fundamental ingredients: the pagan rites and the idolatrous gods integral to them. In other words,

---

[31] For some interpretations of the characteristics of Hellenism and Hellenization see U. Rappaport, 'On the "Hellenization" of the Hasmoneans'; Smith, *Palestinian Parties*, 76–8; S. J. D. Cohen, *From the Maccabees*, 34–45; Moore, *Judaism in the First Centuries*, 19–21. Grunebaum, 'The Problem of Cultural Influences', distinguishes between *orthogenetic* change and *heterogenetic* change, and uses this classification to evaluate the Hellenistic influence on Islamic thinking and its impact in the 9th and 10th cc. in contrast to Western influences in the 19th c. and their impact. Goitein poses four interrelated questions in order to obtain a balanced view of the scope and quality of the influence of the heritage of Greece on Islamic culture: (i) 'How did Islam look before its direct contact with the Greek sciences . . . what is Islam without the Greek ingredient?' (ii) 'Why was Arabic Islam so much more receptive to the Greek heritage than Germanic Europe?' (iii) 'Which features of Hellenic civilization were adopted by Islam and which remained unknown to them or were refused admittance?' (iv) 'How far and how well was the Hellenic tradition absorbed by Islam and how did it contribute to the latter's substance and permanent character?' ('The Intermediate Civilization', 60). Rajak rightly observed that 'Hellenization can mean several different things: in its full sense, it would be the suppression of a native culture and language and its replacement with a fully or mainly Greek style . . . or it might be the creation of a truly mixed, hybrid form . . . or, again, we might see the addition of Greek elements to a persisting culture whose leading features remained visible and relatively constant' ('The Hasmoneans', 265). On the different views concerning the debt of Islam to Hellenism and the nature of the Hellenistic influences on Islam, see Kraemer, *Humanism in the Renaissance of Islam*, 141–5: Kraemer argued that the two cultures were fundamentally distinct; Franz Rosenthal asserts that Islamic civilization as we know it would simply not have existed without the Greek heritage, while C. H. Becker spoke of Islamized Hellenism. These views are similar to the different views on the nature of 'Jewish Hellenism' or 'Hellenistic Judaism'.

apostatism means assimilation in the fullest sense of the word. Hellenizing Jews who wished to become assimilated and absorbed into Hellenistic culture and religion, for reasons of convenience or ideology, could be found among the aristocracy and the priestly classes in Jerusalem and among the educated Jews in Alexandria, but were, it appears, an insignificant minority. On the other hand, it is impossible to know how deep the process of non-ideological assimilation was among the 'common people' as a result of the close contact they had with their neighbours and their culture. There is evidence to show that in different places during the Hasmonean era, and even more so afterwards, there were also such spontaneous manifestations of assimilation: the consequence of social contact, the enticements of a foreign culture, and the like.[32]

(ii) Hellenistic influences, meaning the permeation and infiltration of many traits of Hellenistic culture, in different forms, into various areas of Jewish culture, without jeopardizing contemporary normative Judaism or the symbols of Jewish existence and identity (e.g. the nature of the Temple service and the obligations involved in it, the ritual of circumcision, and so on). In this case, one must always examine each Hellenistic cultural trait, its influence and the nature of its integration, both by itself and in the different historical contexts. The question arising is to what extent influences must accumulate and persist in order for the affected culture to undergo change. No less important is the fact that influences conform to different patterns: a Hellenistic trait could be added to the existing Jewish cultural totality; or it could become part of the total Jewish culture by changing its substance and function; or it could be adopted through the process of inverted acculturation, that is to say adopted precisely for the purpose of grappling with the Hellenistic influence. Indeed, as Goodenough noted, Hellenistic elements could be copied, not in order to move away from the faith of the Fathers, but to strengthen it by new means so that it could endure; just as Orthodoxy in the nineteenth century and after adopted various modern and secular means in order to strengthen itself, such as the widespread use of portraits of rabbis and sages, which had formerly been regarded as an improper Christian custom and as idolatry.[33]

[32] According to Fergus Millar 'what was significant about the Jewish community of the third and second centuries B.C. was the superficiality of its Hellenism . . . We should not look for the intellectual background of a syncretistic reform movement within Judaism, because we have no clear evidence that such a movement existed' ('The Background to the Maccabean Revolution', 20–1).

[33] R. I. Cohen, 'And your Eyes shall See your Teachers'. According to J. A. Seeligman, 'Jerusalem in Jewish Hellenistic Thought'. the conception of the Temple in Jerusalem as the navel of the world was derived from the corresponding Greek belief about the temple of Apollo Pythius at Delphi; but see Roscher, *Der Omphalosgedanke*; Hermann, *Omphalos*; and Weinfeld, *From Joshua To Josiah*, 124–8. Daniel

(iii) Hellenization, meaning the all-inclusive penetration of key Hellenistic values into the existing cultural system and into the cultural tradition, which is regarded as original and distinctive. The assimilation of this new aggregate has a far-reaching influence on the image and the content of the entire borrowing culture, not only on its periphery. This refers primarily to influences upon the system of concepts and values. The fine line between Hellenization and Hellenistic influences is often blurred, just as it is between assimilation and acculturation. Nevertheless, there is a fundamental difference between interspersing isolated traits within an existing cultural system and assimilating those that make substantive and basic changes in the system that absorbs them.

Jews during the Second Temple era and later displayed an independent national and religious awareness, living their lives according to a singular code. They did not assimilate into their surroundings to the point of blurring this singularity; they established unique institutions of their own, completely different from those of the foreigners; and they lacked the characteristic institutions of the general contemporary culture. The extent of openness, tolerance, and liberality exhibited by contemporary Jewish culture, particularly as projected by its spokesmen, changed from time to time and from issue to issue. We have already seen, and shall see again, that the Sages demonstrated liberality, and more than liberality, towards Greek wisdom, but were apathetic and hostile toward traits of other cultures; both strict and lenient opinions could be heard at one and the same time, and there is in no case a declared ideology determining the permissible and the forbidden areas of this acculturation. In the Hellenistic and Roman period, there was a difference between a process like the acculturation that perhaps took place in Egypt, where Jews lived as an urban minority within a foreign urban society, and the process in Palestine, where the encounter with the Hellenistic population was not a meeting between a dependent minority and a ruling political and cultural majority.

The permeation of elements from the Hellenistic and Roman world into the social and cultural texture of Jewish life is described at length by adherents of the so-called anti-normative school, which sought to revise the distorted picture drawn by historical tradition, and in its wake by advocates of a conservative historical outlook. However, they are describing a

Schwartz, 'Temple and Desert', argues that the spiritualization of the temple, namely the idea that a place which is not a temple will be regarded as a temple, developed in Judaism (Philo, Qumran, and Paul) under the influence of Hellenism (see Stephen's speech in Acts 7), but one may also assume that this was a further development of an idea found e.g. in Isa. 66: 1, which may, for various reasons, have become topical at the end of the Second Temple period.

necessary cultural process that signifies not Hellenization but rather being subject to influences. These influences did indeed change Second Temple Judaism, but did not make it an inseparable part of the surrounding Hellenistic world, and did not cause it to become integrated into that world to the point of obfuscating its own identity and singularity. To be sure, Judaism is Hellenistic in the sense that its Hellenization motivated and generated in it extensive internal processes that altered it in comparison with the Judaism of the pre-Hellenistic era. Accordingly, the new picture of cultural history does demonstrate that the normative authority of the Sages after the destruction of the Temple was not as complete or as inclusive as we might infer from canonical tradition. On the other hand, it is clear that the range of its power was extensive and that it had no rival.

From the above we can conclude that the norms of any culture can be judged by what it forbids and what it permits—and no less by the grey area between the two. But another claim can be made, that the cultural reality does not show that what are called rabbinical norms were not actually the ruling norms, but rather that during the Second Temple and the mishnaic and talmudic eras they did not decisively forbid reciprocal relations with Hellenism. Hence there were restrictions, some of which developed out of differing world-outlooks and values, and some out of cultural conservatism, but these were not absolute and all-inclusive restrictions. This was not only because Jewish society was not monolithic, but also because those who set the tone in it—theoretically, the Sages and the Pharisees—issued no decree against reciprocal relations and by implication did not see in Hellenistic culture an impure, repugnant culture. That is the reason why traits of Hellenistic culture can be found in all segments of Jewish society, including the Pharisees.[34]

In an article called 'Jewish Acceptance and Rejection of Hellenism', Jonathan Goldstein maintains that reservations about and opposition to Hellenism were not general and all-encompassing, but limited—and that in Palestine they were motivated by political considerations. Writing of such Hellenic institutions as theatres, stadia, and hippodromes, he states that God had never demonstrated His opposition to participation by the Jews of the Diaspora; as to other aspects of Hellenism, He 'had shown no opposition either in Judea or in the Diaspora, and we find Jews throughout

[34] For the many studies on this subject see n. 31 and also Baron, *Social and Religious History*, i. 165–211, ii. 3–56; Lieberman, *Greek in Jewish Palestine* and *Hellenism in Jewish Palestine*; id., 'How Much Greek'; Sevenster, 'Do you Know Greek?' Hengel, *Jews, Greeks and Barbarians*; M. Stern, 'Judaism and Hellenism in Eretz Yisrael'; Kasher, 'Some Remarks and Insights'; Herr, 'Hellenism and the Jews'; Tcherikover, *Hellenistic Civilization*; Sandmel, 'Hellenistic Judaism'.

regarding them as permitted'.[35] Goldstein greatly plays down the significance of the rejection and opposition, and overlooks the fact that opposition may be grounded on social concerns without necessarily resulting from properly formulated rules of the permissible or the forbidden. In any event, it is important to note here that Jewish tradition dealt primarily with the permissible and the forbidden, but in matters of culture did not impose its own explicit halakhot. The halakhah established censorship and required the adaptation of various items so that they should not clash with halakhic obligations, but it never set out binding rules, and certainly it was unacquainted with the modern idea that each item of culture must be stamped with a specific national imprint.

FIVE HISTORICAL MODELS

We can now summarize the gamut of historiogaphical images of the relationship between Judaism and Hellenism in the Second Temple era current in modern times:

(i) As in the model of Greekness versus Judaism, Judaism and Hellenism are two completely different, antagonistic cultural entities existing side by side while evincing eternal enmity.

(ii) Judaism of the Second Temple era was a Hellenistic Judaism or even, in a more radical version, a Jewish branch of Hellenism, and all forms of Judaism were forms of Hellenistic culture. Hence it is an error—or even a deliberate distortion—to speak of Judaism and Hellenism separately, when in actuality we are talking about a close partnership within the same comprehensive cultural system, not about a Jewish position outside and segregated from it. Consequently, it is also incorrect to speak of 'borrowing' and 'assimilating' from one system to another, if we are referring to the same cultural system itself, comprising Judaism and Hellenism.

(iii) Although Judaism and Hellenism were engaged in an intense struggle,

---

[35] Goldstein, 'Jewish Acceptance and Rejection'; Schalit, *The Hellenistic Age*. In a lecture at Tel Aviv University in March 1996 Professor Erich Gruen claimed that the fact of the Temple priests' attending the athletic competitions proves the absence of a religious prohibition, so that the opposition to 'Hellenization' in the Maccabean books is the expression of a conservative and puritanical attitude. One might counter that while no religious objection is recorded to sport as such, the nakedness of the Greek athlete seems to have offended against the Jews' ethical code; and the fact is that there were no athletic competitions in Jerusalem before 'Hellenization', nor were they revived after the Hasmonean revolt until the time of Herod (not to mention the fact that, according to 1 Macc. 1: 15, competitors 'made themselves uncircumcised' by pulling the foreskin forward). On Alexandrian Jews' attitude to the gymnasium see Kasher, 'The Jewish Attitude to the Alexandrian Gymnasium'.

they also maintained a continuing and stratified interrelationship in various spheres. Judaism was and still is a unique and sovereign culture. In various periods, however, it borrowed and assimilated various elements of the outside culture, even while in principle repudiating and rejecting it. It behoves historical research to consider these spheres of influence and connection in a thorough, precise, and empirical manner.

(iv) The confrontation between Judaism and Hellenism was at the hub of Jewish history in the days of the Second Temple, around which Jewish life revolved. It is possible, therefore, to propose a historical model to examine and evaluate the different eras according to the way Judaism maintained cultural contact with its surroundings and in light of the results of this encounter.

(v) Judaism was a Hellenistic Judaism, which means no normative Judaism existed; it is not only an a-historical concept but an ideological one that took hold at a later time, and was cast into the animated and diversified reality of the Second Temple era. On this view, it is the multifarious nature of Judaism in its broad Hellenistic context that demonstrates normative Judaism to be a theological and ideological concept, not a historical phenomenon. The aims, whether open or concealed, of this historiographical tendency are clear: by questioning whether the notion of one normative Judaism is valid, to legitimize the existence of various streams in modern Judaism, and utterly to repudiate Orthodoxy's claim that it is the faithful and exclusive representative of historical Judaism. In contrast, a pluralistic, dynamic, and shifting picture of the history of the Jewish spirit is designed to shatter its fossilized or frozen image. At the same time, it shows that Judaism is capable of preserving its independence and its distinctive qualities, even while exhibiting spiritual and cultural openness, and advisedly borrowing and absorbing elements of the external culture. Borrowing does not necessarily impair exceptionality or uniqueness; at times it is a clear expression of the character of the absorbing culture. Judaism is not a closed culture, but rather an open one, perhaps indeed by far the most open.

10

JUDAISM AND HELLENISM IN PALESTINE AND ALEXANDRIA: TWO MODELS OF A NATIONAL AND CULTURAL ENCOUNTER

> What is Plato but Moses speaking in Attic Greek?
> *Numenius of Apamea*

APOSTASY AS A TOTALLY NEGATIVE MODEL

THE period that began when Alexander the Great conquered Palestine ended when paganism gave way to Christianity. Notwithstanding the political and cultural changes that took place from 322 BC until the fourth century AD, Jewish literature did not differentiate between the Hellenistic and the Roman cultures in the East. As a matter of fact, although Rome represented the mighty power of the empire, Hellenism continued to represent major components of its culture. In Palestine—just as in Egypt—Hellenistic culture continued to flourish under Roman rule, and there the confrontation-cum-encounter with the Jews took place with Rome as the political authority—and with Hellenism as the culture.

This period saw many upheavals. The Hasmonean rebellion brought about the establishment of a Jewish state, which was a unique phenomenon in the Hellenistic East and a once-only occurrence in Jewish history between the end of the Kingdom of Judah and the establishment of the State of Israel. After the collapse of the state, Herod came to power under Roman protection, and Palestine later became a province of Rome. These violent political vicissitudes had a strong impact on the character of the encounter between Judaism and the different layers of Hellenistic culture, and in consequence on the nature of the Hellenization of regime, society, and culture.

I shall focus here on the way in which this period served as an inclusive historical paradigm, and on the way in which different parts of it were symbols of historical phenomena. As we know, the encounter with Hellenism, particularly in the Hasmonean era, had a powerful and influential impact, and its effects on future generations—and on Jewish historical consciousness—were profound. That is precisely why it functioned as a model of the nature of the encounter between Judaism and other cultures.

Hardly anyone disagrees that from c.200 BC one can find different types of Hellenistic influences on Jewish society in Judaea and Galilee, especially among the upper classes. Knowledge of the Greek language was not unusual.[1] The author of the 'Letter of Aristeas', for example, maintained that there was at least one group of scholars in Jerusalem able to translate the Torah, and it is known that at the close of the second century BC a Jerusalemite priest translated the Book of Esther into Greek. In the course of time, the ethical and metaphysical notions of Greek philosophers posed a challenge that had to be addressed (while some of their concepts were internalized). The difference in principle between 'influences' of this type and the phenomenon of apostasy is eminently clear: there is no parallel or similarity whatsoever between, on the one hand, the influence of philosophical ideas, which permeated Jewish society through various channels (as we may see in Ecclesiastes or the Wisdom of Ben-Sira), or the influx of Greek words into Second Temple Hebrew, and, on the other hand, the introduction of pagan rites into Jerusalem and the Temple, the establishment of a gymnasium, the desire to turn Jerusalem into a *polis*, or the renunciation of ritual circumcision by the apostatizing Jews and their faction. In the former context, we are dealing with influences in the intellectual and literary domain; in the latter, with influences in the realm of religion and ritual, and with the substitution of pagan traditions and rites for Jewish patriarchal customs. The first two Books of Maccabees and the *Antiquities* of Josephus present different descriptions of the Hellenistic elements that were introduced into Jerusalem. In any case, all three sources regard the apostates' actions as a grave renunciation of the ancient customs and the way of life prescribed by them.[2]

It is not surprising that in the collective historical memory of the Jews and in their multifarious historical literature, the apostates (*mityavnim*) are despised and condemned; they become the reflection of all 'Greeks', morally corrupt, bestial, degenerate and the like, contriving to eradicate Judaism. One can even say that the rejection of Hellenistic apostasy as a historical phenomenon became the common denominator of all currents in modern Judaism. They regarded it as a union of contemptible paganism and total moral licentiousness, and saw in it an imitation of the external, inferior, vulgar side of Hellenistic culture, rather than of its positive aspects.

---

[1] Rajak, *Josephus*, 46–64; Hengel, 'The Interpretation of Judaism and Hellenism in the Pre-Maccabean Period'.

[2] M. Stern, 'Antioch in Jerusalem'.

The advocates of acculturation (i.e. the absorption of a foreign 'higher culture') customarily say in an apologetic tone that Antiochus Epiphanes had no desire to propagate in Judaea the loftier Hellenistic culture—the Hellenistic *paideia*—but rather its low, cultic, popular layers. Hence, in their view, there is no connection between 'Hellenization' and acculturation in the modern context.

Until the nineteenth century, the Jewish apostates were likened to the 'cruel' or 'evil ones of our people' (*Yosippon*, xiii. 5–9), to 'wicked scoundrels' who forsook the 'holy covenant'; 'setting at nought their hereditary distinction, they put the highest value on Greek honours' (2 Macc. 4: 15). The apostate priests were 'forsakers of the Torah' who desecrated the Sabbath, sacrificed pigs and impure animals, did not circumcise their sons, and wanted to 'change all the precepts'. They wished to introduce into Jerusalem the Hellenistic cult of kings and the institutions of the *polis*, with their pagan way of life. It is difficult to perceive in them an upper class imbued with the 'classical Greek spirit', as some wished to portray them, for Antiochus was not the disciple of philosophers and did not disseminate 'classical culture'. In Jerusalem, they wanted to introduce, not Greek thought, but Greek games. No wonder the Christian church, and Christianity as a whole, sanctified the Maccabean revolt as a war of religious zeal. Had the apostates not been defeated, wrote Bickerman, then the verdict pronounced on monotheism would have been a harsh one, and in consequence Christianity would never have seen the light of day.[3]

Unquestionably, the champions of Hellenism in modern times ignored many of its manifestations, depicting it as a humanistic and philosophical movement, and consequently describing the Hellenizers as a type of liberal Jew, and the Hasmoneans as narrow-minded nationalistic fanatics, 'echte jüdische Fanatiker' in the words of Eduard Meyer, who had no hesitation in turning their 'wilde Brutalität' against internal opposition and their own families.[4] The fact is that Jewish apostasy would have meant not only the assimilation of the Jews into their foreign environment to the point where they ceased to be a people, but also the disappearance of monotheism from the face of the earth. The attempt to Hellenize Jerusalem

[3] Bickerman, *From Ezra*, 178–82, who declares that 'The Maccabees preserved the Judaism of the Greek period from both dissolution and ossification', but at the same time that one of the historical significances of the Maccabean period is to be found in its 'Hellenization', which enabled Judaism (or Hellenistic Judaism) to be influential on a universal scale: 'If today the West and Islam believe in resurrection, the idea is one which Maccabean Judaism took over from Hellenism and then passed on to Christianity and Islam' (p. 182).

[4] Eduard Meyer, *Ursprung und Anfänge*, ii (*Die Entwicklung des Judentums und Jesus von Nazaret*), 277, quoted by Hoffmann, *Juden und Judentum*, 152.

was an effort by an outside power to exert cultural coercion, even if this had been invited by a certain group within. In modern terms, we are speaking not of a phenomenon of assimilation or even of 'government-sponsored enlightenment', but rather of an attempt to bring about religious conversion by means of brutal religious and economic oppression. Thus it was substantially different from the spread by elements of Hellenistic culture among the generations living after the revolt.

The utterly negative image of the apostatizing Jew changed somewhat during the nineteenth century. The unfounded comparison between Seleucids and ideal Hellenism turned the apostates, at least in the eyes of some Protestant historians, into the most praiseworthy reformers, whose world was firmly moored in Greek philosophy. Paradoxically, historians who had been the enthusiastic spokesmen of German nationalism were those who, out of their anti-Jewish sentiments and their admiration of a Hellenism that neither possessed nor desired the political unity they cherished, were those who considered the anti-nationalist Hellenists an eminently laudable group. They ignored the fact that the Greek philosophers, in their time, had already exhibited an attitude of contempt and derision towards the pagan and mythological cults that the Hellenist apostates wished to adopt.

Our source of knowledge about the apostates is of course the literature that fervently supported the Hasmonean dynasty.[5] Even if some of the vituperation is exaggerated, it was absolutely clear, from the Jewish point of view, that the introduction of idols into the Temple was intolerable—a case of 'prefer death and do not commit that sin!' At any rate, in nineteenth-century Christian historiography, the Hellenists were occasionally depicted as liberal 'men of culture', who wanted to stir up and awaken the Jewish religion, to break through its narrow ethnic confines, to return it to a universalistic orientation, thus integrating it into its cultural environment. They believed that a religious-nationalist theocracy was a utopia, and that the Jewish people would have to pay a very high price in the effort to achieve it. In this Christian historiography, the Hasmoneans were portrayed as a group fighting a fanatical religious war which annihilated its Hellenist foe. This is in total contradiction to the historical tradition of Christianity, which viewed the Hasmoneans as fighting for the religion (the inscription written in 1118 on the tomb of Baldwin I, the Crusader king of Jerusalem, in the Church of the Holy Sepulchre, which was destroyed in 1808, reads 'Judas Maccabaeus II').

Jewish historiography, and along with it the historical novel and novella, presented a totally different picture. It showed an organic society of Jewish

---

[5] Shatzman, 'The Hasmoneans in Graeco-Roman Historiography'.

farmers, cleaving to its heritage and religion, deeply rooted in the land, which the 'city of iniquity' and the deviants among the high society and the mighty priesthood rose up against and attempted to corrupt. According to this view, the Hellenists were responsible for destroying the idyllic and organic unity that had existed since the reforms of Ezra and Nehemiah. The Hasmoneans led a religious and nationalist rebellion 'for our people and for the sanctuary' (1 Macc. 3: 43) and against the foreigners who tried to steal 'their Torah and country and holy temple' (2 Macc. 13: 10). The Jews were called upon to risk their lives 'for their Torah and for their country' (2 Macc. 8: 21) and to fight for liberty, which, according to the speech that Josephus puts in Judas Maccabaeus' mouth, is loved by all mankind for its own sake, and grants the Jews the right to worship the Lord (*Antiquities*, xii. 302–4). The Hasmonean revolt generated a glorious religious, nationalist, and cultural revival movement, which is preserved in Jewish historical memory as an exemplary event.[6]

The first Jews to be labelled 'Hellenists' in modern times were the earliest 'secular' Jews who made an appearance in the eighteenth century. Their growing affinity for their social and cultural environment prompted them to abandon their religion. Later, the members of *Wissenschaft des Judentums* were called 'Hellenists' by their opponents and by those who favoured emancipation through rejecting their national identity. The criticism levelled by the nationalists against 'assimilationist' emancipation was especially harsh, and made no distinction between different types of acculturation. Thus, inadvertently perhaps, these critics also attacked their own foundations. There is nothing new under the sun, declared Peretz Smolenskin, who vigorously attacked the Haskalah and *Wissenschaft des Judentums* in Germany. The Jews of Germany, he contends, like Hellenists in the past, also claim that 'we are not a nation'. These 'lovers of the Greeks and their ways', *Hellenisten* as he called them, 'intensified their wickedness to violate the covenant of brotherhood' and cast off the ethics of the Torah. To Smolenskin and others who agreed with his stand, Hellenism could be likened to anti-nationalism.[7] Smolenskin also described Orthodoxy as Hellenist for its opposition to the unity of the nation.

---

[6] See G. Alon, 'Have the Nation and its Sages Erased the Memory of the Hasmoneans?'; Flusser, 'The Memory of the Maccabees', who writes (p. 54) that the author of the Book of Yosippon bases his description of the heroism of the Maccabees in the war on the status of the Maccabean war in the consciousness of Christian Europe; Joshua Efron, 'The Maccabean Revolt'. Goldstein goes so far in his radical interpretation as to claim that 'there had been good religious reasons for pious Jews to tolerate the Hellenizers . . . The Hellenizers could claim that the letter of the Torah permitted their practices' (*II Maccabees*, 87). For a different view see Millar, 'The Background', 12–20, and Rajak, 'The Hasmoneans'.

[7] Smolenskin, 'Am olam', 93; cf. id., 'Et lata'at', 171.

Lilienblum too drew a parallel between anti-nationalist outlooks and 'Gentile abominations' like wrestling, the sport that the Hellenists wished to instate on Mount Zion: 'And this calamity was not unique in the records of our history. In the generation of Friedländer and Henriette Herz, we also saw such a spectacle, which in many ways resembled the generation of Jason and Menelaus—all that was missing were the Hasmoneans.'[8] And in the same spirit, Nathan Birnbaum (1864–1937), a Zionist who in 1918 became an activist in the orthodox Agudat Yisrael, depicted the Hellenistic era as a time of malignant assimilation, like that of modern times.[9] Ahad Ha'am drew a distinction between the 'Hellenists' in Palestine, who sought, through Hellenism, to discover the singular spirit of Judaism, and those who wanted to assimilate into Hellenism, while rejecting and effacing their Jewish self-identity.[10] Graetz gave a characteristic portrait of Jewish Hellenization:

Hellenism, which the pensive poet of the Divan [Judah Halevi] strikingly characterized as bearing only blossoms but no fruits, steadily attracted ever more admirers from among the Temple officials. Refined paganism was no longer abhorrent in the eyes of many and they gladly welcomed it . . . But precisely as a result of this friendly reception of paganism did the people fathom the extraordinary danger which threatened their spiritual treasure . . .[11]

In its own estimation, the new nationalist Jewish intelligentsia was comparable with the Hasidaeans and the Hasmoneans of antiquity.

Once the term 'Hellenization' had been recognized as a brand of shame for both religious and nationalist libertinism, it became the common currency of the new Jewish historical consciousness. Religious and 'freethinking' Jews alike used it as a battle cry to be frequently hurled at their adversaries: the 'freethinking' nationalists used it against the anti-nationalist secular (or Reform) Jews; the ultra-Orthodox, against their freethinking nationalist opponents. One of the inevitable results of the double use of this sign was to kindle the debate on the essence of the festival of Chanukah that flared up in the 1880s between the different camps in the Hibbat Zion movement. The freethinking members of this movement claimed that the Orthodox were treating Chanukah as a part of Diaspora folklore and obscuring its national dimension; the Orthodox argued that the free-

---

[8] Lilienblum, 'Chomer veruach', 94, cf. 'Al techiyat am Yisrael al admat eretz avotav', 34: redemption did not come to Israel from Jerusalem when Antiochus sentenced it to extinction, but rather from the Hasmonean village of Modi'im. In other words, no support could be expected from the wealthy Jews of Jerusalem, and the Zionists resembled the Hasmoneans in their mettle.

[9] Doron, *The Zionist Thinking of Birnbaum*, 34.   [10] Ahad Ha'am, 'Imitation and Assimilation'.

[11] H. Graetz, *Structure of Jewish History*, 88–9.

thinkers were totally disregarding the religious aspect of the holiday and turning it into a popular national festival.[12] As far as the Orthodox were concerned, 'freethinking' nationalism was, to all intents and purposes, Hellenism save only the formal departure from the bounds of Judaism. The concept of a sovereign Jewish state, for example, which is an indisputable keystone of Zionism, was described as a consummately 'Hellenic' idea that was the exact opposite of a 'halakhic state' according to Mosaic law. How absurd it is, religious writings repeatedly claimed, that the 'freethinking' Jew should celebrate Chanukah, which symbolized the victory over Hellenism, when he himself lived like an out-and-out Hellenist. A secular Jew, therefore, is not allowed to view himself as a 'descendant of the Maccabees'.[13]

I shall only cite a few examples to show how prevalent the use of 'Hellenists' is today as a symbol to serve diverse and bizarre purposes. At the end of 1991, when the Labour party adopted a resolution (rescinded only a short time later) on the separation of religion and state, Chief Rabbi Avraham Shapira stated that this act was perpetrated by a 'handful of people following in the path of the Hellenizers and trying to adopt as their slogan revolt against the people and the unity of the nation'.[14] The most extreme proponent of the idea that non-religious nationalistic Zionism is 'Hellenism' was Rabbi Meir Kahane, who declared that secular Judaism places all Jews in danger of collective punishment.[15] Typical of the unbridled use of this analogy was an article written at the end of 1993 by Shmuel Schnitzer, a leading journalist, in which he asserted that Israelis who were prepared to give up territory or those adhering to liberal (secular) cultural and political positions are even worse than the classical Hellenizers, for the latter

were prepared to belittle themselves in the face of a great, erudite culture that reached artistic heights. The modern Hellenizers appeal to us in the name of a dissolute subculture, a culture of money and glamour, hedonism and permissiveness, a culture which produces hardly any values of its own . . . has no Olympus of its own peopled by a group of gods, who no matter how debauched they are, nonetheless observe rules of good and bad, permitted and forbidden. The gods of the new culture are not heroes of a Greek tragedy, they are representatives of decadence. Their culture is the cult of drugs and pornography, addiction and exhibitionism. Long ago they did away with all shame and from Greek culture they adopted mainly perversion.

---

[12] E. Luz, *Parallels Meet*, 170–1.

[13] Benyamin Tzvieli, 'Historical Dissonance' (Heb.), *Ha'aretz*, 5 Nov. 1988.

[14] *Chadashot*, 22 Nov. 1991. See Y. Shahak's response in *Ha'aretz*, 27 Nov. 1991, entitled 'Kulanu mityavnim' ('We are all Hellenizers').   [15] *Jewish Press*, 31 Aug. 1984.

Between such a culture and Jewish culture, he states, there can be no coexistence, for the world cannot contain them both![16]

The use made by 'freethinking' nationalists of the sign 'Hellenism' was beset with pitfalls. Ahad Ha'am, for instance, described Herod's kingdom as a totally Hellenistic state, while directing his barbs at the portrait of the future Jewish society drawn in Herzl's *Altneuland*, which in his eyes was also nothing but a Hellenistic state.[17] 'Hellenization' came to characterize the diverse manifestations in the development of 'national *kulturah*'. For example, when members of the Yishuv (the pre-State Jewish community in Palestine) spoke foreign languages, it was unhesitatingly defined as a display of 'modern Hellenism'. Any cultural trait identified as negative was described as 'imitation' and 'assimilation', and therefore 'Hellenization'. Integralist nationalist or puritanical cultural outlooks grasped at the image historical tradition offered them and used it to stigmatize the foundations of a culture that had become a thorn in their flesh. Thus the Zionist right wing increasingly described the Zionist left as a 'Hellenistic' movement, which sought to transplant cosmopolitan and internationalist values and world-outlooks into the national culture. For example, as a result of the victory of political liberalism, Abba Achimeir asserted,

the ancient concept of Hellenism has prevailed in Israel. The foreign way of life attracts the Jewish heart no less today than did the Hellenic way of life in the days of Judah the Maccabee . . . The new Hellenism has wrought havoc in the ranks of our people, and in modern times, it embraces a new ideal, in the name of socialism . . .

But at the same time, he described the 'Hellenizers' party' as idealists who wished to bring the wisdom and beauty of Greece to Israel, and he compared Menelaus to Peter the Great: Menelaus sought the good of his people (like Peter) and sought to endow it with the 'wonderful spiritual values of Greece'; he bore the spirit of Homer, and against him rose Mattityahu the priest mouthing psalms. In the same breath, he stated that the Hellenizers were the counterpart of the Jewish internationalist

[16] Schnitzer, 'The New Kulturkampf', *Ma'ariv*, 17 Dec. 1993. In other articles, by contrast, the writers identified with the Hellenizers, who seemed to them 'sane cosmopolitans' in comparison with the 'Hasmonean ague of fundamentalism', or lamented that the analogy between the State of Israel and the Hasmoneans is waning outside the walls of the kindergarten. It is interesting that at the end of the twenties, handbills of the Jewish Palestinian Communist party compared Mattathias and his sons to the Arab fellahin rising against the Arab *effendis* and British imperialism. I thank Dr S. Dotan for this reference.

[17] Laskov, 'Altneuland'. Those defending Herzl's vision asserted that his critics wished to establish an 'Asiatic Jewish state'.

communists, whom he detested.[18] Even the use of English in public life in Israel was characterized as an act of Hellenization.[19]

'Hellenism' as a slogan and as an idea is a striking example of the perverted use of a historical symbol. Religious and 'freethinking' Jews both used it for their own purposes in their quarrel: one side to denote 'forsaking religion', the other 'abandoning the original Jewish culture'. Such improper use of the term could also turn things upside-down. On the fringes of the Israeli political and ideological scene there are harsh critics of Zionism and of Orthodoxy who regard them both as zealous and narrow-minded movements contrary to the spirit of modernism and cultural pluralism. They describe the Maccabeans' victory as the triumph of monotheistic dogmatism over pluralistic, tolerant, and liberal polytheistic paganism; they describe the Hellenists in the manner of the Christian writers cited above, as fostering pluralistic and liberal outlooks.[20] However, the most common image is still that of collaborators with the foreign enemy, while the Maccabees are the symbol of a national war of liberation and of Jewish singularity.[21]

FROM REBELLION TO STATE

If the Hellenists and the Hellenist movement served, for the most part, as negative signals, the attitude towards their victorious enemies—the Hasmoneans—was at times ambiguous. Historians conducted an ongoing polemic on whether 'the Sages tried to repress the memory of the Hasmonean revolt and what content rabbinic Judaism imparted to the rebellion and its aftermath'.[22] To the modern Jewish national movement, this historical dispute had a topical ideological significance: what were the initial objectives of the rebellion? Did the Hasidaeans indeed dissociate themselves from the faction of Judas Maccabaeus after the attainment of religious autonomy? How did the tradition of the Sages depict the revolt?

[18] Achimeir, 'Arba'at hapituyim hagedolim bahistoriah shel am Yisrael', 12–13.

[19] An article in Beitar, 1–5 (Jan.–June 1933), 193.

[20] See Or, 'And Now, Sons, Be Zealous', and Uri Avneri's editorial in Ha'olam hazeh, 31 Dec. 1987. Here the Hasmoneans are likened to the members of Gush Emunim and Meir Kahane is depicted as the successor of Judas Maccabaeus. In a newspaper devoted to a 'different' (sc. liberal humanistic) education there recently appeared an article rejecting the accepted dichotomy 'Greeks bad, Jews good': 'In reality, as we all know, the Greeks developed a magnificent culture on which our foundations rest, which we study to this very day . . . children in the sixth grade, in which ancient Greek culture is taught, often find it difficult to make the connection between what they are taught and the "bad Greeks", who defiled the Temple, against whom the "heroic Maccabees" fought' (Chinukh acher, 12 Dec. 95).

[21] In recent demonstrations against the Israeli withdrawal from the West Bank, much use was made of the comparison between the Israeli government and the mityavenim.

[22] Alon, 'Have the Nation and the Sages'. See also Joshua Efron, 'Bar-Kokhva', 63–7.

When Issachar Baer Schlesinger, in his drama *The Hasmoneans* (1816), sought to glorify the heroism of the Maccabee, he equated him with the great Greek military leaders Epaminondas, Leonidas, and Miltiades. Thus the parallels he chose were strictly from the 'national' history of Greece. More than anything, the revolt of the Hasmoneans was unique:

> Not for the sake of glory did he lead
> his men to massacre, like a murderer,
> But only to remove the bonds of iniquity
> from the neck of a holy and peculiar people . . .

The Hasmonean rebellion was the most apt parallel for those who tried to find in Jewish history symbolic national uprisings that they could equate with similar symbolic events in the history of European nations. Nevertheless, even if Jewish tradition had not downplayed the rebellion, it certainly had neither concerned itself with the detailed course of the war, nor recognized the political aspect of the struggle—the achievement of an independent Jewish state—but only the religious motivation of preserving Jewish life according to halakhah. However, our concern here is not the cause or the ideology of the rebellion, but the debate about the various processes that influenced the character of the Hasmonean state during its lifetime. There are some who see in it the model of an ideal Jewish national state—one which organically integrates 'religion', 'nation', and 'secular policy'. In contrast, others point to the processes of 'Hellenization' that were rapidly generated in the Hasmonean state as an inevitable outcome of its being a state. According to this view, moderate Hellenistic elements in the early Hasmonean period blossomed into full, almost total 'Hellenization' by the time the state came to an end. Key elementary issues of modern Jewish life were seen to be embedded in the way of life of the Hasmonean state, which was the last Jewish state from that time until the modern era.

Pari passu with the controversy about the objectives of the rebellion, debate continues about the make-up of the Hasmonean state that had been created as a result, and about the extent of its 'Hellenization'. This debate is rooted in a basic question: must every Jewish 'state' sooner or later become a 'secular' entity? What is the content of the state's 'Jewishness'? Is there a contradiction between 'state' and 'religion' in Jewish history? This controversy is frequently linked to the pictures of 'normative Judaism' drawn in literature and does not actually constitute an attempt to clarify and reconstruct a real political and cultural existence. Often enough writers compare the Hasmonean period not with the kingdoms of Judah

and Israel, but with Jewish life during the Persian era. It is true that the
Hasmonean kings clearly saw the 'golden age' of the House of David and
Solomon as a historical model, but they acted more out of a desire to
reconquer the divinely granted territories that those kings had ruled.

In the last analysis, the Israelite monarchy could not be considered
the realization of an ideal, for the kings of Israel and Judah were known
to have sinned. Josephus devoted a long description to the portrayal of
King Solomon's reign, in order to condemn the 'Gentile customs' he had
adopted, and even to assert that he had sinned against the precepts of the
Torah and had deviated from the customs of his forefathers (*Antiquities*, viii.
182–208). Even if the descriptions of Solomon's royal behaviour seem to be
taken from the Hellenistic royal courts, there is no fundamental disparity
with the description in the Book of Kings. The conventional historical
doctrine, after all, holds that until the Hasmonean rebellion the Jews existed
as a religious community, which was satisfied with religious autonomy and
lacked political aspirations of any kind. It was only the Hasmoneans, it is
claimed, who transformed this community into a state, which, because
of its needs and pressures, had to be 'secular', that is, 'Hellenistic'. The
tension that exists between 'religion' and 'state' in the modern world was
transplanted to antiquity; but since the ancient world completely lacked
the ideological tension between 'religion' and the 'secularity' on which
the modern state relies in its contest with religion, it was interpreted as the
result of the process by which the Jewish community during the Second
Temple Period became a state rather than a mere community, and as the
main reason for this state's collapse. Against this notion one may point out
that even under Persian rule the life of the Jewish community in Judah
adapted to the prevailing political conditions, and the Israelite monarchy
had also followed a pattern of government taken from the ancient East of
its time.

According to F. E. Peters, the Hasmoneans blocked the spread of cultural
Hellenism, but accepted political Hellenism.[23] Daniel Schwartz writes that
the first Hasmoneans fought against Hellenism, whereas their successors
tried to integrate themselves into the Hellenistic world.[24] Samuel K. Eddy
maintains that Judah and his brothers had no choice but to adopt 'secular
Hellenism',[25] and this opinion is fairly widespread. The distinction, although it transplants to the Hasmonean period the term 'secularism', a

---

[23] Peters, *The Harvest of Hellenism*, 287. Ferguson writes: 'The Maccabean revolt was not in origin a
revolt against Greek Culture but against Idolatry' (*The Heritage of Hellenism*, 18).

[24] Daniel Schwartz, *Agrippa I*, 145–7.

[25] 'Actually, the rebellion led by the Maccabees does not seem to have been entirely a reaction to
Hellenism *per se*': Eddy, *The King is Dead*, 331.

concept alien to its way of life, clearly indicates the trends of Hellenization at that time.

Indeed, there is no doubt that the establishment of the Hasmonean kingdom necessitated many changes in the administration of government and authority, imposing upon its rulers responsibilities that typified an independent state. Not only was the Hasmonean state a new political framework, it was also situated on the extensive front lines of conflict with the Hellenistic political and cultural world around it. Accordingly, what is often described as the adoption of 'ingredients of Hellenism' cannot be deemed a one-dimensional and uncontrolled espousal of Hellenistic cultural features. No less important is the distinction between the Hasmonean government and Jewish society. The Hasmoneans, both as a dynasty and as the governing authority, were functioning according to a new set of rules, while society, for the most part, was not faced with the same pressures. In any event, the ingredients of Hellenization found in the Hasmonean state are primarily the product of processes and developments in the royal court and its organs (the army, for example) and were not a consequence of changes in society. There is clear evidence for this in the tension between the Jewish public at large and Herod together with his court, which frequently erupted into extreme violence.

The dual face of the Hasmonean kingdom is clear: using Greek as the language of diplomacy was an unavoidable necessity and not to be regarded as a manifestation of 'Hellenization', for at the same time the Hasmoneans revived the Hebrew language as the national tongue. The early Hasmoneans revealed iconoclastic cultural puritanism in proceeding to destroy all traces of pagan culture, because to them all the layers of that culture symbolized and were identified with the bitterest enemies of biblical times. Even if we reject the descriptions in Hellenistic historiography of horrifying Hasmonean deeds, we must concede that the first Hasmoneans tried to undermine the foundations of the political and cultural way of life of the Gentile population, and to leave it without institutions and without a culture.[26] The Hellenistic *polis* could not exist without its civic institutions, without religious rites, without the gymnasium, and so on. The later Hasmoneans could relinquish the extreme fundamentalist line out of a sense of power and security, and not necessarily because of a tendency towards assimilation. The traits of political and material culture available to them were primarily those of Hellenistic civilization. Their integration into this culture did not result from a tendency to assimilate, but rather was an outcome of the very existence of the new Jewish entity as an inseparable

[26] Kasher, *Jews and Hellenistic Cities*, 2–13, 122–4.

part of, as well as an influence on, its environment.[27] The Hasmoneans certainly did not function as the rulers of a 'religious community'.

One can find in the Hasmonean state conspicuous components, not only of assimilation, but also of 'inverted acculturation', i.e. an answer to the Hellenistic challenge by nurturing anew the historical biblical tradition, heightening interest in the classical national tongue, reviving biblical history as an active and vital historical memory, and so on. 'Nationalist' anti-Hellenistic trends and tempers developed in the Hasmonean state that paralleled or even drew their inspiration from the opposition of the indigenous 'Eastern' (particularly Egyptian and Persian) populations to the imported Hellenism, from tendencies towards national messianism, which was rooted in the glorification of the ancient monarchy and conveyed images of the historical golden age, and the like.[28] The adoption of Hellenistic genres and motifs in order to contend with Hellenism, or the adoption of 'Eastern' genres and motifs for the same purpose, was a well-established practice in the spiritual life of the Jews during this period.

If the early Hasmoneans consolidated Jewish nationalism as a reply to the Hellenistic challenge, then the later Hasmoneans and the various Jewish sects during the Second Temple era developed various types of reactions and subjects with which to respond to the Hellenistic and Roman challenge—at times by adopting 'Hellenistic themes' and inverting their meaning and content. One should equate occurrences of clearly anti-Hellenistic messianism, such as those which abound in and motivate revelation literature (astrological and apocalyptic), with the 'Hellenistic elements' appearing on coins, in architecture, in the structure of the army and the state, and the like. In any event—and this is the decisive fact—in the 'established religion' of the Hasmonean era, one can find only a few 'Hellenistic elements', although in the opinion of some scholars it too had absorbed and assimilated several Hellenistic influences. Moreover, many of those same popular cultural traits that are labelled 'Hellenistic' were in fact utterly 'Eastern' in their derivation.[29]

The apt parallel between the Hasmonean state and the Herodian monarchy during the Second Temple era proves that the existence of a state obligated its rulers to expand the range of functions of the 'national culture'. In both periods this culture did what was inevitable: it borrowed the components it needed for a normal existence in its political and cultural

---

[27] Kasher, *Jews and Hellenistic Cities*, 136–7; cf. Mendeles, *The Land of Israel*.

[28] According to Momigliano, apocalypticism was one of the two forces (the other was the Pharisaic movement) which separated and drew a line between Judaism and Hellenism ('Jews and Greeks', 22–3).

[29] For an interesting example of the encounter between 'East' and 'West' in the Hellenistic era, see Holt, *Alexander the Great and Bactria*, and Tarn, *The Greeks in Bactria*.

environment, and achieved this without allowing its borrowing to blur the difference between it and the other contemporary entities. Yet despite this resemblance between Hellenizing trends in the Hasmonean state and those in the Herodian state, the differences are substantive: Herod's government was thoroughly Hellenistic in character and the Hellenization of Palestine, through Hellenistic cities and governmental institutions, was intensive. A long series of clashes between Herod on the one hand and the Pharisees and the common people on the other illustrate the extent of the opposition to these trends, which was often fanatically expressed in both word and deed.

Against this background, the question arises whether the splits and controversies in Jewish society, in the Second Temple period, stemmed first and foremost from the need to respond to the Hellenistic challenge. Were the different sects shaped according to the manner in which they reacted to, adapted to, or rejected this challenge? Were those groups whose spiritual and cultural worlds show clear traces of Hellenistic assimilation influenced intentionally and consciously, or are we dealing here with a 'spontaneous' social and cultural process? Did the Jews have the power consciously to select what they wished to borrow and what they wished to reject out of hand? Were they able to put into effect an ideology of picking and choosing?

THE JEWISH SECTS AND THEIR 'HELLENISM'

Quite often, the two key groups in mainstream Judaism—the Pharisees and the Sadducees—have been described and evaluated according to their relations with the Hellenistic world.[30] Daniel Schwartz observed that a central manifestation of intellectual Hellenization was the very assumption that it is important to argue about questions of belief and practice, an assumption which is patently Hellenistic.[31] Consequently, new points of controversy were added to the Jewish intellectual agenda that had never arisen in biblical times, and presaged debates in later periods. The Pharisees and the Sadducees are usually portrayed as the two main factions active within the normative community until the destruction of the Temple. Hence it was possible to use this portrait for divergent, even contradictory,

---

[30] For part of the extensive literature on this subject see: Schürer *et al.*, *The History of the Jewish People*, ii. 52–80, 404–14; Hengel, *The 'Hellenization' of Judea*; Neusner, *The Rabbinic Tradition*; id., *From Politics to Piety*; Rivkin, 'Defining the Pharisees'; Baumgartner, 'Rivkin and Neusner on Pharisees'; L. I. Levin, 'The Political Struggle between Pharisees and Sadducees'.

[31] Daniel Schwartz, '"Kingdom of Priests"—a Pharisaic Slogan?'.

ideological purposes. An examination of the extent to which these groups were 'open' or 'closed' to Hellenistic culture was a touchstone by which they were evaluated, and influenced the way in which they functioned in the modern historical and ideological controversy.

Generally speaking, in Jewish historiography the Pharisees represented the way of normative Judaism.[32] This, I might add, is the source of the difficulty, particularly for 'nationalist historians', in explaining the Pharisees' attitude towards the Hasmonean state.[33] In I. M. Jost's opinion, the Pharisees were influenced by false pagan beliefs, while the Sadducees were influenced by liberal Epicureans (and the Essenes by the Stoics).[34] Abraham Geiger in his *Sadducäer und Pharisäer* regarded the Pharisees as reformers who wished to simplify Judaism and introduce religious and social reforms. In his view, they were a democratic popular group. Simon Dubnow described them as the 'most nationalistic and most powerful party' and said they were 'anchored in the original culture of the people'. In Smolenskin's view, the Pharisees were in fact philhellenes, but not as extreme as the Sadducees. They are described in modern scholarship as a new class that absorbed 'Hellenistic' elements, and some scholars even go so far as to view them as a Hellenistic Jewish sect that shaped the Oral Law on the basis of the Hellenistic Greek model. 'The Pharisees . . . adopted the Hellenistic doctrine of resurrection, but subsumed it under the principles of the Torah', wrote Bickerman.[35] Some scholars view the Pharisees as a school that crystallized under the influence of the Graeco-Hellenistic example and shaped a unique Jewish form of the Hellenistic common culture.[36] Thus opinions vary, some viewing the Pharisees as a sect of a Hellenistic Jewish nature, and others as representing the pure orthogenetic essence of Judaism.

These few examples illustrate the fact that each writer invented Pharisees and Sadducees to fit and justify his own world-outlook. It is paradoxical that both the nationalists and the reformists generally preferred to depict themselves as the modern counterparts of the Pharisees. In Christian historiography, they were a theological faction that personified normative Judaism, and from which Christianity, after clashing with it, had developed. On the other hand, the Sadducees, the adversaries of the Pharisees, were preferred by modern Christian historiography, in diametric contrast to

---

[32] On Salvador's *Histoire de la domination romaine et de la ruine de Jérusalem* (3 vols., Paris, 1847) see M. Graetz, 'The Place of Salvador', 52.

[33] The democratic image of the Pharisees was based on Josephus' account in *War*, ii. 162–6, *Antiquities*, xviii. 12–17.

[34] On Jost's image of the sects see Michael, *I. M. Jost*, 30–1, and Baron, 'I. M. Jost the Historian', 250.   [35] Bickerman, *From Ezra*, 94–7.

[36] Daniel Schwartz, '"Kingdom of Priests"—or Pharisaic Slogan?'

the attitude towards them in the New Testament, and they were viewed as a model of reformist and liberal Judaism. The Sadducees' Judaism was considered more 'open', tolerant, and rational: it rejected metaphysics and folk religions. From time to time, the Sadducees represented 'cultural progress' and Judaism's affinity to Hellenism. The Pharisees represented the rabbis, who immersed themselves in sterile casuistry and *Werkheiligkeit*.

In contrast to this image, an opposite notion was also taking shape in scholarly literature, according to which it was the Sadducees who represented and expounded 'theocratic Orthodoxy'. They were the guardians of the canonized Law who were against the Oral Law, against openness and flexibility, against adapting to the changing conditions of life, and in consequence, also against the systems of logic which the Pharisees, according to some scholars, had adopted from Greek philosophy. The Sadducees were portrayed as the champions of ethnic religion, who vigorously opposed conversion and guarded the purity of the nation. According to this parallelogram of contrasts, it was the Pharisees who embraced the liberal position, and it was they who transformed the national ethnic God into a supreme, universal, and individualistic deity, although they were internally divided between the more 'liberal' (the school of Hillel) and the less 'liberal' (the school of Shammai). In the world of the Pharisees, one may discover numerous 'Hellenistic' elements (which is why they, and not the Sadducees, became the teachers of Jesus), while among the Sadducees— the putative 'philhellenes'—total cultural fundamentalism reigned. Thus an unbroken line extended from the Pharisees to Reform Judaism (and even to Protestantism).

By contrast, the ultra-Orthodox deployed the comparison with the Sadducees as a weapon against the German neo-Orthodox, who held that cultural synthesis was not only traditionally sanctioned, but also the only proper course to save Orthodoxy:

These are the Sadducees	They cling to the sake of heaven
Embrace an alien bosom	Advocate alien tongues
Say, 'Revive Religion!	Make righteous of sinners!
Join Torah and the Secular!'	And cut short the souls of babes and infants.[37]

There was also a political aspect to the repertoire of images. The Pharisees were seen as satisfied with religious autonomy and 'civil rights', as articulating the immanent tension between 'religion' and 'state'. The Sadducees, on the other hand, were portrayed as having broader political ambitions and supporting the Hasmoneans and their policies. The Pharisees

[37] A. Schlesinger, *Lev ha'ivri*, vol. ii, fo. 80b, trans. Silber, 'The Emergence of Ultra-Orthodoxy', 68.

were presented as the internalizers of beliefs, viewpoints, and techniques of Hellenistic culture. Those who viewed the Pharisees as the embodiment of historic Judaism could not accept an image depicting them as a rigid group of fundamentalistic scholars, alienated from 'culture'. Thus their image flourished as spokesmen of the people, who expressed the 'organic unity' of the Jewish way of life in this aspect of the relationship between 'internal' and 'external' as well. 'Hellenism' was also possible within 'Pharisaic-rabbinic Judaism', and was actually a cardinal element of it, except that the Pharisees succeeded in absorbing Hellenism into Judaism rather than espousing it superficially like their adversaries, the Sadducees. The essential difference between the Pharisees and the Sadducees, on this view, lies not in the phenomenon of Hellenism itself, but rather in its substance and its objectives! In any case, as another approach would have it, neither the Pharisees nor the Sadducees reflect the social and cultural life of the overall Jewish population, and the real Hellenization was to be found outside the limited circle of the sects in Jewish society.

One extreme trend, which did not generally acquire a prominent place in historical consciousness—although it happens to fit the pattern of antinomy better than all the others—was crystallized in the apocalyptic literature of the first century AD. This literature cast the political and religious struggle between the Jews and the 'Greeks' and between Judaism and Hellenism as an eternal war that would culminate before the Redemption. In the apocalyptic picture of the present and the future, Hellenism represents the satanic powers of evil, whereas Judaism personifies the divine powers of justice. The struggle between the two is a fateful one, which will decide the way in which the world will be conducted. One finds such an expression of the rejection of Graeco-Hellenistic culture in the *Oracula Sibyllina* (written in Greek by Jewish authors who knew Greek mythology), in which Homer is described as an 'old writer of falsehoods' who led intelligent men astray (iii. 419–32). The Sibyl is also familiar with the Homeric hymn to Apollo, in which the poet is described as blind. It becomes clear, therefore, that familiarity not only does not cause one to be receptive to influence, but on the contrary, it nourishes one's negative attitude to the familiar. (Or as the saying goes: 'familiarity breeds contempt'.)

ORGANIC JUDAISM AND CULTURAL UNIQUENESS

The extensive Jewish historical literature on the extent to which the Pharisees and the Sadducees were Hellenized judges them by modern criteria, that is, criteria that place the question of 'influence' squarely at the centre of the historical debate. Hence those who regarded the Pharisees as the representatives of historic and organic Judaism, and concomitantly considered Judaism an open and dynamic culture that absorbed outside influences and was even shaped by them, were required to find the link between 'Jewish organic culture' and 'openness'. This was provided by the concepts of individuality and distinctiveness.[38] Esteem for the Pharisees established a basis for the most part common to the historical world-view of observant Jews and of 'freethinkers': to them, the Pharisees represented 'average', i.e. normative Judaism, which is also the embodiment of Jewish individuality in history, whereas the Sadducees or the Essenes represented fanatical Judaism. The Pharisees then, stood for ideal, harmonious Judaism: an amalgam of religion and culture, guided by the principle of 'open individuality', i.e. open to selective absorption.

Ahad Ha'am's ideas can serve as a typical example of the positive attitude towards Pharisaism from this point of view, as gauged by the new criteria. He too saw in the Pharisees and the Sadducees two schools that had to answer the eternal question about the relationship between body and soul, and at the same time to answer the question about the relationship between nationalism and Torah. In his opinion, the Sadducees tried to revive the ancient (biblical) Jewish outlook and opposed belief in life after death, in the resurrection of the dead, and so on. But they also were addicted to the pleasures of this world. The Essenes laid emphasis on the eternality of the spirit and its superiority over temporal life on earth. In contrast to these two groups, the Pharisees, in his opinion, exemplified not only 'normative Judaism' but also well-balanced Judaism. Hence they became 'the teachers and guides of the people, . . . who upheld the Jewish view which was handed down by the Prophets; that is, the combination of flesh and spirit'. They brought about the elimination of dualism, not only on the metaphysical philosophical plane, but also within nationalistic life. The Pharisees—argued Ahad Ha'am—in contrast to the Sadducees and the Essenes, fully understood that the spirit of Judaism needed a secure and enduring political body in which the spirit 'could find concrete expression'. A political body, however, is not an end in itself. The exemplary inner balance that the Pharisees achieved enabled them to continue to exist and to be an influence even after the destruction of the Temple, while the Sadducees and the Essenes disappeared from the face of the earth. According to Ahad Ha'am's simplistic sketch, the Pharisees were the torchbearers of a nationalism 'which hung in mid-air', that through the centuries aimed at being incarnated and transfigured into a national body;

[38] See Ch. 16.

a nationalism that was a fusion of the 'spiritual' and 'physical'. Orthodoxy is the counterpart of the Essenes, and national-political Zionism is the counterpart of the Sadducees.[39]

To freethinking nationalists, the Pharisees were an example of a 'living national culture', changing and flexible according to inner principles, but responding to the circumstances of the times. This positive attitude towards Pharisaism results not only from interpreting it as a manifestation of 'popular' and 'organic' Judaism, but also from another mode of interpretation relevant to the issue at hand. We know that the biblical verse 'And ye shall be unto Me a kingdom of priests and a holy nation' (Exod. 19: 6) was interpreted as expressing an explicitly Pharisaic and anti-Sadducee posture that endorsed religious democracy. From the standpoint of the Reformists, the Pharisees were an example not of rabbinic Judaism, but of its opposite, a group that did not hesitate to change the received religion according to its own spirit and the spirit and needs of the nation. What these Reformists and others seeking change regarded as a vehicle for demanding flexibility and openness of rabbinic authority, dialectically became, in the view of the freethinkers, the content of democracy in Judaism and a basis for repudiating rabbinical and Torah-based authority.

A clear example of using the 'Pharisee model' for such a purpose can be found in Peretz Smolenskin, who drew a parallel between 'Pharisaism' and English democracy, seing the latter as rooted in the 'Athenian model' of democracy, based on the sovereignty of the people, the law, and patriarchal tradition. In the 'Pharisaic model', he maintains, the credo 'a kingdom of priests and a holy nation' vests the authority in the hands of all the people, or in the hands of their elected representatives, to decide upon laws and precepts and to change the character of Judaism in line with the times. In Smolenskin's view, it is not the rabbis who hold title to tradition and authority, but rather the 'people' and its representatives—the new national élite. Thus the new Jewish national intelligentsia could see itself as the continuation of the Pharisaic tendency in Judaism and not, as it really was, as a radical break with it.[40] This is also one of those ever-present ironies: Peretz Smolenskin, the arch-enemy of modern Hellenic Judaism, defends the Pharisees for 'affinity to British democracy rooted in Greek ideals'!

---

[39] Ahad Ha'am, 'Flesh and Spirit', 148–51. He follows Graetz, who writes: 'The characteristic traits of Pharisianism are a careful observance of the Laws, an exaggerated concern with ritual purity, tradition . . . and finally the dogma of a future life and resurrection' ('The Structure of Jewish History', 90–2).

[40] Smolenskin, 'Am olam', 98, 110–12.

HELLENISM IN THE SECOND TEMPLE PERIOD

Some scholars believe that Hellenistic culture had already spread among Palestinian Jewry in the Hasmonean era, and that it further deepened its penetration in the time of Herod and under Roman rule. In other words, they assert that Hellenism in the Second Temple period was in the process of gradually increasing and deepening its influence. According to others, knowledge of Greek was not so widespread, and in general, Jewish literature was not written in Greek within the boundaries of Palestine; Greek (and Eastern) art was absorbed only in certain sectors and for defined purposes, particularly in popular art, and Jews were not truly familiar with Greek literature and philosophy.[41] In the Second Temple literature written in Palestine (with the exception, perhaps, of that of 'the Fourth Philosophy')[42] there is no trace of any distinct philosophical terminology. In particular, they argue, Jews did not take part in the pagan rites or in the Greek institutions of culture, education, and the like. In other words, this is a case in which interferences occurred mainly in the peripheral areas of culture.

In his extensive recent study, *Jews and Gentiles in the Ancient World*, Louis H. Feldman reduces to a minimum any Hellenistic influences on Judaism in Palestine (and in the Diaspora), and wherever there were any, he regards them as part of the shared Oriental culture, not necessarily as Hellenistic influences. According to him, Judaism did not only hold its own against Hellenism, preserving its singularity; it also completely or partially Judaized many pagans. In his view 'the net effect of assimilation of the Greek language and culture by the Jews was not defection from Judaism, but rather, on the contrary, the creation of a common bond of communication with gentiles, through which at least some non-Jews were won over to Judaism'.[43] But the Jews in Palestine rejected philosophy as a meaningful study to be applied to their traditional religious literature because they identified it with the pagan lifestyle of the Greeks. Only when Greek philosophical texts were

---

[41] See Herr's discussion ('External Influences') of Hengel's view, expressed in *Judaism and Hellenism*, that the Jews in Palestine produced works in Greek in order to reduce the variance between the Jews of Palestine and those in the Diaspora (cf. Schürer et al., *The History of the Jewish People*, iii/1. 517–21, on Eupolemus). He writes that the view that the dissemination of the Greek language and Hellenistic culture among the Jews in Palestine reached its peak in the 2nd and 3rd cc. BC is groundless, and that the contrary is true. Hengel's position is set out in *Judaism and Hellenism*; Herr cites M. Stern's review of the German original (*Judentum und Hellenismus*, Tübingen, 1969), at *Kiryat Sefer*, 46 (1971), 94–9.

[42] M. Luz, 'Clearchus of Soli'; Stern, 'The Suicide'.

[43] L. H. Feldman, *Jews and Gentiles*, 83.

used by the monotheistic Arabs were the rabbis motivated to pursue its study.[44] On the other hand, some scholars have posited a Greek origin for the practice of allegory and the hermeneutic rule of the *gezerah shavah*.[45] Orthodox Judaism, writes Momigliano, 'was not impervious to Greek influences. The very organization of traditional Jewish education is inconceivable without the example of the Greek *paideia*.'[46] Indeed, on the same line of thought, some scholars do point to the borrowing and assimilation of patterns and techniques—but also of ideas—particularly in the Herodian era and thereafter. The Second Temple period is also characterized by the conflict of 'scholarly Judaism' with Hellenism and its constant confrontation with the Hellenist population in Palestine.

Can we draw the 'real' picture of Jewish life during the Second Temple period? How far was Jerusalem from Athens and Alexandria?

It seems right to claim that the Jews in Palestine of that time lived within the Hellenistic world, but were not an integral part of it. The Jewish village (or city) was different from the Hellenistic village (or city): it contained no temples, altars, or idols, but rather a synagogue and a house of study; it had no gymnasium or stadium. The daily routine, the rhythm of the year, public life, the historical consciousness, the legal system—all these were palpably different in essence and form. There were no mixed marriages; laws of impurity and purification effectually separated or determined clear lines of demarcation between the populations. The function of the 'Oral Law' in Hellenistic and Jewish society was totally different. Jews had a different calendar, different festivals, a different cosmology, and different historical traditions. Regardless of the gap between the norms prescribed by religious authority and the actual conduct of the people, Jewish life was distinctive and separate from the life of the Gentile neighbours. To the outside observer, Judaism looked like a homogeneous unit, and he failed to note its diversity. The Jews, wrote Tacitus, generally do not eat of the bread nor drink of the beverages of the Romans (*Histories*, v. 5. 2 *separati epulis, discreti cubilibus*).[47] No matter how blurred the boundaries may be between Jews and non-Jews in various matters, even pagan polemic against Christianity, in its discussion of Jews and Chris-

---

[44] See Ch. 4 and Kaufmann, *The Religion*, i/1. 240.

[45] *Gezerah shavah* is a mode of arguing from the appearance of the same word in two texts. See Herr's summary, *The Roman–Byzantine Period*, 152–203; Alexander, 'Quid Athens et Hierosolymis?'; S. Stein, 'The Influence of Symposia Literature'; L. H. Feldman, loc. cit.

[46] Momigliano, 'Persian Historiography, Greek Historiography, and Jewish Historiography', 26.

[47] See Herr, 'The Hatred towards the Jews in the Roman Empire'; M. Stern, 'The Hatred of the Jews in Rome'.

tians, actually emphasizes the deep chasm that existed between Judaism and pagan Hellenism.[48]

THE IMAGE OF ALEXANDRIAN JUDAISM

As early as the eighteenth century a distinction was accepted between 'Jewish Hebrews', namely the Pharisees and the Sadducees, and the Hellenistic Jews in the generation before Jesus. According to this distinction, the Hellenistic Jews gave the Bible an allegorical and universalistic interpretation, thus preparing the ground for the spiritual revolution wrought by Jesus and his disciples;[49] Alexandrian Judaism was an exemplary model of liberal Judaism living in symbiosis with its environment. However, Bickerman declared: 'The dichotomy between rabbinic and Hellenized Judaism is an invention of German theology of the nineteenth century',[50] and repudiated the dichotomy for two reasons: first, because in his view, the Jews of Palestine were 'Hellenists'; secondly, because the Jews of Egypt were religiously observant. They found the middle way between Hellenization and narrow concentration on the Commandments.[51]

In an effort to study the special character of Jewish Hellenization in Egypt, modern historical scholarship has addressed this dichotomy—rooted in a unidimensional image of Hellenism in Egypt—at length. Were the Jews of Alexandria really cut off from the sphere of influence of normative Judaism in Palestine? How culturally stratified was Jewish Hellenism? Is it not worthwhile, in the context of Egyptian Judaism as well, to discriminate between disparate levels and qualities of 'Hellenization?' To what extent were the Jews of Egypt 'Orthodox', and how many of them were 'atheists'?[52] What social class do Philo and the Hellenistic Jewish writers represent and who was their target audience?

It is not my intention here to summarize the major views in relation to the essence of Alexandrian Jewry as a social body,[53] and certainly not

---

[48] On the pagan view see Rokéah, *Judaism and Christianity*, and Gager, *The Origins of Anti-Semitism*, 39–115.

[49] Reill, *German Enlightenment*, 169–70. Alexandria could also be praised from a Jewish point of view; see H. Gross, 'Olymp und Sinai', 620.

[50] Bickerman, 'Symbolism in the Dura Synagogue', 222.

[51] Yet another view is that in Alexandria the Jews lived in an environment in which Greek religion had lost its ideal element and become 'a mixture of universal scepticism and empty show, of gross superstitious beliefs in magic and astrology, and Oriental mysticism and human abasement' (Bentwich, *Hellenism*, 66).

[52] See Kasher, 'Some Remarks and Insights'.

[53] Among the vast literature on this subject, see Kasher, *The Jews in Hellenistic and Roman Egypt*; id., 'Some Remarks and Insights'; L. H. Feldman, 'The Orthodoxy of the Jews'; Collins, *Between Athens and*

the writings about Hellenistic Jewish philosophy, particularly those about Philo. What should be remembered is that Alexandrian Jews lived through-out the entire period even as a *politeuma* within the Hellenistic and Roman *polis*, as an ethnic and religious minority within a hostile Hellenistic and Egyptian society, physically cut off from worship in the Temple, the centre of religious life. Their dependence on their cultural milieu and their ties to it were of necessity more intense than those of the Jewish community in Palestine, which was a majority group. A knowledge of Greek was im-perative for them, and in any case it exposed them to all the layers of the surrounding Hellenistic culture. However, it seems that their Helleniza-tion did not lead to assimilation or syncretism but rather created a form (or forms) of acculturation.

It is hard to imagine that the general Jewish public in Alexandria did not absorb traits of Hellenistic culture and did not share in some parts of it. The extent of cultural symbiosis in the various levels of the 'popular culture' is not known, but is seems logical that like the entire surrounding culture, the Jewish culture also embraced 'popular beliefs' in demons, amulets, astrology, and the like. However, such popular beliefs need not impair 'orthodoxy' and the observance of the Torah and the commandments. As to Jewish Hellenistic literature, is was driven to take both an apologetic and a 'missionary' stand since it was addressed to the alien public in a language they understood when it sought to defend 'Judaism' or to glorify its name and praise its contents and messages. The Hellenistic Jewish élite were called upon to explain or justify to foreigners their faith in one god, and since they were unable to find such a rationale in their heritage, and in any case 'had no philosophy at their disposal other than the Greek', they needed Greek philosophy.[54]

The attitude towards Hellenistic Jewish literature in the talmudic tradi-tion is a negative one: the Sages speak of 'evil waters' in *Mishnah Avot*, 1: 11. They described it as heretical writing, and forbade Jews to read it.[55] However, there are hints that at least some part of this literature was known to the Sages and perhaps also to a wider Jewish public. It was the sixteenth century that rediscovered Philo,[56] and the entire corpus of Hellenistic Jew-

---

Jerusalem; Tcherikover, *Hellenistic Civilization*; Sandmel, 'Hellenistic Judaism'; Wolfson, *Philo*, i. 3–86. The Jews who according to Philo, *De virtutibus*, 182 rejected the laws of the Torah, i.e. assimilated Jews such as Ti. Julius Alexander, are regarded by most scholars as a small minority.

[54] Amir, 'Monotheistic Problem'. Azariah de' Rossi, in his *Sefer me'or einayim*, called Philo 'Jedidiah the Alexandrian'.

[55] See Gruenwald, 'Polemical Attitudes towards the Septuagint'.

[56] Weinberg, 'The Quest for Philo'; Momigliano, 'Jews and Greeks', 26–8. The writings of Philo were first translated into German in 1909–19.

ish literature; a second rediscovery followed in the nineteenth. Momigliano pointed to the irony that the Wisdom of Ben-Sira, written 'by the man who had repudiated Greek wisdom, lived on through the centuries in the Greek version made by his grandson'.[57] And it took the *maskilim* of the early nineteenth century to rediscover Hellenistic Jewish literature,[58] the Books of the Maccabees, and Josephus; ironically the very books that describe the victory of the Maccabees over the Hellenizing Jews and the 'Greeks' were also preserved in the language of the 'vanquished'. The texts thus rediscovered did not, for the rediscoverers, merely constitute an ancient, forgotten literature that had came to light in rare manuscripts for the use of scholars, but sketched a new portrait of Second Temple Judaism that brought about an intellectual renaissance.[59] Krochmal wrote that Hellenistic Jewish literature had been condemned to oblivion for not being written in Hebrew.[60] The *maskilim* disregarded this sentence and infused this lost literary corpus into the circulatory system of Hebrew literature. Although they had a negative attitude towards Jewish mysticism, they included not only the wisdom literature but also eschatological literature in the Hebrew literary corpus.[61] But only in the late nineteenth century did the entire body of Hellenistic Jewish literature become available to the educated Hebrew reader.

That literature (including the historical works) made Alexandrian Jewry a complete social and cultural entity. The essence of Alexandrian Jewry was not captured only in the literary corpus it left behind. Rather it became a unique Jewish society, which could also serve as a positive or negative historical model. Alexandrian Jewry was often regarded as a paradigm far

---

[57] Momigliano, *Alien Wisdom*, 96.

[58] On the discovery of the Apocalyptic literature see Koch, *The Rediscovery of Apocalyptic Literature*. On the Jewish rediscovery see Chana's general introduction to the books of the Apocrypha, i, pp. vi–xvii. In his article 'Hasefer ha'ivri', Bialik wrote that 'Hellenistic Jewish literature was created in the spirit of the people'; thus the apocryphal books must be regarded as an integral part of the Hebrew literary canon (p. 38).

[59] Geiger, *Urschrift und Übersetzungen*, 10–19. And see Eisenstein, *The Printing Revolution*, 111–47.

[60] Krochmal, *Moreh*, xxii. 165–7. See also de' Rossi's view in *Me'or einayim*, in Bonfil, *Azariah de' Rossi*, 215–33. S. D. Luzzatto wrote that Aristeas' letter is a 'blatant lie' and that the Septuagint is full of 'frightful errors'; that it was meant for Jews who know no Hebrew and ought not to be relied upon (*Igrot Shadal*, ii. 173, letter to S. L. Rapoport, dated 22 Oct. 1830). We may note that soon after the traditional date of the Septuagint translation (and the likely date of the Greek Pentateuch) the Greek freedman L. Livius Andronicus translated the *Odyssey* into Latin. See too Bickerman, 'The Septuagint as a Translation'.

[61] Kalman Schulman wrote that the author of the Wisdom of Solomon was a Hellenistic Jew from Alexandria who had been influenced by Greek philosophy, and that the spirit of the work is close to that of the New Testament, in his Introduction to Wessely's *Divrei shalom ve'emet*, 13. In his introduction to the translation of the *Wisdom of Solomon* (*Die Weisheit Solomon's*, Prague, 1853) Mendel Stern writes that Solomon is arguing against the pagans who did not recognize the truth.

more suited to the needs of the *maskilim* than those of the Sadducees and the Pharisees. The Pharisees and Sadducees were, after all, distinctly Palestinian creations, whereas Alexandrian Judaism was a product of the Diaspora. The Jews of Alexandria were not embroiled in a political power-struggle, but rather immersed in a struggle for the perpetuation of a unique cultural and civic existence.

This depiction of Alexandrian Jewry as liberal, imbued with freedom and universalistic values, open to and tolerant of the surrounding culture, in contrast to particularistic, insular, legalistic Pharisaism, is baseless, and there is no similarity between it and 'Emancipation Judaism'.[62] However, owing to this analogy, it could serve as a more fitting model of coexistence through symbiosis with its surroundings, while renouncing the national-istic 'earthly' elements of Judaism. From the standpoint of the Mission Theory, the Jews of Alexandria provided the resolute historical answer to the prevalent Christian universalistic ideal. They, not the Christians, em-bodied the universal mission of the people of Israel 'loftier than corporeal existence', and epitomized the universal mission of Judaism, so different in essence from that of the Greeks. Both the Pharisees and the Sadducees failed to meet the challenge of the existence of state and country. Alexan-drian Jewry, which was exempted from the burden of the 'material', was open to outside influences that enriched its creative talents and inspired it to establish lofty humanistic values of liberty and ethics. Alexandria became a sublime model of cultural symbiosis, inducing its Jews to cre-ate a consciousness of their uniqueness based on a foundation of universal meaning. This model was at times even regarded as preferable to the model of the 'Golden Age' in Spain.[63]

Immanuel Wolf (1799–1841), for example, wrote in the first issue of the *Zeitschrift für die Wissenschaft des Judentums* (1822), that Alexandria was the scene of a fertile encounter between two universal elements, Judaism and Hellenism, of which the latter had already celebrated its victory over the previously dominant world of Asia. Judaism contained the idea of the divinity as revelatory; in Hellenistic thought, the source

[62] M. Graetz, *From Periphery to Center*, 239–46.

[63] B. Lewis, 'The Pro-Islamic Jews', 113–16. In Heine's view (*Pariser Berichte*, 'Ludwig Marcus', 22 Apr. 1844), the members of the Society for the Culture and Science of Judaism (*Verein für Kultur und Wissenschaft der Juden*) had attempted to repeat the bad experience from the days of Hellenistic Alexandria and to effect a reconciliation between historical Judaism and the new science. Aby Warburg is an example of a liberal German Jewish scholar who wrote of the persistence of the classical tradition in the Renaissance and feared the victory of the daemonic, dark Dionysian side of the psyche over reason (the Apollonian side). In Athens he saw the symbol of Enlightenment and reason, in Alexandria the symbol of the irrational and the daemonic; hence Athens must always be saved from Alexandria (Mosse, 'Intellectual Authority and Scholarship', 51).

of all knowledge was the human spirit itself. These two ideas, each in its own way, are the most important and fundamental factors in the historical formation of the human spirit. These different principles are hostile to one another. They stand counter to one another, each aspiring to encroach upon the other and consume it.[64] Wolf uses this idealistic, a-historical description to explain how it happened that from this meeting of opposites, which in his view was tempered by the existence of the third, mediating, element—the Egyptian—new world-outlooks were constructed of three components: the philosophy of Philo, Gnosticism, and Neoplatonism. He shows how, through this confrontation, the Jewish people was split into different religious sects, allowing Christianity to turn the idea of overall unity into an accepted concept.

The rediscovery of Hellenistic literature, which the Talmud counted among the forbidden books, was thus not merely the discovery of a forgotten and hidden literary corpus, but an expression of a tendency, a renewed desire to explain and interpret Judaism in the concepts of contemporary philosophy—this time in terms of the new European philosophy. But at the same time, the Alexandrian model was based on a number of tendentious misconceptions. To give one example, it disregarded the political struggle of Alexandria's Jews to attain a special status within the *polis* (of whose 6,500,000 inhabitants they constituted about 1 million), nor the tensions with the Greeks that culminated in the revolt of 115–17;[65] it ignored the fact that Jewish 'atheism' was a marginal phenomenon, and that Jewish philosophy was apologetic rather than addressed to the general Jewish public. The model also overlooked the fundamental difference between the confrontation with Hellenism on the philosophical and theoretical plane and assimilation into the Hellenistic-Egyptian cultural reality—just as it overlooked the confrontation between Greek and demotic in Egyptian society itself.[66] However, ideologues of emancipation and of complete cultural openness found an ideal in the history of Alexandrian Jewry—a yearned-for imaginary type worthy of veneration; an ideal of Judaism as a 'culture', that could provide an underpinning for Jewish existence in the Diaspora in symbiosis with the high culture of the surrounding society.

Not all concurred with this anti-national position, which opposed the idea of a national and cultural revival in Palestine, or fostered Jewish integ-

---

[64] See I. Wolf, 'On the Concept of a Science of Judaism'.

[65] Mendeles, *The Rise and Fall*, 13–54; Eddy, *The King is Dead*, 257. However, Eddy concludes that in the East 'there was no opposition to Hellenism in its totality, and there was no effort made by anybody to destroy Hellenism entirely', 333.

[66] See Rokéah (ed.), *Jewish Revolts*. During the riots (*stasis*) of AD 115–17 both Jewish synagogues and pagan temples were destroyed.

ration with the German (or some other) culture. This was not the view
taken, for example, by Graetz, in whose eyes Alexandrian Jewry was nearly
equated with self-effacement; that is, apostasy. He described it as 'a wild
offshoot of the spirit of Judaism', and stated that those Jews had infused a
watered-down and specious spirit of Judaism into the Greek culture that
they adopted.[67] From this spirit, Graetz stated, one may vividly conjure
up a picture of the abyss into which emancipation and acculturation are
likely to sink. He in no way deemed their 'missionary' function as worthy
of esteem.

It was Ahad Ha'am who proposed a more realistic appraisal. He saw the
Hellenization of Alexandrian Jews as a practical necessity. The translation
of the Bible into Greek, towards which the Sages exhibited an ambivalent
attitude, was in his view necessitated by the existence of a large Diaspora whose tongue was Greek. We did not find—he noted—that a large
movement of assimilation arose in Alexandria:

On the contrary, they employed their Greek knowledge as an instrument for
revealing the essential spirit of Judaism, for showing the world its beauty, and
vindicating it against the proud philosophy of Greece. That is to say, starting from
an Imitation which had its source in self-effacement before an alien spiritual force,
they succeeded, by means of that Imitation, in making the force their own, and
in passing from self-effacement to competition.

The historic Jewish mistake, in his view, lies in the fact that the most sublime spiritual works of classical Greece were not translated into Hebrew
until the Middle Ages, when their appropriation by the Jews took place
on foreign soil. As a result Hellenic philosophy could not be 'positively'
assimilated into Palestinian Judaism. In the Diaspora the laws of dialectics began to operate again: imitation gave way to spiritual competition,
and medieval Judaism discovered its individuality through the medium of
Muslim-Greek philosophy. This is the basis of his conclusion that historical necessity compels the Jews to turn eastwards, to 'the land that was our
centre and our pattern in ancient days'. Ahad Ha'am believed that the Jews
of Alexandria were worthy of esteem because they preserved their faith
under intolerable conditions, and at the same time acted to enhance its
glorification and veneration among the Gentiles. Philo, who on more than
one occasion had been depicted as the forerunner of Mendelssohn, the Jew
who sated himself with 'Greek enlightenment', and sanctioned all those
who wished to cast off the 'yoke of legalism that hung on their necks',

[67] H. Graetz, 'The Structure', 73–4. And see Dubnow, *The World History of the Jewish People*, ii. 63–8,
194–7, 204–11.

was also described by him as desiring to endow Judaism with new validity by grappling with prestigious opinions and beliefs current in his time.[68]

Alexandrian Jewry, often an admired model of a struggle for existence and identity in the Diaspora, also served as a model for searing self-criticism. In a satiric poem written in 1892, entitled 'Simchah vesason layehudim' ('Gladness and Joy for the Jews'), Judah Leib Levin likened the oppression of Russian Jews to that of the Jews of Alexandria. A Greek is found dead outside the city and an unruly mob gathers to vent its fury against the Jews. Fortunately, at the very last moment, it turns out that the victim is not a Greek, but 'just' a Jewish pedlar. The Jews express their joy—not their sorrow—about the dead man:

> Our brother the victim is a Jew, not a Greek—
> Rejoice, you people, so pathetic, so weak![69]

Alexandrian Jewry is not only a model for imitation (one with apologetic tendencies) or a model of Judaism struggling to preserve its spiritual uniqueness. It can also be a model of a miserable and pathetic Jewish existence.

Today, the tension between the Jewish centre in Palestine (the State of Israel) and the Jewish centre in the United States inevitably leads to the use of the historical paradigm of the relationship between 'Jerusalem' and 'Alexandria'. American Judaism was more often described as 'Alexandria on the Hudson' than as being like the Jewish centre in Babylonia. The historical parallel was sometimes used to draw a direct analogy between the situation of US Jewry and the relationship and ties developed by the Jews of Egypt with Jerusalem and the Temple; at other times it served to point to the putative preferred status of one of these two historical entities—as well as of their modern parallels. In other words, it was employed to place in opposition a Diaspora, like American Jewry, grappling with its problems of identity, and a nation-society grappling with its specific problems. The historical polemic of American Jews often carries on the line of argument of European liberal Judaism while the polemic from the Israeli side carries on the anti-Diaspora nationalist line. One cannot avoid noting that the American Jewish polemic views the Alexandrian

---

[68] Ahad Ha'am, 'Imitation and Assimilation', 178. Bentwich writes that the Jews were in close contact with the Hellenistic world, 'and by the assimilation of the general culture of the age could express their message in an intelligible form' (Hellenism, 135). Thus 'The outward expansion of Hellenistic Judaism was greater than its inward cohesion, and became in time a danger. In order to appeal to the Gentile people, Jewish law and Jewish belief were re-interpreted in terms of Greek thought' (ibid. 188). 'While the Palestinian teachers sought to defend Judaism against Hellenism, the Alexandrian teachers to defend it with Hellenism' (ibid. 195).

[69] In Y. L. Levin, Zikhronot vehegyonot, 155–8.

class of *maskilim* as representative of the entire Jewish society in Alexandria and in Hellenistic Egypt, and thus totally ignores the nature of Jewish history there—including the ongoing, even violent, confrontation between Alexandrian Jewry and its surroundings.[70]

Nevertheless, the Jewish situation in modern Europe may clarify the complexity of the Jews' situation in Alexandria.

German Jews employed a wide variety of terms to express the array of changes that occurred in their cultural status or their expectations. They used vague terms such as *Annäherung, Anpassung, Eingliederung, Verschmelzung, Aufgehen, Auflösung*, etc.,[71] in order to describe their complex relationship with German society and culture. Eastern European Jews lacked such a broad vocabulary, so that in many texts the boundary between the notion of assimilation and the notion of acculturation is very vague. It ranges from an attraction to types of culture defined by Jewish polemic as non-Jewish (opera, music, theatre)[72] to changes in the value-system of the orthogenetic culture, which constitute radical acculturation. It seems to me therefore right to argue that we can find fundamental lines of similarity between the nineteenth century and Alexandria. In both cases, the cardinal point to be stressed is the difference between the cultural processes when they apply to Jews in the Diaspora, where they are a sociocultural minority, and the same processes taking place in the framework of a national society in which the entire sociocultural (and political) complex is Jewish. Cultural changes occurring in a group may change the identity of the entire group. As we shall see, this was the root of the national ideology's desire to oversee these changes; precisely because it aspired to far-reaching changes, it wished to exercise absolute control over them.

THE SECOND TEMPLE PERIOD AS A MODEL

The Second Temple period is characterized by the multidimensional encounter of the Jews and Judaism with Hellenism. This took place on the plane of national existence, a clash not only between populations with opposing interests, but between cultures; hence its special and fateful nature

[70] G. Shaked, 'Alexandria'; Kimmirling, 'Between "Alexandria-on-the-Hudson" and Zion'; Gorny, *The State of Israel*, 66.

[71] Y. Toury, 'Emancipation and Assimilation'. Cf. Bickerman's remark that 'Like the Emancipation of the nineteenth century, that of the second century B.C.E. must have necessarily led to religious "reforms". But nineteenth-century Emancipation could in the end escape this necessity, for Occidental civilization as a whole had in the interval become secularized' (*From Ezra*, 107–8).

[72] The enthusiam of the Jews in 19th-c. Odessa for theatre, music, and opera led a Russian visitor to the city in 1839 to speak of the Jewish people as 'fanatico per la musica'. See Zipperstein, 'Jewish Enlightenment in Odessa', 26–7.

and its great significance in Jewish history for generations to come. Second Temple Judaism provides a variety of models, exemplars, and symbols, and is mainly depicted as a dynamic, pluralistic culture and society, which was open to outside influences, capable of rejecting or adopting them, while at the same time maintaining its individuality. This was the nature of Judaism in the Hellenistic period in the mirror of the nineteenth and twentieth centuries; and this was the way modern Judaism wished to be seen. It exposed the complexities of cultural interferences and cultural borrowing and the dangers they posed and the profits they promised. The borrowing process in the modern period, as we shall see in Chapter 16, should be evaluated and judged in the light of Bickerman's illuminating observation that 'discoveries of borrowing and influences have only a modest heuristic value unless we can learn why and to what purpose the new motif was woven into the traditional design',[73] to which we may add, unless we can describe their function and what was the extent and nature of their impact on the receiver.

The three main models provided by the experience of the Second Temple period in Palestine were as follows:

(i) The Second Temple period was a time of unceasing spiritual ferment, resulting from the encounter and confrontation with Hellenism. However, this was Israel's second heyday, an organic period that created a fabric of Jewish life, whole, deeply rooted in its homeland, totally committed to and steadfast in its faith; a union of religion and state, life and halakhah. Since it was this ideal Judaism that encountered Hellenism, its individuality was not impaired. It kept and preserved its purity. Judaism was a strong, organic culture of life, and so sure of itself and its superiority that Hellenism did not exert a strong influence on it; Judaism, it turns out, was so attractive that it influenced great numbers of pagans.

(ii) The Judaism of this period was strong enough to assimilate foreign components and turn them into elements that accelerated and generated its immanent development. The strength of Judaism enabled it to digest and incorporate the alien elements, and to place Hellenistic elements at the service of the ideal society of the Sages. Although there were compromises and 'assimilations', those were made through altering the essence and function of the assimilated traits. There were also external influences of mystery rites and folk beliefs, which operated on the periphery of the 'culture'. Proponents of this view can accept that some Hellenistic influences penetrated the very heart of normative Judaism, because they believe

---

[73] *Jews in the Greek Age*, 304.

in its natural power, in its ability to cull and sift, to adopt and reject, and to pass every received trait through the filter of its unique spirit. This was the Golden Age of Judaism: an era of harmony between the 'external' and the 'internal', which was achieved by virtue of the vitality of the 'internal'. Later on, cultural forces caused rents in this fabric, which led to internal weakness and destruction. The conclusion arrived at by founders of the idea of modern Jewish national culture was that only in its third heyday—the revival of nationalism in Palestine—would organic Judaism become once again receptive to stimulating and enriching influences. The paradox here is that organicity became a precondition for openness.

(iii) There was no normative Judaism during the Second Temple period (or after it). The Pharisaic and rabbinic tradition does not describe the existing reality: in actual fact, Judaism was fragmented into various currents and split into different cultural layers, each of which absorbed and assimilated Hellenistic influences in its own way. There is no one normative Judaism, but a multifaceted Hellenistic Judaism. Therefore the Judaism of the third century onwards should be defined as *hellenistisches Judentum*, or even a Jewish type or branch of Greek religion.[74] The conclusion was that if the Jews of the Second Temple lived outside the sphere of influence of Pharisaic and rabbinic Judaism,[75] then modern secular Judaism, which also lives outside the sphere of halakhic Judaism, is legitimate. If the majority of the Jews in the Second Temple period and thereafter were not halakhic Jews in the rabbinical sense of the term, then there is no truth in the claim that it is halakhic Judaism in the rabbinic or Orthodox sense that is the legitimate heir and sole representative of historical Judaism.

A totally different encounter took place between the Jews and Judaism and the various layers of Hellenism in the centuries following the destruction of the Temple and the destruction of the Jewish community in Alexandria.

---

[74] Hengel, *Judaism and Hellenism*, 193; Bickerman, *Jews in the Greek Age*, 145; id., *From Ezra*, 162–5; Ferguson writes that 'Hellenistic Judaism is Hellenized Judaism', *The Heritage of Hellenism*. 18.

[75] Bowker, *The Targum*, 36–7. Bowker believes that 'the gap Goodenough found between Hellenized Judaism and pharisaic/rabbinic Judaism is in some respects too wide and rigid, and the term "Hellenistic Judaism" can be applied to any form of Judaism which accepts, however partially, Hellenistic ideas and images as a legitimate method of interpetation. Thus, "Hellenism" was also possible within pharisaic/rabbinic Judaism itself'; Goodenough, *Jewish Symbols*, 3–35.

II

HOMERIC BOOKS AND HELLENISTIC CULTURE IN THE WORLD OF THE SAGES

Says Rabban Simeon the son of Rabban Gamaliel the Patriarch: 'There were a thousand young men in my father's house, five hundred of whom studied the [Jewish] law, while the other five hundred studied Greek wisdom.'   *Bava kamma*, 83a

Let him teach him Greek at a time when it is neither day nor night, for it is written 'Thou shalt meditate day and night' (Josh. 1: 8).

jSotah, 9: 24c; j*Pe'ah*, 1: 15c

HELLENISM IN THE WORLD OF THE SAGES

IF the Second Temple period reflected a time of struggle in which the political and cultural dimensions were merged, talmudic literature clearly reflects above all the spiritual and cultural dimension of Hellenistic Jewish discourse. Indeed, the modern reading of talmudic literature regarded it as an expression of the entire field of Jewish culture. In it scholars look for evidence that the Sages were not only familiar with Greek philosophy and literature but also borrowed from and drew upon it. Talmudic literature was described as a 'sea', in whose depths lay deposits of the heritage of Greek literature—open to streams and currents of Greek culture with which one might become familiar without any dogmatic fear.

This image strongly motivated the first generations of the nineteenth century to reread the Talmud. If they found no influence of Greek culture in it, at least it reflected various manifestations of knowledge and familiarity with it, or even the permeation of Hellenistic influences into certain layers of Jewish culture, either through expressions of disapproval or through representation of social and cultural reality. A more modern approach in reading the Sages was not only to seek a diversity of views in their sayings, but also to question their authority: did they really represent the cultural reality, or was Judaism a composite of different types of 'Judaism'? Was it a historical fact that all the Jews lived under the authority of the rabbis? What was the extent of this authority and its power to control the religious cultural norms? Through the emergence of these new questions, the relationship between the 'normative values', the authority of the rabbis and the spiritual and cultural reality became an open historical question of topical significance. Those who explored the 'talmudic sea' found not only different opinions and views in relation to the nature of 'Greek wisdom', but more besides: signs of an open or veiled encounter with it, and a gap or disparity between the reflection of reality in the Talmud and the 'real' reality. Life, it seemed to them, was stronger than the normative system. One conclusion was that talmudic literature reflected only part of the real culture. Various ties were revealed between 'Judaism' and 'Hellenism' in various domains of life, which the Talmud failed to express in concrete fashion or even chose to ignore.[1]

This radical model of Jewish cultural reality gave a stamp of approval not only to modern Liberal Orthodoxy, or to Reform Judaism, but also to secularism. If historic Judaism is not only the Judaism reflected in the Talmud, then Jewish history proves there is no basis for the claim that rabbinic Judaism is the sole and exclusive historic Judaism. Others claim that the world of the Sages reflects the outcome of interaction between the religious norms and a flexible cultural practice, which took into account the needs of life, or was expressed by 'liberal' outlooks.

Modern research has shown that the literature of the Sages was rich in idioms and terms, in techniques of interpreting texts, in literary genres and motifs and more, all of which came into it from the outside. The world of the Sages, studied in breadth and in depth, revealed a certain knowledge of classical and Hellenistic literature as well as various patterns of social and cultural organization that developed under the influence of the cultural milieu: the Passover *seder*, for example, is described as having taken shape under the influence of the Greek symposium; the organization of the Pharisees into 'houses' has also been described as being based on the structure of the Greek 'schools'.[2] Greek culture generally exerted its influence through the oral tradition. However, in speaking of cultural influences or borrowings we should not restrict ourselves to the realm of literary parallels or to real or alleged influences of philosophical ideas,[3]

---

[1] Goodman, 'Jews and Judaism in the Mediterranean Diaspora'. He asserts that 'no authority exists within Diaspora Judaism to impose rules of practice and belief' (p. 222). However, in the world of Babylonian Jewry such authority did exist.

[2] See S. Stein, 'The Influence of *Symposia* Literature'; I. Malkin, 'The Influence of the Greek Symposium on the Passover Seder'; Herr, 'External Influences'; id., *The Roman–Byzantine Period*, 195. For a contrary view see Bokser, *The Origins of the Seder*, 50–66.

[3] See Sandmel, 'Parallelomania'. Among the instances of real parallelism due to direct or indirect influence is R. Aibu's distinction, in *Midrash Tehilim* on Ps. 8: 6, between three kinds of person, those content to contemplate the Creator's work, those who seek a reward in the world to come, and those who seek it now. Sh. Pines and Harvey compare the statement of the first attitude, 'If I had only been

but treat culture as a complex reality. This will enable us to gain a better understanding of the question of cultural borrowing in the modern era.

Therefore one ought to make a clear distinction between three issues: (i) how *familiar* the Sages were with Greek culture and through which agents of culture they learned about it; (ii) to what extent they were *influenced* by it or how many different elements they adopted from it; (iii) how tolerant the Sages were regarding the use of Hellenistic elements by the Jewish public. Complex cultures are characterized by multifariousness and stratification. An ideological outlook would prefer a description of the desirable and the opportune. In contrast, the history of culture reveals a wide diversity of needs and tendencies, expressed in the social context, and the power or weakness of the mechanism for screening and supervision to control all aspects and layers of the cultural system. Any attempt to limit the scope of Judaism as a religious way of life assumes that the Jews were somehow unlike all other human beings or that they had the same cultural needs as all humanity but were able to satisfy and answer these needs by themselves, totally independent of any outside help or influence.

The prevailing view is that when Christianity emerged as a triumphant religion, Jewish fears about the influence of Hellenistic culture decreased. But much earlier than that, from the first century AD, and particularly in the third and fourth, adaptation to Hellenistic and Roman culture increased; so did the latter's influence on all circles of Jewish society from the first century to the Byzantine era. The reason for this was the completion of the process of Hellenization among the foreign inhabitants of Palestine. However, this process did not arouse fears that this influence would lead to idolatry, since Hellenism was not a political force nor was the clash with it political, as in the past. The great Hellenistic influence was expressed in the field of art, architecture, magic, and the like, as well as in the domain of halakhah. In other words, in the very same period when the Sages were the leaders and mentors of the people and Judaism was being reshaped, the influence of Hellenistic culture, in its various manifestations, penetrated into all levels of Jewish society, more so than in the days of the

---

created in order to look upon the heavenly bodies and the stars, that would suffice for me, for it is written, "When I look at thy heavens, the work of thy fingers, the stars and the heavenly bodies which thou hast established" [Ps. 8: 3]', with Anaxagoras (*Fragmente der Vorsokratiker*, 59 A 30 Diels and Kranz), as cited by Aristotle in *Eudemian Ethics*, i. 5. 9 (1216ᵃ10–14) and *Protrepticus*, fr. 19 Düring = Iamblichus, *Protrepticus*, 51. 11–15; they suggest that Aibu, who lived in Palestine at the end of the 3rd c. and the beginning of the 4th, and was a contemporary of Iamblichus, could have been familiar with the contents of Protreptius from reading the text or from conversations with people interested in philosophy ('To Behold the Stars'). There are many parallels of this kind, but one must differentiate between verbal influences and those concerning basic concepts, as that the notion of Jerusalem as the navel of the world was adapted from Greek conceptions; see Ch. 9 n. 33.

Hellenistic kingdoms, the Hasmonean kingdom, or Roman rule prior to the destruction of the Temple in AD 70.

Some scholars claim that the patterns of contact between Jewish and foreign society underwent a deep change. The foreign society also changed. Sages living in Babylon did not pursue their studies in the framework of Hellenistic culture but were far removed from it. The cultural constraints and dangers in Sasanian Babylon were different from those facing the Jews in Palestine, where social intercourse with the Hellenistic neighbours was forbidden.[4] Contact with Greek culture was never entirely suspended in Babylon; that is the reason for the paradox that in the writings of the Babylonian Sages—who lived outside the immediate orbit of Hellenism—one can find many traces of the Hellenistic heritage. 'Perhaps because the danger of contamination by foreign influence was less strong than in Palestine, the mystical and allegorical teachings of the Hellenistic epoch were not as severely repressed in the Babylonian schools.'[5]

That Jews during this period (especially the third and fourth centuries AD) were more exposed to Hellenistic influences in almost every sphere gradually became a commonplace amongst historians. Thus, 'normative Judaism' was seen now in a different light, and at the same time the image of the Jewish society and culture at large underwent radical changes in scholarly literature.

In his previously mentioned lecture, 'Über die Spuren des griechischen und römischen Altertums', Israel Levy, combining his knowledge of the classical world and with that of talmudic literature, paved the way for an understanding of the relationship and the affinity between the two worlds:

Hellenistic views and the Roman way of life were rejected by the Sages, who waged a bitter war against them if they appeared in pagan attire, as alien and hostile to the spirit of Judaism and its mode of life. But not everything that came from Hellas and Rome was of a religious nature. In their everyday contacts and the life they shared with pagan peoples, the Jews became adapted to their customs and even readily accepted them. The advance of culture, we may say, takes place on the international and interreligious plane; sooner or later it gains the recognition of all nations and religious communities, even becoming their property. However, in the case of the Jews, whose halakhah dominates all spheres of life, the changing conditions of culture inevitably also affected religious life and determined its very nature. One may therefore conclude that the influence of Greece and Rome on Judah . . . was of enormous significance, and this conclusion is fully affirmed if we delve deeply and properly into the talmudic literature.[6]

[4] Gafni, *The Jews of Babylonia*, 150–1.
[5] Bentwich, *Hellenism*, 313.
[6] I. Levy, 'Über die Spuren', 77–8. Cf. E. E. Urbach, 'Attempts', 15–16.

In later years, many Jewish scholars followed in Levy's footsteps and delved deeply into the talmudic literature. First and foremost among these scholars was Saul Lieberman. He drew particular attention to its permeation by elements of 'popular Hellenism', and of words, terms, and motifs, thus demonstrating that the Sages did not prohibit the adoption of cultural items that in their view did not seem to contradict the laws of the Torah. In this way, the Sages became the optimal model for modern rabbis. They obtained a knowledge of the alien culture but were not influenced by it. In the world of thought of the Sages, Lieberman found almost no significant Hellenistic influence that helped shape Judaism.[7] E. E. Hallewy even went so far as to assert that the roots of talmudic Judaism lay in the classical world and that talmudic culture absorbed enough of it to create a foundation that would be shared by Judaism and European culture in the future. Hallewy proposed a broad panoply of resemblances from various literary genres, without however establishing hard and fast rules to distinguish independent parallel developments from direct or indirect influence. He firmly believed that without the influence of Greek culture on the East, neither Philo, Hillel, nor the talmudic literature in its entirety would have come into the world in their present form.

We shall first examine the declared policy towards various components of Hellenistic culture.

R. Akiba says: Also he who reads the extra-canonical books such as the books of Ben Sira and the books of Ben La'anah [has no share in the world to come], but he who reads the books of Homer and all other books that were written beyond that is considered like one who is reading a secular document, for [it is written]: 'And furthermore, my son, beware of making many books, and much study [of them] is a weariness of flesh' (Eccl. 12: 12). Hence casual reading is permissible but intensive study is forbidden. (jSanh 10: 1, 28a.)

The expression *sifrei hamiros* or *sifrei hamirom* (literally 'Homeric writings') is a different term from 'Greek wisdom'. In dealing with the character of

---

[7] Lieberman, *Greek in Jewish Palestine*, and *Hellenism in Jewish Palestine*; Bergman, 'The Sages of Eretz Yisrael and Greek and Roman Culture'; E. E. Urbach, *The Sages*, 188–9, 201–5; Wasserstein, 'Greek Elements in Ancient Jewish Literature'; Ben-David, *Biblical Hebrew and Mishnaic Hebrew*, 135–52. Neusner writes that Lieberman 'proved in a most masterful manner that Talmudic literature evolved in creative symbiosis in the Hellenistic-Roman world' (*Early Rabbinic Judaism*, 140). However, the word 'symbiosis' certainly is not a correct interpretation of Lieberman's view, nor is his finding certain realms in the literature of the Sages (its scientific knowledge, for example) or in the popular culture (magic) to be influenced by Hellenistic culture evidence of such a symbiosis. Lieberman was far away from the view that Judaism was profoundly shaped by Graeco-Oriental thought, in particular its mystical and magical thinking (Morton Smith, 'Observations on Hekhalot Rabati', 153–4). See also Charlesworth, 'Jewish Astrology'; Nave and Shaked, *Magic Spells and Formulae*; Margalioth, *Sefer harazim*.

these books, one needs to separate the question whether the Sages knew Homer (i.e. Greek mythology) or even mentioned its motifs, from the question of what *sifrei hamiros* stood for in the broad cultural context. The Sages single out only *sifrei hamiros* and mention no other type of Greek literature. According to Lieberman, the books of Homer were probably not included in the category of Greek wisdom but were considered 'innocuous writings'. We can 'safely assume that the content of Homer's books was well known in certain Jewish circles in Palestine and they were probably not included in the category of Greek wisdom, and they were employed as exercises for those children who in any case did not study Torah'. However, he continues, 'it is very hard to prove that the rabbis made direct use of the Odyssey or the Iliad'.[8] It is also very possible that by the term *sifrei hamiros* the Sages did not intend to allude specifically to the *Iliad* or the *Odyssey* but rather to all written Greek literature, or to 'secular literature'.[9] One cannot conclude from a few isolated mentions and the absence of any others that the Sages were not familiar with Homer just because there is hardly any quotation from his works in their writings. Homeric motifs were an integral part of the education and culture of that period, not only through literature but also through art; moreover, anyone who had a formal education in Greek (even in Rome), began with Homer, and knew Homer even if he knew nothing else, a state of affairs that continued throughout the Byzantine era. It is dangerous to assume that the Sages, who were familiar with their cultural surroundings, had no knowledge of Homer, just because there is no direct quotation from his work in their literature, or that they had only very scant knowledge of Greek mythology because only a few traces of mythological motifs (for example, the Promethean legend) can be found in their writings; in fact there are several allusions in their works: Centaurs (Gen. Rabbah 23: 6, ed. Theodor–Albeck, 227), Sirens (*Sifra*, ed. Weiss, 49*d*), the Sun's chariot (*Avot deRabbi Natan*, 56: 1, ed. Schechter, p. 6), Narcissus (*Nedarim*, 9).

The fact remains that although the world of Greek mythology might have enriched the Sages' writings, which include folktales, legends, fables, and fantasies, not only with tales about gods, but with stories carrying a human message, or idle reading for amusement, motifs from Greek mythology make only a sporadic appearance in the Midrashim. Saul Lieberman suggests that the absence of specific allusions to Homer in rabbinic literature is due to the absence of Greek mythology from the Bible, so that the

[8] Lieberman, 'The Alleged Ban', 105–14; id., 'Rabbinic Polemics against Idolatry'.
[9] Gordis, 'Homeric Books'; Hengel, *Judaism and Hellenism*, 75–7.

rabbis 'found no occasion to utilize Homer';[10] but Midrash was not the only context in which mythological motifs could have appeared in the Talmud. It seems that religious and cultural prohibitions prevented their use in rabbinic literature, but not in art.

Nevertheless, there is a fundamental difference between traces of Homeric motifs and the claim of Alexander and others that the homiletic interpretations of the Hagiographa, for example, are a direct adoption of the commentaries on Homer.[11] Is there really an analogy between Hellenistic hermeneutics, on the one hand, and the homiletic interpretations and the talmudic aggadah, on the other? For, as Hallewy himself states, there was no similarity between the status of mythology in Greek culture and the weight and presence of biblical mythology and biblical legends in the world of the Sages. We have already noted the ambivalent attitude of the Sages towards the aggadah. Even when they referred to it positively, their attitude was most aptly expressed in the statement: 'Those who expound lore [aggadot] say, "If you want to know the one who spoke and brought the world into existence, study lore [aggadah], for out of that you will truly know the one who spoke and brought the world into existence and cleave to his ways"' (*Sifre on Deuteronomy*, 49, ed. Finkelstein, 115). Thus, even if, as Alexander argues, rabbinic midrash, which is a phenomenon of Late Antiquity, employed the same hermeneutic techniques as the hermeneutics of the Graeco-Roman world, and both cultures were 'classicizing', that is largely based on a body of canonical text, and in both cultures the Graeco-Roman schools and the yeshivot, were parallel institutions,[12] still the status of the 'classical text', and far more importantly the purpose of the hermeneutic literature was different.[13]

Consequently, *sifrei hamiros* could have represented the entire corpus of secular literature in Greek, not only Homeric epic or other literature connected with Greek mythology. There can be no doubt that the Sages were familiar with this rich and varied literature, or at least knew of its existence. But it seems they probably were referring primarily to Hellenistic philo-

[10] Lieberman, 'Rabbinic Polemics against Idolatry', 126–7.

[11] Amir, 'Wie verarbeitete das Judentum fremde Einflüsse in hellenistischer Zeit?'; Herr, 'External Influences'; Alexander, 'Quid Athenis et Hierosolymis?', 103: 'The hermeneutics of the Rabbis can be paralleled in all essentials from the hermeneutics of the Greco-Roman world. Rabbinic hermeneutics is thoroughly of its time and place: it is a form of the hermeneutical code which prevailed throughout the world of antiquity' (p. 103). Philo was very familiar with Greek mythology, whose authors 'have put together fables skilfully contrived to deceive the hearers' (*The Decalogue*, 55, trans. Colson vii. 35). On the other hand he used mythology to illustrate moral teachings (*On Providence*, 2. 7). The authors of the *Oracula Sibyllina* were also very familiar with mythological literature.

[12] Alexander, 'Quid Athenis et Hierosolymis', 119–20.

[13] But see Feldman's and Lieberman's opinions, cited in Ch. 10.

sophical literature, which aroused less concern on their part than heretical literature, towards which they could not adopt a merely disparaging or indifferent attitude. According to Maimonides, in his commentary on the Mishnah (*Yadayim*, 4), *sifrei hamiros* are books that dispute the Torah and differ with it, and hence are given that name because they are books that God rejects and spurns. In any event, even if we find mythological motifs or Greek adages in the literature of the Sages, these are not the determining factors; what really counts is the overall cultural system into which the motif is absorbed and which endows it with spiritual significance. The crucial question is whether Hellenistic philosophical concepts seeped into the literature of the Sages, which is generally regarded as the authentic Jewish literature.

Scholars generally agree that no philosophical concepts permeated the Talmud under the Greek influence, despite the fact that the rabbis certainly knew some philosophy. There is no Stoic influence in the Talmud, states Lieberman, and the rabbis never read Plato or Aristotle. Wolfson writes that there is no philosophical influence, nor are there any philosophical concepts, in talmudic literature; there is hearsay knowledge, but not influence.[14] It is also generally accepted that there are no influences from Epicureanism or Platonism in the Talmud. Even though we may find Hellenistic philosophical motifs in it, we shall not find any philosophical influence or a single philosophical concept;[15] an allusion or reference, yes, but no assimilation. The few allusions to philosophical terms do not mean that the Sages were philosophers or that they had found any need to employ the philosophical method of thought. However, some scholars detect in the Talmud a muted debate with various philosophical views—with the Gnostic or Marcionite heresies, with Cynicism and Stoicism—for these ideas were not only part of the teaching of an established philosophical school; they were also part of the popular cultural world. Hence the Midrash, and later the public sermons, could not avoid reacting in one way or another to these prevalent views.

One thing is clear: the world of Jewish philosophy, which was based on Aristotelian methods and interpretation, was totally separate from the world of the Sages in so far as its recourse to the world of Hellenistic thought is concerned. The aggadot and the Midrashim of the Sages are far removed from philosophical abstraction. The prophets and the Sages, according to Kaufmann, do not wage war against anthropomorphism in

---

[14] Wolfson, *Philo*, i. 91–2. See Kadushin, *Conceptual Approach to the Mekhilta*, 29.

[15] Lieberman, 'How Much Greek'; Feldman, 'How Much Hellenism', 106. For a different view see Fischel, Tabor, *Things Unutterable*.

the manner of Greek philosophy, or even avoid it as much as the Hellenistic Jewish writers had done. Deeper influence on Judaism from the abstract, anti-anthropomorphic trend did not begin till the Muslim period, in the time of R. Saadiah Gaon, or more precisely, in the time of Maimonides, about seven hundred years after the canonization of the Talmud.[16]

THE SAGES' VIEWS ON THE DIFFERENT DOMAINS OF CULTURE

In preaching to the Jews, the rabbis' main concern was to fight the ritual practices of idolatry (*avodah zarah*). But what of the social and cultural sphere which is not involved in practising idolatry? It appears that the Sages themselves were aware that Gentile culture was not confined to idolatrous rites. They were well aware of the great temptation that lay in the alien culture, and by struggling against it actually revealed the strength of the influence it exerted on broad social strata. This is, according to one interpretation, the reason why in Palestine they forbade social intercourse with their Hellenistic neighbours.[17] When the Sages repeatedly cautioned: 'Nor shall you follow their laws, the things engraved in their hearts, such as theatres and circuses and stadia' (*Sifra*, 'Acharei mot', 13: 9, ed. Weiss, 86a), or stated that 'He who goes up into Gentiles' amphitheatres—it is forbidden on grounds of idolatry' (*Tosefta Avodah Zarah*, 2. 5–7), one can safely assume they were employing these warnings in their battle against social tendencies to visit forbidden places (a struggle that in a non-conservative society often necessitates finding suitable substitutes), which was certainly a widespread tendency in everyday life. The Sages' struggle was focused on those cultural manifestations that involved idolatry, bloodshed, indecency, and the like. The injunction against wearing a long fringe of hair or a Roman toga, for example, is a sign of conservatism and an attempt to emphasize cultural separateness.[18]

According to Lieberman, all rabbinic literature displays

wide knowledge and thorough understanding of the gentile cultural world. More than that, the lower Jewish classes adopted their neighbors' beliefs in magic, astrology and all kinds of superstitions in defiance of Written and Oral Laws. This is the reason why the rabbis exerted themselves to the utmost in their struggle against that part of the foreign influences on the life of the Jewish people,

---

[16] Kaufmann, *The Religion*, i/3. 240–1.

[17] Bentwich, *Hellenism*, 305. The author of the Letter of Aristeas warned the Jews in Alexandria against 'intermingling with the Gentiles, to avoid being exposed to temptations' (Herr, 'External Influences', 88–9).   [18] See Sperber, *Material Culture*, 134–6 n. 16.

which, in their view, threatened the existence of the Jewish religion and the Jewish nation . . . but their fundamental work was that of Judaizing the foreign elements.[19]

Against this background one may conclude that the Sages and the rabbis were able to control the social and cultural contacts: to forbid and reject negative influences while at the same time to absorb, by means of 'Judaization', those many elements of popular culture (the so-called 'little tradition') that mainly tempted the lower classes of society.

It seems correct to say that the Sages never formulated an overall concept of Jewish culture. Their literature contained prohibitions against the adoption of various cultural traits, those that were contrary to the halakhah or posed a danger to the values of Jewish society. In this literature there were also indications of indifference, namely a neutral attitude towards various traits which were not perceived as endangering Judaism. On the other hand, the Sages showed great understanding of cultural dynamics and cultural needs; hence, instead of fighting different traits, they tried to assimilate them, by 'Judaizing' them.

A few rabbis forbade giving Jews Greek and Roman names, yet in practice we may easily find them; the giving of a name is not evidence of Hellenization or the converse, and can signify both a positive and a neutral attitude. On the other hand, in many domains there are no halakhic rulings. When the Midrash interpreted the instruction 'Nor shall you follow their laws' (*Sifra*, 'Acharei mot', 13: 9), it quoted an example from matrimonial affairs. The Sages interpreted the commandment as applying to matrimonial laws and not, for example, to matters of architectural fashion and the like. The distinction between Jewish culture and alien culture focuses mainly on negative social phenomena. Against this background, it is difficult to accept the view that by 'Greek wisdoms' the Midrash refers to language, literature, and art (painting, sculpture, and music),[20] since the Midrash itself clearly states to which domains of 'culture' it alludes. (Incidentally, among the Hellenistic élite there were many severe critics and naysayers who objected to participation in these spheres, and many more among the Church Fathers).[21]

Pagan influence on Jewish material civilization have given rise to two interpretations. The first, and prevailing, view is that the Sages knew how to single out the aesthetic (or functional) side of art and separate it from

[19] Lieberman, 'Pleasures and Fears', 91–2.

[20] Herr, 'External Influences'; Sperber, *Material Culture*. Items of material culture that were associated with a halakhic prohibition were altered to adapt them to the prohibition.

[21] See, for one example, Tertullian, *De spectaculis*, 17.

its 'religious' significance. The second interpretation holds that there was no longer any reason to be concerned about the danger that art would impart the values it symbolized to its viewers and users.[22] One might ask then why figurative art employing pagan elements was permitted, while theatres were forbidden—and this in a time when Hellenistic culture was declining, along with idolatry and its rites. The answer probably lies in the fact that attending the theatre or the circus involved intimate social contact and exposure to constituents of vulgar popular culture.[23] In contrast, decorating a synagogue or a cemetery (even with the assistance of a pagan artist) did not involve any social contact of this kind, which would be difficult to control or supervise. One may thus assume that in the period in question there was no consensus among the Sages, and in regard to these issues, some were 'conservative' while others were 'liberal'; the attitude taken towards the various cultural elements did not necessarily derive from a clearly formulated and mandatory norm, but was also an expression of a 'conservative' (or, on the other hand, of a tolerant and 'liberal') cultural position, which originated from, among other things, the value assigned not to the signifier but to the signified. Seen in this light, the weight given to the existence of allegorical and symbolic Jewish art seems rather exaggerated. It results from perceiving this cultural facet as definitive evidence that a large portion of Jewish life was conducted 'outside the circle of rabbinic authority'.

The discovery of the Dura-Europos synagogue in 1932 was a landmark in the history of research and polemic on this issue. Although archaeology has also uncovered a great deal of evidence about the central place of the halakhah in Jewish life, and about the widespread distribution of synagogues, houses of study, and ritual baths in Jewish towns and villages, the Dura-Europos synagogue, according to Goodenough, shows that many Jews lived outside the rabbinic authority, and read their Bible in a mystical spirit that not only encouraged allegorized representations of biblical motifs, but found a meaning for their Judaism in 'mystical victory, a victory reached by two paths, the cosmic and the abstractly ontological';[24] it was

---

[22] L. I. Levin, *The Rabbinic Class in Palestine*, 12–22.

[23] But Herr, in 'Synagogues and Theatres', shows that the Sages often knew how to use the artistic (moralistic and satiric) method of the Roman theatre.

[24] Goodenough, *Jewish Symbols*, 259; see too his conclusion, pp. 264–5, and L. I. Levin, *The Synagogue in Late Antiquity*. The main artistic motifs in synagogues of the mishnaic and talmudic period are distinctly Jewish. The use of pagan motifs in the mosaic in Leontis' house in Beit She'an could be regarded as the use of pagan elements to transmit a 'universal' message or allegory. See Foerster, 'Christian Allegories', 204; Rahner, *Greek Myths and Christian Mystery*, 286–328. Boman asserts that the mosaics in Dura retain Jewish uniqueness: 'Where the pagan paints his god or forms him out of stone, the Jew paints the symbol of God's word: the Torah shrine and lamp or else the *action* of his God and so the sacred history' (*Hebrew*

this mystic strand of Judaism that laid the foundation for the emergence of Christianity.

It is generally agreed that the design and decoration of this synagogue show a Hellenistic or Eastern influence; however, the conclusions drawn from that fact have been somewhat speculative and resulted from the exaggerated status and value assigned to 'plastic art' in the Jewish life of the time. Bickerman seems to offer a reasonable solution for the presence of pagan motifs in Jewish synagogues and private homes: the use of such symbols is not related to the rabbis' ability to censor and exert control, but rather to the drive to decorate synagogues so they could compete in their splendour with the places of pagan rites. He also asserts that each symbol may fulfil diverse functions and carry diverse messages. A culture whose 'normative' canonical literature did not hesitate to personify the Deity had no reason to shrink from using figurative art depicting famous scenes from its own writings as well as from a repertoire of well-known scenes belonging to the surrounding culture. When Jewish artists painted Orpheus, or rather a biblical figure in the guise of Orpheus, they were not alluding to 'Orpheus' but to the biblical figure.[25] Orpheus could symbolize a musician or music itself, and not necessarily the Orphic mysteries. Hercules, for instance, could symbolize not only a muscular hero, but also a wise man who restrains his desires and defends the oppressed. The mythological repertoire was generally subjected to a process in which it was divested of its previous meaning, although in some cases mythological symbols did appear without such depletion or change of meaning. In other words, writes Bickerman, there is a difference between an idol and an image,[26]

Thought, 113). As for the mosaics recently uncovered in Zippori (Sepphoris) containing mythological scenes, there is no evidence that the house they were found in was a Jewish home. If these were the homes of wealthy and respected Jews, even if we assume the artists were non-Jews who painted scenes familiar to them from Greek mythology, one still has to ask why the owners did not ask them to paint parallel scenes from the Bible (Noah, Lot, Samson); and also whether they not only attributed any significance to the mythological scenes featuring Heracles, Dionysus, and the like, but also saw nothing morally wrong in them. However that may be, it is abundantly clear that the Jewish inhabitants were very familiar with them and hence that they also knew the central motifs of Greek mythology through art (Netzer and Weiss, 'Byzantine Mosaics'; Netzer, 'New Mosaic Art'.)

[25] See Ovadia and Mucznik, 'The Jerusalem Orpheus', and Torenheim and Ovadia, 'Dionysus in Beth-Shean'.

[26] Bickerman, 'Symbolism in Dura Synagogue'. Momigliano, in a critical essay on Goodenough's monumental study discusses the problems confronting any effort to suggest a 'grand theory' concerning the essence of Hellenistic Judaism and its 'mystical nature' based on figurative and symbolic materials ('Problems of Method in the Interpretation of Judeo-Hellenistic Symbols'). He accepts Bickerman's view (expressed also in 'The Historical Foundation of Postbiblical Judaism') and concludes that the symbols Goodenough studied 'should be interpreted in the context of a superficial process of Hellenization against which both Philo and the rabbis reacted rather than in terms of a mysteriosophic religion not otherwise documented' (p. 57). Goodman writes that the hope that archaeological evidence can act as an

or, as was the case in modern Hebrew literature, the pagan heroes became heroes with a universal message.

One may enlarge on the penetration of Hellenistic elements into the literature of the Sages, on the one hand, and into Jewish life, on the other, as well as on the nature of the use made of them.[27] However, what interests me is one important fact: in the third and fourth centuries AD, a wide variety of Hellenistic elements permeated various sectors of Jewish society. In other words, precisely in those times when Jewish society was subject to the authority of the halakhah, the presence of Hellenistic culture in Jewish life was far greater than in earlier generations. Hence this question was asked over and again: was this due to the reduced danger of Hellenism as paganism and the ability to neutralize various elements of its pagan message, to the weakness of rabbinical authority, or to the tolerance and openness shown by both society and its teachers? Or was it perhaps due to the ability of the Jewish culture to absorb foreign elements without any apprehension, even to assimilate many of them? (And, again, one ought not forget that Hellenistic influence on spiritual life in Palestine in the Roman and Byzantine periods was not the influence of Athens, but of the Hellenized cities of the country.[28]) In any event, the central question that remains is whether the substantial presence of Hellenistic elements in all layers of Jewish culture changed the real content of Judaism and of Jewish life. For example, did pagan elements in the decoration of synagogues in any way impair their unique Jewish nature as an institution of prayer or a house of assembly?

It appears that even if we find Jews who attended the theatre, or who went so far as to adopt techniques of the mime,[29] in the final analysis the institutions of pagan society had no counterparts in Jewish society. The Jews had no amphitheatre, gymnasium, or theatre, no local deities or local rites. The synagogue as an institution had no parallel in the pagan world,

---

objective, untainted corrective to literary traditions is in many cases over-optimistic ('Jews and Judaism in the Mediteranean Diaspora', 220).

[27] The literature on this subject is so vast that there is no point in citing even a part of it.

[28] J. Geiger, 'Greek Intellectuals of Ascalon', 'Greek Orators in Palestine', and 'Athens in Syria'.

[29] Herr, 'Synagogues and Theaters', cites the story in ySanh. (2: 20c–d) and the parallel in Gen. Rabbah (80: 1, ed. Theodor–Albeck, 951–2) about Yose from Maon (near Tiberias) who preached in the synagogue against the corruption raging around R. Judah HaNasi. R. Shimon ben Lakish (a gladiator in his youth) argued in his defence against R. Judah HaNasi that one ought to learn from the Roman-Hellenistic world, in which the mime contained criticism and satire directed against the authorities, and that this was permitted because it released 'pressure'. In other words, the *beit midrash* was a totally different world from the world of the theatre and the circus, and yet they had something in common. Criticism of theatre, stadium, and circus, similar to that of the Sages, was voiced by the Fathers of the Church, in particular Tertullian, *De spectaculis*; note esp. the description of athletes as 'bred for the leisure of Greece' (*propter Graeciae otium altiles*, §18).

which knew only temples. And unquestionably there was no parallel in the pagan world for the function of public prayer and sermons that existed in Jewish society. Hence pagan symbolism in art does not indicate that the Jews did not observe the laws of the Sabbath and purity, nor that they had different calendars. Their legal system was radically different, and almost entirely cut off from the system of the surrounding peoples. If one wishes to argue that it was not the rabbinic authority that supervised most spheres of Jewish life, one has to point to another authority that could have filled the large void created by the absence of the halakhah. The fact that Jewish artists employed pagan motifs is mainly an indication that these motifs were readily available and that the Jews did not shrink from utilizing them.

BETWEEN HELLENIZATION AND SECULARIZATION

As a basis for our historical reappraisal of the influences of alien culture on Judaism in the late Roman period, we can now turn back to the questions posed by Goitein (see Ch. 9).

Judaism in the period after the destruction of the Temple was different from that of the Second Temple period. However, it is impossible to break 'Judaism' down into various components or conduct an attitude survey on the hierarchy of beliefs and the observance of the Commandments in order to define the nature of the Jewish identity, as modern scholars do.[30] The Judaism of late antiquity cannot provide the modern secular Jew with ancient 'forebears', since the Europeanization of modern Jewish culture is not equivalent to any type of Hellenization in the Hellenistic or Roman period.

Second Temple Judaism was heterodox in its ideology, rather than orthodox, or generally orthopractic. While the authority of Torah and halakhah did not in any case disappear, this authority did not preclude cultural openness, and the life of historical Judaism was not totally derived from the world of halakhah: there were many broad cultural needs which prompted all strata of Jewish society to develop diverse cultural components, not all of them gleaned from the halakhah or from some closed internal tradition. In other words, normative Judaism does not mean a Judaism whose whole world is sealed off by halakhah and the Commandments. It means a Judaism whose centre of authority and centre of gravity is halakhah.

On the other hand modern secular Judaism is characterized by both heterodoxy and heteropraxy. Acculturation leads to a radical change in

[30] Herman, *Jewish Identity*.

the nature of Jewish identity. A 'Hellenistic' way of thinking, 'Hellenistic' traits, a 'Hellenistic' way of life became the core of the modern secular Jewish identity. 'Athens' and 'Alexandria' became central features of 'Jerusalem'. The emergence of secularism—national and a-national—expresses a deeper-seated change in Jewish intellectual and cultural history than any type of 'Hellenization' in Jewish society in late antiquity, than any signs of Greek influence on rabbinic literature, and even than Jewish philosophy using Greek philosophical categories.

Thus, we may ask, what was (and still is) the impact of the Hellenistic-Roman era or Late Antiquity as model, image, and mirror, on the making of modern Judaism. The Jews of the Hellenistic age, wrote Bickerman, 'were people of their own times, and Hellenistic civilization offered them an almost endless variety of experiences'.[31] The discovery of these many experiences by modern scholarship, and hence by the collective historical memory and by public discourse, which drew on this complex period for historical paradigms, had a great effect on the new evaluation of Judaism. Not only did this period provide the modern nationalist with a story (or myth) of heroic national revolt, or later a historical analogy for the complexities created by the existence of a sovereign Jewish state; it also enabled modern Jews to draw a complex picture of Judaism and Jewish life in late antiquity. For some the new picture of this period became a proof that 'normative Judaism' was but a rabbinical invention, or that rabbinical Judaism and Jewish society at large were a more 'liberal' open culture than had been portrayed in the Jewish traditional historical conception and image. Thus this new perception was used on behalf of ideologies that called for moderate, or radical, changes in traditional Judaism, and sought legitimation in the Jewish experience in that past. For others, Jewish openness, Jewish knowledge of alien culture, and the Jewish encounter with the dominant surrounding culture was but a proof that Judaism was able to resist and survive. 'The question', writes Feldman, 'is not so much how greatly Jews and Judaism in the Land of Israel were Hellenized, as how strongly they resisted Hellenization. In other words, what was the power of Judaism that enabled it to remain strong despite the challenge of Hellenism and later of Christianity? The answer may lie in its paradoxical self-confidence and defensiveness, its unity and diversity, its stubbornness and flexibility.'[32]

Historical scholarship provides different, even contradictory, answers—of which our discussion has been only summary—in relation to the scope

---

[31] Bickerman, *Jews in the Greek Age*, 299.
[32] Feldman, 'How Much Hellenism', 111.

and depth of the influence that Hellenistic culture exerted on contemporary Judaism.[33] On the other hand, there can be no doubt as to the scope and depth of the influence of Western culture on all streams of modern Judaism. The historical model of the complex encounter with the Hellenistic culture not only opened up a broad vista for study of the nature of the encounter between Judaism and the modern world; it also enabled scholars to elucidate, from a comparative standpoint, the nature of the latter encounter and its influence on the formation of modern Judaism. It demonstrated, on the one hand, that even in Judaism under halakhic authority, there were various currents and undercurrents that apparently took shape under the impact of foreign cultures, on the other, that the world of Judaism was a broad, diversified world that went beyond that of Commandments and halakhah, whether with the approval of the halakhah, in coexistence with it, or in opposition to it. Nevertheless, it was the halakhah that shaped the world of Judaism in the period of the Mishnah and the Talmud; this is borne out by the fact that the mystical currents we may presume to have existed did not weaken the halakhah or normative Judaism (their influence on the development of Christianity is another matter). However, the appearance of a new Jewish culture outside the world of halakhah and even in conflict with it in the modern era led to very different results.

This will be the subject of the next four chapters. Through these two disparate mirrors—that of classical Greece and that of the Hellenistic civilization (and Late Antiquity), we shall try to understand the nature of modern Jewish culture, and above all the national culture.

---

[33] Naturally I have not attempted either to list all the supposedly Hellenistic features in the various spheres of Jewish culture throughout that long and dynamic period, or to cite all the numerous works on this subject. Nor should one forget the influence of Sasanian Persian culture on the culture of Babylonian Jews in the talmudic era.

PART III

ATHENS IN JERUSALEM

Our sons, since their youth, have been living their
lives in a different spirit . . . Most of their concepts
and emotions come from the teachings of Japheth.
AHAD HA'AM, 'Al devar otzar hayahadut balashon ha'ivrit'
('On the Treasury of Judaism in the Hebrew Language')

12

BACK TO HISTORY: THE SECULARIZATION OF THE ANCIENT JEWISH PAST

> Remember the days of old,
> Consider the years of many generations
> DEUTERONOMY 32:7

> History limits itself to a description of events based on observable causes along with the results that evolve from them according to the laws of nature.
> I. M. JOST, *Geschichte der Israeliten*

> I myself am convinced that in the course of Jewish history, the hand of God is in control . . . however, this hand ought not always to be exhibited openly, rather, the writer of history need only hint at the finger of God, as the author of the Book of Esther did, in presenting the miraculous rescue without divine intervention.
> HEINRICH GRAETZ, in a letter dated May 1880

> Homer and the Bible are different books, fundamentally different in outlook, aim and construction. Yet of each the same can be said—the book built a race.
> J. R. GLOVER, *The Challenge of Greek*

THE REVIVAL OF A HISTORICAL SENSE

'IF a faithful Jewish writer, who knows intimately his people's ways and language, its ideas and accomplishments, will undertake faithfully to write the history of his people and their ways', asserted Peretz Smolenskin in 1869, 'he will succeed in illuminating the path of those who grope in darkness and will exalt his people.'[1] Smolenskin was, of course, speaking in a language common to many of his nineteenth-century contemporaries: a strong belief in the redemptive powers of History and in History as a rehabilitative, constructive—not destructive—force. By 'History' they meant not only the knowledge of the national chronology, but the collective experience of the people, its past and future, its aspirations, hopes

---

[1] Smolenskin, 'Even Yisrael', 5: 3; cf. Feiner, 'Smolenskin's Confrontation with the Haskalah'. In 1893 Dubnow wrote: 'at present the fulcrum of Jewish national being lies in historical consciousness' (*Nationalism and History*, 256), since for many secularized Jews the turn to history gradually created an ethnic attachment that might—and should—replace the religious content.

and destiny. History was the cohesive power; in it the unity and uniformity of the people, the product of its genius, were manifested. In order to recognize and understand—and use—these great powers of History, one must first discover and recover one's own history. The call for a return to history meant both changing the nature of Jewish activities and attitudes and reconstructing the people's self-awareness; namely, the creation of a new historical consciousness. The chronicles of the Jewish people, its collective experience, faith, and destiny in history, its perceptions and myths, became the core of its self-definition and identity. Jews in modern times not only 'returned to history', they also related to their history as the principal manifestation of their identity.

But if historical consciousness is so vital and if modern historical understanding constitutes a radical departure from the Judaeo-Christian tradition and a turning back to Greek (that is, pagan) historical conceptions, could the new Jewish historical consciousness be founded on this basis—on the basis of a view of history that knew nothing of Scripture and a philosophy that was trying to free itself from Scripture?[2] The answer to this question is inextricably related to the question whether there really are—as the prevailing view asserts—fundamental differences between a Greek and a Jewish understanding of history.

As we saw in Chapter 7, the claim that there is a fundamental and unbridgeable difference between the conception and meaning of history in Judaism and in classical antiquity is a major component of the antinomical pattern. The possibility that Greek historiography had an influence on some of the biblical books, which, according to this view, were written at the beginning of the Second Temple era,[3] does not necessarily imply any influence on the way the essence of history was understood. Moreover, the focus of the antinomy was not historical motifs or historical methods or the histories' literary merits, but historical world-views: the notion of

[2] See Wolfson, *Philo*, ii. 455–60. On this view any history that denied revelation and the authority of sacred historical tradition, and favoured free inquiry, is based on pagan (Greek) conceptions; as Momigliano writes, 'The History of Salvation was not a Greek type of historiography in pagan days' ('History and Biography', 178).

[3] Mendel and Freedman, *The Relationship between Herodotus' History*; van Seters, *In Search of History*; id., 'The Primeval Histories of Greece and Israel'. Van Seters argued that the list of nations in Genesis combines Eastern flood legends and Western genealogical traditions, products of 'Western' antiquarian interest. See Momigliano's comment in 'Persian Historiography, Greek Historiography, and Jewish Historiography', 9; id., 'Eastern Elements in Post-Exilic Jewish and Greek Historiography'; Weinfeld, *From Joshua to Josiah*, 13–14, arguing that the biblical stories of the Patriarchs were written during the reign of David, when ties were established with Aegean peoples, through whom a tradition of stories about foundations and origins of cities may have reached the Israelites. One should bear in mind that the anthropological dimension, well represented in classical literature, is almost totally absent in biblical historiography.

laws that govern history, concepts of time or of the meaning of historical events, and the place of the people of Israel in world history.

Here is one example of this conventional wisdom:

> The Greeks were ultimately interested in contemplation, the Hebrews in action. . . . The dynamic approach of the Hebrews to reality is expressed in their interest in history. Their God is characteristically one who acts in history, and these actions in history are the core of the religious tradition of Israel . . . The fact that the Greeks also wrote history is not felt to be an obstacle to describing history as a distinctive interest of Hebrew thought. The highest philosophical developments of the Greeks were interested in an unchanging reality and paid no attention to action in history. Greek history was akin to anecdote or to tragedy; it did not see in historical process a higher power than fate or necessity. For ultimate reality the Greeks turned away from history into the unchanging. Typically, therefore, it is held, their view of time became cyclic in the philosophical refinements of thought.[4]

According to these theological (and racial) notions, 'the Jews did not possess the linguistic instruments to think historically'; 'the Hebrew language has no specific word for time'; 'the Greeks conceived of time as a cycle, whereas the Hebrews and the early Christians conceived of it as a progression *ad finitum* or *ad infinitum*'.[5] While Greek historical thought has no place for teleological purposes and causes, or for an explanation based on the truth of religious revelation, these are the underpinnings of Jewish thought: 'The Greeks, wedded to a cyclical theory of development, denied the historical teleology. History simply repeated itself with appropriate variations; it did not lead anywhere. By contrast, Jewish writers have since biblical times viewed world history as moving towards an ultimate consummation.'[6] Karl Löwith, for example, under the inspiration of Hermann Cohen, claimed that the Jews were interested in the past and fused past and future into one entity, whereas the Greeks were interested only

---

[4] Barr, *The Semantics of Biblical Language*, 10–11. But Barr rejects this theological viewpoint and its ethnopsychological presuppositions, which start from a theoretical basis and work from there to linguistic forms, 23–4. See also Boman, *Hebrew Thought Compared with Greek*; Momigliano, 'Time in Ancient Historiography', 179–82.

[5] Momigliano, 'Time', 181–2; he continues: 'It is perhaps not difficult to show that none of these three main differences between Jewish and Greek thought about time can stand up to close examination.' Popper writes that 'What the Homeric interpretation shares with the Jewish is a certain vague feeling of destiny, and the idea of power behind the scenes. But ultimate destiny according to Homer, is not disclosed; unlike its Jewish counterpart, it remains mysterious' (*The Open Society*, i. 11). According to van Seters, 'no cyclical view of time is evident in the Greek histories, whatever the philosophers might say, and there is no eschatology in the Israelite histories, whatever prophets and apocalyptists might propose' (*In Search of History*, 8–9). However, even in the historical books of the Bible Israelite history is conceived as a sacred history of a chosen nation and 'history' as acting according to God's design.

[6] Michael A. Meyer, *Ideas of Jewish History*, 3. See also Jacobson, 'Visions of the Past'.

in the past; he also asserted that Greek history is invested with a cyclical concept while the Judaeo-Christian concept is fundamentally teleological in its belief that history moves towards a predetermined purpose.[7] From this vantage-point, then, when Jews began to write modern history their historical writing became 'Hellenic' both in method and nature.

It is worth taking note of the dimension of time in the two world-views—the Greek and the Jewish. According to Ismar Schorsch the introduction of time marks a revolutionary change in the perception of Jewish history since it was an alien dynamic factor.[8] In contrast, Boman believes that the difference between Jewish and Greek thought lies in the concept of time. The Hebrews' concept of time was dynamic; it described occurrences in time, whereas the Greeks' concept of time was static. According to him, the paradox is that while the Hebrews are a people whose language has no expression for the notion of time and whose verbs [Zeitwörter, literally 'time-words'] lack tenses, the Greeks, whose verbs can distinguish past, present, and future with accuracy, who developed delicately shaded expressions for the notion of time, and whose thinkers reflected profoundly on the content of a time-notion, selected space as their thought-form and never evinced any real sense of historical development. His solution to this problem is this: 'it is the Hebrews who have the adequate understanding of time, not the Greeks and we Europeans'.[9]

One may well doubt whether Boman is correct in drawing this distinction, and if so whether there was any difference between the Jew's sense of time in the biblical period and in the talmudic period or later, in the Middle Ages. But what Schorsch was referring to by the 'dimension of time' is a new awareness of the fact that Judaism underwent changes in the course of time, that it is not the same Judaism which was forged in its formative years and has remained unaltered throughout its history. The dimension of time in modern Jewish consciousness is new and revolutionary because it recognizes the evolutionary or dynamic nature of Jewish

---

[7] Karl Löwith, *Meaning in History*.

[8] Schorsch, 'The Emergence of Historical Consciousness', 415.

[9] Boman, *Hebrew Thought*, 143–4. Good evidence for these polar views as 'conventional wisdom' is to be found in the Unesco Press volume *Cultures and Time*. Neher writes: 'Time, in its strong and true meaning was never perceived as reality in Greek philosophy, for which the word remained essentially cosmos, a changeless and orderly universe, a regular and numbered, space . . . the rift between Hebraic and Greek thought is nowhere more sharply and emphatically demarcated than in the sphere of history' ('The View of Time and History in Jewish Culture', 150, 153). Against such generalizations G. E. R. Lloyd writes: 'there is no such thing as the Greek view of time. In particular the attempts to contrast a Greek with a Jewish view of time, and to see the former as essentially cyclical, the latter as essentially linear is—at least so far as the Greek material is concerned—quite misconceived' ('Views of Time in Greek Thought', 117).

values, concepts, and customs, and consequently, that this change is the product of historical circumstances.

Was this also the case when Jews wrote history in the Hellenistic and Roman period (and I refer to historiography, not to other types of reactions to historical events)? It seems that in this period the reaction was twofold: a return to the past and, at the same time, a retelling of the past. While the Hasmonean kings turned to the biblical past, under the impact of the national and religious struggle against Hellenism, Josephus wrote his *Antiquities* as a nationalistic reply to the Hellenistic historiographical challenge and under its influence. At almost the same time, Hellenistic Jewish historiographers wrote history in Greek and according to the Hellenistic Greek conception, in order to incorporate Jewish history into the framework of universal history,[10] turning not to the historical past but to the mist-enshrouded legendary past. This historiography, however, belongs to the Hellenistic heritage and did not become part of the Jewish intellectual heritage until the nineteenth century.[11] Not only the apologetic motifs were borrowed from the local Hellenistic literature: other devices were taken up as well, such as the extension of the scope of biblical history, namely, the tendency to go beyond the biblical narrative and extend it to other spheres, as well as the adoption of the genre of 'pathetic' or 'tragic' history in order to arouse the readers' emotions, exactly like Romantic historical writing from the eighteenth century onwards.[12] Hellenistic literature attached much weight to literary merit, and laid great emphasis on the role of great personalities with their virtues and their genius. In the same vein Josephus tells us that before his death Mattathias instructed his sons to observe the customs of their forefathers and to restore the ancient order, but also reminded them that the memory of good deeds—those virtues that the classical biography sought to represent—would grant them immortality: 'it is this which I wish you to be in love with, and for its sake to pursue glory and undertake the greatest tasks' (*Antiquities*, xii. 279–83). And we have already seen how Hellenistic Jewish writers (and to some extent the talmudic historical aggadah as well) imitated this genre, and described the fathers of the nation as war heroes and great commanders.

Modern works of hagiography and biography (as well as autobiography), and the Jewish historical novel of the nineteenth century, followed this trend of reinstating the individual to his former status in history. The

[10] Sterling, *Historiography and Self-Definition*; Millikovski, '"Seder olam" and Jewish Chronography'; Wacholder, 'Biblical Chronology in the Hellenistic World Chronicles'.

[11] Momigliano, 'Persian Historiography', 24; see above, Ch. 10.

[12] R. Doran, 'II Maccabees and "Tragic History"'; Geiger, 'The History of Judas Maccabaeus'; M. Stern, 'Maccabees'.

heroic history of Israel was perceived as more exalted than that of Greece:
as Schlesinger wrote in his drama *Hachashmona'im* (1817):

> More than any Athenian, the Maccabee was a man of glory;
> Now you, my friend, in measured verse, can read his story.

The fact remains, however, that Jewish historical writings of the Second
Temple period, which were mostly written in Greek, vanished from Jewish
culture and were rediscovered only at the end of the eighteenth century
and later. The rediscovery of the literature of the Second Temple was also
the rediscovery of its historical literature. Josephus was rediscovered and
regarded as the historian who wrote a faithful version of Jewish history; the
periodical *HaKarmel* (published in Vilna) wrote in 1862 that anyone who
loves his own history and wishes to hear it from a reliable source ought to
turn to the books of Josephus, which merit inclusion with the Holy Books.
The return to history was a return to Second Temple historical literature—
or to historical writing in the Second Temple style—and through it to the
Second Temple period as a central era in Jewish history: a paradigmatic
period. However, Hellenistic Jewish historiography did not propose a new
concept of Jewish history, and certainly not a new Jewish philosophy of
history with a new concept of time.

If we return to the fundamental issue with which I opened this chapter,
it is important first to note that the many works drawing analogies between
Jewish and Greek historical consciousness misconstrue several aspects of
the matter: the analogies overlook changes in the historical consciousness that occur in the Bible itself, and certainly in the time between the
Bible and the post-biblical literature. They posit an inescapable similarity
between the literary text and the consciousness of the common Greek
or the common Hebrew. However, there are differences between them:
according to Momigliano, the intention of the Greek historian was 'to
preserve the memory of important past events and to present the facts in a
trustworthy and attractive way',[13] while to the Hebrew historian, historiography 'soon became a narration of the events from the beginning of the
world such as no Greek historian ever conceived'.[14] And most important
of all: Greek historical philosophy was not familiar with the concept of
revelation or with the belief in a deity who directs the entire course of
history, national and universal, towards a defined end, nor did it have the
concept of God judging the nations or the idea of reward and punishment.

It is doubtful whether such an unequivocal characterization of the Greek
concept of history as against the Jewish concept is irrefutably valid. The

---

[13] Momigliano, 'Persian Historiography', 18.   [14] Ibid. 19.

Greeks may not have had a messianic concept, but they told stories of a utopian past (in the age of the Golden Race), and some had notions of a utopian future. The convention about the substantive opposition between these two historical concepts overlooks the fact that both Jewish and Greek literature proposed different types of historiographies and different historical world-views. Belief in a golden age is common to both Jewish and Greek idealism and the Bible expresses the idea of Return and the 'cyclicity' of national history.[15] In the Bible the *Urzeit-Endzeit* conception frequently appears;[16] on the other hand, the cycle is not a central theme in either Greek mythology or Greek historiography.[17] In Jewish eschatology during the Hellenistic and Roman periods, alongside the belief in the divine guidance of history as a whole, the central theme was a conception of history as consisting of mythical and allegorical cycles.

The major difference is between the status of history, on the one hand, and its constant presence in public life and its influence in shaping it, on the other; that is, between the 'writing of history' and life according to an internalized and guiding 'historical myth'.[18] According to Momigliano, the Greeks liked history, 'but never made it the foundation of their lives', while for the biblical Israelite, 'history and religion were one'. The irony, then, is that the 'Greeks never lost interest in history and transmitted this interest as part as their cultural inheritance', while the Jews, 'to whom history meant so much more, abandoned the practice of historiography almost entirely from the second to the sixteenth century and returned to historical study only under the impact of the Italian Renaissance'.[19] In fact, only when the Jews revived their interest in history in its pre-rabbinic conception did the Greek type of historical tradition become a recognized

[15] Japhet, *The Ideology of the Book of Chronicles*, 326–7, on the comparison of Exodus in some prophetic books with the return to Zion; see in particular Isa. 40–60, assuring the returnees that their way back to Palestine will be easy and miraculous, with no wandering in the desert. And some of their deeds after the Return were a result of a sense of 'Return of History' (Rudolph, *Esra und Nehemia*, 6). Needless to say, restorative messianism is a type of 'Returning of History': 'the booth of David that is fallen' (Amos 9: 11).

[16] Childs, *Myth and Reality*, 75–84. He writes that the theory of cycle is not central to mythical thinking, but it is one form that myth takes (p. 75). He gives many evidences of an *Urzeit-Endzeit* pattern (which 'within Israel is overwhelming'): a returning chaos (Jer. 4: 23), a new creation (Isa. 65: 17), God's re-election of Israel (Isa. 14: 1; Zech. 1: 17), the rebuilding of Judah 'as at the first' (Jer. 33: 7), her cities restored 'as in the days of old' (*kimei olam*, Amos 9: 11), etc. However, he notes important alterations in the *Urzeit-Endzeit* scheme within the Old Testament (pp. 77–8).

[17] 'The often-repeated notion that the Greek historians had a cyclical idea of time is a modern invention': Momigliano, 'Persian Historiography', 18.

[18] On the historical education of the Athenian public see Pearson, 'Historical Allusions', who notes that only a few orators were willing to give lessons in history to their audience. On the place of history and allusions to historical *paradeigmata* in the development of Greek *paideia* see Jaeger, *Paideia*, iii. 101–3.

[19] Momigliano, 'Persian Historiography', 20.

part of Jewish life. If modern historiography is the offspring of Greek and Roman, then whenever a Jewish historian writes history, he inevitably follows the path paved by the great historians of the classical period and not the tradition of the biblical writers. When a Jewish historian revived interest in history this designated a break with the a-historical approach of the Sages and rabbinical tradition,[20] and a return to the Bible and Second Temple period. However, when a Jewish historian stopped believing in God's intervention in history but did believe that history has meaning, he at one and the same time cut himself off from the biblical heritage but still adhered to it in another form.

Some scholars believe the new approach to history that emerged in seventeenth- and eighteenth-century Europe to have constituted a confrontation between the Greek (or rather Graeco-Roman) and the Judaeo-Christian conceptions of history; thus, when Jews in the nineteenth century began to think in terms of historical categories, they entered an arena completely alien to them. This was a turning-point in the Jewish vision of the past, since from the moment a Jew fell under the influence of this critical tradition, he found himself a new man, gone astray and seeking salvation in a totally alien world.[21] Modern historical thought was an alien wisdom that denied the existence of historical teleology and rationalized the Bible; but even more radical, according to this view, was the new understanding of the meaning of history. The Jewish (and Christian) historical conception linked the human world to transcendental objectives, while the Hellenic conception placed man in the centre of the universe. The principal and profoundest difference between the traditional and the new approach to history is to be found not in historical theories (with Greece representing a critical approach), but rather in the philosophy of history, in a consciousness of the world.

It is sometimes asserted that Jewish historical consciousness underwent no actual rupture, but continued to adhere to the basic line of a mission-directed history; thus an 'inner accord' could be established between the

---

[20] Herr, 'The Conception of History among the Sages', who suggests that the Sages showed no interest in what 'really happened' in the past, used events and heroes from the past mainly as *exempla*, and never considered the purpose of writing history. In E. E. Urbach's view the halakhah contains expressions of awareness of historical development and a 'sense for history' and never 'lost its attachment to the past' ('Halakhah and History'); but it seems that Urbach understands 'history' and 'historical awareness' in a very narrow sense.

[21] Arieli, 'New Horizons', 149–50; Glatzer, 'The Beginnings of Modern Jewish Studies'; Schorsch, 'The Emergence of Historical Consciousness'. He also writes that 'to rethink Judaism in terms of the historical canons of the German university was no less of a rupture in Jewish continuity than it had once been to rethink Judaism in terms of Greek philosophy under the impetus of Islam' ('The Ethos of Modern Jewish Scholarship', 162–3).

idea of universal rational progress on the one hand, and the prophetic messianic tradition and the idealistic philosophy of Kantian and post-Kantian history on the other. *Maskilim*, reformers, and members of the *Wissenschaft des Judentums* school—and for that matter, nationalistic thinkers from the late nineteenth century as well—were able, without any hesitation, to adopt the idea of progress, because they found an 'inner accord' between it and the prophetic tradition, which speaks of history as a process of advancement towards a new golden age on earth. No wonder, then, that in their historical consciousness it was not the Pentateuch, but the prophetic books, understood as carrying a universal human message, that were seen as representing the Jewish idea of history; biblical prophecy and the Pentateuch were thus perceived as two separate authorities. Hence, before the new Jewish historical consciousness could merge with the universal idea of progress, it was an essential precondition to convert the prophetic tradition into a central Jewish tradition of historical philosophy. It seems plausible to argue that this was done in order to create a true or imagined symmetry between it and the historical philosophy of universal rationalism. In the modern historical consciousness, destiny, fate, or some other metahistorical power replaced God Almighty.

The change of direction in Jewish historical writing can be found not in the consciousness of a mission or in the messianic schema but elsewhere. Even if there is a similarity between the idea of progress and the idea of a messianic prophecy, the emphasis on continuity in the philosophy of history obscures the revolutionary change expressed in the secular view of Jewish history. Believing in an all-embracing purpose for humanity is not the same as believing in God's intervention in history for His people's sake or in the doctrine of rewards and punishments.[22]

It is not my intention to give an outline of the history of modern Jewish historiography, the circumstances and the manner in which it cut itself off from the patterns of ecclesiastical history, the different Jewish approaches to history, the various historical schemata that have been proposed, and the relationship between historiography, historical consciousness, and historical memory. This has been done, and done well, by other writers.[23] I shall

[22] Philo makes the persecutor Flaccus cry out: 'so then Thou dost not disregard the nation of the Jews, nor do they misreport Thy Providence, but all who say that they do not find in Thee a Champion and Defender, go astray from the true creed' (*Flaccus*, 170, trans. Colson, ix. 395).

[23] See Finley, 'Myth, Memory and History'; R. Horowitz, *Zacharias Fraenkel*; B. Lewis, *History Remembered, Recovered, Invented*; L. Segal, *Historical Consciousness and Religious Tradition*; Yerushalmi, *Zakhor*; Funkenstein, 'Collective Memory and Historical Consciousness'; Feiner, *Haskalah and History*; Feiner, 'Nineteenth-Century Jewish Historiography'; Michael, *Jewish Historiography*; Melamed, 'The Perception of Jewish History'; Bonfil, 'How Golden was the Age of the Renaissance'; Frankel, *Reshaping the Past*.

confine myself to a few instructive parallels between Jewish and Greek historiography in order to shed some light on the new—even revolutionary—character of modern Jewish historiography and the modern Jewish historical consciousness and collective memory.

HISTORY: PRAGMATISM AND ROMANTICISM

The appeal by the Jewish *maskilim* to history was an outcome of the eighteenth century's growing passion for history, the enlargement of the scope of historical knowledge, and the secularization of the historical mind.[24] To revive the knowledge of Jewish history and to renew Jewish interest in general history was seen as a victory over centuries of indifference, ignorance, and banishment. 'History' now included more than some formative events constituting the essential core of collective memory, a schematic chronology of human events, or 'ecclesiatical history'. Its scope was enlarged, and as a result the range of historical memory became broader; once historical knowledge entered the public domain, Jews began to know more of their own history than ever before.

During the nineteenth century, Jewish interest in history mounted. Gradually adopting the prevailing historiographical genres and methods, they searched for a way to create a correspondence between current views of history and historical philosophy and the traditional Jewish conception of Jewish history as the unique chronicle of a Chosen People, which does not abide by the 'universal laws' of world history. Consequently, modern Jewish historical awareness became imbued with an inescapable tension between rationalistic universalism and Romantic particularism, resulting in new emphasis on the multiplicity and diversity of historical phenomena. This turnabout in historical thought and this new interest in history and historical developments created the need for various legitimations.

The primary legitimation at the beginning of the modern era for interest in history and the study and writing of history was to relate the wonders and words of God in history and to draw a moral lesson from them:

> Truly, the books of the chronicles
> Tell the glory of God: from time immemorial.

---

[24] Gay, *The Science of Freedom*, 368–96; Reill, *German Enlightenment*. We shall recall that the German *Aufklärer* were far more conservative with regard to sacred history than their counterparts in France and England.

A generation comes, a generation goes—
and God's wisdom endures.[25]

This kind of legitimation was needed because traditional society regarded the study of history as an unwarranted waste of time, since history is not the key to the truth. A moderate *maskil* like Wessely, in his fourth epistle in *Divrei shalom ve'emet*, asserted that there was no point in studying the histories of various nations, for this occupation is 'fit for idlers, bad for those engaged in worldly affairs, and even worse for wise men versed in the Torah'. Here Wessely was retracting his description of the practical benefits to be gained from a study of history, which suggests he was not sufficiently sure about the value of this new branch of science. On the other hand, radical *maskilim* of the second half of the nineteenth century gave preference to the study of science, not of history. In their search for legitimacy, the first *maskilim* found supportive arguments in the biblical commands to 'remember' and the fact that many books of history are mentioned in the Bible that were later lost for ever (see e.g. Num. 21: 14, Josh. 10: 13).

Another traditional claim, as we have seen, was that history presents a broad vista of all the wonders worked by God in human experience. This was accompanied by a utilitarian justification: it is important for the *maskil* to have at least some general knowledge about the history of the peoples among whom he lives. Using Wessely's view as a point of departure, Isaac Euchel in his article 'Davar el hakoreh mito'elet divrei hayamim hakadmonim' of 1783 ('A Word to the Reader about the Benefits of Ancient History') went much further in defining the understanding of the past as a vital category of thinking and set out four possible uses of history: a philosophical use (*ein philosophischer Nutzen*), more in the sense of 'understanding' than of 'knowledge', by which he meant its use in a rational investigation in order to verify the tradition; a literary use (*ein literarischer Nutzen*), leading to a deeper understanding of the Holy Scriptures against the background of universal history; a political use (*ein politischer Nutzen*), which was a practical use; and an ethical use (*ein moralischer Nutzen*), through which man might reach spiritual perfection, upon acquiring moral discernment through intelligence.[26] This was both a traditionalist and a pragmatic approach to history, but it also had radical implications.

This new appeal to the past entailed several dangers. It opened the

---

[25] Fritz Baer, *Sefer toledot Yisrael*, ii. 1, poem entitled 'Edut hashem ne'emanah ('The Statutes of the Lord are right', Ps. 19: 8).

[26] I am following here Feiner's excellent study, '"History" and "Historical Images"', 39–40.

way for a process of selection of events and periods, because writers of history could choose those times and topics that interested them and adapt them as they liked. It constituted a deviation from the a-historical halakhic standpoint, as well as from medieval rationalism, which preferred philosophy to history; it encouraged the use of external sources, which did not necessarily conform to tradition. It created the option to employ different historical doctrines such as positivism and materialism, which offered different 'laws' of history, including Jewish history. And finally, it planted the seed of the tendency that flourished at the turn of the twentieth century, to see the Jewish people first and foremost as a 'historical entity', whose history—that is to say, the total scope of its historical experience—is the embodiment of its existence.

Under the influence of Romanticism and nationalism, a knowledge of history became a primary element in strengthening the modern Jewish national consciousness and in consolidating its romantic and heroic foundations.[27] Thus a contemporary religiously observant writer, Judah Loeb Landau, could in his play *Herodes* (Lemberg, 1899) compare the publication of the Hebrew translation of Graetz's *Geschichte der Juden* in 1890–9 to the victory of the great liberator:

> Like Judah the Maccabee, Graetz raised the flag—
> Not with a sword, but with a chronicle.

As early as 1821 Eduard Ganz suggested the name 'Die Makkabäer' as the most suitable name for the Verein für Cultur und Wissenschaft der Juden.[28]

It was not only scholarly literature, particularly monumental works like Graetz's, which was highly esteemed. Great value was also placed on the historical novel as a genre to waken sleepers from their slumber. Under the influence of the Romantic approach to historical writing, the emotive Hellenistic historiography was regarded as preferable to pedantic historical research, which could not bring the past back to life. Although one can find a few instances of historical *belles-lettres* in previous generations, such as the Hebrew version of the Alexander Romance, *Ma'aseh Alexander Mokedon*, only in the nineteenth century did the historical novel acquire the status of a creator of collective consciousness, a key partner in creating identity and affinity.[29] It was then that historical writing was seen as a vital ingredient

---

[27] There are some similarities between Hellenistic 'tragic' or 'pathetic' historiography and the Romantic historical writings of the 18th c. onwards. On the influence of 'tragic history' see J. Geiger, 'The History of Judas Maccabaeus'.

[28] Schorsch, 'Breakthrough', 207.

[29] Stoneman, *The Greek Alexander Romance*; J. Dan, *The Story of Alexander*. On Scott, the 'inventor'

in the creation or rehabilitation of national identity; its purpose was not merely to broaden and deepen the understanding of history, but to make the historical past alive and active in the present. In the case of Judaism as well, a knowledge of the past—and not only the spiritual past—was meant to provide paradigms and precedents that should serve the present. In this manner, the new historiography and historical insights filled many functions in Jewish history in the modern era.

Thus, from the end of the eighteenth century, a new Jewish historical consciousness emerged. Its motivation for turning to the historical past was different from that which had moved earlier periods and it produced totally different results. 'History' was perceived as a real expression of the people's spirit, demonstrating its historical purpose, which could serve as a guide not only in matters of moral conduct. Although this approach had its precedents in earlier periods, only in the nineteenth century did it become a major force that shaped the self-awareness and collective experience of the Jews.[30] It was this new consciousness that fragmented Judaism on the one hand, while creating new groups within it on the other. As a result of these processes of change in Jewish society, new understandings emerged of the forces governing and shaping human history in general, and Jewish history in particular. Along with them, new pictures of the past took shape and new historical world-outlooks came into being. The appeal to the past was also intended to provide legitimation for the processes of change. Every current in Judaism attempted to anchor itself in a continuum of Jewish history, to represent itself as an expression of a central stream of historical development, and to embrace and hold fast to precedents from the past.[31]

Historiography also gave legitimacy to the differences of opinion and controversy in the present, as well as to the current condition of multiplicity and divisiveness, while simultaneously offering a new unified framework. Even the most radical currents in Judaism turned to the historical past in order to interpret themselves and to mould their identity as part of a unified Jewish history, despite its multiplicity and diversity. It seems paradoxical that sometimes the more radical these currents were, the more they turned to the distant past for support. Knowledge of history (especially of the rabbinic past) challenged sanctified traditions and at the same time

---

of the genre of the historical novel, see Kerr, *Fiction against History*, 1–17. On the development of the Jewish historical novel in Germany see Ben-Ari, *Historical Images*.

[30] Needless to say, modern European thought also offered traditional and teleological historical explanations.

[31] See Yerushalmi, *Zakhor*; Almog, *Zionism and History*; Feiner, *Haskalah and History*.

provided such substitutes as a consciousness of togetherness and of identity, which served as a basis for defining the new Jewish identity. And no less important, the image of the past was an impetus and a driving force in history. The 'past' was a call to the colours: it served as a mobilizing force that prompted social and political movements, created a consciousness of unity and cooperation, and issued the call to active duty, in order to realize shared goals.

In other words, Jewish history was simultaneously perceived as both a source of controversy and a source of new self-definition. In the course of the nineteenth century, a knowledge of history and a historical conscious-ness became a central and crucial constituent of the cultural, intellectual, and political world of the Jews. These factors were instrumental in helping them to find their place in society, to determine their identity, and to identify their cultural essence.[32]

LEGEND AND HISTORY: DO PARALLELS MEET?

The Jewish historian of the Second Temple period had a deep and strong sense of the historical tradition of the Bible and regarded it as sacred. He had learnt some historical-literary methods from the Greeks, but this did not change his basic outlook. Historical records were regarded by him as reaffirming the biblical tradition and hence he thought they warranted preservation. As the author of 2 Maccabees tells us (2: 14), one of the first things Judas Maccabaeus did after the purification of the Temple was to collect all the books (and official documents) that had been dispersed over the years. Even more significant is Josephus' insistence, in *Against Apion*, that the Jews are to be praised for knowing how to preserve their sacred writings. This, according to him, was one sanctified historical tradition, and not, as in the case of the Greeks, a myriad of traditions conflicting with each other (i. 6–46).[33] Indeed, the Hebrews and the 'Greeks' recognized the fact that they were new nations, that is to say that their appearance on

---

[32] A. D. Smith, *The Ethnic Origins*, 191–208.

[33] Note especially i. 10, in which the reference to 'countless catastrophes (*phthorai*), which have obliterated the memory of the past' echoes the Egyptian priest's words at Plato, *Timaeus*, 22 c. Needless to say, Josephus overlooked the fact that the Bible itself is composed of different traditions, but what he really meant is that once these traditions had been combined and edited they constituted the only canonical Jewish historical tradition. Cardozo wrote that the nations have no more ancient and glorified book than that of Homer, as Josephus testifies, but Homer lived in the days of the Judges, and in any case it is clear that the Torah was far older and was preserved in one sanctified copy (*Las Excelencias*, 128–9). In praising the antiquity of Homer, Cardozo intended to underscore the antiquity of the Bible and its status as an unchallenged tradition, to which no alternative traditions existed. However, he was speaking about the Pentateuch and not the entire Bible.

the stage of history as a people with self-awareness began long after other peoples had already existed, but, according to Josephus, while the Greeks were incapable of crystallizing a historical tradition acceptable to all, the Hebrews had one sole historical tradition.

The question whether every critical history must be secular is a matter of controversy.[34] From a secular point of view it is possible to believe in the uniqueness and chosenness of the Jewish people as well as in the unprecedented nature of its history. But a secular historian cannot see the guiding hand of Providence in all the realms of history. He views fundamentals of faith and the Law not as the fruit of revelation but as a product of individual inspiration and collective genius, and as a creation of gradual progress, stemming from changes in historical circumstances and from human decisions. No longer eternal truths, they become the fruit of the people's spirit, the testimony of its peculiar genius, internalized in its consciousness and its mode of existence, becoming 'historical truth' as well as an active, shaping force. Inevitably, a distinction was created between the history of the people of Israel and the birth of the monotheistic idea. Even those who thought it possible to prove the historical truth of the biblical narrative from the time of the Exodus from Egypt found it difficult to accept the revelation at Mt. Sinai as a historical fact, since that would mean they had to become believers. Hence the solution was to view the appearance of monotheism as a miraculous historical event (basically parallel to the appearance of philosophy in Greece), which began with revelation understood as an idea emerging in the mind of one great figure (Moses) that caused an awesome revolution in the mind of an entire people.[35]

It was not the history of the revelation at Mt. Sinai that had to be proved, but rather Moses' historicity. And if scholars seemed to have difficulties in proving Moses' historicity, then the solution was to claim that the figure of Moses was a spiritual creation of the Jewish people, one that testified to the unique nature of that people's consciousness. 'I care not whether this man Moses really existed', wrote Ahad Ha'am in his famous essay 'Moses' (1904). What he really cared about was that the Jewish people's belief in him was a powerful force that guided their history and that the ideal of Moses 'has been created in the spirit of the Jewish people, and the creator creates in his own image'.[36] From here one need only go one step further

[34] O. Chadwick, *The Secularization*, 189–228. Yerushalmi offers the argument that 'history' became 'the faith of fallen Jews' (*Zakhor*, 86).

[35] Kaufmann, *The Religion*, i/1. 9.

[36] Ahad Ha'am, 'Moses', 208–9. According to Kaufmann, Moses was the first of the emissary prophets and the forerunner of this brand of prophecy, i/iii. 720–1.

to claim that the idea of God was also the creation of the people, in the image of that people.

All this shows clearly that it is no problem to consider the post-biblical history of the Jewish people in secular terms. But what about the *heilige Geschichte*, the biblical history? Does Judaism really depend on the historicity and accuracy of the biblical historical narratives?

The Sages never questioned the biblical historical tradition, nor did they ever attempt to write a different tradition or rectify the existing one. They did make various uses of the biblical traditions and figures: as anachronisms, as exemplars, and even as myth. But they never deviated from the framework, and most important of all they cast no doubt on the actual occurrence of the constitutive events in Jewish history.[37] Critical history wrought a complete change in this situation. Mendelssohn's view was not far from Ahad Ha'am's indifference to the historicity of the biblical stories. He wrote that the biblical historical accounts of formative events

disclose the fundamental purposes of the people's national existence. As historical truth they must, because of their very nature, be accepted on faith. Authority alone can provide evidence of their historicity. Besides, the nation found that these historical accounts were also confirmed by miracles and supported by an authority sufficiently strong to make their faith immune to all doubts and mental reservation.[38]

It is clear that he saw no need to find any verification for the formative events (the stories of the Patriarchs, the Exodus from Egypt, the revelation at Mt. Sinai, etc.) in extra-biblical sources or to grapple with higher criticism of the Bible. Graetz, on the other hand, did feel compelled to contend with the challenge of this criticism and of the historical scholarship that relegated the biblical story to the realm of myth and legend. His reply was that Judaism does not depend on the truth of one or another story, unlike Christianity, which was totally dependent on the dogma of Christ's resurrection from the dead. Even if it is proved that any one of the stories is not historically true, Judaism will not collapse. Although Graetz did not reply emphatically when asked if he believed the story of the revelation

---

[37] Bickerman, *Jews in the Greek Age*, 179: 'The remarkable fact, however, is that Jewish exegetes seem never to have known a historical tradition independent of the Bible.' It should be noted that some of the biblical Midrashim were a reaction to the use Christianity made of the Bible for its own purposes. On both sides, this was a case of legendary, a-historical interpretation.

[38] Mendelssohn, *Jerusalem*, 96. See E. Breuer, 'Haskalah and Scripture'. For an analysis of Mendelssohn's arguments about the validity of the historical truth of the Bible, see Z. Levy, *Judaism in the World View*, 44–51.

at Mt. Sinai was true,[39] the historicity of the formative events in Jewish history was called into question.

The secular Jew, however, was not preoccupied with the issue of whether the Torah is a 'Torah from heaven', but rather was concerned about whether his ancient history was historical fact or nothing but a collection of legends. Moreover, the challenges of modern historiography, and indeed the demands and needs of the new historical awareness, were too strong to be met by indifference or an a-historical outlook. Again, this was not the first time Jews had to respond to this kind of challenge. In the Hellenistic era, pagan philosophers and historians had raised serious doubts in this regard, questioning the accuracy of the biblical tradition (and some had offered a counterhistory of the Jewish people).[40] During the nineteenth century this issue engaged the attention of a large and growing portion of the Jewish public, not only of a handful of philosophers and historians. Religious as well as 'freethinking' Jews increasingly felt the need to respond by using the same tools as their adversaries, above all the external evidence of archaeological finds. Jewish historians and philosophers in the Hellenistic era and the Middle Ages often used alien histories in order to defend the veracity of biblical chronology or the authenticity of miracles; Josephus in *Against Apion* is the foremost example. Maimonides argued for the validity of the biblical chronology by dismissing Indian chronology as pure fiction. The latter, he stated, contains many preposterous legends and hence its tradition is untrustworthy. Spinoza's retort to this kind of argument was that the Jews also have legendary traditions that are about as credible as the Indian legends or the Greek myths—that is, extremely dubious.[41] In an era of historical awareness and of history as science, it was impossible to accept these kinds of answers.

Referring to biblical history as mythology was not at all like referring to the chapters of Genesis as mythology. When George Grote wrote in 1846 that mythology is a story expressing the spirit of the Greeks rather than historical truth, his words were then regarded as outright heresy; however, they were soon accepted without impairing the Greek ideals.[42] From a traditional Jewish point of view, it was unthinkable to negate the validity

---

[39] Graetz, *Jewish Chronicle*, 5 Aug. 1887.

[40] On these pagan writers see Rokéah, *Judaism and Christianity*; Wolfson, 'Verification'. It was Saadiah Gaon who, in the 10th c., laid down the dogma that the revelation at Mt. Sinai meets the test of verification by historical fact.

[41] Wolfson, 'Verification'.

[42] Thompson, *A History of Historical Writing*, ii. 491–5; Turner, *The Greek Heritage*, 83–4. Kitto writes that 'Grote's admirable history had not passed through many editions before Schliemann went to Mycenae and Troy' (*The Greeks*, 16–17).

of the biblical stories, as Pericles negated the Homeric epics, asserting
that the Athenians had no need of Homer or any epic poet to delight
his listeners for the moment, only for the truth to blast the reputation
of his words (Thucydides ii. 41. 4). The historical truth of the Bible was
self-evident; on this point Jews and Christians shared the same view. Thus,
when the critical approach turned from Homer to the Bible and biblical
criticism made its appearance, they were alarmed.

In 1827 Goethe clearly noted the difference between biblical criticism
and the attitude towards Homer: 'Thus they are now pulling to pieces
the Five Books of Moses; and if an annihilating criticism is injurious in
anything, it is so in matters of religion—for there everything depends
upon faith, to which we cannot return when we have once lost it.'[43] And
indeed there is a close connection between F. A. Wolf's *Prolegomena ad
Homerum* (1795), an epoch-making work of philological scholarship, and
Wellhausen's *Prolegomena zur Geschichte Israels* (1878). Wolf relied on a tradition that it was Peisistratus, tyrant of Athens, who collected Homer's
poems. (When his monumental book appeared, Wolf was grateful to
Mendelssohn for his support, against the views of many others.)[44] The
same critical methods were employed in both cases to expose the evolutionary development of the text, but in the case of the Bible they were
used to expose the evolutionary development of the Israelite faith and law.
Some scholars also suggested that Blackwell, Lowth, Wood (the author of
Essay upon the Original Genius and Writing of Homer, 1765)[45] and others, in
their pioneering research on Homer and on the Bible, understood both
works as manifestations of the unique spirit of the people who produced
them.[46] There is indeed no doubt that these works and other later ones
signified a revolution in the understanding of Homer and the Bible. This
was not a revolution in understanding their spiritual message, but rather
in understanding the poetical merits resulting from their links to the natural surroundings in which they were written. The Bible was seen as a
manifestation of the 'unique spirit of the people' who produced it, not as
divine revelation.

During the nineteenth century the Homeric epic was regarded as a

[43] Goethe, *Conversations with Eckermann*, 172.

[44] Wolf, *Prologomena*, 3–35, cf. Altmann, *Moses Mendelssohn*, 423–4. On 8 May 1795 Wolf wrote to
Mendelssohn: 'Assuming that a nation has yet nothing in writing, and assuming that it was customary to
publish by way of recitation nothing but cantos lasting from four to six hours, would a bard—be he
even the greatest and most extraordinary man imaginable—ever have been able to hit upon the idea of
constructing such a tremendous edifice as the *Iliad* and the *Odyssey* without a basis on which the human
mind must rest itself in such cases?' Mendelssohn answered drily: 'No!'

[45] See B. Feldman and Richardson, *The Rise of Modern Mythology*, 99–103, 144–6, 191–2.

[46] Manuel, *Eighteenth Century*, 309; Arieli, 'New Horizons'.

secular Bible, and parallels were drawn between these two books.[47] Indeed, some critics saw a connection between the 'anti-Christian conspiracy against the Bible' and Wolf's attempt to break down the unity of the Homeric epos, the 'Bible of the Greeks'. But in the case of the Bible not only the unity of the book was called into question, but sacred history itself. If the Bible's intention was not to relate legendary traditions but to tell the truth, in accordance with Cicero's prescription for history, *ne quid falsi dicere audeat* ('that it shall not dare say anything false', *De oratore*, ii. 62), then the sacred historical traditions are not exempt from historical scrutiny. The English scholar A. H. Sayce described this rather simplistically in his book *The 'Higher Criticism' and the Verdict of the Monuments*, which sought the high road between hermeneutic criticism and external evidence:

Inevitably, therefore, the scientific criticism of the Old Testament followed upon the scientific criticism of the Greek and Roman historians, and if its tendency was destructive in the case of the one, it was only because it had already been destructive in the case of the other. The same canons of criticism that had relegated the story of Mycenean power and the Trojan war to mythland, relegated also the earlier narratives of the Bible to the same unhistorical region. Abraham only followed Agamemnon, and if the reputed ancestor of the Hebrew race was resolved into a myth, it was because the 'king of men' had already submitted to the same fate.[48]

For the true believer, a comparison such as this was an out-and-out distortion. In the introduction to his seven-volume geographical and historical description of the Holy Land, the French scholar and traveller Victor Gurein quotes Cicero's words 'Quacumque enim ingredimur, in aliqua historia vestigium ponimus.'[49] After studying the antiquities of Asia Minor, Egypt, Greece, and other ancient lands, he reached the conclusion that 'in Palestine you are surrounded on all sides by a glorious past, but it is wonderful that its stamp is truth', not like the glorious past in other countries of the Orient, or in Greece.

And indeed the resemblance between Abraham and Agamemnon is merely external. Although the Homeric epic is regarded in Western culture as a secular Bible and Homer as the 'educator of Hellas',[50] the Homeric ideals were not inextricably linked to the credibility of the events it described, that is, to the *Iliad* and the *Odyssey* as history.[51] The validity and the

---

[47] Turner, *The Greek Heritage*, 135–86.   [48] Sayce, *Higher Criticism*, 17.

[49] 'For whichever way we go, we are walking in some saga' (*De finibus bonorum et malorum*, v. 5), cit. *Description géographique*, i. 1.

[50] Muller, 'Troy: The Bible of Greece'; Turner, *The Greek Heritage*, 140–86; Finley, *The World of Odysseus*, 15–25.

[51] Broshi, 'Troy and Jericho'; Muller, 'Troy: The Bible of Greece'; Finley, *The World of Odysseus*, 159–77; Glover, *The Challenge of Greek*, 216; Lorimer, *Homer and the Monuments*.

plausibility of the story of Troy does not carry the same meaning and value as the accuracy of the story of the Exodus from Egypt. Nor was the siege of Troy equivalent to the revelation at Mt. Sinai; the far-flung voyages of Odysseus and his comrades were not equivalent to the wanderings of the children of Israel in the desert. In the eyes of the believer, this was sacred history, which depicted formative events that occurred in history under the guidance of the one and only God. Thus, even though Mendelssohn, Graetz, and other writers argued that the Bible's spiritual message did not rely on the historicity of the events, for the true believer these historical events were a result of God's intervention in history. He believed that God transmitted His messages through these events; hence their historicity was of vital importance.

The Bible, then, became a history and the core of modern Jewish national awareness. In many ways, modern Hebrew culture, in its many spheres, was a new 'translation' of the Bible into reality.

It was the Berlin Haskalah that gave the Bible its predominant position in Hebrew culture. In so doing, the *maskilim* were following the Lutheran interest in the Bible and seeking to establish a common ground between themselves and the Protestants. The Bible was conceived as a common spiritual heritage with universal messages. While the Talmud represented the insularity, legalism, and dissociation from 'life' of the 'old Judaism', the Bible was seen as a great intellectual and moral contribution to mankind. But there were other decisive reasons for the revival of the Bible: it was written in Hebrew, the classical and national language of the Jews, and it was a genuine manifestation of the literary merits and poetic genius of the Hebrews.[52] Turning back to the Bible meant breaking away from the authority of the rabbis and rabbinic literature. The Bible was national history: the national history of the Jews in their homeland, the history of the link between the people and its country. It also was viewed as the main spiritual, cultural, and national heritage. This was indeed a breakthrough, since in traditional Jewish society the Bible had occupied only a marginal place. Biblical narratives and heroes were known through talmudic exegesis that dressed them in a new and anachronistic garb in order to impart moral lessons. Indeed, one of the first aims of the Haskalah was to revive the reading of the Bible and to assign it a central place in Jewish education not only as a treasury of moral examples, but also as a history.

If the Bible is the history of the people it is clear why it was so important to verify its historical accounts. While many endeavoured to verify the biblical cosmogony (the story of Creation), or the antiquity and unity of the

---

[52] See Ch. 8.

Torah, for the freethinking Jew what needed to be confirmed was first and foremost the history of the nation since the Exodus. The enlightened or secular Jew focused more on the verification of historical traditions linked to the secular history of the Jewish people, and not necessarily to the history of its religious faith. As for more ancient historical traditions or the biblical cosmogony, they were perceived as reflecting the people's world-outlook. Less importance was attributed to the revelation than to the antiquity of monotheism: the former was regarded as a religious outlook itself the fruit of a unique collective consciousness. In this way, the freethinking, enlightened Jew assimilated the basic premises of idealistic ethnocentrism, separating the layer of faith from that of history, and assigning greater value and importance to the latter.

In a certain sense, the modern Jewish historical consciousness was following in the path of certain Jewish historical apologetics of the Hellenistic and Roman era. It too attempted to validate the historical description of the Bible, to repudiate anti-Jewish legends, to underline the unbroken and special ties of the Jews to their country, and to sketch the entire sweep of the Jewish presence in the land. The emphasis on the political and national dimensions of this presence was a counterweight to the previous stress laid on religious history. The desire to emphasize the continuity and antiquity of Jewish settlement can of course be found in the Bible, in the Book of Chronicles, but there it is a secondary theme. Circumstances made it absolutely necessary to stress and heighten these aspects in the modern Jewish historical consciousness. Anyone unable to adopt the theological history that views Palestine as a Promised Land, accorded that status by revelation, was compelled to emphasize the ties of actual life, and to turn the biblical Palestinian *realia* into a central and crucial element of his historical awareness.

'THOSE THAT SLEPT IN THE DUST OF THE EARTH AWOKE'

Near Eastern and biblical archaeology has much in common with the archaeology of Greece, but it also has its singular features. In both cases archaeology was linked with national revival, but only biblical archaeology was linked with questions of faith and religious doctrines. Viewing the Bible as equivalent to the histories of Herodotus or Thucydides was indeed a radical turnabout in Jewish thought. Relying on finds dug up from Egyptian or Babylonian soil as evidence of the truth of the Holy Scripture was also a striking innovation. In the mid-nineteenth century, it seemed that science was placing itself at the service of faith.

For those seeking external evidence, a miracle had come to pass! As if with the wave of a magic wand, by the second half of the nineteenth century, classical and biblical archaeology had produced incontestable evidence of the veracity of ancient Greek historical traditions as well as of biblical cosmogony and the primeval history of the Bible.

Schliemann's excavations at Hisarlık, identified as Troy, in 1870–2 appeared to reveal to an astounded world that there was evidence for a historical background to the Homeric epic.[53] The no less amazing excavations in Mesopotamia and Egypt resonated throughout the world, for, as they seemed to bring forth from the earth marvellous evidence for the credibility of the biblical tales, they seemed to give the lie to all the sceptics.

The year 1872 marked the turning-point. On 3 December in that year, George Smith announced in London that he had deciphered the missing fragment of what would later be known as the Gilgamesh Epic; it was a summary of the Babylonian Flood story (the tale of Atrahasis), which had been dug up at Nineveh. The newspaper *Hamagid*, published in the small border town of Lyck, hastened to report the discovery to its readers in January 1873 and enthusiastically concluded: 'Understandably, the above account made a deep impression because it offers us very ancient evidence of the veracity of what is written in our holy Torah, and this will seal the lips of those who do not believe its truth.' Those who wished to challenge the sacred truths in the name of science were terribly disappointed; science itself, the newspaper wrote, had now proved that the heresy was grounded on false premises. This development forged a constructive approach to archaeology: through it, Abraham became a historical figure, who lived and functioned in an authentic historical background and was part of a concrete geographical and cultural background. The scholars of that generation, said *Hamagid* in amazement, had succeeded in opening the bolted doors of time, in deciphering the stone tablets inscribed in dead languages, and awakening those who had been asleep for almost two thousand years. The wonders of archaeology, therefore, were not inferior to the wonders of chemistry or of physics. They enabled this optimistic, or simply naïve, writer to cry out exultantly 'Truth shall spring out of the earth' (Ps. 85: 12). Now, he announced, none other than the science of archaeology was

---

[53] Schliemann stated: 'I have proved the Iliad to be based upon real facts.' Thomas, 'The Modern Discovery', 73–4. See also Avgouli, 'The First Greek Museums'. On the role of archaeology in modern Arab countries see Sivan, *Arab Political Myths*; Gershoni and Jankovski, *Egypt, Islam, and the Arabs*, 164–90.

'discrediting all the heretical sceptics and shutting their mouths!' Thus began an enthusiastic pursuit of new archaeological discoveries and their resultant historical conclusions throughout the Jewish world—by believers and secular Jews alike.[54]

Of course, there were also many who described the archaeological finds as 'unreliable witnesses'. They found it inconceivable that an Assyrian or Chaldean tablet, made of wood or stone—the cultic material of idolaters— could be considered equivalent to the holy Torah! However, the influence of Bible criticism was so strong that even those who did not see an 'internal' value in archaeology considered it one of the wonderful acts of the Creator, meant to put an end to the 'delusions of Bible criticism'. 'Those that slept in the dust of the earth awoke from a slumber of two millennia', wrote Ze'ev Jawitz. Thus Wellhausen and those who thought as he did were toppled from their lofty positions and stripped of their influence. The parochial Jewish *maskilim* of eastern Europe who had devoutly embraced biblical criticism as infallible were regarded as 'empty vessels' who had purchased damaged goods in the marketplace of the Gentiles.[55]

There were several reasons for this favourable reception. One was the existence of a larger enlightened public in the second half of the century than in the first, a public that had already internalized the new historical insights; another was the certainty that it was impossible to refute eternal historical truths. However, the main reason was probably the belief that archaeology possessed the power to contradict and denounce, one by one, the scientific dogmas of the prevailing school of biblical criticism. Since that same biblical criticism was regarded as the greatest enemy of the historical tradition of the Jewish people, any means of humbling it and repudiating its logic was thought both fitting and desirable. The outcome is once again a case of reverse acculturation: the use of an external cultural element to help defend a cultural tradition.

Archaeology did not delay its entry into the world till biblical criticism had reached the height of its prestige and the peak of its influence. From the 1840s and 1850s, Mesopotamia began to yield up its secrets; the works by P. E. Botta, H. Rawlinson, and A. H. Layard were published before Wellhausen's *Prolegomena*.[56] Criticism of the historical truth of the biblical narratives was familiar to the educated Jewish public by the first half of the nineteenth century.[57] Thus, when Julius Wellhausen and Ernest Renan

---

[54] Y. Shavit, 'Truth shall Spring'.   [55] Jawitz, *Toledot Yisrael*, i. 39–40.

[56] Layard's *Nineveh and its Remains* was published in 1849 and became a bestseller. In the 1920s Leonard Woolley's excavations in Ur were thought to have 'uncovered the Flood'. See Seton Lloyd, *Foundations in the Dust*.

[57] See Soloweitschik and Rubascheff, *The History of Biblical Criticism*; Shelly, *The Study of the Bible*.

endowed biblical criticism with scientific prestige and wide dissemination, archaeology was thought to be the most effective weapon against its destructive tendencies. This prompted the enthusiasm of Jews in diverse circles upon hearing the astounding news of archaeological discoveries. Many segments of the enlightened Jewish public, from the 1870s onward, showed a keen, unceasing interest in the finds of archaeology, and they made uninterrupted use of these finds in the context of the argument about history and faith. The findings of Mesopotamian archaeology were believed to confirm the theory of the 'theft of wisdom', by proving that the source of all culture is in the ancient East. They showed that the widespread claims of the Semitic peoples' cultural inferiority were absurd. They were also supposed to demonstrate that the contemporary theory of progress was baseless, for the ancient peoples were well versed in sciences and technologies that the nineteenth century made a vain pretence of having fathered. Archaeology also refuted a succession of widespread anti-Jewish theories: the source of wisdom lay not in Egypt, but rather in Semitic Mesopotamia. There was now incontrovertible evidence that all the sciences and fine arts did indeed reach Greece through Babylonia and not through Egypt. In consequence, the antiquity and superiority of Semitic wisdom was confirmed.

The archaeological discoveries, stated *Hamelitz* in July 1896, turned the tables on the model prevailing among all historical scholars who had been 'trained in the halls of Greek and Roman enlightenment, which had its source in the wisdom of the sons of the East . . .'. The new-found ancient past also bestowed a new sense of self-confidence in the value and even the superiority of Jewish antiquity and its contribution to mankind. But primarily it was believed that archaeology proved the antiquity of the laws of Moses: the Torah. The finds also seemed to confirm and verify the constitutive stories of the creation of the Jewish nation: the deeds of the Patriarchs, the Exodus from Egypt, and so on. They underscored the terrestrial aspects of the Jewish presence in Palestine and created a tangible, concrete link with the historical past. In this way, archaeology endowed the new Jewish presence in the country with a dimension of continuity and a structure of real depth; and no less important, it provided the historical consciousness and the culture with symbols that granted it historical legitimacy. It also made the past concrete and shortened the distance between it and the present. 'The antiquities of Greece and Rome made their past tangible and hence biblical archaeology will have a similar effect on the Jewish past in Palestine, turning it from an "idea" and "literature" into reality.[58]

In Greece and Palestine, the distant historical past was not a vehicle for cultural archaization or conservatism, but for modernization. The classical past was depicted as being rife with astounding and wondrous cultural achievements, as the source of all the human culture that came in its wake, and as already mentioned—as a past of secular culture. As archaeologists reconstructed the spiritual treasures of the past and brought them vividly to life, that same remote past was endowed with a current presence and existence, one that possessed validity and was a source of inspiration. Byzantine Greece was present and active in Greece in the form of the Greek Orthodox Church, while classical Hellas existed only by virtue of books, and—from the nineteenth century—by virtue of the many vestiges left behind by that same culture in the Greek motherland and throughout the lands of the Aegean and the Mediterranean seas. For modern Greece, archaeological finds attested to the continuity of history, as a means of shaping self-identity, and as an entry ticket into Europe. Through archaeology, the Greeks recovered and appropriated Hellas as it had been moulded by the European spirit.[59]

MYTH AND HISTORY

In summing up this chapter, we now return to the Greek Hellenistic mirror. In *Against Apion*, Josephus compared the Greek historical memory with that of the Jewish people. While the Greeks had many books, each of which told a divergent historical story, the Israelites took care to record their chronicles and to preserve their sacred historical books, which tell a single, reliable historical tale (i. 4–8). In saying this, of course, Josephus emphasized the importance he attributed to an unvarying (and reliable) national historical narrative. He himself, we recall, expanded this narrative in his *Antiquities* and added to it from various sources, including external sources. However, he did not question any historical truths nor did he propose an alternative account for any of the events.

Jewish historiographers from the sixteenth and seventeenth centuries followed a similar course. They rejected the traditional view that historical writing is an 'alien wisdom'. However, in the main, this historiography

---

[58] Soloweitschik, *Sekhiyot hamikra*, 206. St Jerome notes the value of antiquarian knowledge for understanding both profane and sacred history ('Alia Praefatio', *Biblia Sacra iuxta vulgatam versionem: Liber Verborum Dierum*, Papal Commission edn., pp. 7–8 = *PL* 29. 401).

[59] Dakin, *The Unification of Greece*, 253–8.

retained its links to the old historical formula, and only gradually became open to new historical thought. As far as it was concerned, the driving force in history was the Divine factor, but it also took into consideration 'natural causes' operating in history, made use of external sources and recognized the dimension of development in Jewish history.[60] From the time of the Haskalah, the writing of history became a legitimate scholarly and intellectual occupation, and historical consciousness became a basic element of Jewish identity.

However, the awareness that historical time is fluid and dynamic, and that values and norms are the products of their time and the circumstances in which they are formulated, shattered the unified historical picture. The inevitable result was that the situation Josephus had ascribed to the Greeks—the simultaneous existence of diverse and even contradictory historical traditions—came to typify the Jewish historical consciousness. This unavoidably led to the unceasing discourse between disparate historical narratives, and beyond that, between a historical myth—a uniform and accepted picture of the past—and a critical view that challenged this picture.

[60] Melamed, 'The Perception'.

13

THE CHILDREN OF JAPHETH (ARYANS) AND THE CHILDREN OF SHEM (SEMITES): RACE AND INNATE NATIONALISM

Science has now made visible to everybody the great and pregnant elements of difference which lie in race, and in how signal a manner they make the genius and history of an Indo-European people vary from those of a Semitic people. Hellenism is Indo-European growth; Hebraism is Semitic growth.

MATTHEW ARNOLD, *Culture and Anarchy*

. . . the two great races to whose existence is due all, or nearly all, which makes man distinctively man: the stately thoughtful Semitic race . . . and the noble, ever-progressive Aryan race . . .

F. W. FARRAR, *Families of Speech*

THE NATURAL TRADITION IN JUDAISM

THE new historical awareness put the *people* in the centre of the stage. But if it is the people which created its own identity, who is this people and by what force did it create its individuality and shape its history?

In a short story, 'Shem and Japheth on the Train', published in 1890, the author Mendele Mokher Seforim (Shalom Jacob Abramowitsch, 1835–1917), tells about a trip on a train. In the railway car, the narrator hears from his fellow passenger, Moshe the tailor, the life-stories of two men—a Jew and a Pole—whose fate brought them together when they were deported from Bismarck's Germany back to Poland. During the conversation his companion tells him about the new racial concept that prevails in Germany: a combination of ethnography, racial morphology, and religious and popular prejudices.

'But the Germans think otherwise', said Reb Moshe quietly. 'The Germans who perform miracles of science, have turned the clock back a thousand generations, so that all of us at this day are living in the time of the Flood. Nowadays they call the Jew "Shem" and the Gentile "Japheth". With the return of Shem and

Japheth the customs of that far-off age have turned too, and the earth is filled with violence. The non-Semites are hostile towards the Semites . . .'[1]

Why was the East European Jewish narrator so surprised to hear of these concepts, which divide the peoples into races? To explain that, it is necessary to clarify the difference between ethnic stereotypes and the theory of race. The former are sociocultural and literary conventions about 'national character', oversimplified mental pictures of such and such a people (including one's own); the latter is a doctrine claiming that every human group (in particular the so-called races of mankind) has interrelated physiological and mental traits that characterize it as a result of heredity. This is accompanied by the view that these traits create a hierarchy of 'high' and 'low' races. Mendele cannot be surprised by stereotypes, but by the view that endows them with a deterministic biological and genetic source.

Ethnic stereotypes had always been part and parcel of anti-Jewish literature,[2] nor was there anything new about stamping racial attributes on the Jewish people. The labelling of Jews with recognizable traits of character was already a common practice in Hellenistic-Roman literature and from there it passed into medieval and modern Christian literature, where it was expanded to include physiognomical features as well. As far back as 1679, Isaac Cardozo in his *Las excelencias de los Hebreos* tried to give scientific answers to some of the widespread claims about the physical ugliness of the Jews, but these continued to be pervasive in Christian European society. About one hundred years later, in 1787, Henri Baptiste Grégoire, addressing the same issue, explained several signs of the physical ugliness and wretchedness of the Jews as being the result of objective patterns of life rather than an organic flaw. The stereotypes prevalent in anti-Jewish literature described the Jews as an inferior and aesthetically repulsive race. Furthermore, writers such as Lavater sought to establish a link between physiognomical features and character traits, and the image of the body was widely perceived as an external physical expression of psychological traits. Physical repugnance was clearly seen to reflect internal psychologi-

---

[1] Translated by Walter Lever in Alter, *Modern Hebrew Literature*. The story was written after the expulsion of Jews and Poles from eastern Prussia in 1890; thus the Jewish tailor and the Polish shoemaker share the same fate. See now Werses, 'Polish–Jewish Relations'.

[2] Gilman, *The Jew's Body*; cf. Daniel, 'Anti-Semitism'. However, in the ancient world it is beliefs and practices, not physical peculiarities, that are mocked; Dr Holford-Strevens would, on purely literary grounds, disallow the reference at Ammianus Marcellinus xxii. 5. 5 to 'stinking and rioting Jews', *Iudaeorum fetentium et tumultuantium*, since the two qualities do not make a pair and stench is irrelevant to the context; *fetentium* should be emended to *ferventium* ('in a ferment') as proposed by Cornelissen, 'Adversaria', 267–8.

cal ugliness. On the other hand, Haskalah literature developed a system of stereotypical features to describe Gentile society. Ukrainian and Polish peasants usually appear as violent, stupid, vulgar drunkards. They are disparagingly called 'Esau' or 'Ivan': but although 'Esau' suggests a rugged physical type, physiogonomy plays a small part in these stereotypes compared with psychological, social, and mental qualities. 'Ivan' is always a drinker, thief, and murderer.[3]

However, Mendele's narrator ought not to have been surprised by the stereotypical description of national traits. This phenomenon already existed in Greek and Jewish literature.

The division of peoples into races according to their physical characteristics can already be found in ancient literature. In the literature of the Near East physical features were given much attention and consideration; see, for example, the famous 'Great Hymn to the Aten' of the revolutionary King Akhenaten (1379–1362 BC):

[You made] The lands of Khor [Syria and Palestine] and Kush [Ethiopia]
The land of Egypt.
You set every man in his place,
You supply their needs;
Everyone has his food.
His lifetime is counted.
Their tongues differ in speech,
Their character likewise;
Their skins are distinct,
For you distinguished the peoples.[4]

Greek literature dealt extensively with ethnological questions and showed great interest in the origins of the different human races and their various physical (and mental) differences. The Greeks treated the barbarians as a human type opposite to them, but also portrayed particular barbarian nations—and other Greek communities—with specific characteristics; these were later adopted by the Romans, whose own moral characterization of the Greeks is not always flattering.[5] Although they recognized that

[3] Bartal, *Non-Jews and Gentile Society*, 102–15.

[4] Lichtheim, *Ancient Egyptian Literature*, ii. 98.

[5] On this subject see Baldry, *The Unity of Mankind*; Hall, *Inventing the Barbarian*; Tyrrell, *Amazons*; Snowden, *Blacks in Antiquity*; id., *Before Color Prejudice*. On the quasi-science of natural physiognomy in antiquity see Evans, *Physiognomics in the Ancient World*. Against the charges of Jewish exclusiveness, Josephus appealed to Plato's desire to keep his citizens' blood pure (*Against Apion*, ii. 257; cf. Rawson, *The Spartan Tradition*, 98). This may be read as an apology for the Jewish rejection of mixed marriages, but it is misleading to compare the actual ideology and policy of Ezra and Nehemiah to the ideas of Plato, which remain in the realm of philosophy.

human culture is a product of the ability, resourcefulness, and inventiveness of the creative personality, the Greeks none the less attributed great importance to the origin of nations and to explaining the nature of their distinctive cultures. The Hellenistic ethnographic typology sought the ancient core of cultures, and the ancient origin of the *ethnos* was always a central component in it. The *barbaroi* were given not only specific physical characteristics but also mental characteristics: they were emotional, stupid, cruel, subservient, and cowardly. Only during the Hellenistic era was the difference between barbarians and Greeks glossed over, and supplanted, as Eratosthenes noted, by the difference between good people and bad people.[6] From this humanistic concept also follows the idea that all men are, in theory, equal in nature, or more correctly, that all can be educated and become men of culture.

Biblical historiography did not pride itself on the ethnic purity of the primordial Israelite people. On the contrary, in many instances, it even deliberately stressed its inferior origin from a 'house of slaves' or a collective grouping of homeless nomadic peoples: 'Your father was an Amorite and your mother a Hittite' (Ezek. 16: 3). In the Bible, one can find many universalist expressions claiming that all human beings have a common origin since they were all created in the image of God: 'For God made man in His own image' (Gen. 9: 6), and the prophets foretold the redemption of the entire human race. The Gentiles were chastised for their crimes against Israel and their moral degeneracy, not for any innate character traits. True, the Bible also contains the curse against Canaan son of Ham, but this was aimed against the Canaanites as the national enemy. However, the Bible takes almost no interest in the physical features of the nations (the *goyim*), nor is there much physical description or stereotyping as there is of barbarians in Greek literature. The hostility towards the *goyim* and the division of the world between Jews and non-Jews is not expressed in such terms since the biblical authors took no interest in ethnology. It is for idolatry and for moral offences that the *goyim* are condemned.

When Josephus wished to wipe out the insult flung at the Jewish race and to emphasize its antiquity and purity, he declared: 'I have, I think, made sufficiently clear to any that may peruse that work [the *Antiquities*] the extreme antiquity of our Jewish race, the purity of the original stock . . .' (*Against Apion*, i. 1). The Sages based the difference between the people of Israel and the nations of the world not on origin but on a general and all-embracing spiritual opposition; the pre-eminence of Israel is contingent

---

[6] Hall, *Inventing the Barbarian*, 17; Baldry, *The Unity*, 167–71. Cf. Isocrates, *Panegyricus*, 50 (above, Ch. 3 n. 3).

upon the study of the Torah and the observance of its commandments. If there was any concept of the Jews as an ethnic group, it was based on the notion of a common father of the Jewish people. Nevertheless, although the Sages placed the main emphasis on the spiritual pre-eminence of Judaism, in the course of time an ethnic distinction did develop in the aggadic literature.[7] In medieval philosophy there are clear echoes of a theory endowing the Jews with a superiority in natural properties and establishing a metabiological difference between Jews and the nations, which found its basis in the naturalistic approach in the aggadah and kabbalah.[8] Maimonides, for example, wrote that the 'The people who are abroad are all those that have no religion, neither one based on speculation nor one received by tradition. Such are the extreme Turks that wander about in the north, the Kushites who live in the south, and those in our country who are like these. I consider these as irrational beings, and not as human beings; they are below mankind, but above monkeys' (*Guide of the Perplexed*, III. li).[9] What he meant here was to draw a general distinction between cultured peoples and barbarians, not a distinction between Jews and Muslims, for example.

Judah Halevi subscribed to a different view. His national, racial, indeed cosmic approach was the most influential philosophical treatment of racial singularity in medieval Jewish literature. He claimed that the Jews are the only descendants of Adam, through Noah, Abraham, and Moses:

All of them represented the essence and purity of Adam on account of their intimacy with God. Each of them had children only to be compared to them

[7] Oppenheimer, 'Ethnic Groups and Religious Context'; J. Katz, *Exclusiveness and Tolerance*, 13–23.

[8] J. Katz, *Tradition and Crisis*, 26–7; I. Heinemann, 'The Controversy on Nationalism'; id., *The Ways of the Haggadah*, 48–9, quoting several Midrashim in which the different nations are ascribed negative collective ('racial') characteristics, as essentially wicked, violent, corrupt, amoral, etc., whereas the people of Israel are noble, wise, even handsome; ibid. 52–3, comparing the ambiguous attitude of the Sages regarding race with the Greek debate about whether it is possible to endow barbarians with the true culture (wherever national pride grew, there was often a tendency towards the racial motif). In the Zohar and *Sefer Habahir*, there are references to the Jew's innate qualities as well as to his cosmic value, and this became a prevalent notion. It appears often in the hasidic literature which asserts that Jews are endowed with a *neshamah yeterah* (literally, an oversoul, or extra soul). Recently, the former Chief Sephardi Rabbi, Ovadiah Yosef, ruled that a religious Jew is prohibited from receiving a blood transfusion from a Gentile, since the latter eats non-kosher food, which introduces harmful substances into the bloodstream, and from there to the soul. (Note too the ambiguous attitude implied towards converts.) However, in the Talmud the uniqueness of Jewry depends not on character traits but rather on observance of the Torah and ethics. One may detect a close parallel between the Greek *nomos* and the Torah, since a barbarian can learn the Greek *nomos* and a Gentile can accept the Torah (even if he is not a descendant of one who was present at the Revelation on Mt. Sinai). However, Jews undoubtedly took the stress on *physis*, understood as inherited traits, from classical literature. Maimonides waived the 'natural qualities' in so far as they related to differences between Jews and Muslims (and Christians), but did differentiate between these and those who are below mankind!

[9] Maimonides, *Guide*, trans. Friedländer, 384.

outwardly, but not really like them, and, therefore, without direct union with the divine influence. The chronology was established through the medium of those sainted persons who were only single individuals, and not a crowd, until Jacob begat the Twelve Tribes, who were all under this divine influence. Thus the divine element reached a multitude of persons who carried the records further. The chronology of those who lived before these has been handed down to us by Moses.[10]

Unlike the Sages, who regarded the spiritual heritage embodied in the Written and Oral laws as the essence of Judaism, Judah Halevi stressed hereditary spiritual qualities. (It is no wonder that *The Kuzari* was revived, and won popular acclaim, in the nineteenth century.) He attributed the conflict between Israel and the nations of the world to character traits, of which he naturally endowed the Jews with the best. In the sixteenth century, the rabbi and philosopher Judah Loew b. Bezalel of Prague (known as Maharal, 1525–1609) employed similar organicist conceptions of an ontological opposition between Israel and the nations of the world. He stated that each people 'has its own essence and its own form'.[11]

However, there was a more decisive factor in the spiritual history of the Jewish people than orderly systems of thought. That was the use in the Middle Ages of various legends, interpreted as displaying the religious and spiritual superiority of the Jews, as an element in disputations with Christians. These sources were also, and perhaps mainly, designed to encourage and bolster the Jews' consciousness of their self-valuation, in a historical era in which they were depicted as despicable and contemptible, and lived in conditions of humiliation and oppression.[12]

In the nineteenth century, race became vitally important, and an ethnocentric dogma based on a naturally determined biology became widespread in Europe. As a result, any ethnic elements that could be uncovered in the Jewish literary tradition were intensified. Even those who sensed that these views were dangerous still clung to them out of their need and distress, and because they uplifted their spirits;[13] Graetz and his like stressed the spiritual and moral inheritance of the Jews, but the fact remains that they

[10] *Kuzari*, i. 47, 49; it was under Halevi's influence that Heinrich Graetz wrote: 'The Hebrews, the descendants of Eber, are not only qualitatively but also genetically different from other nations. . . . As a result of this inherited nature they were qualified and worthy to receive God's word at Sinai for humanity' ('Structure of Jewish History', 113).

[11] On Maharal's nationalist doctrine, see M. Stein, 'National Uniqueness and Human Unity'; B. Gross, *The Messianism of the Maharal*; Kulka, 'The Historical Background of the National and Educational Teaching'.

[12] J. Katz, *Tradition and Crisis*, 26–7.

[13] Gosset writes: 'The usual response to a racist attack has been for the victim to reply in kind against the race of his opponent—not to question the dogma of racism' (*Race*, 410).

accepted its 'genetic' origin. Well aware of the danger of this conception, the English lady warned Graetz: 'The miracle of the continued existence of the Jewish race despite the war of extermination against it can in any case be accounted for physiologically in terms of race. That is the hobbyhorse of our Disraeli, who even as Prime Minister was proud of his descent and in several of his novels intoned the vigor of the Jews. But that is a dangerous precipice. We approach the point of materialism, which is inherently exclusive and intolerant.'[14] Her ominous prophecy was that the use of concepts of race might provide the peoples of Europe with a justification for swallowing up the Jewish race.

THE DIVISION OF THE WORLD
AND THE DIVISION OF PEOPLES

We have already seen that from a Western point of view the antinomy between Jews and Europeans was also based on a racial division. This, again, was not an innovation: the traditional European ethnography was based on the biblical genealogies[15] until it gained a new, pseudo-scientific foundation.[16] Mendele's narrator, then, ought not to have been surprised by a conceptual framework that divided peoples into children of Shem and children of Japheth. For the Jew well versed in the historic Jewish ethnographical tradition there was also nothing new about the division of the nations into families (or races). Jewish intellectuals found this division compatible with the ancient historical tradition upon which it drew. Therefore Mendele's seemingly naïve character whose words appear at the beginning of the chapter ought not to have been surprised that the Greeks in his time had turned into Indo-Europeans, and that the Jews had become the representatives of the 'Semitic race' in world history. The division of the world into the families of nations is anchored in the genealogies of Genesis and appears in the Book of Jubilees (viii–ix),[17] whose *imago mundi* is derived from Hellenistic ethnographical and geographical literature.

In consequence, when Kalman Schulman, in the introduction to his *Divrei yemei olam* ('World History'), transposed into Hebrew the division of the nations and the map of their distribution from Weber's *Allgemeine Weltgeschichte*, he knew full well that his readers would not view his ethnic

---

[14] H. Graetz, 'The Correspondence', 206. See also M. Graetz, *From Periphery*, 229–30.

[15] Allen, *The Legend of Noah*, 113–37; Reill, *The German Enlightenment*, 75–99.

[16] Mallory, *In Search of the Indo-Europeans*, 266–72; Poliakov, *The Aryan Myth*.

[17] Charlesworth, *The Old Testament*, 71–5. See F. Schmidt, 'Jewish Representations of the Inhabited Earth' and Hay, *Europe*, 7–15. Josephus and the author of *Jubilees* adapted the biblical picture to the Hellenic view of the *oikoumenē* as comprising three continents, Europe, Asia, and 'Libya', i.e. Africa.

map of the world as an extraordinary innovation: the children of Japheth, who had lived in Asia Minor, spread throughout Europe; the children of Ham settled in Africa. And, in the spirit of the time, he added the various traits of the races: these 'heads' (as Schulman translated the German *Rassen*) were, from ancient times, 'different from each other in their temperament, in all their faculties, in their intelligence, in their bodily structure, in the shape of their heads, and in the appearance of their faces'. The children of Japheth were people of refined tastes who excelled in every art and craft, whereas the peoples of Asia were characterized by a 'religion filled with adages, imaginings, and visions'. The children of Ham lacked an 'inner feeling', a lively imagination, and poetic skill. Since the children of Japheth lived in a temperate climate, they developed an inquisitive nature and delved into the roots of phenomena external to man, in nature, and gave to the world 'eternal laws, crafts, and a knowledge of the beautiful and the sublime'.[18]

In his *Ideen zur Philosophie der Geschichte der Menschheit* (1784–91), Herder wrote that the Jews continue to be an Asiatic people in Europe 'foreign to our part of the world, inextricably the prisoners of an ancient law given to them under a distant sky'. Some hundred years later, this alienation—now based no longer on cultural and religious differences, but on racial differences as well—provided an explanation for the Jews' inexorable status as strangers in Europe. In 1882, in Odessa, M. L. Lilienblum recorded an inspiration that he said came to him 'at night as I lay in bed':

Yes. We are strangers . . . We are strangers not only here, but in the whole of Europe, for it is not the homeland of our people. . . . Now I have found an explanation for the word 'antisemitism'. . . . When our faith was strong, we were strangers in Europe on the basis of our beliefs, and now, when nationalism is strong, we are strangers on the basis of our race . . . Yes, we are Semites . . . among Aryans; the children of Shem among the children of Japheth, a Palestinian tribe from Asia in the countries of Europe . . . It is true that the peoples of Europe also came from Asia, but then they had no history, and were not particular peoples. And since the day they came of age and gained a historical life, they have been the peoples of Europe, and we, the children of Shem among the children of Japheth, have been foundlings, uninvited guests.

And in this spirit he wrote to the poet J. L. Gordon in 1888 (a letter quoted at length in Chapter 7), stating that when he addressed the question of modern antisemitism,

this investigation led me to a well-known path, of which I, so preoccupied by

[18] Schulman, *Divrei yemei olam*, i. 11–12.

everyday matters, had till then taken little note. This is the natural difference between the children of Israel (and perhaps all the children of Shem) and the children of Japheth, at that time the Aryan family, the first of which were the Greeks, whose brethren later followed in their footsteps.[19]

This racial division became, in the course of the nineteenth century, a standard fixture of the intelligent and educated Jew. In this manner, nation was associated with race in the Jewish conceptual world. Race was perceived as being parallel to nation, or as endowing the nation with greater immanent historical depth.

THE SEARCH FOR A NEW JEWISH PHYSIQUE

The first reaction to the anti-Jewish stereotypes was to amend the physical image of the Jew and to propose new ways to improve it.

Even Mendele's narrator, who reacts so sarcastically to the new racial concepts, is himself not free of stereotypes. As soon as he sees his fellow traveller entering the railway car, he instantly knows he is a Jew. Why? Because he was 'so Jewish in every detail: a lean man, with a scrawny neck, a bent back, and a long nose'. In other words, the stereotypical physiognomy of the European Jew was taken for granted by the narrator, himself an East European Jew. However, Mendele Mokher Seforim nowhere hinted that there is any link between body and soul: that the Jew's physiognomy tells us anything about his inner nature.

The modern Jew, who saw himself in the mirror of the Other—in keeping with the ideal norms of Europe—could not but shrink from his physical image as portrayed in this European mirror and consequently in antisemitic literature. In many Jewish writings we find this negative portrait of the Jewish type seemingly internalized and adopted, and a resulting attempt not to refute the portrait but to change it, to change the Jewish physiognomy and to create a new Jew from the standpoint of physical traits as well. In actual fact, he contrasted himself not with his real, flesh-and-blood European neighbour, but with the portrait of the ideal man: the outwardly perfect European man.

The idealized portrait of the Greek in European culture was one of the models for shaping the idealized portrait of the new Jew—and in particular the Hebrew Palestinian Jew. In fact, in modern Hebrew literature, two models contended with each other in shaping the ideal Jew: the Greek model, which describes the ideal man as tall, blond, and blue-eyed, and

---

[19] Lilienblum, *An Autobiography*, ii. 196, and see *Igrot Lilienblum*, ed. Brieman, 200.

the Russian model, which describes the new Jew as black-haired and dark-eyed. In some Romantic literature, in particular the Russian, the dashing and courageous hero always had black hair and dark eyes. Nevertheless, the new Jewish *persona* was depicted as the exact opposite of the Jewish *persona* of the Diaspora. He is erect ('as sturdy as a cedar'), he is tanned by the sun, has beautiful eyes and a thatch of black hair; he is healthy, physically strong and vigorous, undaunted by hard work and exertion, and so on. These physical attributes reflect the new mental and psychological attributes: the new Jew is close to nature, self-confident, dynamic, courageous, laughing, singing, and dancing; he loves hard work. He is the fruit of two vital rejuvenating forces: on the one hand the nationalist ideology, which motivates the Jew to change his physical appearance through physical training, manual work, and the like, and on the other the national rebirth in Palestine, where the new social atmosphere creates a new man. To this utopian and romantic idealization of reality, which described types that were the height of perfection, were added anthropological studies that investigated whether changes in their environment and human circumstances—life in Palestine, changes in diet, in climate, physical activity, and the like—did in fact create a new Palestinian type.[20]

A direct link was established between the mind and the body. The new Jew was meant to be 'healthy in body and soul', and the Zionist revolution was conceived as an aesthetic revolution. Almost all the Zionist movements, from the left to the right, internalized and fostered the negative attitude towards the Jewish type in the Diaspora—the Jew with a 'scrawny neck, a bent back, and a long nose'—and the positive portrait of the Jew possessed of inner and outer splendour, endowed with the new aesthetics and new virtues of the revisionist ideology and of the born-and-bred Palestinian Jew rooted in the life of nature and labour, in the ideology of the Labour movement. These images became a central motif in the educational system, in socialization, and in all layers of culture. At no time in the past were the Jews so troubled by the question of their physical appearance as in the modern era. The remaking of the Jew, even from the physiognomic and aesthetic viewpoint, became a key feature in the national ideology. It became a demand for an overall metamorphosis and the creation and moulding of a Jew in total contrast to the Diaspora Jew, a new Jew who would meet the aesthetic requirements and ideals prevailing in contemporary Western culture.

[20] On this subject see Gilman, *The Jew's Body*; id., *Jewish Self-Hatred*, 270–86; B. Even-Zohar, *The Emergence of the Model*; Patai and Patai, *The Myth of the Jewish Race*.

RACE—DETERMINISM AS A LIBERATION FROM METAPHYSICS

However, the use of the term 'collective character traits' based on 'race' had a deeper significance than the desire to present an aesthetic and physically healthy Jewish image or to replace the set of accepted ethnic stereotypes. Beyond that, the deeper change in self-consciousness and self-definition was anchored in the very definition of the Jews as a race with characteristics peculiar to it, and in making the natural essence of the Jews the foundation and source of their identity and culture. It was neither the revelation at Mt. Sinai nor the forty formative years of wandering in the desert that created Jewish distinctiveness; it was the product of the special inner essence (spirit and energy) of the Jewish collective. This inner collective spirit was considered the manifestation of the Jews' racial traits. Jews became a 'race' in the modern sense of the term and Jewish nationalism an 'innate' nationalism. This last concept, *innate nationalism*, was revolutionary in its essence and was regarded by traditional Jews as heresy.

The concept of race was absorbed into the Jewish intellectual world from the second half of the nineteenth century.[21] It had two major strands. In one, the more prevalent, the notion of purity of race was rejected as a-historical. A race is a human creation in history, a composite of a mixture of peoples in historical circumstances that, like a melting-pot, has fused them all into one major group. This does not mean a race has a homogeneous ethnic origin but rather that it has a collective psyche, crystallized in a certain time-period, that creates an immanent collective individuality informed by characteristic spiritual traits. It is, in the language of the time, a psychological recipe. Ze'ev Jabotinsky, who, like others of his day, addressed the issue of race quite extensively, stated that what is generally known as race is always the product of the fusion of different peoples. There is no European race in the sense of one racial origin, and all the peoples of Europe are in fact different races, i.e. separate nations, each with its own peculiar psychological recipe. The Jews, too, are a product of a mixture of peoples, fused together in the circumstances of time, who by adopting a cohesive world outlook became a race, i.e. a nation characterized by particular spiritual qualities; for it is not the Jew's ethnic origin but his religious idea that is the determining factor. The Jewish essence is determined by the realization of this religious idea. In this sense, Jabotinsky was actually adhering to the approach of the Sages;

---

[21] See, for example, M. Graetz, *From Periphery*, 225–63.

the difference was that in his eyes the realization of the religious idea did not necessarily mean the observance of the commandments.[22]

In the other, more radical, strand, the principle of racial purity was adopted. The claim was made that from the earliest stages of history, racial traits were moulded and have since been preserved intact. Ethnic purity of origin is regarded as essential for the purity of the spiritual qualities. However, it is important to note that in speaking of a Jewish race, the Jewish polemicist of the nineteenth century was not referring to a racial hierarchy that ranked certain races and peoples as inferior or superior.

Secular Jewish intellectuals could not escape the influence of the theories and teachings so prevalent at the time. Once they had discarded the idea of divine chosenness and revelation, idealism was their sole refuge from crude historical positivism. This idealism attributed the unique national genius to an inner inspiration and revelation, for the Jews as well as for the Greeks.

The pioneers of the idea of innate nationalism were in fact divided over which approach was preferable—the idealistic or the positivistic. When Heinrich Graetz tried to explain the disparate natures of the Jewish and the Greek 'spirits', he employed a Greek source:

An ancient Greek maxim expresses pointedly the relation between strength and weakness. Nature has given to each creature different means of defence: the lion his jaws, the ox his horns, the bee its sting, and woman her beauty. An artistic picture of early date represents, in a striking manner, how weakness conquers strength, Venus riding on the lion's back, and taming it. The human spirit, which seems but a breath compared with the mighty powers of nature, yet rules them, and makes them subservient to its interest.[23]

From this Greek maxim, Graetz concluded that the intrinsic spirit of a people determines the national ideal, the power that creates the national energy and its product. He continued: 'The ideal of the Greeks was beauty and science; but this ideal only served them for comfort, pleasure, and enjoyment. Did they ever show any self-sacrifice or produce any martyrs for these ideals?' It is not the parallel that is important to us here, but the source: the characteristics of the nation, and in particular its creative ideal, are a creation of nature. What does this new emphasis on nature as the creator of the national ideal stem from?

The aspiration for liberation from metaphysics and the search for a tangible natural ontological basis for the historical unity and distinctiveness of the Jewish people are among the more striking expressions of the change

---

[22] Jabotinsky, 'Race'.   [23] H. Graetz, 'Historical Parallels', 264–5.

in Jewish thought in modern times. They were born in response to the challenge of the Romantic, *völkisch*, racial and even racist conceptions that were prevalent during the nineteenth century, which identified the Jews as a nation possessed of collective ontological characteristics.[24] This response took the form of inverted acculturation; that is to say, the adoption of concepts and assumptions from the outside in order to reach conclusions opposite to those arrived at by the original users of these assumptions. I do not mean to claim that this concept became the dominant one, but it can be found in many texts as an axiom or 'topic', and its use was taken for granted. The semantic field of prevalent terms such as 'Jewish mentality', 'national character', 'Jewish genius', 'Jewish brains', and the like, stemmed from it. Even in many Jewish circles it is almost an a priori idea that Judaism as a historical entity is based on innate traits.

There were at least two compelling needs and motives for the penetration of these terms and the frequent use made of them in the new Jewish intellectual world:

(i) to provide a defence against the accusations that ascribed the negative character and traits of their religion, their culture, and their society to the negative 'racial' characteristics of the Jews;[25]

(ii) to provide an objectivistic foundation for the authentic essence of Judaism and the Jews, and to serve as a substitute for the identification of Judaism with Torah.

Leon Pinsker (1821–91), the harbinger and then the first leader of Hibbat Zion, had stressed in his famous pamphlet *Autoemancipation* (1882) that the Jew was alien and inferior owing to his Semitic origin. This led him to the conclusion that those who refrain from speaking about their Semitic origin in Aryan society do so to no avail. The racial distinction, Pinsker wrote, is the Achilles' heel of the Emancipation. To this, Jellinek, the chief rabbi of Vienna, retorted that the Jews are Germans, French, etc., for 'we no longer have completely Semitic blood, and have lost all sense of Hebrew nationality'.[26] The spirit of Israel, wrote Peretz Smolenskin,

[24] See Stephan, *The Idea of Race*; Macdougall, *Racial Myth*; Bowler, *The Invention of Progress*, 59–71; Poliakov, *The Aryan Myth*; Mallory, *In Search of the Indo-Europeans*; Bacharach, *Racism: The Tool of Politics*; Mosse, 'Influences of the "Volkish" Idea'; Olender, *The Languages of Paradise*; John M. Efron, *Defenders of Race*; Beller, *Vienna and the Jews*.

[25] Heinemann, 'The Attitude'; Kasher, 'The Propaganda Purposes of Manetho's Libellous Story'; Gager, *The Origins of Anti-Semitism*. It is ironic that Heinrich Lowe, in criticizing broad strata of the Jewish people as representing the 'any-Jew' in Judaism, used this Hellenistic anti-Jewish argument and wrote that they are descendants of the riffraff and *hoi polloi* that were not part of the Hebrew nation. Quoted in Doron, 'Classical Zionism and Modern Antisemitism', 100.

[26] In Yoeli, *Pinsker*, 43. Jellinek is quoted on p. 21. Cf. Nordau, *Paradoxes*, 288.

'has always differed, and still does, from the spirit of the other nations in Europe, because Israel is from another family, from the family of Shem, while they are from the family of Japheth. And the spirit of the families will not change or be weakened unless they become intermingled one into the other; and the family of the Jews has not yet intermingled.'[27]

The paradox was clear. Jews used the concept of race to reject racial concepts about Jews. The new concepts became useful as the basis for the 'German ape' (as Lilienblum called it), i.e. German antisemitism. Lilienblum himself, for example, felt compelled to write an emphatic reply to what he scornfully termed 'Renan's drivel', referring to his pamphlet *The Jews as a Religion and as Race*, which was published in French and German in 1883.[28] Renan tried to prove that from the Second Temple period the Jews were no longer a pure Semitic people, or—in Lilienblum's words—that 'the Jewish people living now are no longer the progeny of ancient Israel, but a mixed multitude of unaccepted proselytes from the nations of Asia and Europe'.[29] Renan believed that owing to the proselytizing and Judaizing movement of the Second Temple period, the Jewish people since then had been comprised of elements of a different ethnic origin, and that a distinct Jewish Semitic type no longer existed. He described the attribution of racial purity to modern Jews as a weird misunderstanding. It was an error, in his view, to regard the ancient Israelite tribes as the forefathers of contemporary Jews.

Can one imagine a more convincing argument than this to counter racist antisemitism? Should not the Jewish intellectual have embraced these words with delight, since they undermined the very foundations of modern antisemitism and showed the 'German ape' to be an empty vessel? However, the response was quite different. Graetz, for example, did feel that Renan's words offered an inoculation against antisemitism, but said this was more in the nature of an epidemic which no vaccine could contain.[30]

---

[27] Smolenskin, 'Et lata'at', 95.

[28] See Y. Shavit, '"Semites" and "Aryans"'.

[29] 'Unaccepted proselytes' (*gerim gerurim*) are people who took upon themselves the Jewish religion but were not accepted by the Jewish community (bAv. Zar. 3*b*).

[30] H. Graetz, 'The Correspondence', 244–5. See too Anatole Leroy-Beaulieu's response in his chapter 'Are the Jews Pure Semites?' (*Israel among the Nations*, 100–22). He accepts the view that Jews are not a 'pure Semitic race' (and argues, on the other hand, that the Christian nations have an admixture of Jewish blood). But he believed in the uniqueness of the Jewish people in both its physiological and psychological features, and in contrast to Renan, he held that 'there is a predominant Jewish type, which may be called Semitic' (112–13). The classical type is: 'A long and generally an oval face, a narrow forehead; thick arched eyebrows, often almost running together; large and sometimes blinking eyes, with heavy lids, that give the eyes a half-closed appearance; a long, curved nose, pinched at the base; rather thick lips, and a somewhat receding chin . . .'. This was based on portraits of Sephardi Jews in Amsterdam by Rembrandt.

Here Graetz reacts as if he understood very well the English lady's words of warning. He was not the only one. Other scholars too recognized the danger, for example Simon Dubnow, who preferred to adopt another view of Renan's contradicting the deterministic view—which Renan himself had expressed on numerous occasions—that a nation is a 'perpetual referendum', and hence the Jewish national consciousness has a subjectivist, not a racial, nature.[31] Lilienblum, on the other hand, responded with rage, reminiscent of the reaction of the Greek intelligentsia about fifty years earlier to the theory of the German scholar J. P. Fallmerayer, who in his *Geschichte der Halbinsel Morea* (1830) asserted that the Greeks were not the descendants of the glorious Hellenes of the past, but rather the offspring of Albanian and Slavonic tribes: there was not a single drop of Hellenic blood in the Christian inhabitants of the new Greece, nor were they descendants of the ancient Greeks; only a romantic could dream about the resurrection of the ancient Hellenes in the nineteenth century and regard modern Greeks as the offspring of Alcibiades, Sophocles, and Plato.[32] These words recall an anecdote about Shelley, who after publishing his dramatic poem *Hellas* was taken to see Greek sailors on a ship anchored in the harbour. Upon his return, he admitted that he had to accept the sad fact that there was no connection between them and the Hellenes of the distant past, and that the latter had long disappeared from the earth. Fallmerayer's theory struck a blow at the Greeks' sense of self-esteem, based on their claim of being the direct heirs of classical Greece, a claim that was also the underpinning of Western philhellenism.

To Lilienblum, similarly, Renan's theory was ignorant, perverse, and antisemitic; indeed the very words designed to free the Jews from racist categories were for him a blatant expression of an ethnocentric antisemitism that would supplant theological antisemitism and negate the singularity and individuality of the Jewish people—that same racial individuality which was the substitute for the theological definition. Hence his determined attempt to prove that Jewry was not a disorderly mixture of peoples, but rather a pure people, constituting a direct genetic and ethnic continuation of the biblical Israelites. The radical spiritual conclusion was that it was impossible to blur the traces of race; these would always crop up again. And the radical practical conclusion was that there was no chance of integrating

---

[31] Dubnow, 'Autonomy—The Basis of the National Plan', 79.

[32] On Jakob Philipp Fallmerayer (1790–1861), his *Morea während des Mittelalters* (1830–6), and the Greek responses to his theory see Herzfeld, *Ours Once More*, 75–96, who observes, 'Both Fallmerayer and the Greek nationalists saw the modern Greek "racial" origins as the key issue and ethnographic and historical evidence as the means of resolving it' (p. 77); also Ankori, 'Origins and History of Ashkenazi Jewry'.

the Jews into the peoples of Europe—the 'children of Japheth'—as equals among equals; physical and geographical separation between the two races was imperative. Hence each race must dwell in the locale of its historical origin, and the historical origin of the Jewish people is in the East.

In the epilogue to *Rome and Jerusalem*, Hess states that the Jews were among the most ancient races:

Jewish noses cannot be reformed, and the black, wavy hair of the Jews will not change through conversion into blond, nor can its curves be straighended out by constant combing. The Jewish race is one of the primary races of mankind that has retained its integrity, in spite of the continual change of its climatic environment, and the Jewish type has conserved its purity through the centuries. . . . Jews and Jewesses endeavor, in vain, to obliterate their descent through conversion or intermarriage with the Indo-Germanic and Mongolian races, for the Jewish type is indestructible. Nay more, the Jewish type is undeniable, even in its most beautiful representatives, where it approaches the ancient Greek type.[33]

In keeping with his genetic and organic conceptions, Hess believed that the primordial organicity of the Jewish race was preserved throughout the generations, shaping the patterns of its social and spiritual life; he also accepts the prevailing view that the 'ancient Greek type' represents the pattern of human beauty. Although he rejected Renan's negative view about the nature of the ancient Jewish historical religion, he adopted his notion that primitive languages are racial creations:

History corroborates the story of anthropology, that there were originally different human races and tribes. If the various races and peoples that still exist were not primal, then, in such places as Western Asia, Northern Africa and Europe, where peoples have lived together for thousands of years, commingling through intermarriage and influenced by common climatic conditions, there should have been produced a type, in which there is no trace of their foregone ancestors.[34]

In contradiction to the view of the 'unity of the human species' upheld by radical rationalism, Hess believed that the division of the human species into 'races' was part of the divine plan. Universal unity in the utopian future does not mean a blurring of differences, but rather the creation of a multiracial mosaic existing in harmony and unity.

'Hess was an outspoken race theoretician . . . But [he] was far from following Gobineau, Chamberlain, or even the Slavophile theorist', wrote Syrkin. 'For them there were worthy and worthless races and nations . . .

[33] *Rome and Jerusalem*, trans. Waxman, 59–61. Hess adopted this theory from Gobineau's *Essai sur l'inégalité des races humaines* (1853). See Buber's introduction to the Hebrew translation of *Rome and Jerusalem*, 9–21, and Avineri, *Moses Hess*, 201–8.

[34] Hess, *Rome and Jerusalem*, trans. Waxman, 182–3.

But with Hess all nations are in fact chosen people.'[35] It is therefore easy to acquit him of racism as defined at the start of this chapter; moreover, in respect of modern conditions he spoke not of races or peoples, but of civilizations and genuine human types.

Racial theories permeated the world-view of the radical Jewish intelligentsia from various sources, sometimes without due consideration of the conclusions that might be drawn from them. For example, Nathan Birnbaum, under the influence of Houston Stewart Chamberlain and his infamous book, *Die Grundlagen des 19. Jahrhunderts* ('The Foundations of the Nineteenth Century', 1899), adopted as axiomatic the continuity of races and the biological determination of thought. The difference between them lay in the fact that Birnbaum assigned the Jews, as Semites, to the 'white race' and consequently to European civilization. He believed that a human being's disposition (*Gemüt*) is rooted in biology.[36] Nachman Syrkin argued that the Jews are a specific race, a group possessing special 'psychic and physical properties', it being these that determine the foundations of thought and feeling and express themselves in different modes of relating to the world and to life. These are innate properties, passed down from generation to generation.[37] The socialist thinker Chaim Zhitlowsky expressed a similar opinion in a book written in Yiddish, *Thoughts about Changes in the Historical Fate of the Jews* (1887). In order to buttress the Jews' right to live in multinational Russia, he treated 'nationality' as a racial phenomenon characterized by shared psychophysical traits inherent in each and every individual who belongs to a certain grouping. A nation, according to his definition, is a human group whose spirit is rooted in the hereditary traits of the race and evokes the forces of spiritual creativity that characterize it and determine its role in history. Race served as a new historical and psychological principle, a basis for the self-definition of belongingness and continuity, a shield against assimilation.

Many were alerted to the latent dangers in the racial recipe. Graetz, for example, preferred the dualistic concept of struggle and reconciliation between 'the faculties of the body' and 'the faculties of the soul', between Jewish ontology and Jewish phenomenology. The uniqueness of the Jewish people was, in his view, the harmonious interaction between these faculties. The inordinately talented Hellenic and Latin nations perished from the earth because they had not assimilated this happy balance. Within the context of Judaeo-Christian polemic, it was the famous controversy with

---

[35] Frankel, *Prophecy and Politics*, 297.
[36] A. Schlesinger, *Lev ha'ivri*, ii, fo. 80b, trans. Silver, 'The Emergence of Ultra-Orthodoxy', 68.
[37] Doron, *The Zionist Thinking of Birnbaum*, 63–4.

Treitschke that motivated Graetz to emphasize, under the influence of Hess, the value of the ontological racial factor as a creator of 'essence'. One might well doubt whether the racial principle was really capable of explaining the Jews' obstinate and miraculous will to survive. Graetz's reply was vague and characteristic: indeed, he views the Jewish will to survive as a miraculous fact, which attests to their vigour for life (the 'will-to-live', in the language of Ahad Ha'am). He never overlooks the dangers, but it is impossible for him not to adopt an explanation that is both natural and miraculous—positivistic metaphysics—of the unquenchable and everlasting vital force of the Jews. He assigns more weight to the explanation itself than to the heavy and dangerous shadow that it is liable to cast on the Jews and their survival. And let us not forget, this will-to-live is meant to explain the historical perseverance of a national minority—and not to justify more than a sense of spiritual superiority that compensated the Jews for their miserable life.

Idealism, vulgar positivism, and conservative mystic Romanticism often intermingled. An interesting example is Arthur Ruppin's four-volume *Sociology of the Jews*, which was based on his earlier work *Die Juden der Gegenwart* (Berlin, 1904). Since Ruppin (1876–1943) was Professor of the Sociology of the Jews at the Hebrew University of Jerusalem, the book merits discussion. In the first volume, which deals with the racial position (*Rassenstellung*) of the Jews,[38] Ruppin stated that the issue of the race and traits of the Jews played a significant role in the argument about the 'Jewish question', and that it was therefore important to clarify the definition and traits of the 'Jewish race'. He adopted the view that races were created out of a mixture of ethnic groups, but once the various races were fused into one nation, they were imbued with permanent and immutable qualities of spirit and character. Hence the Jews are a branch of the white race, which evolved mainly from the group of peoples of the Mediterranean (*homo mediterraneus*) and of central Europe and eastern Asia (*homo alpinus*)—which are branches of the white race.[39]

Ruppin did not accept the conventional tripartite division (Semites, Aryans, Hamites); in his breakdown, Semites and Aryans belong to the 'white race', into which he places all sorts of imaginary types that appeared

---

[38] Syrkin, 'Geza, amamiyut vele'umiyut'.

[39] Ruppin, *The Sociology of the Jews*, i. His extensive dependence on German anthropology (dealing with *Rassenzusammenstellung*), especially on F. von Luschan (e.g. *The Early Inhabitants of Western Asia* and *Völker, Rassen, Sprachen*), is shown in his notes. The irony is that one of Ruppin's sources identifies a Greek type as a component of the Jewish race and claimed it was a result of the fusion of the 'Aegean element' (Philistine) with the Jewish people. On Ruppin see Reuveni, 'Sociology and Ideology' and John M. Efron, *The Defenders of Race*, 123–74.

in contemporary ethnographic and anthropographic racial morphologies. He attempts to delineate the complex and dynamic changes of the 'racial' structure in which Jews were mixed over the centuries with the different branches of the white race. The genetic dynamics of the Jewish people within the bounds of the white race thus challenges the validity of the Semitic myth by exchanging one genetic ethnic map for another. The flight from Semitism served here, as it did for others, as an escape from the negative traits that had been attached to the Semitic race as well as from the not always convenient proximity of Jews and Arabs within the same race. An amorphous white or Eastern race devoid of any historical or geographical boundaries was the way out of this quandary.

Thus, according to Ruppin, the Jewish race, after being fused, forged, and shaped, kept its psychological uniformity throughout all the centuries. Nevertheless, he was unwilling to accept a static view—to conclude that the Jews, as soon as they were moulded, became a closed, frozen community, impervious to change. He was not concerned with the primal qualities of the Jews, but rather with their modern attributes. He therefore attributed to the Jewish 'soul' traits such as shrewdness, diligence, ease of mobility, quick-mindedness in theoretical matters, rationalism in religious matters, and so forth. The Jews, according to Ruppin, have a quick grasp and a good sense of orientation. Since mystery and mysticism are alien to them, they have always been urban dwellers and entrepreneurs and tended to maintain the existing social and political order. They are a dynamic human species because at one time they tend to maintain the existing social and political order, and at another are dynamic and capable of adapting to, and even being in the vanguard of, historical changes; here, ironically, his Jewish type was akin to the depiction of the Jew in antisemitic literature, which described him as a pioneer of destructive and divisive modernism! Ruppin's Zionism was an outcome of his fear that in an era of radical change, the Jewish race would have difficulty in preserving its traits and would become assimilated; therefore it required a country of its own.[40]

THE JEWS AS A NATION:
FROM JUDAISM TO JEWISHNESS

Belonging to the Semitic race caused a problem, because the ancient Semites were pagans, and the modern Semites were Arabs. Consequently, the prevailing position was not to attribute the traits of Jews to an overall

---

[40] Ruppin, *The Sociology*, i. 33–4.

Semitic race, but to a special separate race, or, in other words, to regard the Jews as a singular people with singular traits. In this there was next to no disagreement between secular and observant Jews; the fundamental debate was about the source of values, not their content. There was agreement on a shared system of values between those who believed in their revelation and those who believed in their immanent (anthropocentric) development; but the proposition that the Revealed Law is not the source of unalterable values, but rather that a human essence (reason) gives rise to values that can be changed in changing circumstances, bore an enormous revolutionary potential.

For example, Philo asserted that, at the Passover sacrifice, the children of Israel were not a mere multitude or nation or people, but a congregation that came together not only in body but also in mind to sacrifice with one character and one soul.[41] But the mind was not man-made, based on political constitution (or culture), but on divinely revealed laws.[42] Secular Jews also shared the belief in the unity of body and soul, or spirit, but the spirit was not created by a revelation that shaped a group of people into a nation with a specific system of values; rather, it was a historical creation, the outcome of historical development. Thus, in Lilienblum's view:

The nature of men does not change, but the appearance of their inner virtues takes on a new form and the things we define take on new names. In the Middle Ages, religion was a sign of the alien, and now nationality and race. These are the household gods (*lares et penates*) that are now taken up by the peoples of Europe replacing the ideal of religion in bygone times. The Jew is not the Teutonic child of the German people, nor is he a Mongol-Magyar of the Hungarian people, nor Slavonic man, but one of the sons of Shem, and is by necessity a stranger.[43]

In contradiction to this view, Pinchas Razovsky, one of the rabbis who supported Hibbat Zion against Orthodox opposition, wrote:

The innate nationalists known as the intelligentsia are those whom science and learning have misled by teaching them to see in every reality orderly natural laws, and who were induced by a knowledge of ethnography to find a 'national spirit' . . .[44]

These two views express the polarity of basic assumptions. Rabbi Razovsky, like other rabbis of his time, clearly discerned the nature of secular

---

[41] *Questions and Answers on Exodus*, i. 10; 'congregation' (Armenian *zolov*) presumably represents *sunagōgē* in LXX Exod. 12: 6 *pan to plēthos sunagōgēs huiōn Israēl*, 'the multitude of the congregation of the sons of Israel' (though for *plēthos sunagōgēs* the Armenian Bible has *bazmut'iwn zolovrdean*, combining two of the words used to render the rejected terms: 'the multitude of the people').

[42] Wolfson, *Philo*, ii. 395.   [43] Lilienblum, 'Al techiyat am Yisrael'.

[44] Razovsky, *Shivat Tzion*, i (1892), 38.

nationalism, which he, of course pejoratively, labelled as 'innate' (le'umiyut tivit).[45] Observant Jews viewed it as a serious deviation from the spirit of Israel, but they were well aware of the reasons that motivated the secular intelligentsia to adopt the concept of innate nationalism. This understanding did not of course prevent the deep inner opposition that arose between Torah Judaism and natural Judaism from the last quarter of the nineteenth century;[46] these Jews were well aware that the concept of innate nationalism was heretical in nature, and constantly spoke about secular nationalism as innate nationalism in order to emphasize the heresy of rejecting the traditional stance that it is the 'Torah from heaven' that created the Jews as a people—and not vice versa. On the other hand, freethinking Jews accepted the concept of 'innate nationalism' as the correct description of their outlook. In no case did they regard naturalness as some sort of savage state, but rather, as we have seen, as an immanent source of national traits, including moral ones. The new concepts enabled its users to view Judaism as a profound and singular spiritual manifestation, not dependent on a faith in the Revelation, on the chosenness of the Jewish people, or the eternality of the Written and Oral laws, but an inner manifestation arising from the nature of the people and the ideas it engendered.[47]

In other words, in their polemic with secular nationalism, observant Jews renounced—although only in practice—the ethnic, immanent conception. This was because this conception made the people, not the revelation and the Torah, the source of ethics. In truth, however, the dispute concealed an agreement in principle. And there was further agreement in the definition of the product of the ethnic singularity of Judaism—its moral and spiritual supremacy (which we discussed in Chapter 6)—regardless of whether its source lay in the revelation and chosenness of the Jews or in the innate Jewish genius. This agreement in no way blurs the revolutionary character of the concepts of immanency, of the spirit of the people, and of the collective psyche in defining the source of Jewish ethics and in assigning a historical explanation for Jewish monotheism.

In the final analysis, these two basic assumptions—that the Jews are a special people because they belong to the Semitic race and that they are a unique people in their own right—raised the very same question:

---

[45] The intention was not to claim that 'innate' means 'primitive' or 'savage', but rather to claim an ontological origin of the characteristics and ideas; i.e. an anthropocentric claim.

[46] See the detailed study in E. Luz, *Parallels Meet*.

[47] On the development of the idea of national spirit see Reill, *German Enlightenment*, 161–89, and Iggers, *The German Conception of History*, 3–62; Barker, *National Character*; A. Smith, *The Ethnic Origins of Nations*.

is there any link between race, or a specific nationality, and culture? If such a link does exist, then however greatly the Jews are influenced by European culture, it is alien to them; their quest for contact with it can lead only to catastrophe. If such a link is not inevitable, and origin, race, or ethnic singularity do not absolutely determine cultural patterns and affinity to other cultures, then the reciprocal relations between the Jews and European culture remain open.

14

THE PEOPLE AND ITS LAND: COUNTRY, LANDSCAPE, AND CULTURE

I greet you sun and sea!
Do I not see Greece—Greece, the cradle of beautiful and noble souls?
No, for under this splendour, these roaring breakers,
the melodies of Homer blossomed,
the plays of Sophocles were composed.
SAUL TCHERNICHOWSKY, 'Sirtutim' ('Sketches')

The land of Egypt—only if you work over it with mattock and spade
and give up sleep for it [will it yield produce], if you do not, it will
yield nothing. The Land of Israel is not like that—its inhabitants sleep
in their beds while God sends down rain for them.
Sifre on Deuteronomy, 38 (ed. Finkelstein, 77)

. . . in battle no other exhortation of the marshalled men is so effective
as 'You are fighting for your native land!'
LUCIAN, Patriae encomium, 14 (trans. A. M. Harmon)

THE USES OF CLIMATOLOGY

MODERN Jewish nationalism was not only a return to history, or a re-discovery of the people and the nation, but also a return to geography, or rather to the natural native geography. According to the historical perception of the Zionist idea, the Jewish people had been uprooted from its natural geographical environment and had lived ever since in different surroundings, 'against nature'; that is, without a natural environment of its own.[1] In the Diaspora, the Jewish people adapted itself to the changing patterns of the 'host civilizations' and to the different natural environments, but nowhere did it develop a 'natural' attachment to the land and to its landscape. It is as if the course of Jewish history had run against the maxim that 'a civilization cannot simply transplant itself, bag and baggage'.[2] This Jewish alienation from Nature became a major theme in the Haskalah literature. While it usually described Gentile peasants as an almost integral part of the landscape, the Jews were described as strangers, alien to the land;

[1] Baron, 'Emphases in Jewish History'.   [2] Braudel, The Mediterranean, ii. 770.

they have no true feeling for the forest, the trees, the rivers, or the fields, a natural human feeling which all Gentile peasants possess. In contrast to this image, one of the main motifs in the literature of the national revival movement was the return to the soil and to the land, and, as an almost inevitable conclusion, the return to the natural homeland of the Jewish people: Palestine (Eretz Yisrael). Not all Jewish nationalists believed that the return to Palestine was a real possibility, and many rejected the idea, for different reasons. Some, the territorialists, were convinced that Jewish nationalism could be revived in some other land, whether in Eastern Europe itself or on some other continent; Jews, they argued, could change their geography since there was no imperative linkage in their existence and experience between geography and history. Leon Pinsker wrote in *Autoemancipation* that it was not the Jordan River or the city of Jerusalem that inspired the creation of the Torah of Judaism; thus Jews could transplant their laws and customs, their civilization, bag and baggage, to another territory.[3]

Hess's view was ambivalent, even contradictory: he believed that the climate of Palestine had a formative influence on the nature of the Jewish race, but at the same time wrote (in his Fourth Letter) that 'The Jewish race, throughout the world, possesses the ability to acclimatize itself more than all other races. Just as in the native land of the Jews, Palestine, there grow plants of the southern and the northern zones, so does this people, of the temperate clime, thrive in all zones.'[4]

In other words, the contradiction is resolved by characterizing the Palestinian climate as 'universal', one that enables Jews to adapt to any climate anywhere. This theory made it easier both for territorialists (who held that a Jewish autonomous entity could be established anywhere in the world), and for Dubnow and other autonomists (who held that a national–cultural autonomy could be created in eastern Europe), to make use of positivistic reasoning. Franz Rosenzweig took Heine's idea to an extreme, asserting that the myth of the Jewish people is not an autochthonous myth, and hence is free of the restrictive attachment to the land.[5]

From a Zionist point of view, by contrast, the only place where the Hebrew nation could return to history and revitalize its national spirit was the land of their ancestors, their motherland: Eretz Yisrael or Palestine. This

---

[3] Pinsker, *Autoemancipation*, 53. Ironically Heine wrote that the example of European Protestantism proves that 'the morality of ancient Judaism will bloom forth in those countries just as acceptably to God as, in the old time, it blossomed on the banks of Jordan and on the Heights of Lebanon. One needs neither palm trees nor camels to be good . . .' (*The Prose Writings of Heine*, ed. Ellis, 313).

[4] Hess, *Rome and Jerusalem*, trans. Waxman, 61.

[5] Rosenzweig, *Star of Redemption*, 300.

Zionist Palestinian orientation gave rise to many different questions and dilemmas, which the Zionist ideology had to confront and answer.[6] Among them was the need to give convincing reasons why the national revival could take place only in Palestine as the historical-national homeland of the Jewish people. A second need was to prove that the Jews had an innate emotional relationship to Palestine and its soil. A third was to provide non-theological reasons for the historical link between the Jewish people and its country, that is to say for the existence of an affinity not based on the idea of the Covenant or the observance of the commandments,[7] but rather an affinity constituting a natural link between environment, nation, and culture. To these one must add the desire to prove that the traits of the Jewish people were shaped in Palestine, and in this way to provide a positivistic historical explanation for the enigma of the creation and crystallization of the Jews as an ethnic and cultural unit. If the aim of Zionism was to realize a cultural revival, then such an authentic revival was possible only in the historical homeland in which the original Israelite culture was forged, because a national culture is an authentic collective creation inextricably linked to the natural landscape in which it was created.

One such reason was provided by the theory of climate, which enjoyed a great revival in the nineteenth century under the influence of Romanticism and the science of geography. This theory became necessary, or at least useful, because in the eyes of many, a return to geography—to Palestine—was perceived not as a return to history but as an act against the course of history.

It is well known that the people of Israel since antiquity had a clear vision of the geography of their land (as a matter of fact, they had different visions of it). A vast literature was devoted, from the Bible down to the aggadah and medieval Jewish tradition, to praising the fine nature of the land, attaching to it all kinds of good properties ('land of milk and honey').[8] But it should be noted that there is a basic difference between literature dedicated to a celebration of the land and its properties and the literature of *la géographie humaine*. The former sings the praises of the landscape and its features and all the good it lavishes on its inhabitants; the latter deals with the way in which the landscape moulded the psyche of the people. The former is firmly planted in the soil of literary convention; the latter in climate theory.

The ethnographic excursuses in Hellenistic historical literature, follow-

[6] See Vital, *Zionism: The Formative Years*, 267–347.
[7] Weinfeld, 'Inheritance of the Land'.
[8] See Bialik and Ravnitzky, *The Book of Legends*, 356–71.

ing the example of Herodotus,[9] usually opened with a description of the natural environment. This physical character was regarded as an essential background for an understanding of the people's traits. The proponents of climate theory all averred a causal link between the climate and collective character traits.[10] According to Hippocrates in *Air, Water, Places* (ch. 23), 'A variable climate produces a nature which is coupled with a fierce, unsociable, and hot-headed temperament . . . Conditions which change little lead to slackness; variations to toughness of body and mind.' According to Aristotle (*Politics*, vii. 7, 1327^{b}23–33) the men of the cold north are full of spirit but wanting in intelligence, those of the hot east are clever but wanting in spirit; the Greeks are all three, and hence are free, have the best government, and could rule everyone else if they had a single state.[11] On the other hand, there were those who found the people of the East wise in the art of astronomy, owing to the expanse of their plains. This Hellenistic climate theory, which became a *topos*, has its echo in the writings of Philo, who believed that 'Greece alone can truly be said to produce mankind . . . and the cause of this is that the mind is naturally sharpened by the fineness of the air' (*De Providentia*, ii. 66).[12] According to the Book of Jubilees (viii. 29–30) the heritage of Japheth is cold, that of Ham hot, but that of Shem (including the land of Israel) 'is neither hot nor cold but a mingling of hot and cold', and thus (§ 21) is 'a blessed and spacious land, and all that is in it is very good'.[13] However, Jubilees did not associate the characteristics of the land with the traits of the people, but intended only to praise the land.

From the Middle Ages onwards climatology met with ever greater success.[14] Judah Halevi's ethnology bears the imprint of the Hellenistic climate theory, which he utilizes to explain the unique nature of Hebrew prophecy. According to him, Palestine is singled out by its air, its soil, and its skies,

---

[9] See his geographical excursus at *Histories*, iii. 106–17.

[10] See J. O. Thomson, *History of Ancient Geography*, 106–10, with sources at p. 108 n. 1; J. H. Levy, 'Tacitus on the Antiquities of the Jews'; G. E. R. Lloyd, *Hippocratic Writings*, 167. On the place of such arguments in ordinary Greek thought see Dover, *Greek Popular Morality*, 83–98, esp. 86, and in general Cochrane, *Christianity and Classical Culture*, 469–72, who writes that for the Christians 'the failure of classical historiography was the result of its inability to discover the true "cause" of human being and motivation' (p. 472). Here we find a clear distinction between Jewish and Christian historiography and classical historiography. Needless to say, when a Jew turns to 'positivist causes', he moves away from traditional thought and 'revives' classical concepts.

[11] G. E. R. Lloyd, *Polarity and Analogy*, 345–60; Tyrrell, *Amazons*, 60–1. See also in Lucretius, *On the Nature of Things*, vi. 1110–13.

[12] Trans. Colson, ix. 503. And see Plato, *Laws*, vii. 747 D; Heinemann, 'The Controversy on Nationalism'. According to Ptolemy, *Tetrabiblos*, 2. 3 (64), 'The inhabitants of Hellas, Achaia, and Crete . . . have a familiarity with Virgo and Mercury, and are therefore better at reasoning, and fond of learning, and they exercise the soul in preference to the body' (trans. Robbins, 139).

[13] Charlesworth, *The Old Testament Pseudepigrapha*, ii. 74.

[14] Kimble, *Geography in the Middle Ages*, 151–60.

which are invested with a quality like that of prophecy;[15] it belongs with
the 'equable' or temperate climates, the cradle of human civilization. Maimonides believed that settlement in Palestine would guarantee the proper
linguistic development of Hebrew and prevent the corruption of the language,[16] but he did not accept the claim that Palestine had any natural or
metaphysical value: its holiness stemmed from the presence of a Torah-
observing Jewish society. To be sure he repeated the theory he had learnt
from Galen and al-Fārābī, that people living in the middle zones were of
superior intellect, but Palestine had no special status in the climate zone
to which it belongs.[17]

Moses Ibn Ezra (1055–1135), in his *Kitāb al-muḥāḍara wa 'l-mudhākara*,
cites Galen's view that 'if you check, you will find that the physiognomy
of most people as well as their character and their habits are the results of
the country which is theirs'. On the basis of this approach Ibn Ezra found
a direct relationship between the nature of a language and the physical
features of the country in which it was created. His words are relevant to
our discussion, and the example he cites as evidence is the language and
culture of Greece:

The exemplary Galen thought that the language of Greece is the most pleasant and
lucid of all tongues, the most like the language of humans and the most suitable
to men of logic, whereas the tongues of other nations are like the squealing of
pigs and the croaking of frogs, and moreover, are harsh and unpronounceable.
However, al-Ḥarīzī rejected these words of his, in a statement supported by
common sense, among the other conclusions he reached at the end of his work
known as the Book of Doubts; *quod vide*. But the truth is that this people, I refer to
the Greeks, displayed a true interest in the subjects of wisdom and philosophy, and
the study of exact sciences and logical and natural writings, as well as the divine
wisdom, the end purpose of whose loftiness lies in its power to bequeath the
next world. And this nation possessed such political and economic manners and
enlightened and wondrous philosophical treatises that the names of all philosophy
are Greek names. Thus the *rishonim*, the 'early authorities', of blessed memory,
said that God bestowed beauty on Japheth as an allusion to the wisdom of the
Greeks, who are among the children of Japheth.[18]

In the fourteenth century, Ibn Khaldûn provided a very systematic
foundation in his *Muqaddimah*. In his division of the inhabited world

---

[15] See Altmann, 'Climate Theory according to Judah Halevi'; Heinemann, 'The Controversy on
Nationalism'; Melamed, 'The Land of Israel'; Silman, 'The Earthliness of the Land'; Twersky, 'Land and
Exile'; Y. Shavit, 'The Characteristics of the Land'.

[16] Levinger, *Maimonides as Philosopher*, 90–4; Twersky, 'Maimonides and Eretz Yisrael', 361–71.

[17] Kreisel, 'The Land of Israel and Prophecy in Medieval Jewish Philosophy', 46–7.

[18] Ibn Ezra, *Sefer ha'iyunim*, 30–1. See Rosenthal, *The Classical Heritage*, 43–4.

into seven zones, Syria is part of the middle zones whose inhabitants are 'temperate in their physique and character and in their ways of life. They have all the natural conditions necessary for a civilized life . . .'.[19]

Nor did climate theory perish with the Middle Ages. Isaac Cardozo, in his *Las excelencias de los Hebreos*, writes in the same vein as Ibn Ezra that 'the Hebrews are natives of Syria, which lies in a torrid, arid region, which is not humid or wet . . . the air is fresh and healthy and the land of Palestine is good for one's health, and its clime is moderate and perfect, as is fitting for a land chosen by God for His beloved people'.[20] Thomas Blackwell, starting from similar assumptions to those of Ibn Khaldûn, attributed the nature and language of Homeric poetry to the environment in which it took shape (as well as to the influence of the culture in which it was created):

It is not so fat and fruitful as the Plains of Babylon or the Banks of the Nile, to effeminate the inhabitant and beget laziness and inactivity, but the purity and benignity of the air, the varieties of fruits and fields, the beauty and number of the rivers, and the constant gales from the happy Iles of the Western Sea, all conspire to bring its productions of every kind to the highest perfection.[21]

According to this view, the exalted Greek concepts of nature and beauty were formed under the influence of the country's mild climate, and its broad, clear, enchanting, and gently rolling landscapes. Travellers saw the landscape of Greece with the eyes of Homer, Thucydides, Herodotus, and other ancient writers, the land seen being prefigured in Classical legend and ancient history.[22] Needless to say, the Holy Land was seen with the eyes of the Bible. For hundreds of years, these ideas served as an explanation for the special character of Greek poetry in contrast to biblical literature—an explanation rooted in a wrong image of the Greek landscape, and no less in an imaginary portrait of the Palestine landscape.

The new Jewish interest in the nineteenth century in the physical nature of Palestine and the characteristics of the land was first motivated by the desire fully to understand the tenor of biblical poetry. Solomon Loewisohn in *Melitzat Yeshurun* followed the example of Lowth, Blackwell, Herder, and others in stating that one cannot understand the poetic language of the Bible without a knowledge of the landscape that furnishes its symbols and

---

[19] Ibn Khaldûn, *An Introduction to History*, i. 167–73 (Third Preparatory Introduction); he was influenced by Ptolemy's *Geography* and al-ʾIdrīsī's *Book of Roger* (1154).

[20] Cardozo, *Las excelencias*, 53.

[21] Blackwell, *Inquiry*, 4–7.

[22] See Pemble, *Mediterranean Passion*, 113–64.

imagery.[23] The growing interest in the reality of Palestine was motivated by the notion that it is also impossible to comprehend the meaning of many ancient laws and customs without a proper understanding of the natural environment in which they were developed. Not only the Bible, but also parts of the talmudic text were not sufficiently comprehensible without a proper knowledge of the fauna and flora of Palestine. But again there is a fundamental difference between taking an interest in the nature of the land in order to understand the origins of poetical images or the meaning of certain laws, and turning the natural environment into a category of causal explanation and understanding it as a factor shaping the social order,[24] or going even further and turning it into a metahistorical explanation and understanding it as the main factor shaping the nation's world-view and 'collective psychology', i.e. the spiritual and psychological quintessence of a people.

Modern milieu theory (a term coined by Comte under the influence of Lamarck and the *géographie humaine* and *Anthropogeographie* of the eighteenth and nineteenth centuries) provided an explanation for the special character of ancient and modern civilizations. It also aspired to interpret the source of the multiplicity and diversity of the different human cultures.[25] During the first half of the nineteenth century, Jewish intellectuals became acquainted with the writings of Montesquieu, Herder, Wilhelm and Alexander von Humboldt, and Carl Ritter, and in the second half with those of H. T. Buckle, Hippolyte Taine, Gustave Le Bon, Friedrich Ratzel, and others.[26] In the course of the nineteenth century this theory gained far greater significance from a Jewish point of view than before. It was seen as capable of providing an objectivistic explanation for the unique spirit (*Geist*) of Israel. 'Since we do not believe in theological or metaphysical causes, we must assume that the cause of the growth of individuality was natural,' Klausner wrote, and 'the closest natural cause is the geographical environment and the historical circumstances.'[27] The power attributed to the physical landscape and its special quality offered an alternative explanation to belief in revelation and election. From a traditional point of view, it could be used to explain what made Palestine the locus of

---

[23] See T. Cohen's introduction to *The* Melitzat Yeshurun *of Shlomo Levinsohn*, 7–116.

[24] On the causal explanation in the *Aufklärung* see Reill, *The German Enlightenment*, 127–60.

[25] Stoddart, 'Darwin's Impact on Geography'.

[26] See Broek and Webb, *A Geography of Mankind*, 23–37. On the influence of Buckle see Y. Shavit, 'The Works of Buckle'. The influence of Herder's *Ideen zur Philosophie der Geschichte der Menschheit* (1784–91), Montesquieu's *De l'esprit des lois* (1748), A. von Humboldt's *Ansichten der Natur* (1808), Ritter's *Erdkunde* (1822–59), and Ratzel's *Anthropo-Geographie* (1882) passed through different channels. On Montesquieu see Aron, *Main Currents in Sociological Thought*, 31–76.

[27] Klausner, 'Ha'arakhim haruchaniyim shelanu', 146–52.

prophetic revelation. From a national point of view, it provided an a priori conception that every culture is attached to a distinct geographical area, which is itself one indispensable element of its composition.

According to this latter view, a nation or people is shaped within certain geographical borders, in a certain land and its natural environment. A strong imprint is left on the nature of the primal group by the geographical background in which it was formed. The natural environment is perceived as shaping the character of the people as well as its world-view. This is so because every particular type of myth which each nation invented is dependent upon the climate, the landscape, and the environmental condition. From a Jewish point of view, the primeval force of nature was essential since it could support an argument that the imprint of this primal formative period had survived unchanged throughout all the generations.

Before continuing our discussion of the milieu theory in the modern Jewish context, a distinction should be made between the search for a sense of belonging to the *moledet*[28] in Israel's ideological and cultural tradition, and the geohistorical placement (*Lage*) of Palestine within a larger region. Furthermore, one needs to distinguish both of these from the alleged deterministic relationship between the natural landscape and the human and cultural essence taking shape in it: a relationship that supposedly determines and creates a defined collective personality and a distinctive culture. A 'natural' affiliation to a country ('nativism') means an awareness (and a sense) of a link and a belonging to a defined territory, which is expressed not only in literature but also in the collective sentiments of the entire population. Consequently, a separate discussion should be dedicated to the premiss that the Jewish people has an innate 'natural' relationship to Palestine, as well as to the issue of the link between 'consciousness' and 'place'.

Another important distinction to be made is between a positivist view and an organicist view. The former regards 'geography' as a framework that calls for special patterns of adaptation and response to the conditions of physical nature; in a view of this kind, the physical conditions are seen as shaping mainly the orders of society and government. The latter posits a relationship of 'body' and 'soul' between geography and culture, and deterministic influences of the environment on the essence and consciousness of the social body.

Herder, in his *Ideen zur Philosophie der Geschichte der Menschheit*, believed that the relationship between *Volk* and *Klima* exerted by far the greatest

---

[28] One might render *patria, patrie, Vaterland*, emotive words of which English has no real counterpart (Hertz, *Nationalism*, 146–53).

influence on the creative drive of the *Urvolk*, affecting and modifying its innate tendencies. However, he asserted, they do not determine the original character since it is the *Geist* and the *Seele*, the inventive faculties of the *Volk*, that create its unique *Genius*.[29] More than a hundred years later, Oswald Spengler described this link between national culture and land as resembling that between a plant and the soil in which it grows:

A culture is born in the moment when a great soul awakens out of the proto-spirituality of ever-childish humanity, and detaches itself, a form from the formless, a bounded and mortal thing from the boundless and enduring. It blooms on the soil of an exactly-definable landscape, to which plant-wise (*pflanzenhaft*) it remains bound. It dies when the soul has actualized the full sum of its possibilities in the shape of peoples, languages, dogmas, arts, states, sciences, and reverts into the proto-soul.[30]

The environment was perceived as a concrete being that gave rise to growth and identity, determined orientation with respect to the world, and linked the world here with the world beyond.[31]

We shall see that Herder's conception was in the final analysis the most acceptable solution for Jewish thinkers as well. In any event, it is often difficult to distinguish between the two approaches since positivists like Buckle also dealt with the influence of the environment on society's mental skills, those that enabled it to create a social organization of one kind or another.

HOMER'S SUN

Und die Sonne Homers, siehe! sie lächelt auch uns.[32]

SCHILLER, 'Der Spaziergang'

The milieu theory was used to explain the emergence of the unique 'Greek spirit' or 'Greek miracle'; that is, to explain the historical wonder of the emergence of Greek classical culture. This inspired the comparison between Palestine and Greece: those two countries were depicted as two unique countries, whose disparate physical character produced two uniquely different peoples with two unique geniuses.

I have already mentioned the theory prevailing in the nineteenth century that the uniqueness of the Greeks stemmed from their Indo-European racial origin. But this theory came up against a thorny problem: there was

---

[29] Herder, *Reflections on the Idea of Philosophy of History*, ch. 1 (3–78). See Manuel, *Eighteenth Century*, 291–309.   [30] Spengler, *The Decline*, 106 (*Der Untergang*, 143).
[31] Eliade, *The Sacred and the Profane*, 56–7.   [32] 'See, the sun of Homer smiles upon us too.'

a great difference between the Greeks and other Indo-European peoples. Hence the theory of climates seemed to be more valid. Thus, for example, Carl Philipp Funke (1752–1807) in his popular book, *Mythologie für Schulen und zum Selbstunterricht* (1824) explains:

Every people, insofar as its gradual cultural development is not a product of another culture, has its own mythology. Even so most of them share certain images and ideas. However, in not a single one of the Classical peoples shall we find them in so refined and well-defined a form as among the Greeks. This is primarily a result of the felicitous geographical and climatic conditions under which they lived, the natural landscape, and the accidental circumstances.

Hegel, for example, believed—as did many others before and after him—that the peculiar spirit of the Greeks, as they developed from a mixture of peoples, was shaped by the geography of Greece. This did not impose uniformity on them, but the reverse: diversity and multiplicity. Therefore the Greeks' attention was more largely directed to themselves and to the extension of their mature capabilities.[33] The scenery of the Greek peninsula, and its symbolic heart Attica, gave rise in European literature to popular *topoi* of the landscape and its furnishings—the mountains, the sea, and the pure air. It was supposed that the clear, luminous light glowing over Attica moulded elegant philosophical concepts and inspired sculpture, which sees things in terms of patterns and reliefs, not as painting does in terms of space and surface. On the shores of the sea, at the foot of the mountains, in conditions that forced the inhabitants to labour strenuously to eke out their livelihood, a daring and courageous people developed, characterized by qualities of clarity, youthfulness, inner tranquillity, a wonderful sense of beauty, and an aptitude for rational thought, a joyful radiance of sun.[34] These qualities of character and soul are reflected in all aspects of its art and literature. Here again, one can find a combination of an organicist view and a positivist view; the first speaks about the influence of landscape on psychology, the other about its influence on social organization. According to this, the Greek city and Greek democracy are products of a society that was able to conduct its public life openly in broad daylight.[35]

Although the real nature of Greece was very remote from its idealized image, its idealistic depiction as 'Arcadia' in popular imagination since

---

[33] Hegel, *Philosophy of History*, part II, ch. 1, p. 236.

[34] Kohn, *The Mind of Germany*, 33. And see Cary, *The Geographical Background*; A. Philippson, *Das griechische Klima*.

[35] 'The climate of Greece was instrumental in making such a life possible and even its architecture reflected openness': Thomas, 'The Modern Discovery', 183. Some see the dependence of Greek agriculture on rainfall as a source of the freedom of spirit of the Greek society in the city-state—and the origin for the development of scientific thinking. See Harold Doran, *The Geography of Science*, 68–73.

the Renaissance was enshrined in the literature and became a popular *topos* received as an incontrovertible truth, and as an explanation of the source of Greek culture.[36] In the popular imagination it was stamped as a placid pastoral land of peasants, covered with forests and meadows: a young and for ever happy country, a land not visited by turbulent natural phenomena like earthquakes and volcanoes that stir the soul and induce it to believe in mysterious forces. It is mild and serene, imparting a feeling of security, and inspiring a sense of beauty, moderation, and logic. Even though Boeotia is a more fertile land than the average in Greece, Hesiod, a farmer and a Boeotian (and thus familiar with its qualities), portrays his Boeotian home of Ascra in his *Works and Days* as a hard country to live in and from which to eke out a livelihood.[37] This not so cheerful picture is much more appropriate for the real Greece. Other writers sang its praises, just as the literature of the Sages extravagantly praised the Land of Israel as a flourishing land, a land of milk and honey, despite the 'reality' of a constant shortage of water and frequent droughts; this contrast is still found in nineteenth-century Christian travel writings.

In speaking of Greece, writers, of course, were referring mainly to Attica, which is, in an ancient poet's words, 'the Hellas of Hellas';[38] even though Greece is a land of great variety, its main characteristics were said to be light, youthfulness, calm.[39] The *topos* that links landscape to psychological and intellectual traits was so pervasive that even the reliable description of the landscape and conditions of life in Greece could not expunge it. Thus Buckle wrote about the abysmal disparity between the two great Indo-European peoples—the Hindus and the Greeks:

The tendency of the surrounding phenomena was, in India, to inspire fear; in Greece, to give confidence. In India, Man was intimidated; in Greece he was encouraged . . . In Greece, opposite circumstances were followed by opposite results. In Greece, Nature was less dangerous, less intrusive, and less mysterious than in India. In Greece, therefore, the human mind was less appalled, and less superstitious . . . It is, thus, that in Greece everything tended to exalt the dignity of Man.[40]

This *topos* of Greece's landscape, so frequent in European literature, was also absorbed into Hebrew. The best-known example is Saul Tcher-

---

[36] Muller, 'The Romantic Glory', 104–5; Jenkyns, *The Victorians*, 165–74; Crook, 'The Arcadian Vision'. [37] Kitto, *The Greeks*, 35.

[38] *Palatine Anthology*, vii. 45, cf. Toynbee, *A Study of History*, i. 114–15.

[39] Kitto, *The Greeks*, 28–43. He writes that Greece 'in fact, is one of those countries which have a climate, and not merely weather'. For the Victorian vision of Greece see too Jenkyns, *The Victorians*, 164–74.

[40] Buckle, *Introduction*, 78–83.

nichowsky's poem 'Deianira', written in Heidelberg in 1901, which was obviously inspired by Schiller's poem, 'Die Götter Griechenlandes' (1788), the most famous German poem on Greece. Tchernichowsky describes an ideal Greece as a country surrounded by azure seas, a land of rolling hills covered with pine forests and olive groves that look like emerald gems set in gold and purple embroidery. Wheat and barley grow in its fields; many rivers and springs flow through its plains. Its skies are likened by the poet to deep blue eyes. He depicts the Greeks themselves in the same imaginary idealistic vein as 'men of the earth, merry and naïve, strong and sinewy; they are possessed of wisdom and courage and are very much like gods themselves'.[41]

BETWEEN SINAI, PALESTINE, AND ATTICA

The adoption of the milieu theory and its application to the history of the people of Israel raised some fundamental problems: where in fact was the spirit of Israel shaped—in Palestine or in the Sinai Desert? The sanctified Jewish tradition believes it was in the wilderness of Sinai, but the modern national ideology found it difficult to accept the tradition that the Jewish people was shaped in a place not part of the Promised Land. That claim attenuated the natural link between a people and its country. The milieu theory could be applied to explain the traditional story. Maharal of Prague, for example, argued that Sinai was selected as the place of revelation because it symbolized desolation, and a people without Torah is like a wasteland; the Torah was given to Israel to make it whole, to turn it into soil that should bring forth trees and plants. The desert is also a no-man's land in which the Torah could be given without any hindrance or intervention. It is spiritual, free of any influences by the physical environment, while a settled area is 'natural'.[42] Others believed that the desert was chosen as the place in which the Torah should be given and the people shaped because it had low and thorny mountains and was not a paradisiacal garden, for sanctity and wisdom do not come forth in pleasure or vain luxuries, but rather in torments and miseries.

According to Syrkin, 'The spirit of the desert is a monotheistic spirit . . . And the nomadic God is social. In the nomadic life there is no private land

---

[41] Tchernichowsky, *Shirim*, i. 106.

[42] See Philo's explanation in *The Decalogue*, 2–17 (trans. Colson, vii. 7–15). Soloweitschik, 'The Desert in the History and in the World-View of the People of Israel'; Kariv, *The Writings of the Maharal*, 50–1; Talmon, 'The Desert Motif'; Achimeir, 'Milchemet ha'or vehachosekh baNegev'. See also Cardozo, *Las excelencias*, 84. But according to him, Sinai was a low, not a high, mountain, for the Torah is associated with modesty, not haughtiness.

and the animals and goods belong to the tribe as a whole.'[43] Nevertheless, from a nationalist point of view, a basic change in this formative and sacred tradition was necessary in order to move the location of the constitutive shaping and forging of the people to Palestine. For the Zionist writers this theory provided a historical explanation for the eternal quintessence of the Jewish people as it took shape in its formative years when it wandered in the Sinai desert. Thus they altered the tradition and adapted a Palestinian milieu theory which revealed a necessary historical link between the land and the Hebrew national culture as it developed in Palestine.

Such an understanding of the influence of the nature of Palestine and the properties of the land is frequently found in the geographical and historical literature about Palestine that flourished in the nineteenth century. To give two examples out of many: the Scottish scholar George Adam Smith (1856–1942) stated in *The Historical Geography of the Holy Land* (1894) that conditions in which fertility comes from heaven, not the soil, is part cause of Israel's doctrine of providence.[44] Earlier, the Revd H. B. Tristram (1822–1906), a great contributor to the study of Palestinian natural history, stated in his *Land of Israel: A Journal of Travels* (1863–4) that Palestine was made the birthplace and cradle of monotheism by the amazing and wonderful variegation of its scenery, its produce, and its climate. He added another reason—because there is nothing 'romantic' about it that is likely to inflame the imagination or strengthen superstitions born of the dread that nature evokes in human beings. Both Tristram and Smith described the distinctive properties of the land in order to provide an explanation for the character of the religious history that took place in it. The prevailing idea in nineteenth-century Christian literature was that the landscape of Palestine was the soil from which universal monotheism sprang forth.

The milieu theory made it imperative on the one hand to characterize the physical character of Palestine, and on the other to determine how nature and climate affected the world-view and culture of the tribes of Israel.

Isaac Marcus Jost, the pioneer of modern Jewish historiography, depicted Palestine as a 'land of milk and honey', a country of plenitude. In place of

---

[43] In 'Die jüdische Volksstimme', 1 (1900), quoted in Frankel, *Prophecy and Politics*, 305; translated in *Kitvei N. Syrkin*, 25–7.

[44] G. A. Smith, *Historical Geography*, ch. 3; but at p. 55 he declares that the land's variety of climate permitted the coexistence of various cultures and religions: 'Palestine is almost as much divided in petty provinces as Greece, and far more than those of Greece are her divisions intensified by differences of soil and climate.' See also Baly, *The Geography of the Bible*; Ben-Arieh, 'Characteristics of Nineteenth-Century Historical Geographical Literature'; id., 'Nineteenth-Century Western Literature on Travel to Eretz Yisrael'.

the Spartan life of the desert, the children of Israel enjoyed the bountiful days of the farmer and the tiller. In Palestine, the power of imagination began to exert its influence, sapping the power of reason. The monotheistic faith born in the desert weakened, and under the effect of Palestinian nature the children of Israel grew fond of imaginary tales and vain enchantments (i.e. mythology and idolatry). Hence anyone who sees Jewry's mission as spreading prophetic morality among the nations is cautioned against returning to that territory which leads man astray. Graetz, on the other hand, in chapter 2 of his *History of the Jews*, recapitulated geographical approaches like those of Smith and Tristram, and imputed a totally different result to the influence of the varied configuration of Palestine. Graetz's Palestine is a 'land of lofty peaks and undulating crests of mountains, seen in alternation with verdant plains . . . their images are reflected upon the glittering surfaces of many waters. These towering heights . . . call forth cheering and elevating emotions.' It is also a land

of beautiful and extremely diversified landscapes . . . The climate was made salubrious by the sea breezes and the free currents of mountain air . . . Here were no miasmatic swamps to poison the atmosphere. Diseases and the ravages of plagues are to this day of rare occurrence, and only caused by infections imported from elsewhere.

This multifaceted vision can be apprehended in its entirety:

Whilst the eye surveyed, from a prominent standpoint, the objects encircled by an extensive horizon, the soul was impressed with the sublime idea of infinitude . . . Single-hearted and single-minded men, in the midst of such surroundings, became imbued with a perception of the grandeur and infinity of the Godhead, whose guiding power the people of Israel acknowledged in the early stages of its history. Sensitive hearts and reflecting minds may well be said to perceive 'the finger of God' in this region.

It is no wonder that 'from the varied charms of scenic beauty the most gifted men of this land drew their inspiration for their pensive poetry . . . which has its root in a deep consciousness of the greatness of the Creator'. Based on this view, monotheism and prophetic ethics were founded in the days when Israel dwelled on its land in Canaan, under the influence of its moderate, temperate climate, and not during the years of its wanderings in the desert.[45]

Solomon Judah Leib Rappoport, known as Shir (1790–1867), a *maskil*

---

[45] H. Graetz, *History of the Jews*, i. 45–9. On Jost see Michael, *Jost*, 22–3. Jost was influenced by Ritter and von Humboldt; in his *Geschichte der Israeliten* (1820–8) he dedicated 100 pages to the geography, topography, and climatology of Palestine.

and scholar, from 1840 chief rabbi of Prague, wrote in 1831 that the various peoples were classified according to character traits determined by their natural environment. Thus the eastern and southern peoples lived in a hot climate that weakened the intelligence and intensified instinct, but among the western and northern peoples, who lived in a cold or temperate climate, intelligence outweighed instinct; herein lay the explanation for the flowering of Graeco-Roman culture. However, the pre-eminence of intelligence and the absence of emotion led to political instability and finally to downfall; by contrast the location of the Land of Israel between these two climates resulted in a balance between the forces of passion and those of reason. A return to Eretz Yisrael, on this argument, would restore to the people of Israel the balance between reason and emotion.[46]

Members of the Russian Jewish intelligentsia—Eliezer Ben-Yehuda, Nachman Syrkin, Jabotinsky, Klausner, and others—accepted the milieu theory and used it frequently. In his famous essay 'She'elah nekhbadah' ('A Weighty Question', 1879) Ben-Yehuda wrote:

Is nationalism an empty thing? Is it the invention of humans who devised it to console their spirit? Why is this people different from any other in its temperament, the qualities of its spirit, its language and its virtues? For after all, all of these are from Nature, natural causes such as the differences between countries, their appearance and the various traits of their climes—mountains and valleys, seas and rivers, cold and warmth, humidity and dryness—all these will have an effect. And if so, do we have it in our power to change all these according to our desires? Can we order nature to change?[47]

Nature, he added, rules over man, and man is powerless to cancel the division into nations possessing disparate traits and capabilities which result from the natural environment in which they were shaped and in which they live.

Ze'ev Jabotinsky's version of the milieu theory in the national territorial context was:

The physical as well as the psychological nature of man—these are such sensitive and fine mechanisms that even the slightest difference in natural environment must exert its influence on them. The mountainous horizon must leave its special imprint on the soul of a man who was reared in the mountains, in contrast to the soul of a man reared in the plains. And thus it is in every thing; even if the only difference between two places, similar in the structure of the terrain, etc., is no more than two or three degrees in average annual temperature, even this minute difference will inevitably, over several generations, give rise to a parallel

[46] S. J. L. Rappaport, introduction to *Toledot rabenu Chananel*.
[47] Ben-Yehuda, *She'elah nekhbadah*, 39–40.

difference between the typical representatives of the two places. . . . Only if one takes a one-sided and nearsighted view of things can one deny the vast influence of natural elements on the body and psyche of man, the influence which shapes the various races . . .

In yet another article he carried this idea further:

The changing social factors exert a sharp, clear, and recognizable influence on the body and soul of man. However, far deeper than that is the influence of the slow, constant pressure, which does not let up for a minute, exerted on man by the natural landscape of the homeland, the climate of the homeland, the flora of the homeland, and the winds of the homeland. The psychological structure of the people is forged only by the elements of nature . . . Before we came to Palestine we were not a people, we did not exist. On the soil of Palestine, the Hebrew people was forged out of the fragments of other peoples. On the soil of Palestine, we grew up, on it we became citizens; we fortified our monotheistic faith; we breathed deeply of the winds of the land . . .[48]

Of all the Jewish scholars who later adopted the milieu theory that drew a detailed comparison between Palestine and Greece, Simon Berenfeld (1860–1940) in the introduction to his book on Jewish history (*Koré hadorot*, 1888) presents the most elaborate one. He traces the origin of the antinomy between Greeks and Hebrews in the effects of their different landscapes. In his view, the nature and culture of a people are a product of material and spiritual actions affected by the climate of the country, its flora, its topography, and 'many other fine details of the place'. Self-awareness and a world-view start with observing nature and interpreting the forces operating in it.

The nations that held their gods to be deleterious powers and instruments of evil for creatures in general and for the human race in particular no doubt lived in a country whose climate was mightily ruled by the forces of nature. A nation that dwelt by a sea of turbulent waters—that would flood and destroy the harvests of the land, man and beast, or make it the victim of hail and kindred forces—looked upon their god as a malevolent god, a lover of evil, who would bathe his actions in blood, trampling and tearing asunder, and there is no redeemer . . . As for the settler in a land where the climate is good and gives him his food in due season, when he begins to delve into the origins of the natural forces, he will come to know that there is a Creator and a Maker of all. Then in his soul, he will imagine a benevolent power who favours his creatures.

This basic assumption renders it easy to adopt the antithesis and its themes:

---

[48] Jabotinsky, 'Tziyonut ve'Eretz Yisrael', 120–3; 'Al teritorializm', 133–4.

The climate of Greece was entirely suited to a different conception in matters of belief. The land of Greece was the most fortunate of all lands in regard to its climate and nature, and only the Greeks dwelling in that country could bring forth the celebrated culture that affects all enlightened peoples. They observed no harmful and injurious forces, but also had no need for the magnanimity of the Creator, because the nature of their land provided them with all that their spirits desired, and more. Their physical needs were few, but their spirit was not sated by the enjoyment of spiritual delights under the cloudless skies in the vineyards of Greece. The people became accustomed to finding boundlessly great happiness in the forces of nature, created just for their pleasure. Unlike them, the Jews living in the land of Canaan would lift up their eyes to the rains of the heavens. If the rain did not fall, they felt their weakness and their need of the Creator who made rain for them from the heavens, and in the innocence of their hearts they expressed a prayer to the living God to give them rain in its proper season. They also felt that they were only flesh and blood and if God would not pour out his treasure for them, then they could not exist in the land. The Greeks did not feel any of these. The forces of nature were only for their pleasure; their entire lives were only amusement, and their entertainment was most important to this nation; who won the racing competition and the like, was a very serious question to them, a national question.

In Berenfeld's view, the Greeks esteemed the forces of nature only for two advantages found in them. The first was the perfection of power. The sun radiates its clear light in total perfection; its heat in total perfection; the rain will give moisture in total perfection; the land its harvest, and so on. The second advantage is the perfection of the attributes. The sun loses neither its light nor its heat. Thus, the Greeks did indeed materialize these powers into gods, but did not feel any great distance between themselves and the powers. They did not believe in one great power that invented everything; the gods indeed represented individual powers exalted over them, but in a sense they were merely creatures who had reached greater perfection. Human beings, in the Greek view, could also reach that level of perfection. Because of this, people from amongst their own who were exceedingly outstanding for some deed or power were revered as if they were gods. The gods depicted by Homer are the natural forces in corporeal form. However, their appearance and inner form were modelled upon human beings who had attained total perfection in their physical powers, for—as we shall learn from the history of this people—the Greeks greatly esteemed the physical powers, as well as the spiritual.[49]

Other Jewish authors espoused similar views. It was the temperate climate of Greece, they believed, that imbued the Greeks with philosophical

[49] Berenfeld, *Koré hadorot*, 7–8.

curiosity and the admiration of beauty. We have already seen that Kalman Schulman, who attributed to the Greeks pre-eminence over all other ancient peoples, ascribed the singular Greek spirit to the temperate climate that produced a culture which admittedly was unable to rise above the limitations of a 'false religion', but did make a great contribution to humankind in many important spheres.

AN APOLLONIAN AND A DIONYSIAN COUNTRY

The disparate portraits painted of Palestine gave rise to two opposite conclusions. On the one hand, it was seen as a land of plenty and profusion, which explains the attraction for the Children of Israel of idolatry expressing a belief in multiplicity. On the other hand, this plenty and profusion were seen to exist in one unified, cohesive, and harmonious framework that explained the creation of a universal monotheism connecting opposites and establishing order amongst them. These are two disparate historical interpretations of the spiritual and cultural essence of the Jewish people in the biblical era, which lead to totally different conclusions about its optimal future.

One way of resolving this contradiction was by applying Nietzsche's distinction between the Apollonian element and the Dionysian element to the nature of Palestine. According to this view, in the Israelite spirit, as well, there was constant vacillation between these two extremes. The desert period of the Jewish people created the Apollonian element in its consciousness, whereas its settlement on the land created the Dionysian. Hence the Janus-faced character of the Jewish people. The biblical scholar Menahem Soloweitschik contended that this was why the desert period is depicted by the prophets as a romantic time, as the 'golden age' of the link between the people and its God. The desert was not a barren, forbidding wilderness, but the base for the yearned-for days of innocence and purity. This idealization of the desert is the response of the historical (and social) consciousness to the intensification of the Dionysian element in the days when the people was settled on its land.[50]

This view enabled Abba Achimeir to offer a differentiation not between 'land' and 'desert' but between two separate formative regions within Palestine. Paradoxically, Achimeir, in distinguishing between the Galilee and Judaea, took up a view that originated in Protestant historical pseudo-science, which he himself regarded as one of the sources of

---

[50] Soloweitschik, 'The Desert in the History and in the World-View of the People of Israel', 26.

modern scientific antisemitism. The Galilee, he asserted, remained pagan owing to its natural environment. Judaea, mountainous and desert-like, was the stronghold of fanatical and militant national monotheism. Or, in the terms used by Arnold, the Galilee was Catholic while Judaea and the Negev were Puritanical.[51] The desert imbued the Jews with the nomadic spirit, but also with intransigence, cruelty, and other anti-pacifistic traits. Even Ben-Yehuda, who like Smith described Palestine as a land containing a great diversity of natural configurations, landscape, and climate, followed Renan's line (in *La Vie de Jésus*, 1863) in drawing a distinction between the Galilee and Judaea in regard to the nature of their inhabitants.[52]

'*Athens* and *Thebes*', wrote David Hume,

were but a short Day's Journey from each other; tho' the *Athenians* were as remarkable for Ingenuity, Politeness, and Gaiety, as the *Thebans* for Dulness, Rusticity, and a phlegmatic Temper. *Plutarch*, discoursing of the Effects of Air on the Minds of Men, observed that the Inhabitants of the *Piræeum* [sic], possest very different Tempers from those of the higher Town of *Athens*, which was distant about four Miles from it. But I believe no one attributes the Difference of manners, in *Wapping* and St. *James's*, to a Difference of Air or Climate.[53]

We have already seen that in Herder's eyes it was the genius of the people that was the most creative force. According to Buckle, European civilization was able to rise to its advanced state of progress since man was not entirely subordinate to the 'external forces' of nature. In Europe, as well as in Palestine, it was man who modified nature, and not nature that modified man.[54] As in the case of the concept of Jewish history and of Jewish ethnicity, the metaphysical and theological dogmas were rejected; instead an idealistic concept prevailed. It is the genius of the people, or

[51] Achimeir, 'Milchemet ha'or vehachoshekh'. Contrast Gross, 'Olymp und Sinai', 596, who describes the kingdoms of Israel and Judah as respectively the Hebraic Boeotia and the Hebraic Attica.

[52] Ben-Yehuda, 'He'arah me'otzar hasifrut'.

[53] Hume, 'Of National Characters', 275–6; Thebes was the chief city of Boeotia, a region associated by other Greeks ancient and modern with boorish peasants. See too ibid. 276–7 (incidentally rebutting Hippocrates' unfavourable account of Asians): 'Where any Accident, as a Difference of Language or Religion, keeps two Nations, inhabiting the same Country, from mixing with each other, they will preserve a distinct and even opposite Set of Manners for several Centuries. The Integrity, Gravity, and Bravery of the *Turks* form an exact Contrast to the Levity, Deceit, and Cowardice of the modern *Greeks*.' See Snyder, *The Dynamics of Nationalism*, 57–8; Fyfe, *The Illusion of National Character* and Barker, *National Character*. According to Gervase of Tilbury, *Otia imperialia*, ii. 3 (p. 912), as a result of the differences of the air, the Romans are grave, the Greeks flighty, the Carthaginians sly, the Gauls naturally fierce, the English distinguished by power of intellect, the Germans by vigour; cf. J. K. Wright, *The Geographical Lore*, 186. Some scholars (see Wittfogel, *Oriental Despotism*) hold that the dependence of Greece on rain, as opposed to irrigation as in Egypt or Mesopotamia, made the peasant in the hill country comparatively free from political control by the lowlands and helped to develop free societies. See J. P. Brown, *Israel and Hellas*, 22–5, and note that the rainfall in Palestine was described as 'showers of blessing' (Ezek. 34: 26).

[54] Buckle, *Introduction*, 11.

the genius of great figures, which creates new notions, new ideas, new concepts, and new culture. This was the case in Greece as well as in Palestine.[55] Anyone who did not speak in organicist terms of a mystical link to the landscape, and of the shaping influence of landscape on mind, spoke in the language of Montesquieu, who stated that the laws men enact must suit the nature of the land, its climate, the quality of its soil, and so forth. If we replace 'laws' with 'culture', we find that according to this view, men create their culture, but must adapt it to the environment, to the country in which they live. Needless to say, they must know well the nature of the habitat; the ways to adapt to it, as we have seen, can be subject to various interpretations.

GREEKS, JEWS, AND THEIR HOMELANDS

Nevertheless, since climatology was only a *topos* or a pseudo-science, it was of little help, and the problem of defining Jewish links to Palestine still remained.

The idea of nationalism was foreign to ancient Greece. The 'Hellenic alliance' was depicted in idealistic terms as a partnership of culture, not of nationality. 'Again, there is *to Hellēnikon*—being united in of blood (*homaimon*) and language, sharing temples and ritual and a common way of life' (Herodotus viii. 144); the term 'Hellene' had no political connotation, but only intellectual, spiritual, and moral meaning.[56] In the Hellenic world, local patriotism prevailed, umbilically linked to the city-state, not to a 'Greek homeland'. Greek cities joined forces against a common enemy from the outside but fought each other constantly and fiercely. The concept of an extended cultural *Hellas* existed at least by the beginning of the seventh century BC;[57] however, when a Greek spoke about 'our city, our land', what he meant by 'land' was the region in which he lived, not a defined Greece with its defined borders (such as the biblical borders, 'from Dan even to Beer-sheba'). Greek literature shows a deep sense of emotional ties to a 'native land' in the sense of a birthplace. 'Those who have a real mother-country love the soil on which they were born and bred, even if they own but little of it, and that be rough and thin, though they be hard put to it to praise the soil, they will not lack words to extol

---

[55] Klausner, 'Hamaterializm hahistori vehatenuah hale'umit' ; Kaufmann, introduction to *The Religion of Israel*, i. 21–44. Obviously from a Jewish point of departure it was impossible to link the expressions of the Jewish genius to geographical circumstances.

[56] See Finley, 'The Ancient Greeks and their Nation'.

[57] Hall, *Inventing the Barbarian*, 8.

their country', wrote Lucian; '. . . if immortality be offered him he will not accept it, preferring a grave in his native land, and the smoke thereof is brighter to his eyes than fire elsewhere.'[58] Patriotism was a powerful force in the cities of Greece (though it did not always transcend class or ideology), but it was given to the city, or at most to the regional league, not to 'Hellas' in any defined historical (and political) boundaries. The limits of the native land were the city, or the region, and not the 'country' in any defined historical (and political) boundaries.[59]

The word *patris* is often translated into Hebrew by the modern concept of *moledet*, but more accurately it should be translated as *nachalat avot* (the heritage of one's fathers) or *eretz avot* (the land of one's fathers). Here Greeks and Jews share the same notion. It appears in 2 Maccabees, when Judas Maccabaeus, after telling his men tales of the past to raise their spirits, 'made them ready to die in defence of their laws and their country' (8: 21). He is alluding to the ancestral heritage, a concept employed later by Simon in replying to claims that he had conquered a foreign land: 'We have not taken land that is not ours nor have we conquered anything that belongs to others, but rather the heritage of our fathers (*tēs klēronomias tōn paterōn hēmōn*), which had for a time been unjustly conquered by our enemies' (1 Macc. 15: 33). According to Bickerman, this term (representing *nachalat avotenu*), instead of the 'Promised Land', was adopted by the Maccabees from Hellenistic legal terminology as an alternative to the theological terminology. This new concept, which was directed against the Hellenized native population, combined ethnographic, historical, topographical, and legal arguments. Bickerman believes this to be an illuminating instance of an adoption of a Hellenistic legal conception. It appears also in Philo's *Hypothetica* (*Apology for the Jews*, 6. 1) where he speaks of the 'ancient fatherland' (*tēs patriou kai archaias gēs*) of the Jewish nation.[60] At 1 Kings 21: 3, the term *nachalat avotai* (translated as 'the inheritance of my fa-

---

[58] Lucian, *Patriae encomium*, 10–11, trans. Harmon, i. 217–19. These passages are full of allusions to the *Odyssey*: Odysseus longs 'to see the smoke leaping up from his land' (i. 57–8), and declare that 'nothing is sweeter than one's native land or one's parents' (ix. 34–5). By contrast, Abraham, commanded by an oracle to leave country, [*patrida*], kinsfolk, and ancestral home, 'hastened eagerly to obey, not as though he were leaving home for a strange land but rather as returning from amid strangers to his home' (Philo, *De Abrahamo*, 62–3, trans. Colson, vi. 35).

[59] It should be recalled that *Hellēnes* (once it had transcended its Homeric use for the inhabitants of Phthiotis in Thessaly) denoted the peoples of the whole Greek-speaking world, not merely of Greece, just as 'the People of Israel' denoted the whole Jewish Diaspora.

[60] Trans. Colson, ix. 415. No Jew during the Second Temple period would have defined his membership of the community like Cleocritus in Xenophon, *Hellenica*, ii. 4. 20–1, by shared sacrifices, feasts, choruses, military expeditions, relations by kinship and marriage, and clubs (*hetaireiai*). On the other hand, the laws of the *polis* formulate the citizens' rights and the constitution of the state, concepts missing in the Torah and halakhah.

thers' in the King James version) refers to privately owned land, not to national sovereignty.[61] On the other hand, we should not forget that the Hasmoneans turned to the Bible in order to support their arguments about their right to conquer the land from its pagan population.

The concept of *moledet* (homeland) in its modern Hebrew sense was borrowed from modern European languages and context. But this does not mean that the Jews of the Second Temple period lacked a sense of belonging or national attachment to their land, and based their claims only on theological arguments. In the Hellenistic East, many of the ethnic peoples maintained their individual character and their historical claims to their native land. In that sense, the people of Israel were no different. Hellenized Egyptian historiography, for example, lauded the land of Egypt as the cradle of human civilization, and quite a few indigenous peoples of the East tried to preserve their self-identity based on their love of country, a common origin, a common language, a traditional religion and its institutions, temples, priests, and the like.[62] However, the political and cultural unity of the various Hellenistic kingdoms was not based on a common territorial political consciousness, but on a cultural and political (incomplete) unity, which was founded on a link to the Hellenistic ruler. The unifying factor was local and municipal patriotism rather than the modern concept of the sovereignty of a people in its historical homeland, or the notion of citizenship. The Greeks and the indigenous populations had separate legal systems.[63] The Jews of that era were no less a nation than other historical nations of the time and showed their love for and natural bond to their land. The defined territory was an important and central constituent in the Jewish nationalism of the Second Temple era, and the Jewish religion of the time—unlike Christianity—was not a 'spiritualistic' religion cut off from its native territory.[64]

Just as the Hellenistic challenge motivated and prompted the Hasmoneans both to return to the Bible and to use Hellenistic concepts, so the nineteenth century, and the appearance of modern nationalism, motivated and prompted Jews to formulate a new national historiography and a new national ideology based both on biblical (and post-biblical) traditions and modern concepts. It was important to prove that beyond

---

[61] On this subject see Bickerman, *From Ezra*; Heinemann, 'The Relationship'; Mendeles, *The Land of Israel*; J. H. Levy, 'A Dispute over the Land'; Kasher, *Jews and Hellenistic Cities*, 112 n. 175. On the concept of 'historical rights' in Zionist ideology see Almog, *Zionism and History*, 181–5.

[62] In detail see Mendeles, *The Rise and Fall*.

[63] Avi-Yonah, *Hellenism and the East*; J. Geiger, 'Local Patriotism'; Hadas, 'From Nationalism to Cosmopolitanism'.

[64] Mendeles, *Jewish Nationalism*, 243–66.

the official theology there was in Jewish history a thick layer of natural and emotional bonds to the land. Consequently, a rich literature in Hebrew was devoted to this matter, motivated by the desire to prove that the Jews—like the Greeks—loved their country, felt for it as for a mother, yearned for it, and were nourished by it. From the end of the nineteenth century, a new Hebrew literature emerged for the sole purpose of nurturing national-territorial emotions—the view of man and nation as a product of the earth—and an experience of homeland. Key national ideologies of the nineteenth century were attired in Hebrew garb (the tactic of disguise). The generation born in Palestine was likened by Jabotinsky to Antaeus, the mythical Libyan giant, son of Poseidon, who was invincible when he was in contact with the earth, and whom Heracles could overcome only by lifting him off the ground (Apollodorus, *The Library*, ii. 5. 11). In his short story, 'Ba'al bayit kezayit' ('The Little Homeowner'), written in 1910, Jabotinsky describes a small Jewish boy in Palestine who had a direct link to the country and felt no need for a Zionist ideology as justification. He used the Greek mythological paradigm: 'What a marvellous Antaeus-like power is growing and ripening in this small creature, tied by a thousand hidden roots to this sacred soil; how this power will yet thrive and flourish and how many miracles and wonders has it yet to perform!'[65] In fact, the giant Alcyoneus was better suited to Jabotinsky's purpose: he was immortal as long as he fought in the land of his birth, for the soil of his homeland gave him life (Apollodorus, ibid. i. 6. 1).[66]

One intriguing example of this effort to prove the existence of natural links is the controversy between the renowned Polish classical philologist Tadeusz Zieliński and the Polish Jewish scholar Menahem Stein. In his *Hellenizm a Judaizm* of 1927, Zieliński Christianized pagan Greekness in order to Graecize Christianity, but described Judaism and the Jews as totally lacking in any natural link to country and soil. Menahem Stein, a representative *par excellence* of Jewish classical scholarship in Poland between the two world wars, responded in an extensive and vigorous essay. If Zieliński was a contemporary Apion, Stein confronted him like a modern Josephus. Among other arguments, Stein produced persuasive evidence to show that the Greeks were not the only people to

---

[65] Jabotinsky, 'Ba'al bayit kezayit', 216. *Hercules and Antaeus* is a well-known painting by Antonio del Pollaiuolo (1481). Karl Rosenkranz (1805–79), a professor in Berlin and a follower of Hegel, compared the Jews with the giant Antaeus, 'except that the giant was strengthened whenever he touched the earth, while the Jews gain new strength whenever they touch heaven' (cited by Heine in *Ludwig Börne*, book iv; Ewen, *The Poetry and Prose*, 669).

[66] See I. Malkin, *Myth and Territory*, 181–7.

revere Mother Earth.[67] He maintained that the Jews regarded the Earth as a nursing mother, endowed the land of Palestine with occult cathartic powers, and attributed to it wondrous natural qualities. Stein found such expressions of intimate ties not only in Hellenistic Jewish writings but also in the literature of the Sages: 'R. Eleazar further stated: Any man who owns no land is not a proper man; for it is said, The heavens are the heavens of the Lord; but the earth hath he given to the children of men' (bYev. 63a); 'Your brother left the bosom of his mother and embraced the bosom of a Gentile woman' (jMoed Katan 3: 81c).[68]

Quotations stressing a natural attitude towards country, earth and soil, and midrashim that spoke of the marvellous powers in the soil of the homeland began to occupy an increasingly prominent place in the new national Jewish mind-set and experience. This served as a counterweight to the dominant ideology of stipulation and reward. At their extreme pole, these concepts also gave rise to premises about a mythic monotheism (or monotheistic myth) that endows the earth with powers of creation and interprets the relationship between Israel and its land as a mystical 'sacred copulation', not as the natural and national relationship expounded in the prevalent version.[69]

This mystic-romantic ideology, as formulated, for example, by Buber or the poet Uri Zevi Greenberg, claimed to be inspired only by Jewish intellectual tradition, but it evolved under the mystic and conservative influence of European Romanticism.[70] A revealing letter in this regard was written by the philosopher S. H. Bergman to his friend Buber in 1915: 'It was only thanks to Fichte that we found parallel currents in Jewish culture, and learned to understand Judaism.'[71] What he meant was

---

[67] See A. Dietrich, *Mutter Erde*; Philo, *De plantatione*, 14—15. Stein accepted the controversial equation *Demeter* = *Gē mētēr* (Cicero, *De natura deorum*, ii. 67).

[68] See also Zieliński, *Historja kultury antycznej*; M. C. Stein, 'Mother Earth in Ancient Jewish Literature'.

[69] Almog, 'Redemption in Zionist Rhetoric'; Buber, 'Land and People'.

[70] Shapira, 'Buber's Attachment to Herder'; Buber, op. cit. For more literature on Jewish attitudes towards 'land' and 'soil' (*eretz, adamah, karka*), see Rosenberg, 'The Link with Eretz Yisrael'; Weinfeld, 'Inheritance of the Land'; Almog, 'The Land to its Workers'; Davies, *The Territorial Dimension*; Schweid, *Homeland or a Land of Promise*; Y. Shavit, *The New Hebrew Nation*; Z. Zohar, *Chinukh benuach hamoledet*. See also Walicki's chapter 'Return to the Soil', *The Slavophile Controversy*, 531–58, and A. D. Smith, *The Ethnic Origins*, 183–200. On the theory of climate in modern Egyptian nationalism see the chapter 'The Egyptian Image of Egypt: I', in Gershoni and Jankovski, *Egypt, Islam, and the Arabs*, 130–42. The Pharaonic movement spoke about an 'Egyptian mentality', 'Egyptian genius', and 'Egyptian spirit' shaped by the Nile Valley.

[71] Shapira, *Between Spirit and Reality*, 105.

that Fichte's concept of nationalism had led him to search for similar ideas in the Jewish tradition.[72]

But there were some dissident voices: those who accepted the view that Jewish monotheism had desiccated and rendered barren the Jews' natural link to the soil. The poet Tchernichowsky, for example, stated in his poem 'Ba'al ha'emek' ('The Ba'al of the Valley'):

> For Zion will be redeemed with the spade
> And its fields with labour
> With the blessing of a new god.[73]

Judaism was seen as a religion needing no territory of its own in order to exist; on the contrary, it preferred to exist without its own territory, as a religious testament, not as a nation. Not only had the Jewish religion no need of its own territory, but it was apprehensive of territory.[74] For Judaism, Palestine was a Holy Land or a Promised Land, not a national homeland. The call for a return to the ancient past, to biblical times or even pre-biblical time, was a call for the revival of a past, in which the gods symbolized a defined place, and were not a universal divinity without ties to any particular place.

However, mainstream Zionism could find in the Jewish tradition, mainly in the aggadot and midrashim, a wealth of motifs and themes on which to base an ideology that viewed Zionism as an unbroken continuation of the traditional Jewish national and territorial consciousness but with new form and new content. Lilienblum even argued that it was the Bible that had first created a national consciousness by assigning each nation its own tract of land, its laws, and its own particular gods.[75] As evidence of this, he quoted from the Song of Moses:

> When the Most High gave to the nations their inheritance,
> when he separated the sons of men,
> he fixed the bounds of the peoples
> according to the number of the sons of Israel
>
> (Deut. 32: 8)

The Bible itself, then, was the origin of nationalism and the Jewish historical consciousness. In contrast, the Hellenistic–Roman world created the universal consciousness (inherited by Christianity) that seeks to blur the natural differences between human beings and to establish one law for all; it was from this idea that universal rationalism and modern cosmopoli-

---

[72] See also Y. Shavit, 'Politics and Messianism'.
[74] Y. Shavit, *The New Hebrew Nation*, 104–20.
[73] Tchernichowsky, *Shirim*, 501–5.
[75] Lilienblum, 'Al techiyat am Yisrael'.

tanism sprang. The world of the nineteenth century and the world of the future, Lilienblum believed, were marching confidently along the ancient path mapped out by the Bible, not on the modern Hellenistic path!

The attempts to find in the Bible and in later Jewish literature evidence attesting to the existence of Jewish national-territorial self-awareness that would fit the notion of modern nationalism occupied much of the modern national Jewish intellectual endeavour. Some believed that the relationship between the people of Israel and its country was not derived from modern nationalism, but is a unique phenomenon.[76] A more radical claim was that the Hebrews were the indigenous population of Palestine. According to Johanan Levy, Hellenistic and Roman ethnography was occupied in searching for the *origo* of a people, since it perceived it as the source of its *mores* and *virtus*; it praised the *indigenae*, those who were born within, and not the *advenae*, those who came from outside.[77] The Greeks were very well aware that they were outsiders (Thucydides, i. 2) and that some Greek cities had been founded by migrants from abroad (Argos, Thebes).[78] Nevertheless, Athenian orators describe the citizens of Athens as people who were born of the earth, which gave them a mother's nourishment.[79]

The need for a new political and territorial ideology dictated the description of the Jews as *indigenae*. The ideology of the 'remnant' (Jews who were left in Palestine after the Babylonian Exile), who claimed that their link to the land was not a result of divine promise but of their remaining in the land, had been denounced in the Bible: 'Son of man, they that inhabit those wastes of the land of Israel speak, saying, Abraham was one, and he inherited the land: but we are many; the land is given us for inheritance' (Ezek. 33: 24). In 1 Chronicles 1–9 one can find the perception of the Jews as insiders and not outsiders, but it seems that this does not represent the main ideology of the book.[80] The dominant conception in the Bible and post-biblical sources was and remained one that made the right to the land depend on the divine promise and to the doctrine of reward. Before the

---

[76] Buber, *Israel and Palestine*; Tal, 'Myth and Solidarity'.

[77] J. Levy, 'Tacitus', 130–1. However, stories of outside origins are not peculiar to ancient Israel: Diodorus writes (i. 9. 3): 'Now concerning the antiquity of each race, not only do the Greeks differ, but also many of the barbarians, all declaring themselves to be autochthonous' (trans. Murphy, *The Antiquities of Egypt*, 12).

[78] Compare the story of Abraham with that of Cadmus: 'He knelt before Apollo's oracle | and asked what country he should make his home' (Ovid, *Metamorphoses*, iii. 8–9, trans. A. D. Melville, 51).

[79] Thuc. i. 2. 4, ii. 36. 1, cf. Tyrrell, *Amazons*, 114–17. From the 6th c. autochthony in Athens was part of the self-definition of the Athenians.

[80] Tadmor, 'The Relation of the Jewish People to the Land of Israel'; Japhet, *The Ideology of the Book of Chronicles*, 326–33 and a different interpretation in Machinist, 'Outsiders or Insiders'. Maimonides stated that neither a biological right nor an ancestral right ensures ownership of the land (Levinger, *Maimonides as Philosopher*, 90–4).

nineteenth century, it was unthinkable to suppose that the right to settlement on the land might be detached and separated from the obligation
to observe the Torah and the commandments. However, some proposed
an autochthonous version of the history of Israel in its land (among other
reasons, in response to the claim of Palestinian Arabs, an echo of claims
made by the pagan population, that they are the descendants of the ancient Canaanites). For example, Itamar Ben-Avi, called 'the first Hebrew
child' because he was the son of Eliezer Ben-Yehuda, widely renowned as
the foremost figure in the revival of Hebrew as a spoken language, wrote
in his book *Kana'an artzenu* ('Canaan Our Land—5,000 Years of Israel
Uninterruptedly in its Land' (1932):

the whole issue of our leaving Ur of the Chaldees to take over a country which did
not belong to us and to drive out its original inhabitants is basically unsubstantiated,
a devious lie perpetrated by the enemies of Israel in ancient times . . . do not say,
I have read 'Get thee out of thy land and out of thy birthplace and out of the
house of thy fathers to the land which I shall show thee', but rather 'Get out of
thy land and out of thy birthplace and out of thy father's house to the land which
is thy land . . .'.[81]

In the early 1960s David Ben-Gurion proposed a theory (which was his
own invention) that only one Hebrew family had left Palestine and gone to
Egypt. This caused political unrest and public debate, but his real intention
was to disseminate the autochthonous theory and thus to turn the Diaspora
from a historical concept into an ideological one.[82] The paradox of the new
Jewish nationalism in Palestine was that it asserted the historical continuity
of Jewish nationalism in Palestine, the divine assignment of land, and a
national affinity with and belongingness to the land; at the same time, it
saw itself as a society of immigrants that needed, in diverse ways, to renew
this affinity, which was not inherent.

As a result of new attitudes towards the land, mainly the secularization
of the traditional theological conception,[83] and the need of the newborn Jewish society in Palestine,[84] an enormous effort was invested in
nurturing the sense of country and the creation of an authentic link to the
landscape: namely, in creating a homeland. The new Hebrew, as a son of
this homeland, became the central theme of the Zionist educational system
and of Hebrew literature. The ancient Hebrew of the biblical period—
and at his side the east European peasant rooted in his land—became the

[81] See Y. Shavit, *The New Hebrew Nation*, 14–18.
[82] See Keren, *Ben-Gurion*, 100–7.
[83] T. Cohen, *From Dream to Reality*; Almog, 'Redemption in Zionist Rhetoric'; 'Land and People'.
[84] For a small part of this literature see n. 61.

prototype of a native son of a country firmly fixed in his land, with which he maintains an essentially mystical link. However, the east European (and the Greek) peasant had become tied to the soil and to the region through generations of attachment to the land, to the rhythm of its folklore and folk customs. These qualities, which made him 'plant-like', were all lacking in the Jewish immigrant who came to Palestine in the 1880s; he lacked, in the language of the time, 'the environment of country'. Hence the vast importance of the Bible (and archaeology) in creating the new link. The aim of imparting a knowledge of the land (*yediat ha'aretz*) and organizing hikes across the country[85] was to translate the literary landscape into a real and concrete landscape. A new popular culture and a new folklore were forged in order to supplant the popular Jewish culture in the Diaspora. Furthermore, the ethos of the return to the land was not a mystical link, but one expressed in working the land.[86]

LANDSCAPE AND CULTURE

Obviously, allusions to the milieu theory in a group of texts fail to provide any evidence of the extent of its distribution or influence. One cannot argue that the modern Jewish national ideology was seriously in need of this theory as a basis for its claim that a national Jewish revival could take place in Palestine and that only there could the Jewish people be renewed. The appearance of the theory of milieu in various texts reveals the manner in which nineteenth-century theories seeped into the mental world of the Jewish intelligentsia. However, in one sphere this theory had a deeper impact. I refer to the widespread claim that it is necessary to adapt the cultural environment to the natural. From the early 1880s, nativistic views came to the fore, asserting that the new Jewish society needed to replace its old world-picture, whose intimate natural scenery was moored in the landscape of Europe (mainly eastern Europe), with a new one rooted in the natural landscape of Palestine. By using symbols drawn from a European landscape, the Jews showed they were foreigners and had the consciousness of immigrants, unable to cut themselves off from their former world and acclimatize themselves to the new landscape.

The desired authenticity was perceived as a state of direct affinity between man, society, and their natural environment. The native differs from

---

[85] 'Wandering by foot through the Fatherland', wrote Friedrich Ludwig Jahn (Turnvater Jahn, 1778–1852), in his *Das deutsche Volkstum* (1810), 'awakened slumbering virtues, the sense of belonging, a common spirit and a love for humanity' (Snyder, *The Dynamics of Nationalism*, 151–3).

[86] Sh. Katz, 'The Israeli Teacher-Guide'.

the immigrant in that his perception of the landscape is a primal one; he does not perceive it as a new phenomenon that needs to be acquired and translated according to a prior system of concepts, but as the most fundamental and natural thing in the world. This was the basis for the ongoing argument about the nature of art in Palestine, for example, its close rapport with the landscape and the purported special light of the country.

From a less extreme standpoint, there were those who spoke about a harmony with Mother Nature in all branches of material culture, in organizing the new physical space of Palestine, in using raw materials, in relating to light and shadow, and so forth. For example, the forms of agricultural cultivation had to be adapted to the type of soil and the seasons of the year, and the design and construction of buildings suited to the climate. The yearning for a native culture and for integration into the landscape was a deep-seated longing in Hebrew culture in Palestine from 1882.

15

A 'POLIS' IN JERUSALEM: THE JEWISH STATE

And because of all this we make a firm covenant, and write it, and our princes, our Levites, and our priests set their seal to it.

NEHEMIAH 9: 38

. . . they jointly chose Solon as arbitrator and Archon and entrusted the government to him . . . And he established a constitution and made other laws . . . They wrote up the laws of the Boards and set them in the Royal Colonnade, and all swore to observe them . . .

ARISTOTLE, *Athenian Constitution*, 5. 2, 7. 1 (trans. by H. Rackham)

THE DUAL POLITICAL HERITAGE

THE return of the Jews to history was also their return to the realm of politics and statesmanship, whether as participants in European politics in various countries or as a new emerging political entity in Palestine from 1882. The idea of a Jewish state could be nourished by the memories of Jewish independence and Jewish sovereignty in biblical and post-biblical times, or by the messianic prophecies, but no one seriously thought of a revival of a Jewish kingdom. Thus it was the European political experience which was the political school of the Zionist movement.[1] When Jews of the late nineteenth century lost faith in absolute enlightened monarchies (or after monarchies gave way to other types of government), the liberal-democratic paradigm of state that they adopted was closer to the political heritage of classical antiquity than to the Jewish political heritage. In that they followed the course taken by Western civilization.

Christian political tradition was based on biblical foundations. When the Carolingian emperors gave the law (a positive law) to the whole Christian people, writes Christopher Dawson, they did it 'in the spirit of the kings and judges of the Old Testament' and used the Book of Divine Law as their manual of government. As a result, a complete break was made with the Roman or barbarian past, and 'Christendom enacted its own laws, which covered the whole field of social activity in Church and State . . . This was inspired neither by Germanic nor [by] Roman precedent.'[2] Later

---

[1] Halpern, *The Idea of a Jewish State*.   [2] Dawson, *Religion and Culture*, 90–1.

in the Middle Ages, theological and political thinking was influenced by
Roman political theory (taken mainly from Cicero, Seneca, and Plutarch's
purported *Institutio Traiani* in John of Salisbury's *Policraticus*) and then by the
political theories of Plato and Aristotle, but basically it was a theological
theory. The rift between the *sacerdotium* and *regnum*, between sacred and
profane, the Investiture controversy that convulsed Western Christianity
was foreign to the world of Greece and the Hellenistic civilization. Christian writers, for example, used the organic analogy in order to describe
the structure of society, but it was the world of the Bible which was the
source of the analogy of the struggle between the good and bad ruler as
well as the source of the authority of his power.

'Did not Samuel pass sentence of deposition against Saul by reason of his
disobedience and supersede him on the pinnacle of kingly rule with the
lowly son of Ysai [Jesse]?', asked John of Salisbury;[3] vain is the sanction of
all laws, if it does not bear the image of the divine law.[4] The situation in
Greece was different. Certain Greek states indeed claimed a divine sanction
for their laws; but the Greek and Hellenistic governments were thoroughly
secular, and ritual activity never affected political decisions.[5] The break-
away of the Renaissance from the Middle Ages, and the heritage it left
to Western civilization, was expressed, among other things, in the 'cult
of constitutional government, which was eventually to confer upon itself
the Hellenic title of Democracy'.[6] Rousseau popularized the Plutarchean
version of Hellenism, and the French revolutionists, wrote Toynbee, 'were
never tired of allusions to Solon and Lycurgus'. The Athenian ideals of
equality before the law (*isonomia*), of participation by the citizenry in public life, of government by open discussion,[7] became the guiding political

---

[3] 'Nonne Samuel in Saulem ex causa inobedientiae depositionis sententiam tulit, et ei in regni
aspicem humilem filium Ysai subrogauit?' (*Policraticus*, iv. 3 = *The Statesman's Book*, trans. Dickinson, 10).
Cf. Bolgar, *The Revival of Roman Law*.

[4] 'Omnium legum inanis est censura si non diuinae legis imaginem gerat' (ibid. iv. 6). See also
the purported 'Letter of Plutarch to Trajan' in book v. 1 and the *Institutio Traiani* following, with the
comment 'His point of departure is from reverence for a supernatural being; ours is from God' ('Porro
ei initium a reverentia numinum est, nobis a Deo', v. 3; trans. Dickinson, 66). According to Philo, the
king is rightly called father, 'for what the father in family life is to the children the king is to the state and
God is to the world' (*On Providence*, 2. 3, trans. Colson, ix. 461). Also see Copleston, *Medieval Philosophy*,
Part I; Ullmann, *A History of Political Thought*; Carlyle and Carlyle, *A History of Medieval Political Theory*.

[5] Finley, 'Politics and Political Theory', 23–4.

[6] Toynbee, *A Study of History*, 269.

[7] On the origins and nature of Athenian democracy see, amongst the many studies of the subject,
Ostwald, *From Popular Sovereignty*; Vernant, *The Origins of Greek Thought*, 82–118; Finley, *Democracy
Ancient and Modern*; Starr, *The Birth of Athenian Democracy*. It is not suggested that modern Western
democracy resembles Athenian democracy or that the latter is its source or sole model. Many forces
played a role in shaping it; this is not the place to discuss them in detail, but unquestionably Athens
served as an inspiration and frequently as a historical exemplar of democracy.

principles of the modern liberal tradition, as well as its inspiration. Under this influence, during the Renaissance there were also Jewish circles that preferred a republic to an ideal king. But Athenian democracy also served as a warning—as a *topos* of an unstable society which led in the end to tyranny and collapse: 'the debate over the Athenian constitution was primarily a debate over the conservative image of democracy and not over democracy itself.'[8] On the other side of the ocean, in eighteenth-century American political thought, the ancient world was seen as useful in providing guidelines, parallels, analogies, mainly in a very simplistic way. But when Alexis de Tocqueville, in his *De la démocratie en Amérique* (1835), compared Greek democracy with the American, he wrote: 'when I think of all the attempts that are made to judge the modern by the aid of those of antiquity, and to foresee what will happen in our time by what happened two thousand years ago, I am tempted to burn my books in order to apply only new ideas to so new a condition of society.'[9]

THE TORAH AS A CONSTITUTION

Athens and Jerusalem differed not only when it came to the relationship between the religious and secular authorities. The main difference lay in the source of the laws. Solon (594/3 BC) and Ezra and Nehemiah (444 BC) gave respectively the Athenian citizen body and the Jewish community in Jerusalem written and public laws. Basing himself on this resemblance, Bultmann believes that Solon is a counterpart of the Old Testament prophets: 'Under the reign of law, sanity and wisdom prevail ever among men.'[10] But the differences between Solon's legislation and that of Ezra and Nehemiah are evident. The covenant made in Jerusalem was indeed sealed by the princes, Levites, and priests of their own free will, but the constitution that they vowed to uphold was the Mosaic law. In other words, they took a public oath of allegiance to the age-old sanctified law (Neh. 10: 30–40). Solon, on the other hand, having been elected to an existing office (Plutarch, *Life of Solon*, 14), introduced new laws and reformed the

---

[8] Turner, *The Greek Heritage*, 263; and see the whole chapter: 'The Debate over the Athenian Constitution', 187–263.

[9] In Reinhold, *Classica Americana*, 109. According to Tocqueville, the American system, in which all political power is held by elected representatives, brings the United States closer to the Athenian model; the difference lies only in the number of citizens participating in the political process (book 1, ch. 21). On the Greek and Jewish roots of American democracy see Mandelbaum, 'The Flowering of American Democracy'.

[10] Bultmann, *Primitive Christianity*, 103–18.

constitution.[11] The citizens of Athens replaced the existing laws of Draco with those introduced by Solon; he 'established a constitution and made other laws . . . And he fixed the laws to stay unaltered for a hundred years' (Aristotle, *Athenian Constitution*, 7. 1–2). His code dealt with the political organization of the city, not with the ritual of the temples and the priests or the observance of religious commandments;[12] on the other hand, the 'unwritten laws' of fundamental ethics and social *mores* said by Athenian writers of the fifth and fourth centuries BC to be of divine origin (Sophocles, *Antigone*, 453–5; Xenophon, *Memorabilia*, iv. 4. 19) are very far from a comprehensive code governing all aspects of daily life. In other cities, too, even if the fundamental laws of the state were ascribed to a divinely approved lawgiver such as Lycurgus, they were considered his laws and not the gods'.

The case was quite otherwise with the Jewish community in Judah. Ezra and Nehemiah were also depicted in the Bible as men who by force of their personality and authority brought the Jewish people back to the Torah. But their Torah was not only the 'ancestral laws' but the law of God. By divine command, the Jews were subject to the laws of Moses. These laws, and only these laws, were designed to regulate their lives, and the laws of Moses are the Torah from heaven; 'Holding that the laws are oracles vouchsafed by God and having been trained in this doctrine from our earliest years, they carry the likenesses of the commandments enshrined in their souls.'[13] As Josephus (*Antiquities*, xiii. 297) notes, there was a distinction between regulations not written in the Torah (*nomima*), and the written laws of Moses (*nomoi*); indeed, the main point of conflict between the Pharisees and the Sadducees was their different view of the unwritten law. However, both stemmed from the same source, the unwritten law being an interpretation of the written by religious authorities and not by the citizen body or the holders of political power; as between Athenians— or Greeks at large—and Jews, so different are the sources of law, and the relation of the written law to the unwritten, that any similarity is purely verbal.

The comparison between the Athenian and the Mosaic constitutions is

---

[11] 'Solon, in fact, is regarded as the one man who in his own person and enactments personifies the Athenian democratic ideals' (Pearson, 'Historical Allusions', 221–2).

[12] For the purported details of his laws see Aristotle, *Athenian Constitution*, 6–10, and Plutarch, *Life of Solon*, 17–25.

[13] Philo, *The Embassy to Gaius*, 210 (trans. Colson, x. 109), cf. §115 (x. 57): 'trained . . . even from the cradle, by parents and tutors and instructors and by the far higher authority of the sacred laws and also the unwritten customs, to acknowledge one God who is the Father and Maker of the world'. This is utterly different from any residual association of *nomos* with the gods (Vernant, *The Origins of Greek Thought*, 86).

not, of course, my own innovation. Such a comparison was already drawn
in the Hellenistic era. For the Athenians, the most significant 'cultural'
difference between themselves and the barbarians was in *politeia* ('the life
of the polis').[14] Living in a world where Greek political ideals were seen as
the supreme model of political life and values, writers such as Josephus and
Philo found it vital to compare the 'Jewish constitution' with the Greek
one. This was done in order to combat negative Hellenistic descriptions
of the Mosaic law, and at the same time to see the Torah as a constitution,
as the Hellenistic writers did. Hecataeus of Abdera, for example, devoted
considerable space in his book *On Egypt* to a description of the history
of the Jews, and to Moses, whom he considered the creator of the Jewish
people's polity and laws; his account has been interpreted as a counterpart
to Plato's *Laws*.[15] Hellenistic Jews had no trouble using Greek concepts
such as *politeia* ('republic', 'citizenship', or 'civic constitution') for the
'laws of the Torah'; in particular, Josephus not only uses it on his own
account to describe the Mosaic code but puts it in Moses' mouth (*Antiquities*, iv. 184, 191). The constitution of Moses was the ideal constitution
which philosophers had been looking for: a harmonious combination of
monarchy, aristocracy, and democracy.[16]

In *Hypothetica*, 6. 9, Philo praises his people for not having changed even
one word of the laws written by Moses (whether they were the fruit of
his own reasoning or came to him from a supernatural source), for strictly
upholding the laws and not taking a permissive attitude towards them. The
difference between the laws of a *polis* and the laws of the Hebrews lies not
only in the way they are implemented, since implementation refers to the
pragmatic sphere, but mainly in the fact that the laws of Moses are revealed
by God, and God is the real ruler (and here he presents the argument that
was the source and core of the medieval Investiture controversy). Thus
the laws of Moses alone remain secure from the day when they were first
enacted until today.[17]

The interpretation of Judaism as a political constitution was renewed in
the nineteenth century. Influenced by the positivistic language of Montesquieu's *L'Esprit des lois*, J. Salvador, the French Jewish scholar (1796–
1873), in his book *Histoire des institutions et du peuple hébreu* (1862), described
the Mosaic law as an ideal political constitution existing in historical re-

---

[14] Hall, *Inventing the Barbarian*, 191.

[15] Fr. Jacoby, *FGrH* 264 F 6; Y. Gutman, 'Hecataeus'; Momigliano, 'An Apology of Judaism', 65; J.
Levy, 'Hecataeus', 44–59.

[16] Wolfson, *Philo*, ii. 375, 382–3.

[17] 'This [the retention of God's laws] is due to the recognition that the divine tribunal is superior to
the human': Philo, *De Providentia*, ii. 35–6 (trans. Colson, ix. 483–5).

ality and directing people's lives in all spheres, including the political. He viewed Judaism not only as an idea or a system of religious commandments, but as a political doctrine and a political constitution. This was in contrast to the views of other liberal Jews of his generation, who regarded the Mosaic law as a high wall separating the Jews from their surroundings that ought to be torn down.[18] The fundamental similarity between his view and the Hellenistic interpretation is very striking: in both cases, the Mosaic law is described in terms of the Greek theory of state. Salvador's book is an outstanding example of the 'tactic of correspondence': while Hecataeus interpreted the Mosaic law according to Platonic conceptions, Salvador interpreted it against the backdrop of French post-revolutionary political history and under the influence of the contemporary positivistic theory. His purpose was to prove that Moses did not found a theocracy like the Eastern theocracies; in other words, that Judaism was not insulated from the winds of political change blowing over western Europe. Salvador went even further; in his view, Moses founded a moderate democracy, a government based on the natural rule of reason. The Mosaic law was a law freely accepted by the nation (the will of the people). It was accepted by the entire people (a 'contract') and written in a book, hence it became a public law equal for all. It is therefore surprising, Salvador writes, that Bossuet, in his *Discours sur l'histoire universelle*, did not compare the Mosaic law with Greek laws. In other words, Mosaic law is no less democratic than the Greek laws, and consequently, the political tradition of the Jewish people is not alien to the spirit of Western liberal democracy, which is rooted in the Greek political tradition. In this manner, Salvador was carrying on the tradition of Jewish Hellenistic literature.

Salvador was not the only one—nor was he the first or the last—to try to present the political theory of Judaism. Earlier, Azariah de' Rossi sought to prove the superiority of the Jewish people's polity in its land.[19] He was preceded in the fifteenth century by Judah Messer Leon, who, in his *Sefer nofet tzufim* (1475), wrote that Jewish political doctrine was far superior to those of the Gentiles: 'How great has grown the pre-eminence of the Israelite nation over all human beings, how goodly are her tents and her dwellings and how beautiful her stately bearings!'[20] Views such as this reappear in modern Jewish literature. One example is Ze'ev Jawitz's essay *Olamot overim*, in which, in a rather derisive tone, he described French

---

[18] Salvador; I used the Hebrew translation, *Toledot mosedotav shel Moshe veshel am ha'ivrim*, 22.

[19] Bonfil, 'Expressions of Uniqueness', 39.

[20] *The Book of the Honeycomb's Flow*, ii. 18. On Jewish political thought during the Renaissance, see Melamed, *Wisdom's Little Sister*.

political literature as having led to upheavals and revolutions and hence to perversity and waywardness. These revolutionary ideas are different from the eternal basic values of Judaism. Thus the Torah must be the ideal guide for government and political culture.[21] Again, this new image of the political history of the Jews opposed the Renanian view that they lack any kind of *esprit public* and were never a *politeia* in the Greek sense.[22]

JEWS AS LOYAL CITIZENS AND THE CALL FOR REFORM

In the course of the nineteenth century, Jews found themselves urged to adjust to different types of political regimes and were motivated by the need to prove there was no contradiction between a Jew's adhering to his faith and being as loyal and productive as his fellow citizens. They felt impelled to prove that the Jews' loyalty to the halakhah and the principles of faith does not contradict their loyalty to the state in which they live and to its laws: a Jew can be a patriot and a productive citizen. The Haskalah approach, calling on the Jews to adhere faithfully to the religion of their forefathers, but to accept the laws of the country in which they live, found support in the words of Jeremiah: 'But seek the welfare of the city where I have sent you into exile . . . for in its welfare you will find your welfare' (29: 7). The Haskalah literature of the nineteenth century is replete with statements, declarations, and evidence for the fact that there is no immanent opposition between a man's Jewishness and his patriotism, and that a Jew is, by his very nature and the conditions of his existence, a loyal, obedient, and useful subject-citizen.[23] The question of dual obedience to the Natural Laws (the laws of the state) and the Revealed Laws was seen as a dilemma which could easily be solved. Moreover, it is the Jew's duty to demonstrate his loyalty and to prepare himself to be a loyal subject-citizen.[24] This is the root of the unequivocal preference shown by most of the nineteenth-century *maskilim*, at least until the 1880s, for enlightened absolutism, and the suspicion—even deep-seated apprehension—they showed towards some of the key manifestations on the scene of the French revolution, particularly the

[21] Jawitz, 'Olamot overim', 48.

[22] Renan, *Histoire générale*, 13.

[23] Wessely, *Divrei shalom ve'emet*, 13–14. And see Cardozo's apologia in refutation of the calumny that Jews are not loyal to their princes, *Las excelencias*, 93–104.

[24] On the French Jewish case see Berkowitz, *The Shaping of Jewish Identity*, 57–84. Also see Funkenstein, 'The Threshold of Modernity', 220–3. Indeed, according to Spinoza, because the idea of a political constitution was foreign to the Torah, after the Exile the Torah became invalid, whereas in traditional—and secular—thought, it was regarded as the constitution that safeguarded the Jews in the Diaspora as well. See too Graff, *Separation of Church and State*.

appearance of the mob and the principle of popular representation.[25] It would be true to state that the Haskalah linked its destiny to enlightened absolutism; it hoped and expected it would bring about emancipation.

The failure of these expectations led to Jewish political radicalization on the one hand, and to the emergence of the national political idea on the other. Kalman Schulman, for example, in his *Divrei yemei olam*, went to great pains to make a sharp distinction between the great revolt against the Romans and the French Revolution and its various forms.

A radical *maskil* like Peretz Smolenskin adopted Edmund Burke's approach, praising the evolutionary and traditionalist manner in which political change took place in England, which seemed inordinately preferable to the French revolutionary and radical way.[26] Smolenskin did not reject the principle of the sovereignty of the nation, but used it in the internal Jewish arena. His objective was to prove that the 'reform' of Judaism is compatible with the desire to change old orders not by dramatic revolution but by internal reform. One of the points of his criticism of Maimonides was that he had not only interpreted Jewish faith 'in the way of the Greeks', but also had collected all the halakhic rules into one book, thus blocking any possibility of changing this binding codification. In this way, Smolenskin opined, Maimonides had given boundless authority to the *posekim*, authors of the Responsa, and precluded any possibility of rejuvenation. According to him, Maimonides had turned the Torah into a 'deep trough' or a 'stagnant swamp'.[27] The national and traditionalist dimension in his thinking was expressed in his justification of change not from abstract political theories to justify the need for change, but from the Jewish tradition itself. Like so many others before and after him, he turned to the distant past to search for fitting precedents:

The times change from generation to generation, the activities, wishes, and spiritual attributes of one generation differ from those of the generations that preceded it . . . but since the times change from generation to generation it is no wonder then that they sometimes retrace their steps, for it has been said: what is new for the generation that has just now passed was already a perennial feature in the generations that had gone before in bygone days, even though not in all its laws and decrees.[28]

Smolenskin used the principle of the sovereignty of the people as the source of authority for changes in the normative religious system. With this in mind, he gave a modern interpretation to the saying that all the

[25] Feiner, '"Rebellious French"', 230–6; see also Kolat, 'The French Revolution's Impact'.
[26] Smolenskin, 'Am olam', 39–41; Feiner, *Fuenn: From Militant to Conservative Maskil*, 34–7.
[27] Smolenskin, 'Et lata'at', 209–10.   [28] Ibid. 84.

children of Israel are 'a kingdom of priests and a holy nation'. The people's sovereignty is limited; it does not pave the way for a total revolution of values, but only facilitates a mechanism of changes that will make the 'religion' suitable to 'life', thus meeting the needs of life expressed by the people's representatives. Since the rabbinical authority does nothing to address the need for change, and the rabbis who 'dwell in their panelled houses, and have nothing to do with the workers in the land, will never know or understand the distress brought about by their many laws',[29] so it is the people who must wield the authority to introduce changes, to 'reform and rescind' the burdensome laws. Smolenskin finds support for his argument in the claim that many laws and customs are the product of time and place and differ from locality to locality, and hence do not constitute immutable halakhah. The Torah is a doctrine of life and 'a court has not the power to nullify the opinion of another court unless it was greater than the other in wisdom, in numbers, and in tradition' (e.g. Mishnah Eduy. 1: 5). Thus it is possible to set up a court greater than its predecessors to introduce the required changes into halakhah and tradition. Another support he found was the statement that the Torah is the inheritance of the Congregation of Jacob and was not given into the hands of the rabbis:

In the House of Israel, the Torah was not given to the priests but to the Congregation of Jacob, and it may do with its legacy as it wishes, and the rabbis are only elected by the people and must do whatever is requested of them, and if the entire people will desire to reform or rescind, it has the authority to do so and no one can protest.[30]

Furthermore, Smolenskin even asserted that many of the accepted customs were not the fruit of Jewish internal tradition but just 'alien corn' that the Jews adopted from the peoples around them. In other words, the reform of Jewish life is legitimized through describing it not as an imitation but as a 'purification' of customary lifestyles that are not originally Jewish. It was the British historical model, not the French one, which provided him with irrefutable evidence that it is possible to introduce changes without impairing time-honoured tradition. Here we have the use of modern political terms to explain the need for religious reform, not for the purpose of proposing a future political form of government. Neither Smolenskin nor other national thinkers of his time proposed any concrete political structure.

In the last quarter of the nineteenth century the radical *maskilim* faced a

---

[29] Smolenskin, 'Am olam', 26.   [30] Ibid. 32.

twofold disappointment: they were disillusioned with the existing political structures, and despaired of the possibility of reforming Jewish society from within. Some radical *maskilim* joined revolutionary movements; others were attracted by nationalism. It was the latter who had to begin thinking about concrete political solutions.

THE NATURE OF THE JEWISH STATE

At its inception, the Zionist movement was preoccupied with questions about what its political organization would be like and how it would act on the political level, but practical discussions on the character of the political structure of the new Jewish society in Palestine had already begun in the early 1880s. In the blueprints of Zionist utopias, hardly any attention was paid to the structure of government. The writers were engrossed in describing the portrait of the future Jewish society—but not that of the future Jewish state.[31] Proposals such as the 'renewal of the Sanhedrin' of the Second Temple era failed to strike a resonant chord in the Jewish public and had no basis in reality. The writings of Herzl, the father of political Zionism who envisioned the Jewish state, furnish a striking and classic example of the political thought of his time. In his political writings, Herzl demonstrated profound hostility towards parliamentary democracy, describing it in the most pejorative terms.[32] In his utopian novel *Altneuland*, however, the ideal Jewish state is the consummate democratic liberal state. What really matters is not ideas expressed in various writings but two facts: that the Zionist organization founded by Herzl was based on a quasi-democratic foundation, and that from the 1880s onwards the new Yishuv (the Jewish community in Palestine) established its own institutions on a secular basis.[33] This shows that liberal 'Western' political values were deeply internalized and that the preferred form of government was representative democracy, which had a distinctly secular character.

The principle of representative democracy was accepted and implemented despite expressions of opposition by some influential groups. From the outset there were quite a few comments in Zionist political literature that democratic processes were ineffectual or opposed to the revolutionary, vital spirit of Zionism and the avant-garde conception of the minority.

---

[31] Elboim-Dror, *Yesterday's Tomorrow*, i. 117–20.

[32] His abhorrence of the parliamentary system, as giving power to the mob and the demagogues, is expressed in his *Palais Bourbon* and in his plan for the future Jewish state.

[33] Kaniel, 'Religion and "Community"', 190–1; Y. Shavit, 'Regulations of the First Colonies'.

From the point of view of a revolutionary socialist ideology, for example, the parliamentary system was regarded as a tool of the 'despicable bourgeoisie' ('the refuse of alien parliamentarianism'),[34] which is opposed to the pioneering leadership of the vanguard on the one hand, and to class collectivism on the other. From the point of view of a conservative right-wing ideology, representative parliamentarianism was a 'non-Jewish' system that impaired the organic nature of the nation. These views sprang from current antiliberal European thought, and Plato's and Aristotle's negative attitude towards Greek democracy was frequently cited in support of these views.

In reality, the rules of the game adopted by the Zionist movement and the Jewish polity in Palestine were those of formal democracy.

When the new Jewish polity in Palestine was first organized after World War I, many spokesmen emphasized the 'spirit of democratization in the establishment of our parliamentary life', the adoption of the formula of free and secret general elections, and the like.[35] In view of the lack of democratic tradition and the opposition to the democratic system it is surprising that democratic principles were accepted by most segments of the Jewish population, including the religious and ultra-Orthodox, during the Mandatory period.[36] They accepted the fact that Jewish self-rule, and later the Jewish state, were basically and essentially secular. In religious thought, the connection between repentance and redemption is unequivocal: 'Anyone who throws off the burden of the Torah, which is likened to fire, is given the burden of government, which is likened to fire' (*Mekhilta of R. Shimon B. Yochai* 19: 18, ed. Epstein–Melamed, 143–4). According to this, a state of Jews whose Jewish citizens throw off the yoke of the commandments is a state living in sin. The existence of a secular Jewish state in the land of Israel has indeed posed dire dilemmas for the Orthodox public, but in historical reality a complex system of exchange and coexistence has been forged between that public and the secular state. The radical anti-Zionist Orthodox find the secular foundation of the Jewish state repugnant; but even they participate in parliamentary and political party life subject to the laws of the state, enacted by a secular body, and they often speak in the name of democratic values and laws that the democracy has passed in order to protect the rights of minorities. Among some national-religious circles, the state has even acquired a character of sanctity, although it is not a halakhic state and its life is not conducted according to the laws

---

[34] Gorny, *Achdut Ha'avodah*, 161–81.
[35] Gil-Har, *The Organization and Self-Government*, 58–61.
[36] See Horowitz and Lissak, *Origins of the Israeli Polity*.

of the Torah (that is, it is sanctified yet imperfect); within different ultra-Orthodox circles this fact has given rise to an ambivalent attitude or to harshly extreme opposition to the very existence of the state.[37]

Political pragmatism, opportunism, and a theology separating the state from religious life, or viewing the secular state as the dawn of redemption, were the solutions the various strata of religious society found for its dilemma. The fact that a binding status was assigned to religious authority in several spheres of life, in particular in relation to the laws of matrimony, made it easier to accept these solutions. Beyond that, an ongoing struggle raged over the dimensions and degree of the involvement of the religious authorities in the life of the state and society.

Many people view this involvement as a sign that Israel is not a secular liberal state. These critics question the democratic nature of Israel and claim that the state is not a true Western-liberal democracy but rather a theo-democracy (or an ethno-democracy).[38] From my point of view, however, the important fact here is that this struggle takes place within a patently secular framework, and the ultra-Orthodox public accepts the rules of the game and plays the game, despite its fundamental objection. This criticism also fails to see the revolutionary nature of the Jewish democracy from a historical perspective, and its fundamental democratic features. These critics look at the political reality from a secular vantage-point. In their view, 'Jerusalem' prevails over 'Athens'. However, from a different vantage-point, the very fact that there is an 'Athens' in 'Jerusalem' points to a radical change in Jewish history.

A JEWISH STATE, JEWISH VALUES

The attempt by the High Priest Jason to turn Jerusalem into a Hellenized city called Antiochia was regarded as an attempt to transform it into a *polis* and integrate it into Greek municipal civilization. This attempt was one of the major causes of the Maccabean revolt. According to the Books of Maccabees, as well as Josephus, the purpose of the Hasmonean revolt

---

[37] Among the many studies on the tension between religion and state in Israel see: Ravitsky, *Messianism, Zionism and Jewish Religious Radicalism*; Friedman, 'The State of Israel as a Theological Dilemma'; Kolat, 'Religion, Society and State'; Belfer, *'Malkhut shamayim' and the State of Israel*. In the view of national religious Zionism, the (secular) state took on a measure of sanctity and its laws were regarded as a substitute for the 'law of the king', but in recent years the state has lost much of this dimension of sanctity.

[38] This claim states that Israeli democracy is a Jewish democracy that does not apply to the Arab population. I do not intend to address this claim here, nor to discuss the interrelationship between formal democracy and the actual focal points of authority and power.

was to ensure freedom, which meant not only political independence but also the freedom to keep Jewish laws. The freedom demanded by Zionism was not the freedom to live according to the Torah, but the freedom to establish a state in which the Jews could enact laws as they saw fit, based on the tradition of their forefathers, but also on a new system of values. In this sense, those who established Israel's independence in 1948 were more like Solon or Pericles, the members of the National Assembly in Paris, or the signers of the United States' Declaration of Independence, than they were like Ezra and Nehemiah or the Sanhedrin.

The argument about whether Judaism can establish a democratic government is a fruitless debate. Judaism has no preferred political system; it can adapt to any system and exist within its framework. Nowhere in the Scriptures is there a definite statement as to what form of government the Jewish state should take;[39] the Sages had no systematic political thought and no preference for any type of political order.[40] The monarchic regime founded by Samuel the prophet was based on the model of the monarchies of the ancient East; he even took the trouble to warn the people that the change from a tribal system to a kingdom was a radical departure from their former way of life, and that nothing good would come to them from a monarchy. The tension between rulers and the laws of the Torah was the cause of the conflict between the kings of Judah and Israel and the prophets, as well as between the Hasmonean kings and the Pharisees.[41] Prophecy and the messianic tradition sanctified the monarchy, but only after the monarchy had disappeared, as part of the longing for a 'golden age' that had supposedly existed and was no more. In Jewish literature on the subject there are spheres in which the king's rule is secular—'all the king's matters' (2 Chron. 19: 11)—and is based on a 'temporary provision', according to the discretion of the earthly authority. But this is a very limited sphere; there is no doubt that the religious system is the dominant one and that in speaking of the 'secular' sphere, the reference is not to a separate legislative system, certainly not one that contradicts the religious values. Moreover, even when the king's authority is anchored in public consensus, it is derived from a divine source and is restricted by religious law.[42]

[39] According to Kaufmann, Jewry never knew a theocratic priestly ideal; the kingdom of God was not meant to be realized by priests, but by kings who upheld the laws of the Torah and by prophets who acted as spritual guides. *The Religion of Israel*, i/3, 686–708.

[40] Wolfson, *Philo*, ii. 325. And see Funkenstein, 'The Image of the Ruler'.

[41] D. Schwartz, 'On Pharisaic Opposition'.

[42] Kaufmann, *The Religion*, v. 371–400. See also Blidstein, *Political Concepts in Maimonidean Halakhah*; Ravitsky, 'On Kings and Statutes in Jewish Thought'.

Ostensibly Judaism, like Christianity, was aware of the inner tension between the two authorities, and various spheres of life were shaped not according to the halakhah or the laws of the Torah but by lay representatives of the public. We have already mentioned the debate about whether the Jews really lived under the authority of the halakhah after the destruction of the Temple. In Jewish communities, the lay leaders possessed various powers, enacted regulations, and deliberated issues, not always on the basis of halakhah. In various spheres of life, the Jewish community formulated regulations not derived from the halakhah, and the community leadership was chosen in elections that granted special prerogatives to the rich. As a matter of fact, one can argue that a quasi-democratic institution existed that gave expression to the lay dimension of community life, and in many respects was not subordinate to rabbinical authority.[43]

There were others who, from a no less radical position, argued for far-reaching reform in religious rules and defended changes not only in the Oral Law but also in the Revealed Law, namely in the laws of the Torah. However, nowhere and at no time was an alternative and overall legal system created that did not draw its authority from the halakhah or operated outside it, at times even in opposition to it, as was to happen in the State of Israel, whose laws have expropriated many spheres from the halakhah. They do not merely constitute a system supplementing the laws of the Torah; they are the dominant system. Hence it is no wonder that the Orthodox response to modernity, and all the more to the secular Jewish state, was not necessarily self-isolation within enclaves in which they lived according to the Torah, cut off from the secular world; rather it was an attempt to expand the terms 'laws of the Torah' and 'knowledge of the Torah' and to impose rules in all spheres of life, many of which neither the Torah nor the halakhah had ever previously been called upon to regulate.

A discussion about the feasibility of a sovereign state based on the Torah and halakhah is merely a theoretical one. The fact is that there has never been a Jewish state that lived according to the halakhah (a theocracy), and the notion that such a state will ever exist is a matter of wishful thinking or speculation. One thing is clear: such a state cannot be a democracy. On the other hand, the question whether a democratic state can be a Jewish state touches upon its basic values, not the nature of its political

[43] J. Katz, *Tradition and Crisis*, 91–102. See the articles in H. H. Ben-Sasson, *The Medieval Jewish Community* and Ettinger's Introduction to I. Halperin, *The Records of the Council of the Four Lands*, 15–24; also Landman, *Jewish Law in the Diaspora*. On the effort to find a democratic dimension in biblical tradition see Gordis, 'Democratic Origins in Ancient Israel'.

system.[44] Hence the leaders of the State of Israel saw fit to draw a fundamental distinction between the pattern of government and the sources of its binding norms, on the one hand, and its declared values on the other. Public political polemic in Israel often turns to biblical prophecies, seeking there a specific code of Jewish political and especially moral conduct. Indeed, one may learn political ethics from the prophets, but they had nothing to say about the form of government; for example, they did not object to the institution of monarchy but preached a vision of enlightened messianic monarchy. Moreover, there is a basic difference between a political and social ethos on the one hand, and a political framework (the operating system, so to speak) on the other. The claim that Judaism proposes an ideal sociopolitical ethos—that is, a lofty system of values and rules of conduct—says nothing about the structure of the political system and the principles of its operation. In the immediate political context, certain criticism of the allegedly non-Jewish nature of the state is intended as a demand that more space be allotted to the religious norms in the (secular) legal system, whereas in the more ideological context, the intention is to propose an ideal or utopian 'halakhic state'.

The system of values operating in the social (and constitutional) reality of Israel in part conforms with what is regarded as the 'spirit of Judaism' and stems from Jewish law, and in part originates from norms and rules of conduct that differ from, and sometimes fundamentally contradict, the 'spirit of the Torah'. The main argumentation in public polemic is centred on the source of the values and not necessarily on their content. But there is a radical potential inherent in the assumption that if the source of values is not the revealed laws, but man, then man can change them. And in many instances, social (and legal) norms do contradict the 'spirit of Judaism' as it is reflected in the halakhah.[45]

It is, indeed, an irony of history: in 1949, Jerusalem became the capital of the State of Israel, a country proclaimed as a state of the Jews, or as a Jewish state. This state, founded in 1948, was an 'Athens' in Jerusalem; in its political structure it more closely resembles a *polis* than it does the Jewish community in the days of Ezra and Nehemiah or even the Hasmonean kingdom.

---

[44] Schweid, *Democracy and Halakhah*; Elazar and Aviad, *Religion and Politics in Israel*; Elazar, 'Towards a Jewish Definition of Statehood'.

[45] The continuing debate about the authority of the Supreme Court is evidence of the inner tension between two legal systems anchored in different value-systems. In the debate in 1994 about the legal status of homosexual couples, the norms laid down by the court blatantly contradict the halakhah and the Jewish norm and are similar to those which prevailed in the Graeco-Roman world.

SPARTA OR ATHENS?

In *Against Apion*, Josephus painted a utopian picture of Jewish life as a harmonious and ideal fusion of the finest attributes of Greece or, put another way, the best of the two polar opposites Athens and Sparta (cf. Philo, *De Vita Mosis*, ii. 19): whereas the Spartans (and Cretans) trained their citizens in approved conduct, but not in the principles on which it was based, and the Athenians (along with most other Greeks) laid down laws but neglected to inculcate them in practice, Moses knew how to teach by using the Torah and the commandments, both precept and practice (ii. 171–81). He paid particular attention to the contrast between the Jews, who had steadfastly adhered to their laws through all their sufferings and who welcomed all those who wished to join them, and the Spartans, who had abandoned their traditions in defeat and who regularly expelled all strangers from their midst (ii. 227–8, 259–61).[46]

The Greek experience and Western perceptions of Athens and Sparta as two different political entities provided the political debate in Israel with yet another political *topos*. Is Israel more like Sparta or more like Athens? We have already seen that Josephus represented Israel as the best of both worlds. The Hasmoneans, for political reasons, claimed genealogical ties to Sparta. However, Athens, as a centre of spiritual and intellectual creation, became in the nineteenth century the true representative of Greece and the Greek heritage. It was only after the establishment of the State of Israel, with the existence of a sovereign Jewish political entity that employs military strength, that the question of its similarity to Sparta or Athens arose.

'Athens' and 'Sparta' became models of two polar regimes and political cultures. Writers employing the image of Athens portrayed it in its ideal form, making it easy for those more sympathetic to Spartan elements to underscore the dark side of the Athenian reality: slavery, imperialism, and the like. However, the Israeli system of political images generally adopted the prevalent European typology permeating modern Western political thought and educational theory. Sparta in this argument represented a totalitarian method of state education that regards military education as the supreme, as distinct from Athens in which the method of education was open and liberal: 'The prevailing style of education, described by Plato in the dialogue *Protagoras*, brings to mind the method of the *cheder* that was practised among the Jews of eastern Europe . . .'.[47] This statement is

---

[46] On Josephus' and Philo's perceptions of Athens and Sparta see Rawson, *The Spartan Tradition*, 94–8.
[47] A. E. Simon, 'Sparta or Athens?', 55.

of course hyperbole, for in the *cheder* there was no physical education, no violin lessons, and the like. Hence the proponents of military education employed images that did not originate in the political or military history of Second Temple Jewry but rather raised the cry 'bring us a sixty-fourth part of Sparta!'[48]

On the other hand, criticism of the so-called Spartan atmosphere in the State of Israel was based mainly on the claim that this 'Spartan education'—namely, education for militarism, which changes the character of the Israeli Jewish man—stems from a flawed nationalistic policy. While the Spartans fostered their educational system in order to preserve their minority rule over the majority of the conquered population, in the State of Israel that approach is also necessitated by the circumstances of its existence, in the view of some, or by a misconceived national policy, in the view of others. It is not surprising that A. E. Simon (1899–1988), an educator and thinker, repeated Second Temple apologetics in his attempt to propose the ideal harmonious blend: Josephus described the education of the Jews as a successful blend of Spartan halakhah and Athenian aggadah. The fact is that it was awkward to give 'Sparta' a positive image since it lacked any spiritual content. Thus, while for some the Athenian collapse was due to the inept way in which a democracy conducts its foreign affairs, others emphasized the military dimension in Athenian history (as did the Athenian orators themselves) and turned Athens into *the* historical model of a democratic state, able not only to defeat its mighty enemy (the Persian Empire), but also to establish its hegemony in the Greek world. The use of this political *topos* was of course really an echo of the debate in European political thought.

In this way, the Israeli political scene added another dimension to the more profound dichotomy between the 'Dionysian' and the 'Apollonian' in Israeli life: the Spartan merged with the Dionysian, the Athenian with the Apollonian, and the resulting amalgam was an ideal harmony between these two.

---

[48] Ariel Sharon, quoted in A. E. Simon, 'Sparta or Athens?', 68. In 18th-c. American political thought Sparta was considered a model of freedom and order, 'a stable, long-lived commonwealth', but Rome served as the republican archetype (Reinhold, *Classica Americana*, 95).

16

THE NEW JEWISH CULTURE:
IDEAL AND REALITY

One merely has to utter from the podium that awful word *kul'tura*—
perhaps the loftiest and most sublime word in the human vocabulary—
and immediately the air trembles with voices raised from both right and
left, as if the final Day of Judgement has arrived, on which Zionism
will be sentenced to life or death.

AHAD HA'AM, 'The Spiritual Revival' (1902)

All of us have thirstily imbibed the Hebrew opium from the very same
well.   URI ZEVI GREENBERG, *Heroica*

CULTURE AND ACCULTURATION

IN 1899, the young Martin Buber read the first volume of Jacob Burckhardt's monumental *Griechische Kulturgeschichte*, which appeared in four
volumes between 1898 and 1902. In a letter to the friend who had sent
him the book as a gift, Buber wrote how deeply impressed he was by the
description of the inner life of the Greeks and commented: 'I ask myself
when we shall have such a book, *A History of Jewish Culture*.'[1] Almost
a century has passed since then, and we still have no all-encompassing
and comprehensive book on the history of Jewish culture. Nor is there a
comprehensive book describing the one hundred years of Jewish culture
in Palestine. Much literature exists on various aspects of the history of
Jewish culture, but not one comprehensive summary like Burckhardt's
great books on the culture of Greece and of the Renaissance. There are
many attempts to trace the components of Jewish identity and draw a
distinction between practice and faith, and numerous studies deal with
modern Jewish political and national value culture. However, what Buber
meant was an all-inclusive account of the total fabric of Jewish life, in
which the history of the culture should reveal the latter's underlying idea—
and itself be informed by an ordering principle.

Burckhardt himself regarded 'culture' as a multifaceted and dynamic
phenomenon, so that it was possible to reconstruct the uniformity and
unity of a closed culture—one that has already ceased to exist—but not of

---

[1] Mendes-Flohr, 'Hale'umiyut shebalev', 34; the title represents German *Nationalismus der Innerlichkeit*.

a living one. We may assume that what Buber wanted was really not a comprehensive description of all the manifestations of the Jewish culture, but rather a description of the idea of the culture in its classical manifestations, or its Great Tradition. He, like others of his time, was searching for what might be considered the permanent manifestations and characteristics of Jewish culture. Based on the model of the Hellenic ideal, they sought for 'Jewishness' as it is reflected in its culture and its values.

The reason for the lack of an all-inclusive work on Jewish or Hebrew culture stems not only from the state of scholarship, but also from the nature of Jewish culture. It is too pluralistic, or even too heterogeneous, to permit a sweeping panoramic and synthetic picture totally derived from one key idea. Hence we find innumerable works dealing with the essence of Jewish and Israeli culture, but only a few attempts to draw an overall map of this cultural space. This situation is in stark contrast to the centrality of the concept of culture in Jewish life and in Jewish polemics in the last two centuries, and all the more so in the chronicles of Jewish nationalism and of the Jewish society in Palestine in the last one hundred years.

My interest in this chapter is not in the significant phenomenon of Jewish acculturation; in other words, in processes through which the modern Jew became an active consumer of the goods offered on the foreign cultural market. Jewish acculturation is a complex historical phenomenon; we have seen already that Jews in all periods were consumers of a variety of foreign cultural traits. Gazing in the Hellenistic mirror we have seen that the question of which items in Jewish culture were a product of authentic internal creation and which had been absorbed from the outside became a cardinal question in understanding the period.

In modern times, the possibilities of being consumers in the general cultural market (as well as active participants in its creation) greatly increased as a result of the secularization of European society. This process—the creation of a culture devoid of religious content (although, as we have seen, frequently with neo-pagan wrappings)—made it easier for the Jews to become its consumers. Thus, from the time of the Renaissance and thereafter, one can find writings harshly criticizing the trend towards acculturation—perceived as a clear expression of licentiousness—through participation in the culture (usually the popular culture) of the Gentiles. Graetz's rhetorical question: 'Will "culture" be the grave of Judaism?' became crucial from the beginning of the modern era, when a segment of Jewry left the enclosed domain of its religious culture and stood at the gates of the secular West. This raised the questions of the future relation between the Jewish and foreign cultures, and the impact that Jews' consumption of a foreign culture would have on Jewish culture. We have noted that the spokesmen of the Haskalah were aware of the need for acculturation and hence were also aware of the need to control and monitor its dimensions and content. In both cases, different tactics were adopted to prevent negative accultur- ation and to achieve harmony and reconciliation between the inside and the outside. A preference was assigned to those items of culture considered 'neutral' or 'suitable' for the Jewish system of values, and prohibitions and reservations were set up in relation to those items perceived as negative in character.

In the context of the modern Jewish society in Palestine, this topic took on a new dimension. At one and the same time, a new Jewish culture was created, which absorbed and internalized a plethora of new traits from the outside, and a new cultural environment came into being, in which the market of imported culture played an important role. In both spheres, an attempt was made to exert control, to screen the traits taken into Jewish culture, and to censor the imported cultural market. The identity and the content of the new culture were determined according to the degree of success or failure that met attempts to govern these two spheres on the basis of a predetermined pattern.

Furthermore, *culture* is not only a system of values but also of practice, of modes of behaviour. The Hellenizing Jew, we recall, was accused, not of having adopted the principles of Greek philosophy, but of having emulated and adopted Hellenistic cultural practices. Hence the basic question in relation to the content of a culture is not necessarily what its declared system of values is, but rather what its actual modes of behaviour are.

THE MEANING OF CULTURE

'The word *kul'tura* is, after all, an indeterminate word which says nothing, or even worse than that, one that says too much. Wherever they can- not precisely designate some spiritual concept, they take the vague word *kul'tura* and sport with it before us . . .'.[2] These caustic remarks of the Heb- rew author David Frischmann aptly reflect the evolution of the word and its unclear and diverse usages. But the fact that the concept of *culture* was so vague did not prevent it from becoming a subject of endless controversies and disputes within Hibbat Zion and the Zionist movement.[3] One only has to utter from the podium the word *kulturah* in order to arouse tremendous

---

[2] Quoted by Brenner in *Bachayim ubesifrut*, 65–6.

[3] For a detailed description of the debate about 'culture' in Hibbat Zion and in the early days of the Zionist movement see E. Luz, *Parallels Meet*.

excitement as if the Day of Judgement had arrived, wrote Ahad Ha'am in his essay 'Techiyat haruach' ('The Spiritual Revival', 1902).[4] He, of course, was referring to what is known in Zionist terminology as the 'polemic of *kulturah*', namely, the dispute about the character and content of Judaism, which some Zionists tried to place on the agenda of the Zionist movement and which Herzl tried his utmost to prevent from becoming a *Kulturkampf* likely to preclude any co-operation between secular and observant Jews. It is important to take note of the language in which Ahad Ha'am described the term 'culture': 'perhaps the loftiest and most sublime word in the human vocabulary'. It is significant that *culture*—not Torah—is, in his view, the loftiest and most sublime word! Bialik, his disciple, spoke in the same vein in his address at the inauguration of the Hebrew University of Jerusalem in 1925: 'in the consciousness of the nation, the term culture, in its comprehensive and human sense, has replaced the theological term Torah'.[5] And indeed, in using the word 'culture' they were both alluding to Jewish culture ('which incorporates within itself universal values in total harmony'). However, in the eyes of observant Jews, the replacement of Torah by 'culture' was a clear expression of the Hellenic or 'Hellenizing' and heretical character of the 'cultural Jewry' (*yahadut hatarbut*) that aspires to take the place of Torah Jewry.

What did those using the term 'culture' in the Jewish polemic from the days of the Berlin Haskalah have in mind?

The term *tarbut* (culture), having appeared only a few times in Jewish literature, was thus an innovation in modern Hebrew (just as the term *yahadut* was in its time); moreover, its meaning in modern Hebrew was different from that in the ancient sources, where it always bore a negative connotation: *tarbut anashim chata'im* ('a brood of sinful men') (Num. 32: 14). Elisha Ben Avoya is a man who *yatza letarbut ra'ah* ('fell into bad ways') (bHag. 15a) etc. The Talmud, as we have seen, speaks of Greek wisdom, but it has no word for 'culture' even as *paideia*. Until the last quarter of the nineteenth century, the spokesmen of the Hebrew revival still preferred to speak about *kul'tura* (in Russian), and not about *tarbut* (in Hebrew), owing to the negative associations of that word with idolatry in the historical memory.[6]

When the term *Kultur* first appeared in the world of the German Jewish Haskalah in the late eighteenth century, a limited meaning was ascribed to it. To a great extent, it encompassed the same meanings as what were

---

[4] Ahad Ha'am, 'The Spiritual Revival'; cf. Rubenstein, 'The Concept of Culture in Ahad Ha'am'.

[5] Bialik, 'Lepetichat haUniversitah haIvrit beYerushalayim', 131.

[6] A. E. Simon, 'Ha'im od yehudim anachnu?', 22–4.

known in traditional language as *chokhmot to'altiyot* or *chokhmot nimusiyot*. *Kultur* was regarded as an array of professional and useful skills, helpful in amending the image of Jewish society and in cultivating virtues, fostering good taste, and promoting a certain degree of enlightenment.[7] The aim of the Haskalah movement was, as we remember, to 'cultivate' the Jews; that is, to 'civilize' them. However, the criteria applied to culture in this sense were borrowed from the cultural environment, and the aim in meeting these criteria was to bring Jewish society closer to it. For it is important to bear in mind that the Haskalah hoped to be able to control the process of acculturation and to determine a new normative system that should create a balance between Judaism and the external culture.

A new and broader definition, in the spirit of German idealism, was the one proposed by the *Wissenschaft des Judentums*. In the programme he drew up in 1822 for the Society for Jewish Culture and Science, called 'Über den Begriff einer Wissenschaft des Judenthums', Immanuel Wolf defined Jewish culture as the concentrate of all the circumstances, traits, and achievements of the Jews in religion, philosophy, history, law, general literature, public life, and all other human endeavours. Wolf had in mind the complex whole of the cultural works of the past, and made an attempt to examine the ways in which the idea of Judaism, over the centuries, had taken diverse forms, embracing all shades and layers of Jewish history and literature. He also aspired to assemble this complex whole into a unity of meaning.[8] Zunz adopted the same view in compiling a complete bibliography of Jewish creative writing (the *Volksliteratur*) from the classic to the ephemeral; it was engendered by its fundamental ideas and modes of consciousness, which gave it content, meaning, and cohesiveness. Zunz never doubted that what was involved was a religious–national idea, which lay at the very foundation of Judaism in all its ramifications. His aim was to provide a complete picture of the branches that sprung from that same idea, and to describe the multifariousness which that religious idea was capable of creating, through the incorporation of foreign elements. The fundamental principle of Judaism possessed the power and capacity to assimilate and fuse any element that it absorbed.[9]

Wolf's intention, and that of his colleagues, was not to create a new Jewish culture in Germany, but to represent the Jews as a *Kulturvolk*

---

[7] Sorkin, *The Transformation*, 71–3.

[8] Wolf, 'On the Concept of a Science of Judaism', 203.

[9] Zunz, *Etwas über die rabbinische Literatur* (1818). See Wieseltier, '*Etwas über die judische* [sic] *Historik*'; Mendes-Flohr, 'The Jew as a Man of World Culture'; Schorsch, 'Breakthrough into the Past', Glatzer, 'The Beginnings of Modern Jewish Studies', 27–45. In contrast to Zunz, Geiger believed that the sciences do not form part of the national cultural heritage.

whose spiritual identity is not determined by religion alone. In this way, they hoped to prove that Jews could be full partners in the European-German culture of their time. They were looking for a new definition of *Jüdischsein* (Jewish existence) in order to reconcile some elements of *Volkstümlichkeit* (the authentic culture of the people) with German secular culture (*bürgerliche Kultur*).[10]

While Wolf, Zunz, Geiger, and others spoke of a culture which belonged to the past, the ideologues of the Hebrew revival spoke of and foresaw a culture that did not yet exist, which they hoped to structure, create, or even 'invent'. They desired not only the compilation and canonization of all the works produced in the past, but also the creation of a new 'living culture' that would be the foundation of the new Jewish national identity and commonality. Their aim was to study Jewish cultural history not in order to prove that in the past Jews had been active in all spheres of culture, but to search in the literary works of bygone eras for expressions of the Jewish spirit which could be revived to serve as inspiration for the new national culture. The ideology of the Hebrew revival alluded to re-creation of an integrative whole and sought out its organizing principle and cultural code in order to preserve its distinctiveness, but at the same time also acknowledged the imperative, and the value, of remaining open to the surrounding cultures. This acknowledgement of the need for openness only strengthened the need for a strong organizing principle.

In the language of the period, the term 'culture' might be understood on three levels.

(i) As what was then called the 'cultural condition' (*matzav kulturi*) or 'civilization'. So used, it meant the patterns of Jewish existence. While the patterns of existence in the European Diaspora and in the Levant were perceived as non-cultural, as expressing an old or backward culture, far removed from the civilizing progress that marked the developed 'Europe', the new culture in Palestine was intended to be modern and progressive in every sphere. This involved technological progress, relations of production, material culture, methods of education, the social structure, and much else. In fact, this involved a process of 'Westernization' or modernization—which are synonymous terms, since all the constituents of modernization were derived from a Western, European source.

(ii) As the totality of literary and artistic creation, the 'Great Tradition'. We have already seen (in Chapter 8) that when the Jews looked into the Greek mirror, they saw language, literature, music, and art as the main

---

[10] Schorsch, 'Breakthrough'; id., 'German Judaism: From Confession to Culture'.

manifestations of national genius and culture. Thus the Hebrew revival meant a new golden age of cultural creativity: first and foremost the creation of Hebrew literature, a Hebrew theatre, Jewish (or Palestinian) art, Jewish (or Palestinian) music, and the like. Consequently, the question of the content and style of creative works in all these spheres became a cardinal issue.

(iii) In the manner of German idealism, as the inner spiritual world of a society, not only its external manifestations. It was perceived as originating in the inner creative force of the collective, a manifestation of the a-personal dimension of the community's spiritual existence giving expression to the new content of life.[11]

This German holistic concept of *Kultur* placed special stress on national differences and on national identity; it was therefore very influential in central and eastern Europe.[12] Jewish thinkers and men of letters borrowed from German Romanticism and Hegelianism,[13] directly and indirectly, the concept of culture as a product of the distinctive national genius and as an organic totality expressing one total, central national idea (*ein besonderer Volksgeist*). From it they learnt that a nation was not a superficial entity but a deep-rooted collective,[14] an organism with a specific personality—dreams, fears, a mentality, complex values, and a philosophy of life.[15] Culture was described not as a mere collective being but as the dynamic power that shapes a people's psyche and arises from a central constitutive core—its *Idee*—originating in its singular spirit: a manifestation of distinctiveness (*Eigentümlichkeit*) and authenticity (*Echtheit*). Culture is also a code by which to understand and describe the world, a code of behaviour and of creation, which provides legitimacy, determines order, a hierarchy, and so forth. Most of the proponents of the idea of Hebrew culture were consummate Hegelians, and their world-outlook was shaped by the idealistic notion of culture as constituting a complete and unified system of values, norms, symbols, material works of art, etc. It was culture, then, that differentiated between one people and another, one nation and another. This culture, however, was not folklore or popular culture, but high culture; a *Kulturnation* could exist

---

[11] Mendes-Flohr, 'Hale'umiyut shebalev', 34–9.

[12] Elias, *The Civilizing Progress*, 3–13; Braudel, 'The History of Civilization'; Kroeber and Kluckhohn, *Culture*; Kroeber, *The Nature of Culture*. E. B. Tylor's definition still holds: culture is 'that complex whole which includes knowledge, belief, art, morals, customs, and any capabilities and habits acquired by man as a member of society' (*Primitive Culture*, 1).   [13] Gombrich, *In Search of Cultural History*.

[14] Iggers, *The German Conception of History*, 29–43.

[15] Walicki, *Philosophy and Romantic Nationalism*, 64–85.

and fulfil itself only if its culture met the accepted criteria. It was according to these that the cultural past was judged, and the cultural future portrayed.

A nation (these writers maintained) is also a living whole that grows and is cultivated. It is high culture which transforms a people into a nation or a *Kulturvolk*.[16] Hence the intention was, by the 'work of *kul'-tura*' (*avodat hatarbut* or *avodat hakulturah*), to raise the level of education and to produce a literature based on highly regarded Western models. Just as the model of Greek culture as representing the Greek genius became a cliché, the model of Jewish culture, similar in character, was contraposed to it. Judaism was depicted as a complete and unique culture with a glorious past, and by the ideologues of the national revival as a complete and unique culture that would also in the not too distant future represent the Jewish genius and its original creations. Culture now became a full and legitimate alternative to the Jewish religious essence, a complete substitute for religion. What was revolutionary here was the pronouncement that Judaism is a historical and cultural essence, a product of the spirit and innermost soul (*Gemüt*) of a nation whose uniqueness was expressed and encapsulated in its culture, not in its religion. Culture was depicted as determining the suprapersonal nature of the human collective, as an expression of its vitality and its power of creativity.

The emergence of the concept 'Jewish culture', and all the more so the emergence of the term 'secular Jewish national culture', marked a great revolution in Jewish history.[17] It was an expression of the deep rupture within the traditional normative system, to which it constituted a new alternative. Furthermore, a dialectical process ensued because in order to represent secular national Judaism as legitimate, it was necessary to challenge the outlook of so-called normative historical Judaism, which understood normativeness as a certain form of religious life and faith. This challenge led to a demand for a new normativeness, which questioned the normativeness of other outlooks in Judaism. Those who spoke about a 'new Jewish culture' or a 'Hebrew culture', were actually proposing a new type or ideal of normative Judaism, and since they were conscious of the rupture and the revolution, they felt impelled to point not only to change but also to elements of continuity in the cultural tradition. A

---

[16] On the Russian case see Walicki, *The Slavophile Controversy*, 394–455.

[17] See Brinker, *Narrative Art and Social Theory*; I. Even-Zohar, 'The Emergence of a Native Hebrew Culture'; Schweid, *Judaism and Secular Culture*; id., *The Idea of Judaism as a Culture*; Y. Shavit, 'Ahad Ha'am and Hebrew National Culture'; id., 'A National Society and National Hebrew Cultures'.

process ensued of selecting the symbols and values of a tradition, in order to formulate a new tradition.

As a result of this, the historical controversy within Zionist circles centred on the issue of the nature of this singular 'innermost soul' and on how it should be translated into a code of values and norms. This was an urgent need, since a national movement building a new society cannot. restrict itself to one dimension of the concept of culture, and certainly not only to philosophical studies on the nature and scope of the concept. It had to deal with a real culture, that is to say, with the new value system of the new society and its reality in almost every sphere. The Zionist movement was a political movement that grew out of an idea and a cultural platform; as in other national movements, writers, teachers, and artists were called upon to create a culture through *Kulturpolitik*[18]—for 'there is only one path that leads to nationhood and sovereignty, and its name is "culture"', in Jabotinsky's words. The term 'culture', as he and others used it, meant schools, textbooks, adult education, kindergartens, science books, playgrounds, Hebrew theatre, dictionaries, scientific terminology, physical maps, topographical maps, a university, technical colleges, as well as children's songs, idioms, games, leisure culture, ways of living, styles of furniture, manners, and so forth and so on. 'Culture' in this sense was the veritable embodiment of 'pure Hebrew life in the home, the street, and public institutions'.[19]

This perception of culture as a new cosmos was characteristic of the radical national ideology that regarded the new Jewish culture as a total, complete, and organic system, given expression in every sphere of society—thought, art, economy, the understanding of history, and so forth. It was considered a 'new translation' of Judaism and of Jewishness. Again and again one finds in contemporary literature phrases like: 'pure Hebrew life', 'original Hebrew culture', 'an individual style of life', 'a natural Hebrew culture'. These general phrases were made specific through a repertoire of physical and mental attributes, images, items of material culture, and the like. The Hebraist radicals, the spokesmen of the notion of the Hebrew revolution, motivated by the desire to create a total cultural world as well as by an organicist and idealistic world-view, became utopians—ideologues of a normative Hebrew culture for which they laid down rigid, even élitist rules. As a matter of fact, they established very harsh rules—a cultural halakhah—and attributed to Hebrew culture the status of sanctity,

---

[18] Y. Shavit, 'The Status of Culture'.

[19] Jabotinsky, 'Avodah umatzav ru'ach' (1919), and see Berl Katznelson, 'Likrat hayamim haba'im' (1919). Quoted in Shavit, 'The Status'.

of a *Kulturreligion*. Moreover, since they were ideologues of a culture of which only the basic elements existed and were active—a culture in the making, becoming crystallized and institutionalized in a defined social and historical context—they attempted to predetermine its normative system. They sought to define the permissible and the forbidden in nearly every sphere of life. They regarded cultural nationalism as a tool with which they could develop the spirit of the people, improve its qualities, shape its world-outlook in all spheres—intellectual, emotional, aesthetic—and build its material world. They believed that the role of the national movement and its institutions was to discharge all these tasks. To do so, they needed clear guidelines about what belonged and was appropriate to this new framework, and what was alien and unnecessary; in other words, a set of rules for a cultural halakhah.

THE SEARCH FOR AN IDEAL HEBREW CULTURE

Alas, it was easier to set forth the ideal of Hebrew culture than to determine and shape its concrete contents. There were several reasons for this: first, culture—unlike institutionalized religion—can have no obligatory books of rules; its accepted and internalized canon of values, symbols, and patterns of behaviour becomes crystallized in the course of history, not as a one-off constitutive event.[20] Second, Jewish culture from its inception was changing and diversified, and the major, and most striking, feature of nineteenth-century Jewry was the creation of many diverse cultural centres. Third, Judaism laid down various prohibitions in the realm of culture, but had no overall cultural conception; and we have already seen that many of the prohibitions were the outcome of social policy, not of halakhic rules. Consequently a broad area was left open to outside influences, depending on historical circumstances and social and cultural needs. This presented an objective difficulty for any attempt to set up a uniform cultural model that should apply both to the past and to the future.

Nevertheless, the ideologues of the new Hebrew culture believed they could design it on the basis of the model they found desirable. Indeed, given their approach they could assume no otherwise. Hence this rupture with tradition, combined with the desire to propose a new model of normative Judaism, produced a severe and fundamental inner tension that can be easily discerned in the writings of many scholars and men of letters. It is markedly reflected in the words of Berdyczewski, a representative of

[20] Lotman and Uspenski, 'Binary Models', 30–1.

the radical, historicist Hebrew world-view. He believed that there is no such thing as one sole normative Judaism ('There is no Judaism common to all the generations . . .'), and that throughout the centuries, Judaism had undergone deep-seated changes. Judaism is the creation of the Jews (and not vice versa, as the religious outlook would have it). Berdyczewski asked the rhetorical question: 'Is there any need to say that the God of the Song of Songs is not the God of Ben-Sira . . .?'[21] He held the radical view that one can totally change the content and values of Judaism and still remain a Jew, since a people can begin a new spiritual life. But when Berdyczewski attempted to define culture, he did so as:

a historical and spiritual property that encompasses all of human spiritual life and casts it into a permanent historical-popular form peculiar to a specific grouping. To put that into simplistic language: culture is the eternal remnant of ephemeral life and ephemeral needs, a remnant passed down from father to son and from generation to generation.

In his view, then, the Jews have no common religious system, but they do have a common metaculture. They have also internalized a psychological core and a consciousness that are both permanent and peculiar to them. Thus when Berdyczewski addresses the issue of culture, he becomes a historicist with a distinctly organicist world-view. The reason is clear: in his opinion, culture is a system of views, experiences, and values that is handed down from generation to generation. Each people has its own special system. Had he thought otherwise, he would have had to conclude that in the framework of Jewish culture there could be no normativeness: either several types of Jewish culture existed at one and the same time, of which Hebrew culture was one; or Hebrew culture had severed itself from the national spiritual continuity and a 'new people' had come into being.

Yehezkel Kaufmann faced the very same dilemma. He believed that in reality there is an infinite multiplicity of works of culture, not only in the diachronic, but also in the synchronic dimension. It is from this point of departure that Kaufmann, the critic of philosophical idealism, also had to determine what his chosen form of normativeness was for the new historical era, and what 'form of culture' was the desirable normative model that ought to be selected out of this 'multiplicity of forms'.[22] Since he believed that culture is a product of diverse historical circumstances, he was forced to believe in the existence of a 'latent creative spirit' with crystallized values, not transient but eternal, as well as a unique characteristic style;

---

[21] Berdyczewski, 'Shinui arakhim', 37–8.
[22] Y. Kaufmann, 'Bekivshonah shel hayetzirah hale'umit', 11–33.

that is to say, the distinctive content and pattern of creativity resulting from a long historical process. Thus the process of creating shared values causes these values to leave their imprint on all areas of creative work, producing a stylistic uniformity that clearly identifies the specific culture. But nowhere did he state what the distinctive style of the new national culture should be like. He probably believed that it could not be predetermined and that the historian can only observe the process and determine its character after it has crystallized. This inability to translate general concepts into an overall cultural system with delineated features is characteristic of nearly all the Zionist and nationalist literature. Kaufmann rejected what he termed the 'symbolic idealism in Hegel's teachings', and did not believe that one constitutive principle was dominant in every culture. Such a principle, in his view, symbolized nebulous entities, but not a cultural reality. A people has no one spiritual essence, he claimed, but is governed by diverse styles: 'There were different and opposed entities in the Greek nation, such as Athens and Sparta.' The question that arises from this assumption is whether one cohesive and uniform Jewish culture or Greek culture ever existed.

Another interesting example of this inner conflict between the diversified nature of Jewish culture and the search for a unified normative culture can be found in Buber's writings. In an article entitled 'Medinah vetarbut' ('State and Culture'), Buber expresses his concern about the prospect of the state's intervention in shaping cultural life and tells his readers how, in classical Athens, Pisistratus established one large festival in honour of the god of the peasants, Dionysus, but did not dictate the topics of art or of poetry. In this way, spontaneous works were created in Greece and the freedom of culture was preserved. In ancient Egypt, on the other hand (as Buber learnt from Plato), the state (and the religion) dictated the topics of art. According to his view, which is based on the popular ideal image of the Greeks, even though they had no books of law, they possessed a unified culture. Concerned about the long arm of the state, Buber spoke in the name of spontaneous creativity without any obligatory rules, but at the same time he spoke of the need to set cultural norms that draw upon the unique psychic mechanism of the people.[23]

Here, then, lies the inner tension at the core of the new idea of culture. How could harmony be achieved between the freedom of cultural creativity and the uniformity of content and style? How would it be pos-

---

[23] Buber, 'Medinah vetarbut'. See also his article 'Yahadut vetarbut'. He wrote that the citizens of Israel should be proud to be citizens of a state whose heritage is similar to that of Athens, and not, Heaven forbid, to that of Egypt.

sible to achieve such uniformity in the context of Jewish culture? The cultural past, as we have seen, could not serve as a suitable guide. No other way remained than to attempt to identify and define the character of the 'Jewish genius' and to believe that in Palestine, in a 'natural' and sovereign framework, communal life would create a new cultural style. However, the ideologues of culture were too apprehensive about cultural disarray and pluralism to rely on the force of some hidden mechanism. As a result, they all sought to put forward a cultural programme and to engage in *Kulturpolitik*. This utopian pretension engendered on the one hand a cultural eschatology, a belief in the creation of a new, distinct, and integrative culture as a vital element in national redemption, and on the other a perpetual feeling of dissatisfaction and disappointment. For this reason, then, it was difficult for these ideologues to arrive at an agreed description of an ideal or model. It was even more difficult for them to translate abstract concepts into a concrete repertoire.

HEBREW CULTURE
FROM AN ORTHODOX POINT OF VIEW

Whereas the ideologues, promoters, and creators of Hebrew culture found it difficult to define that Hebrew culture, the replacement of the concept of Torah by the concept of culture was glaringly reflected in the mirror of Jewish Orthodoxy. Orthodox Jews also understood very well the nature of the radical change that had taken place in Judaism during the nineteenth century, and they defined freethinking Judaism, as soon as it came upon the scene, as based upon immanent nationalism and upon Judaized Greek culture. It was not only licentiousness (*hitpakrut*), a form of forsaking Judaism, but rather a conscious attempt to construct an all-encompassing new Judaism. The secular Jew is a 'forsaker of the Torah, a heretic', and even more dangerous than the heretic of former periods, since the modern secular national Jew does not quit Judaism but wants to change its nature from within to a Judaism without Torah and commandments. In the eyes of a religiously observant Jew, freethinking nationalistic Judaism means, as we have seen, a new Judaism 'built on foundations of chaos'; the secular Jew is a 'forsaker of the Torah, a heretic'.[24] For example, Y. M. Pines (1843–1913), an observant Jew and a leader of Hibbat Zion and the Yishuv, considered the totality of constituents in modern Jewish culture as 'a Judaized Greek culture'. It was, in his eyes, analogous to a 'new heresy',

[24] Hirschberg, 'Be'eretz hamizrach', 163–73. Malachi, 'The War of the Old Yishuv against Ahad Ha'am'.

a licentious culture of heresy and illusion. In its schools the students did
not learn Torah, only Hebrew and history; it was a culture containing
'Sabbath desecration, immorality, and dancing', that turned the theatre
into a 'regular occurrence in Israel and in Eretz Yisrael', whose way of life
was similar to that of all the nations.[25] In 1912, Chaim Tchernowitz (Rav
Tza'ir), following his visit to Palestine, wrote that some Hebrew teachers
'try to . . . create a Jewish type based on the period of the First Temple, on
Jephthah . . . or on Samson, who lived by his sword and his courage. . . .
most of the teachers . . . arrange excursions and games on the Olympic
pattern'.[26] These are not mere 'deviations from the norm', or found only
among the 'ignorant', the *am ha'aretz*, he wrote, for they are defined by the
freethinkers as the very essence and substance of Jewish culture. The fact
that both observant and secular Jews drew upon the same reservoir of values
and symbols occasionally narrowed the gap between them, but could not
bridge it. The paradox is that secular nationalism, by reinterpreting Jewish
tradition to meet its needs, overturned the foundation of the religious
interpretation and downplayed religious elements; instead of constituting
common ground between the two groups, the fact of drawing on the
same reservoir of values exacerbated internal tension, since here different
interpretations of the same cultural heritage were vying with each other,
laying claim to legitimacy, if not exclusivity.

What made the conflict inevitable was the new secular Hebrew society's
refusal to accept halakhah as the normative code of behaviour, and the
centrality of foreign culture to its existence. And if that were not enough,
as we shall see further on, secular culture interprets its Judaism in Graecized
terms. Contrary to the religiously observant society, the free society no
longer lived according to the Torah, but turned its perception of the essence
of Jewish culture into a constitutive element that moulded its identity
and quiddity. This society exhibited its Hellenization by making radical
changes in its consciousness of identity and self-definition in relation to
its past and heritage. This was not merely a change in its way of life, or
the annexation of a neutral cultural system; this was an exchange of one
cultural system for another. Because this culture was in fact saturated with
foreign elements, the freethinking Jew found himself required to meet his
adversaries' arguments in matters that touched upon his link to the past.
He also felt obliged to find answers to questions about the nature of his

[25] Pines, 'Ahavat hachikui'. For examples of the emulation of Greek ways in Palestine of the 1880s,
Pines cited the secular schools, amateur theatricals, and dances in which both men and women participated. To him, Ahad Ha'am was a modern Menelaus, the 'high priest' of Hellenistic licentiousness.

[26] Tchernowitz, 'Rishmei Eretz Yisrael', 3–4, quoted in Frankel, 'The "Yizkor" Book of 1911', 376
n. 58. See Ch. 8.

identity. He had to define his Judaism and claim legitimacy; he had to clarify for his adversaries and critics where he stood within the Jewish historical continuity, whose existence he did not deny, and to explain what gave him the right to change the essence of Judaism and why his new Judaism was entitled to be regarded as Judaism.

BORROWING AND DISTINCTIVENESS

We have seen that, in the past, 'culture' had been an indivisible part of the Jewish religion, and that religion and religious tradition determined, in most areas of life, what was permissible and what was forbidden in the development and adoption of various constituents of culture. This system of religion and culture was established by leaders who possessed halakhic authority. That does not mean that the religious system of rules controlled everything, or that it was always uniform, but it was the dominant system. The penetration of cultural elements from the outside was, throughout the entire course of Jewish history, a complex and multifaceted process that generally required religious legitimation, or at the very least could not be opposed to the accepted religious and cultural norms. Those elements from the outside that penetrated into the religious system and were internalized were primarily in the sphere of custom and folklore, and the processes of indigenizing and Judaizing these elements were manifested in diverse ways.[27]

Scholars disagree about how many of these customs were the corollary of inner development and how many developed by way of borrowing and adoption. But there is no doubt that key customs, which became an inseparable part of the religious culture, were the result of borrowing and assimilation. This assimilation took place both in the domain of the Great Tradition (high culture) and the Little Tradition (low or folk culture). The chronicles of Jewish culture are an unceasing tale of processes of adoption and assimilation accompanied by an effort to create an inner reconciliation between internal and external components and to find a correspondence between them.[28] For many components assimilation was accompanied by controversies and a need for legitimation, while others were assimilated

[27] See e.g. Ta-Shema, *Early Franco-German Ritual*, 13–105; Wexler, *The Ashkenazic Jews*, 83–180; Pollack, *Jewish Folkways in Germanic Lands*.

[28] Bonfil, *As by a Mirror*, 123–32; J. Dan, *Hebrew Ethical and Homiletical Literature*, 183–201. M. Singer writes: 'For a foreign import . . . to enter the hallowed realm of the traditional, it must become old, must conform to customary or scriptural norms, and must have an origin in myth, in which it is linked to a great traditional set of ancestors or precedents . . . As a result of this process of "traditionalization", the new turned into something old' (*When a Great Tradition Modernizes*, 397, 399).

in a 'natural' way, that is to say, almost unnoticed; many of them became an indivisible part of Jewish culture. However, in no period before the nineteenth century were all these elements represented as an inseparable part of Jewish culture or as a manifestation of its nature. It was only from the nineteenth century, when religious precepts no longer determined the limits of the permissible and the forbidden, when their authority was challenged and rejected, that the system of Hebrew culture was called upon, with greater authority and urgency, to determine a normative system of its own. In the modern era, in other words, numerous items of culture are borrowed, since the modern Jew is a consumer of non-Jewish culture to an extent that has no precedent in the past. Hence an attempt was made to control the patterns of the consumption of the foreign culture and to define what was regarded as 'licentiousness' and the like. And—most important of all—since the borrowing and adoption of foreign elements were regarded as an essential, legitimate process, the mechanisms that should control borrowing and the criteria that should apply to the process became a cardinal question. As a result, an attempt was made to formulate a programme and policy for the selection of specific foreign and indigenous elements out of which a new cultural identity could be forged.

In the previous chapters, I described how several modern Western categories of thought were internalized into the Jewish intellectual world. The interaction between Jewish and Christian (and Muslim) thought is so complex that it is not always possible to follow the transformations these ideas underwent from the time of Philo, through Saadiah Gaon and Maimonides, until the modern era. The difference between these borrowings and the history of the general Jewish world-view and Jewish culture is clear: the latter is not a case of reciprocal influence between Jewish and non-Jewish élites, but rather the internalization of concepts by broad segments of the population. Hence the arguments about the elements of foreign cultures that were absorbed into Jewish culture were more trenchant than arguments on a more philosophical level.

The Greek case can serve as a point of departure for a discussion of this issue. The Greeks, as we have seen, never tried to conceal the fact that many elements of their culture came from foreign sources. But they—and nearly all the later literature dealing with the source of key items of Greek culture—understood the Greek miracle as the fruit of the Greeks' unique capacity to absorb and recreate these borrowed items. The assumption was that the Greeks' genius transformed what they learnt into something new. Traditional Jewish literature, in contrast, usually tried to represent Jewish culture as a singular product, free of any foreign influences. It was generally accepted that the history of Jewish culture was a history of an inner tradition living by its own laws and that every external influence was a fundamentally invalid phenomenon. Y. M. Pines, for example, condemned the 'destructive tendency of imitation' that held so many in thrall. He suggested a conservative historical schema, according to which the growth of trends of cultural imitation (or of universalist and cosmopolitan trends) within the Jewish people was the result of an increasing love of imitation.[29]

These charges were sometimes countered by outright denial of external influence: the phenomenon in question was said to have developed autonomously within Judaism itself. When this was impossible, and pagan borrowing could not even be classified as neutral 'wisdom', recourse might be had to the 'cunning of Providence' (as one may term it), classically illustrated by Maimonides' account of Temple sacrifice:

But the custom which was in those days general among all men, and the general mode of worship in which the Israelites were brought up, consisted in sacrificing animals in those temples which contained certain images . . . It was in accordance with the wisdom and plan of God, as displayed in the Whole Creation, that He did not command us to give up and discontinue all these manners of the service, for to obey such a commandment would have been contrary to the nature of man, who generally cleaves to that which he is used to . . . He transferred to His service that which had formerly served as a worship of created beings, and of things imaginary and unreal, and commanded us to serve Him in the same manner.[30]

Such a notion could bestow retrospective legitimacy on the phenomenon of borrowing and appropriating pagan elements into the practice of Judaism. Islam too had need for a similar principle of legitimations; and so had the forgers of the new national culture. In their view, the history of Jewish culture is a history of an unending process of borrowing and rejection, of interaction between internal forces of creativity and external influences, which shaped the contours of this culture.

Since secular, nationalist Jews, unlike Orthodox Jews, accepted foreign cultural influences as a fact, they had in consequence to differentiate between positive and negative influences. The distinction was between the borrowing of traits of the low, popular culture and customs regarded as unsuitable on the one hand, and the borrowing of cultural traits regarded as high and positive on the other. The definition of traits of low

---

[29] Pines, 'Ahavat hachikui'.

[30] Maimonides, *Guide of the Perplexed*, iii. 32 (p. 323). Unquestionably Maimonides was familiar with the ways in which Islam 'neutralized' and 'appropriated' pagan customs, including those associated with the Kaʿba in Mecca.

acculturation varied from generation to generation according to the conservative or liberal stance of those who determined the cultural ideology and the criteria to be applied.[31] Owing to the deep concern aroused by the danger of negative acculturation, all parties—Orthodox, *maskilim*, and nationalists—were impelled, each in its own way, to try to formulate rules of prohibitions and injunctions that should direct and regulate cultural contacts and influences:

The Jews have always been ready and willing to receive from the nations they dwell amongst, in antiquity from the Canaanites, the Babylonians, and the other nations, and in later years, from the Greeks, the Romans, the Arabs, and others . . . But then, while the Spirit was still mighty upon them, a new and holy spirit, a spirit zealous for unity, they received with open eyes only what was acceptable to their faith, and what was alien to them, they dispersed further; go, go, they said to it.[32]

The Galician scholar Joshua Heschel Schorr (1818–95), who wrote thus in 1865, was one of the pioneers of Jewish scholarly research into Persian influences on Jewish culture from the time of the Return to Zion. His article was one of the first attempts to find the patterns of the positive link between the Jewish and alien cultures. In the same vein, in an article entitled 'Min hachutzah ha'ohelah' ('From Outside into the Tent'), Nachman Syrkin drew a distinction between the periods when Jewish culture took in and absorbed outside elements, and those when it closed itself off from the world around it and arrested its development. A positive and fruitful encounter is created when a culture has an inner, vital power that allows it to show openness and to absorb elements from without. Isolation is a demonstration of weakness and instability. In that event, the most productive periods in the history of the Jewish spirit were times of great openness—such as the Second Temple era—that did not impair Jewish singularity, but rather infused it with new content.

In his well-known essay 'Slavery in Freedom', Ahad Ha'am also tried to offer a key to a positive pattern of borrowing. In his scheme, Judaism does not lock its gates against alien cultures, but on the contrary opens them wide. However, it can only work properly and positively in those circumstances when culture (the spirit) is able to incorporate the borrowed elements. The nature of the spirit of individuality is revealed mainly through its ability to absorb and internalize. The Jewish people is entitled to receive whatever it lacks from the outside, wrote Rabbi Abraham Isaac

---

[31] Zipperstein, 'Jewish Enlightenment in Odessa'; Feiner, 'The Modern Jewish Woman'.
[32] Schorr, 'HaTorah vedat Zaratustra'.

Kook, but 'influence is dictated by the inner essence'. In other words, the beauty of Japheth when it comes into the tents of Shem is there refashioned by the inner force of Shem.[33] According to this concept, individuality is not the cultural product, but rather its crucible. Therein lies the difference between 'imitation and assimilation' on the one hand, and the borrowing and absorption of positive elements and values, on the other. Thus individuality, a mystic metacultural entity, became strengthened and intensified as a selective mechanism, which works according to an inner code of unequivocal rules. This is the 'hidden hand' of culture, and one must recognize its laws and then work according to them.

The belief in the power of individuality to assimilate and naturalize foreign elements was shared by all currents of Judaism. For the most part, however, all those who believed it possible to determine a new normative system had to believe in the existence of individuality. No ideology and no mechanism of cultural control could work if it did not arise from within the same hidden inner strength that is actually the prime regulator of the cultural mechanism and determines the criteria according to which it works. If no such hidden inner strength exists, then there is no chance whatsoever for any kind of cultural mechanism to work, for without that strength it is liable to create a non-authentic, artificial, alien, heterogeneous culture.

However, since Jewish cultural tradition could not provide the ideologues of Hebrew culture with valid and clear criteria for the permissible and the forbidden, they had to use vague concepts about values that expressed the 'spirit of the nation' or the 'spirit of Judaism'. These vague terms could not define the value culture of Hebrew culture, and certainly not the real culture of the new Jewish society. Quite often it appeared as if those who spoke of Hebrew culture as the essence of Judaism and an expression of Jewish singularity and distinctiveness believed that it would spring up miraculously from the newborn Jewish collective 'self' in Palestine, and would, through the new patterns of life there, create a revitalized Jewish society, a nation of Jews new in body and soul. Such conditions— thought many of the philosophers of the Hebrew revival—would be fully realized in Palestine as part of a national and territorially based Jewish society. Only then would Jewish culture be able once again to be open and organic at one and the same time. 'Without organicism . . . there is no vital culture'; organicism, an inner creation whose parts are all interwoven, means integrativeness stamped with the impress of the idiosyncratic synthesizing principle.[34]

[33] Kook, *Orot*, 152.   [34] Zur, *Kehiliyatenu*, 156.

FROM AN IDEAL CULTURE TO A REAL CULTURE

Only rarely does a complete system of beliefs and customs pass from one society to another, and it is even rarer to find one cultural layer disappearing in its entirety and being replaced by another without leaving any traces. However, elements tend to be transmitted from one society to another and from one culture to another. The question to be asked, then, is not only what was transmitted, but how it was absorbed and what the results of that absorption were. Or, in the words of Ashley Montague: 'Diffusion is the process by which cultural traits have been transmitted from one group to another—to be distinguished from acculturation, the process during which cultural traits are actively being transmitted from one people to another.'[35] Therefore, from the historical point of view, the question is how the Jewish cultural system culled what it absorbed and injected new content into the borrowed elements. At this point, the cohesiveness of a cultural system determines the impact made on it by the acceptance of outside influences. A society with a complete and well-established cultural system can accept, incorporate, and assimilate cultural values from the outside without being weakened, or it can refuse to accept them.

The cultural system of the Yishuv and its repertoire were created in several simultaneous processes. Many of these were controlled: various cultural mechanisms initiated, planned, culled, and disseminated items of culture in the society. Some others were items created in the 'free market' of the culture, frequently to the chagrin of those responsible for the various cultural mechanisms.

However, the influx of cultural elements transmitted from one system to another as direct borrowings—what may be termed 'active taking'[36]—was determined first of all by need, by the function that the materials of culture had to fulfil. Since the new cultural system was in need of many elements it had previously lacked, and since at least some parts of it were crucial for the construction of the new culture and society, the repertoire of the required materials was very large. Thus the process of transmission and reception was determined by the availability, accessibility, and in particular the suitability of cultural components, which were preferred if they were regarded as suitable to the spirit of the new society, and were selected as the foreign segment of the Hebrew culture if they were regarded as congruent or compatible with it. For example, since those who set the tone regarded

---

[35] Montagu, *Man: His First Two Million Years*, 218.

[36] For the term see I. Even-Zohar, 'Cultural Interferences'; cf. id., 'Laws of Literary Interference', 'Relations between Primary and Secondary Systems', 'Russian and Hebrew'.

realistic literature as more appropriate than modernistic literature, for a long time mainly realistic literature was translated, and original Hebrew works were written according to the realistic literary model.

In a short time the ideologues of culture developed patterns of argument closely resembling those employed by the old Jewish tradition. They distinguished between 'good' and 'bad', between the permitted and the forbidden in the repertoire of borrowing. Through their cultural mechanisms they sought to control the cultural system in three ways:

(i) by choosing elements from within the high and the popular Jewish culture while changing their meaning and function, in particular with regard to those from the religious tradition;

(ii) by selecting those elements from among other cultures that seemed worthy of being received and absorbed into the Hebrew culture and making some of them an inseparable part of it and its 'authentic' culture (for example, popular Russian songs and music were adapted and absorbed, becoming popular Hebrew songs; the same was true of folk dances from eastern Europe);[37]

(iii) by selecting those elements of an 'alien' identity that could be permitted to exist as a non-Hebrew subsystem alongside the Hebrew system.

The first two ways involve the selection and absorption into Hebrew culture of outside elements; the third involves elements that remain clearly imported. The process of culling and absorption may be a product of a functional need; since this was an intensive process of creating a culture and of filling a void by supplying any cultural elements that were lacking, there was hardly an element that was not judged according to its correspondence to a predetermined model. The national ideology tried to lay down rules on what was permitted and forbidden in every part of the realm of cultural consumption, even in material culture. However, its main concern was with value culture.

It sought, for example, to determine what should be the character of education in the schools, which works of world literature merited translation,[38] and which were forbidden;[39] what films should be shown and what

---

[37] D. Segal, 'The Impact of Russian Literature'. The national anthem *Hatikvah* is a very good example: its melody originated in a Romanian folk-tune.

[38] Z. and Y. Shavit, 'Translated vs. Original Literature'.

[39] Kaniel, 'Continuity and Change'; M. Singer, *When a Great Tradition Modernizes*, 405; I. Even-Zohar, 'Relations Between Primary and Secondary Systems'; Schweid, 'The Jewish Pluralistic Culture in Israel'; Liebman, 'The Jewish Religion'; Liebman and Don-Yehiya, *Civil Religion in Israel*. Needless

plays should be staged; which style of music, which school of art was most suitable to the spirit of the Jewish society in Palestine, and so forth. Many cultural agents participated in the creation and dissemination of values, patterns of behaviour, new symbols, and ceremonies—all with the aim of creating a shared Hebrew culture. This process entailed elements of subordination, neutralization, compartmentalization, vicarious ritualization, typological stylization, reinterpretation, archaization, and much else.

Does this multiplicity of borrowed items in the repertoire of Hebrew culture and the significance of imported culture in the overall cultural system mean that the Hebrew culture of Israel lacks any singularity or individuality? In order to answer this question, one has to compare this new culture both with Jewish cultures in previous generations and with the non-Jewish cultures from which Israeli culture borrowed many items. This comparison will point to many differences in both instances. The major difference, it seems to me, lies in the composition of the many subcultures that make up Israeli culture; this is an unprecedented pluralism, which exists in a social and political framework whose like there has never been before in Jewish history.

Every civilization, Kroeber wrote, is 'a composite of different elements, some of them borrowed from other cultures'. However, 'In spite of the foreign origins [of] the bulk of their cultural inventories . . . most cultures succeed in working and organizing these elements into a distinctive overall pattern or style.' Once crystallized, a total pattern or style gives a culture its distinctive character.[40] In other words, the absorption of materials of culture is an inevitable and necessary process in the creation of any culture, and need not impair its identity. Its content may change, but only in extreme cases of cultural conversion is the link between past and new identity severed.

A Jewish traveller from the Middle Ages or even the eighteenth century, not to speak of one from the Hellenistic era, would find in twentieth-century Israel many cultural elements—patterns of society, institutions, customs, and values—that he would recognize as familiar to him: synagogues, the Hebrew calendar, the Sabbath, the seder, and holidays that represent the continuation of the Jewish way of life but for a non-religious Jew are part of his tradition or 'Jewishness', not an integral part of a re-

---

to say, the literature, both polemical and scholarly, concerning the relationship between the Jewish state and the Jewish religion is vast indeed.

[40] Kroeber, *An Anthropologist Looks at History*, 40. On the Kroeber–Redfield models see M. Singer, *When a Great Tradition Modernizes*, 251–2.

ligious way of life. But he would be surprised to discover a great many others that were new and totally unfamiliar. He would find it difficult to define the culture, just as people today often have trouble in characterizing it in an unambiguous way. There is no way of knowing how our imaginary traveller would react or what his impressions might be, but anyone who is part of the present-day secular Israeli Jewish culture and knows he has a cultural identity of his own still has a hard time defining it. Paradoxically, it is its special syncretistic nature that makes this culture unique in relation to others and in relation to the Jewish culture of the past. Within this complex, all the things branded by rabbinical society as alien or Greek were added to the Jewish cultural system, becoming an integral part of it. The classical heritage and Hellenism, transmitted through Western culture, became an inseparable and essential part of secular Israeli Jewish culture and shaped its image. The 'ancient culture of Jerusalem', the ideal of religiously observant Jews, has in Israel been replaced to a great extent by the 'culture of Greece'. In contrast to the situation in earlier generations, 'Greek' institutions, values, and patterns of behaviour—theatre, plastic arts, *belles-lettres*, academe, sport—are not merely tolerated phenomena, but a major part of Jewish life.

A secular Jew is not merely a *Hellēnistēs*, one who behaves like the Gentiles by participating in the foreign culture: the foreign culture is an inalienable part of his own new culture and provides him with the concepts and definitions with which to test his old Judaism, define his new identity, and form his cultural life.

CONCLUSION: WHAT HAS ATHENS TO DO WITH JERUSALEM?

W E might have gone on travelling in this Jewish and Greek Hellenistic land of mirrors and inverted mirrors, which could reflect additional aspects of modern Jewish history. Would it not have been appropriate, for example, to discuss the continuity between Hellenistic antisemitism and modern secular antisemitism? And ought we not to compare the Jewish and Greek attitudes towards women, or towards love and sex? Should we not find a similarity in the relationship that exists between the Greek and Jewish diasporas and their homelands? Or in the relation between religion and state in Judaism and the State of Israel, and in Greece? Do the Jewish and Greek cultures both belong to the realm of Mediterranean culture, with its shared contents and traits? And what of the parallel between the development of the modern Greek and modern Hebrew languages? We could, indeed, go further in this vast realm of analogies, but it seems that at this point it is time to reach some conclusions.

More than fifty years ago, Gershom Scholem stated that Maimonides' Judaism was closer to the Christianity or Islam of his own time than it was to the Judaism of today. What he probably had in mind was the Judaism of a secular Jew.[1] Maimonides, according to this observation, would have felt more at home in contemporary Cairo and Rome than in modern-day Jerusalem. Scholem was, to a great extent, exaggerating, but he caustically pointed to the revolutionary historical change the Jewish people had undergone since the twilight of the eighteenth century. And this observation leads us back to the two mirrors—the Greek and the Hellenistic—and to the way Judaism is reflected in them.

The fact that Athens is an integral and essential part of the modern Jerusalem has, I hope, been well established in this study. If this is so, and if, as proposed by the model of antimony, Athens and Jerusalem are two antipodal entities, how can these hostile and contradicting spiritual and cultural entities exist together? If we look in the Greek mirror, or better said, in the mirror of the ideal Greece, the answer is that modern Judaism, namely secular Judaism, inspired by Athens and shaped by the heritage of classical antiquity (and Western values), is a different type of Judaism from the Judaism of previous generations; therefore, the conflict between Athens

[1] Scholem, 'Zikaron ve'utopiyah', 95.

and Jerusalem *in* Jerusalem was and is inevitable. This conflict is the core of the struggle over the identity and content of modern Judaism in Palestine. On the other hand, if one accepts the historical model that stresses the existence of Hellenic and Hellenistic cultural ingredients in Judaism from the time of the Second Temple, and their influence on the nature of Judaism through the ages, then by looking into the Hellenistic mirror one may conclude that once again Judaism is a dynamic and multifaceted phenomenon in which different alien traits are absorbed and that, as in antiquity, the interchange between these and the indigenous traits creates the core and essence of modern Jewish life and Jewish identity.

Let us persist with the language of mirrors, in which Jerusalem and Athens (as well as Alexandria and Antioch) serve as metaphors for various models of Judaism. In the public consciousness in Israel, the two cities of Tel Aviv and Jerusalem symbolize the polarity in Israeli culture: Tel Aviv, the secular, hedonistic, dynamic, liberal city, versus Jerusalem, the religious, even ultra-religious, frozen, conservative city. This antithesis depicts Jewish Jerusalem as a monotonous entity, whereas in fact it is a microcosm (*tevel*, in the language of the Midrash) of modern Jewry.

The Hellenization of Jerusalem before the Hasmonean revolt was manifested, we shall recall, in its transformation into a *polis*, and in the erection of a *gymnasium* and *ephebeia* on the Temple Mount, institutions that to the author of 2 Maccabees (4: 13) were 'the height of Greek fashions, and increase of heathenish manners'. Hellenism came to Jerusalem again in the days of the Hasmonean kings, and with greater impetus and intensivity during Herod's reign. Josephus tells how Herod violated the ancestral laws in Jerusalem (*Antiquities*, xv. 267–76) and began, with alien customs, to disrupt the ancient order of life, which he was forbidden to encroach upon. He built a theatre, a hippodrome, and a stadium in which wrestling-matches, stage-entertainments, and wild-beast fights in the Roman manner were held; even more offence was caused by the erection of trophies, which the Jews took to be idols. By common consent, says Josephus, 'he was closer to Greeks than to Jews', in contrast to Agrippa, who scrupulously observed ancestral custom in Jerusalem even though he furthered Graeco-Roman culture in Beirut (ibid. xix. 328–37). This pagan Jerusalem existed alongside the Jewish Jerusalem of the Second Temple with its ritual of sacrifices, pilgrimages, schools of study, Sages, and spiritual creation. From Josephus' description, one could conclude that all the Jews of Jerusalem viewed this 'Hellenization' of the city as an appalling affront to the ancestral laws and a desecration of its purity, but in fact Herod himself and the Herodian circles often displayed a large measure of sensitivity for the Jewish position and curtailed their own Hellenistic tendencies, particularly in Jerusalem, whereas the Jews did not spurn all the manifestations of Hellenistic culture, certainly not in its material form. Although we do not know what plays were performed in the Herodian theatre in Jerusalem, even if these were works by Euripides and Sophocles, rather than mime, one may assume that for most of the Jews this was not Athens in Jerusalem but rather Antioch in Jerusalem.

This tense co-existence of 'Judaism' and 'Hellenism', which led, among other things, to the Great Revolt, cannot fully characterize the nature of the historical model I have called 'Athens in Jerusalem'. For in addition to the reciprocal relations and the enormous rising tensions between the two cities considered as symbols, there were various channels of influence between Hellenism and Judaism. And we have already seen that the processes of 'Hellenization' bore a more complex nature than the adoption of different components of material culture. Quite a few important elements of Hellenistic culture were adopted and internalized by layers and factions of Jewish society and culture, and in diverse ways these affected the shape taken by this society and culture. Hellenism served as a rival, a challenge, and an inspiration that aroused diverse reactions in different Jewish groups. Without the influence of 'Athens' (or 'Alexandria'), Second Temple Judaism would have been quite different, and the legacy of Jerusalem to the generations to come would also have been different. After the pagan Aelia Capitolina had become first a Christian and then a Muslim city, its inhabitants, adherents of all these religions, as well as all its rulers, Christians and Muslims alike, strictly maintained its religious and conservative nature, forbidding the existence of any cultural institutions alongside the religious ones. The appearance of the café as a cultural-social institution in the eighteenth century was an exception that proved the rule.

The creation of the new Jewish Jerusalem outside the city walls from the end of the nineteenth century, which was greatly accelerated after the British conquest in 1917, was attended by the establishment of cultural institutions which were here metaphorically defined (but non-metaphorically by their critics) as 'Greek Hellenistic'. These included an academy of music, an art school (Bezalel, 1906), a sports organization (which was called, of course, Maccabee, just as a soccer team that played on Saturdays, even in Jerusalem, was called, nothing more and nothing less, than Makabi-Chashmona'i or 'Hasmonean Maccabee'!), a theatre, cinemas, a university (1925), and a sports stadium. The British authorities wished to perserve Jerusalem's unique character as a conservative and religious (and 'oriental') city, but paid special attention to what was taking place inside the walls, whereas outside them a new city was taking shape.

Thus the struggle over the character of Jerusalem was renewed, reflecting world-views and lifestyles, a struggle that has been waged ever since then on an almost daily basis. The nature and contents of the cultural institutions have very little in common with real Greek or Hellenistic culture; thus the university is a product of the Middle Ages.[2] This is obviously true in relation to the lifestyle and accepted norms of the city's inhabitants. But in the eyes of the observant Jew, as in the eyes of those who feared injury to the 'ancestral laws' in the Second Temple period, all these manifestations were—and are—a desecration of the holy city and a clear expression of Hellenization. They are described as Hellenization, rather than as apostasy, to make it clear that they refer not only to the failure to keep the religious commandments or to accept the articles of faith, but to the adoption of the offensive norms of an alien culture. From this standpoint, everything defined as 'Greek' is negative, without any distinction being drawn between positive and negative traditions. However, from a non-religious standpoint, one can say that, in this new Jerusalem, 'Apollonian Athens' and 'Dionysian Athens' live in harmony, that in it there is an expression of the values of the high culture symbolized by Athens in its days of glory, as well as of its 'low' popular pagan culture; or, to use another metaphor, that 'Athens' and 'Antioch' abide in it side by side.

Alongside this Jerusalem, there is of course the traditional ultra-Orthodox Jerusalem, in which numerous synagogues and yeshivot replace the Temple. The presence in Jerusalem of this normative religious Jewry, with all its factions and its sects, its world-view and its norms of living, its studious and its popular culture, is particularly strong; it now leaves a greater imprint than at any time since the Second Temple period. So now, once again, Hellenistic Jerusalem and Jewish Jerusalem exist side by side, with reconciliation and intense strain, as they did during a considerable part of that period.

But, again, such a description of a divided Jerusalem and of tense co-existence cannot exhaustively depict the complex reality. Broad circles of religious society are also consumers of secular culture, both Israeli and Western, and their world-view and lifestyle have internalized values and norms that cannot be defined as Jewish in origin. And I have already claimed that the world-view and lifestyle of the secular groups are shaped

---

[2] Nevertheless the spirit of free enquiry, the classification of sciences, the spirit of the Alexandrian library, and the scientific tradition of the same city's Museum all played their part in its development (Sarton, *Hellenistic Science*, 29–34; 141–57); Judaism (and Islam) lacked institutes for 'secular' learning.

to a great extent by values and norms defined here as 'Hellenistic'. In other words, they are, at one and the same time, consumers of Hellenistic (i.e. Western) culture, while values defined as Hellenistic are internalized in their Jewish-Israeli intellectual and cultural world. One might almost say that this Jerusalem, in which Jerusalem and Athens are entwined, is Alexandria in Israel—Alexandria in the sense of the cultural symbiosis that it represents, if Alexandria could also be a symbol of a non-nationalistic, territorial existence.

All this having been said, it is now clear that Athens is an integral and essential part of the modern Jerusalem. Looking in these two mirrors we can also ask whether it is at all possible to characterize a certain culture according to one constitutive set of ideas and norms. Is not every society and every culture an open, multifaceted, dynamic system, which changes with the passage of time, and not a closed, tightly sealed, and static one? According to the model of antinomy, national culture is a uniform set of values, while according to the Hellenistic model it is always a diversified entity. On the face of it, we could say that Jewish secular culture is a blend of Hellenistic Judaism and talmudic Judaism. Like the former, it adopted 'foreign' philosophical categories of thought in order to redefine Judaism; like the latter, it revealed openness and readiness to incorporate many elements of foreign culture (or did so in practice). Such an argument might have been valid if secular Judaism had preserved the essential core of Judaism— observance of the commandments and living according to the halakhah. But that is not the case, and it is the modern addition—secularism—that makes modern Jewish 'Hellenism' an entirely new phenomenon.

Ahad Ha'am believed that the modern Jew could write a *Mishneh Torah* or a *Guide of the Perplexed* in which the value of Judaism would be explained in the concepts of Japheth's school of thought, and through which the intellectual content and the lofty ethics of Judaism would be revealed.[3] And indeed Judaism was not only interpreted but also reconstructed on the basis of Western concepts. If Ahad Ha'am, as one typical example, thought that the only result of applying the concepts of Japheth would be to strengthen the old Judaism and adapt it to the modern world, it turned out that these concepts also created a Judaism with entirely new values and a content far from any connection with the old Judaism.

Historical analogies bring into sharp focus the things they compare, and it seems to me that in the case before us the analogies are instructive in relation to the distinctly new aspect of modern Israeli culture: syncretism

---

[3] Ahad Ha'am, 'Al devar otzar hayahadut', 213–14.

in the framework of a sovereign national and territorial society. This syncretism is the unique feature of Israeli culture, the key expression of the
complex and multifaceted pluralism that exists within a uniform framework, just as it is also a source of unceasing tension and a potential source
of even greater tension.

Our discussion should, I believe, lead us to the conclusion that culture
is an elusive phenomenon; none the less, it is not a mere set of images and
generalizations but also a defined reality. It is the sum total of components,
and at the same time it is also their integration. Judaism, in every historical
period until the modern era, was a totally different entity from the Greek
and Hellenistic (or Muslim and Christian) entities. A Jew would never have
questioned that, and to a Hellene or someone living in Hellenistic times
there was not even the shadow of a doubt. Were a stranger to both of them
to come upon a Jew and a Hellene, would notice at once the differences
in their way of life, their faith, their code of behaviour and its source
of authority. Even the indistinct boundaries between these historical and
cultural entities, as well as the details common to both, were they many or
few, could not dim the difference and the contrast (except, perhaps, in cases
of radical syncretism). They were clearly dissimilar in their substance, even
if there were various areas of contact between them and even if we should
discover contents and components they both shared. Thus, whether we
adopt the opinion of those who exaggerate the depth of the Hellenistic
influence on Judaism in the Hellenistic-Roman period or accept the views
of those who understate it, the main point of our concern is this: what
we call a religious way of life, as distinct from culture, was the centre, the
pivot, and the compass of Jewish society and of Jewish existence in that
period and later.

In the past, innumerable spheres of alien culture were absorbed and
taken over by the religiously controlled society, often becoming integral
parts of the Jewish way of life. Borrowing and absorption were the fruits
of the activities of various social and cultural mechanisms, but a decisive
consideration was their adaptation or non-adaptation to religious norms,
according to which their status and functions were established. We saw that
the incorporation of Hellenistic elements into Jewish culture in Palestine
did not divert the Jews from their faith and their religious observance.
Using philosophical categories did not divert the philosophers from faith,
and more importantly the philosophical thought of the Middle Ages did
not become an integral part of the world-view of the overall Jewish community.

In contrast, the ideas of the Haskalah penetrated more and more, becoming increasingly prevalent and internalized throughout the nineteenth century in the world-view of a broad Jewish public. In actual fact, there is no Jewish group of any kind that did not internalize, in one way or another, something of the spirit of modernism, and did not undergo an intensive process of Europeanization and modernization. In the Jewish case as well, 'Enlightenment was for the few. Secularization was for the many.'[4] The main difference between borrowings in previous ages and in the modern period lies in the fact that in the modern era the new borrowed components of culture were not assimilated into a life controlled by religion, but rather were crystallized into an autonomous—even sovereign—way of life. Culture became an alternative system of values and the essence of a new identity, a composite of traditional and traditionalist components, Jewish components 'translated' into Greek, and a wide array of alien traits. To the secular Jew, culture is the all-inclusive replacement of religion. In this culture, not only were 'Western' elements, (i.e. those borrowed from 'European culture') added and incorporated into the mainstream and the fringes of the previous system, but they became an integral part of it. What we have here is a totally new being in Jewish history: the 'secular Jew', a Jew who creates for himself a 'Judaism of another kind', a Judaism which is neither Hellenistic nor one that a medieval Jewish philosopher could accept as Judaism.

This gulf between modern secular Judaism and the earlier Jewish world is manifested, paradoxically, in efforts by the former to interpret the past in a way that will generate continuity. Thus, as we saw, as they gazed into the Greek mirror, the secular Jews tried to redefine the essence of ideal Judaism. By looking into this mirror, they hoped to design their ideal culture, and since the visible 'border guards'—a traditional way of life and religious observance—had disappeared, the new guards they invented were cultural norms, values, and lifestyle. Here the historical paradox was revealed: as the clear-cut and absolute lines of contrast between the Jews and the alien world blurred, it became necessary to draw new ones, but these were faint and imperceptible!

As a result of this need to define the borders and the content of Hebrew culture three cultural utopias or ideals appeared.

(i) The utopia of choice and selection: Hebrew components and Western components would exist within the Hebrew culture as two different systems. The modern Jew, a member of the Hebrew culture, would be a consumer of such Western cultural components as he should select.

---

[4] O. Chadwick, *The Secularization*, 9.

(ii) The utopia of harmony: Hebrew and Western components would attain absolute harmony, reconciling the two worlds. The disparity between the Jewish and the universal human being would be eradicated through the assimilation of Western values into Hebrew culture, instead of this culture's standing alongside Western culture as a separate system.

(iii) The utopia of isolation and exclusivity: Hebrew culture would consist of every cultural trait needed; these would all be drawn from immanent sources and stamped with the idiosyncratic Jewish or Hebrew seal. Thus there would be no need to borrow material from an outside culture, either as a supplementary system or as a source of borrowed and assimilated values and traits.

When these three utopias are reflected in the real mirror, modern Jerusalem is seen as 'Hellenistic' in nature. First, because it includes more 'alien' elements than ever before, and these elements are an integral part and the core of its identity. Second, because cultural reality is more diversified than at any time in the past. In modern Jerusalem, there are more Jewish factions than ever before. And the web of conservatism and tradition, revived tradition, modernism, secularism, and many other cultural forces is entangled and complex. To a large extent, this is a syncretistic culture, whose characteristics defy definition, and which certainly cannot be described in terms of an ideal type. 'Jerusalem' is an amalgam of 'Yavneh' and 'Athens', of 'Alexandria' and 'Sparta' and 'Antioch', and other symbolic cities.[5] Nevertheless, this syncretism exists not in a heterodox and heterogeneous religious society, but rather within the framework of a secular society that enables it to exist and operate.

'Quid Athenis et Hierosolymis?', asked Tertullian. We can answer this question in three ways. First, Athens served as an inverted image of Jerusalem. Second, Athens served as a model for Jerusalem, and third, as I hope to have demonstrated in this study, Athens is an integral part of Jerusalem. Without it, Jerusalem, namely the modern secular Jew and modern secular Jewish life in Israel, would not be what they are today.

---

[5] It was in Yavneh that the *beit midrash* or house of study was established by R. Yochanan ben Zakai, with Roman permission, after the destruction of the Second Temple. There the principles and foundations of post-Destruction normative Jewry were laid down by the Sages of the Torah, the heirs of the Pharisees. Thus it became a symbol of Judaism without the Temple, and for some, with a more radical view, also as Judaism that could exist without a territory of its own.

BIBLIOGRAPHY

Dictionaries and Reference Works

BRÜGGEMANN, T., and EWERS, H. H., *Handbuch zur Kinder- und Jugendliteratur von 1750 bis 1800* (Stuttgart, 1982).

DECROT, O., and TODOROV, T., *Encyclopedic Dictionary of the Science of Language*, trans. C. Porter, 13 vols. (Baltimore, 1983).

Encyclopaedia Judaica, 16 vols. (Jerusalem, 1971).

The Encyclopedia of Islam, 2nd edn., ed. B. Lewis *et al.* (Leiden and London, 1960–).

Ha'entziklopediah ha'ivrit ('Hebrew Encyclopaedia'), 32 vols. (Tel Aviv and Jerusalem, 1949–81).

Lexikon der Kinder- und Jugendliteratur, ed. Klaus Doderer, 3 vols. (Weinheim and Basle, 1975–9.)

The Oxford Classical Dictionary, 2nd edn., ed. N. G. L. Hammond and H. H. Scullard (Oxford, 1970).

PRINCE, GERALD, *A Dictionary of Narratology* (Lincoln, Nebr., 1987).

The New Princeton Encyclopedia of Poetry and Poetics, ed. Alex Preminger and T. V. F. Brogan (Princeton, 1993).

Reallexikon für Antike und Christentum, ed. Theodor Klauser (Stuttgart, 1950–).

Rabbinic Literature

Avot deRabbi Nathan, ed. S. Schechter, 2nd edn. (New York, 1967).

The Babylonian Talmud, trans. ed. Dr I. Epstein, 35 vols. (London, 1935–59).

Mekhilta of Rabbi Shimon bar Yochai, ed. J. M. Epstein and E. Z. Melamed (Jerusalem, 1955) (Heb.).

Midrash Genesis Rabbah, ed. I. Theodor and H. Albeck, 2nd edn. (Jerusalem, 1965).

Midrash Sifre on Numbers, trans. P. Levertoff (London, 1926).

Midrash on Psalms, trans. William G. Braude, 2 vols. (New Haven, 1959).

Midrash Rabbah, trans. ed. Rabbi D. H. Freedman and Maurice Simon, 10 vols. (London, 1939).

The Minor Tractates of the Talmud, trans. ed. Rev. Dr. A. Cohen, 2 vols. (London, 1965).

Pirkei Avot/Ethics of the Fathers (Artscroll Mesorah Series; Brooklyn, NY, 1984).

Sifra, ed. I. H. Weiss (Vienna, 1862). (Heb.)

Sifra: An Analytical Translation, trans. Jacob Neusner, 4 vols. (Brown Judaic Studies, 138–40, 142; Atlanta, Ga., 1988).

Sifre on Deuteronomy, ed. L. Finkelstein, 2nd edn. (New York, 1969). (Heb.)

Sifre: A Tannaitic Commentary on the Book of Deuteronomy, trans. Reuven Hammer (Yale Judaic Studies; New Haven, 1986).

The Talmud of Babylonia: An American Translation, trans. Jacob Neusner, 36 vols. (Brown Judaic Studies; Atlanta, Ga., 1984–90).

The Talmud of the Land of Israel: A Preliminary Translation and Explanation, ed. Jacob Neusner, 35 vols. (Chicago, 1982–91).

The Tosefta—The Order of Nezikim, ed. S. Lieberman (New York, 1988). (Heb.)

Other Works

ABRAMSON, GLENDA, 'Hellenism Revisited: The Use of Myth in Modern Hebrew Literature', *Prooftext*, 10/2 (1990), 237–56.

ACHIMEIR, A., 'Aman venavi' ('Artist and Prophet'), in *Kri'at hagever* ('The Crowing of the Cock') (Tel Aviv, n.d.), 64–5.

——— 'Arba'at hapituyim hagedolim bahistoriyah shel am Yisrael' ('The Four Great Temptations in the History of the People of Israel'), in *Berit habiryonim*.

——— *Berit habiryonim* ('The Covenant of the Ruffians'; Tel Aviv, 1972).

——— 'Milchemet ha'or vehachosekh baNegev' ('The War between the Light and the Darkness in the Negev'), in *Berit habiryonim*, 1–13.

——— '"Yavan" beYehudah ve"Yehudah" beYavan' ('"Greekness" in Judaea and "Judaism" in Greece'), in *Hatziyonut hamahapkhanit* ('Revolutionary Zionism') (Tel Aviv, 1966), 235–39.

AHAD HA'AM, 'Al devar otzar hayahadut balashon ha'ivrit' ('On the Treasury of Judaism in the Hebrew Language'), in *Al parashat derakhim*, i. 205–46.

——— *Al parashat derakhim* ('At the Parting of the Ways: Writings'), 4 vols. (new edn., Berlin, 1930).

——— 'Derekh haru'ach' ('The Way of the Spirit'), in *Al parashat derakhim*, i. 68–114.

——— 'Flesh and Spirit', in *Selected Essays*, 139–58.

——— 'Halashon vedikdukah' ('Language and its Grammar'), in *Al parashat derakhim*, i. 196–241.

——— 'Hamusar hale'umi' ('National Morality'), in *Al parashat derakhim*, iv. 111–43.

——— *Igerot* ('Letters'), iv (Tel Aviv, 1956).

——— 'Imitation and Assimilation', in *Selected Essays*, 107–24.

——— 'Iyov vePrometeus' ('Job and Prometheus'), in *Al parashat derakhim*, iii. 66–8.

——— 'Kohen venavi' ('Priest and Prophet'), in *Al parashat derakhim*, i. 178–84.

——— 'Moses', in *Selected Essays*, 306–30.

——— 'Past and Future', in *Selected Essays*, 80–90.

——— *Selected Essays by Ahad Ha'am*, trans. Leon Simon (Philadelphia, 1944).

——— 'Shilton hasekhel' ('The Reign of Reason'), in *Al parashat derakhim*, i. 1–37.

——— 'Slavery in Freedom', in *Selected Essays*, 171–94.

——— 'The Spiritual Revival', in *Selected Essays*, 253–307.

——— 'The Transvaluation of Values', in *Selected Essays*, 217–40.

ALEXANDER, PHILIP, '"Quid Athenis et Hierosolymis?" Rabbinic Midrash and Hermeneutics in the Greco-Roman World', in Davies and White (eds.), *A Tribute to Geza Vermes*, 101–24.

ALLEN, DON CAMERON, *The Legend of Noah: Renaissance Rationalism in Art, Science, and Letters* (Urbana, Ill., 1949, repr. 1963).

ALMOG, SHMUEL, 'From "Muscular Jewry" to the "Religion of Labour"', *Hatzionut*, 9 (1984), 137–46. (Heb.)

—— 'The Historical Dimension of Jewish Nationalism', *Zion*, NS 53/4 (1988), 405–21. (Heb.)

—— 'Land and People in Jewish Nationalism', *Contemporary Jewry: A Research Annual*, 1 (Jerusalem, 1983), 53–67. (Heb.)

—— '"The Land to its Workers" and the Conversion to Judaism of the Fellahin', in Ettinger (ed.), *Nation and History*, ii. 165–75. (Heb.)

—— 'The Racial Motif in Ernst Renan's Attitude towards Judaism and the Jews', *Zion*, NS 32/3–4 (1967), 175–200. (Heb.)

—— 'Redemption in Zionist Rhetoric', in Ruth Kark (ed.), *Redemption of the Soil of Eretz Yisrael: Ideology and Practice* (Jerusalem, 1990), 13–32. (Heb.)

—— *Zionism and History* (Jerusalem, 1982). (Heb.)

—— et al. (eds.), *Israel and the Nations: Essays Presented in Honor of Sh. Ettinger* (Jerusalem, 1987). (Heb.)

ALON, GEDALYAHU, 'Have the Nation and its Sages Erased the Memory of the Hasmoneans?', in *Studies of Jewish History in the Land of Israel in the Period of the Mishna and the Talmud*, i (Tel Aviv, 1957), 15–25. (English trans. by I. Abrahams: *Jews, Judaism and the Classical World*, 1977).

ALON, ILAI, *Socrates in Mediaeval Arabic Literature* (Leiden, 1991).

ALTER, ROBERT (ed.), *Modern Hebrew Literature* (New York, 1962).

ALTMANN, ALEXANDER, 'Climate Theory according to Judah Halevi', in *Mililah: A Volume of Studies* (Manchester, 1944), 1–17. (Heb.)

—— *Moses Mendelssohn: A Biographical Study* (London, 1973).

—— (ed.), *Biblical and Other Studies* (Cambridge, Mass., 1963).

—— (ed.), *Biblical Motifs: Origins and Transformation* (Cambridge, Mass., 1966).

—— (ed.), *Jewish Medieval and Renaissance Studies* (Cambridge, Mass., 1967).

AMIR, YEHOSHUA, 'The Monotheistic Problem of Hellenistic Jewry', *Da'at: A Journal of Jewish Philosophy and Kabbalah*, 13 (Summer, 1972), 13–27. (Heb.)

—— 'The Term *Ioudaïsmos*: A Study in Jewish Hellenistic Self-Definition', *Immanuel*, 14 (1982), 34–41. (Heb.)

—— 'Wie verarbeitete das Judentum fremde Einflüsse in hellenistischer Zeit?', *Judaica*, 38 (1982), 150–63.

al-'ANDALUSĪ, ṢĀ'ID, *Science in the Medieval World: Book of the Categories of Nations*, trans. and ed. Sema I. Salen and Alok Kumar (Austin, Tex., 1991).

ANI, MARIMBA, *Yurugu: An Afrocentric Critique of European Cultural Thought and Behavior* (Trenton, NJ, 1994).

ANKORI, ZVI, *Encounter in History: Jews and Christian Greeks in their Relations through the Ages* (Tel Aviv, 1984). (Heb.)

—— 'Origins and History of Ashkenazi Jewry (8th to 18th Century)', in Richard M. Goodman and Arno G. Matulski (eds.), *Genetic Diseases among Ashkenazi Jews* (New York, 1978), 19–46.

Anon., *Bible Folk-Lore, a Study in Comparative Mythology* (London, 1884).

APOLLODORUS, *The Library*, with an English translation by Sir J. G. Frazer, 2 vols. (The Loeb Classical Library, New York and London, 1921).

ARIELI, YEHOSHUA, 'New Horizons in the Historiography of the 18th and 19th Centuries', in Salmon *et al.* (eds.),*Studies in Historiography*, 145–68 = *History and Politics* (Tel Aviv, 1992), 34–63. (Heb.)

ARISTOTLE, *The Athenian Constitution*, English trans. by H. Rackham (Loeb Classical Library, rev. and repr., Cambridge, Mass., and London, 1981).

—— *Protrepticus*, ed. Ingemar Düring (Studia Graeca et Latina Gothoburgensia, 12; Göteborg, 1961).

ARMSTRONG, A. H., 'Greek Philosophy and Christianity', in Finley (ed.), *The Legacy of Greece*, 347–75.

ARNOLD, MATTHEW, 'Culture and Anarchy', in *Selected Prose* (London, 1982), 202–300.

—— 'Heinrich Heine', in *Essays in Criticism* (First Series) (New York, 1983), 119–47.

—— 'On the Modern Element in Literature', in Harold Bloom (ed.), *The Nostalgia of Classicism* (Essays in Criticism, 3rd ser.; New York, 1983), 35–83.

ARON, RAYMOND, *Main Currents in Sociological Thought*, trans. C. Perelstein (Tel Aviv, 1993). (Heb.)

ASHERI, DAVID, 'In Memory of A. Momigliano, 1908–1987', *The Israeli Academy of Sciences* (Jerusalem, 1992), 11–25. (Heb.)

ATHANASSIADI-FOWDEN, POLYMNIA, *Julian and Hellenism: An Intellectual Biography* (Oxford, 1981).

AUERBACH, ERIC, *Mimesis: The Representation of Reality in Western Literature*, trans. Willard R. Trask (Princeton, 1953).

AUGUSTINE, *De doctrina Christiana*, ed. and trans. R. P. H. Green (Oxford, 1995).

—— *The City of God*, trans. H. Bettenson (Harmondsworth, 1984).

AVGOULI, MARIA, 'The First Greek Museums', in Flora E. S. Kaplan (ed.), *Museums and the Making of 'Ourselves': The Role of Objects in National Identity* (London and New York, 1994), 246–65.

AVINERI, SHLOMO, *Moses Hess: Prophet of Communism and Zionism* (New York, 1985).

AVI-YONAH, MICHAEL, *Hellenism and the East: Contacts and Interrelations from Alexander to the Roman Conquest* (Jerusalem, 1978). (Heb.)

BACHARACH, ZEVI, *Racism: The Tool of Politics. From Monism towards Nazism* (Jerusalem, 1985). (Heb.)

BAER, FRITZ, *Sefer toledot Yisrael* ('Book of Jewish History'), i (Prague, 1796); ii (Vienna, 1808).

BAER, YITZHAK F., 'The Historical Foundations of the Halakhah', in *Studies in the History of the Jewish People*, i. 305–59. (Heb.)

—— 'Problems of Religion in the Hasmonean Period', in *Studies in the History of the Jewish People*, i. 49–77 (= 57–84). (Heb.)

—— *Studies in the History of the Jewish People*, i (Jerusalem, 1985). (Heb.)

BAIRD, JAMES, *Ismael: A Study of the Symbolic Mode in Primitivism* (New York, 1960).

BAKHTIN, M. M. B., 'Response to a Question from Novy Mir Editorial Staff', in *Speech Genres and Other Late Essays*, trans. V. W. Macgee, ed. C. Emerson and M. Holquist (Austin, Tex., 1960), 1–7.

BALDRY, H. C., *The Unity of Mankind in Greek Thought* (Cambridge, 1965).

BALY, DENIS, *The Geography of the Bible: A Study in Historical Geography* (London, 1951).

BARAS, ZEVI, *et al.* (eds.), *Eretz Yisrael from the Destruction of the Second Temple to the Muslim Conquest*, i: *Political, Social, and Cultural History* (Jerusalem, 1982). (Heb.)

BARASH, MOSHE, *Winckelmann as a Theoretician of Art* (Jerusalem, 1991). (Heb.)

—— 'The System of Arts from Schlegel to Baudelaire', in Kristeller and Barash (eds.), *The Western System of the Arts*, 59–116. (Heb.)

BAR-ASHER, M. (ed.), *Studies in Judaica* (Jerusalem, 1984). (Heb.)

BAR-EL, JUDITH, 'The National Poet: The Emergence of a Conception in Hebrew Literary Criticism (1885–1905)', *Prooftext*, 6 (1986), 205–20.

BARKER, ERNEST, *National Character* (2nd edn., London, 1939).

BARON, SALO W., 'Azariah de' Rossi's Historical Method', in *History and Jewish Historians*, 239–65.

—— 'Emphases in Jewish History', in *History and Jewish Historians*, 65–88.

—— *History and Jewish Historians* (Philadelphia, 1964).

—— 'I. M. Jost the Historian', in *History and Jewish Historians*, 240–63.

—— *A Social and Religious History of the Jews*, 2nd edn., rev. (New York, 1966).

BARR, JAMES, *The Semantics of Biblical Language* (Oxford, 1961).

BARRETT, WILLIAM, *Irrational Man: A Study in Existential Philosophy* (New York, 1958).

BARTAL, ISRAEL, 'Non-Jews and Gentile Society in East European Hebrew and Yiddish Literature, 1856–1914' (Ph.D. thesis, Hebrew University, 1986).

BARTLETT, JOHN R., *Jews in the Hellenistic World: Josephus, Aristeas, the Sibylline Oracles, Eupolemus* (Cambridge, 1985).

BAR-YOSEF, HAMUTAL, 'The Heine Cult in Hebrew', in M. H. Gelber (ed.), *The Jewish Reception of Heine*, 127–38.

BARZILAY, ISAAC E., 'The Italian and Berlin Haskalah (Parallels and Differences)', *American Academy for Jewish Research: Proceedings*, 34 (1960–1), 17–54.

——*Joseph Solomon Delmedigo (Yashar of Candia)* (Leiden, 1974).

BASIL THE GREAT, *De legendis libris Gentilium = Saint Basil on Greek Literature*, ed. N. G. Wilson (London, 1975).

BAUMGARDT, DAVID, 'The Ethics of Lazarus and Steinthal', *Leo Baeck Year Book*, 2 (1957), 205–17.

BAUMGARTNER, A. I., 'Rivkin and Neusner on the Pharisees', in Richardson (ed.), *Law in Religious Communities in the Roman Period*, 109–27.

BECKER, CARL L., *The Heavenly City of the Eighteenth-Century Philosophers* (New Haven, 1932).

BEHLER, ERNEST, 'The Force of Classical Greece in the Formation of the Romantic Age in Germany', in Carol (ed.), *Paths From Ancient Greece*, 118–39.

BELFER, ELLA, *'Malkhut shamayim' and the State of Israel: Studies in the Political Aspects of Jewish Thought* (Ramat Gan, 1991). (Heb.)

BELLA, MOSHE, *The World of Z. Jabotinsky* (Tel Aviv, 1972). (Heb.)

BELLER, STEVEN, *Vienna and the Jews, 1867–1938: A Cultural History* (Cambridge, 1989).

BEN-ARI, NITSA, 'Historical Images and the Emergence of a New National Literary System' (Ph.D. diss., Tel Aviv University, 1993). (Heb.)

BEN-ARIEH, YEHOSHUA, 'Characteristics of Nineteenth-Century Historical Geographical Literature on Eretz Yisrael', in Yosi Katz *et al.* (eds.), *Historical-Geographical Studies in the Settlement of Eretz Yisrael*, 13–27. (Heb.)

BEN-DAVID, ABBA, *Biblical Hebrew and Mishnaic Hebrew*, i (rev. edn., Tel Aviv, 1967). (Heb.)

BENEDICT, RUTH, *Patterns of Culture* (Boston and New York, 1934).

BEN-GURION, DAVID, *Medinat Yisrael hamitchadeshet* ('The Restored State of Israel'), i (Tel Aviv, 1968).

—— *Yichud veye'ud* ('Unity and Destiny') (Tel Aviv, 1971).

BEN-PORAT, ZIVA, '"Japheth's" Appearance in Shem's Tents: Literary Allusions and other References to European Texts in Modern Hebrew Literature', *Hasifrut/Literature*, 29 (VIII/3; Dec. 1979), 34–43. (Heb.)

BEN-SASSON, H. H. (ed.), *The Medieval Jewish Community* (Jerusalem, 1976). (Heb.)

BEN-SASSON, MENAHEM, *et al.* (eds.), *Culture and History in Medieval Jewry: Studies Dedicated to the Memory of Y. H. Ben-Sasson* (Jerusalem, 1989). (Heb.)

BENTWICH, NORMAN, *Hellenism* (Philadelphia, 1919).

BEN-YEHUDA, ELIEZER, 'Ha'adon Pines vehaginuto' ('Mr Pines and his Fairness'), *Hazevi*, 20 (31 May 1895).

—— 'He'arah me'otzar hasifrut' ('Notes from the Treasure of Literature') *Ha'or*, 14 January 1896.

—— 'She'elah nekhbadah' ('A Weighty Question'; 1879), in *Hachalom veshivro: Mivchar ketavim be'inyanei lashon* ('The Dream and its Fulfilment: Selected Writings'), ed. with an introduction and notes by Reuven Sivan (2nd edn., 1986), 37–48.

BEN-ZE'EV, J. L., *Beit hasefer*, i: *Mesilat halimud*; ii: *Limudei hameisharim* (1802) (6th edn., Vienna, 1820).

—— *Chakhmei Yavan: Hu sefer divrei chakhamim* ('The Sages of Greece') (Munkács, 1869).

BERDYCZEWSKI, M. J. [Y.], 'Divrei bikoret' ('Criticism'), in *Kitvei M. Y. Berdyczewski: Ma'amarim*, 245–80.

—— *Kitvei M. Y. Berdyczewski: Ma'amarim* ('Collected Writings: Articles') (2nd edn., Tel Aviv, 1960).

—— 'Machshavot' ('Thoughts'), in *Kitvei M. Y. Berdyczewski: Ma'amarim*, 32–6.

—— *Me'otzar ha'agadah/Aus dem jüdischen Sagenschatz*, 2 vols. (Berlin, 1913); i: *Mini kedem* ('From Antiquity' [Ps. 78: 1]).

—— 'Mishnei ha'avarim' ('On Both Sides'), in *Kitvei M. Y. Berdyczewski*, 99–140.

—— 'Shinui arakhim' ('A Change of Values'), in *Kitvei M. Y. Berdyczewski*, 27–55.

—— 'Tziyunim' ('Notes'), in *Kitvei M. Y. Berdyczewski*, 49–53.

BERENFELD, SIMON, *Koré hadorot* ('Calling the Generations' [Isa. 41: 4]), i (Warsaw, 1888).

BERGMAN, I., 'The Sages of Eretz Yisrael and Greek and Roman Culture', in N. H. Tortshiner (ed.), *Sefer Klausner* (Tel Aviv, 1937), 146–53. (Heb.)

BERKOWITZ, JAY R., *The Shaping of Jewish Identity in Nineteenth-Century France* (Detroit, 1989).

BERLIN, ISAIAH, *The Magus of the North*, ed. Henry Hardy (London, 1993).

BERNAL, MARTIN, *Black Athena: The Afroasiatic Roots of Classical Civilization*, i: *The Fabrication of Ancient Greece 1785–1985* (London, 1987).

—— *Black Athena*, ii: *The Archaeological and Documentary Evidence* (New Brunswick, NJ, 1991).

BIALE, DAVID, *Eros among the Jews: From Biblical Israel to Contemporary America* (New York, 1992).

BIALIK, H. N., 'Al hasifrut ha'ivrit hatze'irah' ('On Young Hebrew Literature'), in *Devarim shebe'alpeh* ('Talks'), ii (Tel Aviv, 1935), 9–18.

—— *Divrei sifrut* (2nd edn., Tel Aviv, 1965).

—— 'Hasefer ha'ivri' ('The Hebrew Book'), in *Divrei sifrut*, 32–52.

—— 'Lepetichat haUniversitah haIvrit beYerushalayim' ('On the Inauguration of the Hebrew University in Jerusalem') (1925), in *Divrei sifrut*, 127–35.

—— and Ravnitzky, Y. H., *The Book of Legends: Legends from the Talmud and Midrash*, trans. W. G. Braude (New York, 1992) = *Sefer ha'agadah* (Odessa, 1900–10).

BICKERMAN, E. J., 'The Colophon of the Greek Book of Esther', in *Studies in Jewish and Christian History*, i. 225–45.

—— *Four Strange Books of the Bible* (New York, 1967).

—— *From Ezra to the Last of the Maccabees: Foundation of Post-Biblical Judaism* (New York, 1962).

—— 'The Jewish Historian Demetrius', in *Studies in Jewish and Christian History*, ii. 347–58.

—— *The Jews in the Greek Age* (Cambridge, Mass., 1988).

—— 'Origines Gentium', *Classical Philology*, 47 (1952), 65–81.

—— 'The Septuagint as a Translation', in *Studies in Jewish and Christian History*, i. 167–206.

—— *Studies in Jewish and Christian History*, 3 vols. (Leiden, 1976–86).

—— 'Symbolism in the Dura Synagogue', in *Studies in Jewish and Christian History*, iii. 225–44.

—— 'The Historical Foundation of Postbiblical Judaism', in Louis Finkelstein (ed.) *The Jews, Their History, Culture and Religion*, 2 vols. (New York, 1970–1, 4th edn.), i. 70–114.

BIDERMAN, S., and SHARFSTEIN, BEN-AMI (eds.), *Interpretation in Religion* (Leiden, 1992).

BIN-GORION, EMANUEL, *The Path of Legend: An Introduction to Folktales* (2nd rev. edn.; Jerusalem, 1970). (Heb.)

BIRNBAUM, NATHAN, 'Judaismus und Hellenismus', *Die Zeit*, 18 July 1896 = *Ausgewählte Schriften zur jüdischen Frage* (Czernowitz, 1910), i. 131–9.

BLACKALL, ERIC A., *The Emergence of German as a Literary Language, 1700–1775* (Cambridge, 1959).

BLACKHAM, HAROLD J., *The Fable as Literature* (London, 1958).

BLACKWELL, THOMAS, *An Inquiry into the Life and Writings of Homer* (1735; repr. Hildesheim, 1976).

BLIDSTEIN, GERALD J., *Political Concepts in Maimonidean Halakhah* (Ramat Gan, 1983). (Heb.)

BOAS, GEORGE (ed.), *The Greek Tradition* (Baltimore, 1939).

BOKSER, BARUCH M., *The Origins of the Seder: The Passover Rite and early Rabbinic Judaism* (Berkeley, 1984).

BOLGAR, R. R., 'The Greek Legacy', in Finley (ed.), *The Legacy of Greece*, 429–72.

—— 'The Revival of Roman Law in Medieval Europe', in Bolgar (ed.), *The Classical Heritage*, 138–49.

—— (ed.), *The Classical Heritage and its Beneficiaries* (Cambridge, 1954).

—— (ed.), *Classical Influences on European Culture, 500–1500* (Cambridge, 1971).

—— (ed.), *Classical Influences on European Culture 1500–1700* (Cambridge, 1976).

BOMAN, THORLEIF, *Hebrew Thought Compared with Greek*, trans. J. L. Moreau (London, 1970).

BONFIL, ROBERT [REUVEN], *Jewish Life in Renaissance Italy* (Berkeley, 1994).

—— 'Expressions of the Uniqueness of the Jewish People in the Period of the Renaissance)', *Sinai*, 76 (1975), 36–46. (Heb.)

—— 'How Golden was the Age of the Renaissance in Jewish Historiography?' in David Ruderman (ed.), *Essential Papers on Jewish Culture in Renaissance and Baroque Italy* (New York, 1992), 219–51.

—— 'Preaching as Mediation between Elite and Popular Cultures: The Case of Judah del Bene', in David B. Ruderman (ed.), *Preachers of the Italian Ghetto*, 67–88.

BORGES, JORGE LUIS, 'Averroes' Search', in *Labyrinths: Selected Stories and other Writings*, ed. A. Yates and J. E. Irby (Harmondsworth, 1974), 148–55.

BOROCHOV, DOV BER, 'O charaktere evrejskogo uma' ('On the Nature of the Jewish Mind'), *Illustrirovannyj sionistkij al'manach*, 1902–3, 316–37 = *Kitavim filosofi'im* ('Philosophical Writings'), ed. D. Ben-Nahum and A. Yasur (Haifa and Tel Aviv, 1994), 27–53.

BOSWELL, JAMES, *Life of Johnson*, ed. G. B. Hill and L. F. Powell, iv (Oxford, 1934).

BOWEN, JAMES, 'Education, Ideology and the Ruling Class: Hellenism and English Public Schools in the Nineteenth Century', in G. W. Clarke (ed.), *Rediscovering Hellenism*, 161–86.

BOWERSOCK, G. W., *Hellenism in Late Antiquity* (Ann Arbor, 1990).

BOWKER, JOHN, *The Targum and Rabbinic Literature: An Introduction to Jewish Interpretation of Scripture* (Cambridge, 1969).

BOWLER, PETER J., *The Invention of Progress: The Victorians and the Past* (Oxford, 1989).

BOWRA, C. M., *The Greek Experience* (London, 1957).

BRANDES, GEORGE, *Main Currents in Nineteenth-Century Literature*, trans. [by Diana White and Mary Morison], 6 vols. (London, 1901–5), from *Hovedstrømninger i det 19de Aarhundredes Litteratur* (Copenhagen, 1873–90).

BRAUDEL, FERNAND, 'The History of Civilization: The Past Explains the Present', in *On History*, trans. Sarah Matthews (Chicago, 1980), 177–218.

—— *The Mediterranean and the Mediterranean World in the Age of Philip II*, trans. Sian Reynolds, 2 vols. (New York, 1966).

BRENNER, J. H., 'Bachayim ubesifrut' ('In Life and in Literature'), in *Kol kitvei Y. H. Brenner*, ii. 52–96.

—— 'Bimkom retzentsia: Mitokh hapinkas' ('Instead of Criticism') in *Kol kitvei Y. H. Brenner*, ii. 153–4.

—— *Kol kitvei Y. H. Brenner* ('Collected Writings of J. H. Brenner'), 3 vols. (Tel Aviv, 1964–7).

—— *Sedeh hasifrut*, in *Kol kitvei*, ii. 329–68.

—— 'Tiyul be'olam hamashal veha'agadah' ('Journey in the World of Fable and Legend'), in *Kol kitvei*, iii. 445–9.

Breuer, Edward, 'Haskalah and Scripture in the Early Writings of Moses Mendelssohn', *Zion*, ns 59/4 (1994), 445–65. (Heb.)

Breuer, Mordechai, *Jüdische Orthodoxie im Deutschen Reich: 1871–1918: Sozialgeschichte einer religiösen Minderheit*, Hebrew trans. (Jerusalem, 1986).

Brieman, Shlomo, 'A. U. Kovner and his Place in the History of Hebrew Criticism', *Metsudah*, 7 (1954), 416–57. (Heb.)

Brink, C. O., *English Classical Scholarship* (Cambridge and New York, 1986).

Brinker, Menachem, *Narrative Art and Social Theory in J. H. Brenner* (Tel Aviv, 1990). (Heb.)

—— et al. (eds.), *Baruch de Spinoza: A Collection of Papers on his Thought* (Tel Aviv, 1979). (Heb.)

Broek, J. O. M., and Webb, J. W., *A Geography of Mankind* (New York, 1968).

Broshi, Magen, 'Troy and Jericho', *Bulletin of the Anglo-Israeli Archeological Society*, 7 (1987–8), 3–8. (Heb.)

Brown, John Pairman, *Israel and Hellas* (Berlin and New York, 1995).

Brown, Robert, *Semitic Influence in Hellenic Mythology* (London, 1899).

Browning, Robert (ed.), *The Greeks: Classical, Byzantine and Modern* (New York, 1985).

Brüggemann, Theodor, *Kinder- und Jugendliteratur 1498–1950: Kommentierter Katalog der Sammlung Brüggenman* (Osnabrück, 1986).

—— 'Zur Rezeption antiker Mythologie in der Kinder- und Jugendliteratur der Goethezeit', *Imprimatur*, nf, 12 (1987), 93–116.

Buber, Martin, *Am ve'artzo* ('A People and its Land') (Tel Aviv, 1944; repr. 1984); English trans., *Israel and Palestine* (London, 1952).

—— 'Myth in Judaism', trans. Eva Jospe in *On Judaism*, 95–107.

—— 'Medinah vetarbut' ('State and Culture'), in *Tikvah lesha'ah zo* ('Hope for the Present Hour') (Tel Aviv, 1992), 89–90.

—— *On Judaism*, ed. Nahum N. Glatzer (New York, 1967).

—— *Penei ha'adam* ('The Face of Man') (Jerusalem, 1962).

—— 'The Spirit of the Orient and Judaism', trans. Eva Jospe in *On Judaism*, 56–78.

—— *Te'udah veye'ud*, i: *Te'udah veye'ud*; ii: *Am olam* (Jerusalem, 1984).

—— 'Tevi'at haruach vehametziut hahistorit' ('The Demand of the Spirit and Historical Reality'), in *Am olam* (*Writings on Current Events*), ii (Jerusalem, 1961), 49–62. (Heb.)

—— 'Yahadut vetarbut' ('Judaism and Culture'), in *Te'udah veye'ud*, i. 226–36.

Bucaille, Maurice, *The Bible, the Qur'an and Science*, trans. from the French by A. D. Pannell and the author (Indianapolis, 1978).

Buckle, Henry Thomas, *Introduction to the History of Civilization in England* (new and rev. edn. (London, 1857–61).

Bultmann, Rodolf, *Primitive Christianity in its Contemporary Setting*, trans. R. H. Fuller (London, 1983).

BULWER-LYTTON (Edward Lord Lytton), *The Last Days of Pompeii* (1834) (London, 1964).

BUNO, JOHANNES, *Bilderbibel* (Hamburg, 1680).

BURCKHARDT, JACOB, *The Civilization of the Renaissance in Italy*, trans. S. G. C. Middlemore with a new introduction by P. Burke and notes by P. Murray (Harmondsworth, 1990).

—— *Griechische Kulturgeschichte*, 4 vols. (Berlin and Stuttgart, 1898–1902).

BURKERT, WALTER, *The Orientalizing Revolution: The Near Eastern Influences on Greek Culture in the Early Archaic Age*, trans. M. E. Pinder and W. Burkert (Cambridge, Mass., 1992).

BURSTEIN, STANLEY M., 'The Greek Tradition from Alexander to the End of Antiquity', in Carol (ed.), *Paths from Ancient Greece*, 27–50.

BURY, J. B., *The Idea of Progress: An Inquiry into its Origin and Growth* (repr. New York, 1960).

BUSSLER, E., *Hiob und Prometheus: Zwei Volkskämpfer der göttlichen Gerechtigkeit* (Hamburg, 1897).

BUTLER, E. M., *The Tyranny of Greece over Germany: A Study of the Influence Exercised by Greek Art and Poetry over the Great German Writers of the Eighteenth, Nineteenth and Twentieth Centuries* (1935; Boston, 1958).

BUTCHER, S. H., 'Greece and Israel', in *Harvard Lectures on Greek Subjects* (London, 1904), 1–43.

—— *Some Aspects of the Greek Genius* (London, 1891).

CAMUS ALBERT 'L'Exil d'Hélène', in *Essais* (Paris, 1965), 851–7.

CARDOZO ISAAC *Las Excelencias de los Hebreos* (Amsterdam, 1679); Heb. trans. with introduction and notes by Yosef Kaplan (Jerusalem, 1971).

Carmina Anacreontea, ed. Martin L. West (Leipzig, 1984).

CARLYLE, R. W. and A. J., *A History of Mediaeval Political Theory*, 6 vols. (Edinburgh, 1903–36).

CAROL, G. Thomas (ed.), *Paths from Ancient Greece* (Leiden, 1988).

CARY, M. R., *The Geographical Background of Greek and Roman History* (Oxford, 1949).

CASSIRER, ERNST, *An Essay on Man: An Introduction to a Philosophy of Human Culture* (New Haven, third printing, 1945).

CASSUTO, DAVID, (ed.), *Jewish Art: Collected Studies* (Jerusalem, 1991). (Heb.)

CASSUTO, M. D., *A Commentary on the Book of Genesis* (8th edn., Jerusalem, 1983).

CHADWICK, HENRY, *The Early Church* (Harmondsworth, 1957).

CHADWICK, OWEN, *The Secularization of the European Mind in the 19th Century* (Cambridge, 1990).

CHAKHAM, NOACH, 'Shorshei hadramah: Mechkar histori-sifruti' ('The Origins of the Drama: Historical-Literary Study'), *Ha'ezrach*, 1 (Mar.–Apr. 1919), 91–101.

CHAMBERLAIN, HOUSTON STEWART, *Foundations of the Nineteenth Century*, trans. John Lees, 2 vols. (London, 1913).

CHAMBERS, ROGER R., 'Greek Athletics and the Jews (165 B.C.–A.D. 70)' (Ph.D. diss., Miami University, Oxford, Ohio, 1980).

CHARLES, R. H., Introduction to *The Book of Sirah* in *The Apocrypha and the Pseudepigrapha of the Old Testament in English* (Oxford, 1913), i. 268–315.

CHARLESWORTH, JAMES H., 'Jewish Astrology in the Talmud Pseudepigrapha, the Dead Sea Scrolls and Early Palestinian Synagogues,' *Harvard Theological Review*, 70 (1977), 183–206.

——— (ed.), *The Old Testament Pseudepigrapha*, i (New York, 1985).

CHERNISS, RUTH, 'The Ancient as Authority in Seventeenth-Century France,' in Boas (ed.), *The Greek Tradition*, 137–170.

CHEYETTE, BRIAN, *Constructions of 'the Jew' in English Literature and Society: Racial Representations, 1875–1945* (Cambridge, 1993).

CHILDS, B. S., *Myth and Reality in the Old Testament* (Studies in Biblical Theology, 27; London, 1968).

CICERO, *De Natura Deorum (The Nature of the Gods)*, trans. Horace C. P. McGregor, with an Introduction by J. M. Ross (Harmondsworth, 1972).

CLARKE, G. W. (ed.), *Rediscovering Hellenism: The Hellenic Inheritance and the English Imagination* (Cambridge, Mass., 1989).

CLARKE, MARTIN L., *Classical Education in Britain 1500–1900* (Cambridge, 1959).

——— *Greek Studies in England 1700–1830* (Cambridge, 1945).

COCHRANE, CHARLES NORRIS, *Christianity and Classical Culture: A Study of Thought and Action from Augustus to Augustine* (Oxford, 1940, repr. New York, 1957).

COHEN, HERMANN, *Deutschtum und Judentum* (Giessen, 1915).

——— 'The Social Ideal as Seen by Plato and the Prophets', in E. Jospe (ed. and trans.), *Reason and Hope: Selections from the Jewish Writings of Hermann Cohen* (New York, 1971), 66–77.

——— *Writing on Judaism*, trans. to Heb. from the German by Zvi Wislawsky (Jerusalem, 1935).

COHEN, RICHARD I., '"And your Eyes Shall See your Teachers": The Rabbi as an Icon', *Zion*, NS 57/4 (1993), 407–52. (Heb.)

——— 'The Visual Image of the Jew and Judaism in Early Modern Europe: From Symbolism to Realism', *Zion*, NS 57/3 (1992), 275–340 (Heb.)

COHEN, ROBERT S., and WARTOFSKY, MARK W. (eds.), *Epistemology, Methodology, and The Social Sciences* (Boston and London, 1983).

COHEN, SHAYE J. D., *From the Maccabees to the Mishnah* (Philadelphia, 1987).

COHEN, TOVA, *From Dream to Reality: Descriptions of Eretz Yisrael in Haskalah Literature* (Ramat Gan, 1992). (Heb.)

——— *The Melitzat Yeshurun of Shlomo Levinsohn: The Work and its Author* (Ramat Gan, 1988). (Heb.)

COLLINS, JOHN J., *Between Athens and Jerusalem: Jewish Identity in the Hellenistic Diaspora* (New York, 1983).

CONZELMAN, HANS, *Gentiles, Jews and Christians: Polemics and Apologetics in the Greco-Roman Era*, trans. M. Eugene Boring (Minneapolis, 1992).

COPLESTON, FREDERICK S. J., *A History of Philosophy*, ii: *Mediaeval Philosophy*, Part I: *Augustine to Bonaventure* (New York, 1962).

CORNELISSEN, J. J., 'Ad Ammianum Marcellinum adversaria critica', *Mnemosyne*, 2nd ser., 14 (1886), 234–304.

COWAN, H. M., *An Anthology of the Writings of Wilhelm von Humboldt: Humanist without Portfolio* (Detroit, 1966).

CROCE, BENEDETTO, *History of Europe in the Nineteenth Century*, trans. from the Italian by Henry Furst (London, 1939).

Cultures and Time (Unesco Press, Paris, 1976).

CURTIUS, ERNST ROBERT, *European Literature and the Latin Middle Ages*, trans. W. R. Trask (New York, 1953).

CURTIUS, LUDWIG, *Winckelmann und seine Nachfolge* (Vienna, 1941).

DAHL, ERHARD, *Die Entstehung der phantastischen Kinder- und Jugenderzählungen in England* (Paderborn, 1986).

DAKIN, DOUGLAS, *The Unification of Greece (1770–1923)* (London, 1972).

DAMON, PHILIP, 'Troy and Canaan: The Near Eastern Context of Homeric Legend', *Hasifrut/Literature*, 17 (V/1; Sept. 1974), 8–19. (Heb.)

DAN, JOSEPH, *Hebrew Ethical and Homiletical Literature (The Middle Ages and Early Modern Period)* (Jerusalem, 1975). (Heb.)

—— *The Story of Alexander the Great* (Jerusalem, 1969). (Heb.)

DAN, YARON, *The City in Eretz Israel during the Late Roman and Byzantine Periods* (Jerusalem, 1984). (Heb.)

DANIEL, JERRY L., 'Anti-Semitism in the Hellenistic-Roman Period', *Journal of Biblical Literature*, 98 (1979), 45–65.

DARNTON, ROBERT, 'The Social History of Ideas', in *The Kiss of Lamourette: Reflections in Cultural History* (New York, 1990), 219–52.

DAVID, Y., *Moshe Chayim Luzzatto's Theory of Rhetoric and Poetry: A Comparative Study* (Tel Aviv, 1978) (Heb.)

DAVIDSON, THOMAS, *The Education of the Greek People and its Influence on Civilization* (New York, 1894; repr. 1971).

DAVIES, P. R., and WHITE, R. T. (eds.), *A Tribute to Geza Vermes: Essays on Jewish and Christian Literature and History*, Journal for the Study of the Old Testament, Supplement Series 100 (Sheffield, 1990)

DAVIES, W. D., *The Territorial Dimension of Judaism* (Berkeley and Los Angeles, 1982).

DAVIS, IRWIN, *English Neo-Classical Art* (London, 1966).

DAVIS, MOSHE (ed.), *Israel: Its Role in Civilization* (New York, 1956).

DAWSON, CHRISTOPHER, *Religion and Culture* (London, 1948).

DELAURA, DAVID J., *Hebrew and Hellene in Victorian England: Newman, Arnold and Pater* (Austin, Tex., 1969).

DELMEDIGO, ELIJAH, *Sefer bechinat hadat* ('Examination of Religion'), ed. with introduction, notes, and commentary by Jacob Joshua Ross (Tel Aviv, 1984). (Heb.)

DEMOS, R., 'The Neo-Hellenic Enlightenment, 1750–1820', *Journal of Ideas*, 19 (1958), 523–41.

DICK, MEIR, *Sipurei chakhmei Yavan* ('Stories of the Greek Sages') (Vilna, 1864).

DIETRICH, ALBRECHT, *Mutter Erde: Ein Versuch über Völksreligion* (Leipzig and Berlin, 1903).

DIETRICH, W., *Cohen and Troeltsch: Ethical Monotheistic Religion and the Theory of Culture* (Providence, RI, 1986).

DI LELLA, A. A., introduction and commentary to *The Wisdom of Ben Sira*, trans. Patrick W. Skehan (New York, 1987).

DILTHEY, W., *Weltanschauung und Analyse* (Leipzig, 1914).

DINUR, BEN-ZION, *A Documentary History of the Jewish People from its Beginning to the Present*, Second Series: *Israel in the Diaspora*, Vol. II, Book VI (Jerusalem, 1972). (Heb.)

DIODORUS SICULUS, *The Antiquities of Egypt*, a translation with notes of Book I of the *Library of History*, rev. and expanded trans. by Edwin Murphy (New Brunswick, NJ, and London, 1990).

—— *Library of History*, trans. C. H. Oldfather (Loeb Classical Library, repr. Cambridge, Mass., and London, 1960).

DIOP, CHEIKH ANTA, *Civilization or Barbarism: An Authentic Anthropology*, trans. from the French by Yaa-Lengi Meema Ngemi (Brooklyn, NY, 1991).

—— *The Cultural Unity of Black Africa* (3rd edn., Chicago, 1978).

DISRAELI, BENJAMIN, *Lord George Bentinck: A Political Biography* (London, 1852).

DITHMER, REINHARD, *Das Fabel* (Paderborn, 1974).

DODDS, E. R., *The Greeks and the Irrational* (Berkeley and Los Angeles, 1951).

DON-YEHIYA, ELIEZER, 'Hanukah and the Myth of the Maccabeans in Zionist Ideology and in Israeli Society', *The Jewish Journal of Sociology*, 34/1 (June 1992), 5–24.

DORAN, HAROLD, *The Geography of Science* (Baltimore and London, 1991).

DORAN, R., 'II Maccabees and "Tragic History"', *Hebrew Union College Annual*, 50 (1979), 107–14.

DORON, JOACHIM, 'Classical Zionism and Modern Antisemitism (1883–1914)', *Hatziyonut*, 8 (1983), 57–101. (Heb.)

—— *The Zionist Thinking of Nathan Birnbaum* (Jerusalem, 1988). (Heb.)

DOVER, K. J., *Greek Popular Morality in the Time of Plato and Aristotle* (Oxford, 1974).

DOWDEN, KEN, *The Use of Greek Mythology* (London and New York, 1992).

DRAPER, WILLIAM JOHN, *History of the Intellectual Development of Europe*, i (1861; rev. edn., New York and London, 1896).

DREIFUS, T., and ELSTEIN, Y. (eds.), *Contemporary Jewish Culture: Crisis or Revitalization* (Ramat Gan: 1983). (Heb.)

DROGE, ARTHUR J., *Homer or Moses? Early Christian Interpretations of the History of Culture* (Tubingen, 1989).

DROYSEN, JOHANN GUSTAV, *Geschichte Alexanders des Großen* (1833, 2nd edn., 1877; Munich, 1980).

—— *Geschichte des Hellenismus*, 2 vols., Hamburg 1836–43; 2nd edn., 6 vols. (Gotha, 1877–8).

DUBNOW, SIMON, 'Autonomy—The Basis of the National Plan', in *Nationalism and History*, 131–43.

—— *The World History of the Jewish People*, ii (*Divrei yemei am olam*; Hebrew trans. of *Die Weltgeschichte des jüdischen Volkes*, 1925–1929) by B. Kropnik (5th edn., Tel Aviv, 1949).

—— *Nationalism and History: Essays on Old and New Judaism*, ed. K. S. Pinson (Philadelphia, 1970).

DÜLMEN, RICHARD VAN, *Die Gesellschaft der Aufklärer: Zur bürgerlichen Emanzipation und aufklärischen Kultur in Deutschland* (Frankfurt am Main, 1986).

DYKMAN, SHLOMO, 'Check-List of Greek and Classics Rendered into Hebrew', *Ariel*, 12 (1965), 94–6.

EDDY, SAMUEL K., *The King is Dead: Studies in the Near Eastern Resistance to Hellenism 334–31 BC* (Lincoln, Nebr., 1961).

EDELSTEIN, L., *The Idea of Progress in Classical Antiquity* (Baltimore, 1967).

EDMUNDS, LOWELL (ed.), *Approaches to Greek Myth* (Baltimore, 1990).

EDWARDS, RUTH B., *Kadmos the Phoenician: A Study in Greek Legends and the Mycenaean Age* (Amsterdam, 1979).

EFRAT, GIDEON, 'The Idyll and Palestinian Painting', *Davar*, 9 Apr. 93. (Heb.)

EFRON, JOHN M., *Defenders of Race: Jewish Doctors and Race Science in Fin-de-Siècle Europe* (New Haven, 1994).

EFRON, JOSHUA, 'Bar-Kokhva in the Light of the Palestinian and Babylonian Talmudic Tradition', in Aharon Oppenheimer and Uriel Rappaport (eds.), *Bar-Kokhva Revolt: A New Approach* (Jerusalem, 1984), 47–104. (Heb.)

—— 'The Maccabean Revolt in Modern Historiography', in *Studies of the Hasmonean Period* (Leiden, 1987), 1–27.

EICHENDORFF, JOSEPH FREIHERR VON, *Das Marmorbild*, in *Werke*, ed. Wolf Dietrich Rasch (Munich and Vienna, 1971).

EIDELBERG, PAUL, *Jerusalem vs. Athens: In Quest of a General Theory of Existence* (Lanham, Md., 1983).

EISENSTEIN, ELIZABETH L., *The Printing Revolution in Early Modern Europe* (Cambridge, 1992).

ELAZAR, D. J., 'Towards a Jewish Definition of Statehood', *Judaism*, 27/2 (Spring 1978), 233–44.

—— and AVIAD, J., *Religion and Politics in Israel: The Interplay of Judaism and Zionism* (New York, 1981).

ELBAUM, JACOB, *Openness and Insularity: Late Sixteenth-Century Jewish Literature in Poland and Germany* (Jerusalem, 1990). (Heb.)

ELBOIM-DROR, RACHEL, *Yesterday's Tomorrow*, i: *The Zionist Utopia* (Jerusalem, 1993). (Heb.)

ELDAD, ISRAEL, 'Nietzsche and the Bible', *Zehut*, 3 (Summer 1983), 73–86. (Heb.) Eng. trans., 'Nietzsche and the Old Testament', in J. O. Flaherty, T. F. Sellner, and R. U. Helm (eds.), *Studies in Nietzsche and the Jewish–Christian Tradition* (London, 1985), 47–68.

—— 'Tarbut ha'ayin beYavan vehashemiyah beYisrael' ('The Art of Sight in Greece and of Hearing in Israel'), in *Hegiyonot Yehudah* (Tel Aviv, 1982), 150–7.

ELIADE, MIRCEA, *The Sacred and the Profane: The Nature of Religion*, trans. William R. Trask (San Diego, Calif., New York, and London, 1959).

ELIAS, NORBERT, *The Civilizing Progress: The History of Manners and State Formation and Civilization*, trans. E. Jephcott (Oxford, 1982).

ELIAV, MORDECHAI, *Jewish Education in Germany in the Period of Enlightenment and Emancipation* (Jerusalem, 1960). (Heb.)

ELIZUR, SHULAMIT, *et al.* (eds.), *Knesset Ezra: Literature and Life in the Synagogue. Studies Presented to Ezra Fleischer* (Jerusalem, 1994). (Heb.)

ELKOSHI, G., 'Y. L. Gordon as a Critic', *Metsudah*, 3 (1954), 458–89. (Heb.)

ELSCHENBROICH, ADALBERT, *Die deutsche und lateinische Fabel in der Frühen Neuzeit*, 2 vols. (Tübingen, 1990).

EMDEN, YAACOV (Jacob), *Megilat sefer* (Warsaw, 1896).

ERLICH, VICTOR, *The Double Image: Concepts of the Poet in Slavic Literature* (Baltimore, 1964).

ETKES, IMANUEL, 'The Gaon of Vilna and the Haskalah: Image and Reality', in id. and Salmon (eds.), *Studies in the History*, 192–214. (Heb.)

—— 'The Question of the Forerunners of the Haskalah in Eastern Europe', *Tarbiz*, 57/1 (Oct.–Dec. 1987), 95–114. (Heb.)

—— (ed.), *The East European Jewish Enlightenment* (Jerusalem, 1993). (Heb.)

—— and SALMON, Y. (eds.), *Studies in the History of Jewish Society in the Middle Ages and in the Modern Period* (Jerusalem, 1980). (Heb.)

ETTINGER, SHMUEL, 'Jews and Judaism as Seen by English Deists of the Eighteenth Century', *Zion*, NS 24 (1964), 182–207.

—— (ed.), *Nation and History: Studies in the History of the Jewish People*, ii (Jerusalem, 1985). (Heb.)

EUCHEL, ISAAC, 'Davar el hakoré mito'elet divrei hayamim hakadmonim', *Hame'asef*, 1 (1783–4), 9–14, 25–30.

——— *Hakdamah lesefer Mishlei, meturgam vemevuar al pi hamefarshim vehama'atikim harishonim vegam ha'acharonim, hukhan al yedei Wolf Meier* ('Introduction to Book of Proverbs') (Prague, 1834), 10–18.

——— 'Igrot Meshulam ben Uriyah ha'eshtemo'i' ('Letters of Meshullam son of Uriah of Eshtemoa'), *Hame'asef*, 6 (1790), 38–50, 80–5, 171–6, 245–9.

EVANS, ELIZABETH C., *Physiognomics in the Ancient World* (Transactions of the American Philosophical Society, NS 59/5; Philadelphia, 1969).

EVEN-ZOHAR, BASMAT, 'The Emergence of the Model of "The New Hebrew" in Modern Hebrew Literature, 1880–1930' (MA thesis, Tel Aviv University, 1988). (Heb.)

EVEN-ZOHAR, ITAMAR, 'Cultural Interferences and the Creation of Hebrew Culture', in N. Geretz (ed.), *Perspectives on Culture and Society*, 129–40. (Heb.)

——— 'The Emergence of a Native Hebrew Culture in Palestine 1882–1948', in *Polysystem Studies*, 175–91.

——— 'Laws of Literary Interference', in *Polysystem Studies*, 53–72.

——— *Papers in Historical Poetics* (Tel Aviv, 1978).

——— *Polysystem Studies: Poetics Today*, 11/1 (Spring 1990).

——— 'Relations between Primary and Secondary Systems', in *Papers in Historical Poetics*, 14–20.

——— 'Russian and Hebrew: The Case of Dependent Polysystems', in *Polysystem Studies*, 97–110.

——— 'System, Dynamics and Interferences in Culture: A Synoptic View', in *Polysystem Studies*, 85–94.

EVRON, BOAZ, 'Atuna ve'eretz Utz' ('Athens and the Land of Utz'), *Iton* 77, 77 (June 1986), 24–7.

——— *A National Reckoning* (Tel Aviv, 1988). (Heb.) Published in English as *Jewish State or Israeli Nation* (Indiana, 1995).

EWERS, H. H., *Kindheit als poetische Daseinsform* (Munich, 1989).

AL-FAKHAR, *Igrot hakana'ut* (Leipzig, 1859; repr. Jerusalem, 1957).

FARRAR, F. W., *Families of Speech: Four Lectures Delivered before the Royal Institution of Great Britain* (London, 1870).

FEINER, SHMUEL, *Haskalah and History: The Emergence of a Modern Jewish Awareness of the Past* (Jerusalem, 1995). (Heb.)

——— ' "History" and "Historical Images" in Jewish Haskalah 1782–1820' (MA diss., Hebrew University, 1984). (Heb.)

——— 'Isaac Euchel—Entrepreneur of the Haskalah Movement in Germany', *Zion*, NS 52/4 (1987), 427–69. (Heb.)

——— 'The Modern Jewish Woman: A Test-Case in the Relationship between Haskalah and Modernity', *Zion*, NS 57/4 (1993), 453–99. (Heb.)

——— 'Nineteenth-Century Jewish Historiography: The Second Track', in Jonathan Frankel (ed.), *Reshaping the Past*, 17–44.

FEINER, SHMUEL, '"Rebellious French" and "Jewish Freedom": The French Revolution in the East European Haskalah's Image of the Past', in R. I. Cohen (ed.), *The French Revolution* (Jerusalem, 1991), 215–47. (Heb.)

—— 'Smolenskin's Confrontation with the Haskalah Movement and the Roots of Jewish Nationalistic Historiography', *Hatzionut*, 16 (1991), 9–32. (Heb.)

—— (ed.), *S. J. Fuenn: From Militant to Conservative Maskil* (Jerusalem, 1993). (Heb.)

FEIRE, ERNEST, 'The Greek Tradition in Germany', in Boas (ed.), *The Greek Tradition*, 171–91.

FELDMAN, BURTON, and RICHARDSON, ROBERT D., *The Rise of Modern Mythology 1680–1860* (Bloomington, Ind., 1972).

FELDMAN, LOUIS H., 'Hellenization in Josephus' *Jewish Antiquities*: The Portrait of Abraham', in L. H. Feldman and G. Hata (eds.), *Josephus, Judaism and Christianity* (Detroit, 1987), 133–53.

—— 'Hengel's Judaism and Hellenism in Retrospect', *Journal of Biblical Literature*, 96 (1977), 371–82.

—— 'How Much Hellenism in Jewish Palestine?', *Hebrew Union College Annual*, 57 (1986), 83–111.

——*Jews and Gentiles in the Ancient World: Attitudes and Interactions from Alexander to Justinian* (Princeton, 1993).

—— 'The Orthodoxy of the Jews in Hellenistic Egypt', *Jewish Social Studies*, 22 (1960), 212–37.

—— 'Torah and Secular Culture: Challenge and Response in the Hellenistic Period', *Tradition*, 23/2 (Summer 1987), 1–15.

FELDMAN, W. H., *Rabbinical Mathematics and Astronomy* (London, 1931).

FERGUSON, JOHN, *The Heritage of Hellenism* (London, 1973).

FINLEY, MOSES I., 'The Ancient Greeks and their Nation', in *The Use and Abuse of History*, 120–33.

—— 'Christian Beginnings: Three Views of Historiography', in *Aspects of Antiquity: Discoveries and Controversies* (London, 1968), 167–84.

—— *Democracy Ancient and Modern*, 2nd edn. (London, 1985).

—— 'Generalizations in Ancient History', in *The Use and Abuse of History*, 61–74.

—— 'Myth, Memory and History', in *The Use and Abuse of History*, 11–33.

—— 'Politics', in *The Legacy of Greece*, 22–36.

—— *The Use and Abuse of History* (London, 1975; rev. edn. 1986).

—— *The World of Odysseus*, 2nd edn. (London, 1977).

—— (ed.), *The Legacy of Greece: A New Appraisal* (Oxford, 1981).

FISCHEL, HENRY A., *Rabbinic Literature and Greco-Roman Philosophy: A Study of Epicurea and Rhetorica in Early Midrashic Writings* (Leiden, 1973).

FISCHER, ERIC, *The Passing of the European Age: A Study in the Transfer of Western Civilization and its Renewal in Other Continents* (Cambridge, Mass., 1943).

FLORIAN, JEAN-PIERRE CLARIS DE, *Fables complètes* (1792; repr. Étoile-sur-Rhône, 1991).

FLUSSER, DAVID, 'The Memory of the Maccabees among Medieval Jews', *Cathedra*, 75 (Apr. 1995), 36–54. (Heb.)

—— 'The Proverbs of Jesus and the Proverbs in the Literature of the Sages', in *Jewish Sources in Early Christianity: Studies and Essays* (Jerusalem, 1979), 150–209. (Heb.)

FOERSTER, GIDEON, 'Christian Allegories and Symbols in the Mosaic Designs of Sixth-Century Eretz Yisrael Synagogues', in D. Jacoby and Tzafrir (eds.), *Jews, Samaritans, and Christians in Byzantine Palestine* (Jerusalem, 1988), 198–206. (Heb.)

FORTENBAUGH, WILLIAM W., HUBY, PAMELA M., SHARPLES, ROBERT W., and DUTAS, DIMITRI, *Theophrastus of Eresus: Sources for his Life, Writings, Thought and Influence*, 2 vols. (Philosophia Antiqua, 54. 1–2; Leiden, 1992).

FOWDEN, GARTH, *The Egyptian Hermes: A Historical Approach to the Late Pagan Mind* (Princeton, 1986).

Fragmente der Vorsokratiker, ed. H. Diels and W. Kranz, 6th edn., 3 vols. (Berlin, 1951–2).

FRANKEL, JONATHAN, *Prophecy and Politics: Socialism, Nationalism and the Russian Jews, 1862–1917* (Cambridge, 1988).

—— *Reshaping the Past: Jewish History and the Historians* (Studies in Contemporary Jewry, 10; New York, 1994).

—— 'The "Yizkor" Book of 1911—A Note on National Myths in the Second Aliya', in H. Ben-Israel *et al.* (eds.), *Religion, Ideology and Nationalism in Europe and America* (Jerusalem, 1986), 355–84.

FREEMAN, EDWARD A., *Greater Greece and Greater Britain* (London, 1886).

FREYNE, SEAN, *Galilee from Alexander the Great to Hadrian 323 B.C.E. to 135 C.E.: A Study of Second Temple Judaism* (Wilmington, Del., 1980).

FRIEDENWALD, HARRY, *The Jews and Medicine*, 2 vols. (1944; repr. New York, 1967).

FRIEDLÄNDER, DAVID, *Lesebuch für jüdische Kinder*, new edn. with introduction and appendix by Zohar Shavit (Frankfurt am Main, 1990).

FRIEDLANDER, Y., *Hebrew Satire in Europe in the Nineteenth Century*, iii (Ramat Gan, 1994). (Heb.)

—— 'Hebrew Satire in Germany in the Late Eighteenth Century: Dissertation of a Critique', *Zion*, NS 52/4 (1987), 510–23. (Heb.)

—— 'The Status of the Haskalah in the Literature of the Haskalah: The Attitude towards Maimonides' Codification', *Jerusalem Studies in Jewish Thought*, 5 (1986), 349–62. (Heb.)

FRIEDMAN, MENACHEM, 'The State of Israel as a Religious Dilemma', *Alpayim*, 3 (1990), 24–68. (Heb.)

FRIEDMANN, BOSCHWITZ, *Julius Wellhausen* (Tel Aviv, 1982). (Heb.)

FRISCHMANN, DAVID, *Kol kitvei David Frishman vemivchar tirgumav* ('Collected Works of D.F. and a Selection of his Translations') (Warsaw, 1914).

FUENN, SHMUEL, *Divrei hayamim livnei Yisrael* ('The Chronicles of the Children of Israel') (Vilna, 1893).

FUKS, GIDEON, *Scythopolis: A Greek City in Eretz Yisrael* (Jerusalem, 1983). (Heb.)

FUNKENSTEIN, AMOS, 'Collective Memory and Historical Consciousness', in *Perceptions of Jewish History*, 3–21.

—— 'Haskalah, History, and the Medieval Tradition', in *Perceptions of Jewish History*, 234–46.

—— 'History and Accommodation: Ibn Ezra', in *Styles in Medieval Biblical Exegesis*, 88–97.

—— 'The Image of the Ruler in Jewish Sources', in *Perceptions of Jewish History*, 155–68.

—— *Perceptions of Jewish History* (Berkeley and Los Angeles, 1993).

—— *Styles in Medieval Biblical Exegesis: An Introduction* (Tel Aviv, 1990). (Heb.)

—— 'The Threshold of Modernity', in *Perceptions of Jewish History*, 220–56.

FYFE, HAMILTON, *The Illusion of National Character* (London, 1946).

GABBA, EMILIO, *Greek Knowledge of Jews up to Hecataeus of Abder: Protocol of the Fortieth Colloquy, 7 December 1980* (Center for Hermeneutical Studies in Hellenistic and Modern Culture; Berkeley, 1981).

GAFNI, ISAIAH, *The Jews of Babylonia in the Talmudic Era* (Jerusalem, 1990). (Heb.)

—— Oppenheimer, Aharon, and Stern, Menahem (eds.), *Jews and Judaism in the Time of the Second Temple, the Mishnah, and the Talmud: Studies in Honour of Shmuel Safrai* (Jerusalem, 1993). (Heb.)

GAGER, JOHN G., *Moses in Greco-Roman Paganism* (Nashville, Tenn., 1972).

—— *The Origins of Anti-Semitism: Attitudes Toward Judaism in Pagan and Christian Antiquity* (Oxford, 1985).

GANS, EDUARD, *Das Erbrecht in weltgeschichtlicher Entwicklung*, 4 vols. (Berlin, 1824–35).

GAON, SAADIAH, *Emunot vede'ot: The Book of Beliefs and Opinions* (Berlin, 1789; Leipzig, 1869; New Haven, 1948).

GARDINER, EDWARD NORMAN, *Athletics of the Ancient World* (Oxford, 1930).

GAY, PETER, *The Enlightenment: An Interpretation*, i: *The Science of Freedom*; ii: *The Rise of Modern Paganism* (New York and London, 1977).

GEIGER, ABRAHAM, *Urschrift und Übersetzungen der Bibel in ihrer Abhängigkeit von der innern Entwicklung des Judentums* (Breslau, 1857).

—— *Sadducäer und Pharisäer* (Breslau, 1863, 2nd edn. 1924).

GEIGER, JOSEPH, 'Athens in Syria: Greek Intellectuals of Gedera', *Cathedra*, 35 (Apr. 1985), 3–16. (Heb.)

—— 'Greek Intellectuals of Ascalon', *Cathedra*, 60 (June 1991), 5–16. (Heb.)

—— 'Greek Orators in Palestine', *Cathedra*, 66 (Dec. 1992), 47–56. (Heb.)

—— 'The History of Judas Maccabaeus: One Aspect of Hellenistic Historiography', *Zion*, NS 59/1 (1985), 1–8. (Heb.)

—— 'Local Patriotism in the Hellenistic Cities of Palestine', in Kasher *et al.* (eds.), *Greece and Rome*, 141–56.

—— 'On the History of the Term *Apikoros*', *Tarbiz*, 42/2 (1972–3), 499–500. (Heb.)

GELBER, C. F., 'Heine, Herzl and Nordau', in M. H. Gelber (ed.), *The Jewish Reception of Heine*, 139–52.

GELBER, MARK H. (ed.), *The Jewish Reception of Heine* (Tübingen, 1992).

GELLERT, CHRISTIAN FÜRCHTEGOTT, *Fabeln und Erzählungen*, ed. K. H. Falbacher (Stuttgart, 1986).

GERETZ, NURITH (ed.), *Perspectives on Culture and Society in Israel* (Tel Aviv, 1988). (Heb.)

GERSHONI, ISRAEL, and JANKOVSKI, JAN, *Egypt, Islam, and the Arabs: The Search for Egyptian Nationhood (1900–1930)* (Oxford, 1989).

GERVASE OF TILBURY, *Otia imperialia ad Ottonem IV*, in *Scriptores rerum Brunsvicensium illustrationi inservientes*, ed. G. W. Leibniz, 3 vols. (Hanover, 1707–11), i. 881–1005.

GILBERT, M., 'Wisdom Literature', in M. H. Stone (ed.), *Jewish Writings of the Second Temple Period* (Compendia Rerum Iudaicarum ad Novum Testmentum pertinentium, 2; Assen, 1984), 283–324.

GILBOA, MENUHA, *Between Realism and Romanticism: A Study of the Critical Work of David Frischmann* (Tel Aviv, 1975). (Heb.)

GIL-HAR, YITZHAK, 'The Organization and Self-Government of the Yishuv in Palestine from the Beginnings of the British Rule to the Ratification of the Mandate (1917–1922)' (Ph.D. thesis, Hebrew University, 1972). (Heb.)

GILMAN, SANDER L., *Jewish Self-Hatred and the Hidden Language of the Jews* (Baltimore, 1986).

—— *The Jew's Body* (New York, 1991).

GILON, MEIR, 'Hebrew Satire in the Age of Haskalah in Germany: A Rejoinder', *Zion*, NS 52/4 (1987), 524–30. (Heb.)

—— *Mendelssohn's* Kohelet musar *in its Historical Context* (Jerusalem, 1979). (Heb.)

GINOSSAR, PINHAS, 'Bialik, Berl and Brenner: Law and Narrative ("Halakhah ve'agadah") and Responses', in id. (ed.), *Hebrew Literature and the Labour Movement* (Beersheva, 1989), 54–86. (Heb.)

GINSBURG, M. S., 'Sparta and Judea', *Classical Philology*, 28 (1934), 117–27.

GINZBERG, LOUIS, *On Halakhah and Agadah* (Tel Aviv, 1960). (Heb.)

—— *The Legends of the Jews*, 7 vols. (Philadelphia, 1946–59;. Hebrew trans., 2nd edn., Ramat Gan, 1966).

GLANVILLE, D. (ed.), *The Legacy of Egypt* (Oxford, 1942).

GLASER, HERMAN, *The German Mind of the 19th Century: A Literary and Historical Anthology* (New York, 1981).

GLATZER, NAHUM, 'The Beginnings of Modern Jewish Studies', in Alexander Altman (ed.), *Studies in Nineteenth-Century Jewish Intellectual History* (Cambridge, Mass., 1964), 27–45.

—— *Leopold Zunz: The Man, His Life and Creation*, trans. from the German by Dov Kvestler (Jerusalem, 1989).

GLINERT, L. (ed.), *Hebrew in Ashkenaz: A Language in Exile* (Oxford, 1993).

GLOVER, T. R., *The Challenge of Greek* (Cambridge, 1942).

GODWIN, J., *Athanasius Kircher: A Renaissance Man and the Quest for Lost Knowledge* (London, 1976).

GOETHE, J. G. VON, *Aus meinem Leben: Dichtung und Wahrheit*, 2 vols. (Basle, 1949).

—— *Conversations of Goethe with Eckermann*, trans. John Oxenford, ed. J. K. Moorhead (Everyman's Library, 851; London, 1951).

GOITEIN, S. D., 'The Intermediate Civilization: The Hellenic Heritage in Islam', in *Studies in Islamic History and Institutions* (Leiden, 1966), 54–69.

GOLAN, DAVID, *A History of the Hellenistic World* (Jerusalem, 1983). (Heb.)

GOLB, NORMAN, 'The Music of Obadiah the Proselyte and his Conversion', *The Journal of Jewish Studies*, 18 (1967), 43–63.

GOLDSTEIN, JONATHAN A., 'Jewish Acceptance and Rejection of Hellenism', in Sanders *et al.* (eds.), *Jewish and Christian Self-Definition*, ii. 64–87.

—— *I Maccabees: A New Translation with Introduction and Commentary* (Garden City, NY, 1976).

—— *II Maccabees: A New Translation with Introduction and Notes* (New York, 1983).

GOLDZIHER, IGNAZ, *Mythology among the Hebrews and its Historical Development*, trans. from the German by R. Martineau with additions by the Author (London, 1877; New York, 1967).

GOLOMB, JACOB, 'Nietzsche's Image of the Jews, Judaism, and Zionism', *Jerusalem Studies in Jewish Thought*, 2/3 (1973), 439–71.

GOMBRICH, E. H., *In Search of Cultural History* (Oxford, 1969).

GOODENOUGH, ERWIN R., *Jewish Symbols in the Greco-Roman Period*, 13 vols. (New York, 1953–1968); ed. and abridged by Jacob Neusner (Princeton, 1988).

GOODMAN, MARTIN, 'Jews and Judaism in the Mediterranean Diaspora in the Late Roman Period: The Limitation of Evidence', *Journal of Mediterranean Studies*, 4/2 (1994), 208–42.

—— *State and Society in Roman Galilee, A.D. 132–212* (Totowa, NJ, 1983).

GORDIS, ROBERT, 'Democratic Origins in Ancient Israel—The Biblical Edah', in *Alexander Marx Jubilee Volume* (New York, 1950), 369–89.

—— 'Homeric Books in Palestine', *Jewish Quarterly Review*, 38/4 (1948), 359–68.

—— *Kohelet—The Man and His World: A Study of Ecclesiastes* (3rd edn., New York, 1968).

GORDON, CYRUS H., *Before the Bible: The Common Background of Greek and Hebrew Civilization* (New York, 1962).

—— *Ugarit and Minoan Crete: The Bearing of their Texts on the Origin of Western Culture* (New York, 1966).

GORDON, Y. [=J.] L., 'Mishlei Yehudah', in *Kitvei Y. L. Gordon: Shirim* ('Collected Writings: Poetry') (3rd edn., Tel Aviv, 1956), 175–9.

GOR-GRASOVSKY, YEHUDA, *Me'agadot hayevanim* ('From the Greek Legends') (Tel Aviv, 1916).

GORNY, YOSEF, *Achdut Ha'avodah 1919–1930* (Tel Aviv, 1973).

—— *The State of Israel in Jewish Public Thought: The Quest for Collective Identity* (London, 1994).

GOSSET, THOMAS F., *Race: The History of an Idea in America* (New York, 1963).

GOTTSCHALK, YEHIEL ALFRED, *Ahad Ha'am and the Jewish National Spirit* (Jerusalem, 1992). (Heb.)

GOVRIN, AKIVA, *Be'ikvei hamesimot* ('In the Wake of the Tasks') (Tel Aviv, 1974).

Graecogermania: Griechichstudien deutscher Humanisten: Die Editionstätigkeit der Griechen in der italienische Renaissance (1469–1523) (Wolfenbüttel, 1989).

GRAETZ, HEINRICH, 'Biblical Criticism and its Meaning', in *Essays, Memories, Letters*, trans. Y. Tolkes (Jerusalem, 1969), 235–40. (Heb.)

—— 'The Correspondence of an English Lady on Judaism and Semitism', in *The Structure of Jewish History*, 191–258.

—— 'Historical Parallels in Jewish History', in *The Structure of Jewish History*, 259–74.

—— *The History of the Jews*, 5 vols. (Philadelphia, 1967).

—— 'The Significance of Judaism for the Present and the Future', in *The Structure of Jewish History*, 275–302.

—— 'The Structure of Jewish History', in *The Structure of Jewish History*, 63–124.

—— *The Structure of Jewish History and Other Essays*, trans. and ed. Ismar Schorsch, The Jewish Theological Seminary of America (New York, 1975).

GRAETZ, MICHAEL, 'The Formation of the New "Jewish Consciousness" in the Time of Mendelssohn's Disciples—Shaul Asher', in *Studies in the History of the Jewish People and the Land of Israel*, iv (Ramat Gan, 1978), 219–37. (Heb.)

—— *From Periphery to Center: Chapters in the 19th-Century History of French Jewry—From Saint-Simon to the Foundation of the 'Alliance Israélite Universelle'* (Jerusalem, 1982). (Heb.)

—— 'Joseph Salvador's Place in the Emergence of Jewish Consciousness', *Zion*, NS 37 (1972), 41–65. (Heb.)

GRAFF, G., *Separation of Church and State: Dina de-Malkuta Dina in Jewish Law, 1750–1848* (Tuscaloosa, Ala., 1985).

GRANT, FREDERICK (ed.), *Hellenistic Religion: The Age of Syncretism* (New York, 1953).

GRÄTZ, MANFRED, *Das Märchen in der deutschen Aufklärung: Vom Feenmärchen zum Volksmärchen* (Stuttgart, 1988).

GREEN, PETER, 'Victorian Hellas', in *Classical Bearing: Interpreting Ancient History and Culture* (London, 1980), 31–44.

—— (ed.), *Hellenistic History and Culture* (Berkeley and Los Angeles, 1993).

GREENBERG, MOSHE, 'Mankind, Israel and the Nations in Hebraic Heritage', in Nelson (ed.), *No Man is Alien*, 15–40.

—— 'The Sages and Alien Wisdom', in Bar-Asher (ed.), *Studies in Judaica*, 117–26. (Heb.)

GREENBERG, URI ZEVI, *Klapei tishim vetishah* ('Against Ninety-Nine') (1929; new edn., Tel Aviv, n.d).

GREENSPAHN, F. E. (ed.), *Essential Papers on Israel and the Ancient Near East* (New York, 1991).

GRÉGOIRE, HENRI BAPTISTE, *Essai sur la régénération physique et politique des Juifs* (Paris, 1789); trans. into Hebrew by Lea Zagagi (Jerusalem, 1989).

GREGORY THE GREAT, *In Canticum canticorum; In librum primum Regum*, ed. P. Verbraken (Corpus Christianorum, Series Latina, 144; Turnhout, 1963).

GREGORY OF NYSSA, *De vita Moysis*, ed. M. Musurillo (Gregorii Nysseni Opera, vii/1: Leiden, 1966).

GRIFFITH, G., 'Classical Greece and the Italian Renaissance', in Thomas, *Paths from Ancient Greece*, 92–117.

GROSS, BENJAMIN, *The Messianism of the Maharal of Prague* (Tel Aviv, 1977). (Heb.)

GROSS, HEINRICH, 'Olymp und Sinai', *Allgemeine Zeitung des Judentums*, 55 (1891), 595–7, 606–8, 619–20.

GRUEN, ERICH S., *The Hellenistic World and the Coming of Rome* (Berkeley and Los Angeles, 1986).

GRUENWALD, ITAMAR, 'Polemical Attitudes towards the Septuagint', *Te'udah* (The Chaim Rosenberg School of Jewish Studies Research Series, 4; Jerusalem, 1976), 65–78. (Heb.)

GRUNEBAUM, GUSTAV E. VON, 'Acculturation and Literature', in *Modern Islam: The Search for Cultural Identity*, 355–90.

—— 'An Analysis of Islamic Anthropology', in *Modern Islam: The Search for Cultural Identity*, 40–8.

—— 'The Concept of Cultural Classicism', in *Modern Islam: The Search for Cultural Identity*, 98–128.

—— *Modern Islam: The Search for Cultural Identity* (New York, 1964).

—— 'The Problem of Cultural Influences', in *Modern Islam: The Search for Cultural Identity*, 19–40.

GÜNZBURG, MORDECAI AARON, *Galut ha'eretz hachadashah* (Vienna, 1823) = Hebrew translation of J. H. Campe, *Die Entdeckung von Amerika* (1781/2).

GUREIN, VICTOR, *Description géographique, historique et archéologique de la Palestine*, 7 vols. (Paris, 1869–80).

GUTMAN, JOSEPH, 'The Dura-Europos Synagogue Painting: The State of Research', in I. L. Levin (ed.), *The Synagogue in Late Antiquity*, 61–72.

GUTMAN, YEHOSHUA, 'Aristobulus', in *The Beginnings of Jewish Hellenistic Literature*, i. 186–220.

—— *The Beginnings of Jewish Hellenistic Literature*, i (Jerusalem, 1958; 2nd edn., 1969). (Heb.)

—— 'Clearchus', in *The Beginnings of Jewish Hellenistic Literature*, i. 91–102. (Heb.)

—— 'Demetrius the Chronographer', in *The Beginnings of Jewish Hellenistic Literature*, i. 132–48. (Heb.)

—— 'Hecataeus of Abdera', in *The Beginnings of Jewish Hellenistic Literature*, i. 39–73. (Heb.)

—— 'The Negotiation with Sparta', in *The Beginnings of Jewish Hellenistic Literature*, i. 108–11. (Heb.)

—— 'Pseudo-Allusions to Israel in Greek Literature prior to the Hellenistic Era', in *The Beginnings of Jewish Hellenistic Literature*, i. 265–73. (Heb.)

GUTTMANN, JULIUS, *Philosophies of Judaism*, trans. David W. Silverman (New York and London, 1964) from the revised and enlarged Hebrew trans. by Y. L. Baruch (4th edn., Jerusalem, 1951) of *Die Philosophie des Judentums* (Munich, 1973).

HADAS, MOSES, 'From Nationalism to Cosmopolitanism in the Greco-Roman World', *Journal of the History of Ideas*, 4 (1943), 105–11.

—— *The Greek Ideal and its Survival* (New York, 1966).

—— *Hellenistic Culture: Fusion and Diffusion* (New York, 1959).

HALAMISH, MOSHE, and RAVITSKY, AVIEZER (eds.), *The Land of Israel in Medieval Jewish Thought* (Jerusalem, 1991). (Heb.)

HALEVI, JUDAH, *The Book of the Kuzari* (*Kitab Al Khazar*), trans. from the Arabic with an Introduction by Hartwig Hirschfeld (London and New York, 1905).

HALL, EDITH, *Inventing the Barbarian: Greek Self-Definition through Tragedy* (Oxford, 1989).

HALLE, AHARON WOLFSOHN, *Avtalyon* (Berlin, 1790).

HALLEWY, E. E., *The Biographical-Historical Legends in the Light of Greek and Latin Sources* (Tel Aviv, 1975). (Heb.)

—— 'Concerning the Ban on Greek Wisdom', *Tarbiz*, 41/2 (1982), 274–69. (Heb.)

—— *The Values of the Aggadah and the Halakhah in the Light of Greek and Latin Sources*, 4 vols. (Tel Aviv, 1979–82). (Heb.)

—— *The Gates of the Aggadah*, 2 vols. (Tel Aviv, 1963). (Heb.)

—— *The World of Aggadah in the Light of Greek Sources*, 2 vols. (Tel Aviv, 1972). (Heb.)

HALPERIN, I. (comp. and annot.), *The Records of the Council of the Four Lands*, i: *1580–1792*, rev. and ed. I. Bartal (Jerusalem, 1990).

HALPERN, BEN, *The Idea of a Jewish State* (2nd edn., Cambridge, Mass., 1969).

HAMEIRI, AVIGDOR, *Sodo shel Socrates* (*The Secret of Socrates: A Novel from Ancient Greece*) (Tel Aviv, 1955).

HAMILTON, EDITH, *The Greek Way to Western Civilization* (1930; 13th edn., New York, 1961).

—— *Mythology* (Boston, 1940).

HARNACK, ADOLF, *History of Dogma*, 4 vols. (London, 1895–1906).

HARRÁN, DON, *In Search of Harmony: Hebrew and Humanistic Elements in Sixteenth-Century Musical Thought* (Stuttgart, 1988).

HARRIS, HAROLD A., *Greek Athletes and Athetics* (London, 1964).

—— *Greek Athletics and the Jews*, ed. I. M. Barton and A. J. Brothers (Cardiff, 1976).

HARRIS, W. T., Editor's Introduction to Davidson, *The Education*, pp. v–xi.

HARSHAV, BENJAMIN, 'Essay on the Revival of the Hebrew Language', *Alpayim*, 2 (1990), 9–54. (Heb.)

HARTMAN, DAVID, *Maimonides: Torah and the Philosophic Quest* (Philadelphia, 1985).

HARVEY, W. Z., 'Maimonides and Aquinas on Interpreting the Bible', *Proceedings of the American Academy for Jewish Research*, 55 (1988), 59–77.

HASKINS, CHALED HOMER, *The Renaissance of the Twelfth Century* (Cleveland, Ohio, 1957).

HATFIELD, HENRY I., *Aesthetic Paganism in German Literature, from Winckelmann to the Death of Goethe* (Cambridge, Mass., 1964).

—— *Winckelmann and his German Critics, 1755–1781: A Prelude to the Classical Age* (New York, 1943).

HAVELOCK, ERIC A., *The Liberal Temper in Greek Politics* (New Haven, 1957).

HAY, DENYS, *Europe: The Emergence of an Idea* (2nd edn., Edinburgh, 1968).

HAYKAL, MUHAMMAD HUSAYN, *The Life of Muhammad*, trans. from the 8th edn. by Isma'īl Rāgī A. Al Fārūqī (Indianapolis, 1976).

HAYS, JOHN, *Old Testament Form Criticism* (San Antonio, Tex., 1974).

HAZARD, PAUL, *European Thought in the Eighteenth Century* (Cleveland and New York, 1967).

HEGEL, W. G., *The Philosophy of History*, trans. J. Sibree (New York, 1956).

HEINE, HEINRICH, *Sämtliche Werke*, ed. H. Kaufman, 14 vols, (Munich, 1961–4).

—— *Heine on Shakespeare*, trans. Ida Benecke (Westminster, 1895).

—— *Not a Kadish Will They Say: On Jews, Judaism and Freedom*, trans. and ed. Y. Eloni and Shlomo Tanny (Tel Aviv, 1994). (Heb.)

—— *The Poems of Heinrich Heine*, trans. Louis Untermeyer (London, 1938).

—— *The Poetry and Prose of Heinrich Heine*, Selected Edition with introduction by Friedrich Ewen (New York, 1959).

—— *Prose and Poetry by Heinrich Heine*, ed. Ernest Rhys (London and New York, 1934).

—— *The Prose Writings of Heinrich Heine*, ed. Havelock Ellis (New York, 1973).

—— *Selected Verse*, introduced and trans. Peter Branscombe (Harmondsworth, 1986).

HEINEMAN, YOSEF, *Aggadah and its Development* (2nd edn., Jerusalem, 1954). (Heb.)

HEINEMANN, ISAAC, 'The Attitude of the Ancient World toward Judaism', *Review of Religion*, 4 (1940), 385–400.

—— 'The Controversy on Nationalism, in Aggadah and of the Middle Ages', in Baer *et al.* (eds.), *Sefer Dinaburg* (Jerusalem, 1949), 131–50. (Heb.)

—— 'The Relationship between the Jewish People and the Holy Land in Hellenistic Jewish Literature', *Zion*, NS 12–14 (1948), 1–9. (Heb.)

—— 'The Unity in Mendelssohn's Philosophy', *Metsudah*, 7 (London, 1954), 197–219. (Heb.)

—— *The Ways of the Haggadah* (Jerusalem, 1970). (Heb.)

HELLER, JOSEPH, *Lehi: Ideology and Politics, 1940–1949*, 2 vols. (Jerusalem, 1989). (Heb.)

HENDERSON, G. P., *The Revival of Greek Thought 1620–1830* (Albany, NY, 1970).

HENGEL, MARTIN, *The 'Hellenization' of Judea in the First Century after Christ* (London and Philadelphia, 1989).

—— 'The Interpretation of Judaism and Hellenism in the Pre-Maccabean Period', in *Cambridge History of Judaism*, ii (Cambridge, 1989), 167–228.

—— *Jews, Greeks and Barbarians: Aspects of the Hellenization of Judaism in pre-Christian Period*, trans. J. Bowden (Philadelphia, 1980).

—— *Judaism and Hellenism: Studies in their Encounter in Palestine during the Early Hellenic Period*, 2 vols. trans. John Bowden (London and Philadelphia, 1974).

HERBERG, WILL, *Judaism and Modern Man: An Interpretation of Jewish Religion* (New York, 1951).

HERBERT, CHRISTOPHER, *Culture and Anomie: Ethnographic Imagination in the Nineteenth Century* (Chicago, 1991).

HERDER, J. G., *Reflections on the Idea of Philosophy of History of Mankind* (Chicago, 1968).

HERMAN, SIMON N., *Jewish Identity: A Social Psychological Perspective* (Jerusalem, 1979). (Heb.)

HERMANN, H. V., *Omphalos* (Orbis Antiquus, 13; Münster, 1959).

HERR, M. D., 'The Conception of History among the Sages', *Proceedings of the Sixth World Congress of Jewish Studies*, iii (Jerusalem, 1977), 129–42. (Heb.)

—— 'External Influences in the World of the Sages', in Kaplan and Stern (eds.), *Acculturation and Assimilation*, 83–106. (Heb.)

—— 'Greek Wisdom', *Ha'entziklopediah ha'ivrit*, xix (1968), 625–7. (Heb.)

—— 'The Hatred towards the Jews in the Roman Empire in the Light of Literature', in *The Hellenistic Views of the Jews: Collected Essays* (Jerusalem, 1974), 33–44. (Heb.)

HERR, M. D., 'Hellenism and the Jews of Eretz Yisrael', *Eshkolot*, 2–3 (9–10) (1987–8), 20–7. (Heb.)

—— 'Hellenistic Influences in the Jewish City: The Fourth and Sixth Centuries CE', *Cathedra*, 8 (July 1978), 90–4. (Heb.)

—— *The Roman-Byzantine Period: The Mishnah and Talmud Period and the Byzantine Rule (70–640)* = Y. Shavit (ed.), *The History of Eretz Yisrael*, vol. v (Jerusalem, 1985). (Heb.)

—— 'Synagogues and Theatres (Sermons and Satiric Plays)', in Elizur *et al.* (eds.), *Knesset Ezra: Literature and Life in the Synagogue*, 105–20. (Heb.)

HERSEY, G. L., 'Aryanism in Victorian England', *Yale Review*, 66 (1976), 104–13.

HERTZ, FREDERICK, *Nationalism and Politics: A Psychology and Sociology of National Sentiment and Nationalism* (London, 1951).

HERZFELD, MICHAEL, *Anthropology through the Looking-Glass: Critical Ethnography in the Margins of Europe* (Cambridge, 1987).

—— *Ours Once More: Folklore, Ideology, and the Making of Modern Greece* (Austin, Tex., 1982).

HESCHEL, ABRAHAM JOSHUA, 'The Heresy of Yafet in the Tents of Shem', in *Theology of Ancient Judaism*, i. 102–4.

—— *Theology of Ancient Judaism*, 2 vols. (London, 1962).

HESIOD, *Theogony; Works and Days*, trans. M. L. West (Oxford, 1988).

HESS, MOSES, 'Briefe über Israels Mission in der Geschichte der Menschheit', in *Jüdische Schriften*, 16–19.

—— 'Ein charakteristischer Psalm', in *Jüdische Schriften*, 241–3.

—— 'Die drei großen mittelländischen Völker und das Christentum', in *Jüdische Schriften*, 70–8.

—— *Jüdische Schriften*, ed. Theodor Zlocisti (Berlin, 1903).

—— *Rome and Jerusalem: A Study in Jewish Nationalism*, with Introd. by Melvin J. Urofsky (Lincoln, Nebr., 1995).

—— *Rome and Jerusalem and Other Jewish Writings*, trans. into Hebrew from the German by Y. Keshet (Jerusalem, 1983).

HIGHET, GILBERT, *The Classical Tradition: Greek and Roman Influences on Western Literature* (Oxford, 1970).

HILPERIN, PINECHAS MENACHEM, *Teshuvot anshei aven* ('The Replies of the Wicked Men'; Frankfurt, 1854).

HINKS, ROGER, *Myth and Allegory in Ancient Art* (London, 1939; repr. Liechtenstein, 1968).

HIRSCHBERG, A. S., *Be'eretz hamizrach* ('In Oriental Lands') (Vilna, 1910; repr. Jerusalem, 1990).

HIRSCHBERG, H. Z., and MARMELSTEIN, A., *The Attitude of the Aggadah to the Halakhah* (Vienna, 1929). (Heb.)

HIRSHMAN, MARC, and GRONER, ZVI (eds.), *Rabbinic Thought* (Proceedings of the

First Conference on the Thinking of our Sages, held at the University of Haifa, Dec. 1987; Haifa, 1990). (Heb.)

HOFFMANN, CHRISTHARD, *Juden und Judentum im Werk deutscher Althistoriker des 19. und 20. Jahrhunderts* (Leiden, 1984).

HOLT, FRANK L., *Alexander the Great and Bactria: The Foundation of a Greek Frontier in Central Asia* (Leiden, 1988).

HOLZMAN, AVNER (ed.), *Ginzei Mikhah Yosef*, vi (Holon, 1995).

HOROWITZ, DAN, and LISSAK, MOSHE, *Origins of the Israeli Polity: Palestine under the Mandate*, trans. Charles Hoffman (Chicago, 1978).

HOROWITZ, RIVKA, *Zacharias Frankel and the Beginnings of Positive-Historical Judaism* (Jerusalem, 1984). (Heb.)

HUCH, E. L. D., *Aesopus oder Versuch über den Unterschied zwischen Fabel und Märchen* (Wittenberg and Zerbst, 1769).

HUMBOLDT, ALEXANDER VON, *Kosmos*, 5 vols. (Stuttgart, 1845–62).

HUME, DAVID, 'Of National Characters', in *Essays and Treatises on Several Subjects*, 4 vols. (1753–4), i. 267–88.

HUNT, H. A. K., *The Humanism of Cicero* (Melbourne, 1954).

HURSHOVSKI, BENJAMIN, *The Theory and Practice of Rhythm in the Expressionist Poetry of U. Z. Greenberg* (Tel Aviv, 1987). (Heb.)

IBN EZRA, MOSHE BEN YA'AKOV, *Sefer ha'iyunim vehadiyunim: Liber Discussionis et Commemorationis (Poetica Hebraica): Kitāb al-muḥāḍara wa 'l-mudhākara*, trans. into Hebrew by A. S. Halkin (Jerusalem, 1975).

IBN ISHAK, HONEIN (Ḥunayn ibn 'Isḥāq), *Musre Haphilosophim* (*Sinnsprüche der Philosophen*), trans. Jehuda ben Salomo Alcharisi (Judah ben al-Harizi), ed. A. Löwenthal (Frankfurt am Main, 1896).

IBN KHALDÛN, *The Muqaddimah: An Introduction to History*, 3 vols. trans. from the Arabic by F. Rosenthal (New York, 1958).

IDEL, MOSHE, 'The Journey to Paradise: The Jewish Transformation of a Greek Mythological Motif', *Jerusalem Studies in Jewish Folklore*, 2 (1982), 7–16. (Heb.)

—— 'Prometheus in Hebrew Dress', *Eshkolot*, NS 5–6 (12–13) (Jerusalem, 1980–1), 119–27. (Heb.)

IDELSOHN, A. Z., *Neginatenu hale'umit* ('Our National Music') (Tel Aviv, 1924).

IGGERS, GEORGE G., *The German Conception of History: The National Tradition of Historical Thought from Herder to the Present* (rev. edn., Middletown, Conn., 1983).

IRWIN, DAVID, *English Neo-Classical Art* (London, 1966).

ISAAC, BEN, 'Ethnic Groups in Judea under Roman Rule', in Kasher and Oppenheimer (eds.), *Dor ledor*, 201–8. (Heb.)

ISH-HURWITZ, SHAI, 'Leshe'elat kiyum hayahadut' ('On the Question of the Existence of Judaism'), *Hashiloach*, 13/4 (Apr. 1904), 287–303.

ISOCRATES, *Panegyrikos*, trans. G. Norlin in Loeb Classical Library edn., i (1928; repr. Cambridge, Mass., and London, 1961), 121–241.

ISSERLES, MOSES (Rema), *Responsa* (Kraków, 1640). (Heb.)

JABOTINSKY, ZE'EV, *Al tarbut ve'omanut* ('On Culture and Art') (Jerusalem, 1948)

—— 'Al teritorializm' ('On Territorialism'), in *Ketavim tsiyonim rishonim*, 131–61.

—— 'Aseret hasefarim' ('The Ten Books'), in *Al tarbut ve'omanut*, 13–45.

—— 'Avodah umatzav ru'ach' ('Work and Spiritual Disposition'), in *Chadashot miha'aretz*, 27 Oct. 1919.

—— 'Ba'al bayit kezayit' ('The Little Homeowner'), in *Sipurim* ('Stories') (Jerusalem, 1952), 207–18.

—— 'Dr Herzl', in *Ketavim tzioniyim rishonim*, 75–106. (Heb.).

—— 'Geza' ('Race'), *Umah vechevrah* ('Nation and Society'; Tel Aviv, 1950), 123–43.

—— *Ketavim tsiyonim rishonim* ('First Zionist Writings') (Tel Aviv, 1949).

—— 'Tsiyonut ve'Eretz Yisrael' ('Zionism and Eretz Yisrael'), in *Al tarbut ve'omanut*, 107–29.

JACOB, MARGARET C., *The Cultural Meaning of the Scientific Revolution* (Philadelphia, 1988).

JACOBS, JOSEPH (ed.), *The Fables of Aesop* (1894; New York, 1966).

JACOBSON, HOWARD, 'Visions of the Past: Jews and Greeks', *Judaism*, 35/4 (Fall 1986), 467–82.

JACOBY, FRIEDRICH, *Die Fragmente der griechischen Historiker* (*FGrH*) (Berlin and Leiden, 1923–57).

JAEGER, WERNER, *Early Christianity and Greek Paideia* (Cambridge, Mass., 1962).

—— *Paideia: The Ideals of Greek Culture*, trans. G. Highet, 3 vols. (Oxford and New York, 1939–44).

—— *The Theology of the Early Greek Philosophers* (Oxford, 1947).

JAMES, GEORGE G. M., *Stolen Legacy* (New York, 1954, repr. 1989).

JAMES, WILLIAM, *The Varieties of Religious Experience* (New York, 1902).

JAPHET, SARA, *The Ideology of the Book of Chronicles and its Place in Biblical Thought* (Jerusalem, 1977). (Heb.)

JAWITZ, ZE'EV, 'Hashirah vehachakirah beYisrael uba'amim' ('Poetry and Inquiry in Israel and in the Nations'), *Keneset Yisrael*, 1 (Warsaw, 1886), 1001–6.

—— 'Olamot overim ve'olam omed' ('Worlds Pass and a World Stands'), in N. Sokolov (ed.), *Sefer hashanah*, i (Warsaw, 1900), 43–54.

—— *Sichot mini kedem*, with introductions by S. J. Fuenn and S. P. Rabinowitz (Warsaw, 1887).

—— *Toledot Yisrael* ('History of Israel'), 14 vols. (Warsaw, 1895; Tel Aviv 1940).

JELLINEK, ADOLF AHARON, *Der jüdische Stamm: Ethnographische Studien* (Vienna, 1868).

JENKYNS, RICHARD, *The Victorians and Ancient Greece* (Cambridge, Mass., 1980).

JOHN OF SALISBURY, *Policraticus*, ed. C. C. J. Webb, 2 vols. (Oxford, 1909), bks.

i–iv; also K. S. B. Keats-Rohan (Corpus Christianorum, Continuatio Mediaevalis, 118; Turnhout, 1993); partial English translation by John Dickinson, *The Statesman's Book of John of Salisbury (Policraticus)* (New York, 1927).

JONES, TOM B., 'Graecia Capta', in Carol (ed.), *Paths from Ancient Greece*, 51–75.

JOSEPHUS, trans. H. St. J. Thackeray *et al.*, 10 vols. (Loeb Classical Library, New York/Cambridge., Mass., and London, 1926–65): i: *Against Apion*, ii–iii: *The Jewish War*, iv–x: *Jewish Antiquities*.

JULIAN (Emperor), trans. William Cave Wright, 3 vols. (Loeb Classical Library, New York and London, 1913–23).

KADUSHIN, MAX, *Conceptual Approach to the Mekhilta* (New York, 1969).

—— *The Rabbinic Mind* (3rd edn., New York, 1972).

—— *Worship and Ethics: A Study in Rabbinic Judaism*, 3rd edn., with an appendix by S. Greenberg (New York, 1963).

KAGAN, ZIPORA, *Halakhah and Aggadah as Code of Literature* (Jerusalem, 1989). (Heb.)

KAHANAH, ABRAHAM, introduction to *Hasefarim hachitsoniyim* (*The Apocrypha*), i (repr. Jerusalem, 1970), pp. vi–xvii.

KAHN, JEAN-GEORGES, 'Philo on Secular Education' (review of A. Mendelson, *Secular Education*), *Tarbiz*, 54/2 (Jan.–Mar. 1985), 306–14. (Heb.)

—— 'The Status of General Education in Judaism—the View of Philo', in M. Stern (ed.), *Nation and History*, 51–4. (Heb.)

KAMENKA, EUGENE, *The Philosophy of L. Feuerbach* (London, 1970).

KAMIN, SARA, 'The Polemics against Allegory in the Commentary of Rabbi Joseph Bekhor Shor', *Jerusalem Studies in Jewish Thought*, 3/3 (1984), 367–92. (Heb.)

KAMINKA, AHARON, 'Hamusar hayevani vehamusar hayehudi' ('Greek Morality and Jewish Morality'), in *Seneca: Selected Writings* (Tel Aviv, 1962), 359–69.

—— 'Mavo leshirat haYevanim' ('Introduction to the Poetry of the Greeks'), *Kenesset Yisrael*, 2 (Warsaw, 1887), 128–52.

—— *Zemorot nokhriot* ('Alien Twigs') (Paris, 1888).

—— (ed. and trans.), *Ideas of Marcus Aurelius Antoninus* (Warsaw, 1923). (Heb.)

KANIEL, YEHOSHUA, *Continuity and Change: Old Yishuv and New Yishuv during the First and Second Aliyah* (Jerusalem, 1981). (Heb.)

—— 'Religion and "Community" in the Outlook of the Immigrants of the First and Second Aliyha (1882–1914)', *Shalem*, 5 (Jerusalem, 1987), 189–205. (Heb.)

KAPITZA, PETER K., *Ein bürgerlicher Krieg in der gelehrten Welt: Geschichte der Querelle des Anciens et des Modernes in Deutschland* (Munich, 1981).

KAPLAN, Y., and STERN, M. (eds.), *Acculturation and Assimilation: Continuity and Change in the Cultures of Israel and the Nations. Collected Essays* (Jerusalem, 1989). (Heb.)

KARIV, AVRAHAM (ed.), *The Writings of the Maharal of Prague* (Jerusalem, 1972).

KASHER, ARYEH, *Jews and Hellenistic Cities in Eretz-Israel: Relations of the Jews in*

Eretz-Israel with the Hellenistic Cities during the Second Temple Period (332 BCE–70 CE) (Texte und Studien zum antiken Judentum; Tübingen, 1990).

KASHER, ARYEH, 'The Jewish Attitude to the Alexandrian Gymnasium in the First Century A.D.', *American Journal of Ancient History*, 1 (1976), 148–61.

—— *The Jews in Hellenistic and Roman Egypt: The Struggle for Equal Rights* (Tel Aviv, 1978) (English translation: Tübingen, 1985).

—— 'The Propaganda Purposes of Manetho's Libellous Story about the Base Origin of the Jews', *Studies in the History of the Jewish People and the Land of Israel*, 3 (University of Haifa, 1974), 69–84. (Heb.)

—— 'Some Remarks and Insights on Expressions of the Assimilation of Jews in Ancient Alexandria', in Kaplan and Stern (eds.), *Acculturation and Assimilation*, 71–82. (Heb.)

—— and OPPENHEIMER, AHARON (eds.), *Dor ledor: From the End of Biblical Times up to the Redaction of the Talmud. Studies in Honour of J. Efron* (Tel Aviv, 1995). (Heb.)

—— RAPPAPORT, URIEL, and FUKS, GIDEON (eds.), *Greece and Rome in Eretz-Israel: Collected Essays* (Jerusalem, 1990).

KATZ, DAVID S., *Philo-Semitism and the Readmission of the Jews to England 1603–1655* (Oxford, 1982).

KATZ, JACOB, *Exclusiveness and Tolerance: Studies in Jewish–Gentile Relations in Medieval and Modern Times* (London, 1961).

—— 'Halahkah and Kabalah as Competitive Subjects of Study', in *Halahkah and Kabbalah*, 52–69. (Heb.)

—— *Halakhah and Kabbalah: Studies in the History of Jewish Religion, its Various Faces and Social Relevance* (Jerusalem, repr. 1986). (Heb.)

—— *Tradition and Crisis: Jewish Society at the End of the Middle Ages*, 2nd edn., trans. Bernard Dov Cooperman (New York, 1993).

KATZ, SHAUL, 'The Israeli Teacher-Guide: The Emergence and Perception of a Role', *Annals of Tourism Research*, 12 (1985), 49–72.

KATZ, Y., et al. (eds.), *Historical-Geographical Studies in the Settlement of Eretz Yisrael* (Jerusalem, 1991).

KATZNELSON, BERL, 'Likrat hayamim haba'im' ('Towards the Future', 1919), in *Ketavim* ('Writings') (Tel Aviv, 1950), 68–87.

KAUFMAN, DAVID, 'The Dispute about the Sermons of David de Bene of Mantua', *Jewish Quarterly Review*, 8 (1886), 513–24.

KAUFMANN, WALTER, *Nietzsche: Philosopher, Psychologist, Antichrist* (3rd edn., Princeton, 1968).

KAUFMANN, YEHEZKEL, 'Bekivshonah shel hayetzirah hale'umit' ('In the Kiln of the National Creation') in *Toledot ha'emunah hayisraelit*, 6 vols. (Jerusalem and Tel Aviv, 1976), i/2. 1–44.

—— *The Religion of Israel: From the Beginning to the Babylonian Exile*, 8 vols. (Chicago, 1960).

KELLNER, MENACHEM, 'Inadvertent Heresy in Medieval Jewish Thought: Maimonides and Abrabanel vs. Crescas and Duran?', *Jerusalem Studies in Jewish Thought*, 3/3 (1983/4), 393–403. (Heb.)

—— 'Attempts at Reviving Civic Sentiment at the Beginning of Jewish Nationalism' in: Etkes and Salmon (eds.), *Studies in the History of Jewish Society* (Jerusalem, 1980), 208–29. (Heb.)

KENT-HILD, DOROTHY, 'Archaeology and the Idea of Classical Antiquity', in Boas (ed.), *The Greek Tradition*, 15–74.

KEREN, MICHAEL, *Ben-Gurion and the Intellectuals: Power, Knowledge, and Charisma* (De Kalb, Ill., 1983).

KERR, JAMES, *Fiction Against History: Scott as Story-Teller* (Cambridge, 1989).

KESHET, YESHURUN, 'Al Heine: Me'ah shanim lepetirato' ('On Heine: On the Centenary of his Death'), *Shenaton Davar* (1957), 415–42.

KIMBLE, GEORGE H. T., *Geography in the Middle Ages* (New York, 1968).

KIMMERLING, Baruch, 'Between "Alexandria-on-the-Hudson" and Zion', in *The Israeli State and Society*, 237–64.

—— (ed.), *The Israeli State and Society: Boundaries and Frontiers* (Albany, NY, 1989).

KINGSLEY, CHARLES, *The Heroes* (Cambridge, 1956).

KIRK, G. S., *Myth: Its Meaning and Function in Ancient and Other Cultures* (Cambridge, 1970).

—— *The Nature of Greek Myths* (Harmondsworth, 1974).

KISCH, GUIDO (ed.), *Das Breslauer Seminar: Gedächtnisschrift* (Tübingen, 1963).

KITTO, H. D. F., *The Greeks* (Harmondsworth, 1962).

KLATZKIN, JACOB (Ya'akov), 'Al Herman Kohen' ('On Hermann Cohen)', *Hatekufah*, 11 (Warsaw, 1921), 493–502.

—— *Kera'im: Midrashim filosofiyim* ('Philosophical Exegeses') (Jerusalem and Berlin, 1923).

KLAUSNER, YOSEF, 'Ben hekhrach veratzon—leshe'elat hayahadut' ('Between Necessity and Desire: On the Question of the Existence of Judaism'), in *Judaism and Humanity*, i. 187–213.

—— 'Ernest Renan vetorat hageza' ('Ernest Renan and the Theory of Race'), in *Yahadut ve'enoshiyut*, i. 107–38.

—— 'Ha'arakhim haruchaniyim shelanu' ('Our Spiritual Values'), in *Yahadut ve'enoshiyut*, i. 145–86.

—— 'Hamaterializm hahistori vehatenuah hale'umit' ('Historical Materialism and the National Movement'), in *Yahadut ve'enoshiyut*, i. 81–106.

—— *History of Modern Hebrew Literature*, 5 vols. (Tel Aviv, 1968). (Heb.)

—— 'Jeremiah', in *The Prophets: Essays on the Nature of Prophecy and the World-View of the Israeli Prophets* (Jerusalem, 1954), 113–36. (Heb.)

—— 'Milchemet haruach' ('The War of the Spirit'), *Hazeman: Yalkut sifruti* (Warsaw, 1896), 67–72.

Klausner, Yosef, 'Tefisat ha'olam shel Tchernichowsky' ('Tchernichowsky's World View'), in *Meshorerei dorenu* (Jerusalem, 1956), 61–112.

—— *Yahadut ve'enoshiyut* ('Judaism and Humanity'), 2 vols. (4th edn., Jerusalem, 1955).

—— 'Yehudah veYavan—shenei hafachim?' ('Judah and Greece—Two Opposites?'), in *Yahadut ve'enoshiyut*, i. 214–30.

Klein, Charlotte, *Anti-Judaism in Christian Theology*, trans. E. Quinn (Philadelphia, 1978).

Koch, Klaus, *The Rediscovery of Apocalyptic Literature*, trans. from the German by M. Koch (Naperville, Ill., 1970).

Kohn, Hans, *The Mind of Germany: The Education of a Nation* (New York, 1960).

Kolat, Israel, 'The French Revolution's Impact on the Jewish National Movement', in R. I. Cohn (ed.), *The French Revolution and its Impacts* (Jerusalem, 1987), 287–314. (Heb.)

—— 'Religion, Society and State During the National Home Period', in S. Almog *et al.* (eds.), *Zionism and Religion* (Jerusalem, 1994), 329–72. (Heb.)

Kollmann, E. D., and Roisman-Maslovski, H., 'Hebrew Translations of Greek and Roman Literature: A Bibliography', *Hasifrut/Literature*, 4 (Oct. 1973), 753–70. (Heb.)

Könneker, Barbara, 'Die Rezeption der aesopischen Fabel in der deutschen Literatur des Mittelalters und der frühen Neuzeit', in August Buck (ed.), *Die Rezeption der Antike: Zur Problematik der Kontinuität zwischen Mittelalter und Renaissance. Vorträge gehalten anläßlich des ersten Kongresses des Wolfenbütteler Arbeitskreises für Renaissanceforschung in der Herzog August Bibliothek Wolfenbüttel vom 2. bis 5. September 1978* (Wolfenbütteler Abhandlungen zur Renaissanceforschung, 1; Hamburg, 1981), 209–24.

Kook, Abraham Isaac, *Orot* (Jerusalem, 1950) (English trans. by Rabbi Bezalel Naor, Northvale, NJ, 1993).

Kraemer, Joel L., *Humanism in the Renaissance of Islam: The Cultural Revival during the Bayid Age* (2nd rev edn.; Leiden, 1992).

Krauss, Shmuel, *Persia and Rome in the Talmud and the Midrashim* (Jerusalem, 1948). (Heb.)

Kreeft, Peter, *Socrates Meets Jesus* (Downers Grove, Ill., 1987).

Kreisel, Howard, 'The Land of Israel and Prophecy in Medieval Jewish Philosophy', in Halamish and Ravitsky (eds.), *The Land of Israel in Medieval Jewish Thought*, 40–51. (Heb.)

Kristeller, Paul Oskar, 'The Modern System of the Arts', *Journal of the History of Ideas*, 12 (1951), 496–527, 13 (1952), 17–46.

—— *Renaissance Thought: The Classic, Scholastic, and Humanistic Strains* (New York, 1961).

—— and Barash, M. (eds.), *The Western System of the Arts* (Jerusalem, 1990). (Heb.)

KROCHMAL, NACHMAN, *Moreh nevuchei hazeman* ('The Guide of the Perplexed of our Time') (Lvov, 1852).

—— *Werke: Erste vollständige Ausgabe*, ed. S. Rawidowicz (Berlin, 1924). (Heb.)

KROEBER, A. L., *An Anthropologist Looks at History* (Berkeley and Los Angeles, 1963).

—— 'Explanations of Cause and Origin', in *The Nature of Culture* (Chicago, 1952), 12–19.

—— *The Nature of Culture* (Chicago, 1952).

—— and Kluckhohn, C., *Culture* (Cambridge, Mass., 1952).

KUHRT, AMÉLIE, and SHERWIN-WHITE, SUSAN (eds.), *Hellenism in the East: The Interaction of Greek and Non-Greek Civilizations from Syria to Central Asia after Alexander* (London, 1987).

KULKA, DOV, 'The Historical Background of the National and Educational Teaching of Rabbi Judah Loew Bezalel of Prague: A Suggested New Approach to the Study of the Maharal', *Zion: Jubilee Volume* (50) (Jerusalem, 1985), 277–320. (Heb.)

LACH, DONALD, *Asia in the Making of Europe*, ii: *A Century of Wonder*; iii: *The Scholarly Disciplines* (Chicago, 1971).

LACHS, SAMUEL TOBIAS, 'The Pandora–Eve Motif in Rabbinic Literature', *Harvard Theological Review*, 67 (1974), 341–5.

LACHOWER, YERUCHAM, *History of Modern Hebrew Literature*, 3 vols. (Tel Aviv, 1936–7). (Heb.)

LANDMAN, LEO, *Jewish Law in the Diaspora* (Philadelphia, 1968).

LANGE, NICHOLAS R. M. DE, 'Shem and Japheth—On the Jews and the Greek Language', in *Pe'amim: Studies in the Heritage of Oriental Jewry*, 38 (Jerusalem, 1989), 2–20. (Heb.)

LANGLOIS, G. (ed.), *The Persistent Voice: Essay on Hellenism in French Literature since the 18th Century* (Geneva, 1971).

LASKOV, SHULAMIT, 'Altneuland', *Hatzionut*, 15 (1990), 35–54. (Heb.)

LATEINER, DONALD, *The Historical Methods of Herodotus* (Toronto, 1991).

LAYARD, A. H., *Nineveh and its Remains*, 2 vols. (London, 1849).

LAZARUS, MORITZ, *Die Ethik des Judentums*, 2 vols. (Frankfurt am Main, 1898) = *Ethics of Judaism*, trans. Henrietta Szold (Philadelphia, 1900).

LEBENSON, MICAH JOSEPH (Mikhal), *Shirei Mikhal: Letters and Translations*, ed. J. Fichman (Tel Aviv, 1974).

LECKY, W. E. H., *History of the Rise and Influence of the Spirit of Rationalism in Europe*, 2 vols. (London, 1865).

LEFKOWITZ, MARY, 'The Myth of a "Stolen Legacy"', *Fraud*, 27 (Mar.–Apr. 1994), 27–33.

—— *Not Out of Africa: How Afrocentrism became an Excuse to Teach Myth as History* (New York, 1996).

LEROY-BEAULIEU, ANATOLE, *Israel among the Nations: A Study of Jews and Anti-semitism*, trans. Frances Hellman (New York, 1895).

LEVENSON, JOSEPH R., *Liang Ch'i-ch'ao and the Mind of Modern China* (Berkeley and Los Angeles, 1967).

LEVIN, LEE I., 'The Political Struggle between Pharisees and Sadducees', in Oppenheimer *et al.* (eds.), *Jerusalem in the Second Temple Period*, 61–83. (Heb.)

—— *The Rabbinic Class of Palestine in Late Antiquity* (Jerusalem, 1986).

—— (ed.), *The Synagogue in Late Antiquity* (Philadelphia, 1984).

LEVIN, MORDECHAI (Marcus), *Social and Economic Values: The Idea of Modernization in the Ideology of the Haskalah Movement* (Jerusalem, 1975). (Heb.)

LEVIN, YEHUDAH L., 'She'elot hazeman' ('Questions of Our Time'), in *Zikhronot vehegyonot*, 140–3.

—— 'Simchah vesason laYehudim' ('Gladness and Joy to the Jews'), in *Zikhronot vehegyonot*, 155–8.

—— *Zikhronot vehegyonot* ('Memories and Studies'), ed. Y. Sluzky (Jerusalem, 1968).

LEVINE, HILLEL, 'Paradise not Surrendered: Jewish Reactions to Copernicus and The Growth of Modern Science', in R. S. Cohen and Wartofsky (eds.), *Epistemology, Methodology, and the Social Sciences*, 203–23.

LEVINGER, JACOB S., *Maimonides as Philosopher and Codifier* (Jerusalem, 1989). (Heb.)

LEVINSOHN, ISAAC BAER, *Te'udah beYisrael* ('A Testimony in Israel') (Photocopy of the Vilna and Grodno edn., 1828, introduction by I. Etkes (Jerusalem, 1977)).

LEVY, ISRAEL, 'Über die Spuren des griechischen und römischen Altertums in talmudischen Schriften', *Abhandlungen der 33. Philologenversammlung* (Gera, 1878).

LEVY, JOHANAN (Hans Lewy), 'Aristotle and the Jewish Sage', in *Studies in Jewish Hellenism*, 15–43. (Heb.)

—— 'Hecataeus of Abdera', in *Studies in Jewish Hellenism*, 44–59. (Heb.)

—— 'New Ways in the Study of Jewish Hellenism', in *Studies in Jewish Hellenism*, 209–20. (Heb.)

—— 'A Quarrel over the Land of Eretz Yisrael', in *Studies in Jewish Hellenism*, 60–78. (Heb.)

—— *Studies in Jewish Hellenism* (2nd edn., Jerusalem, 1962). (Heb.)

—— 'Tacitus on the Antiquities of the Jews and their Virtues', in *Studies in Jewish Hellenism*, 115–96. (Heb.)

LEVY, ZE'EV, 'Esthetical Values and the Jewish Religious Tradition', in Dreifus and Elstein, *Contemporary Jewish Culture*, 25–36. (Heb.)

—— *Judaism in the World View of J. G. Hamman, J. G. Herder and W. V. Goethe* (Jerusalem, 1994). (Heb.)

—— *Shem and Japheth: The Relationship between Jewish and General Philosophy* (Tel Aviv, 1984). (Heb.)

LEWIS, BERNARD, *History Remembered, Recovered, Invented*, 2 vols. (Princeton, 1976).

—— *Islam in History: Ideas, Men and Events in the Middle East* (London, 1973).

—— 'The Pro-Islamic Jews', in *Islam in History*, 123–37.

—— 'Semites and Anti-Semites', in *Islam and History*, 138–57.

LEWIS, D. M., 'The First Greek Jew', *Journal of Semitic Studies*, 2 (1957), 264–6.

LICHTHEIM, MIRIAM, *Ancient Egyptian Literature*, 3 vols. (Berkeley and Los Angeles, 1973–8).

LIEBERMAN, SAUL, 'The Alleged Ban on Greek Wisdom', in *Hellenism in Jewish Palestine*, ii. 110–14.

—— 'The Greek of the Bible', in *Greek in Jewish Palestine*, i. 15–28.

—— 'Greek and Latin Proverbs in Rabbinic Literature', in *Greek in Jewish Palestine*, i. 144–60.

—— *Greek in Jewish Palestine* (i) and *Hellenism in Jewish Palestine* (ii), with a new introduction by Dov Zlotnick (new edn. in 1 vol.; New York, 1994).

—— 'How Much Greek in Jewish Palestine?', in *Texts and Studies* (New York, 1974), 123–41.

—— 'The Natural Sciences of the Rabbis', in *Greek in Jewish Palestine*, i. 180–91.

—— 'Pleasures and Fears', in *Greek in Jewish Palestine*, i. 91–114.

—— 'Rabbinic Polemics against Idolatry', in *Hellenism in Jewish Palestine*, ii. 115–27.

LIEBES, YEHUDAH, *The Sin of Elisha: The Four who Enter the Orchard and the Nature of Talmudic Mysticism* (2nd rev. and enlarged edn.; Jerusalem, 1991). (Heb.)

LIEBESCHÜTZ, H., *Das Judentum in deutschen Geschichtsbild von Hegel bis Weber* (Tübingen, 1961).

LIEBMAN, CHARLES, 'The Jewish Religion in Contemporary Israeli Nationalism', *Zemanim*, 13, nos. 50–1 (Tel Aviv, 1995), 132–46. (Heb.)

—— and DON-YEHIYA, E., *Civil Religion in Israel* (Berkeley and Los Angeles, 1993.

LILIENBLUM, M. L., *An Autobiography*, 3 vols. (Jerusalem, 1970). (Heb.)

—— 'Al techiyat am Yisrael al admat eretz avotav' ('On the Revival of the People of Israel in the Land of its Fathers') (Odessa, 1884) = *Derekh ge'ulim*, 3–35.

—— 'Chomer veruach' ('Matter and Spirit'), in *Derekh ge'ulim*, 90–4.

—— *Derekh ge'ulim* (*The Path of Redemption*) (Tel Aviv, 1935).

—— *Igrot M. L. Lilienblum le Y. L. Gordon* ('Letters of Lilienblum to Gordon'), ed. with introduction and notes by Shlomo Brieman (Jerusalem, 1968).

LIVINGSTONE, R. W., *The Greek Genius and its Meaning to Us* (Oxford, 1912).

—— *Greek Ideas and Modern Life* (Oxford, 1935).

—— (ed.), *The Legacy of Greece* (Oxford, 1921).

LLOYD, G. E. R., *Polarity and Analogy: Two Types of Argumentation in Early Greek Thought* (Cambridge, 1966).

—— *The Revolution of Wisdom: Studies in the Claims and Practice of Ancient Greek Science* (Berkeley and Los Angeles, 1987).

—— 'Views of Time in Greek Thought', in *Cultures and Time*, 117–48.

—— (ed.), *Hippocratic Writings*, trans. J. Chadwick and W. N. Mann (Harmondsworth, 1978), 9–63.

LLOYD, SETON, *Foundations in the Dust: The Story of Mesopotamian Explorations*, rev. and enlarged edn. (London, 1980).

LLOYD-JONES, HUGH, *Blood for the Ghosts: The Classical Influences in the Nineteenth and Twentieth Centuries* (London, 1982).

—— *Classical Survivals: The Classics in the Modern World* (London, 1982).

—— 'Tacitus': introduction to *Tacitus: The Annals and the Histories*, trans. A. J. Church and W. J. Brodribb (Chalfont St. Giles, 1966) = *Classical Survivals*, 146–65.

LOEWE, R. (ed.), *Studies in Rationalism, Judaism and Universalism, in Memory of Leon Roth* (London and New York, 1966).

LONGINUS, *On the Sublime*, trans. with an introduction by T. S. Dorsch in *Classical Literary Criticism* (Harmondsworth, 1965), 97–158.

LORIMER, H. L., *Homer and the Monuments* (London, 1950).

LOTMAN, IURI M., and USPENSKI, BORIS A., 'Binary Models in the Dynamics of Russian Culture (to the end of the Eighteenth Century)', in *The Semiotics of Russian Cultural History*, trans. from the Russian with an Introduction by Boris Gasparov (Ithaca, NY, 1985), 30–66.

LOVEJOY, ARTHUR, 'Herder and the Enlightenment Philosophy of History', in *Essays in the History of Ideas* (Baltimore, 1948), 166–82.

LOW, ALFRED D., *Jews in the Eyes of the Germans: From The Enlightenment to Imperial Germany* (Philadelphia, 1979).

LOWENSTEIN, STEVEN M., *The Berlin Jewish Community: Enlightenment, Family and Crisis, 1770–1830* (New York and Oxford, 1994).

LOWTH, KARL, *Meaning in History* (Chicago, 1949; repr. London, 1976).

LOWTH, ROBERT, *Lectures on the Sacred Poetry of the Hebrews* (1753), repr. with an introduction by V. Freimarck (Hildesheim, 1969).

LUCIAN, trans. A. M. Harmon *et al.*, 8 vols. (Loeb Classical Library, New York/Cambridge., Mass. and London, 1921–67).

LUCRETIUS, *On the Nature of Things*, trans. Charles E. Bennett (New York, 1951).

LUSCHAN, F. VON, *The Early Inhabitants of Western Asia* (London, 1911).

—— *Völker, Rassen, Sprachen* (Berlin, 1922).

LUZ, EHUD, *Parallels Meet: Religion and Nationalism in the Early Zionist Movement (1882–1904)* (Tel Aviv, 1985). (Heb.)

LUZ, MENACHEM, 'Clearchus of Soli as a Source of Eleazar's Deuterosis', in U. Rappaport (ed.), *Josephus Flavius*, 79–90. (Heb.)

LUZZATTO, MOSES CHAYIM, *Layesharim tehilah* ('Praise to the Righteous') (Amsterdam, 1743; repr. Jerusalem, 1949).

—— *Mesilat yesharim* (Amsterdam, 1740; *The Path of the Upright*, trans. M. M. Kaplan (2nd edn., Jerusalem, 1964).

—— *Sefer leshon limudim* (Mantua, 1727).

LUZZATTO, SAMUEL DAVID, 'Ahavat haberiot bayahadut' ('The Love of Mankind in Judaism'), in *Selected Writings*, i. 57–68.

—— 'Atticisme et judaïsme', *Ozar nechmad*, 4 (1863), 108–32 (Heb., French; Hebrew also in *Mechkarei hayahadut*, ii. 237–47).

—— *Betulat bat Yehudah* ('The Virgin Daughter of Judah', Prague, 1840).

—— 'Derekh eretz o Atikismus', in *Selected Writings*, ii. 41–73.

—— 'Ha'emunah beTorat Moshe' ('Faith in the Torah of Moses'), in *Mechkarei hayahadut*, i/2. 5–30.

—— *Igrot Shadal be'ivrit (Hebräische Briefe)*, ed. S. E. Graber, 9 vols. (Przemyśl and Kraków), 1882–94.

—— 'Lezioni di teologia dogmatica' ('Lessons in Dogmatic Theology'): Heb. trans. in *Selected Writings*, i. 69–103.

—— *Lezioni di teologia morale Israelitica* ('Lessons in Jewish Ethical Theology'; Padua, 1862).

—— 'Mahut hayahadut' ('The Essence of Judaism'), in *Selected Writings*, i. 47–56.

—— *Mechkarei hayahadut* ('Studies in Judaism'; Warsaw, 1873).

—— 'Perush leBereishit 1–2' ('Commentary on Genesis 1–2'), in *Selected Writings*, ii. 135–76.

—— 'Perush lesefer Yeshayahu' ('Commentary on the Book of Isaiah'), in *Selected Writings*, i. 217; ii. 206–16.

—— 'Perush leShemot 15' ('Commentary on Exodus 15'), in *Selected Writings*, ii. 177–205.

—— *Selected Writings*, 2 vols., ed. with introduction and notes by M. E. Artom (Jerusalem, 1976). (Heb.)

—— 'Yesodei haTorah' ('The Foundations of the Torah'), in *Mechkarei hayahadut*, i/1. 9–49.

MAASS, ERNST, *Goethe und die Antike* (Berlin, Stuttgart, and Leipzig, 1912).

MCCRINDLE, M., *The Invasion of India by Alexander the Great* (2nd edn.; New Delhi, 1978).

MACDOUGALL, HUGH A., *Racial Myth in English History: Trojans, Teutons, and Anglo-Saxons* (Montreal, 1982).

MCGRATH, WILLIAM J., *Dionysian Art and Populist Politics* (New Haven, 1974).

MACHINIST, PETER, 'The Question of Distinctiveness in Ancient Israel' in Greenspahn (ed.), *Essential Papers*, 420–42.

—— 'Outsiders or Insiders: The Biblical View of Emergent Israel and its Context', in L. J. Silberstein and R. L. Cohen (eds.), *The Others in Jewish Thought and History: Constructions of Jewish Culture and Identity* (New York, 1994), 35–50.

MACK, HANNEL, *The Aggadic Midrash Literature* (Tel Aviv, 1989). (Heb.)

MACY, JEFFREY, 'Hellenistic Influences on Islam and Judaism in the Middle Ages', in Kaplan and Stern (eds.), *Acculturation and Assimilation*, 118–34. (Heb.)

MAHLER, RAPHAEL, *Hasidim and Haskalah in Galicia and the Congress Kingdom of Poland in the First Half of the Nineteenth century* (Merhavya, 1961). (Heb.)

MAIMONIDES, MOSES, *The Guide of the Perplexed: An Abridged edition*, trans. from the Arabic by Chaim Rabin (London, 1952).

—— *Moreh nebuchim: The Guide for the Perplexed*, trans. from the original Arabic text by M. Friedländer (2nd rev. edn.; London, 1956).

MALACHI, A. R., 'The War of the Old Yishuv against Ahad Ha'am', in *Studies in the History of the Old Yishuv* (Tel Aviv, 1971), 346–84. (Heb.)

MALEČKOVÁ, JITKA, 'Ludwig Büchner versus Nat Pinkerton: Turkish Translations from Western Language, 1880–1914', *Mediterranean Historical Review*, 9/1 (1994), 73–99.

MALKIN, IRAD, *Myth and Territory in the Spartan Mediterranean* (Cambridge, 1994).

—— 'The Influence of the Greek Symposium on the Passover Seder', *Free Judaism*, 2 (1994), 30.

MALKIN, YAACOV, 'Moses and Aaron—Founders of the Tradition of the Art of Sculpture in Israel', *Free Judaism*, 5 (1995), 93.

MALLORY, J. P., *In Search of the Indo-Europeans: Language, Archaeology and Myth* (London, 1989).

MANDELBAUM, BERNARD, 'The Flowering of American Democracy: Greek Branches and Jewish Roots', *The Samuel Friedland Lectures 1960–1966* (Jewish Theological Seminar; New York, 1966), 21–93.

MANUEL, FRANK E., *The Eighteenth Century Confronts the Gods* (New York, 1967).

MARCUSE, LUDWIG, *Heinrich Heine: A Life between Love and Hate* (New York, 1933) (translation of *Heinrich Heine: Ein Leben zwischen gestern und morgen* (Berlin, 1932).

MARGALIOTH, MORDECHAI (ed.), *Sefer harazim: A Newly Recovered Book of Magic fron the Talmudic Period* (Jerusalem, 1966). (Heb.)

MARGALITH, O., 'The Parallels between the Legend of Samson and the Legends of the People of the Aegean Sea', *Beit Mikra*, 11 (1966), 122–30. (Heb.)

—— *The Sea Peoples in the Bible* (Tel Aviv, 1988). (Heb.)

MARR, WILHELM, *Der Sieg des Judenthums über das Germanenthum* (Berne, 1879).

MARROU, H. I., 'Education and Rhetoric', in Finley (ed.), *The Legacy of Greece: A New Appraisal* (Oxford, 1981), 185–201.

—— *A History of Education in Antiquity*, trans. George Lamb (Madison, Wis., 1956).

MARSDEN, GEORGE M., *Fundamentalism and American Culture: The Shaping of Twentieth-Century Evangelianism 1876–1925* (Oxford, 1982).

MARTHAN, ABRAHAM A., 'The Question of the Hellenism in Tchernichowsky's Poetry: Summary and Conclusions', in Waldman (ed.), *Community and Culture*, 17–36.

—— 'Tchernichowsky's Response to Myth', in S. Nash (ed.), *Migvan*, 265–86. (Heb.)

MEBURAH, BARUCH, *Napoleon and his Age: Hebrew Contemporary Chronicles and Testimonies* (Tel Aviv, 1968). (Heb.)

MEEKS, WAYNE A., *The Origins of Christian Morality: The First Two Centuries* (New Haven and London, 1993).

MELAMED, ABRAHAM, 'The Land of Israel and Climatology in Jewish Thought', in Halamish and Ravitsky (eds.), *The Land of Israel in Medieval Jewish Thought*, 52–78. (Heb.)

—— 'The Perception of Jewish History in Italian Jewish Thought of the Sixteenth and Seventeenth Centuries, A Re-Examination', in *Examination: Italia Judaica* (Rome, 1986), 139–70.

—— 'Philosophical Commentaries on Jeremiah 9: 22–3', *Jerusalem Studies in Medieval and Renaissance Thought*, 41–2 (1984/5), 31–82. (Heb.)

—— 'Wisdom's Little Sister: The Political Thought of Jewish Thinkers in the Italian Renaissance' (Ph.D. diss., Tel Aviv University, 1976). (Heb.)

MENDEL, SARA, and FREEDMAN, DAVID NOEL, *The Relationship between Herodotus' History and Primary History* (Atlanta, Ga., 1993).

MENDELES, DORON, 'Acculturation and Assimilation among Egyptian Intellectuals in the 3rd and 4th Centuries B.C.', in Kaplan and Stern (eds.), *Acculturation and Assimilation*, 61–70. (Heb.)

—— 'Hecataeus of Abdera and a Jewish *Patrios Politeia* of the Persian Period (Diodorus Siculus XL, 3)', *Zeitschrift für die alttestamentliche Wissenschaft*, 95 (1983), 96–110.

—— *The Land of Israel as a Political Concept in Hasmonean Literature: Response to History in the Second Century BC* (Tübingen, 1987).

—— *The Rise and Fall of Jewish Nationalism* (New York, 1993).

MENDELSON, ALAN, *Secular Education in Philo of Alexandria* (Cincinnati, 1982).

MENDELSSOHN, MOSES, *Jerusalem and Other Jewish Writings*, trans. and ed. Alfred Jospe (New York, 1969).

MENDES-FLOHR, PAUL, 'Buber between Nationalism and Mysticism', *Iyun: A Hebrew Philosophical Quarterly*, 29 (1980), 71–91. (Heb.)

—— '*Fin de siècle* Orientalism and the Aesthetics of Jewish Self-Affirmation', in *Jerusalem Studies in Jewish Thought*, 3/4 (1983/4), 623–81. (Heb.)

—— 'Hale'umiyut shebalev' ('Nationalism of the Heart'), in *In Memory of M. Buber on the Tenth Anniversary of his Death* (Jerusalem, 1987), 37–50.

—— 'The Jew as a Man of World Culture', *Proza*, 87 (Oct. 1986), 30–4. (Heb.)

—— *Modern Jewish Studies: Historical and Philosophical Perspectives* (Jerusalem, 1979). (Heb.)

MEYER, EDUARD, *Ursprung und Anfänge des Christentums* (Stuttgart, 1921–3).

—— *Geschichte des Altertums*, 5 vols. (Basle, 1953–8).

MEYER, MICHAEL A., *Response to Modernity: A History of the Reform Movement in Judaism* (New York and Oxford, 1988).

MEYER, MICHAEL A. (ed.), *Ideas of Jewish History* (New York, 1974).

MICHAEL, REUVEN, *I. M. Jost—Founder of Modern Jewish Historiography* (Jerusalem, 1983). (Heb.)

——*Jewish Historiography from the Renaissance to Modern Times* (Jerusalem, 1993). (Heb.)

—— 'Solomon Lewinsohn—His Approach to Jewish History', in Ettinger (ed.), *Nation and History*, ii. 147–62. (Heb.)

MIESIS, J. L., *Kinat ha'emet* ('Zeal for the Truth') (Vienna, 1829), repr. in Friedlander, *Bemisterei hasatirah: Hebrew Satire*, iii. 17–144.

MILL, J. S., *The Spirit of the Age*, ed. F. A. Hayek (Chicago, 1942).

MILLAR, FERGUS, 'The Background to the Maccabean Revolution: Reflections on Martin Hengel's *Judaism and Hellenism*', *Journal of Jewish Studies*, 2/1 (Spring 1978), 1–21.

MILLIKOVSKI, CHAIM, '"Seder olam" and Jewish Chronography during the Hellenistic Period', in Salmon *et al.* (eds.), *Studies in Historiography*, 59–71. (Heb.)

MIRON, DAN, '*Razei lailah*: Imagination and Myth in Ch. N. Bialik's Poetry', *Hasifrut/Literature*, 1/33 (Summer 1984), 57–112. (Heb.)

—— *When Loners Come Together: A Portrait of Hebrew Literature at the Turn of the Twentieth Century* (Tel Aviv, 1987). (Heb.)

MIRSKI, A., *et al.* (eds.), *Exile and Diaspora: Studies in the History of the Jewish People* (Jerusalem, 1988). (Heb.)

MISHORI, ALIK, 'The Rebirth of Hebrew Art: Ideology, Utopia, Search', in Geretz (ed.), *Perspectives on Culture and Society*, 175–94. (Heb.)

MITELPONSKI, A., *Hagadot Yavan: Mivchar sipurei hamitologiah* ('Greek Legends') (Warsaw, 1921).

MODRZEJEWSKI, JOSEPH MÉLÈZE, 'L'Image du juif dans la pensée grecque vers 300 avant notre ère', in Kasher *et al.* (eds.), *Greece and Rome in Eretz-Israel*, 105–18.

MOMIGLIANO, ARNALDO, *Alien Wisdom: The Limits of Hellenization* (Cambridge, 1978).

—— 'An Apology of Judaism in the *Against Apion* by Flavius Josephus', in *Essays on Ancient and Modern Judaism*, 58–66.

—— *The Classical Foundations of Modern Historiography* (Chicago, 1990).

—— 'Eastern Elements in Post-Exilic Jewish, and Greek, Historiography', in *Essays in Ancient and Modern Historiography*, 25–35.

—— *Essays in Ancient and Modern Historiography* (Oxford, 1977).

—— *Essays on Ancient and Modern Judaism*, ed. and with introduction by Silvia Berti, trans. Masella Gayley (Chicago, 1994).

—— 'The Fault of the Greeks', in *Essays in Ancient and Modern Historiography*, 9–23.

—— 'Greek Culture and the Jews', in Finley (ed.), *The Legacy of Greece*, 325–46.

—— 'Hellenism', *Encyclopaedia Judaica*, viii (1972), col. 291.

—— 'History and Biography', in Finley (ed.), *The Legacy of Greece*, 155–84.

—— 'Introduction to the *Griechische Kulturgeschichte* by Jacob Burckhardt', in *Essays in Ancient and Modern Historiography*, 295–305.

—— 'J. G. Droysen between Greeks and Jews', in *Essays in Ancient and Modern Historiography*, 307–23.

—— 'Jews and Greeks', in *Essays on Ancient and Modern Judaism*, 10–28.

—— *On Pagans, Jews, and Christians* (Middletown, Conn., 1987).

—— 'The Origins of Universal History', in *The Classical Foundations of Modern Historiography*, 31–57.

—— 'Persian Historiography, Greek Historiography, and Jewish Historiography', in *On Pagans, Jews, and Christians*, 5–28.

—— 'Problems and Methods in the Interpretation of Judeo-Hellenistic Symbols', in *Essays on Ancient and Modern Judaism*, 48–57.

—— 'Religion in Athens, Rome, and Jerusalem in the First Century B.C', in *The Classical Foundations of Modern Historiography*, 74–107.

—— review of Martin Hengel, *Judentum und Hellenismus*, in *Journal of Theological Studies*, NS 21 (1970), 149–53.

—— 'Time in Ancient Historiography', in *Essays in Ancient and Modern Historiography*, 179–204.

MONTAGU, ASHLEY, *Man: His First Two Million Years—A Brief Introduction to Anthropology* (New York, repr. 1969).

MONTESQUIEU, *Persian Letters*, trans. with an introduction and notes by C. J. Betts (Harmondsworth, 1973).

MOORE, GEORGE F., *Judaism in the First Centuries of the Christian Era: The Age of the Tannaim*, 2 vols. (Cambridge, Mass., 1927–30).

MOSSE, GEORGE L., *The Crisis of German Ideology: Intellectual Origins of the Third Reich*, with a new preface by the author (New York, 1981).

—— 'Influence of the "Volkish" Idea on German Jewry', in *Germans and Jews* (Detroit, 1987), 77–115.

—— 'Intellectual Authority and Scholarship', in *German Jews beyond Judaism* (Bloomington, Ind., 1984), 42–54.

—— 'Jewish Emancipation: Between *Bildung* and Respectability', in Reinharz and Schatzberg (eds.), *The Jewish Response to German Culture*, 1–16.

MULLER, HERBERT J., 'The Romantic Glory of Classical Greece', in *The Uses of the Past: Profiles of Former Societies* (New York, 1952), 99–113.

—— 'Troy: The Bible of Greece', in *The Loom of History* (New York, 1958), 62–96.

MURRAY, GILBERT, *Hellenism and the Modern World* (London, 1953).

NA'AMAN, SHLOMO, 'Moses Hess Explains his *Rome and Jerusalem*', *Hatzionut*, 17 (1993), 9–38. (Heb.)

NASH, STANLEY, *In Search of Hebraism: Shai Hurwitz and his Polemic in the Hebrew Press* (Leiden, 1989).

—— *Migvan: Studies in Hebrew Literature* (Lod, 1988). (Heb.)

NAVE, JOSEPH, and SHAKED, SHAUL, *Magic Spells and Formulae: Aramaic Incantations of Late Antiquity* (Jerusalem, 1985). (Heb.)

NEHER, ANDRÉ, 'The View of Time and History in Jewish Culture', in *Cultures and Time*, 149–67.

NELSON, J. R. (ed.), *No Man is Alien* (Leiden, 1971).

NETTON, IAN RICHARD, *Al-Farabi and his School* (London, 1992).

NETZER, E., 'New Mosaic Art from Seephoris', *Biblical Archeology Review*, 100 (1992), 36–43.

—— and WEISS, Z., 'Byzantine Mosaics of Seephoris: New Finds', *The Israel Museum Journal*, 10 (1992), 75–80.

NEUMARK, DAVID, 'Hashkafat olam vehashkafat chayim' ('World View and Perspective on Life'), *Hashilo'ach*, 11: 61–4 (Jan.–July 1903), 418–32; 219–31; 129–39; 26–32.

—— *Toledot hafilosofiah hayisraelit* ('The History of Philosophy among the People of Israel'), i (New York, Warsaw, and Moscow, 1921).

NEUSNER, JACOB, *Early Rabbinic Judaism: Historical Studies in Religion, Literature and Art* (Leiden, 1975).

—— *Emergence of Pharisaic Judaism* (2nd edn., New York, 1979).

—— *From Politics to Piety: First-Century Judaism in Crisis* (New York, 1975).

—— *The Rabbinic Tradition about the Pharisees* (Atlanta, Ga., 1994).

—— (ed.), *Jews, Greeks and Christians: Religious Cultures in Late Antiquity* (Studies in Judaism in Late Antiquity, 21; Leiden, 1976).

NIETZSCHE, FRIEDRICH, *Die Geburt der Tragödie* (1871); *The Birth of Tragedy*, trans. W. Kaufmann (New York, 1967).

—— *Götzendämmerung* (1889); *Twilight of the Idols*, trans. R. J. Hollingdale (Harmondsworth, 1990).

—— *Menschliches, Allzumenschliches* (1878–80); *Human, All too Human*, trans. M. Faber and S. Lehmann (Harmondsworth, 1984).

—— *Morgenröte* (1881); *Daybreak*, trans. R. J. Hollingdale (Cambridge, 1982).

—— *Der Wille zur Macht*, ed. Elisabeth Förster-Nietzsche and P. Gast (1906); *The Will to Power*, 175, trans. W. Kaufmann and J. H. Hollingdale, ed. W. Kaufmann (New York, 1968).

—— *Zur Genealogie der Moral* (1887); *On the Genealogy of Morality*, trans. Carol Diethe, ed. K. Ansell-Pearson (Cambridge, 1994)

NILSSON, MARTIN P., *Greek Folk Religion* (Philadelphia, 1978).

—— *Greek Piety*, trans. J. J. Rose (New York, 1969).

NOCK, A. D., *Early Gentile Christianity and its Hellenistic Background* (New York, 1964).

NOEL, THOMAS, *Theories of the Fable in the Eighteenth Century* (New York and London, 1975).

NORDAU, MAX, *Paradoxes* (Leipzig, 1896).

—— 'Yahadut hasheririm' ('Muscular Jewry') in *Ketavim* ('Writings'), i (Jerusalem, 1966), 187–9.

OFEK, URIEL, *Hebrew Children's Literature: The Beginnings* (Tel Aviv, 1979). (Heb.)

O'LEARY, D. LACY, *How Greek Science Passed to the Arabs* (London, 1949).

OLENDER, MAURICE, *The Languages of Paradise: Race, Religion, and Philosophy in the Nineteenth Century*, trans. Arthur Goldhammer (Cambridge, Mass., 1992).

OPPENHEIMER, AHARON, 'Ethnic Groups and Religious Context in the Talmudic Literature', in Kasher and Oppenheimer, *Dor ledor*, 209–14. (Heb.)

—— *Galilee in the Mishnaic Period* (Jerusalem, 1991). (Heb.)

—— et al. (eds.), *Jerusalem in the Second Temple Period* (Jerusalem, 1980). (Heb.)

OR, AMIR, 'And Now, Sons, Be Zealous of the Torah', *Iton 77* (Nov.–Dec. 1988), 106–7. (Heb.)

ORIGEN, *Contra Celsum*, trans. and ed. Henry Chadwick (Cambridge, 1965).

OSTWALD, MARTIN, *From Popular Sovereignty to the Sovereignty of Law* (Berkeley, Calif., 1986).

OVADIA, ASHER, and MUCZNIK, SONIA, 'The Jerusalem Orpheus—A Pagan or a Christian Figure?', in Oppenheimer et al. (eds.), *Jerusalem in the Second Temple Period*, 415–33. (Heb.)

OVID, *Metamorphoses*, trans. A. D. Melville, with an introduction and notes by E. J. Kenney (Oxford, 1987).

PAPERNA, A. M., 'Shirah chadashah' ('New Poetry'), *Sefer hashanah*, 2 (1902), 246–63.

PATAI, RAPHAEL, and PATAI, JENNIFER, *The Myth of the Jewish Race* (rev. edn.; Detroit, 1989).

PATER, WALTER, 'Winckelmann', in *The Renaissance: Studies in Art and Poetry* (Oxford, 1986), 114–49.

PEARSON, LIONEL, 'Historical Allusions in the Attic Orators', *Classical Philology*, 36/3 (July 1941), 209–29.

PELIKAN, JAROSLAV, *Christianity and Classical Culture: The Metamorphosis of Natural Theology in the Christian Encounter with Hellenism* (New Haven, 1993).

PELLI, MOSHE, *The Age of Haskalah: Studies in Hebrew Literature of the Enlightenment in Germany* (Leiden, 1979).

—— 'The Genre of the Parable in Hebrew Haskalah Literature', in *Proceedings of the Eleventh Congress of Jewish Studies*, iii (Jerusalem, 1994), 45–51. (Heb.)

—— *Struggle for Change: Studies in the Hebrew Enlightenment in Germany at the End of the 18th Century* (Tel Aviv, 1989). (Heb.)

PEMBLE, JOHN, *The Mediterranean Passion: Victorians and Edwardians in the South* (Oxford, 1988).

PERUSH, IRIS, 'Judaism and Europeanism in J. Klausner's Literary Criticism', in Shamir and Holzman (eds.), *Turning-Points in Hebrew Literature*, 147–56. (Heb.)

PETERS, F. E., *Aristotle and the Arabs* (New York, 1968).

PETERS, F. E., *The Harvest of Hellenism: A History of the Near East From Alexander the Great to the Triumph of Christianity* (London, 1972).

—— 'Hellenism in Islam', in Carol (ed.), *Paths from Ancient Greece*, 76–91.

PETUCHOWSKI, JACOB JOSEPH, 'The Theology of Hacham David Nieto: An Eighteenth-Century Defense of the Jewish Tradition' (Ph.D. diss., Hebrew Union College, 1954).

PFEIFFER, RUDOLF, *A History of Classical Scholarship from the Beginning to the End of the Hellenistic Age* (Oxford, 1968).

—— *A History of Classical Scholarship from 1300 to 1850* (Oxford, 1976).

PHILIPPSON, ALFRED, *Das griechische Klima* (Bonn, 1948).

PHILIPPSON, LUDWIG, 'Pindar und David: Eine vergleichende Skizze', *Allgemeine Zeitung des Judentums*, 46 (1882), 201–5, 217–21, 269–71.

PHILO JUDAEUS, trans. F. H. Colson *et al.*, 10 vols. and 2 suppl. vols. (Loeb Classical Library, New York/Cambridge, Mass., and London, 1929–53).

PINCZOWER, FELIX, *Der jüdische Läufer* (Berlin, 1931) (Hebrew trans., Tel Aviv, 1994).

PINES, SHLOMO, 'The Philosophical Sources of the *Guide*', in *Studies in the History of Jewish Philosophy: The Transmission of Texts and Ideas* (Jerusalem, 1977), 103–73. (Heb.)

—— and HARVEY, W. Z., 'To Behold the Stars and the Heavenly Bodies', *Jerusalem Studies in Jewish Thought*, 3 (1983/4), 507–11. (Heb.)

PINES, Y. M., 'Ahavat hachikui vepe'ulatah miyom hayah Yisrael legoy' ('The Love of Imitation and its Effect from the Time Israel Became a Nation'), in *Yaldei ruchi* (2nd edn., Jerusalem, 1934), 8–13.

PINSKER, Y. L., *Autoemancipation* (Berlin, 1882), ed. M. Yoeli (Tel Aviv, 1960). (Heb.)

PINSON, K. S. (ed.), *Essays on Antisemitism* (2nd edn., New York, 1946).

PLUTARCH, 'On the Fortune of the Romans', in *Moralia*, trans. F. C. Babbitt, iv (Loeb Classical Library, New York and London, 1936), 319–77.

POLIAKOV, LEON, *The Aryan Myth* (London, 1974).

POLLACK, HERMAN, *Jewish Folkways in Germanic Lands (1648–1606): Studies in Aspects of Daily Life* (Cambridge, Mass., 1971).

POPPER, KARL R., *The Open Society and Its Enemies*, i: *The Spell of Plato* (11th edn., revised; London, 1966).

PRAWER, S. S., *Heine's Jewish Comedy: A Study of His Portrait of Jews and Judaism* (Oxford, 1983).

PRESCOTT, HENRY W. M., 'The Greek Tradition in the Hellenistic Age', in Boas (ed.), *The Greek Tradition*, 1–14.

PRICKETT, STEPHEN, '"Hebrew" versus "Hellene" as a Principle of Literary Criticism: The Hellenic Inheritance and the English Imagination', in G. W. Clarke (ed.), *Rediscovering Hellenism*, 137–59.

PTOLEMY, *Tetrabiblos*, ed. and trans. F. E. Robbins (Cambridge, Mass., and London, 1940).

Proza, Special Issue, 60–3 (1982). (Heb.)

QADIR, C. A., *Philosophy and Science in the Islamic World* (London, 1988).

RAGGIO, O., 'The Myth of Prometheus—Its Survival and Metamorphosis up to the Eighteenth Century', *Journal of Warburg and Courtauld Institutes*, 21 (1958), 44–62

RAHMAN, FAZLAR, *Islam and Modernity: Transformation of an Intellectual Tradition* (Chicago, 1982).

RAHNER, HUGO, *Greek Myths and Christian Mystery* (Cheshire, Conn., 1963).

RAISIN, JACOB S., *The Haskalah Movement in Russia* (Philadelphia, 1913).

RAJAK, TESSA, 'The Hasmoneans and the Use of Hellenism: The Hasmonean State and Hellenism', in Davies and White (eds.), *A Tribute to Geza Vermes*, 161–80.

——*Josephus: The Historian and his Society* (London, 1983).

RALL, YISRAEL, *Shirei romi* ('Roman Poetry') (Odessa, 1867).

RAPOPORT-ALBERT, ADA, and ZIPPERSTEIN, S. J. (eds.), *Jewish History: Essays in Honour of Chimen Abramsky* (London, 1988).

RAPPAPORT, SOLOMON JUDAH LEIB, introduction to *Toledot rabenu Chananel* ('The Life of Rabbi Chananel'), in *Bikurei ha'itim*, 12 (1831), 6–11.

RAPPAPORT, URIEL (ed.), *Josephus Flavius: Historian of Eretz Yisrael in the Hellenistic-Roman Period* (Jerusalem, 1982). (Heb.)

——'The Hasmonean State and Hellenism', *Tarbiz*, 60/4 (July 1991), 477–503. (Heb.)

RAPPEL, DOV, '*Chokhmah Yevanit*: Rhetoric', *Jerusalem Studies in Jewish Thought*, 2/3 (1984), 317–22. (Heb.)

——'Jewish Education' in Yitzhak Refa'el (ed.), *Germany in the Nineteenth Century as Reflected in Textbooks* (Jerusalem, 1986), 205–16. (Heb.)

——*Seven Wisdoms: The Controversy about Secular Studies in Jewish Educational Literature until the Beginning of the Haskalah* (Jerusalem, 1990). (Heb.)

RATZEL, FRIEDRICH, *Anthropo-Geographie, oder Grundzüge der Anwendung der Erdkunde auf die Geschichte* (Stuttgart, 1882).

RAVITSKY, AVIEZER, *Messianism, Zionism and Jewish Religious Radicalism* (Tel Aviv, 1993). (Heb.)

——'On Kings and Statutes in Jewish Thought in the Middle Ages: From R. Nissim Gerondi to Isaac Abrabanel', in M. Ben-Sasson *et al.* (eds.), *Culture and Society*, 469–92. (Heb.)

RAWIDOWICZ, SIMON, 'M. Mendelssohn's Translation of the Book of Psalms', in *Sefer Klausner* (Tel Aviv, 1937), 283–302. (Heb.)

RAWSON, E., *The Spartan Tradition in European Thought* (Oxford, 1969).

RAZLER-BERSHON, NEHAMA, 'Isaac Satanow: An Epitome of an Era', *Leo Baeck Institute Year Book*, 25 (London, 1986), 81–99.

RAZOVSKY, PINCHAS, *Shivat Zion: Kovetz mamarei ga'onei hador beshivchei yeshuv Eretz Yisrael* ('The Return to Zion: A Collection of Essays by Learned Scholars Praising the Settlement of the Land of Israel'), ed. A. J. Slutsky (Warsaw, 1892), 37–9.

REILL, P. H., *The German Enlightenment and the Rise of Historicism* (Berkeley and Los Angeles, 1975).

REINER, E., 'The Etiological Myth of the "Seven Sages"', *Orientalia*, 30 (1961), 1–11.

REINHARZ, JEHUDA, and SCHATZBERG, WALTER (eds.), *The Jewish Response to German Culture* (Hanover, NH, 1985).

REINHOLD, MEYER, *Classica Americana: The Greek and Roman Heritage in the United States* (Detroit, 1984).

RENAN, ERNEST, *Le Judaïsme comme race et comme religion/Das Judenthum vom Gesichtspunkte der Rasse und der Religion* (Basle, 1883).

—— *L'Histoire générale et système comparé des langues sémitiques* (Paris, 1848).

—— *History of the People of Israel till the Time of King David* (London, 1888).

REUVENI, YAACOV, 'Sociology and Ideology in Ruppin's Thinking', *Kivunim*, 23 (May 1984), 25–48. (Heb.)

RICE, E. F., *The Renaissance Idea of Wisdom* (Cambridge, Mass., 1958).

RICHARD, CARL J., *The Founders and the Classics: Greece, Rome and the American Enlightenment* (Cambridge, Mass., 1994).

RICHARDSON, P. (ed.), *Law in Religious Communities in the Roman Period* (Waterloo, Ont., 1991)

RICHE, PIERRE, *Education and Culture in the Barbarian West: Sixth through Eighth Centuries*, trans. from the 3rd French edn. by John J. Contreni (Los Angeles, 1976).

RIST, J. M., *Stoic Philosophy* (Cambridge, 1969).

RITTER, CARL, *Erdkunde*, 19 parts (Berlin, 1822–59); translated and adapted as *Comparative Geography*, 4 vols. (Edinburgh and London, 1865).

RIVKIN, ELLIS, 'Defining the Pharisees: The Tannaic Sources', *Hebrew Union College Annual*, 50 (1979), 205–49.

—— *A Hidden Revolution: The Pharisees' Search for the Kingdom Within* (Nashville, Tenn., 1978).

ROBINSON, ZE'EV, and ROISMAN, H. (eds.), *Sefer Perelman: Thirty-three Studies on Classical Culture and its Heritage* (Tel Aviv, 1989). (Heb.)

ROFÉ, ALEXANDER, and ZAKOVITCH, YAIR (eds.), *Isaac Leo Seeligman Volume: Essays on the Bible and the Ancient World*, ii (Jerusalem, 1983). (Heb.)

ROKÉAH, DAVID, *Judaism and Christianity in Pagan Polemics: Celsus, Porphyry, Julian* (Jerusalem, 1991). (Heb.)

—— (ed.), *Jewish Revolts in the Time of Trajan, A.D. 115–17* (Jerusalem 1987). (Heb.)

ROMM, JAMES S., *The Edges of the Earth in Ancient Thought* (Princeton, 1992).

ROSENBERG, SHALOM, 'The Link with Eretz Yisrael in Jewish Philosophy: Clash of View Points', *Cathedra*, 4 (July 1977), 147–66. (Heb.)

ROSENBLOOM, NOAH H., *Studies in Torah Judaism: Luzzatto's Ethico-Psychological Interpretation of Judaism* (New York, 1965).

ROSENSTEIN, D., *Mi'agadot Yavan* ('Greek Legends: Selection of Mythological Stories') (Warsaw, 1909).

ROSENTAL, YEHUDA, 'On M. Stein', introduction to Stein, *The Relationship Between Jewish, Greek and Roman Cultures*, 5–25. (Heb.)

ROSENTHAL, BERNICE GLATZER, 'Stages of Nietzscheanism: Merezhkovsky's Intellectual Revolution', in ead. (ed.), *Nietzsche in Russia* (Princeton, 1986), 69–94.

ROSENTHAL, FRANZ, *The Classical Heritage in Islam*, trans. from the German by E. and J. Marmorstein (Berkeley and Los Angeles, 1975).

—— *Knowledge Triumphant: The Concept of Knowledge in Islam* (Leiden, 1970).

ROSENZWEIG, FRANZ, *Der Stern der Erlösung*, 4th edn. (The Hague, 1976) = *The Star of Redemption*. trans. William W. Hallo (London, 1971).

ROSCHER, W. H., *Der Omphalosgedanke bei den verschiedenen Völkern, insbesondere den semitischen* (Berichte über die Verhandlungen der Sächsischen Gesellschaft der Wissenschaften, Philologisch-historische Klasse, 70/2; Leipzig, 1918).

ROSS, JACOB JOSHUA, 'Spinoza and the Interpretation of the Bible in our Day', in Brinker *et al.* (eds.), *Baruch de Spinoza*, 116–27. (Heb.)

ROSSI, AZARIAH DE', *Selected Chapters from Azariah de' Rossi's Sefer me'or einayim and Matzref lakesef*, ed. with introduction and notes by Reuven Bonfil (Jerusalem, 1991). (Heb.)

ROTENSTREICH, NATAN, 'Kant's Image of Judaism', *Tarbiz*, 27 (1957–8), 388–405. (Heb.)

ROTH, NORMAN, 'The Theft of Philosophy by the Greeks from the Jews', *Classical Folia: Studies in the Christian Preparation of the Classics*, 31 (1978), 53–67.

ROUTLEDGE, J., *The Dialogue of the Dead in Eighteenth-Century Germany* (Berlin, 1974).

RUBENSTEIN, ARYEH, 'The Concept of Culture in Ahad Ha'am's Thinking', *Melilah*, 3–4 (Manchester, 1950), 289–310. (Heb.)

RUBIN, SHLOMO, *Milchemet hanigleh vehanistar* ('The War between the Concealed and the Revealed') (Newark, 1899).

RUDERMAN, DAVID, *Jewish Thought and Scientific Discovery in Early Modern Europe* (New Haven, 1995).

—— *Science, Medicine and Jewish Culture in Early Modern Europe* (Tel Aviv, 1987).

—— *The World of a Renaissance Jew: The Life and Thought of Abraham Farissol* (Cincinnati, 1979).

—— (ed.), *Preachers of the Italian Ghetto* (Berkeley and Los Angeles, 1992)

RUDOLPH, W., *Esra und Nehemia* (Handbuch zum Alten Testament; Tübingen, 1949).

RUPPIN, ARTHUR, *The Sociology of the Jews*, i: *The Social Structure of the Jews* (Berlin and Tel Aviv, 1930). (Heb).

RYLAARSDAM, J. COERT, *Revelation in Jewish Wisdom Literature* (Chicago, 1971).

SADAN, DOV, 'The Parable of the Parable', in *Shai olamot: Three Hundred and Ten Worlds: Twelve Folkloristic Studies*, ed. with an afterword by Dov Noy (Jerusalem, 1990), 74–106. (Heb.)

SAFRAI, SHMUEL, 'The Attitude of the Aggadah to the Halakhah', in Kasher and Oppenheimer (eds.), *Dor ledor*, 215–34. (Heb.)

SAID, EDWARD, *Orientalism* (New York, 1979).

ST. CLAIR, WILLIAM, *That Greece might Still be Free: The Philhellenes in the War of Independence* (London, 1972).

SALIN, EDGAR, *Jacob Burkhardt und Nietszche* (Heidelberg, 1948).

SALMON, YOSEF, et al. (eds.), *Studies in Historiography: Collected Essays* (Jerusalem, 1987). (Heb.)

SALVADOR, J., *Histoire des institutions de Moïse et du peuple hébreu* (Paris, 1862), trans. into Hebrew by Albert Ben-Naim, with a preface by Michael Graetz (Jerusalem, 1975).

SAMBURSKY, SHMUEL, *The Laws of Heaven and Earth* (Jerusalem, 1987). (Heb.)

—— 'The Term *Gematria*—Source and Meaning', *Tarbiz*, 45/3–4 (1986), 268–71. (Heb.)

SANDERS, E. P., et al. (eds.), *Jews and Christian Self-Definition*, ii: *Aspects of Judaism in the Greco-Roman Period* (Philadelphia, 1981).

SANDMEL, SAMUEL, 'The Confrontation of Greek and Jewish Ethics: Philo *De decalogo*', in Silver (ed.), *Judaism and Ethics*, 163–78.

—— 'Hellenistic Judaism', in *Judaism and Christian Beginnings* (Oxford, 1978), 257–301.

—— 'Parallelomania', *Journal of Biblical Literature*, 81 (1962), 1–13.

SANDROSS, E., *Sokrates and Nietzsche* (Leiden, 1966).

SANDYS, J. E., *A History of Classical Scholarship*, 3 vols. (Cambridge, 1903–8; rev. edn., New York, 1958).

SAPERSTEIN, MARC, *Decoding the Rabbis: A Thirteenth-Century Commentary on the Aggadah* (Cambridge, Mass., 1980).

SARACHEK, JOSEPH, *Faith and Reason: The Conflict over the Rationalism of Maimonides* (New York, 1935).

SATANOW, I., *Mishlei Asaf; Gam eileh mishlei Asaf* ('The Proverbs of Asaph; These are also Asaph's Proverbs') (Berlin, 1794).

SARTON, GEORGE, *The Appreciation of Ancient and Medieval Science during the Renaissance (1450–1600)* (Philadelphia, 1955).

—— *Hellenistic Science and Culture in the Last Three Centuries B.C.* (New York, 1987).

SAYCE, A. H., *The 'Higher Criticism' and the Verdict of the Monuments* (3rd rev. edn., London, 1894).

SCHAECHTER, RIVKA, 'The Revival of Tragedy' ('Hitchadshut hatragediah'), *Maariv*, 12 August 1983.

SCHAECHTER, S. Z., 'The Reasons Given by the Rabbis for their Cooperation with the "Maskilim" in the "Hibbat Zion Movement"', in *Studies in the History of the Jewish People and the Land of Israel*, iv (Haifa, 1978), 239–51. (Heb.)

SCHALIT, ABRAHAM, notes to his translation of Josephus, *Antiquities*, ii (Jerusalem and Tel Aviv, 1967), 1–164. (Heb.)

—— (ed.), *The Hellenistic Age: Political History of Jewish Palestine 322 B.C.E. to 67 B.C.E.* (The World History of the Jewish People; New Brunswick, NJ, 1972).

SCHILLER, FRIEDRICH, trans. Edgar A. Bowring, *The Poems of Schiller* (London, 1880).

SCHIRMANN, JEFIM (ed. with an introduction and appendices), *Tzakhut bedichutah dekidushin* ('*The Comedy of Betrothal* by Jehuda Sommo') (Jerusalem, 1965).

SCHLESINGER, AKIVA, *Beit Yosef Hahadash* (Jerusalem, 1875).

—— *El ha'adarim* (Pressburg, 1863).

SCHMIDT, FRANCIS, 'Jewish Representations of the Inhabited Earth during the Hellenistic and Roman Periods', in Kasher *et al.* (eds.), *Greece and Rome*, 119–34.

SCHMIDT, L., *Die Ethik der alten Griechen* (Berlin, 1887).

SCHNABEL, ECKARD J., *Law and Wisdom From Ben Sira to Paul: An Historical Inquiry into the Relation of Law, Wisdom and Ethics* (Tübingen, 1985).

SCHNEIDER, CARL, *Kulturgeschichte des Hellenismus*, i (Munich, 1967).

SCHNEIDER, HELMUT J. (ed.), *Deutsche Idyllentheorien im 18. Jahrhundert* (Tübingen, 1987).

SCHNITZER, SHMUEL, 'The New Kulturkampf', *Ma'ariv*, 17 Dec. 1993. (Heb.)

SCHOLEM, GERSHOM, 'Zikaron ve'utopiyah' ('Memory and Utopia'), in *Od devarim* ('Explications and Implications: Writings on Jewish Heritage and Renaissance'), ii (Tel Aviv, 1989), 187–95.

SCHORR, JOSHUA HESCHEL (Osias), 'HaTorah vedat Zaratustra' ('The Torah and the Zoroastrian Religion') (1865) = *Selected Essays*, ed. Ezra Spicehandler (Jerusalem, 1972), 174–90.

SCHORSCH, ISMAR, 'Breakthrough into the Past: The *Verein für Cultur und Wissenschaft der Juden*', in *From Text to Context*, 205–32.

—— 'The Emergence of Historical Consciousness in Modern Judaism', in *From Text to Context*, 177–204.

—— 'The Ethos of Modern Jewish Scholarship', in *From Text to Context*, 151–7.

—— *From Text to Context: The Turn to History in Modern Judaism* (Hanover, NH, 1994).

—— 'German Judaism: From Confession to Culture', in *From Text to Context*, 360–7.

—— 'Verein für Cultur und Wissenschaft der Juden', in *From Text to Context*, 205–32.

SCHRÖDER, FRANZ ROLF, *Germanentum und Hellenismus* (Heidelberg, 1924).

SCHULMAN, KALMAN, *Divrei yemei olam* ('History of the World'), 9 vols. (1867; 3rd edn. Vilna, 1880).

SCHÜRER, EMIL, *The History of the Jewish People in the Age of Jesus Christ (175 B.C.– A.D. 135)*, rev. and ed. by Geza Vermes, Fergus Millar, and Martin Goodman, 3 vols. (Edinburgh, 1973–87).

SCHWAB, RAYMOND, *The Oriental Renaissance: Europe's Rediscovery of India and the East (1680–1880)*, trans. G. Patterson-Black and Victor Reinking (New York, 1984).

SCHWARCZ, MOSHE, 'Buber's Conception of Myths and the Problem of *Entmythologisierung* in our Times', in *Language, Myth, Art*, 216–49. (Heb.)

—— *Language, Myth, Art* (Tel Aviv, 1966). (Heb.)

—— 'Mendelssohn's "Jerusalem" and Hamann's "Golgatha and Scheblimini"', in *Language, Myth, Art*, 54–88. (Heb.)

—— 'The Poetry of the "Sublime" and the *Melitzat Yeshurun* of Sh. Levinsohn', in *Language, Myth, Art*, 282–308. (Heb.)

SCHWARTZ, DANIEL, *Agrippa I* (Jerusalem, 1987). (Heb.)

—— '"Kingdom of Priests"—or Pharisaic Slogan?', in *Studies in the Jewish Background*, 57–80.

—— 'On Pharisaic Opposition to the Hasmonean Monarchy', in *Studies in the Jewish Background*, 56–114.

—— *Studies in the Jewish Background of Christianity* (Tübingen, 1992).

—— 'Temple and Desert: Or Religion and State in Second Temple Period Judaea', in *Studies in the Jewish Background*, 29–43.

SCHWARTZ, DOV, '"Greek Wisdom"—A Revised Examination of the Period of Controversy about the Study of Philosophy', *Sinai*, 52/104 (May–June 1989), 149–53. (Heb.)

SCHWARTZ, JOSHUA, 'Ball Play in Jewish Society in the Second Temple, Mishnah and Talmud Periods', *Zion*, 60 (1995), 247–76. (Heb.)

SCHWARZBAUM, HAIM, *The Fox Fables of Rabbi Berechiah Hanakdan: A Study in Comparative Folklore and Fable Lore* (Kiron, 1979). (Heb.)

SCHWARZSCHILD, STEVEN, 'The Legal Foundation of Jewish Aesthetics', *Journal of Aesthetic Education*, 9 (1975), 29–42.

—— 'The Theological-Political Basis of Liberal Christian-Jewish Relations in Modernity', in *Das deutsche Judentum und der Liberalismus* (Sankt Augustin, 1986), 70–95.

SCHWEID, ELIEZER, 'Art as an Existential Problem in Jewish Thinking in the Modern Era', in *New Ways in Jewish Religion and National Thought* (Jerusalem, 1991), 141–80. (Heb.)

—— *Democracy and Halakhah: A Study of the Thought of Rabbi Chaim Hirschensohn* (Jerusalem, 1978). (Heb.)

—— *Homeland and a Land of Promise* (Tel Aviv, 1979). (Heb.)

—— *The Idea of Judaism as a Culture* (Tel Aviv, 1995). (Heb.)

—— 'The Jewish Pluralistic Culture in Israel', in Stempler (ed.), *People and State*, 265–75. (Heb.)

—— *Judaism and Secular Culture* (Tel Aviv, 1981). (Heb.)

—— *Ta'am vehakashah*: Studies in Jewish Thought Literature in the Middle Ages (Ramat Gan, 1970). (Heb.)

SCOTT, WALTER (ed. and trans.), *Hermetica* (repr. Bristol, 1993).

SEGAL, DIMITRI, 'The Impact of Russian Literature and Culture on the Emergence of the Jewish Revival Movement', in Geretz (ed.), *Perspectives on Culture and Society in Israel*, 1–16. (Heb.)

SEGAL, LESTER, *Historical Consciousness and Religious Tradition in Azariah de' Rossi's* Me'or einayim (Philadelphia, 1989).

SEGAL, M. Z., *Sefer Ben Sira hashalem* ('The Complete Book of Ben-Sira') (Jerusalem, 1958).

SELIGMAN, J. A., 'Jerusalem in Jewish Hellenistic Thought', in *Judah and Jerusalem Exploration Society Society, 12th Archaeological Convention* (Jerusalem, 1957), 192–208. (Heb.)

SETERS, J. VAN, *In Search of History: Historiography in the Ancient World and the Origins of Biblical History* (New Haven, 1983).

—— 'The Primeval Histories of Greece and Israel Compared', *Zeitschrift für die alttestamentische Wissenschaft*, 100 (1988), 1–22.

SEVENSTER, JAN M., *Do you Know Greek? How Much Greek Could the First-Century Jewish Christians have Known?* (Leiden, 1968).

SEZNEC, JEAN, *The Survival of the Pagan Gods: The Mythological Tradition and its Place in Renaissance Humanism and Art*, trans. from the French by Barbara F. Sessions (2nd edn., Princeton, 1972).

SHABTAI, A., introduction to his translation of Aeschylus' *Prometheus* (Tel Aviv, 1995). (Heb.)

SHAHAK, Y., 'Kulanu mityavenim' ('We are All Hellenizers'), *Ha'aretz*, 27 Nov. 1991.

SHAKED, GERSHON, 'Alexandria: On Jews and Judaism in America', *The Jerusalem Quarterly*, 94 (Winter 1980), 47–84.

SHAKED, SAUL, 'The Influence of Iranian Religion on Judaism', in H. Tadmor (ed.), *Shivat Tziyon*, 236–50. (Heb.)

—— 'Persia as a Model of Cross-Cultural Encounter', in Kaplan and Stern (eds.), *Acculturation and Assimilation*, 119–34. (Heb.)

—— et al. (eds.), *Gilgul: Essays on Transformation and Permanence in the History of Religion* (Studies in the History of Religion, Supplement to *Numen*; Leiden, 1987).

SHAMIR, ZIVA, 'Bialik and Tchernichowsky', *Motzaim*, 69/4 (1985), 19–22. (Heb.)

SHAMIR, ZIVA, *Love Unveiled: Bialik's Personal World of Ideas. A Study of the Adapted Folktale 'The Legend of Three and Four'* (Tel Aviv, 1991). (Heb.)

—— and HOLZMAN, AVNER (eds.), *Turning-Points in Hebrew Literature and their Relationship to Contacts with Other Literatures* (Tel Aviv, 1993). (Heb.)

SHAPIRA, AVRAHAM, *Between Spirit and Reality: Dual Structures in the Thought of M. M. Buber* (Jerusalem, 1994). (Heb.)

—— 'Buber's Attachment to Herder and German "*Volkism*"', *Studies in Zionism*, 14/1 (Spring 1993), 1–30. (Heb.)

SHAPIRO, GARY, 'Nietzsche contra Renan', *History and Theory*, 21/2 (1982), 193–222.

SHATZMAN, ISRAEL, 'The Hasmoneans in Graeco-Roman Historiography', *Zion*, NS 57/1 (1992), 5–64. (Heb.)

SHAVIT, UZI, *Poetry and Ideology: A Contribution to the Evolution of Hebrew Poetry in the 18th and 19th Centuries* (Tel Aviv, 1987). (Heb.)

—— 'What is Haskalah?' An Examination of the Term 'Haskalah' in Hebrew Literature', *Jerusalem Studies in Hebrew Literature*, 12 (1990), 51–83. (Heb.)

SHAVIT, YAACOV, 'Ahad Ha'am and Hebrew National Culture: Realist or Utopianist?', *Jewish History*, 4/2 (Fall 1990), 71–88.

—— 'Characteristics of the Land of Israel in Modern Jewish Thought', in A. Ravitzky (ed.), *Eretz Yisrael in Modern Jewish Thought* (forthcoming). (Heb.)

—— 'A Duty too Heavy to Bear: Hebrew in the Berlin Haskalah, 1783–1819: Between Classic, Modern, and Romantic', in Glinert (ed.), *Hebrew in Ashkenaz*, 111–28.

—— 'The "Glorious Century" and the "Cursed Century": Fin-de-Siècle Europe and the Emergence of a Modern Jewish Nationalism', *Journal of Contemporary History*, 26 (1991), 553–74.

—— 'Hebrews and Phoenicians: An Ancient Historical Image and its Usage', *Studies in Zionism*, 5/2 (1984), 157–88.

—— *Jabotinsky and the Revisionist Movement* (London, 1988).

—— 'King Herod—Historical Personality Looking for a Writer', *Idan* (Jerusalem, 1987), 168–80. (Heb.)

—— 'A National Society and National Hebrew Culture: Two Perspectives', *Hatziyonut*, 9 (1984), 111–22. (Heb.)

—— *The New Hebrew Nation: A Study in Israeli Heresy and Fantasy* (London, 1987).

—— 'Politics and Messianism: The Zionist Revolutionist Movement and Polish Political Culture', *Studies in Zionism*, 6/2 (1985), 229–46.

—— 'Regulations of the First Colonies', *Cathedra*, 72 (June 1994), 50–62. (Heb.)

—— '"Semites" and "Aryans" in Modern Jewish Polemics', in Almog *et al.* (eds.), *Israel and the Nations*, 215–41. (Heb.)

—— '"The Spirit of France" and "French Culture" in the Jewish Yishuv in Eretz Yisrael (1882–1914)', *Cathedra*, 62 (Dec. 1991), 37–53. (Heb.)

—— 'The Status of Culture in the Process of the Formation of a National Society in Palestine: Basic Position and Concepts', in Z. Shavit (ed.), *The Construction of Hebrew Culture of the Jewish Yishuv in Eretz Yisrael* (forthcoming). (Heb.)

—— '"Truth shall Spring out of the Earth": The Development of Jewish Popular Interest in Archaeology in Eretz Yisrael', *Cathedra*, 44 (June 1987), 27–54. (Heb.)

—— 'Uri Zvi Greenberg: Conservative Revolutionarism and National Messianism', *The Jerusalem Quarterly*, 84 (Fall 1988), 63–72.

—— 'Window on the World', *Kesher*, 4 (Nov. 1988), 3–10. (Heb.)

—— 'The Works of H. T. Buckle and their Application by the *Maskilim* of eastern Europe', *Zion*, NS 49/4 (1984), 401–12. (Heb.)

SHAVIT, ZOHAR (ed.), *The Construction of Hebrew Culture of the Jewish Yishuv in Eretz Yisrael* (Jerusalem, 1996; forthcoming). (Heb.)

—— and SHAVIT, YAACOV, 'Translated vs. Original Literature in the Creation of the Literary Center in Eretz Yisrael', *Hasifrut/Literature*, 25 (7/2) (Oct. 1977), 45–68. (Heb.)

SHELLY, CHAIM, *The Study of the Bible in the Literature of Haskalah* (Jerusalem, 1942). (Heb.)

SHESTOV, LEV, *Athens and Jerusalem*, trans., with an introduction by Bernard Martin (Athens, Ohio, 1966).

SHIMRON, BINYAMIN, *Introduction to Classical Civilization: Greece and Rome* (Tel Aviv, 1993). (Heb.)

—— 'Farewell', in Robinson and Roisman (eds.), *Sefer Perelman*, 380–5. (Heb.)

SHINAN, AVIGDOR, *The World of Aggadic Literature* (Tel Aviv, 1987). (Heb.)

SHMERUK, H., 'A Call to a Prophet: Shneur, Bialik, Peretz and Nadson', *Hasifrut/Literature*, 2/1 (Sept. 1969), 241–4. (Heb.)

SHMUELI, EPHRAIM, 'Diyukano shel historion le'umi' ('Portrait of a National Historian'), *Kivunim* (31 May 1986), 37–62.

SHOHAM, SHLOMO GIORA, *Valhalla, Calvary, and Auschwitz* (Tel Aviv, 1992). (Heb.) (Eng. trans. pub. Tel Aviv, 1995.)

SIDGWICK, HENRY, *Practical Ethics* (London, 1898).

SILBER, M. K., 'The Emergence of Ultra-Orthodoxy: The Invention of a Tradition' in Jack Wertheimer (ed.), *The Uses of Tradition: Jewish Continuity in the Modern Era* (New York and Jerusalem, 1992), 23–84.

SILBERSCHLAG, EISIG, 'Tchernichowsky and Homer', *Proceedings of the American Academy for Jewish Research*, 14 (1944), 253–65.

SILMAN, YOCHANAN, 'The Earthliness of the Land of Israel in the *Kuzari*', in Halamish and Ravitsky (eds.), *The Land of Israel in Medieval Jewish Thought*, 79–89. (Heb.)

SILVER, D. J., *Maimonidean Criticism and the Maimonidean Controversy, 1180–1240* (New York, 1965).

SILVER, D. J. (ed.), *Judaism and Ethics* (New York, 1970).

SIMON, AKIVA ERNST, *Are We Still Jews: Essays* (Tel Aviv, 1982). (Heb.)

—— 'Ha'im od yehudim anachnu?' ('Are We Still Jews?'), in *Are We Still Jews: Essays*, 7–46. (Heb.)

—— 'Sparta or Athens?', in *Are We Still Jews: Essays*, 49–69. (Heb.)

SIMON, MARCEL, *Verus Israel: Étude sur les relations entre chrétiens et juifs dans l'empire romain (135–425)* (Bibliothèque des Écoles Françaises d'Athènes et de Rome, 166; Paris, 1948).

SINGER, AHARON M., 'The Rabbinic Fable', *Jerusalem Studies in Jewish Folklore*, 4 (1983), 79–91. (Heb.)

SINGER, I. J., *Beit Karnovs* (1943), trans. J. Singer, *The Family Carnovsky* (New York, 1969; repr. 1988).

SINGER, MILTON, *When a Great Tradition Modernizes: An Anthropological Approach to Indian Civilization* (New York, 1972).

SINGHAL, D. P., *India and World Civilization*, i (Ann Arbor, 1969).

SIRAT, COLETTE, *A History of Jewish Philosophy in the Middle Ages* (Cambridge, 1990).

SIVAN, E., *Arab Political Myths* (Tel Aviv, 1978). (Heb.)

SLUTSKY, YEHUDAH, *The Haskalah Movement in Russia* (Jerusalem, 1977). (Heb.)

SMITH, ANTHONY D., *The Ethnic Origins of Nations* (Oxford, 1988).

SMITH, GEORGE ADAM, *The Historical Geography of the Holy Land* (1894; 4th edn.; New York, 1974).

SMITH, MORTON, 'Hellenization', in *Palestinian Parties and Politics*, 43–61.

—— 'The Image of God: Notes on the Hellenization of Judaism', *Bulletin of the John Rylands Library*, 40 (1957–8), 473–512.

—— 'Palestine Judaism in the First Century', in Moshe Davis (ed.), *Israel*, 67–81.

—— 'Observations on Hekhalot Rabati', in Altmann (ed.), *Biblical and Other Studies*, 142–60.

—— *Palestinian Parties and Politics that Shaped the Old Testament* (New York, 1971).

SMITH, N. K., *Hume's Dialogues concerning Natural Religion* (London, 1923).

SMOLENSKIN, PERETZ, 'Am olam' ('People of Eternity'), in *Ma'amarim* ('Articles'), (Jerusalem, 1925), i. 1–183.

—— 'Even Yisrael' ('The Jewish Race'), in *Hashachar*, 1 (1869), 3: 4–8, 14: 3–8, 5: 2–7; 11: 72–91.

—— 'Et lata'at' ('A Time to Plant'), in *Ma'amarim* (*Articles*), ii (Jerusalem, 1925), 3–149.

SNELL, B., *The Discovery of Mind*, trans. T. G. Rosenmeyer (Oxford, 1961).

SNOWDEN, FRANK M., Jr., *Before Color Prejudice: The Ancient View of Blacks* (Cambridge, Mass., 1983).

—— *Blacks in Antiquity: Ethiopians in Greco-Roman Experience* (Cambridge, Mass., 1970).

SNYDER, LOUIS S. L., *The Dynamics of Nationalism: Reading in its Meaning and Development* (Princeton, 1964).

SOLOVEITCHIK, JOSEPH B., *The Halakhic Mind: An Essay on Jewish Tradition and Modern Thought* (New York and London, 1986).

SOLOWEITSCHIK, MENACHEM, 'Hamidbar betoledotav shel am Israel' ('The Desert in the History and in the World-View of the People of Israel'), *Dvir*, 2 (Berlin, 1924), 16–45.

—— *Sekhiyot hamikra: Otzar temunot lekitvei hakodesh ulekadmuni'oteihem* '('Treasures of the Bible: A Treasury of Pictures for the Holy Scriptures and their Antiquities'; Berlin, 1925).

—— and RUBASCHEFF, Z. M., *The History of Biblical Criticism* (Berlin, 1925). (Heb.)

SORKIN, DAVID, *The Transformation of German Jewry 1780–1840* (Oxford, 1987).

SPENGLER, OSWALD, *Der Untergang des Abendlandes: Umrisse einer Morphologie der Weltgeschichte* (1923) (Munich, 1986); *The Decline of the West*, trans. C. F. Atkinson (New York, 1926; 1944).

SPERBER, DANIEL, *Material Culture in Eretz Yisrael during the Talmudic Period* (Jerusalem, 1993). (Heb.)

SPIEGEL, NATHAN, *Homer* (Jerusalem, 1989). (Heb.)

—— *The Wisdom of Ancient Greece in Anecdote, Proverb, and Joke* (Jerusalem, 1994). (Heb.)

STARR, CHESTER G., *The Birth of Athenian Democracy* (New York, 1990).

STEIN, MENACHEM, 'Judaism and Hellenism', in *The Relationship between Jewish, Greek and Roman, Literature*, 112–16. (Heb.)

—— 'Mother Earth in Ancient Jewish Literature', in *The Relationship between Jewish, Greek, and Roman Literature*, 189–213. (Heb.)

—— 'National Singularity and Human Unity in the Philosophy of R. Judah Halevi', in *The Relationship between Jewish, Greek, and Roman Literature*, 155–68. (Heb.)

—— *The Relationship between Jewish, Greek, and Roman Literature* (Ramat Gan, 1970). (Heb.)

STEIN, S., 'The Influence of Symposia Literature on the Literary Form of the Pesaḥ Haggadah', *Journal of Jewish Studies*, 8 (1957), 13–44.

STEINHEIM, S. L., *Moses Mendelssohn und seine Schule* (Hamburg, 1840).

STEINTHAL, H., 'Die Erzählkunst der Bibel', in *Bibel und Religionsphilosphie: Vorträge und Abhandlungen* (Berlin, 1890), 1–15.

STEMPLER, S. (ed.), *People and State: Israeli Society* (Tel Aviv, 1989). (Heb.)

STEPHAN, NANCY, *The Idea of Race in Science* (Basingstoke, 1987).

STEPHENS, ANTONY M., 'Socrates or Chorus Person?: The Problem of Individuality in Nietzsche's Hellenism', in G. W. Clarke (ed.), *Rediscovering Hellenism*, 237–60.

STEPHENS, JOHN, *The Italian Renaissance: The Origins of Intellectual and Artistic Change before the Reformation* (London and New York, 1990).

STERLING, GREGORY, E., *Historiography and Self-Definition: Josephus, Luke–Acts and Apologetic Historiography* (Leiden, 1991).

STERN, DAVID, *Parables in Midrash: Narrative and Exegesis in Rabbinic Literature* (Cambridge, Mass., 1991).

—— and MIRSKY, MARC J., *Rabbinic Fantasies: Imaginative Narratives from Classical Hebrew Literature* (Philadelphia and New York, 1990).

STERN, MENAHEM, '"Antioch in Jerusalem": The Gymnasium, the Polis and the Rise of Menelaus', *Zion*, NS 57/3 (1992), 233–4.6 (Heb.)

—— 'Chronological Sequence of the First References to Jews in Greek Literature', in *Studies in Jewish History*, 417–21. (Heb.)

—— *Greek and Latin Authors on Jews and Judaism*, 3 vols. (Leiden and Jerusalem, 1974–84).

—— 'The Hatred of the Jews in Rome', in *Studies in Jewish History*, 536–48. (Heb.)

—— *The Hellenistic Period and the Hasmonean State (332–37 BC)* (Jerusalem, 1981). (Heb.)

—— 'Judaism and Hellenism in Eretz Yisrael in the Third and Fourth Centuries BC', in *Studies in Jewish History*, 3–21. (Heb.)

—— 'Maccabees, Book of Maccabees', in *Studies in Jewish History*, 347–62. (Heb.)

—— 'Philosophers and Men of Science in *The Life of Isidorus* by Damascius', in *Studies in Jewish History*, 556–68. (Heb.)

—— *Studies in Jewish History: The Second Temple Period*, ed. M. Amit, I. Gafni, and M. D. Herr (Jerusalem, 1991). (Heb.)

—— 'The Suicide of Eleazar ben Jair and his Men at Masada, and the "Fourth Philosophy"', *Zion*, NS 47/4 (1982), 367–98. (Heb.)

—— (ed.), *Nation and History: Studies in the History of the Jewish People*, i (Jerusalem, 1983). (Heb.)

STOBART, J. C., *The Glory that Was Greece* (4th edn., New York, 1964).

STODDART, D. S., 'Darwin's Impact on Geography', *Annals of the Association of American Geographers*, 56 (1966), 613–99.

STONE, M. E. (ed.), *Jewish Writings of the Second Temple Period* (Compendia Rerum Iudaicarum ad Novum Testmentum, 2; Assen, 1984)

STONEMAN, RICHARD (trans. with an introduction and notes), *The Greek Alexander Romance* (Harmondsworth, 1991).

STROUMSA, GEDALIAHU, 'Moses' Riddles: Esoteric Trends in Patristic Hermeneutics', in Biderman and Sharfstein (eds.), *Interpretation in Religion* (Leiden, 1992), 229–49.

—— 'Myth into Metaphor: The Case of Prometheus', in S. Shaked *et al.* (eds.), *Gilgul*, 309–23.

SULZBACH, A., *Renan und der Judaismus* (Frankfurt am Main, 1867).

SUTHERLAND, ALEXANDER, *The Origins and Growth of the Moral Instinct*, 2 vols. (London, 1898).

SYLVESTER, JOSUAH, 'Babilon', in id. (trans.), *The Divine Weeks and Works of Guillaume de Saluste, sieur du Bartas*, ed. Susan Snyder, 2 vols. (Oxford, 1979), i. 421–41.

SYRKIN, NACHMAN, 'Geza, amamiyut vele'umiyut' ('Race, Populism and Nationalism'), in *Kitvei N. Sirkin* ('N. Syrkin's Writings'), ed. B. Katznelson and I. Kaufman, i (Tel Aviv, 1939), 263–72.

—— 'Min hachutzah ha'ohelah' ('From the Outside into the Tent'), in *Kitvei N. Syrkin*, i. 134–72.

TABOR, JAMES D., *Things Unutterable: Paul's Ascent to Paradise in its Greco-Roman Judaic and Early Christian Context* (Lanham, Md., 1986).

TABORY, J., ' "The Persian Period" according to the Jewish Sages', in *Milet: Everyman's University Studies in Jewish History and Literature*, ii (Tel Aviv, 1985), 65–78. (Heb.)

TADMOR, HAIM, 'The Relation of the Jewish People to the Land of Israel in the Light of the Babylonian Exile and the Return to Zion', in Mirski *et al.* (eds.), *Exile and Diaspora*, 50–6. (Heb.)

—— (ed.), *Shivat Zion: The Restoration—The Persian Period* (Tel Aviv, 1983). (Heb.)

TAL, URIEL, *Christians and Jews in Germany: Religion, Politics, and Ideology in the Second Reich (1870–1914)*, trans. N. J. Jacobs (Ithaca, NY, 1975).

—— 'Myth and Solidarity in the Zionist Thought and Activity of Martin Buber's Zionism', *Hatzionut*, 7 (1981), 18–35. (Heb.)

TALMAGE, FRANK, 'R. Yoseph Kimhi: From the Dispersion of Jerusalem in *Sepharad* to the Canaanites in *Zarphath*', in M. Ben-Sasson *et al.* (eds.), *Culture and Society*, 315–32. (Heb.)

TALMON, SHEMARYAHU, 'The Desert Motif in the Bible and in Qumran Literature', in Altmann (ed.), *Biblical Motifs*, 31–61.

TANNENBAUM, A., 'Habeniyah vehagizrah' ('The Building and the Courtyard' [Ezek. 41: 12]), *Keneset Yisrael*, 1 (1886), 1013–88.

TARN, W. W., *Alexander the Great* (Cambridge, 1948).

—— *The Greeks in Bactria and India* (Cambridge, 1966).

—— *Hellenistic Civilization*, 3rd edn., rev. with G. T. Griffith (London, 1952).

TA-SHEMA, ISRAEL, *Early Franco-German Ritual and Custom* (Jerusalem, 1992). (Heb.)

TCHERIKOVER, VICTOR, *Hellenistic Civilization and the Jews* (in Hebrew, Jerusalem, 1931, 2nd edn. 1963); English translation by A. Appelbaum (Philadelphia, 1959).

TCHERNICHOWSKY, SAUL, Epilogues to his translations of the *Iliad*, 599–638, and the *Odyssey*, 469–80 (Tel Aviv, 1987).

—— *Shirim* ('Poems'), i (Tel Aviv, 1987).

TCHERNOWITZ, CHAYIM (Rav Tsa'ir), 'Rishmei Eretz Yisrael: Matzav hachinukh'

('Impressions of the Land of Israel: The State of Education'), *Ha'olam*, 11 (19 June–2 July, 1912), 3-4.

TEVETH, SHABTAI, *Ben-Gurion: The Burning Ground 1886–1948* (Boston, 1987).

THOMAS, CAROL G. (ed.), *Paths from Ancient Greece* (Leiden, 1988).

—— 'The Modern Discovery of Ancient Greece', in Thomas (ed.), *Paths from Ancient Greece*, 168–86.

THOMPSON, JAMES W., *A History of Historical Writing*, ii (New York, 1942).

THOMSON, J. A. K., *The Classical Background of English Literature* (London, 1948).

THOMSON, J. OLIVER, *History of Ancient Geography* (Cambridge, 1948).

THRAEDE, K., 'Erfinder', in *Reallexikon für Antike und Christentum*, v (Stuttgart, 1962), 1191–1278.

TORENHEIM, YEHUDIT, and OVADIA, ASHER, 'Dionysus in Beth-Shean', *Cathedra*, 71 (Mar. 1994), 21–34. (Heb.)

TORTSHINER, N. H. (ed.), *Sefer Klausner* (Tel Aviv, 1937). (Heb.)

TOURY, GIDEON, 'An Enlightened Use of Fable: C. F. Gellert in Hebrew Literature', in Shamir and Holzman (eds.), *Turning Points in Hebrew Literature*, 75–86. (Heb.)

TOURY, YAACOV, *Between Revolution, Reaction and Emancipation: A Social and Political History of the Jews in Germany in the Years 1841–71* (Tel Aviv, 1978). (Heb.)

—— 'Emancipation and Assimilation', *Yalkut moreshet*, 2 (1964), 167–82. (Heb.)

TOYNBEE, A. J., *Greek Civilization and Character: The Self-Revelation of Ancient Greek Society* (5th edn., New York, 1965).

—— *A Study of History*, abridgement of vols. vii–x by D. C. Somervell, ii (New York, 1957).

TREVELYAN, HUMPHREY, *Goethe and the Greeks*, foreword by H. Lloyd-Jones (Cambridge, 1981).

—— *The Popular Background to Goethe's Hellenism* (London, 1934).

TRISTRAM, HENRI B., *The Land of Israel: A Journal of Travels in Palestine* (London, 1865).

TSAFRIR, YORAM, *Eretz Yisrael from the Destruction of the Second Temple to the Muslim Conquest*, ii: *Archeology and Art* (Jerusalem, 1984). (Heb.)

TSAMRIYON, TSEMACH, *Hame'asef: The First Modern Periodical in Hebrew* (Tel Aviv, 1988). (Heb.)

TSIGAKOU, FANI-MARIA, *The Rediscovery of Greece: Travellers and Painters of the Romantic Era* (New Rochelle, NY, 1981).

TURNER, FRANK M., *The Greek Heritage in Victorian England* (New Haven, 1981).

—— 'Why the Greeks and Not the Romans in Victorian Britain?', in Clarke (ed.), *Rediscovering Hellenism*, 61–82.

TWERSKY, ISADORE, 'Land and Exile', in Halamish and Ravitsky (eds.), *The Land of Israel in Medieval Jewish Thought*, 90–122. (Heb.)

—— 'Maimonides and Eretz Yisrael: Halachic, Philosophical, and Historical Aspects', in Ben-Sasson *et al.* (eds.), *Culture and Society in Medieval Jewry*, 353–82. (Heb.)

TYLOR, E. B., *Primitive Culture* (London, 1871).

TYRRELL, WM. BLAKE, *Amazons: A Study in Athenian Mythmaking* (2nd edn., Baltimore, 1986).

TZVIELI, BENYAMIN, 'Historical Dissonance', *Ha'aretz*, 5 Nov. 1988. (Heb.)

UHLIG, LUDWIG (ed.), *Griechenland als Ideal: Winckelmann und seine Rezeption in Deutschland* (Tübingen, 1988).

ULLMANN, WALTER, *A History of Political Thought: The Middle Ages* (Harmondsworth, 1965).

URBACH, EPRAHIM E., 'Attempts at Investigating Rabbinic Thought', in Hirshman and Groner (eds.), *Rabbinic Thought*, 13–19. (Heb.)

—— 'Halakhah and History', in Neusner (ed.), *Jews, Greeks and Christians*, 112–28.

—— *The Sages*, tr. Israel Abraham, 2 vols. (Cambridge, Mass., 1987).

—— 'Self-Isolation or Self-Affirmation in Judaism in the First Three Centuries: Theory and Practice', in *Jewish and Christian Self-Definition: Aspects of Judaism in the Greco-Roman Period* (Philadelphia, 1981), 269–98.

—— 'The Three Teachers of the Talmud in the Breslau Seminary' ('Der Einfluß des Seminars auf das Studium des Jerusalemischen Talmuds'), in Kisch (ed.), *Das Breslauer Seminar*, 17–185. (Heb.)

URBACH, PETER, *Francis Bacon's Philosophy of Science* (La Salle, Ill., 1987).

URBACH, SHMUEL, 'Hate'oriah shel Einstein veha'antishemiyut' ('Einstein's Theory and Antisemitism'), *Hedim: Booklets on Literature*, 3/4 (Tel Aviv, 1926), 111–12.

VERNANT, JEAN-PIERRE, *The Origins of Greek Thought*, trans. from the French (Ithaca, NY, 1982).

VITAL, DAVID, *The Origins of Zionism*, i (Oxford, 1973).

—— *Zionism: The Formative Years* (Oxford, 1982).

VITERBO, ARIEL, 'Socrates in the Ghetto of Venice' (MA diss., Hebrew University, 1995). (Heb.)

VOGT, JOSEPH, *Ancient Slavery* (Cambridge, Mass., 1975).

VOLKOV, SHULAMIT, 'Soziale Ursachen des jüdischen Erfolgs in der Wissenschaft', in *Jüdisches Leben und Antisemitismus im 19. und 20. Jahrhundert* (Munich, 1990), 146–65.

VUCINICH, ALEXANDER, *Darwin in Russian Thought* (Berkeley and Los Angeles, 1988).

WACHOLDER, BEN ZION, 'Biblical Chronology in the Hellenistic World Chronicles', *Harvard Theological Review*, 61 (1968), 451–81 = id., *Essays on Jewish Chronology and Chronography* (New York, 1976), 106–36.

WADDELL, HELEN, *The Wandering Scholars* (London, 1944).

WAETZOLDT, WILHELM, *Johann Joachim Winkelmann, der Begründer der deutschen Kunstwissenschaft* (Leipzig, 1946).

WALBANK, F. W., *The Hellenistic World* (Cambridge, Mass., 1981).

WALDMAN, N. M. (ed.), *Community and Culture: Essays in Jewish Culture* (Philadelphia, 1987).

WALICKI, ANDRZEJ, *History of Russian Thought from the Enlightenment to Marxism*, trans. from the Polish by H. Andrews Rusiecka (Stanford, Calif., 1979).

—— *Philosophy and Romantic Nationalism: The Case of Poland* (Oxford, 1982).

—— *The Slavophile Controversy: History of a Conservative Utopia in Nineteenth-Century Russian Thought* (Notre Dame, Ind., 1989).

WALZER, R., *Greek into Arabic* (Cambridge, Mass., 1962).

WARREN, ZE'EV HARVEY, 'Maimonides and Aquinas on Interpreting the Bible', *Proceedings of the American Academy for Jewish Research*, 55 (1988), 59–77.

WASSERSTEIN, ABRAHAM, 'Astronomy and Geometry as Propaedeutic Studies in Rabbinic Literature', *Tarbiz*, 43 (1974), 53–7. (Heb.)

—— 'Greek Elements in Ancient Jewish Literature', in Alexander Rofé and Yair Zakovitch (eds.), *Isaac Leo Seeligman Volume*, ii (Jerusalem, 1983), 483–98. (Heb.)

WEBER, G., *Allgemeine Weltgeschichte*, 15 vols. (Leipzig, 1857–81).

WEBER, MAX, *On the Methodology of the Social Sciences*, ed. E. Shilds and H. A. M. Finch (New York, 1949).

WEHRLI, FRITZ, *Die Schule des Aristoteles*, 2nd edn. (Basle, 1967–9).

WEILER, GERSHON, *Jewish Theocracy* (Tel Aviv, 1976). (Heb.)

WEINBERG, JOANNA, 'The Quest for Philo in Sixteenth-Century Jewish Historiography', in Rapoport and Zipperstein (eds.), *Jewish History*, 163–87.

WEINFELD, MOSHE, *From Joshua To Josiah: Turning-Points in the History of Israel From the Conquest of the Land until the Fall of Judah* (Jerusalem, 1992). (Heb.)

—— 'Inheritance of the Land—Privilege versus Obligation: The Concept of the "Promise of the Land" in the Sources of the First and Second Temple Period', *Zion*, NS 49/2 (1989), 115–37. (Heb.)

WEINTRAUB, VICTOR, *Literature as Prophecy: Scholarship and Martinist Poetic in Mickiewiz's Parisian Lectures* (The Hague, 1959).

WEISS, R., *The Renaissance Discovery of Classical Antiquity* (Oxford, 1988).

WEIZMANN, CHAIM, 'Al darkah shel ha'Universitah ha'Ivrit', ('On the Path to be Taken by the Hebrew University') in id., *Devarim (Speeches)*, iv (Tel Aviv, 1937), 714–16.

WERBLOWSKY, ZVI, 'Greek Wisdom and Proficiency in Greek', in *Paganisme, Judaisme, Christianisme: Influences et Affrontementes dans le monde antique* (Paris, 1978), 55–60.

WERSES, S., 'Echoes of Lucian in the Literature of the Hebrew Haskalah', in *Trends and Forms*, 223–48. (Heb.)

—— 'Nachman's Last Speech and its Sources', *Moznaim Jubilee Issue: 1929–79* (Apr.–May 1979), 280–91. (Heb.)

—— 'On I. Satanow and his Work *Mishlei Asaf*', in *Trends and Forms*, 163–86. (Heb.)

—— 'Polish–Jewish Relations in the Stories by Mendele Mocher Sforim', *Gal-Ed: On the History of the Jews in Poland*, 14 (1995), 137–63. (Heb.)

—— 'The Relationship between Literature and the Study of Judaism', in *Trends and Forms*, 13–49. (Heb.)

—— *Trends and Forms in Haskalah Literature* (Jerusalem, 1990). (Heb.)

—— 'Judah Halevi in the Nineteenth Century', in *Trends and Forms*, 50–90. (Heb.)

WES, MARINUS A., *Classics in Russia 1700–1855: Between Two Bronze Horsemen* (Leiden, 1992).

WESSELY, NAPHTALI HERZ, *Divrei shalom ve'emet* ('Words of Peace and Truth') Berlin (1782–5; Vienna, 1826).

—— *Shirei tiferet* ('Songs of Glory'; Berlin and Prague, 1789–1811; Warsaw, 1858).

WEST, CORNELL, *Prophesy Deliverance: An Afro-American Revolutionary Christianity* (Philadelphia, 1982).

WESTFALL, R. S., *Science and Religion in Seventeenth-Century England* (New Haven, 1958).

WEXLER, PAUL, *The Ashkenazic Jews: A Slavo-Turkic People in Search of a Jewish Identity* (Columbus, Ohio, 1993).

WIESELTIER, LEON, '*Etwas über die jüdische Historik*: Leopold Zunz and the Inception of Modern Jewish Historiography', *History and Theory*, 20 (1981), 135–49.

WIESENBERG, ERNEST, 'Related Prohibitions: Swine Breeding and the Study of Greek', *Hebrew Union College Annual*, 27 (1956), 213–33.

WILAMOWITZ-MOELLENDORFF, ULRICH VON, *History of Classical Scholarship*, trans. Alan Harris, ed. H. Lloyd-Jones (London, 1982).

WILL, ÉDOUARD, *Doriens et Ioniens* (Paris, 1956).

WILLEY, BASIL, *The Eighteenth Century Background: Studies on the Idea of Nature in the Thought of the Period* (Harmondsworth, 1972).

WILLIAMS, R. D., 'The Logic of Arianism', *Journal of Theological Studies*, NS 34 (1983), 56–81.

WILLSON, A. LESLIE, *A Mythical Image: The Idea of India in German Romanticism* (Durham, NC, 1964).

WILSON, N. G., *From Byzantium to Italy: Greek Studies in the Italian Renaissance* (Baltimore, 1992).

—— *Scholars of Byzantium* (London, 1983).

WINCKELMANN, JOHANN JOACHIM, *Gedanken über die Nachahmung der griechischen Werke in der Malerei und Bildhauerkunst* (1755). English translation: Winckelmann, *Writings on Art*, ed. David Irwin (Oxford, 1972).

WINDFUHR, MANFRED, *Deutschen Fabeln des 18. Jahrhunderts* (Stuttgart, 1977).

WISTRICH, ROBERT, 'Radical Antisemitism in France and Germany', in Almog *et al.* (eds.), *Israel and the Nations*, i. 157–84. (Heb.)

WITTFOGEL, KARL A., *Oriental Despotism: A Comparative Study of Total Power* (New Haven, 1958).

WOLF, F. A., *Prolegomena to Homer* (1795), trans., with introduction and notes by A. Grafton, G. W. Most, and J. E. G. Zetzel (Princeton, 1988).

WOLF, IMMANUEL, 'Über den Begriff einer Wissenschaft des Judentums', *Zeitschrift für die Wissenschaft des Judentums*, 1 (1822–3), 1–24; 'On the Concept of a Science of Judaism', trans. Lionel Kochan, in *Leo Baeck Institute Year Book*, 2 (London, 1957), 194–204.

WOLFSON, HARRY A., 'The Classification of Sciences in Medieval Jewish Philosophy', *Hebrew Union College Jubilee Volume* (Jerusalem, 1925), 263–315.

—— 'Notes on Proofs of the Existence of God in Jewish Philosophy', *Hebrew Union College Annual*, 1 (1924), 575–96.

—— *Philo: Foundation of Religious Philosophy in Judaism, Christianity, and Islam*, 2 vols. (rev. 2nd printing; Cambridge, Mass., 1948).

—— 'The Verification of the Holy Scripture from Philo to Spinoza', in *Studies in the History of Philosophy and Religion*, ed. I. Twersky and G. H. Williams (Cambridge, Mass., 1987)

WOOD, JAMES, *Wisdom Literature: An Introduction* (London, 1979).

WOODHOUSE, C. M., *The Philhellenes* (London, 1969).

WRIGHT, ERNEST, *The Old Testament against its Environment* (London, 1950).

WRIGHT, JOHN KIRTLAND, *The Geographical Lore of the Time of the Crusades: A Study in the History of Medieval Science and Tradition in Western Europe*, with a new introduction by C. J. Glacken (New York, 1965).

WÜRTHWEIN, ERNST, 'Egyptian Wisdom and the Old Testament', in Greenspahn (ed.), *Essential Papers*, 129–49.

YADIN, YIGAEL, 'And Dan, Why did he Remain in Ships? (Judges 5: 17)' in Greenspahn (ed.), *Essential Papers*, 294–310.

YASIF, ELI, *The Hebrew Folktale: History, Genre, Meaning* (Jerusalem, 1994). (Heb.)

YAVETZ, ZVI, '"Why Rome?", Zeitgeist and Ancient Historians in Early 19th-Century Germany', *American Journal of Philology*, 97 (1976), 276–96.

YERUSHALMI, YOSEPH H., *Zakhor: Jewish History, Jewish Memory* (Seattle and London, 1982).

YEVIN, Y. H., 'Legion hazarim chozer habaitah' ('The Foreign Legion Returns Home'), in *Ketavim* (Tel Aviv, 1969), 365–80.

YOELI, MORDECHAI (trans. and ed.), introduction to *J. L. Pinsker, Mevaser hate-chiya hale'umit: Ha'autoemantsipatziah vehabikoret aleihah* (*Presager of the National Revival: The Autoemancipation and the Criticism of it*) (Tel Aviv, 1944), 5–35.

YOVEL, YIRMIYAHU, *Spinoza and Other Heretics* (Princeton, 1989).

—— *Dark Riddle: Hegel, Nietzsche, and the Jews* (Jerusalem and Tel Aviv, 1996) (Heb.).

YUVAL, ISRAEL J., 'Rishonim and Acharonim, antiqui et moderni (Periodization and Self-Awareness in Ashkenaz)', *Zion*, NS 57/4 (1992), 369–94. (Heb.)

ZAMOSC, DAVID, *Resisei hamelitzah* (Dyhernfurth, 1821).

ZELIGMAN, A., 'S. Freud: Das Unbehagen in der Kultur', *Achdut Ha'avodah*, 2 (June, 1930), 223–4.

ZEVI'ELI, BENYAMIN, 'Historical Dissonance', *Ha'aretz*, 5 Dec. 1988.

ZIELIŃSKI, TADEUSZ, *Hellenizm a Judaizm* ('Hellenism and Judaism', Warsaw, 1927).

—— *Historja kultury antycznej w zwięzłym wykładzie* ('Concise History of Ancient Culture'; Warsaw, 1922).

ZIFFER, E., *At the Time the Canaanites were in the Land of Canaan* (Tel Aviv, 1990).

ZINBERG, ISRAEL, *History of the Literature of Israel*, iii–vi (Tel Aviv, 1952). (Heb.).

ZIPPERSTEIN, STEVE J., 'Jewish Enlightenment in Odessa: Cultural Charcteristics, 1794–1871', *Jewish Social Studies*, 44/1 (Winter 1982), 19–36.

ZOHAR, NOMI, 'Between Shem and Japheth: A Translation Issue in Haskalah Literature', *Moznaim*, 1 (Apr. 1988), 4–9. (Heb.)

ZOHAR, ZVI, *Chinukh beruach hamoledet* ('Teaching in the Spirit of the Homeland') (Tel Aviv, 1937).

ZUNZ, LEOPOLD, 'Etwas über die rabbinische Literatur' (1818), in *Gesamelte Schriften*, ed. Curatorium der Zunzstiftung, i (Berlin, 1875), 1–31.

—— *Die gottesdienstlichen Vorträge der Juden, historisch entwickelt* (Berlin, 1832). Hebrew translation, *Hederashot beYisrael vehistalshelutan hahistorit* (Jerusalem, 1947).

ZUR, MOKI (ed.), *Kehiliyatenu* ('Our Community') (1922; new edn., Jerusalem, 1988).

INDEX

A

acculturation:
  intellectual, tactics of 77–8
  in Islam 9
  and the modern educated Jew 126
Achimeir, Abba:
  as disciple of Berdyczewski 213–14
  on duality in Judaism 213, 420–1
  on Hebrew literature 247–8
  on Hellenism in Israel 313–14
  on Zionism 213
aggadah:
  aggadic and midrashic tradition, and
    interpretation of biblical stories 60–1
  and pluralistic nature of Judaism 260–1
  and the Talmud 258–9
Ahad Ha'am:
  on cultural borrowing 466
  on culture 451–2
  on Darwinism 114–15
  on ethics and religion 185–6
  on future Jewish state as Hellenistic 313
  on Greek lack of morality 169–70
  on the Hebrew language 236
  on Hellenists 311
  on Hellenization of Alexandrian Jews
    332–3
  on Jewish contribution to art 225
  on Jewish culture 276
  on Jews 7–8; on Judaism 477
  on Moses and belief 369
  on the Pharisees and the Sadducees
    323–4
  on Plato and Aristotle 133
  on Shadal and new nationalistic trends
    168–9
  on Tchernichowsky 245
aesthetics, see beauty
Akiva, Rabbi:
  on Ben-Sira 90
  on sifrei hamiros 341
Alexandria:
  Jews of, and Judaism in Palestine 327;
    political struggle of 331
  as symbol for Hellenistic culture 281–2
Alexandrian Judaism:
  and Hellenistic Jewish literature 329–30
  image of 327–34

  and the Mission Theory 330
American Jewry, tension with State of Israel 333–4
antisemitism 394
  anti-Jewish literature 382–3, 389
  and Athens 54–5
  ethnic stereotypes in Christian Europe
    382–3
  German 394
  Greek elements in 206
  and the Hellenic ideal 50–1
  and nationalist Jews 192–3
Apollo, in Hebrew literature 148–54
apostasy, as negative cultural model for
  Jews 306–14
apostates (mityavnim), in collective Jewish
  historical memory 307–9
archaeology:
  Bible criticism inspires interest in 375–9
Aristoxenus of Tarentum, on Socrates
  140–1
Arnold, Matthew:
  on European civilization 55–6
  on Greek life 10
  on Hebraism and Hellenism 46–7
  on Heine 45
Arnold, Thomas, on Greek and Roman
  history 29
art, architecture, and music:
  classicism v. monumentalism 269–74
  Jewish architectonic perception 272–3
  Jewish art, concept of 271–2; in Pales-
    tine 271
  music, in cultural life of the Jews 273
  see also beauty; creative arts
Artapanus, on Jewish origins of ancient
  Egyptian culture 67
Athens:
  and Jerusalem, as conceptual twins in a
    binary model of Judaism 3, 474
  and Sparta, as models of polar regimes
    and political cultures 447–8
Auerbach, Erich, and biblical narrative 245

B

Baer, Yitzhak (Fritz), on Jewish society
  and the Greek polis 175
Bakhtin, M. M. B., on culture 8

beauty:
absence of, in Judaism 2, 228
discovery of, by *maskilim* 228–34
as distraction from the Torah tradition
231
perfection in, as divine 229–30
Ben-Avi, Itamar, on the Jews and land 429
Ben-Gurion, David:
on ethics and science 212
on the exile in Egypt 429
on Greece and ancient Judaism 212
on Greek philosophy 134; on Socrates
142
on Greek science and art 135
and the Jewish genius 118
Ben-Sira:
Haskalah acceptance of 89
Hellenistic influences on 89 n.
on wisdom 88, 108
Bentwich, Norman, on harmony of Hebraic and Hellenic ideas 216
Ben-Yehuda, Eliezer:
on the Hebrew theatre 252
and the milieu theory of culture 417
Ben-Ze'ev, Judah Leib:
on Aristotle and Simon HaTsaddik (the
Pious) 75
on the fable 254–6
on 'Greek sages' 133
on science 106–7
on Socrates 141–2
on the Talmud and Greek philosophy
173
Berdyczewski, M. J.:
on aggadah 260
and Ahad Ha'am 135
on Apollo 149–50
on Jawitz 167
on Jews as a Hellenic people 2
on Judaism 217, 458–9; as distinct from
Hellenism 217–18
on Prometheus 152, 169
Berenfeld, Rabbi Simon:
on Heine and the Pharisees 163
and the milieu theory of culture 418–19
Bergman, S. H., on the nationalist concept
in the Jewish tradition 426
Bernal, Martin, on *Hellenomania* 23
Bialik, Chayim Nachman:
and aggadah 260
on Semitic languages 237

Bible:
Book of Genesis, and mythological traditions 60
on the emergence of culture 61
as history 374
as the Jews' gift to the world 43
mythological layers in 263–4
prominence accorded to, by Haskalah
374–5
biblical criticism 373
inspires interest in archaeology 377–8
Bickerman, E. J.:
on cultural borrowing 335
on Hellenistic Jewish writers 65
on Jews in classical Greek literature 62
on 'land of our fathers' as Hellenistic
concept 423
on the Pharisees 320
on rabbinic and Hellenized Judaism 327
Birnbaum, Nathan:
on the Hellenistic era as period of 'malignant assimilation' 311
on Jews as part of European civilization
397
on Judaism and classical Greece 215–16
Blackwell, Thomas the younger:
on the environment and culture 408
on Judah Halevi 71
Borges, Jorge Luis, quotes Renan on
Averroes 238
Borochov, Dov Ber, on the Jews and culture 224
Brandes, George, on the German perception of Greece 32
Brenner, J. H.:
on aggadah 262
criticizes translation of decadent literature into Hebrew 246
on Hebrew translation of Plato 135–6
on link between Hebrew and Greek
literature 252
Brüll, Joel, on *maskilim* and literature 256
Buber, Martin:
on Jewish culture, history of 449
on Jews of antiquity 199–200
on Judaism as an Eastern phenomenon
198–9
and search for normative Jewish culture
460
Buckle, Thomas Henry:
on imagination 233

on Indo-European peoples and nature 413

Bultmann, Rodolf, on Solon and the Old Testament prophets 434

Burckhardt, Jacob:
on antiquity 122
on culture 449–50; on history of Jewish culture 449
on history as an essential element in the utopian future 28–9

Bussler, E., on Job and Prometheus 169

Butcher, S. H.:
on Greece and Israel 47–8
on the Hebrews and art 221

C

Cardozo, Isaac Fernando:
attacks antisemitic stereotypes 382
on monotheistic philosophies 71–2

Chakham, Noach, on Jewish origins of Greek drama 250–2

chokhmot hagoyim, see wisdom, secular, classifications of

Christianity 52

Cicero, on Athens 22

classical antiquity:
as a burden on the European mind 27–8
Jewish discovery of 123–31

Clearchus of Soli, on the Jews 1

climatology, theories of, in explaining culture 403–11
Zionist adoption of 403–5

Cohen, Hermann, on Plato and the Prophets 216–17

creative arts, and the Jews 220–4
see also art, architecture, and music

Crescas, Rabbi Hasdai, on Maimonides 93

Croce, Benedetto, on German love of Greece 32

culture:
and acculturation 449–51; tactics of 77–8
common origins, search for 58–65
cultural borrowing 335, 463–7
Great Tradition (high culture), borrowing in 463–4
Haskalah concept of 224–6, 452–8, 478–9
and ideologies 469–70
Jewish contribution to 225–6
levels of understanding of 8, 454–6
Little Tradition (low or folk culture), borrowing in 463–4
meaning of 451–8
19th-cent. Jews and 224–8
norms of 303
as stratified system 296
understanding one's own 5
see also Hebrew culture; Jewish culture; Jewish physical culture; *Kultur*

D

Delaura, David J., on Greece as antithesis of Christianity 34

de' Rossi, Azariah:
as erudite Renaissance Jew 124–5
on rabbinic familiarity with Aristotle 94
on superiority of Jewish polity 437

Disraeli, Benjamin, on Semitism and art 220

Draper, J. W., on the Hellenistic period 284

Droysen, Johann Gustav, on Hellenism 283

Dubnow, Simon:
on the Greek spirit and the spirit of Israel 179
on Jewish national consciousness 395
pessimism of regarding the Jewish condition 181
on the Pharisees as nationalists 320

Dura-Europos synagogue, as evidence of flourishing non-rabbinic Judaism 347–9

E

Ecclesiasticus, *see* Ben-Sira

Eldad (Scheib), Israel, on Greek and Jewish view of history 200–1

Emden, Rabbi Jacob, on science and philosophy 114

Emperor Julian, on the Jews and the sciences 221–2

Enlightenment, and moral corruption 176–84

Enlightenment, Jewish, *see* Haskalah movement; *maskilim*

eretz avot, see patris

Euchel, Isaac:
on history, uses of 365
on Socrates 74, 141
on wisdom, concept of 88

Euhemerus:
    and the mytho-historical tradition 59–
        60
    euhemerism 58–65; in Hellenistic Jew-
        ish literature 61–2
Eupolemus, on Moses 67
Eusebius, on Moses 67

F
Falklash, Rabbi Eliezer, on Jewish reading
    habits 126
Feldman, Louis H., on Hellenistic influ-
    ences on Judaism in Palestine 325
Fischer, Marcus, on Socrates 142
Frischmann, David, on the concept of
    culture 451
Fuenn, S. J.:
    on aggadah 261
    on imagination 232
fundamentalism, Jewish Orthodox 116
Funke, Carl Philipp, on climatic influences
    on the Greeks 412

G
Geiger, Abraham, on the Pharisees 320
Gentiles:
    culture of, Jewish tradition of opposi-
        tion to 188–93
    as 'Greeks' 191
Germanism, cultural heritage of 51
Gilgamesh epic 376
Glaser, Herman, on components of Greek
    culture 35
Goethe, J. W. von:
    on biblical criticism 372
    on the world of ancient Greece 31, 34,
        37, 143, 151
Goldstein, Jonathan, on Hellenism in
    Palestine 303–4 and n.
Goldziher, Ignaz (Yitzhak):
    on Greek literature and theologies 65–6
    on Israelite culture and mythology 264,
        265–6
    and the Jewish imagination 264, 265
Gordon, J. L.:
    on the influence of Aesop's fables on
        the Talmud 257
    and the Jewish contribution to culture
        225–6
Graetz, Heinrich:
    on Alexandrian Jewry 332
    on antisemitism 394–5

on Christianity and paganism 170
on climate and geography of Palestine
    416
on culture 178, 205; and Judaism 450
on disparate natures of Jewish and
    Greek 'spirits' 392
on faith and morality 185
and 'genetic' origin of the Jews 386–7
on Heine 45
on Jewish Hellenization 311
on Jewish history: historicity of events
    in 370–1; in the Bible 374
on Jewish monotheism and ethics 178–9
on Jewish will to survive 397–8
on Judaism and paganism 197
Greece:
    ancient, concept of nationalism foreign
        to 422–3
    as culture and counter-culture 35–9
    culture of: borrowing in 464; and Eu-
        rope 22; as product of reason 37; in
        Second Temple Palestine and there-
        after 124
    dissemination of heritage and ideals of
        25–7
    Greek antiquity v. Christianity 33–4
    Greek language, and Jewish society 295
    'Greek values', and Judaism's value-
        system 5
    'Greekness': European culture a meta-
        phor for 191; and the redemption of
        Judaism 217–19
    idealist depiction of 22–30, 34–5, 38–9,
        412–13
    and Israel 47–8
    in Jewish historical consciousness 4,
        37 n.
    Jewish hostility to idea of 129
    and Judaism, as opposite of 8
    in the Later Prophets 62–3
    literature of: and ethnological questions
        383–4; and Hebrew translations 129–
        31, 134
    mythological symbols of: and the cha-
        lutzim 146–7; in Hebrew 143–54; in
        Hebrew literature 146
    as plurality 36
    as political model 29–30
    religious ideas in 38
    as universal culture 37–8
    see also Hellenism; wisdom: 'Greek'

Greenberg, Uri Zevi:
on classicism 269
on Hebrew poets 244
on Jewish ambivalence towards Europe
182–3
Grégoire, Abbé Henri Baptiste:
on Jewish physical inferiority 382
on the Jews and culture 222–3
Grunebaum, G. E. von:
on classicism 23
on the relevance of acculturation in Islam to Judaism 9
on utilization of 'the other' to understand one's own civilization 5
Gurein, Victor, on the past of Palestine
373

H
Halevi, Judah:
on Greek philosophy 70–1
on Greek wisdom 91–2
on Jewish music 273
on the Jews as descendants of Adam
385–6
on the Jews and science 81
and Palestinian climate 406–7
on the Sanhedrin and secular wisdom
71
Hallewy, E. E., and Greek and biblical
mythology 343
Hamagid (newspaper):
on barbarism of the ancients 177–8
on the Gilgamesh epic 376–7
on wisdom 108–9
Hame'asef (literary periodical):
founders of, and Wessely 125
on limitations of Hebrew 238
publishes Hellenic material 144
and use of Hebrew 235
Hameiri, Avigdor:
on Jewish and Greek culture 75–7
on monumentalism as a Hebrew characteristic 270
Hamelitz (newspaper):
on archaeological discoveries 378–9
on Germany as the nadir of degradation
180
Hamilton, Edith, on the Greeks and religion 38
Hammer, Zevulun, compares Judaism and
Hellenism 82

Haskalah movement:
of Berlin 105, 374
Bible, prominence accorded to by 184,
374
broad impact of 176
and concept of Jewish culture 3, 6,
224–6
and education 109–10
and ethics 185–7
internal disillusionment with 180
literature of 230–69, 383; see also Hamagid; Hame'asef; Hamelitz
and religion 176, 184–5, 438, 479
satirized 268–9
and science 107, 108, 113; zeal for scientific knowledge 83–4
and secularization 479
and social change 176–84
and traditional Jewish society 230
as turning-point in Jewish history 13,
113
and wisdom: lost and forgotten 81; and
the Torah 109–10
see also maskilim
Hasmonean state 317–19
Hasmoneans, revolt of 320
as Jewish historical symbol 315
Hebrew culture:
borrowed elements in 468–71
and the classical heritage 119–54
defined 15–16; as distinct from Jewish
culture 459
ideologies of 469–70
and Jewish Orthodoxy 461–3
in modern Israel 470–1, 479–80
search for 276–7, 458–61
utopias in 479–80
in the Yishuv 430–1, 451, 462–3, 468–9
see also Jewish culture
Hebrew language:
German Jewish scholars regard as dead
236
and Greek, compared 234–7
Haskalah attitude to 234–7
Hasmonean revival of 317
Jewish abandonment of 126
limitations of, for acquiring modern
culture 236, 238
Hebrew literature:
and biblical and mythological symbols
and images 131–2, 153–4
'Hellenization' in 291–3

Hebrew literature (*cont.*):
　and images from classical literary works
　　131–6, 252
　maskilic goals for 247–8
　and nationalism 246, 425
　Persian influence in 291–2
　poetry: discovery of 237–50; expansion
　　of range of 244–5; and Greek poetry
　　240, 246; status of 243–4
　satire in 268–9
　see also Jewish literature
Hebrew theatre:
　Hebrew drama, antiquity of 250–1
　as 'Hellenic' 252
　in Palestine 252
Hegel, W. G.:
　on the Greeks 37; and geography of
　　Greece 412
　on Judaism 53
Heine, Heinrich:
　on the aggadah 259
　on the Bible 43
　on biblical Judaism *v.* talmudic Judaism
　　41
　on European civilization 55–6
　on Greek language 126
　on Greek mythology 143
　on the 'Hellenic soul' 1–2
　intellectual and emotional life of 42
　on the Jewish–Hellenistic dichotomy
　　40–1, 42, 44, 45
　on Moses 43
　on self as Jew 44
　utopian Hellenism of 57
Hellenism:
　and Christianity and Germanism 49–57
　as culture 295–6, 295 n., 316; *v.* political
　　Hellenism 316–17
　defined 16, 283–6
　in Hasmonean era 306–7, 316–19
　and 'Hebraism' as conceptual twins 40,
　　41, 42
　as historical–cultural reality 11
　images of: in Jewish eyes 286–91; in the
　　Jewish historical memory 101, 287–8;
　　misused, by Jewish ideologues 314
　impact of: on Jewish society in Judea
　　and Galilee 307; on Judaism in mo-
　　dern times 9–10; on Pharisees and
　　Sadducees 319–22
　and Judaism 56–7, 289; historiographical

　images of 304–5; in Second Temple
　　period 325–7
　perceived as the enemy of Judaism (*tar-
　　but yevanit*) 10
　and the world of the Sages 337–45
Hellenistic culture:
　concern with Jews 63–4
　and European culture 300
　influence of, on Judaism 300–2
　literature, rediscovery of 331
　presence of in Jewish society 349
'Hellenization':
　defined 16
　in Jewish historical consciousness 311–
　　12
　mityavnim ('Hellenizers'), as enemies of
　　Judaism from within 10
　and secularization 350–2
Hengel, Martin, on Jewish–Greek antithe-
　　sis 286
Herzl, Theodor, political writings of 441
Hess, Moses:
　compares Judaism and Hellenism 194–7
　on Jewish acclimatization in Palestine
　　404
　on the Jewish race 396
　and mythological gods 266–7
Hisarlik, and the Homeric epic 376 and n.
historical consciousness, Jewish:
　alternative modes of 10–11
　apostates in 307–9
　Greece in 37 n.
　Hellenism in 10, 287–8; Hellenization
　　in 311–12
　and the Jewish nationalist movement
　　13–14
　perception of time in 358–9
　religious–secular divide in 479
　revival in 355–68
　sacred books, as source of 368, 379
　among writers and intellectuals 39, 73
historical symbols, misuse of 314
historiography:
　biblical, and ethnic purity 384
　Jewish: change of direction in 363–4; as
　　unifying force 367–8
　modern, challenges of 371
　and national identity 367
history:
　biblical, as mythology 371–2
　as collective experience of the people
　　355–6

as an essential element in the utopian
future 28–9
Greek concept of 360–1
Jewish and classical interpretations of,
compared 356–8
new approach to, in 17th- and 18th-
cent. Europe 362
pragmatism and romanticism in 364–8
secular Jewish view of 369–70
status of, and public life 361–2
uses of 365
Holocaust, metahistorical interpretation of
208–9
homeland:
irrelevance of in Judaism 404
Jewish and Greek concepts of, compared 422–30
as 'land of our fathers' 423
as 'Promised Land' 423
Homeric epic, as secular Bible 372–3
Homeric world, and biblical world 66
Humboldt, Alexander von, on the cosmos
231–2
Humboldt, Wilhelm von, on Greece and
the Greeks as an ideal 23, 31
Hume, David, on Athens and Thebes 421
Hurowitz, Shai (Sha'ul Yisrael), on Greek
philosophers 100

I
ibn al-Fakhar, Rabbi Judah, on Maimonides 93
ibn Caspi, Rabbi Yosef, on Maimonides
and Aristotle 93
ibn Ezra, Moses, on a country's physical
features and language 407
Ibn Khaldun, on the conditions for a civilized life 408
Idelson, Abraham, on Semitic origins of
Greek music 273
imagination:
absence of, in Judaism 228
development and promotion of, by
maskilim 228–34
and the 'Jewish mind' 264–6
Ish-Hurwitz, Shai, on Judaism and Jewish
ethics 185
Israel, State of:
Athens or Sparta as models for 447–8
culture of 477–8, 480
as *polis* 432–46

religious and ultra-Orthodox Jews in
442–3, 476–7
see also Jewish state
Isserles, Rabbi Moses, on the study of the
Greeks 83
Izhar, S., on Hebrew writers and Socrates
142

J
Jabotinsky, Ze'ev:
on culture 457
on the 'Homeric man' as archetype of
the modern Hebrew man 147
on Jewish links to the soil 425
and the milieu theory of culture 417–18
on race 391–2
Jaeger, Werner, on Greece 1, 38–9
James, William, on the Greeks of Homeric
times 35
Jawitz, Ze'ev:
on aggadah 260, 261, 262
on archaeology 377
on European culture 119, 120
on French political literature 437–8
on Greek culture 120–1
on the Jewish essence of poetry 241,
242
on the Jewish–Greek antinomy 166–7
on Judaism 120
Jellinek, Rabbi Adolf Aharon, on absence
of Hebrew nationality 393
Jenkyns, Richard, on the pervasive influence of Greece 24, 32
Jerusalem:
Hellenization of before Hasmonean revolt 308–9, 474
modern, as 'Athens' 475–6, 477;
struggle over character of 476
Jewish culture:
Ahad Ha'am on 276
borrowed elements in 463–7, 478
emergence of 456–8
and Greek culture, opposition of 75–7
and Hellenism 289–91
history of 449–50
influences on in the biblical era 294
metacultural levels of 459
national secular form of 456–8, 462
nature of 450–1, 458, 460
normative 460
and organicism 467
in Palestine 462

Jewish culture (*cont.*):
   and religion, distinction between 478
   as singular 464–5
   see also Hebrew culture; historical con-
     sciousness, Jewish; Jewish physical
     culture
Jewish genius, and the new spirit of research 116–18
Jewish intellectuals and thinkers:
   assert the antiquity of Jewish wisdom
     as source of wisdom of other nations
     66–7, 73–5
   confront the Jewish–Greek antinomy
     191–2
   medieval 73
   seek legitimacy from Jewish past 39, 73
   in 16th–18th cents. 83, 91–5
Jewish literature:
   and Greece 209
   Hellenistic: euhemerism in 61–2; in the
     talmudic tradition 328–30
   see also Hebrew literature
Jewish physical culture:
   Jews and athletics 274–5
   physical attributes of the new Jew 389–
     90
Jewish state:
   Ahad Ha'am sees as Hellenistic 313
   as democracy 441–2
   'Greek' institutions in 475–6
   and halakhah 445–6, 462–3
   Jewish values in 443–6
   nature of 441–3, 474; struggle over 474,
     476, 477
   new culture for 450–1
   as secular 442–3, 473–4
   Torah as constitutional basis for 428–9,
     434–8
   see also Israel, State of
Jewish values:
   and ethics 185
   in Jewish state 443–6
   morals and morality 156–7
Jews:
   dual political heritage of 432–4
   as a Hellenic people 2
   historical consciousness of, *see* historical
     consciousness, Jewish
   Orthodox, *see under* Judaism
   and sciences 221–2
   secular: labelled 'Hellenists' 310; culture
     of 479

Josephus:
   on biblical chronology and miracles 371
   on Greek and Jewish historical memory
     368, 379
   on Herod and Jerusalem 474–5
   on Jewish religion and culture 188–9
   on national antiquity as source of pride
     64–5; Jewish consciousness of 384
   on science: introduction of, to Egypt
     67; and monotheism 102
Jost, I. M.:
   on Palestine as 'land of milk and honey'
     415–16
   on the Pharisees and the Sadducees 320
Judaism:
   biblical *v.* talmudic 41
   v. classical Greece 11; reconciliation
     with 215–16
   'closed' and 'open' 218
   and collective national morality 186
   conflicts within 213
   cultural borrowing in 463–8, 474
   as culture 227–8
   as dialectical exercise 41
   duality in 213–17
   eradication of, in the Aryan world 53–4
   and ethics 185
   'Europeanization' of 4
   external influences on 294–5, 326
   v. Germanic spirit 51
   and Greekness, antinomy with 7, 192
   Heine on 41
   and Hellenism, *see* Judaism and Hel-
     lenism
   historiographical images of 304–5
   introduced as concept in 19th cent. 287
   and Jewishness 399–402
   as living entity 120
   modern: and classical tradition 5; de-
     fined as secular Judaism 473
   morals and morality, as distinguishing
     feature of 156–7
   mystical, as opposed to rabbinic 347–9
   and myth 264
   normative 458–9, 460
   not a religion 53
   Orthodox: and Hebrew culture 461–3;
     and secular wisdom 115–16
   polarizing tendencies of 188–93
   and political systems 444
   rabbinic 327; Jews opposed to authority
     of 347–9

as religion-culture 293–7
as 'the religion of intelligence' 228–9
Second Temple, and Greek philosophical heritage 297
secular, as modern Judaism 478–9
as separating the material from the spiritual 41
spirit of, located in biblical prophecy 184
as spirituality 41; spiritual propensities of 211
talmudic, Jewish animosity towards 213
ultra-Orthodox, and secular wisdom 115–16
Judaism and Hellenism 40–1, 42, 44, 45
antinomy between 5, 7, 56, 57, 194–7, 198, 217–18, 289
and Christianity, respective influences on 50
co-existence of 475
ethics *v.* aesthetics 82
and German Jewish culture 297–9
moral scales of 166

K
Kahane, Rabbi Meir, and Hellenism 312
Kaminka, Aaron:
on Hebrew poetry 242–3
on Roman ethics and Jewish beliefs 174
Kant, Immanuel, on Judaism 53
Kaufmann, Yehezkel:
on culture 459–60
and mythological elements in Judaism 267
on the uniqueness of the Israelite nation 207–8
Klatzkin, Jacob, on Judaism and Hellenism 198, 208
Klausner, Joseph:
on geographical environment and individuality 409
on Hebrew poetry 246
on Jewish ambivalence towards the West 181–2
on Jewish and Greek morality 167
Judaism and humanism, reconciliation of 209–12
and the milieu theory of civilization 417
on Renan 248–50
on the spirit of Greece 211
Kohn, Hans, on Goethe 30–1

Kook, Rabbi Abraham Isaac, on cultural borrowing 466–7
Krochmal, Nachman (Ranak):
on Hellenistic Jewish literature 329
on national differences 193–4
on *sifrei hamiros* 127
Kultur:
in German Haskalah 452–4
German holistic concept of 455–6

L
Land of Israel 423
Jewish right to 428–9
Landau, Judah Loeb, on Graetz 366
Lazarus, Moritz, on the Jewish imagination 264
Lebensohn, Micah Joseph, on mythology 145
legend and myth:
Haskalah rediscovery of 257–67
and Jewish and Hebrew culture 258
Jewish superiority, extolled by 386
Leon, Judah Messer, on Jewish political doctrine 437
Levin, Judah Leib:
on Jews of Alexandria as negative model 333
on science and society 180–1
Levinsohn, Isaac Baer (Ribal):
Berlin Haskalah, follows path of 98–9
on Graeco-Roman literature 128–9
on the Hebrew language 236
on the Jewish contribution to Western culture 74–5
on Jewish tradition and classical antiquity 144–5
opposes Sages' opposition to mythology 262–3
and wisdom as seen in Jewish literature 97–8
Levy, Israel, on Judaism and the Hellenistic way of life 299, 340
Levy, Johanan, and the Hebrews and Palestine 428
Lieberman, Saul:
on knowledge of Homer in Palestine 342–3
on the Sages and 'popular Hellenism' 341
on the Talmud 344
on understanding the Gentile cultural world 345–6

Lilienblum, M. L.:
on antisemitism 388–9
on the biblical Israelites 395–6
and the European Enlightenment 203
on Hellenism 45–6; on Hellenists 311
on the Jew 400; on the educated Jew
129; on the Jewish *maskil* 226; on the
Jews as strangers in Europe 388; on
the Jews and territory 427
on Jewish literature of the 19th cent.
201–3
on the Jewish people, ethnic divisions in
394
on national redemption 204–5
on natural sciences 115
on the poetry of Israel 241
Livingstone, R. W., on Greece and the
Jewish people 48
Loewisohn, Solomon:
on beauty 230–1; in the Bible 240
on biblical language and landscape 408–
9
Löwith, Karl, on the Jews and history
357–8
Lowth, Bishop Robert, on Greek and
Hebrew 235
Lubavicher Rebbe, on Judaism and scientific theory 116
Luzzatto, Moses Chayim (Ramhal):
on imagination (*dimyon*) 228
on natural sciences 104
Luzzatto, Rabbi Simone (Shimon b. Yitzhak Simchah), on Socrates 136–7,
137 n.
Luzzatto, S. D., *see* Shadal

M

Maccabees:
and Hellenization in Jerusalem (Books I
and II) 287
on imposition of Hellenic character
upon Jews (Book II) 2
Maimonides:
on aggadah 259
on cultural borrowing 465
on inferior peoples 385
on Jews and science 81
on *sifrei hamiros* 344
on source of Palestine's metaphysical
attributes 407
on wisdom 92–3
Martyr, Justin, on Socrates 140

maskilim:
and acculturation and borrowing 465–6
and the Bible: biblical chronology, validity of 371; biblical literature 90
and classical antiquity and Hellenism 12
and ethics 155–6, 172, 173; Jewish ethical literature, dislike of 256
and the European Enlightenment 184,
226–7
and the Hebrew language 234, 241
and imagination 229
and Judaism as 'the religion of intelligence' 228–9
literary influences on: classical 127; German 256; Greek 121; Hellenistic Jewish 329
and Maimonides 95
and moral precepts: emphasis on 155,
162–8, 183–4; Greek–Jewish similarities in 173–4
and morality, universal base of 157
and Orthodox Jews 111–12
and reform of Jewish life, need for 440–
1
and religion 176–7
on science and faith 103–4, 111–13
on secular wisdom: 'alien wisdoms' 96;
'neutral knowledge' 86
see also Haskalah movement
Melnikoff, Abraham, on Jewish art 270–1
Mendele Mokher Seforim, on racist antisemitism 381–2
Mendelssohn, Moses:
on aestheticism and perfection 230, 231
on the Bible 42, 370, 374
on the Hebrew language 234, 235
and humanism 171–2
on pagans 171
on Socrates 139
and the Talmud 42
Meyer, Eduard:
on the Hellenizers and the Hasmoneans
308
and Second Temple Judaism 284
milieu theory of culture:
application of, in the context of Jews
and Palestine 414, 415
Berenfeld, Rabbi Simon, on 418–19
Eliezer Ben-Yehuda on 417
modern 409–20
moledet, modern concept of 423–4

Momigliano, Arnaldo:
  on Greek and Hebrew historians 360
  on the Greeks: and history 361; and the
    Jews 62; and Orthodox Judaism 326
  on the Wisdom of Ben-Sira 329
monotheism:
  as incapable of creating culture 223
  philosophies of 71–2
Montague, Ashley, on transmission of cul-
    tural traits 468
morals and morality:
  as distinguishing factor of Judaism 156–
    7
  Greece, as antinomical to Judaism 156
  maskilic emphasis on 155, 183–4
  pagan, viewed by Christians and Jews
    171
  secularization of 184–7
  universality of 168–75
Murray, Gilbert, on Hellenism 284
music, see art, architecture, and music
mythology:
  and the Book of Genesis 60
  in origins of culture 58–65

N

nachalat avot, see patris
nationalism:
  and claims of antiquity 64–5, 384
  concept of, foreign to ancient Greece
    422–3
  as deviation from the spirit of Israel
    400–1
  Hebrew literature as nurturing 256, 425
  Jewish: aims of 13–14; disappearance
    of 393; models for 39; as subjectivist
    rather than racial 395; tradition of
    426
  of Pharisees 320
  see also homeland; moledet; patris
Neumark, David:
  on Judaism's 'life outlook' and the
    Greek 'world outlook' 163, 216
  on philosophy and literature 123
Nieto, David, on Torah as the source of
    wisdom 72
Nietzsche, Friedrich:
  and Apollonian and Dionysian elements
    in Greece 35–6; in Palestine 420
  on Christianity 53; Greek elements in
    49
  on the Jewish heroic character 49

on Prometheus 151–2
Nordau, Max, and Jews in sport 274

O

Origen, on the Jews and Greek literature
    123–4

P

parable and fable, in Haskalah literature
    253–7
patris, concept of 423–4
Paulson, Friedrich, on Hellenizing hu-
    manism 122
Perl, Joseph, on Socrates 141
Perrault, Charles, on significance of the
    classical past 27
Peters, F. E., on Hasmonean opposition to
    cultural Hellenism 316
Pharisees, the:
  in Christian historiography 320–1
  and Hellenism 319, 322
  Jewish views of differ in 19th cent.
    320–4
Philippson, Rabbi Ludwig, on Hebrew
    and Greek poetry 243
Philo of Alexandria, on Egyptian and
    Greek influences on Moses 68
Pines, Y. M.:
  on imitation in culture 465
  on modern Jewish culture 461–2
Pinsker, Leon:
  on geography as irrelevant to Judaism
    404
  on Semitic origins as inferior 393
Plato's Symposium, as symbol of the cha-
    lutzic life 146–7
Pliny the younger, on the Greeks 22
Plutarch, on Athens 22 n.
political systems, Jewish views of 443–6
Prometheus, image of, in Hebrew litera-
    ture 150–4
Pseudo-Eupolemus, on Abraham 67–8

R

Rabban Simon, on study of Greek wis-
    dom 124
Rabinowitz, S. P., on aggadah as Jewish
    national literature 261
race:
  Akhenaten on 383
  concept of, in the Jewish world 387–9,
    391–9

race (*cont.*):
  and the Jews 394, 400
  racial purity: and the Jews 392; as fiction 394
  racial theories, and the radical Jewish intelligentsia 397
radicalism, emergence of, in 19th-cent. Europe 179–80
Rall, Yisrael:
  on classical poetry, value of 233
  on intelligence and imagination 233
  on science and faith 110–11
Ramhal, *see* Luzatto, Moses Chayim
Ranak, *see* Krochmal, Nachman
Rappaport, Meir Eleazar, on the study of Greek philosophy 100–1
Rappoport, Solomon Judah Leib (Shir), on Israel as source of Jewish equilibrium 417
Rav Tza'ir, *see* Tchernowitz, Chayim
Razovsky, Rabbi Pinchas, on nationalism as a deviation from the spirit of Israel 400–1
Reggio, Rabbi Isaac Samuel, on the Sages and Aristotelian philosophy 99
Renan, Ernest:
  biblical criticism, support for 377–8
  and European civilization 53, 55–6
  on the Hebrew language 235–6
  and Jewish racial purity as fiction 394
  on truth and beauty 2
Ribal, *see* Levinsohn, Isaac Baer
Ruppin, Arthur, on the racial structure of the Jews 398–9

S
Sadducees, the 319–23
Sages, the:
  and 'alien wisdoms' 105
  and art 346–7
  Babylonian 340
  on Ben-Sira 90
  and biblical historical tradition 370
  on cultural domains and needs 345–50
  and the Greeks 37, 62; culture 339; as the 'other' 190–1; wisdom 86
  and Hellenism 189–90, 337–45
  and idolatry 345
  literature of, external influences on 338–9
  parables of, and New Testament and Greek philosophy 254–5

and *sifrei hamiros* 131
  on Torah as source of Israel's pre-eminence 384–5
Salvador, J., on Mosaic law 436–7
Satanow, Isaac, on wisdom 74, 81, 110
Sayce, A. H., on scientific criticism of the Old Testament 373
Schiller, Friedrich, on *Greekomania* 22, 23 n.
Schlegel, Friedrich von, and Greece 32
Schlesinger, Akiva, on Torah and external wisdom, incompatibility of 115
Schlesinger, Isaac Baer:
  Greek influence on 132
  on Israel's heroic history 315, 360
  on morals of Christian Europe and Greece 170
Schnitzer, Shmuel, on modern Hellenizers 312–13
Scholem, Gershom, on Maimonides' Judaism 473
Schorr, Joshua Heschel, on cultural borrowing 466
Schorsch, Ismar, on perception of time in Jewish history 358–9
Schulman, Kalman:
  on the Christian faith and Western society 176
  on the Greek spirit and climate 420
  on Jewish contribution: to Western culture 226; to science 116–17
  on *maskilim*: and Orthodox Jews 111–12; and religion 176–7
  on nations, distinctions between 387–8
  and pagan Hellenic culture 132–3
science:
  and faith 101–13
  and the *maskilim* 101–3
  modern, challenges of 113–18
  and philosophy 114
  as route to revealing the Creator 106–7
  and Torah 113–14
Second Temple period:
  as a model for Jewish–Hellenistic encounter 334–6
  religious and national awareness of Jews in 302–3
secularization:
  and Enlightenment, contrasted 479
  Greekness seen as positive model for 218
  and Hellenization 350–2

Shadal (S. D. Luzatto):
  on faith and science 106
  on Greek concept of the sublime in
    biblical poetics 240
  on Greek cultural decadence 145, 162
  on Greek philosophy 163
  on Hellenism *v.* Judaism 158–9, 165
  on Jewish ethics 163, 164
  on Judah Halevi 92
  on Maimonides 100, 164
  on medieval Jewish philosophy 163, 164
  on morality 157–8, 162 and n., 164–5
  on science 102–3
  on Socrates 141
  on the Torah and Atticism 159–61,
    161 n.
  on Western civilization 159
Shapira, Chief Rabbi Avraham, on
    present-day Hellenists 312
Shir, *see* Rappoport, Solomon Judah Leib
Shklov, Rabbi Baruch, argues for learning
    'alien wisdoms' 86–7
sifrei hamiros (Homeric literature):
  character of 341–4
  as corpus of Greek secular literature 343
  reading of 127
Singer, I. J., on Greek philosophy 128
Smith, George Adam, on climatic factors
    in the Jewish doctrine of divine prov-
    idence 415
Smolenskin, Peretz:
  on antinomy of Judaism and Classical
    Greece 206–7
  on German Jewish Hellenists 310
  on Graetz and the Song of Songs 240–1
  on the Greek dimension in Judaism
    205–6
  and Greek spiritual inferiority 179
  and the Hebrew language 126
  on the Hebrew renaissance in Germany,
    influences on 121–2
  on the Jews and the reality of life 206
  on Maimonides 100, 439–40
  on 'Pharisaism' 324
  on the Pharisees and the Sadducees 320
  on the Sages and Greek wisdom 133–4
  on the spirit of Israel 393–4
  on the Vilna Gaon 87 and n.
  on the writing of Jewish history 355
Socrates:
  as hero of the Haskalah 136–42
  and the humanists 138

  as intellectual 138
  Judaization of 139
Soloweitschik, Menahem, and Apollonian
    and Dionysian phases in Jewish his-
    tory 214, 420
Sparta, and Athens 447–8
Spengler, Oswald:
  on the 'Classical' 120
  on national culture and land 411
Spinoza, Baruch, and the Jews' legendary
    traditions 371
Stein, Menahem, and Zielinski, on Jews
    and the soil 425–6
Steinhal, Heymann (Hermann):
  and biblical narrative 245
  and Jewish imagination 264
Stern, Abraham (Yair), as Hebrew Prome-
    theus 152
Syrkin, Nachman:
  on cultural borrowing 466
  on the Greeks and the Hebrews 179
  on Hess 396–7
  on the Jews as a race 397
  and the milieu theory of culture 414–
    15, 417

T

Talmud:
  and Greek philosophy 173, 190
  influenced by Aesop's fables 257
Tannenbaum, Abraham, on Jewish archi-
    tectonic perception 272–3
Tchernichowsky, Saul:
  and Apollo 148
  on the Greeks and nature 414
  as 'Hellenic poet' 245
  on the Jews and the soil 427
Tchernowitz, Chayim (Rav Tza'ir):
  on Jewish culture in Palestine 462
  on sport and Hellenism in Palestine 275
Tertullian:
  on Athens and Jerusalem 1, 480
  on Socrates 140
time, dimension of:
  in Greek and Jewish world-views 358
  in Jewish historiography 359
Torah:
  as constitutional basis for relationship
    between religious and secular author-
    ities 434–8
  as law of God 435
  as source of wisdom 72

Toynbee, A. J., on the political influence of Hellenism on Western life 29
Trezek, I. A., on the Sages and Greek mythology 134
Tristram, Revd H. B., on the landscape of Palestine and religious history 415

V

Vilna Gaon (Elijah of Vilna), and value of sciences 86, 87

W

Weizmann, Chaim, on the humanities and nationalism 117
Wellhausen, Julius, and biblical criticism 377–8
Wessely, Naphtali Herz:
  on Aristotle's metaphysics 99
  on Hebrew poetry 241; foreign deities in 143–4
  on the histories of nations 365
  on Jewish wisdom 81; on wisdom, understanding, and knowledge (chokmah, binah, da'at) 96
  on Moses as pupil of the Greeks 80
  and torat ha'adam ('the Torah of Man') 81
Winckelman, Johann Joachim, on Greek culture 31
wisdom:
  'alien' 84; as wisdom from a non-Jewish source 85–6
  Ben-Sira on 88, 108
  concept of, according to Euchel 88
  as cosmological entity 88 and n.
  'external' 84
  'Greek': and the Jews 224; in medieval literature 94–5; rejection of 116; and the Sages' interpretation of 84–6; unclear meaning of 85 and n.; as wisdom of the occult 85
  in the Haskalah 81, 95–9, 113
  and intellectual challenges 95–6
  in Jewish literature, as philosophy and science 82–3
  literature, and the Bible 87–91
  and man's ability to master things that affect his life 90
  as philosophy 99–101
  secular: as 'Greek wisdom' 80–4; Haskalah attitudes to 81, 96–7, 113;

  medieval, Renaissance, and post-Renaissance Jewish attitudes to 91–5; see also wisdom, secular
  as source of ethics 90–1
wisdom, secular (chokhmot hagoyim), classifications of:
  chokhmot limudiyot (theoretical sciences): as part of intellect 97; as the wisdom of all nations 81
  chokhmot nimusiyot (useful wisdoms), history and geography as 97
  chokhmot nitsrakhot (practical skills) 97, 113
  chokhmot tiviyot (natural sciences): as positivistic sciences 96–7; as the wisdom of all nations 81
  see also Wessely, Naphtali Herz
Wolf, Friedrich August:
  on Homer 372 and n.
  on image of Greece 31
Wolf, Immanuel:
  on Jewish culture 45
  on Judaism and Hellenism in Alexandria 330–1
Wolfson, Harry A., on philosophical influence in talmudic literature 344

Z

Zamosc, David, and scientists 109
Zamosc, Rabbi Israel, on learning 'alien wisdoms' 86–7
Zhitlovsky, Chaim:
  on Jewish and Hellenic modus vivendi 216
  on nationality as racial phenomenon 397
Zieliński, Tadeusz, see Stein, Menahem
Zionism:
  and the national revival in Palestine 405
  and principle of representative democracy 441–3
  see also climatology
Zunz, Leopold (Yom Tov) Lippmann:
  and aggadah 260
  and Jewish culture 227, 453–4
  on Jewish emancipation in Germany 177
  on Judaism and non-Judaism 7–8
  on the Talmud and scientific enquiry 225